ALICE WATERS

&

CHEZ PANISSE

BOOKS BY THOMAS MCNAMEE

The Grizzly Bear

*Nature First: Keeping Our Wild Places
and Wild Creatures Wild*

A Story of Deep Delight

The Return of the Wolf to Yellowstone

THE PENGUIN PRESS

New York

2007

ALICE WATERS

&

CHEZ PANISSE

THE ROMANTIC, IMPRACTICAL,

OFTEN ECCENTRIC, ULTIMATELY BRILLIANT

MAKING OF A FOOD REVOLUTION

THOMAS McNAMEE

Foreword by R. W. Apple, Jr.

THE PENGUIN PRESS
Published by the Penguin Group
Penguin Group (USA) Inc., 375 Hudson Street, New York, New York 10014, U.S.A. • Penguin
Group (Canada), 90 Eglinton Avenue East, Suite 700, Toronto, Ontario, Canada M4P 2Y3
(a division of Pearson Penguin Canada Inc.) • Penguin Books Ltd, 80 Strand, London
WCR2 0RL, England • Penguin Ireland, 25 St. Stephen's Green, Dublin 2, Ireland (a division
of Penguin Books Ltd) • Penguin Books Australia Ltd, 250 Camberwell Road, Camberwell,
Victoria 3124, Australia (a division of Pearson Australia Group Pty Ltd) • Penguin Books India
Pvt Ltd, 11 Community Centre, Panchsheel Park, New Delhi–110 017, India • Penguin
Group (NZ), 67 Apollo Drive, Mairangi Bay, Auckland 1311, New Zealand (a division of
Pearson New Zealand Ltd) • Penguin Books (South Africa) (Pty) Ltd, 24 Sturdee Avenue,
Rosebank, Johannesburg 2196, South Africa

Penguin Books Ltd, Registered Offices: 80 Strand, London WC2R 0RL, England

First published in 2007 by The Penguin Press,
a member of Penguin Group (USA) Inc.

A portion of this book first appeared in *Saveur*.

Grateful acknowledgment is made for permission to reprint the following copyrighted works:
"Food neither good to look at nor to eat" by Fritz Streiff. By permission of the author.
Chez Panisse song, music, and lyrics by Michael Tilson Thomas. © 2001 Kongcha Music.
By permission of Michael Tilson Thomas.
Selections from *California Dish* by Jeremiah Tower (Free Press, 2003). By permission of the
author.
Selections from *Chez Panisse Menu Cookbook* by Alice Waters. Copyright © 1982 by Alice
Waters. Used by permission of Random House, Inc.

Photograph credits appear on page 381.

Library of Congress Cataloging-in-Publication Data
McNamee, Thomas, 1947–
Alice Waters and Chez Panisse : the romantic, impractical, often eccentric, ultimately brilliant
making of a food revolution / Thomas McNamee.
p.   cm.
Includes bibliographical references and index.
ISBN 978-1-59420-115-8
1. Waters, Alice.   2. Restaurateurs—United States—Biography.   3. Women cooks—
United States—Biography.   4. Chez Panisse.   I. Title.
TX910.5.W38M36 2007
641.5092—dc22
[B]
2006050334

Printed in the United States of America
1   3   5   7   9   10   8   6   4   2

DESIGNED BY AMANDA DEWEY

for

ELIZABETH

CONTENTS

FOREWORD

by R. W. Apple, Jr.

By now, everyone in this country who can tell the difference between an éclair and an entrecôte (and quite a few who cannot) knows who Alice Waters is.

She is, of course, the creator of Chez Panisse in Berkeley, California, one of the fountainheads of California cuisine, which some demanding judges consider the best restaurant in the United States. It is indisputably the most influential one. Before Chez Panisse, even the grandest American restaurants relied on imported, often canned or frozen products; today, the Waters credo—fresh, local seasonal, and where possible organic ingredients—is followed by hundreds of farmers' markets, thousands of restaurants, and millions of home cooks.

Her approach wins plaudits abroad as well as at home. I remember a conference at the opulent Manoir aux Quat'Saisons near Oxford, involving leading chefs from the United States, England, and France, where she dazzled her peers. They had arrived with trunks full of raw materials; she brought a few Meyer lemons and not much else, and relied for the rest on the Manoir's wonderful gardens and products on offer in the region, very simply prepared and served. All the chefs whom I asked said that her meal had been their favorite. It made the other meals seem somehow overwrought.

What is little understood, and what Thomas McNamee makes abundantly clear in this penetrating biography, is how unlikely a revolutionary Alice Waters is.

For one thing, she is no chef, at least in the generally understood meaning of the term. She has never attended cooking school and never served the same kind of rigorous apprenticeship, working in a succession of well-established kitchens, as have generations of European and more recently American culinary stars. She cooks, yes, and beautifully, but with some reluctance, and she has run Chez Panisse's kitchen only very episodically.

She isn't much of a businesswoman. Well into its period of ascendancy, Chez Panisse lost money, despite the best efforts of a series of business managers (including Ms. Waters's father) to impose fiscal discipline. Her habitual extravagance made their work hard and often all but impossible. In 1972, when the restaurant had been operating for less than a year, no less than thirty thousand dollars' worth of wine was unaccounted for.

Nor is she really a writer, despite the excellence and enormous success of her cookbooks. Like so much of her work, they are the products of her interaction with a group of friends, even when her name is the only one listed on the title page, as is sometimes the case.

Perhaps most surprising, the restaurant's mature style, marked above all by simplicity, evolved much more slowly than is generally appreciated. It is hard to believe, when one is faced with a trademark Chez Panisse dish like a salad with goat cheese, dependent for its impact on the quality of the greens and the care of the preparation, or a rustic soup of root vegetables, that Chez Panisse once served dishes of extraordinary complexity with no evident connection to northern California.

This was especially true during the tenure of Jeremiah Tower in the kitchen. He reveled in special dinners including surrealistic dishes inspired by Salvador Dalí or haute cuisine extravagances like duck stuffed with oysters, shallots, and its liver. A far cry, those, from the eventual house cuisine, influenced by Alice's experiences in the south of France, based on fresh herbs, newly picked vegetables, garlic, and olive oil.

So what assets did Ms. Waters bring to the project if not the usual skills of the successful restaurateur? Several.

Perhaps most important, what her old friend Eleanor Bertino calls "an iron will." A determination to press on when the staff or her private life was in turmoil, which has not always been visible to the casual observer, disarmed perhaps by her elfin appearance. Eleanor Bertino again: "There has always been this interesting contradiction between the delicate little way Alice looks and how she really is. . . . [She wore] these antique hats, delicate little hats that lay close to her head—she looked just like a Pre-Raphaelite angel."

"Of course it's possible," Ms. Waters would often say when someone told her that something could not possibly work. Another old friend, Greil Marcus, pictured Alice when challenged: "She'll simply smile and without any agitation at all, say, 'It can be done, it will be done, it's going to happen, you'll see.' She really does believe that she can change the world, she can change individual people one by one."

That determination has been hitched to a vision, one that has gripped Ms. Waters from the time of her first visit to France. As she told Mc-Namee: "I wanted civilized meals, and I wanted to wear French clothes. The cultural experience, that aesthetic, that paying attention to every little detail—I wanted to live my life like that."

So she made a restaurant about much more than food, taking infinite pains with flowers and lighting and color, menu design, the sequence of dishes, and the pace of service. An intensely social being, she has always been most at home in the dining room. To borrow a concept from Wagnerian opera, you might call Chez Panisse a *Gesamtkunstwerk,* a unitary work of art in which numerous elements play indispensable parts.

Not that food is slighted. By the testimony of her closest co-workers, Ms. Waters has an almost infallible palate and taste memory. If she tastes a dish and suggests that it needs just a squirt of lemon juice, that nearly always proves to be true. She knows that fava beans will combine well with rosemary, and she knows precisely how to make mulberry ice cream taste best.

And finally, she has that most valuable of leadership skills, the ability to build a feeling of camaraderie among staff members. No matter how turbulent things have become at certain moments in Chez Panisse's history—and they have often become turbulent indeed, fueled by gallons of Champagne, occasional dalliances with cocaine, and ample lashings of sex—Ms. Waters has managed to retain the loyalty of key figures like the chef Jean-Pierre Moullé for many decades, and even the humblest of workers is valued as a member of the Chez Panisse family.

The great triumph of her private life is her daughter, Fanny, named like the restaurant in homage to Marcel Pagnol's films. It was concern for Fanny's well-being, at least in part, that led her mother into her crusades for better food for children (the Edible Schoolyard project) and for college students (beginning with Fanny and her classmates at Yale). They may prove to be Ms. Waters's lasting monuments.

"How we eat," as this diminutive woman of grand dreams said confidently not long ago, "can change the world."

AUTHOR'S NOTE

Cristina Salas-Porras, at the time Alice Waters's assistant, first approached me about writing this book, presumably on her boss's authority, and in that sense it is "authorized," but I have had complete freedom throughout. Alice herself has been extremely generous with her time and resources. I have had unimpeded access to the Chez Panisse archives at the Bancroft Library of the University of California at Berkeley and to the archives stored at the restaurant. Alice has granted me many hours of interviews, and I have been free to interview her friends and colleagues as well.

Because Alice and my other interviewees have often been so well spoken and so candid, I have quoted them extensively. This approach has resulted in a frequent cohabitation of past and present tenses—for example, " 'Amboise and Jean-Didier were their names,' says Alice."

Alice has been kind enough to talk her way through a number of recipes that illuminate certain significant times in her life. Lindsey Shere, the pastry chef of Chez Panisse for twenty-six years, has also provided two of these "narrative recipes."

On a few occasions I have interwoven individual interviews into a sort of dialogue that I believe more fully represents my interlocutors' recollections than presenting them separately would have done.

WHEN I WAS FIRST thinking about this book, I went to the home of Lindsey Shere and her husband, Charles, who has been a partner or director of Chez Panisse throughout its history. When I asked Charles what he thought my biggest difficulty would be, he answered quickly: "Too much information."

And how. Whenever I have mentioned this project to anybody who knows Alice Waters or Chez Panisse, I've been almost certain to hear something like, "Have you talked to Jean-Jacques Quelquechose?"

And I've answered, "Not only have I not talked to Jean-Jacques Quelquechose, I've never heard of Jean-Jacques Quelquechose."

To which the riposte came, "Well, I don't know how you expect to do this book without talking to Jean-Jacques. He was one of Alice's most . . ."

Too much information.

I'm sure I've made significant omissions that I will come to regret, and I'm sure I've made some outright mistakes. All I can say is that I've done the best I could, and I beg the reader's forgiveness for my errors.

1.

OPENING
NIGHT

1971, 2006

Late-summer sun streamed into the dining room, turning every westward surface gold—French gilt mirrors on ivory plaster walls, redwood trim, oak floors and flea-market oak chairs, mismatched flea-market china and flatware on red-and-white-checkered tablecloths, one great vase of flowers with a white-linened table all to itself. On the stairway to the second floor, a woman, on her knees, was nailing down an Oriental runner.

"Alice?" called a waiter from below. "It's six o'clock."

Alice Waters rose and turned and descended the stairs. She was twenty-seven years old but looked much younger, with the skin and guileless mien of a child. She was wearing a tan lace dress, of an earlier day, delicate, fine, exactingly chosen. She was tiny, barely five feet two, with wide-open, wide-set gray eyes and a soft, pensive mouth.

This little restaurant in an old house on Shattuck Avenue in Berkeley, California, was the dream of Alice's life, and tonight, August 28, 1971, was its opening night. She had named the restaurant in honor of Honoré Panisse, the most generous and life-loving character in Marcel Pagnol's film trilogy *Marius, Fanny,* and *César.* Alice wanted Chez Panisse to be an easygoing, unaffected gathering place, like César's Bar de la Marine on the Old Port of Marseille, where friends could laugh, argue, flirt, and drink wine for hours on end. At Chez Panisse, they could also have something simple and delicious to eat.

She threw her shoulders back, lifted her chin, and prepared to smile. She opened the door, and in poured a multitude. "We'd invited friends that first night," she recalls today, "but there was a line out the door and down the block. We just didn't know what to do."

Alice led them to their tables with a confident smile and a flourish of the hand as though she had been running a restaurant all her life. "In fact," she says, "my entire professional experience amounted to one summer making crab salad sandwiches at the tearoom in Bullock's department store, plus a little waitressing here and there."

The menu was chalked on a blackboard:

Pâté en croûte

Canard aux olives

Plum tart

Café

$3.95

And that was it. There was no choice except of wine—Mondavi Fumé Blanc, Mondavi Gamay, and, by the glass, a fine Sauternes, Château Suduiraut.

The dining-room staff had no uniforms and so were hard to distinguish from the customers, but there were a lot of them, in both the kitchen and the dining room. Chez Panisse on its opening night had fifty seats and fifty-five employees.

The pâté arrived promptly. It had been made in advance, and required only to be sliced and plated at the last minute. It was simple, an archetype of French bistro cooking: tightly packed chopped pork and pork fat flavored with Cognac and wrapped in an egg-glazed pastry crust. It was accompanied by the little sour pickles known as *cornichons* and crocks of

Dijon mustard. The customers dug in, and came up smiling. And then the wait began.

Behind the kitchen door was, in Alice's recollection, "sheer chaos." Victoria Kroyer, also twenty-seven, had been laboring at the sauce for the duck for three days, not shortcutting any of the many steps of the classical sequence set down by the imperious nineteenth-century master Auguste Escoffier. She had begun by making a *fond brun,* the classic long-cooked stock of vegetables, beef, and veal. She then thickened her stock with a roux of flour browned in clarified butter and set it to simmer through repeated skimmings of the scum that floated to the top. After six hours of that, she added tomatoes and *mirepoix* (minced carrots, onions, celery, and raw ham, with thyme and bay leaf), and skimmed it some more, reduced it some more, and strained it again, yielding *sauce espagnole,* the base on which many more elaborate sauces are built in French haute cuisine. To the *espagnole* she added more *fond brun* and reduced that combination by half; and then she spiked it with a bit of sherry and again strained the result, a demi-glace, which was still only a base. From the duck bones and trimmings and white wine Victoria then created a second stock, which she cooked for four hours, skimmed, strained, defatted, reduced, and finally combined with the demi-glace. That amalgam, in turn, she cooked with the olives for two hours. The sauce was magnificent, if a bit salty, but the braising of the ducks was now falling desperately behind.

Until Alice hired her as chef a few weeks prior to the opening of Chez Panisse, Victoria Kroyer had been a graduate student in philosophy, at the University of California at Berkeley, who liked to cook at home. She had never made *sauce espagnole* or demi-glace or, indeed, *canard aux olives* before this night. She had never worked in a restaurant kitchen. "Victoria had a certain confidence," remembers Alice, "which I lacked completely."

The ducks were fresh, not frozen, from Chinatown in San Francisco. Most of the produce had come from either the Japanese produce concession at the Usave on Grove Street or the Berkeley Co-op grocery across the street from the restaurant. For the salad, served after the main course though unlisted on the menu, the best they could get was romaine lettuce, and Alice ended up throwing away three-quarters of it. Alice and

Victoria had worried for days about which olives to use in the sauce, and as it turned out, says Alice, "neither of us was satisfied with the ones we ended up buying. Green Sicilian olives. They were much too salty." Alice and Victoria didn't even know that there were such things as restaurant purveyors. Not that it mattered, for the big suppliers didn't have fresh ducks, or beautiful salad greens, or the appropriate French olives either.

In the kitchen, casseroles of duck simmered on every burner and were crowded into the ovens, and still the meat refused to soften to the melting tenderness that Alice remembered from her seven months in Paris during her junior year in college. The dining room grew quieter as the diners' patience waned. Alice was in and out of the kitchen every few minutes, first cheering her crew on, then begging, then, finally, in a serious temper. Luckily, she did not know about the ash that had fallen from Victoria's cigarette into the sauce.

Between the pâté and the first plate of duck to appear in the dining room, a full hour went by. "I was going out of my mind," Alice remembers. "All these people waiting at the tables. More people waiting at the door to be seated. People waiting out on the sidewalk. And we just couldn't get their food out to them. And I was the one who had to talk to them."

At last, at intervals, waiters burst out of the kitchen to rush to a table with a few plates of unctuous, glistening, and delicious duck with olive sauce. At some unlucky other tables, as the kitchen bogged down further, the wait stretched to two hours. It was a good thing that so many of the diners were friends or family. "We had fifteen or more people in the kitchen," says Alice, "way more than we needed. Way more than there was room for. Not one of them professionally trained. Making it up as they went along. Same in the front of the house. Waiters and waitresses who were actually painters or poets or dancers. I hired them all, because I liked them. I didn't want professionals. We were just going to figure it out. That's what we were all doing, making it up as we went along. It was totally insane."

The plum tart—straightforward, almost austere, the plums at their peak of ripeness spread across a light custard and baked in a buttery crust—was the work of Lindsey Shere, a longtime friend of Alice's, who worked in calm isolation in a shack in the backyard and was, therefore, protected from the infectious nervous breakdown that had taken hold of Chez Panisse that night. The tart was perfect: warm, delicate, intensely fragrant, and ready to be served on time.

At the end of the evening, as the last late diners trickled out, Alice stood beaming in the doorway, her heart still pounding. One hundred twenty meals had finally been served. How many of those were actually paid for, no one would ever remember precisely. How much it cost to serve them was certainly much more than what they brought in.

There were still at least fifty people waiting in the street. "I'm sorry," Alice called to them. "We just don't have any more food. Come back tomorrow!"

Past midnight, Alice and the staff and the friends who stayed on opened some wine in the half-finished café upstairs and sat quietly together, exhausted, elated. "We were so happy. We were so young," she reminisces. "We were in love with what we were doing. And we were in the right place at the right time. It was sheer luck, really."

THIRTY-FIVE YEARS LATER, Alice Waters is arguably the most famous restaurateur in the United States, Chez Panisse the best-known restaurant. In 2001, *Gourmet* magazine deemed it the best restaurant in the nation; in the magazine's next assessment, in its October 2006 issue, Chez Panisse fell to number two (behind a Chicago newcomer called Alinea).

How the slapdash, make-it-up-as-we-go-along little hangout and its harried mistress became such icons is a story of adventure, misadventure, unintended consequences, steel will, pure chance, and utterly unrealistic visions. The characters who thread through its history range from hedonists to Machiavellian careerists, from the crazy to the coolly rationalist; nearly all have been driven by passion, passion sometimes so fierce as to be blind. The road Chez Panisse has traveled from there to here is neither straight nor smooth. It is potholed, booby-trapped, cliff-hanging, devil-daring, sometimes not quite a road at all.

In some ways, Chez Panisse today goes no further than Alice's first, modest desires for it. It still occupies the same old house in Berkeley. It is still an easygoing, unaffected gathering place where friends laugh, argue, flirt, and drink wine for hours on end—and have something simple and delicious to eat. Some of the same stoned hippies who were fumbling plates of duck on opening night are now polished professionals and still there—though their practiced manners mask the same antic, cerebral inner lives that attracted Alice to them years ago. There is not a Chez Panisse outpost in Las Vegas, or anywhere else; there is no Chez Panisse frozen pizza; and it is only in the last few years that Chez Panisse has become a genuinely profitable enterprise. Alice is a hero and a celebrity, hounded for endorsements and autographs, but she can still seem the same childlike, slightly out-of-focus dreamer who opened a restaurant without knowing anything about restaurants. Chez Panisse is a place of pilgrimage for gourmets and chefs from all over the world, but it offers no culinary fireworks, no vertiginous architectural assemblages on the plate, no wild combinations of exotic ingredients. It's still just a place to have fun and eat very good food.

But for many people, including many who will never eat there, Chez Panisse is a much larger enterprise than a restaurant. It is a standard-bearer for a system of moral values. It is the leader of a style of cooking, of a social movement, and of a comprehensive philosophy of doing good and living well. It is also a work of art—the work of many, the masterpiece of one.

With eight books, hundreds of talks, dozens of honors and awards, ceaseless media attention, and one not very big restaurant, Alice Waters has transformed the way many Americans eat and the way they think about food. Her insistence on the freshest ingredients, used only at the peak of their season, nearly always grown locally and organically, is now a ruling principle in the best American restaurants and for many home cooks. Her conception of a moral community based on good food and goodwill has helped to spawn a new generation of artisans and farmers. Like her, they are committed to stewardship of the land and waters. They settle for nothing less than the highest quality in what they produce. They see themselves as an increasingly potent force in American culture and politics. Under the leadership that Alice has reluctantly and somewhat awkwardly assumed, this new community has seen its ideals and methods spread across the country. You can now walk into a co-op or a farmers' market, or even a supermarket, in Montana or Mississippi, Ohio or New Mexico, and find fresh, delicious, organic foodstuffs, grown by people who share the values and vision of Alice Waters.

By the time Alice turned sixty years old, in 2004, she had far-reaching ambitions. Already she was seeing students, from grade school to college, being taught to grow and cook their own food. On a larger scale yet, she envisioned the soul-deadening machinery of corporate agriculture supplanted by a profusion of small organic farms, sustainable fisheries, and humane and ecologically benign animal husbandry. She dreamed of the fractured American family coming back together, and back to health, around the dining table. She saw that people worldwide could be drawn by pleasure to a new way of thinking about the earth and a better way of living on it.

Alice today is much changed from the girlish twenty-seven-year-old of 1971; Chez Panisse is in many ways much changed as well. But together—and their identities have become inseparable—they are still making it up as they go along, and every dinner is still a passionate experiment, often changing up to the moment it is served.

2.

SOUP

1944–1965

Alice Louise Waters was born on April 28, 1944, the second of four daughters of Margaret Hickman Waters and Charles Patrick Waters, of Chatham, New Jersey. Hers was an ordinary American suburban childhood, but Alice's experience of it was extraordinarily intense, because her senses were so acute. "Through the senses, always through the senses" is still how Alice Waters describes her lifelong way of knowing the world.

Her earliest memory is of the garden. Bad eyesight had prevented Alice's father, known as Pat, from serving in World War II. His part in the war effort had been to plant a victory garden. One Fourth of July, for a costume contest at the playground, Alice's mother, Marge, dressed Alice as the Queen of the Garden, with a skirt of lettuce leaves, bracelets made from radishes, anklets of red and green peppers, a necklace woven of long-stemmed strawberries, and a crown of asparagus.

Half a century later, Alice vividly recalls her mother's applesauce and apple pies, the strawberry patch, bacon sandwiches slathered with butter, running to the white Good Humor truck for a cherry-lime Popsicle, red on one side, with real pieces of cherry in it, green on the other, each half with its own wooden stick to be licked clean.

"The meal I loved best," she says, "was when my father was grilling a steak outside. The smell of the smoke, the sizzling of the meat and the fat. For my birthday, I always wanted a grilled steak, and we'd have green beans. That was my favorite meal, steak and green beans. Still is one of my favorites."

Alice remembers the aromas of the outdoors—the freshly cut grass on the hill she rolled down in Hacklebarney State Park, the musty smell of her snowsuit when she sledded the same hill in winter, the forsythia hedge in spring, the lilacs and the lilies of the valley beneath them, the newly turned black soil of the garden.

She remembers a good many things she didn't like, among them some elements of her mother's efforts toward good nutrition—brown, dry "health bread," oatmeal, vitamin pills that Alice sneaked into the bathroom to spit out. What becomes clear as she recalls her girlhood is that her senses were almost painfully acute. In the bedroom that she and her older sister, Ellen, shared, Alice was always too hot or too cold. When she complained of the cold, her mother would take her to the basement, stand her shivering in front of the furnace, and stuff her into her snowsuit. Hot summer nights, Alice would lie sleepless on top of the sheets. Then, in the mornings, through the open windows came the murmur of the creek beyond the raspberry brambles, squirrel chatter in the big oaks and maples, birdsong, and all the sounds of a summer morning.

As Pat rose through the ranks of the Prudential Life Insurance Company, the family moved to Indiana and then to southern California, and Alice grew from Mary Janes and cap-sleeved little dresses made by her aunt to pink Capezio pumps with a soft pink sweater and a straight pink skirt, through spin the bottle to serious smooching in the dark. In high school she discovered drinking, and boys—"lots of boyfriends, lots of driving up and down the main street in town, going out with older boys and ones from the other side of the tracks. Guys who had big Bonneville convertibles."

At Van Nuys High, she fell in with the intellectual crowd, and for college her parents urged her to go to the famously intellectual University of

California at Berkeley. But Alice chose U.C. Santa Barbara, which in her recollection is a whirl of skirts and hairstyles, parties, frat boys, and a great deal of drinking. "That was a dark period of my life," she says. "I was just moving from one party to another. There were various people I was involved with, but I don't remember a single person's name. I never got into pot smoking, but alcohol affects your memory too. Especially when you drink enough to pass out."

She was very smart, but she was in danger of becoming an irredeemable party girl. Rescue of a sort came from a fellow Van Nuys graduate, one she hadn't known there, a slim, cerebral beauty named Eleanor Bertino, one of her sisters at Alpha Phi. Eleanor was elegant, soft-spoken, and serious. She wanted to leave Santa Barbara, and she thought Alice would do well to join her. In the fall of their sophomore year, 1963, Eleanor, Alice, and another Alpha Phi, Sara Flanders, all applied for transfer to the University of California at Berkeley.

That moment was an early instance of what came to be a pattern in Alice's life: people stepping in to rescue her at just the right moment, and in doing so drastically altering her world. Although she has always seemed to lead a well-ordered life, Alice still sometimes characterizes herself as more acted upon than purposeful.

When they arrived in January 1964, the campus was nothing like the serene intellectual refuge they had imagined. The quiet, scholarly air of the 1950s had been shattered by the assassination of President John F. Kennedy, by violence against the civil rights movement in the South, by the arms race (indeed, nuclear weapons were being designed right there, at the Lawrence Berkeley Laboratory). That summer of 1964, the Freedom Riders James Chaney, Andrew Goodman, and Michael Schwerner were murdered by Ku Klux Klansmen in Mississippi, and President Lyndon B. Johnson pushed the fraudulent Gulf of Tonkin Resolution through Congress, setting in motion a war that would kill fifty-eight thousand Americans and three million Vietnamese. That year, the Republican Party, at its convention in San Francisco, named Barry Goldwater its presidential candidate. Goldwater wanted a much bigger Vietnam War (including the possible use of nuclear weapons) and much smaller federal defense of civil rights.

Years later, Eleanor Bertino looked back to the signal moment that drew them personally into the Berkeley whirlwind: "The Free Speech Movement erupted at our feet."

"And that changed everything," says Alice. "Changed my life forever."

BERKELEY WAS IN TURMOIL throughout the fall of 1964. Thousands of students were protesting university rules that effectively forbade political activity of any kind on campus. The administration met the protests with repression that grew more extreme by the week. The students' resistance took organized form that October as the Free Speech Movement. The FSM marked the beginning of the wave of political and cultural upheaval that would sweep around the world for the next ten years. Like many another venture in Berkeley, it was a first, and its leaders—some students; some older, long-dedicated activists; some mysterious characters who seemed to have materialized out of nowhere—tended to rely on intuition, improvisation, and a style of expression designed to shock their elders. They were remarkably successful nevertheless, and profoundly disturbing to the University of California system, its Board of Regents, the state legislature, and the governor. The movement made for sensational press, and that fall, emotions on all sides were mounting toward frenzy.

On December 2, 1964, the galvanic orator Mario Savio led some one thousand Free Speech Movement adherents in an occupation of Sproul Hall, the university's main administration building. Nothing like that had ever happened at an American university. That night, hundreds of policemen gathered at the edge of campus. All but a few of the students refused to leave. At three o'clock in the morning, 367 police officers stormed the building, and 773 of the occupiers were arrested. It was the biggest mass arrest of students in American history.

Real violence, southern style—with dogs, tear gas, and beatings—seemed imminent, and many of the students, inflamed with their sense of injury and injustice, were ready to welcome it. Many others were frightened and confused.

Alice had taken part in a few of the demonstrations earlier that fall, and her heart was with the protesters, but when her friend Sara Flanders showed her a brochure describing study at the Sorbonne, it did seem like a fine time to go to France.

ICELANDIC, the favored airline of young Americans traveling to Europe in the mid-1960s, flew crowded, scruffy turboprops from New York to Luxembourg, with a leisurely stop in Iceland to refuel, and a continuous party aloft. On those long and festive flights there was not much sleep to be had.

It was dark when Sara Flanders and Alice Waters arrived in Luxembourg, and they were already exhausted. Paris was another five hours by bus. It was February 1965, and freezing.

Alice had never been abroad. She had not come to France for the food, for she knew little about food, French or otherwise. She liked the idea of learning to speak French. She liked the idea of meeting French boys. She liked the idea of France.

"My rich aunt had told us about a place where we should stay, on the Rue Cambon, in the First Arrondissement, right behind the Place Vendôme," Alice recalls. "It cost ten times what we should have spent. We closed the curtains—the heavy, heavy blue curtains—and we went to bed, and we didn't wake up for a whole day. We missed the whole next day.

"Finally, we woke up. Our second day there, which we really couldn't afford. We went down to the dining room for lunch, and we didn't know what to order, so we just had the soup because it was the cheapest thing. It was a *soupe des légumes*. It wasn't puréed, it was just very finely chopped up, and it was so delicious. It felt like I had never eaten before. And everything that went with it—those big, old, thick curtains and a bed that was made with those sheets that had rolled-up cushions at the head of the bed—it was a sensibility that was not part of my life, had never been."

· WINTER VEGETABLE SOUP ·

You start with real winter vegetables, mostly roots, like carrots and turnips, parsnips, parsley root sometimes. And maybe winter squash and some greens. Maybe a little potato to give it body. You cut the vegetables into equal-size cubes and sauté them with onions and garlic and herbs till they're just starting to soften. Since it's winter, I would probably use a couple of thyme branches and a bay leaf. A little lovage leaf might be nice in there.

Then you add your liquid, just enough to stew the vegetables till they're nice and soft but haven't lost their shape—an hour and a half, or two hours at the most. If you cook them too long, the taste is too strong.

You can use just water, for the pure taste of the vegetables, or a little light chicken stock, but really light, made from uncooked chicken parts and nothing else. It's got to be more about vegetables than it is about the taste of the stock. Don't forget to take out the thyme and the bay leaf.

You don't want to use a blender or a food processor because that would make it too smooth. I use a food mill with the widest holes, so you still have a sense of the liquid in the soup. It's not emulsified. You still have all those different colors—the oranges, the yellows, the whites, the greens.

It might just need a little oil or a little butter right at the end. You want to serve it as soon as it's done. You don't want to keep it overnight in the refrigerator.

There are other sorts of vegetable soups, very long-cooked, with many vegetables, a soup that likes to be reheated. Minestrone, for example. But this one keeps the bright, live taste of the vegetables. I'll never forget that first time I tasted it.

"Well, we had to leave, and so we set out to find a hotel," Alice recalls, "which we found on the Rue des Écoles. It was a seventh-floor walk-up."

In their first days there, Alice and Sara were afraid to go to a restaurant because they thought their French was so poor. The Self Service Latin-Cluny, where you didn't have to speak French to anyone, was their haven. "They had pretty decent pâté, with *cornichons,* and *oeufs mayonnaise,* two hard-boiled eggs coated with mayonnaise. We'd have a glass of wine and a glass of mineral water and yogurt. I can still taste that yogurt."

For their permanent lodgings, the Sorbonne helped Alice and Sara find a studio apartment on the Place des Gobelins, with a bathroom down the hall. "I remember trying to make the true café au lait, with steamed milk," says Alice. Sara, now a psychoanalyst in London, adds, "And we would go out to this wonderful *pâtisserie,* for hot croissants and *pain au chocolat,* and bring them back to the flat."

"We would just sit there in that room," remembers Alice, "and eat this little treat, pastries and café au lait. Then we missed our first class, and it kind of went on like that."

It didn't take Alice and Sara long to overcome their fear of restaurants, and once they'd started going to them, they couldn't stop. Back in Berkeley, Sara had been the one excited about all the French food they were going to eat, while Alice's opinion, as Sara recalls it, was that they should be thinking about gaining some experience with French men. But it was food that Alice fell in love with. "And the culture," she adds now. "And the politics."

The dreary classrooms of the Sorbonne versus a joyous immersion in French cuisine in the sparkling, spotless dining rooms of Paris's restaurants—for Alice it was an easy choice. She reveled in the aromas of onion soup and Gauloise smoke in the bistros, the flowers on the tables, the meticulous geometry of the place settings. Down every Paris street, it seemed, food beckoned to her: roasting chestnuts, glistening oysters at the stands of long-aproned shuckers, the little outdoor markets that bloomed at dawn and were gone before lunch, with their exquisitely arranged fruits, vegetables, eels, chickens, and sausages, and their garrulous, mock-aggressive merchants.

Alice's meals card for the Sorbonne, 1965

She was enchanted by the rhythms, the old and inflexible customs, the sheer charm of Parisian dining. She loved the squiggly handwritten menus on the bistro chalkboards and the fact that the bill of fare changed every day. She loved the unvarying *"Bon appétit!"* and being called *mademoiselle.* Even in the most modest places, the napery was crisp and spotless, the flatware polished bright, the food better than anything she had ever tasted. Nevertheless, she recalls, "that was the time when no matter what we said in French, in a restaurant or to anyone, they said, *'Comment?'* They just refused to understand us. It was so demoralizing, and so painful. *'Comment?'* These good-looking French waiters. And of course I was dressed like a Russian émigré, with thick old boots and a giant huge coat and a huge hat, and it was snowing. These little French girls had on heels and spring coats, and they looked like they weighed about ninety-nine pounds, carrying their purses and eating a hard-boiled egg for lunch. I wanted to dress like them, but I was too cold. I was freezing. I did long for those beautiful French tight-fitting sweaters."

Alice and Sara's enchantment with French food grew into obsession. "We'd get up and have breakfast and figure out where we were going to go for lunch. That took some time, and nearly as soon as we finished lunch, we had to figure out where we were going to go for dinner. It was a wonderful time to be in France. It was real and genuine and honest. And really affordable. We were able to go to restaurants twice a day for five francs."

Sara adds, "I think I cared about the prices far more than Alice, who was—and is—extremely extravagant."

"I was still very intimidated everywhere we went," says Alice. "I didn't want to be gauche and order the red wine with the wrong course or the white with the wrong course, so I just ordered rosé. And I always ordered too much food. The waiters must have all been laughing hysterically in the back room. That's always how we felt, like no matter what we did, we were doing the wrong thing. But sometimes you learn well when you're on your knees, you know?"

Alice did show up for class from time to time, and began to acquire passable French. She remained afraid to use it, however, unless her interlocutor spoke absolutely no English. "Her French was better than mine," Sara Flanders recalls, "but she was paralyzed about talking, and I would be the one who would speak. Not because my French was that good, but because Alice used to start, 'Uh, uh, uh'—she just couldn't get it out."

"But I got the whole French aesthetic, from beginning to end," Alice says. "What those thick curtains looked like, what the fruit bowl looked like, how the cheese was presented, how it was put on the shelves, how the baguettes twisted. The shapes, the colors, the styles.

"Everything in Paris was magical to me. You'd walk past a church and you'd hear music, and you'd walk in and sit down and they'd be playing Bach at lunch. Concerts—we went to so many concerts. And those magnificent museums."

For spring vacation in 1965, Sara and Alice went first to Barcelona, and then to the south of France for three weeks. There Alice discovered the sort of elemental, boldly flavored food that would, years later, be the foundation of the Chez Panisse style: fresh herbs, just-picked vegetables, garlic, olive oil. Olive oil, especially the sharp, aromatic, green, first-pressing oil that was the single most basic ingredient in southern French cooking, was all but unknown in the United States. "I'd hardly even heard of olive oil at all, much less 'extra virgin.'"

After their return to Paris, Alice and Sara met two young Frenchmen. "Amboise and Jean-Didier were their names," says Alice. "They took us out in the country, and that was our real introduction to the food."

"Amboise, who was from Brittany, made an itinerary for our first trip there," Sara recalls. "This little chart, all the places Alice and I should go."

"I'll never forget those mussels in Honfleur," Alice says.

The fishermen brought them in from the boat, rinsed them off for a minute, threw them into this big cauldron, and then scooped them out. And I developed a whole crêpe obsession. I loved the *crêpes Grand Marnier* in Brittany. Buckwheat crêpes. I'd have a couple dozen oysters for lunch and a couple of crêpes, savory and sweet, and a bottle of apple cider. Oh, that cider. The first time we had it, we didn't know it was hard cider, and after lunch we were walking along the road getting sleepier and sleepier, and finally we just lay down in the grass and drifted off to sleep. I don't know how long we must have slept in that grass.

And the *fraises des bois*! I didn't know what they were. Strawberries of the woods. Couldn't imagine somebody out there picking them. We had them with crème fraîche and a sugar shaker. The waiter comes to the table with this big bowl, and you help yourself. Unbelievable.

In Paris, I loved the steak Bercy. All those shallots. *Entrecôte Bercy.* That was very expensive. And the salads and the skinny little green beans. And those big crudité platters. I loved standing at the bar at Au Pied de Cochon. I loved the idea of that restaurant, because it had those oysters out front, and then you'd go into the downstairs part and for four francs fifty you could eat at the bar and have a *blanquette de veau* and a glass of red wine and a basket of great bread.

I remember going to Caen, just to have those famous *tripes à la mode de Caen.* It was a sort of pilgrimage, really. But we set one foot inside that restaurant, took one whiff—augh!—and out we ran.

Late that spring of 1965, at a restaurant in a little stone house in Brittany, Alice had a meal that crystallized her conception of what good food ought to be. "Elsewhere, even when I found the food to be wonderful," she would write years later, the French "would say only that it was 'all right'; but after the meal in this tiny restaurant, they applauded the chef and cried, '*C'est fantastique!*' I've remembered this dinner a thousand times: the old stone house, the stairs leading up to the small dining room, which seated no more than twelve at the pink cloth–covered tables and from which one could look through the open windows to the stream running beside the house and the garden in back. The chef, a woman, announced the menu: cured ham and melon, trout with almonds, and raspberry tart. The trout had just come from the stream and the raspberries from the garden."[1]

After classes ended in June, Alice and Sara got rail passes that for a single price allowed them for the next two months to take the train anywhere in Western Europe on the spur of the moment. They went to England, and then to Italy, and from there on to the Salzburg music festival. Alice was not impressed with the food anywhere they went: "I was a confirmed francophile by then."

In September 1965, Alice and Sara returned to America by sea, sailing from Rotterdam on an old ship crammed with hundreds of students. One of them was a freshly minted Amherst graduate on his way to law school at Berkeley's Boalt Hall, Tim Savinar, who remains a friend of Alice's today.

"Almost immediately it was very rough, and just about everybody was sick as a dog," he says. "I don't get seasick—I'm an old salmon fisherman. And the other person who seemed not to be seasick was Alice. There we were, with this whole ship to ourselves, going to dinner, going to the bar, dancing. Alice said that she was going back to Berkeley, but what she really wanted to do was to operate some kind of a café, or some sort of meeting place that had the food that she had been awakened to, and combine it with people sitting around talking about film or something like that. She was quite romantic."

"When I got back from France," Alice remembers, "I wanted hot baguettes in the morning, and apricot jam, and café au lait in bowls, and I wanted a café to hang out in, in the afternoon, and I wanted civilized meals, and I wanted to wear French clothes. The cultural experience, that aesthetic, that paying attention to every little detail—I wanted to live my life like that."

3.

VERY SIXTIES

1965–1966

lice's experience of Berkeley in the fall of 1965 could hardly have been less like the sweet and decorous life she had known in France. At this midpoint of the 1960s, Berkeley was undergoing all at once the cultural conflicts that would come to the rest of the United States through the later years of the decade. Social protest tended toward the vitriolic in Berkeley. Communal living often took radical forms, driven by ideology and lots of sex, some of it rather defiantly flaunted.

In Paris, Alice and Sara had read the *Herald Tribune* to keep up with the mounting discord in America, and they had heard French antiwar protesters chanting, *"U! S! Assassins!"* but there was a certain abstractness to it all. In Berkeley, the anger and the sense of danger were real. In Alice's absence, the Free Speech Movement sitters-in who had been arrested on December 2, 1964, had gone to trial and had been found guilty en masse. The black neighborhood of Watts in Los Angeles had rioted and burned; thirty-four people had been killed there, a thousand wounded. The first United States troops—thirty-four hundred Marines—had entered the Vietnam War in the spring of 1965, and by the end of the year, there would be nearly two hundred thousand Americans there. Berkeley was seething.

"I'll never forget the time Alice took us to one antiwar session," her sister Ellen Waters Pisor recalls. "We went to hear a speech by William F. Buckley, and afterward we could ask questions from the floor, so Alice immediately stood up. She was outraged by everything Buckley had said, and she said, 'What are you planning to do about the genocide in Vietnam?' Well, *genocide,* that was a pretty heady word for 1966."

"God, it was a wild time," says Alice. "A terrible time in many ways. But it all felt so important. History was being made in Berkeley, and we all felt that we were part of it. I didn't lose my French aesthetics, not at all, but what was going on at Cal seemed bigger, more important."

It was a very exciting time to be young and in Berkeley. The word *revolution* was heard constantly, and it meant not only the political uprising against war and racism but also a social and sexual revolution. While dour radicals debated all night in the dorms about correct and incorrect forms of violence, there was also the Sexual Freedom League holding weekly orgies and demonstrating naked on the campus.

Berkeley has a history of sexual freedom nearly as long as its activist tradition. In 1960, a professor (and Cal alumnus) at the University of Illinois, Leo Koch, advocated "free love" in the student newspaper and was summarily fired, but Berkeley welcomed him home the next spring with an outpouring of jubilation. Long before cohabitation was common anywhere else in the country, unmarried couples were openly living together in Berkeley. They didn't call themselves girlfriend and boyfriend, or companions or partners. They used the word *lovers.*

For Alice Waters, the radicals' romanticizing of violence was something to steer clear of. She and Sara Flanders and their friends were enacting their own sort of revolution, quietly devising a new way of living, grounded less in outrage than in pleasure, while also imbued with ideals of social justice. "I kept drinking my café au lait from a bowl," Alice says, "but I was also seeing the world beyond that now a little more clearly."

In 1966, Alice, Sara, Eleanor Bertino, and another former Alpha Phi sister from Santa Barbara teamed up to take an apartment with a well-equipped kitchen, where Sara and Alice tried to reproduce the French dishes they loved. There was a Frenchman living downstairs who was a good cook and a good teacher. Julia Child's television series on French cooking was in its third year and was a rich source of information. "My specialty," Alice says, "was crêpes with orange zest, just like I'd had in Brittany."

· CRÊPES WITH ORANGE ZEST ·

These were buckwheat crêpes—mostly buckwheat flour, but some white flour, and milk, and some beer, butter, eggs, a tiny bit of sugar. You let it sit in the refrigerator for at least a couple of hours. Overnight is better.

I have my own crêpe pans now. It's possible to use an omelet pan. It's hard to do it just free-form, because it's hard to get the batter very, very thin like you want to have it, and it's hard to pick it up if you have a high-sided pan. You need to have a very low-sided pan. In France, they sort of rake it out on a flat griddle with a little instrument, a little wooden snowplow-like thing, but I've never made them that way. I suppose you could try it, but you just absolutely have to have the right amount of liquid or you can't get it right. The batter's got to be as thin as possible.

You can use butter or oil, not too much, just about medium hot. I put the batter in, and then I pick up the pan and tip it all around so the batter goes out to the edges and forms a very, very thin layer. Then as soon as it bubbles and gets settled a little bit, I lift it up by one edge with my fingers—I don't flip it in the air—and turn it over and cook it another minute, and then stack them in a pile.

You make a kind of butter with orange zest and sugar in it. After you make the crêpes, you spread them quickly with that butter, *et voilà.* Maybe put in a touch of Grand Marnier or Cognac. I think the buckwheat is incredibly delicious, that flavor. Yes, I do.

With girls this pretty and food this good, the apartment was a popular destination for young men. "The door was always open," says Eleanor, "and we always had men who were just friends, which was something a little bit new. Things were open in Berkeley. The sixties started in Berkeley before anywhere else, you know. You could be a nice girl and still sleep with your boyfriend. Everything was kind of expansive. It was like the whole world was brighter and opening up. And of course we were the defining generation."

And for many in their generation, in mid-sixties Berkeley, the defining experience was LSD. Lysergic acid diethylamide was still legal. Its most famous manufacturer, Augustus Owsley Stanley III, universally known as Owsley, plied his trade nearby, in north Berkeley. Sara Flanders announced that it was time for them to give it a try, and Alice was intrigued by what promised to be an entirely new sensory experience. "Owsley was a friend of one of our downstairs neighbors," says Alice, "so we managed to get the good stuff. I had never even smoked dope before that. Well, it blew my mind, as they say. I was up there on the ceiling looking down at Eleanor, who was on the chair. I don't think I came down for three days. The whole world looked different to me after that. I just understood something about another way of thinking. It was an important experience, but it scared me terribly. There was that feeling that I was going to lose my mind. And that I would never ever come down. Never, ever, ever."

This was classic Alice: portraying herself as timid while also daring the high dive; having her adventure never alone, but always in the company of trusted friends; and describing a moment of intense sensory experience as somehow, inexpressibly, life-changing.

Alice's aesthetics and her political commitment came together in her study of the Romantic period in Europe. She was gaining confidence. She created her own major, in French cultural history, focusing on the period between 1750 and 1850—"in other words, the French Revolution. In part, I suppose, because it felt like the moment we were living in."

"She was never a shy person, exactly," says Eleanor, who has made something of a life study of Alice, "but she wasn't very articulate. Then, in 1965, when she was back from France, all this intellectual stuff and the arts gave her a means of expressing herself. She was super-energetic. Not a moment of self-doubt. I mean, if she didn't like your boyfriend, she was not nice to him. She knew who she wanted me to go out with, and I wasn't doing that. She made life very difficult for this poor guy I was going out with.

"She wanted to run things, and she had the strength and energy to do it. When it took two of us to take a mattress and struggle up this flight of stairs, Alice would just throw it over her shoulder and run up the stairs. That's how I always think of Alice, still—lifting things, carrying them, moving things, always moving so quickly.

"There's always been this interesting contradiction between the delicate little way Alice looks and how she really is. There was something very turn-of-the-century-to-1930 about Alice's appearance, and there still is. When you look at the furniture in her house, I think, some of it is from the thirties still. And she started wearing these antique hats, delicate little hats that lay close to her head—she looked just like a Pre-Raphaelite angel. She had this long, wavy hair, and was very, very skinny. Barely five-two. But an iron will. Always."

Eleanor understands Alice deeply enough to make Alice sometimes quite uncomfortable, but her cool take on Alice's foibles is in its way an expression of Eleanor's great affection. To the curious would-be analyst of Alice's complexities, Eleanor responds with unsentimental simplicity: "She has never wanted to stop. She is not a contemplative person. She's not somebody who likes to stop and really think about things. She's not one of those people who need to go off and read a book and be alone."

Alice and Eleanor and most of their fellow students foresaw a changed world in their near future, one they had forged themselves. Sometimes they saw it as generated by political action, and sometimes from within, close to home, in the way people lived.

"In the spring of '66," Eleanor says, "I remember sitting around together and saying, 'You know, we don't have to get married.' All our sorority sisters in Santa Barbara were getting married. And Sara said, 'It's kind of exciting—we can do whatever we want; there are no rules, there's no structure. We have to make them up ourselves, and that's sort of frightening.' And we decided that we wanted to have a restaurant. Well, more than a restaurant. I wanted to call it The Four Muses. We'd get this great big old house, and Sara would make clothes there, and Betsy Danch, our other roommate, would have an art gallery, and I would have the bookstore, and Alice would do the restaurant. Alice had wanted to have a restaurant where a different person would cook each night, but where we would all go to eat. We were starting to think about a more community-oriented, communal way of life—creating a family in that way instead of the traditional mommy, daddy, baby."

Also in the spring of 1966, the editor of the radical magazine *Ramparts*, Robert Scheer, decided to run in the Democratic congressional primary, on an antiwar platform, and Alice volunteered for his campaign. "I didn't really think I could win," recalls Scheer, now a syndicated political columnist. "I just wanted to force the incumbent guy to come out against the Vietnam War. I wasn't a politician. Alice was only twenty-one, but I put her in charge of our press liaison, and she was so good, so unflappable, so passionate, so focused. And then damned if our campaign didn't take off. I lost, but I did come close to winning."

Alice would bring campaign materials to the printers at the Berkeley Free Press, where one of the leaders of the Free Speech Movement, David Lance Goines, was learning the printing trade. David was studious and reserved, with an elegant, rather formal way of speaking. He had been a classics scholar, studying Greek and Latin, until he was expelled for distributing a course catalog "supplement" in which students dared to evaluate their professors. "And now, thirty years later," he says with a laugh, "they're required to do it."

Alice soon learned that David also bore the radical's badge of highest honor: He had gone to jail. He had served a month in the summer of 1965 for his part in the Sproul Hall takeover of December 2, 1964, and would serve another thirty days in the summer of 1967.

David also appealed to her aesthetic sense. He was a very good graphic designer and calligrapher, and Alice found herself fascinated by calligraphy. "She had such a strong, bold hand," he recalls. In the summer of 1966, Alice moved in with David Goines.

Alice and David Goines, 1967

Alice and David loved to cook together. "Alice would try anything," David says.

Sara Flanders, with something of a shudder in her voice, remembers their serving her "these big mushrooms with a snail coiled in them."

"We knew that you were supposed to make soufflés using copper," David says. "You were supposed to whip the egg whites in copper. But we didn't know the copper had to be absolutely clean, so we made this wonderful soufflé that came out grass-green. We figured it would kill us dead if we ate it, which it would in fact have done. So we threw it away and had popcorn for dinner. We had a fair amount of failure. We were willing to fail, which is absolutely essential to any kind of learning. Truly momentous disasters occurred on a regular basis, both in my artwork, which I destroyed, and in her cooking, which she destroyed. All those failures are, needless to say, not around to accuse us at this point."

David and Alice lived on the same block as Charles and Lindsey Shere. Charles was a music critic, a composer, and the music director of the notoriously provocative radio station KPFA, whose printing David did. Charles was a towering presence, intimidating until you realized how soft a heart his bearlike demeanor concealed; David's manner was mild and formal. They made a good pair of friends. Lindsey and Alice both loved to cook. In the fall of 1966, the four of them began to dine together often.

Lindsey shared with Alice a commitment to using only the best ingredients and doing her best at whatever she undertook; like Alice, she had little use for shortcuts; like Alice she was slim and delicately featured. Their voices were both soft, and softest when they were together. They were instant soul mates. Usually Alice would cook the main course at home, and then the two couples would stroll down the street for Lindsey's dessert.

"There was a wonderful Wallace Stevens poem that hung on the wall in Alice and David's kitchen," Charles Shere recalls, "right by the kitchen table where we ate our crêpes ['Cy Est Pourtraicte, Madame Ste Ursule, et les Unze Mille Vierges']. In the text of the poem, Saint Ursula is distracted from the cruelty of the slaughter of the eleven thousand virgins by the beauty of the radishes growing in a field. Alice must have looked at that poem ten times a day.

"Those meals of ours were truly composed, like music," Charles says. "I spent years at KPFA making record concerts, and I was always really interested in how you design a program—how this piece of music goes with that piece of music. That was one of the things that really impressed me about Alice. Every item on each menu had a relation to all the other items on the menu. When you spend a lot of your time composing things, then I think you develop a mind that always looks to see what the interconnections are, what the running threads are. I think that Alice's awareness of interconnection ultimately flowered in her thinking about the whole concept of sustainability"—the idea that any human undertaking should be part of a larger ecology, in which the use of resources can be sustained indefinitely as they are replenished by natural processes.[1]

Alice decided to cook her way straight through Elizabeth David's *French Provincial Cooking*. The book was about more than just good recipes. It portrayed a way of life—honest, elemental, caring—from which a tactile, sense-engaging way of making food emerged as naturally as a plant from the earth. Alice was becoming a very good cook, although she could still curdle a béarnaise sauce. "She didn't even try to save it," David remembers. "Just threw it right in the garbage. I was shocked. She was very demanding, very exacting. Everything had to be, within reasonable limits, perfect, or she wouldn't serve it." They developed a crowd of regular guests, from university intellectuals to a topless dancer, and, though Alice was raised loosely Presbyterian and none of them was Jewish, they also always "set a place for Elijah"—a Passover tradition of welcome to an uninvited guest. In fact, as often as not, somebody would turn up just in time to occupy Elijah's chair.

4.

MONTESSORI AND A DREAM

1967–1971

Because her semester abroad did not count toward her degree, Alice continued at Cal through 1966 and graduated in January 1967. That spring, she took a job at what David Goines describes as a "trying-to-be-French" restaurant in Berkeley named the Quest.

"I was a good waitress, I think," Alice says, "but in that kitchen I wasn't learning anything." She was already a much better cook than anyone there.

"It was an awful place," recalls Charles Shere.

That winter, Eleanor Bertino and Sara Flanders left for an extended sojourn in Paris, to be followed by Sara's psychoanalytic training in London. Alice herself didn't know what she was going to do. She did still daydream of having her own restaurant, but "the restaurant fantasy was still just that," says David. "A fantasy. Lots of people have dreams, and how many of those dreams are ever realized?"

Meanwhile, for the *San Francisco Express Times,* an "alternative" weekly newspaper, David and Alice began collaborating on a food column titled "Alice's Restaurant," after Arlo Guthrie's antiwar story-song. Each column consisted of one of Alice's favorite recipes calligraphed and illustrated by

LA SAUCE MAYONNAISE

it is essential to begin with all the ingredients at room temperature · beat together two egg yolks in a wide bottom bowl
using a fork stuck into half a potatoe with the flat side
exposed · beat in ½ teaspoon dijon mustard · ½ teaspoon of
salt · & ½ teaspoon wine vinegar · & ½ teaspoon of confection-
er's sugar · when the mixture is smooth · begin pouring a
constant thread of olive oil - the better the quality of the oil ·
the better the taste · stir vigourously as the oil is added · when
about ⅓ cup of oil has been poured · the mixture should begin to emulsify · continue · adding a sprinkling of vinegar every so often · after several additions of vinegar · switch to lemon
juice · it is possible to use as much as 2½ cups of oil · adding
lemon when necessary to insure the consistency & taste ·

David. In 1970, David would print them as a limited edition of litho-
graphs titled *Thirty Recipes Suitable for Framing.*

With Alice working nights and David at the print shop all day, their
time together was scarce. Late into the nights, they would cook together.
Alice fed David his first raw oyster. "Everything for us was about taste,"
he recalls. "I'd forgotten what real food tasted like. And I grew up on a
farm, just like Charles and Lindsey. When I was a baby, my mom squirted
milk straight from the cow into my mouth. We were discovering and re-
discovering, always exploring."

But the food Alice was cooking didn't live up to what she had eaten in

France. Was it a trick of memory, a magnification by nostalgia? That was unlikely, because Alice had learned by now that she was possessed of a preternaturally fine palate and a nearly flawless taste memory.

Much of the food that Alice had loved most was *la cuisine du marché*—market cooking. She had seen it in action many times. A French housewife would stroll through a village market, sniffing, appraising, thinking. If some farmer's basket of bristling, just-harvested cardoons struck her fancy, and a particularly nice rabbit was hanging from the butcher's hook, the Frenchwoman would devise in her mind a rabbit-with-cardoons dish and then shop for harmonious accompaniments. The little blue-and-white boats would come into port with nets bulging with dozens of species of wriggling sea creatures, and the fishermen's wives or mothers would spread them, still flopping, on tables at the water's edge: The smells of the sea and the fish and the cries of the circling seabirds merged in an indivisible whole of sensory felicity; and the housewife would compose her *bourride* as she paced along the quay.

In the big French cities, and in the luxurious Michelin-starred establishments of the provinces, such improvisation was either considered unprofessional or not considered at all. A serious restaurant had to be able to turn out a consistent menu day after day. It was true that the grand restaurants' menus changed somewhat with the seasons, bringing game and truffles in fall, tomatoes and eggplant in summer, but their rigid system could not respond to the arrhythmic, unpredictable supply of provender direct from the farm and the sea.

The chefs of more modest restaurants, however, the ones Alice had loved best, were in the markets every day, touching the food, smelling it, talking to the farmers and fishermen. A farmer might have only a half dozen ducks, but if they were really exceptional ducks, the chef would compose his *plat du jour* around them.

If Alice wanted to buy a duck in Berkeley, the only one she could get was a frozen-stiff Long Island duckling exactly like every other frozen-stiff Long Island duckling in the United States. But she soon discovered in the Chinatowns of Oakland and San Francisco ducks that had been raised on nearby farms being sold either still alive or freshly killed, with their heads and feet still attached, just as they had been in France. The Chinese markets were crowded and chaotic, but they had chickens that tasted like chicken, Dungeness crabs still waving their legs and smelling of the cold, clear Alaskan current just offshore, salmon spawned in the Sacramento River delta just a few miles north of Berkeley. There were live rock cod and catfish and sturgeon and prawns in tanks. The fish on ice hadn't been dead long enough to have lost the mucous sheen on their scales, the lively pinkness of their gills, the clarity of their bulging eyes.

"Ingredients!" Alice cries, remembering those first illuminations in the farmers' markets of France. "Sure, you had to know technique. But if you didn't start with great ingredients, you could never make great food."

THE QUEST was a nightly exercise in humiliation—impossible demands from customers and bosses, contempt from the kitchen, lousy tips, lousy food. At the restaurant Alice was dreaming of, the staff would be treated with respect, the food cooked with love. But she had no money, didn't know how to raise it, and had no idea how to run a business. Until she could figure all that out, she was going to have to find something else to do.

Barbara Carlitz had been the college roommate of Alice's sister Ellen, and had become a virtual member of the Waters family. She was also a Montessori teacher, and "I just had a feeling that Alice would love teaching," she says.

"And I did," Alice agrees. "Right from the start."

In the fall of 1967, she began assistant teaching at the Berkeley Montessori School and was enraptured. "Montessori went straight to my heart, because it's all about encountering the world through the senses. That's how kids learn best. The hands are the instrument of the mind— that was how Maria Montessori put it." The excitement of learning new things, growing rapidly into a new world, and doing so through sensory engagement—the Montessori narrative was a recapitulation of Alice's own life story. "Maria Montessori's great idea," says Alice, was to design a curriculum that accommodated the way kids were naturally, and the stage of physical growth they were in, and the emotional stage as well. She designed materials to appeal to kids through all their senses—for instance, these special color tablets or color squares. You begin with the most simple of matching—it's a little game where you're matching the blues, the yellows, and the reds. You have them all scattered out, and the idea is to put the two blues together, the two reds, and the two yellows, each one with a beautiful enameled center and a polished wood frame.

The idea is not to touch the color but to hold it by its side. You're not only teaching them this game, you're teaching them to pick something up carefully. All the games are designed so that the kids will be successful. If you say to a little kid, "Go pick up that glass," and then it's big and heavy and he drops it, and the mother comes over and says, "Why did you spill that on the ground?" the poor kid learns nothing. Maria Montessori would have a little tray of glasses in the classroom, and the child would touch the glass, and then he'd close his hand and feel how weighty it is, how big or little it is. You ask him, "See whether you can lift it up," and you say, "You put your hands like this, all the way around this side and all the way around that side, and you lift it up. And you bring it over, and you put it right here. And you let go." It's an observation that's not just with your eyes. You take a little broom and try to get up every crumb on the floor. You take your little tray and you put that back on the shelf. There's a place for it. You learn about everything in your environment. You become familiar with it. And you begin to really see what its value is.

The International Montessori Centre in London was supposed to be the best place in the world to train in the Montessori method, and Barbara Carlitz and her husband, Michael, had recently moved to London. Barb was teaching in a London Montessori school, and when Alice announced her intention to pursue certification there, they were delighted to put her up. But this meant leaving David behind. He was in the midst of several work and study projects, and he encouraged Alice to go ahead. He might come over and join her later in the fall.

Alice flew to London in August 1968. "I remember the time precisely," Barbara Carlitz recalls, "because it was just at the time of the fall of Dubček, when the Russian tanks rolled into Prague.

"She was working a couple of different jobs while she was going to school," Barb remembers. "She used to give me her money. She's always been quite bad about money. And she would say, 'Now, Barb, don't give it back to me no matter what I say.' Then she'd come and say, 'I've found the most gorgeous coat. Now, this is really important. This is a necessity. I have to have this coat. This is exceptional.'"

When the Carlitzes came home from a brief vacation in October 1968, they were astonished to find David Goines ensconced in their flat with Alice. "Hello," David greeted them, "I'm your certified commie creep."

Alice and David stayed at Barb and Michael's through Christmas, and then Alice went out looking for a place of her own. In Hampstead, her eye was drawn to a tall Victorian house with a turret. "I've always loved turrets," she enthuses. There was a sign out front advertising a room to let, and the room was at the top of the turret! The landlady was suspicious, informing Alice coldly that the room was for one woman only, no visitors allowed. The turret bedroom was barely big enough for the single bed in it. "There was no central heating. You fed a space heater with shillings. The kitchen was in a closet across the hall—a two-burner hot plate with a tiny broiler underneath. I didn't care. I was living in a turret."

In the London of 1968, no matter how "swinging" its international reputation, unmarried couples did not live together. David was going to have to find digs of his own. The flat he found was at least near Alice's. And thanks to the Carlitzes' broad-minded hospitality, Alice and David did manage to spend the occasional night together—and to cook together again.

"I nearly froze to death that winter," Alice recalls, "but I cooked up a storm. I was cooking for anybody who would come over. I'd go down to Harrods and just look at all the beautiful things. I would eat in this Indian restaurant down the street, having the prawn-and-spinach curry for lunch while I was supposedly doing my homework, and reading Keats and thinking about cooking. I loved London.

"And I loved the Montessori work. The thing about Montessori is that every kid has something that he's good at, and you just have to find out what that is, help him open that door to find what he has a passion about. Kids can find that out very early on, and it's what gives them a sense of confidence and gives them a passion about their life. That's what I was getting, too."

Alice and David decided to get married. The wedding would be in February 1969, in London. It would be small—just their parents and the Carlitzes. Neither the Waterses nor David's parents had ever been abroad. Barb Carlitz and Alice went shopping for a wedding dress at the boutique of the famous British designer Biba. "A beautiful mauve crepe," Alice reminisces.

But one day, David and Alice looked at each other and realized that, as Alice puts it, "Somehow we just didn't connect."

What had happened? Barbara Carlitz remembers Alice telling her at the time that it was David who "had gotten cold feet." Years later, when Barb raised the same recollection to Alice, "She looked at me like I was nuts."

Lindsey Shere believes it wasn't a breakup at all: "I'm pretty sure that the real breakup happened after she came back from England, because I remember talking to her in our garage. She was quite upset—it had clearly just happened. I don't remember what she said except that it was David's idea, because he was unhappy about something."

Says David himself, with a shrug, "We were like teenagers. We just changed our minds."

And Alice says, "David's exactly right. We were too young."

On the surface, it was just that casual. But their whole generation was deeply suspicious of established institutions, and not getting married was truer to the do-your-own-thing ethos of the time than long-term commitment would have been. Alice to this day is wary of personal attachments that entail obligation. Her idea of friendship or of love is the voluntary exchange of affection between independent individuals.

Alice and David continued to spend as much time together as possible. After Alice's Montessori studies concluded, they headed for Paris for two weeks of serious eating.

David flew home to California in midsummer 1969. Alice, meanwhile, found a new friend in another American woman studying at the Montessori Centre, Judy Johnson, and together they bought an Austin Mini Cooper and set out across the Continent, on a beeline for Bulgaria. Another friend had introduced Alice to Bulgarian music. "We thought we were going to listen to Gypsy music in Bulgaria, and smell rose essence, or something. And, of course, we found kind of a military state.

"Well, we got to Turkey, and we drove into the interior, and we hooked up with two French guys. They followed us in their little Citroën Deux Chevaux, and we'd set up tents together side by side. It was a great thing, because two women couldn't get into anyplace without men."

In an essay she contributed to a collection called *The Kindness of Strangers,* Alice recalled how deep an impression Turkish hospitality made on her.

We ran out of gas. . . . A shy, big-eyed boy appeared, and he mimed that there was no gas to pump. And we counter-mimed that we supposed we would have to wait. . . . Then, fingers pointing to mouth, where would we get something to eat?

. . . Solemnly the boy leads us indoors and into the back room where there are benches against the wall covered with beautiful old rugs, a brazier in the corner made out of an old gas can, birdcages hanging from the low ceiling, and a baby brother. Clearly the parents are away and the big brother has been left behind to babysit and turn away customers, and to offer us the imperative hospitality of rural Turkey.

The boy builds us a fire out of pinecones, puts on a kettle, and makes us tea. Then he produces a small piece of cheese and painstakingly cuts it into even smaller pieces, which he offers us gravely.

. . . He has given us everything he has, and he has done this with absolutely no expectation of anything in return. A small miracle of trust, and a lesson in hospitality that changed my life forever.

"We went down along the coast and into Greece, and ended up in Corfu. It was like the Garden of Eden," Alice muses. "You just went out and picked things off the tree. We tenderized octopus by throwing it against the wall. We cooked every day. We'd have this beautiful feta cheese with ouzo, and beautiful olives and olive oil. I'd never had olive oil like that. We never used a watch. The people had these big pig roasts, with everybody dancing. There was a certain poverty, certainly, but it was a beautiful way they lived their lives in spite of it. And then we went to Venice, and I fell in love all over again. I'm still in love with Venice."

HER MONEY GONE, Alice returned to Berkeley in the late summer of 1969, now fully qualified to teach at the Montessori school there. She moved back in with David Goines, in a new apartment he'd found on Channing Way. They seemed to their friends to be just as attached as ever. They just didn't want to get married.

A French couple named Claude and Martine Labro had recently moved to Berkeley from Vence, in the south of France. Claude, a mathematician, was teaching at the university. Like David, Martine was a graphic artist— as well as a serious cook, like Alice. A mutual friend urged a meeting, and Alice took to Martine immediately. Alice's notions of French elegance were somewhat general; Martine's were highly specific. Martine knew how to draw the perfect warm bath, just the right temperature, with a perfect little vase of flowers on the windowsill. She knew how to arrange the curtains so that the light filtered through just so. Martine had learned from her mother to search through the *marchés aux puces* for the thing unanticipated but just right, and now she and Alice began to haunt the Bay Area's flea markets together. Martine loved American patchwork quilts, and so did Alice. Martine loved antique dresses of fine and much-worked cloth, gathered, shirred, beaded, pleated, sheer-layered, softly draping, pastel. Alice began to wear such dresses. Martine thought Alice looked fabulous in a beret or a tightly wound cloche. Alice wears such hats to this day.

"I guess you could say I'm extremely impressionable," Alice says. "I've gotten something important from a great number of people in my life. Martine was very important in my whole aesthetic. She was very definitive. About lighting—that was one thing I got from her, an obsession about lighting. I also learned from Martine a certain kind of frugality. I'll never forget Martine serving a chicken for ten people. I bought one chicken for, you know, two or four. That's the American way. And she bought one chicken for ten. I was astonished that she could imagine there would be enough food. She made the most beautiful dinner, and everybody had plenty of everything. It was just that they had a small amount of chicken."

That winter, Alice and David parted again, this time for good— although they have remained close friends ever since. It is in fact a nearly universal principle in Alice's life that any man who has ever been her lover will be her friend forever. No strings, no obligations, no entanglement, no mutual responsibilities—such is Alice's ideal setting for the free exchange of admiration, attraction, affinity, love.

The late sixties and early seventies were the heyday of the French cinema, and the Telegraph Repertory Cinema in Berkeley was a favorite night out for Claude and Martine. They had become friends with its young manager, Tom Luddy, and early in 1970 they introduced him to Alice.

Alice fell hard for Tom Luddy, and for French movies. She moved in with Tom in his little one-bedroom house on Dana Street. She still cooked with Lindsey and Charles Shere, and now Martine and Claude Labro were joining in as well. Frequently, they turned out elaborate, multicourse feasts.

Dinner, cooked by Alice and company, would often be followed by a movie that Tom had brought. "Tom would show maybe a political documentary, or a Bresson film, or some old American film that we had never seen," Eleanor Bertino recalls. "Film was the art form of the moment. And Tom knew so many interesting people. Susan Sontag, Huey Newton, Agnès Varda, Abbie Hoffman, Jean-Luc Godard—Tom was Godard's agent in the United States. If they were in town, they would be invited over to the house. It was, like, this fantastic salon, in this incredibly modest house. Then Alice would serve Cognac and a little French tart in the latter part of the evening. She was completely obsessed with food by that point. I always say that the best year of Chez Panisse was the year before it opened."

Tom took Alice to see the classic trilogy of films written and directed by Marcel Pagnol (and derived from his own stage plays of the same names), *Marius, Fanny,* and *César.* "Alice just cried and cried, cried her heart out, she was so moved," he recalls. All three films revolve around a little bar-café on the Old Port of Marseille and its motley habitués. The Bar de la Marine is an island seemingly outside of time, with its own crusty ways, genial spirit, complex affections, and long afternoons of card games and ancient arguments. César is the irascible but golden-hearted owner of the bar; Marius, his passionate, ne'er-do-well son; Fanny, the lovely and innocent girl whom Marius impregnates and abandons. The emotional climax of the films comes when the much older Honoré Panisse offers to marry Fanny and raise the coming child as their own. The generosity, the sheer goodness, of Panisse struck a deep chord in Alice, and the easy familiarity, trust, and benevolence shared by the waterfront community reawoke her old conviction that a restaurant could exemplify those values.

Through Tom's friends Alice now had had a peek at the world in which things really got done and weren't just dreamed about. As she began to imagine the food, the lighting, the feeling, the communitarian ethos that her restaurant would embody, Alice knew, at last, what she wanted. The Montessori way—direct sensory experience, experimentation, optimism, confidence—would be the way of her restaurant. As for the practicalities, she had no specific ideas. She had never heard of a business plan. She had only faith that things would fall into place.

Alice had good reason to believe there would be a public for her cooking. Nearly everyone who had come to dine at the little house on Dana Street said that hers was some of the best food they'd ever tasted. Even Tom's French friends, not as free-handed with praise as Americans tended to be, called her a genius. The university, with its cosmopolitan and well-traveled faculty, could provide a ready customer base. Many other restaurants in the East Bay—and, for that matter, the majority in the supposedly great dining capital of San Francisco—compromised shamelessly on the quality of ingredients. At many, the service and welcome were indifferent at best. And the cooking ranged from occasionally competent to consistently poor.

Alice's first hope, an inspiration that had come to her in 1969, was for a tiny storefront in an alleyway off Telegraph Avenue, where she would serve the buckwheat crêpes she had loved in Brittany. But a businessman friend of David's did a projection of the best possible financial scenario and showed Alice that in so small a place—especially with people hanging out for hours as she intended they would do—even breaking even, never mind making a profit, was out of the question.

All through the spring, summer, and fall of 1970, Tom and Alice and Claude and Martine tried restaurant after restaurant "to see what we could learn from them," Tom explains. "Usually it was learning what not to do."

Then, in the little town of Bolinas, on the Pacific coast not far north of San Francisco, they discovered the Gibson House. It was a converted Victorian farmhouse, surrounded with flowers, where the chef—a woman—produced such exotic fare as roast duck garnished with nasturtiums from the restaurant's own flower beds. There were flowers everywhere inside as well, and patchwork quilts on the walls, and mismatched china and flatware, and, as Alice remembers the scene, "Nobody cared if you wanted to stay at your table playing poker all evening. I loved the idea of a restaurant in a house. I loved the flowers. I loved that you could stay as long as you liked."

By the end of 1970 Alice knew that her dream could be realized. There were long discussions with Tom Luddy and others about what to name the restaurant. Eventually, they agreed to find a name somewhere in the Pagnol trilogy, but they couldn't agree on what it would be. Then it came to them all at once: The restaurant should be named not after one of the major characters but after sweet old Panisse. Chez Panisse!

Years later, in her foreword to an edition of Pagnol's pair of memoirs *My Father's Glory* and *My Mother's Castle*, Alice wrote that she chose the name "to evoke the sunny good feelings of another world that contained so much that was incomplete or missing in our own—the simple wholesome good food of Provence, the atmosphere of tolerant camaraderie and great lifelong friendships, and a respect both for the old folks and their pleasures and for the young and their passion." There was also the charming fact that a *panisse* was a chickpea-flour fritter sold since time immemorial in the streets of Marseille.

There would be a restaurant downstairs, and a little bar upstairs. You could come for just a cup of coffee, a dozen oysters, a sandwich, an ice cream cone, a bottle of Champagne, a six-course feast. Chez Panisse would be utterly informal, anyone would be welcome, and the food would be superb.

Tom understood that Chez Panisse would have to be an actual business, requiring capital, planning, and discipline. "Among the friends who used to come over for the films," he recalls, "was Paul Aratow, who was a graduate student studying Italian at Berkeley and married to a woman named Connie. They had a little money in their family, and they lived in a nice house, while we were more the poor, starving types. Sometimes we'd also show movies at Paul and Connie's house, and Paul would cook."

At the University of Florence, Paul had learned Italian cooking from some of the faculty wives. "He made pasta from scratch!" Alice says. "That was unheard of." When Connie had a Fulbright to study in Paris, Paul mastered French cooking too. He had no professional experience, but he exuded self-confidence. He also owned a collection of French copper cookware manufactured for Dehillerin, from whom Escoffier himself, the father of modern French cuisine, had bought his pots and pans. Tom told Paul that Alice was looking for backers for a restaurant. Would he be interested in coming in as a partner?

"And I said, 'Why not?' Not knowing then"—his voice trails off. Paul persuaded Alice that Chez Panisse should be open nearly around the clock, like La Coupole in Paris, serving breakfast, midmorning snacks, lunch, tea, ice cream, dinner, and late supper.

Paul also brought in Rosemarie Harriot, who supposedly had some accounting experience. By the time the partnership came together, Paul's marriage had come apart, but he had a girlfriend, from whom he borrowed six hundred dollars to put into the deal. There were several limited partners as well—Alice's old family friends Barbara and Michael Carlitz, the rock critic Greil Marcus and his wife, Jenny, and other friends.

1517 Shattuck Avenue, 1971

There were also some necessarily silent partners—drug dealers. These were not the scary Glock-wielding gangsters one associates with the term *drug dealer* today. These were ordinary gentle Berkeleyites who happened to make their livings by supplying a network of friends with pot and other "soft" drugs. "Well, of course, they were the only people who had money," Alice says. "The only sort of counterculture people who had money. We couldn't get it from a bank, God knows."

Early in 1971, Paul found a two-story down-at-the-heels old stucco house in Berkeley. Alice thought 1517 Shattuck Avenue was perfect.

"It looked like a rundown hippie crash pad that had fallen on bad days from too many students living there," Tom Luddy remembers.

Originally, the two lawyers representing the partnership intended to invest as well, but at the eleventh hour they pulled out. Instead they bought the building, which was a solid, lawyerly, salable asset; they would then lease it to the restaurant, which was a highly speculative asset at best.

Alice's parents mortgaged their house in southern California, to the tune of ten thousand dollars, and put it all at Alice's disposal. Paul Aratow and Alice's dad insisted that the lease include an option to buy the property in two years.

As construction proceeded, friends came and went, hammering, sawing, kibitzing. Paul and his brother learned to hang Sheetrock, put in pipes, build a brick patio. Frequently, the workers' compensation came in the form of lunch, cooked on a grill in the backyard.

Alice thought that Paul's international training and seamless confidence would make him the perfect chef. But as construction progressed, the reality of the unforgiving hours of drudgery that are the sine qua non of a chef began to sink in. When he learned what his salary would be, his mind was made up. Cheffing at Chez Panisse was not to be Paul Aratow's career.

Alice, superb cook though she had become, could not picture herself behind the stoves. She wanted to be in the dining room—with people, personifying the open-hearted hospitality that she saw as fundamental to the restaurant's identity. She also wanted to determine the menus. She would certainly be in the kitchen as well. She alone would dictate how every dish was to be prepared, down to the finest touch of technique: how brown a particular sauté should be, how many shallots to sweeten a sauce, how finely chopped. She knew exactly how she wanted everything to taste, to look, to smell, to feel.

By the spring of 1971, Alice was seeing Chez Panisse as a gestalt: Food would be the center of attention, certainly, but the experience as a whole would depend on a complex of sensations. The room must look a certain way—casual, offhand, warm. From Martine Labro she had learned that light was the key. "Martine," says Tom Luddy, "was the kind of Frenchwoman Alice really admired—not some bourgeois Frenchwoman but an artistic one, not some snobbish Parisian. She was somebody from the south of France who loved the Berkeley scene, as much a bohemian radical as Alice but also very feminine, very artistic. And you know Frenchwomen all have a sense of light. The restaurant has to look good, women have to look good in the restaurant. My wife is French. They're all that way. Women have to look beautiful." Martine recommended that there be many small sources of light, and gilt-framed mirrors to reflect it, so that there would be a warm, seemingly sourceless glow.

Alice wanted every guest to feel welcomed and, most of all, comfortable. There would be no snobbery, nor fawning, none of the fussy formality that characterized most French restaurants in the United States. There would be both waiters and waitresses—at that time, a rarity. They wouldn't even wear uniforms.

"Just something nice and neat" was the extent of Alice's expectation. It would be some years before Chez Panisse would settle on the minimalist "uniform" that persists to this day: plain white shirt, plain black pants or skirt, plain black shoes.

In the flea markets, all through the summer of 1971, Tom and Alice and Martine shopped for mirrors, lamps, cutlery, china, and glassware—much of it Victorian, none of it matching. All of it, however, felt good in the hand. Covering the tables would be red-and-white-checkered oilcloth, not white linen. The tables themselves would be oak, and of various shapes and sizes. The chairs would be oak as well, straight-backed, simple. The oak floors would be polished and uncarpeted. The plaster walls would be painted a soft ivory. The trim would be the most classic of California woods, redwood. The windows facing west would be uncurtained, so that the intense afternoon and sunset light that glittered off San Francisco Bay would pour in unhindered. Alice wanted fresh flowers everywhere, with an enormous, blowsily spilling bouquet given a table all its own (a table, Paul pointed out, that might otherwise have accommodated four paying customers).

The ventilation had to be such that the cool breezes off the Bay would scent the dining room even as the warm aromas from the kitchen curled in from the other direction. The play of fragrances would make entering diners pause and notice, and having paused, they might then see how extraordinary the flowers were. Each bite of the food would be something to savor, something to slow the eater down. Every nuance of the experience would be sensuous, every detail thought through. The surfaces had to be such that voices were clear, while sharp noises were muffled. When she realized that booted feet on the stairs produced a bone-jarring thunder (heavy boots were big in Berkeley in the seventies), Alice started shopping for an Oriental runner.

Her most momentous decision was that the dinner menu would offer no choice whatever. "I wanted it to be like going to somebody's house. Nobody gives you a choice about what to eat at a dinner party." The menu would be new every night, seven nights a week.

Elizabeth David had exerted the strongest influence on Alice's conception of the individual dishes. Richard Olney, the American food writer long resident in the south of France, inspired the Chez Panisse approach of sequencing the dishes into a harmonious whole. In *The French Menu Cookbook,* published in 1970, Olney had written, "A menu composed of preparations that are not themselves French may remain totally French in spirit, for it is the degree to which a menu is based on a sensuous and aesthetic concept that differentiates a French meal from all others. It may be served under the simplest and most intimate of circumstances, but its formal aspect is respected, and its composition—the interrelationships and the progression of courses and wines—is of the greatest importance."

In August 1971, Alice started hiring. There were no job descriptions. Experience was not required. Alice simply knew that she would know who was right for Chez Panisse. One of the first applicants, for a waitress position, was Sharon Jones, who is still a close friend of Alice's. Alice, washing salad greens, didn't even turn around to look at her. As Sharon stammered through her qualifications, which were slim at best—a little waitressing in college—Alice asked her no questions, just listened. At length Alice turned around, gave Sharon a quick look up and down, made intense, searching eye contact, and told Sharon she was hired. Sharon wanted to work part-time, because she was studying theater. Fine, said Alice.

In fact, nearly everyone who applied for work at Chez Panisse was doing something else—poetry, filmmaking, graduate school, pottery—and Alice willingly made room for whatever it happened to be. If you wanted to work every other Thursday, fine. If you needed to take a couple of weeks to go meditate in an ashram, no problem.

The story of another of the original waiters, Jerry Budrick, is prototypical Chez Panisse. Jerry was just the kind of character Alice delighted in. "I was in the used fur coat business, just kind of hanging out in Urbana, Illinois," he recalls, "and this fellow came hitchhiking through from New York back to Berkeley. We stayed up late at night smoking marijuana and singing songs and having a great time, and he said, 'I'm pushing out to California.' I said, 'How are you going to get there?' And he said, 'I'm going to hitchhike.' I said, 'There's a foot of snow outside, and it's zero degrees! Are you crazy?' He said, 'I don't have enough money to pay for a ticket.' I said, 'Well, I can get us a car that somebody wants taken somewhere.' So I got us a drive-away GTO. Thirty-two hours later, we were in Bakersfield. We went on to L.A. in a Cadillac and eventually to Berkeley. He was a drama student at Cal. His housemates became my buddies. They were all graduate students in various departments there. I met this wonderful woman, and she and I took a trip up to Vancouver, Canada, together. She was going to see her boyfriend, but she ended up becoming my wife instead. We took a long trip to Europe and then drove across to India and Nepal and then drove back to Europe. We came back to this little town in Austria, and I got a job as a waiter for about a month and a half in the summer. I spoke enough German to get by, and they needed someone who spoke English. Then we came back to the Bay Area. One of my old friends was a guy named Bob Waks, who ran this cooperative on Shattuck Avenue called the Cheese Board.

"Well, Bob was walking down the street, and I was walking down the street, and he said, 'Where have you been for the last two years?' I needed a job, and I thought, Well, being a waiter might be a good thing to do. Bob told me about this new restaurant that was opening across Shattuck from the Cheese Board. So I went over there and got interviewed for a job at Chez Panisse. This was August of '71. I started the first night."

"He just had a style," Alice reminisces. "I think I hired him because I thought he was an Austrian waiter. He had this fancy wallet that folded out—one of those change wallets that European waiters have. I was so impressed with that wallet. He came for his interview, and he was wearing a black vest and a white shirt, and he just looked like a ready-made European waiter. So I hired him."

Alice's hiring for the Chez Panisse kitchen, following her instinct for who "got it" or didn't, harvested an impressive array of advanced degrees and highly trained intellects. When Paul Aratow declined the invitation to be chef, Alice chose instead Victoria Kroyer, a U.C. Berkeley graduate student in philosophy who had never worked in a restaurant but who had cooked Alice a superb audition meal. Alice persuaded her friend Lindsey Shere, with her Berkeley degree (like Alice's) in French cultural history and her faultless instinct for fruit, to be pastry chef. Charles Shere, the composer and critic, would work in the café upstairs part-time, tending bar and making sandwiches and ice cream cones. Most of the rest of the kitchen brigade had similarly high qualifications for jobs other than the ones they would actually be doing. Alice felt sure that with all those brains, what they lacked in knowledge they could surpass in imagination. What they lacked in experience, Alice would make up with sheer numbers.

As the days ticked down toward August 28, it became clear that Chez Panisse was not going to be ready. Construction on the upstairs café was halted. Alice and her partners were out of money. People were working on the basis of trust, or hope, or desperation.

"Well," says Alice's sister Ellen, "her whole personal approach had always been chaos. We used to say she spent money like Waters. She thought if somebody called her with a credit card offer with a ten-thousand-dollar credit limit, that meant she had ten thousand dollars."

Friends and the staff-in-waiting walked around Berkeley passing out flyers and got an enthusiastic response. The dinners that Alice had been cooking with her friends for the last several years had become a local legend, and people wanted to know if the food could possibly be as good as the hearsay held it to be.

On August 27, 1971, construction and painting began at dawn and continued far into the night. All day August 28, the half-panicked finishing continued. The fragrance of simmering stock mingled with the sharp scents of sawdust and wet paint. Carpenters were still nailing up shelves as six o'clock approached, amid hurrying cooks, jostling waiters, worrying backers, and an exceedingly anxious Alice Waters.

5.

VERY BERKELEY

1971–1973

As the first days and weeks passed, Alice was happy but not satisfied. The yellow-gold light shed by the 1920s Pullman car candlesticks she had found in a flea market seemed to nearly anyone else a marvel of refinement, but Alice didn't like it. "The light on the food should be white," she insisted, "so that it looks the beautiful colors that it is. I didn't like the whole idea of separate tables, either. I'd rather have had just one big table, with the food served from big bowls. But I also loved the idea of a couple of shills in the corner, a couple we'd hire to eat there every night and say, 'Ah, this is the best meal ever!'"

She didn't like the noise that shoes made on the bare wood floor. When the young French waitress Brigitte clomped through the dining room in her wooden clogs, it was deafening. That was not the only grievance against Brigitte. One elderly female customer complained that the young lady was quite clearly not wearing any underwear. Alice didn't care what Brigitte wore or didn't wear.

Above all else, what Alice wanted was that Chez Panisse should be warm, its aural atmosphere a lively but civilized flow of conversation punctuated by the sounds of popped corks and softly clinking cutlery. But she didn't want rugs; spilled food stuck in them. "I wasn't sure I liked the square-cornered tables, either. A circle's such a nicer shape."

The lack of choice on the menu was in part the product of Alice's desire to compose meals like music, and in part an expression of familiality. "But frankly," she says, "it was also a little bit of laziness. And ignorance. I really didn't know how other restaurants turned out all those dishes for so many people all at once."

In Alice's vision, Chez Panisse would never be grand, but it would never compromise on quality. The utmost in craftsmanship and effort would characterize its every creation. If the staff worked as hard as she did, and with the same meticulous care, they would be well rewarded; if they did not, they would not last. It was simple: "No corners cut," she told everyone. "Ever."

Ingredients of the quality that Alice insisted on were expensive. "I was looking for the food that I'd eaten in France. I was on a quest. I remember buying four cases of Kentucky Wonder beans and just taking the little ones out of the bottom and pretending those were haricots verts. I threw all the rest into the compost."

She knew nothing about business and didn't give a damn. If she wanted a certain ingredient, truffles, say, she declined to notice the price. Shaver in hand, she would stroll through the dining room snowing truffles left and right, no charge, "just to see the delight on their faces."

Bills were accumulating on the floor of the grungy little office, mingling with still-unpaid construction bills. Nobody knew what was coming in, how much was going out, and in whose hands or into whose pocket. On September 12, 1971, when the restaurant had been open for all of two weeks, Alice and her partners distributed a memo to the staff reading, in part, "We cannot meet the current payroll. . . . We have $500 to disburse, which is 10% of the payroll, so we are paying 10% of the wages due to each employee. Everyone will have to be paid off as we correct the financial situation. If anyone wants to return his partial payment, it will be put into a fund and redisbursed to other needy employees. . . ."

Alice outside Chez Panisse, 1971

"I had nightmares all the time," Alice recalls. "It was a train out of control, a wreck about to happen."

THOUGH CHEZ PANISSE seemed unable to overcome what seemed to be continual financial crisis, the restaurant gradually began to come together. The food came to the customers within a reasonable time, most of the time. It was more consistently good, often very good. The menu began moving away from three-day stocks and Escoffier. The La Coupole concept died unmourned. "Paul Aratow's idea had been for us to be open twenty-four hours a day. Eventually he settled for seven-thirty in the morning until two a.m., seven days a week. I was very insecure," Alice admits, "so I went along with it. But that didn't last very long. Nobody came before noon. Only dinner was successful at all."

Alice combed through her cookbooks every day, and her half-imagined conception of pastoral France was taking clearer shape. "I always came back to Elizabeth David. Asparagus vinaigrette, cauliflower soup, roast pork with whatever. It definitely was French in spirit, and kind of simple-*sounding*. Not so simple to *do*, in fact."

The first menu that anyone saved was that of Sunday, October 31, 1971. It was rendered in Alice's own calligraphy, which she had learned from David Goines, and in her own dauntless franglais:

hors d'oeuvres variés, including homemade terrine

❧

boeuf en daube provençal

❧

salade

❧

fresh fruit tarte

❧

$4.50

à la carte: desserts .75, coffee .25, tea .30, espresso .30

dining room open 6:00 pm–10:30 every day

For Friday and Saturday nights, the price was raised to $6.00. In Berkeley, California, in 1971, that was not cheap. The amounts equivalent to $4.50 and $6.00 in 1971 are about $22.00 and $29.00 today. But that would still be much less expensive than now: Dinner prices at Chez Panisse in 2006 ranged from $50.00 on Monday nights to $85.00 on Friday and Saturday.

Alice wanted to keep the prices as low as possible, but her native extravagance, and her insistence on the best in everything, sometimes trumped her generosity. When she didn't like the flowers, which she had been buying and arranging herself, she found the equally perfectionist Carrie Wright. Carrie's arrangements might include grasses, dead branches, shriveled berries, old baskets, strange, menacing jungle flowers, but they also spilled forth in profusion, expressing everything Alice loved about abundance, vitality, and finding grace in the unexpected. With Alice's devil-may-care carte blanche, Carrie's artistry was also stunningly expensive.

"We were always scrambling," Alice says. "The menu was decided by what meat we could get on what day. You'd know that one day the sweetbreads came in at Such-and-such Meats, and the freshest ducks were available on Tuesday and Thursday at some place in Chinatown. I was driving all over the place. And the bills, the bills—we just lost track. We were headed for catastrophe."

For help, Alice called on the only friend of hers who had ever actually run a business: "Gene Opton. She ran a store called the Kitchen, in Berkeley, one of the early fancy kitchen equipment stores," Alice says. "I knew her because I went there when I first got back from Europe. I was looking for little *baba au rhum* containers and little porcelain cups for chocolate mousse. She was the one who gave me Elizabeth David's book."

Gene agreed to take a look at the financial situation. "At that time there was a little run-down shack behind the house," she recalls, "with a refrigerator where Lindsey could keep butter. They also had a stand-up freezer back there. All just family-type equipment. There was a desk, and in the middle drawer were receipts from hardware stores and other places where materials had been bought. No one had ever sorted them or added them up. Or paid them."

Having given up the notion of being chef, Paul Aratow was acting as a sort of general manager, though everybody knew that no management decision, no matter how small, would be made by anybody other than Alice. "It was a madhouse," Paul remembers. "Nobody, none of us, had any real experience. We would have heated discussions about putting in more tables. Alice would say, 'No, it has this lovely atmosphere, not too crowded.' And I would say, 'We're losing money! We're turning people away! We could serve another twenty meals a night and break even if we put three more tables in!' She was very stubborn. And we were equal partners, so there was no way that one of us could do anything the other didn't want. Alice had a very pure vision, and she didn't really have the business sense to get the thing off the ground."

When somebody showed up with a bushel of perfect garden-grown radishes with dew still wet on the leaves and soil still clinging to the roots, it was the form at Chez Panisse not so much to pay for them as to make a reciprocal gift—free dinner, for instance. This sort of thing is what people in Berkeley call "very Berkeley." Alice and the waiters were giving away desserts, Champagne, whole dinners, left and right.

"There was too much, too many," recalls Claude Labro, laughing. "Too many friends. Too many service, much too many cooks."

Rosemarie Harriot, the third general partner, who was going to run the business end of things, lasted less than two months. One day in the fall of 1971, she simply disappeared, never to be heard from again—though to this day her name remains on the restaurant's monthly Pacific Gas and Electric bills.

"I knew it was going to be hard work," Alice says. "What I guess I didn't know was that I wouldn't be able to get control of it somehow. I thought, since we had all these people, surely we'd be okay—and because Paul seemed to know so much more than I did. But then, of course, he left."

"I had no idea how complicated it would be, and how difficult it would be to get help that would work. We were really floundering," Paul said years later. "Besides, I'm a filmmaker, and I had never intended to spend the rest of my life at Chez Panisse."

It's hard for Alice or anyone else to say how much the general craziness, including the blithe disregard of financial reality, may have had to do with recreational drugs, because they were so thoroughly integrated with the rest of the Chez Panisse experience. It was quite unremarkable for a waiter lofting a tray to suck back a last-minute toke before plunging through the swinging door to the dining room, exhaling as he plunged. It was hardly remarkable to the customers either, many of whom had arrived already ripped to the gills themselves.

Wine was popular too during work hours. The first time someone bothered to tote up the loss, in 1972, less than a year after the restaurant's opening, thirty thousand dollars' worth of wine was unaccounted for.

Gene Opton recalls, "Alice would say in this overwhelmed way, 'We just really need help.' There was no system for keeping track of the hours. When I said there should be a time clock, it was taken as a really mean-spirited, bureaucratic intrusion on the style that Alice had hoped would be okay. There was talk about running it as a commune. The Cheese Board was successfully setting up its commune across the street, which was a most amazing enterprise. But they understood that the people who belong to the commune have to bring in the equivalent of capital."

One of the most remarkable mysteries in the history of Chez Panisse is how this careless, sometimes intentional ignorance of fiscal discipline persisted through the years, as the restaurant's excellence and reputation rose and rose. It was not until it was nearly thirty years old that Chez Panisse began to behave truly like a business.

"Alice had no interest in these facts, basically," Gene Opton avers. "It's not the way she thinks about things. They were serving meals for four-fifty that cost a minimum of six dollars to prepare, and they had borrowed to cover the construction and hadn't paid that off. But my husband, Ned, thought they were a worthwhile undertaking nonetheless, and he said, 'Why don't we see if we can get involved with this, and make them a loan?' Part of the agreement was that I was named the manager of the restaurant—a combined CEO/CFO. We had a very formal document stipulating that all the financial matters were to be decided by me and paid by me. I mean, physically writing the checks. I was to hire and fire all the personnel. And a plan would be arrived at that would make the restaurant sustainable. For a considerable time I wasn't paid, but then eventually I was paid six hundred a month, as was Alice."

Alice signed the agreement, and then continued to do exactly as she wished. If she wanted truffles, she bought truffles. New china? Hire another friend? Give away bottles of Champagne? No document was going to stop Alice Waters from building Chez Panisse according to her dream. She did not own a majority interest in it, and never would. But no matter what the legal papers said, Chez Panisse, from day one, was Alice's, to be operated, populated, decorated, redecorated, reconceived, fussed over, fiddled with, and loved as Alice saw fit. Nobody else had her zeal, her imagination, her inexhaustible energy, her innate authority.

"If Alice got stubborn," Jerry Budrick remembers, "there was no way to shake her. She would just ramrod things through. But she always had a keen eye, and her palate has always been so wonderful. I'll never forget the time she was invited to participate in a tasting of twenty different foodstuffs that had been frozen. The frozen food industry was having this panel come to taste to see if they could actually freeze things and then claim that they tasted as good as fresh. So they had twenty of the same thing, some fresh and some frozen, and they put them into various dishes and disguised them. Alice got all twenty. Nailed them all."

People meeting Alice for the first time would be struck by her shyness, her uncertainty, her unfinished sentences, the childlike tone her voice often fell into. Her familiars, however, knew that behind Alice's diffidence lay an indomitable will. She drew people out, asked their ideas, freely gave credit for all she'd learned from her worldlier friends—the Sheres, the Labros, Eleanor Bertino, David Goines, Tom Luddy—but once she had made up her mind about what was right, what was best, what was to be, that was that. If Alice said the salad looked tired, Victoria knew not to argue. It didn't matter if it was five o'clock—Victoria threw the salad out and managed somehow to find something better in the hour remaining

Alice, Lindsey Shere, and Victoria Kroyer, 1972

before the tables began to fill. If Alice ran her finger along a molding and frowned, she didn't even have to speak—someone would come running with a damp cloth to dust it. When she moved the big vase of Carrie's flowers a quarter inch to the precise center of the table, someone would be watching and would get it right tomorrow. The cooks would mock Alice behind her back, plucking an infinitesimal leaf from a plate and sniffing, "Too much lettuce!"

SLOWLY, a modicum of discipline asserted dominance over slapdash passion. Lindsey Shere set the tone. Having grown up on a farm in Sonoma County, daughter and niece of food-loving Italians on her father's side, daughter of a pastry-loving German mother, Lindsey had been baking since the age of nine. The farm had a big orchard—prunes, walnuts, peaches, pears, plums, nectarines, figs, Sonoma's celebrated Gravenstein apples— and Lindsey had a passion for perfect fruit. Eight years older than Alice,

Lindsey nonetheless also looked like a girl, wide-eyed, quick to smile. She was consistently calm and meticulous, the epitome of cheerful discipline. Her domain was the little shack behind the restaurant. When it rained, she had to rush her tarts under an umbrella to the kitchen.

Lindsey's desserts looked so simple, and they were. They were also the first dishes fully to embody the elegance and unassuming perfection that were Alice's ideals for Chez Panisse. An unobservant eater could gobble down a slice of Lindsey's pear *tarte Tatin* without a thought, and might also find the serving a bit on the small side. The diner attuned to nuance would feel the puff pastry melting unctuously across his tongue, would recognize the heady essence of pear caught at its fleeting moment of lushest aroma, would sense the precise balance of the fruit's texture between softness and resistance. Gifted with palates of exquisite sensitivity—to a degree perhaps incomprehensible to those who do not possess such power of discrimination—Lindsey and Alice could communicate almost without words. *"Mmm,"* Alice would murmur over something hot from Lindsey's oven, swaying as if to faint. "Oh, Lindsey!" And Lindsey would merely smile.

Lindsey was farm-girl frugal. "If sixty customers were expected," says Alice, "Lindsey would make sixty desserts, and woe to the waiter who dropped one, or, worse, gave in to it."

· LINDSEY'S ALMOND TART ·

What I start with is just a regular short-crust pastry. Basically, flour and butter and a little bit of sugar and a little bit of water and flavoring—grated lemon peel or a little bit of vanilla. The crust gets rolled out thin and put into a nine-inch tart pan and chilled thoroughly. Keep back a little bit of dough for patching later. While that's chilling—you can make it well ahead if you want, and freeze it—the filling is made with three-quarters of a cup of whipping cream, three-quarters of a cup of sugar, and a teaspoon of Grand Marnier. Mix those in a stainless steel saucepan, and then put the saucepan on a moderate burner. Stir till the filling comes to a full rolling boil and it looks thick and bubbly. Then you add a cup of sliced almonds—unpeeled almonds, raw—and set it aside for about fifteen minutes.

Then you prebake the shell in the top third of the oven at about three seventy-five, till it's golden, twenty or twenty-five minutes. You want to bake it all the way, because it won't cook any more once it gets that liquid filling inside it. If there are any cracks that go all the way through the crust, here's where you should patch them, because otherwise the filling will just run out.

Put a piece of foil in the top third of a four-hundred-degree oven, because the filling is probably going to bubble over. Put the dull side of the foil up, because the shiny side can mess up your oven thermometer's sensor.

When you pour the filling into the crust, make sure that the almonds are evenly distributed. Spread them around with a spatula.

Put the tart in the oven and start checking after about fifteen minutes. At a certain point it'll start to make big, thick bubbles—which is what you want it to do—and if the almonds start popping up to the top, push them down into the cream with a spatula. Keep doing that until the top starts to brown. Continue baking till it's a really nice caramelized brown color, with maybe a very few creamy-looking spots, about thirty or thirty-five minutes.

Set it on a rack to cool for about five minutes. Then you need to push the bottom up and free the sides of the tart. If you don't, it'll glue itself to the sides of the tart ring. If you want to take the tart off the tart pan bottom, it's easiest to free it when it's cooled some more, so that it's thoroughly set but not completely cool. If you want to take it off later, you can put it over a burner just enough to melt that layer of sugar and cream.

I would serve it like cookies, basically, because it really is not a fork dessert at all. You want to pick it up and eat it.

You could serve it as a cookie, or with a fruit compote. Whipped cream I can't even imagine, or ice cream—that would be just too, too much.

Lindsey was as frustrated as Alice at the poor quality of ingredients they often had to settle for. It was during those first few months that Lindsey's husband, Charles, observed the growth of what he called "the hunter-gatherer culture of Chez Panisse," which still persists. In an essay called "The Farm-Restaurant Connection," published in 1989, Alice looked back on these days. "Not only did we prowl the supermarkets, the stores and stalls of Chinatown, and such specialty shops as Berkeley then possessed, but we also literally foraged. We gathered watercress from streams, picked nasturtiums and fennel from roadsides, and gathered blackberries from the Santa Fe tracks in Berkeley. We took herbs from the gardens of friends. We also relied on friends with rural connections. The mother of one of our cooks planted *fraises des bois* for us, and Lindsey got her father to grow the perfect fruit she wanted."[1]

This was something that no American restaurant had ever done. Chez Panisse imbued its food with the aromas of its locality, the textures of its place. The French use the word *terroir* to denote a food's or wine's evocation of the whole of a place—the minerality of its soil, the roughness or smoothness of its landforms, its heat or cold, the fragrances carried on its breezes. Alice did not know the word, but her food's expression of its *terroir* was foremost among the qualities that from its earliest days set Chez Panisse apart.

Tom Luddy knew that there was nothing else like Chez Panisse, and he believed that it deserved to be better known. His Telegraph Repertory Cinema programs and his work with the San Francisco Film Festival drew people from worlds beyond Berkeley. Soon he would become director of the prestigious Pacific Film Archive. "Most weeks," he recalls, "I'd have two or three great filmmakers visiting. There were the old masters—Howard Hawks, Douglas Sirk, Satyajit Ray, Akira Kurosawa, Roberto Rossellini—and young masters—Jean-Luc Godard, Werner Herzog. And the up-and-coming American directors—Francis Ford Coppola, George Lucas. Actors and actresses too. I always took them to dinner at Chez Panisse." These worldly visitors recognized that something was going on here unlike anything else in America—amateurish, perhaps; inconsistent, certainly; but nearly always delicious, unique, and fun.

There was fun behind the scenes as well. The kitchen's discipline extended to cleanliness, civility, impeccable technique—but it was never meant to hinder creativity or the high spirits that Alice prized. If a waiter, or even a busser, wanted to try cooking something, that was fine—though it would never appear in the dining room unless it passed Alice's unsparing review. Often Alice came running to Victoria, excitedly waving a recipe she'd found in one of her obscure cookbooks. Alice herself had never made the dish, neither had Victoria, nor had anyone else in the kitchen, but Alice would decree it to be next Monday's main course—a full-dress performance without a minute's rehearsal. The regulars knew to expect the occasional failure, and knew too that if they complained, the kitchen would invent something else on the spot.

Alice brought the Montessori ideal of learning-by-doing to every activity in the restaurant. "I always believed you can't ask somebody to do a job when you don't know what's involved in it. Say you're asking somebody to wash dishes. You can't know how hard that is, or what it's really worth, what people should be paid or how it should be set up, unless you experience it yourself. So when somebody new would start, I'd take them into every little nook and cranny. They'd have to go into the narrow closet to see how narrow it was. They needed to go outside and see how we took care of the garbage. They needed to go into the refrigerator and see how cold it was, and the big carcasses of meat. I wanted them to understand the things that the cooks were using. How hot it was in front of the ovens. How it all felt."

Years later, a longtime Chez Panisse employee reflected on the far-reaching effects of Alice's Montessori indoctrination: "Every single person who works here, including the dishwashers, loves to eat. Go to the Berkeley farmers' market on a weekend, and you see everyone from the restaurant shopping. And these people don't make a lot of money, but they all have dinner parties, and they're spending their money on traveling, and we're all comparing cheap travel notes. It's a common view of life, I think. It's really family-oriented. You just don't find restaurants where people have as many kids as they do here. And where people have solid marriages, and have been married a long time."

The menus for the week were posted every Monday. Lots of people, the clientele still being largely local, just strolled by, took a look at the hand-printed bill of fare in the picture frame on the front of the building, perhaps came in and discussed it with Alice or a cook, and made their plans accordingly.

"You ate what was there," Greil Marcus recalls, "and often it was something you had never had, or cooked in a way that you had never imagined. Very quickly Jenny figured out that the wrong way to go to Chez Panisse was to see what the menus were and pick something you thought you would like. The best way was to pick something that you thought that you didn't like or you had never heard of. We loved having people come from out of town, and taking them to this extraordinary place that didn't meet anyone's expectations of a good restaurant. It wasn't fancy, there were no pretensions, there were no choices, there were none of the dishes associated with fancy restaurants, or very few, and it was just thrilling."

The kitchen staff met early every afternoon. The first order of business was to compare what was on the published menu with what was actually in the house. If salmon was scheduled for Friday night and the salmon that had come in that morning was, in Alice's opinion, anything less than pristine—well, did anyone have a suggestion? A cook might volunteer that she'd seen some excellent halibut at the Japanese market, though it seemed awfully expensive. Alice never asked the price. The staff could eat salmon for the next two days. Someone might then ask, "Wouldn't the halibut go just as well with the chanterelles, garlic, and chervil butter we'd planned for the salmon?" Others would start chiming in. Maybe a vinaigrette instead of butter, to spike up the somewhat tamer flavor of the white-fleshed fish? Maybe shallots instead of garlic?

The new menu would grow through shared creativity and Alice's firm decisions. Alice declared the peas too starchy, but a cook had noticed some beautiful little purple artichokes in a basket someone had dropped off. There weren't enough for a whole course, but someone then suggested they be braised with potatoes and spring onions. Someone else had heard that one of the neighbors up the hill might have spinach in her backyard. The cook made a quick phone call, and the spinach arrived, just picked, at five. The main course had now become halibut with chanterelles, garlic, and a chervil vinaigrette, accompanied by baby artichokes braised with potatoes and spring onions and by a spinach purée.

Alice would write out the new menu. Sometimes the dish would change even in mid-evening, if someone—most often Alice—had a better idea.

At the end of each meeting, there would be a conversation to decide who was going to do what. Members of the kitchen brigade were not classified as sauciers and prep cooks and line cooks and grill cooks. All of them could do anything, or at least were eager to try. Sometimes Alice expressed a preference that a certain person should cook a dish to which Alice thought he was particularly well suited; more often, the cooks worked it out among themselves.

This approach set Chez Panisse radically apart from traditional high-end restaurants. There was no apprentice at a cook's elbow to sharpen her knives, chop her shallots, sweep up her spillage, wash and dry and steam her twenty pounds of spinach and hand-grind it through the food mill. Nobody had to stand at a permanently assigned station wearily flipping the same four things night after night. Every dinner was a new challenge. Certainly cooks pitched in to help one another, but basically the person who chose to do the halibut was expected to butcher it, make the stock, pick through the chervil, emulsify the vinaigrette, and clean up afterward. Whoever volunteered to do the spinach purée had sole responsibility for it.

So if Alice didn't like some tiny something about one of the dishes—and very often she didn't—she knew whom to talk to about it. "The spinach is sandy," she might say, and walk away. Humbly, whoever was doing the spinach would dump it in the compost, find another batch of acceptable spinach, clean it, and start again. Alice would taste it again. "A little lemon?" she might suggest, and that, almost unfailingly, would be just what it needed.

Friends of Alice's were guinea pigs for the kitchen's experiments, and in return they were often the recipients of her generosity. If someone had foraged a few morels, not enough to put on the menu, Alice would just appear at a friend's table and set down a plate of morels fried in butter, saying, "Just something to pick at." When Barbara Carlitz (having moved from London to Palo Alto) brought in her new baby, Alice puréed carrots *à la grecque* for little Natasha.

Alice never went so far as to say that the customer was always right, but she did bend to the reality of some of her customers' insufficient enthusiasm for the likes of sweetbreads, tongue, or kidneys. In November 1971, a little squib was added at the bottom of the otherwise still firmly fixed menu:

steaks and chops

Alice didn't like it when people rejected her chosen menu, so she usually didn't keep the steaks and chops on hand. If a customer ordered one, somebody from the kitchen would be hastily dispatched across Shattuck to the Co-op or to Lenny's meat market.

Change was constant. When seven nights a week proved too wearing, Sunday dinner was dropped. Alice opened a private dining room, then closed it. Toward the end of 1971, the dispiriting sight of people waiting two hours for dinner led her to accept a formality she had hoped to avoid: reservations.

In February 1972, after desultory carpentry and finish work through the fall, Chez Panisse finally opened a modest, kitchenless café upstairs, serving sandwiches, ice cream sundaes, and drinks till midnight. Downstairs, the dining room started serving an informal, modestly priced lunch four days a week. In April 1972, $2.50 would buy the *plat du jour*—perhaps poached chicken with aïoli, blood sausages with apples, or quiche lorraine.

Breakfast soon reappeared as well, very French, evocative of Alice's junior year in Paris—croissants, café au lait in bowls, *pain au chocolat.* In April 1972, concerned that some of her friends couldn't afford Chez Panisse, Alice introduced a cheaper weeknight dinner menu, comprising an appetizer and a main course only, for $3.75, while raising the three-course version by a quarter, to $4.75. House wine was 60 cents a glass, $2.25 a bottle.

In the spring of 1972, an aspiring young restaurateur named Tom Guernsey and his wife, Nancy Donnell, visited Chez Panisse, seeking inspiration for a place of their own. After hearing Tom's ideas, Alice hired him on the spot. Tom established a stylish Sunday brunch in the café, offering a set menu at $2.75. The first:

English chicken & bacon pie

❦

homemade Bath buns

❦

citrus fruit cup

❦

café noir or café au lait

A certain spirit was taking hold at Chez Panisse that spring. The kitchen was turning out delicious food, the service was gracious and precise, and the dining rooms felt effortlessly comfortable. The camaraderie and the sense of belonging among the staff were like nothing any of them had known in their lives. The feeling of belonging extended well beyond the employees, too. Not only they, but also the suppliers and the regular customers, seemed to be thinking of the Chez Panisse circle as a whole, a tribe, a family. Restaurant kitchens were notoriously noisy, uncivil, profane places, but the kitchen at Chez Panisse was orderly, polite, almost serene. Trust and charity and generosity were the norm. Even at the height of service, with everybody working at maximum effort, a newcomer, astonished, might hear:

"Could you hand me that butter, please?"

"Certainly."

"Thank you."

"You're welcome."

Not many new people, as it happened, were coming aboard. The staff in the earliest days had been much too large for the tasks at hand, and gradually, those who didn't quite get it drifted away. The core members of the *famille Panisse* could not imagine leaving. This was a family worth being part of.

Within the first year of the life of Chez Panisse, Alice had created a little world, and peopled it with like-hearted creatures, and now it was alive. After the last customers were gone, some of the staff would stay, usually in the café, to wind down, talk, drink wine, smoke some dope, flirt, maybe fall in love. They would push the chairs and tables to the edge of the room, crank up the rock 'n' roll, and dance. "I've always loved to dance," says Alice, "and oh, we did dance."

For all the fun, however, Alice was driving herself to exhaustion. One night, Tom Luddy arrived at the restaurant to take Alice home, and found

Tom Guernsey dancing with Alice

her in the kitchen sitting on an upturned pot, sweaty, bedraggled, head down.

"What's wrong?" he cried.

"I can't see," answered Alice. Her nervous system had shorted out, and, albeit momentarily, she had gone blind. This happened to her from time to time, and her vision would always return, so it was not cause for a trip to the emergency room, but it certainly upset Tom Luddy.

He waited until Alice could come with him to the car. He walked her up the stairs and into their house, and Alice, once inside, collapsed on the floor. Tom picked her up, undressed her, and put her to bed.

Alice had Sunday off, but for her it was virtually never a day of rest. More and more often, some friend of hers, or would-be friend, would plead, "Oh, my daughter's getting married, and we thought it would be a dream if you'd cater the wedding," or the benefit, or the kid's birthday party, and Alice, again and again, would accede.

Tom Luddy was going out of his mind. "Alice, you have to say no," he said over and over, "learn to say no, you just have to. You can't do it. You just have to say no, say no, say no, say no."

And Alice in her littlest voice would plead, "But I can't. I can't. They're such good customers, they're such good friends. How can I say no?"

Finally, Alice had to choose between Tom Luddy and Chez Panisse. No one was surprised when she and Tom parted ways—she was married to the restaurant, and both she and Tom recognized that she could never give him the time and attention that he (like any other man) required. No one was surprised that Alice and Tom separated without rancor. Nor was anyone surprised that they stayed friends, or that Tom and his movie pals would continue to come to the restaurant, often, down through the years. A pattern was being set: Alice's ex-boyfriends would nearly always remain close to her.

Kermit Lynch, a wine merchant and importer, and a longtime friend of Alice's, remembers, "Right next to my wine shop was a restaurant called La China Poblana, which served Mexican and Indian food. Sometimes Alice would come there bleary-eyed, so tired it was hard to get her out of the car, and then she'd drink a couple of Bohemias and eat some spicy food, and *bang*, she was bright-eyed and ready to go back to work."

Gene Opton and her husband, Ned, had continued to pay off the restaurant's debts as those debts rose and rose. Gene was reviled by some of the staff, who had a very Berkeley disdain for the squalor of mammon. But she did know what she was doing. Although Paul Aratow and Alice Waters were, on paper, the owners of Chez Panisse, they owed considerably more than the restaurant's net worth to Gene and Ned Opton. In effect, the Optons now owned Chez Panisse. And it was eminently clear to them that Chez Panisse was not, and was not likely to become, a profit-making enterprise.

IN APRIL 1972, Chez Panisse had its first review, in a mimeographed newsletter called *À la Vôtre*, published anonymously by Serena Jutkovitz in San Francisco. "There are so many aspects of this new restaurant that are almost touchingly admirable," she wrote,

> that what faults there are seem somehow more tolerable than they might elsewhere. Unfortunately the warm mood is disrupted by chilly drafts.
>
> The soup was called *purée de poix* [*sic*] and, though piping hot and interesting, suffered from what struck us as the only mildly troublesome aspect of the restaurant—talented amateurism. The soup had no pea taste, but was permeated with the flavor of—probably—Madeira.
>
> Our second dinner began with *hors d'oeuvres variés*, each portion of which was brought out and served separately from a platter, a charming though seemingly inefficient system. First came a delicious mixture of marinated broiled green pepper and fennel (!), then a cold lentil salad which was delightful. There were also hard-boiled eggs with homemade mayonnaise and a tasty substance on a buttered crouton that seemed like lamb marrow, but no one could identify it for sure since that particular cook had gone.

In May 1972, the Bay Area's leading restaurant authority, *Jack Shelton's Private Guide to Restaurants,* gave Chez Panisse its first rave:

Right now in an unassuming, circa 1900 wood-frame house on Berkeley's Shattuck Avenue, an exciting experiment in restaurant dining is being carried out. That is how I view Chez Panisse—as a vibrantly alive, ongoing experiment, not always meeting with un-qualified success, but never anything less than stimulating and often positively exhilarating.

Shelton's praise went on for three densely typed pages:

novel and diverse repertory . . . eager efficiency . . . relaxed friend-liness . . . a complete delight. . . . What other restaurant is willing to refute the lengthy menu dictates of the general public and offer an uncompromising, set daily menu? What other restaurant displays the daring of offering such an intriguing variety of dishes over any short span of time? . . . Chez Panisse, even if I found your cooking disappointing, I would openly admire your courageous stand! . . . Don't lose your marvelous aura of adventuresome experimentation, don't bridle the dining room staff's enthusiasm and camaraderie with the patrons. Keep striving to improve and to experiment, but don't change, whatever you do!

Exhorted never to change, Chez Panisse promptly changed. Jack Shelton's ink was barely dry when Victoria Kroyer quit. "I left to go live with a person I thought I was going to marry, in Montreal," she says. "It was one of those serious miscalculations of youth."

"I never wanted to be chef," says Alice, "but there I was. Luckily, I had Barbara Rosenblum, Victoria's sous-chef, who knew what she was doing."

As chef, Alice delved deep into the provinces of France for recipes hardly ever seen on this side of the Atlantic: *cou de canard,* duck neck stuffed with duck meat and foie gras; *jambon en saupiquet,* a very old recipe, ham in a vinegar-piqued cream sauce; *cassoulet,* the laborious white bean casserole with duck or goose confit; *aïllade de veau,* veal stewed with tomatoes and lots of garlic, the sauce thickened with bread crumbs; *ris de veau à la lyonnaise,* scallops of sweetbreads with a sauce of chopped hard-boiled eggs, mustard, capers, *cornichons,* and chives; *choucroute garnie,* the steaming heap of juniper-redolent sauerkraut piled with pork loin, ham, bacon, preserved pork belly, and an omnium-gatherum of sausages; and, with a frequency attesting to its popularity with the Chez Panisse crowd, Victoria's archetypal Parisian bistro dish *lapin à la moutarde.*

There was so much friction between Gene Opton and Alice over Alice's free-spending ways—and so much resentment of Gene by the restaurant's freethinking staff—that Gene's effectiveness was declining toward zero. Basically, nobody was listening to her anymore. As Gene's star waned, Tom Guernsey's rose. Everybody liked him, and his gentle manner was very Chez Panisse.

Tom's marriage to Nancy Donnell had foundered as Tom allowed himself to realize that he was gay. In his self-discovery, Tom seemed to blossom. Nearly everyone who knew the early days of Chez Panisse remembers Tom as the exemplar of its unique esprit. He was the person to go to when something wasn't working right, when a supplier was delivering late, when you were troubled, when you wanted more money, when you wanted out. "Tom was the glue," says Alice. "I was always out on one limb or another, and Tom held the center together. He was friends with the dishwashers, he knew all the gossip, he knew everybody in the restaurant. He had a great good spirit, and had wonderful taste. A really elegant guy. Very sensual. I was in love with him. There were lots of gay men that I fell for. Fritz Streiff, who came later to cook, I fell in love with him too."

"Alice falls in love," says Fritz. "This is the story of Alice's life. She falls in love with a dish. She falls in love with a lamp. She falls in love with a bowl of cherries. She falls in love with a man. Alice loves men." Fritz went on from cooking at Chez Panisse to being a waiter, a host, and ultimately an occasional ghostwriter for Alice. Introductions to her books, the phrasing of recipes, her speeches, even her letters would begin with Alice talking through her ideas as Fritz simply listened. Then he would write up the ideas. Then Alice would edit. Fritz would rewrite. Alice would re-edit. And so on till it was just right.

Alice soon fell in love again. "The first anniversary came, August of 1972," recalls Jerry Budrick, "and that night we had a big party. Everybody had a great time. At the end, it came down to just me and Alice, and Alice seduced me, right there in the restaurant. And we began an affair that went on for eight years."

"One reason the story of Chez Panisse is so complex," says Barbara Carlitz, "is that Alice was involved with so many of the men. And if she wasn't involved with them, then someone else in the restaurant was. Oh, boy."

"Alice's life is driven by passion," says her erstwhile transatlantic shipmate Tim Savinar. "At bottom, I think, it's sexual passion, which sometimes she lets overwhelm her and sometimes she sublimates in the food of Chez Panisse."

IN OCTOBER 1972, Victoria Kroyer's Montreal sojourn ended. "It didn't suit me one little bit. Either Montreal or the guy."

"There was a very unpleasant altercation when Victoria came back," Gene Opton recalls. "I said to Alice, being this terribly literal person—and it is a shortcoming, I am very literal—that if Alice was being paid to do the cooking, there was no money to pay Victoria to do it. We were still running in the red. We weren't anywhere close to getting out of it. I said, 'You're supposed to cook here.' Then Victoria and Barbara Rosenblum came to my house and confronted me. Victoria was quite irate."

"Victoria punched Gene Opton in the nose," says Charles Shere. "I wish I could have seen that."

Victoria promptly resumed her place at the stoves, with Barbara as sous-chef. Alice had won another round. But the Optons still owned the business.

Jerry remembers: "Gene was going to buy Paul out and get Alice as her partner—but a minority partner—and was going to set the direction of the restaurant in a different way from what we had established that first year, which was this joyful place. I went and I talked to Charles Shere first, because I thought of Lindsey as an important member of the group, and I could tell that she didn't like being ruled by somebody either. I said, 'Charles, we can't let this happen. Here's what I think the plan should be. It should be that the principal players in the restaurant become the owners, and we go out and find the money that it takes to pay Gene back out of this.' We needed like thirty-five thousand dollars to do that. I thought it should be Alice, me, Lindsey and Charles as one partner, and Tom Guernsey and Nancy Donnell as one partner, plus the chef."

"It was a great deal more than thirty-five thousand," Gene Opton maintains.

"Anyway," says Jerry, "Gene was pretty resistant to being bought out. But we convinced her. It wasn't easy, because she really believed in what she was trying to do. Here's a typical problem we faced. One of the first things that Paul Aratow had insisted upon, and one of the great things— I'm not sure it was so great, looking back—was that we had to taste the wines. Everybody should be able to talk about the wines to the customers. So we had tastings. Well, it ended up we were drinking a substantial portion of the wine inventory by doing that. You open a bottle from every case, that's eight and a half percent of your wine gone. Gene wanted to abolish that. And then there were the giveaways. That kind of thing was difficult to sustain, but I believed in it. It was a sharing attitude. We were bustling, and we didn't think of ourselves as starving, so we could share it."

"Alice had already made it clear," says Gene, "and I knew enough at that point, having worked with her for a year and a half, that she found me unacceptable. So it became a matter of just extricating myself without additional hassles or hard feelings. What happened was that when the new partners assumed control, we were given a note that was paid off over a period of time at a really modest interest, something like eight and a half percent. Which for a risky loan at that time was very low."

Charles Shere's take on the history of Chez Panisse is often one of amusement. "So we were exercising our option," he quips, "while exorcising our Opton."

The dining room, 1972

FOR ALL THE TUMULT behind the scenes, Alice Waters and Chez Panisse continued to innovate, to surprise, to dazzle. The restaurant's second New Year's Eve dinner, December 31, 1972, was a sharp turn away from the country dishes that Alice and Victoria usually favored. This menu was all Victoria's, and an exercise in pure classicism:

Pâté de poisson à la Guillaume Tirel

❦

Consommé royale à l'oseille

❦

Pigeonnaux farcis, choux rouges braisés

❦

Fromages variés

❦

Gâteau Moka, Paris-Brest, ou tarte aux oranges

❦

Bonbons assortis "Chez Panisse"

The first course was a fish pâté in the style of the chef to the French royal courts of the latter fourteenth century. Guillaume Tirel was also the author of one of the first cookbooks ever written, *Le Viandier,* published under the pen name Taillevent—now the name of one of the greatest restaurants in France.

The soup was a classic of nineteenth-century banquets. It was one of those things that may look easy to the untrained eye, and in many a restaurant may be, entailing little more than opening a can. This consommé was the culmination of hours of preparation—a long-cooked chicken-and-vegetable stock, clarified with egg whites and decorated with tiny floating cutouts of egg custard. At the last minute, Victoria added ribbons of sorrel, a lemony-sour leaf that grows wild in lots of places but was then little known in America.

The main course was roast squab (baby pigeon), another delicacy beloved in France but at that time seldom seen here, its flesh rich, dark red, and liverish, stuffed with its own innards and accompanied by braised red cabbage.

Lindsey Shere's glistening orange tart exalted the only decent local fruit available in the depth of winter. Her second dessert, the Paris-Brest, was a crown-shaped ring of cream-puff pastry, sliced horizontally in half, filled with praline buttercream, and sprinkled with chopped almonds. For the *gâteau Moka,* Lindsey sliced *génoise* cake into thin layers and interleaved them with mocha buttercream, the whole swathed in mocha icing. The chocolates that followed were all handmade by Lindsey as well.

"The price," notes Alice, "was the highest Chez Panisse had ever charged: twelve dollars."

To raise the money to buy the Optons out, Alice turned to a few of her closest friends—Greil and Jenny Marcus (who were already partners), Daidie Donnelly (also one of the original investors), Nancy Donnell (Tom Guernsey's ex-wife), and Barbara and Michael Carlitz. Henceforward, they would be shareholders in a corporation named Pagnol et Compagnie. Up to that point, Paul Aratow and Alice had owned Chez Panisse fifty-fifty.

(It may be more accurate to say that what they owned fifty-fifty was their debt to the Optons.) Paul now sold all but a 10 percent interest to the new stockholders, and with his retained 10 percent, he became another stockholder. Mary Borelli, whom Gene had brought in as bookkeeper, also bought a block of shares. The senior shareholders would constitute the new board of directors of Pagnol et Cie. They would be the people who ran the restaurant: Alice Waters, Jerry Budrick, Charles and Lindsey Shere (acting as one partner), Tom Guernsey, and "the chef"—an ambiguous definition, since Alice had been chef, and Barbara Rosenblum still was chef, and now Victoria was back.

"We decided," says Jerry, "that we had to choose between Barbara Rosenblum and Victoria Kroyer, and we chose Victoria. We told Barbara that she was, I guess, fired, for want of a better word."

"It's not like lowering the boom on someone," says Greil Marcus, the writer who has been a partner in Chez Panisse since the beginning. "Letting someone go is a process. It's usually not like Dr. Doom comes and gives somebody the bad news. But when we've had to, we have cut people loose, we have forced people out, we have bought people out, we have gotten rid of people with utter ruthlessness and boldness. And it's been the right thing to do. Sometimes I marvel at the way we have closed ranks and gotten rid of people who, despite their long involvement with the restaurant, despite the fact the restaurant wouldn't be here, perhaps, if they hadn't done what they had done, when the time came that they became a threat to the stability of the future of the place, we got rid of them."

Alice herself has virtually never been the ax wielder. Someone else would start with a subtle hint or two that Alice wasn't entirely pleased. Sometimes it took a few more hints. Alice's hands were clean: A major dismissal was nearly always voted on by the board. The dismissee, nonetheless, nearly always believed the decision had been Alice's. In many cases that was quite true, and the vote of the board had been just a formality. In this case, anyway, Barbara Rosenblum got the message. The generous spirit of the *famille Panisse* went only so far.

"And, well," recalls Jerry Budrick, "Victoria said, 'You can't fire my best friend! I quit.'"

Victoria soon found a job as personal chef to the director (and Chez Panisse regular) Francis Ford Coppola at his grand mansion in San Francisco.

"So we needed a chef," continues Jerry, "and we put an ad in the *Chronicle*. We couldn't believe it. We had, like, four people come."

Then came a fifth applicant, who would turn Chez Panisse from a very good restaurant into a great one.

6.

JEREMIAH

1973–1975

Jeremiah Tower looked, spoke, moved, and dressed like no one Alice Waters had ever met. His pale cheeks had dark pink rougelike accents at the cheekbones. His thick strawberry-blond hair was swept back from his forehead in a carefully tousled swirl. His head and shoulders were massive, but his hands and feet seemed tiny. He wiggled his fingers as he talked, his words rapid, breathy, florid, in an accent Alice couldn't place. There was something feminine in the way he tossed his hair back, something aggressively masculine in his forward-leaning carriage. There was in his bright blue eyes the jaded look of an old roué, though he was barely thirty years old. If Jeremiah had ever known humility, he did not betray it. He made sure Alice knew right away that he'd gone to Harvard.

What was somebody like this doing answering a classified ad for a chef?

Well, he simply *adored* food. (He did not add that he was flat broke.) He had been cooking forever. He had been taught, he said, by an Aborigine to roast barracuda and wild parrots on an Australian beach; by his mother, in Jean Patou suits and Cartier jewels, to dine in grand hotels and on ocean liners; by an aunt, a Philadelphia Main Line ex-debutante, to love art galleries, emeralds, and no restaurants but the finest; by the head-waiter at London's Hyde Park Hotel to slice smoked salmon paper-thin; by a tweedy English lesbian to smoke a cigarette in an ivory holder and drink gin; by six years in a British boarding school to detest bad food, crave fresh fruit, and love boys; and by a decidedly louche teaching fellow at Harvard to revel in candlelight, drugs, and Champagne. He had been making nasturtium sandwiches at the age of five.

Jeremiah's first job after graduating from Harvard College in 1965 had been as chef of the Horse and Groom, a pub in Surrey, near his parents' former house. He was soon sacked for forcing French food on the shepherd's-pie regulars.

He tried a girlfriend, and a farm in Massachusetts. On the girlfriend's family's island in Maine, he read Euell Gibbons's *Stalking the Wild Asparagus* and gathered mussels, duck eggs, and wild greens. It was there that he saw for the first time beyond fancy cooking to the indispensability of the freshest, most vivid-tasting ingredients.

A return to Harvard in 1967, to study architecture at the Graduate School of Design, offered another opportunity to *épater la bourgeoisie.* In his memoir *California Dish,* Jeremiah writes that for his assignment on public housing, he "decided on a multimedia effort: cooking, film, music, and drugs. My presentation was called 'Champagne While the World Crumbles,' and consisted of a film loop of the atom bomb going off amid footage of the worst public housing projects and urban sprawl I could find. The music was Lou Reed, the food a huge platter of marijuana cookies." He got his master's degree in 1971.

He worked in garden design, and wrote a memoir. For "the World's Fair in Hawaii that I had heard would be on the water," he designed a pavilion that would be half above and half below the ocean surface. In the summer of 1972, he drove with his pavilion plans to San Francisco, where architects turned him away. There never had been going to be a World's Fair in Hawaii, aquatic or terrestrial.

"On my thirtieth birthday," Jeremiah writes, "I was down to twenty-five dollars." He managed, nevertheless, to make himself a New Year's "feast for one": boiled garlic mashed with beef marrow on toast, accompanied by a bottle of Château d'Yquem, the outlandishly expensive sweet white wine.

In January 1973, a friend of Tom Luddy's told Jeremiah about the job opening at Chez Panisse, and asked Tom to introduce Jeremiah to Alice. Jeremiah had eaten there once, and remembered "the most perfect slice of raspberry tart I had ever tasted."

Jeremiah presented Alice with a sheaf of eighteen sample menus—omitting the desserts, which he knew to be still Lindsey Shere's domain. Among the dishes he proposed were *gougères* (Gruyère cheese puffs); *matelote à la normande* (a mélange of several varieties of saltwater fish, poached, then served with a sauce of cream, fish stock, cider, and Calvados and garnished with mushrooms, mussels, oysters, crayfish, and heart-shaped croutons); *cervelles de veau froides à la crème* (cold calf's brains in cream); and "haricot" of oxtail Alice B. Toklas (which despite the name has nothing to do with beans: it is a seventeenth-century dish in which the jointed oxtail is stewed with turnips, chestnuts, and spicy sausage). He also brought Alice an azalea with peach-colored blossoms.

Alice was charmed. It was his panache and his menus that got Jeremiah Tower hired, but the Chez Panisse legend is the soup that Alice asked him to taste and correct.

"I turned to the biggest aluminum pot I had ever seen, twenty gallons, full of a liquid purée of some kind. I stuck a finger in and tasted it. All it needed was salt, but I added a bit of white wine and cream, to show off."

"I, of course, immediately fell madly in love with him," Alice says. "And that was a problem. Yes, he was gay, but that didn't ever stop me from trying. He was incredibly handsome, and he had taste. I was in love with the way he thought about food, the way he handled food, the intellectual approach he had, and the guts. He wanted to make an artistic statement. You know how when you're in love with somebody, you really learn things in a way that you never forget, and you learn everything because you're so interested in that person? We had a collaboration, and I loved that. I would seek out better and better ingredients—he would say, 'Oh, let's do it with live fish!' and I'd find live fish for him. Or go out to Dal Porto Ranch for the little baby lambs he wanted. 'Go get me some wild fennel!' and I'd go find the wild fennel. He was a perfectionist, and so was I, and that's why it worked."

Jerry Budrick says, "I told him, 'Well, there's one rule here. I'm already here, and I'm Jerry'—because he was Jerry Tower. 'What's your real name?' He said, 'Jeremiah,' and I said, 'Okay, do you mind if you become Jeremiah instead of Jerry?' And he said, 'No.'" For Jerry Budrick there was an undercurrent of discomfort in this exchange, despite the fact that it came out as he wished; for Jerry Budrick was still Alice's boyfriend (though they had yet to live together), and her infatuation with Jeremiah Tower was plain.

According to plan, Jeremiah was allotted five hundred senior shares in Pagnol et Cie. As chef, he was paid four hundred dollars a month, which, adjusted for inflation, would be a little over seventeen hundred dollars today. Chefs were not stars in 1973. They were laborers. Jeremiah, however, steeped as he was in the lore of the tyrannical rulers of the French kitchen in the great hotels and manor houses of the nineteenth century, didn't let his puny salary get in the way of his grandeur.

His first sous-chef was a bearded, Brillo-haired renegade hippie and artist named Willy Bishop, who thought that anyone who looked and acted like Jeremiah "could only be an asshole." But Willy, too, in due course, was charmed. To Jeremiah's swagger Willy made an ideal foil—acid-witted, hard-working, hard to gull, resolutely blue-collar.

Willy had been a department store window dresser, a record shop clerk, a poster salesman, a bartender, a drummer in a band, a fruit salad maker, a dishonorable dischargee from the Air Force, and finally a Chez Panisse dishwasher. He would always be a painter. But he had soon shown cooking talent, too. Alice and Jeremiah both loved his raffish style. When Jeremiah's intellectualism and sophistication got "too Harvard," Willy—who had grown up in New Haven in the shadow of Yale without a thought of ever going there—was a ready, foul-mouthed antidote. For the first year and more of Jeremiah's tenure as chef, he and Willy alone prepped and cooked nearly everything that came out of the kitchen except Lindsey's desserts.

Jeremiah began his transformation of Chez Panisse immediately. Loud Led Zeppelin was banned from the kitchen stereo; opera replaced it. Classic stocks were simmering for days once more.

Willy Bishop and Jeremiah Tower

With a modest remodeling, the café upstairs became an extension of the dining room, adding some twenty-five seats to the fifty downstairs. In addition, there was a private room, called the *cabinet,* pronounced as in French, "cabeenay," with a table for six.

Jeremiah was especially fond of dishes that anyone but a French-born historian of gastronomy would have to ask a waiter to explain: from his first week alone, *poulet à la limousine* (chicken stuffed with sausage and roasted with chestnuts), *caneton à la rouennaise* (roast duck stuffed with its own liver, with a bordelaise sauce thickened with duck liver), and *pissenlit aux lardons* (salad of dandelion—"piss-in-bed" in French—with bacon).

Alice continued to write out the menu in French in calligraphy, but in late March 1973, in response to the perplexity that Jeremiah's dishes occasioned, that sheet now came attached to a second, in English, typed. *La flammiche de Flandres* could now be understood as "brioche cheese tarte," *aïgo bouido à la ménagère* as "Provençal tomato and garlic soup," *oeufs durs au gratin Boulestin* as "eggs with mushrooms and tomato sauce"—named for Marcel Boulestin, the world's first TV chef, whose program *Cook's Night Out* began appearing on the BBC in 1937.[1]

"Jeremiah would try anything," Willy Bishop remembers. "It was not that we were confident but that we didn't know better. When we first did chateaubriand, neither he nor I knew which way to cut the top sirloin roast. If we turn it this way, the grain goes this way. How much do we trim the fat? And one end would always be gristle and rind and all that. That was for the well-done people.

"Fuckups? We had a few. More than a few. I remember Jeremiah trying to make fish quenelles. He didn't get the batter right, and of course you're supposed to turn them with spoons and make these little kernels and float them. Well, they kept falling apart in the water, and I didn't know what to do, and he didn't know what to do.

"Another big disaster was a *brandade de morue*, which kept separating. We had hot towels under our mixing machine, the bowl that Lindsey used to make pastry. The bowl was big, and it was thick, and you could not keep the thing hot inside, warm enough so that it would coalesce—the cod and the potatoes and shit—and so it just looked like mashed potatoes. But what can you do? The menu is printed, and there's nothing else in the house, and there you are. Screwed.

"Still, he was such a perfectionist. We had braziers under the work-table, burning charcoal. He would throw spices or herbs on it, and we had to go around with this little mister with rose water. It was theater, in his mind. Of course, he was insecure about what he was doing, so it made him a nervous wreck. But showtime was showtime. Very disciplined. Sometimes we'd run out of food, because Alice would overbook. She couldn't say no."

"Jeremiah was Escoffier," says Alice, "with the whole extravagant, decadent thing. We used to go out after work and have Champagne and caviar, and he'd order the best, spend all our money. Little by little we dressed up the dining room. We were never able to afford very much, but we certainly went from oilcloth to linen.

"I believed in his fantasy, his myths about himself and about the food. And I sold it to the customers—the whole fantasy. Once we were doing grilled salt cod, and he didn't know to soak it. He put it on the grill, and I took it out to the dining room. The first customer said, 'This is inedible.' Jeremiah was dictatorial: 'Tell them to wash it down with a glass of wine. It's supposed to be drunk with red wine.' So I would go right out to the dining room: 'That's the way the chef intends it. Drink lots of red wine with it.' And who knows? They did or they didn't, but I made them believe that's the way it was supposed to be."

Chez Panisse was moving very quickly away from the cozy, easygoing model of Pagnol's Bar de la Marine. Not yet two years old, struggling from paycheck to paycheck, utterly unprofessional at every level, Chez Panisse was becoming a Great Restaurant in spite of itself.

Alice and Jeremiah began seeking out better and better provender to match their ever-more-ambitious cooking. They would rattle across the Bay in Alice's asthmatic 1966 Dodge Dart for ducks and fish in San Francisco's Chinatown. In the Italian delis of North Beach, they bought olive oil, olives, and anchovies. At the wholesale meat market, Jeremiah would plunge his arms into drums filled with blood and calves' livers, picking out only the blondest livers, as the butchers looked on both aghast and impressed. Fishermen would offer them "trash fish"—perfectly good but noncommercial species—with which Alice and Jeremiah would eagerly experiment. Foraging friends would bring in wild mushrooms from Mount Tamalpais, huckleberries from Point Reyes, a better egg from some old farmer's lost race of chickens, an incomparable plum varietal from somebody's brother's backyard.

There were now, and would be thenceforth, two formal seatings: For the first, diners arrived between six and six thirty; for the second, between eight forty-five and nine fifteen. Everyone seemed to object to what in California amounted to a choice between a too-early dinner hour and a too-late one. People are still objecting, but most seem to accept the system as just another Chez Panisse eccentricity. The homey provincial fare that was Alice's hallmark often gave way now to *consommé de veau aux cerises* (veal consommé with cherries), *bouchées à la reine* (sweetbreads, chicken, and mushrooms in Madeira cream sauce, served in a vol-au-vent pastry cup), *meurette bourguignonne* (freshwater and salt-water fish poached in red Burgundy with brandy and leeks, served with garlic croutons).

Ruth Reichl, who would go on to become the restaurant critic of the *New York Times* and editor in chief of *Gourmet* magazine, was a waitress at another restaurant in Berkeley. She remembers:

My parents came to visit my husband, Doug, and me when we were living in Berkeley, and my mother said brightly one night, "You know, I've read about this little restaurant." This was in '73, and we had no money, and the idea of going out to eat was really exciting. This was still in the days when if you didn't like what they had on the menu, you could have a steak. And my mother ordered a steak, and Alice came out and really tried to talk her out of it. I realized later that the steak was frozen and she wasn't proud of it. It was very interesting to me to see these very determined women facing off. Alice was absolutely determined that my mother was not going to order this steak, and my mother, having decided that the steak was more valuable than the *blanquette de veau,* was determined she was going to have the steak. Alice is not used to losing an argument. My mother, however, never lost an argument, and she won this one. For years, my parents sent me twenty-five dollars on my birthday for Doug and me to go to Chez Panisse. It was the one restaurant meal that we had every year.

Alice did find ways to assert her own, simpler taste. For the second birthday of Chez Panisse, August 28, 1973, she instituted the first of many special dinners that emphasized the restaurant's heritage in rustic, non-Parisian cooking. Her ex-lover and still-close friend David Goines designed the menu-cum-poster. That was also the beginning of a tradition of original posters for special occasions at Chez Panisse, many of them, over the years, created and printed by David. The menu, in Alice's distinctive jumble of English and French, read:

Cassoulet

❦

¹/₂ litre of wine & salad

❦

$5.25

❦

Also un film de Marcel Pagnol

Seasonality was not yet a Chez Panisse ideal. Alice was serving the wintriest, heaviest imaginable dish at the height of summer. The price was generously lower than the usual $6.00, but the very next day, regular weeknight dinners rose to $6.50, weekend dinners to $7.50.

On September 4, 1973, at the even stiffer price of $8.25, Alice and Jeremiah presented their first regional French special dinner, in tribute to Alice's beloved Brittany. The menu, as was customary now, was bilingual:

Huîtres
(oysters, on the half shell)

❦

Crêpes de moules
(mussel crêpes)

❦

Canard nantaise
(roast duckling with baby peas)

❦

Salade cressonière
(watercress salad)

❦

Fromage Pont l'Évêque

❦

Le gâteau Bas-breton aux amandes
(almond cake with almond paste and crème Chantilly)

❦

Special regional wines

More than one hundred people came, half again more than the week-night average. On November 27, 1973, the nightly menu began to read, CHEZ PANISSE: FRENCH COUNTRY COOKING.

Two nights later, it was Jeremiah's favorite region, Champagne, that was the focus of another special dinner. The menu was a long way from "country cooking"—and cost an unprecedented $10 a person—but the dishes reflected Jeremiah's researches in old French cookbooks, and they were authentically *champenois*:

Boudin de lapin à la Sainte Ménehould
(white sausage of rabbit, breaded and grilled)

❧

Truites au bleu au Champagne
(fresh trout poached in Champagne)

❧

La brioche de ris de veau au Champagne
(sweetbreads in a brioche pastry with a Champagne sauce)

❧

Salade verte

❧

Plat du fromage[2]
(cheeses from the Champagne region)

❧

Sorbets de poire et de cassis
(fresh Comice pear and black currant sherbets)

Properly done, *truites au bleu* are rather shockingly blue, and for the trout to come out that way, the cook must have not just fresh trout but live ones. A living trout is covered with an invisible, slimy film that protects its skin from infection, and that film begins to deteriorate within seconds of the fish's death. Perfect technique—instantaneous death and evisceration, the gentlest of handling—will yield a trout that on contact with boiling liquid turns bright blue.

The Champagne dinner's trout came from a hatchery in Big Sur. "We brought them back in barrels," says Alice. "We thought we could keep them alive if we aerated the water in the sinks in the kitchen." Jeremiah borrowed a compressor from a garage across the street, "but of course we didn't consider what kind of water was in those sinks. Chlorinated. So the trout were jumping out of the sinks. We were hitting them on the head and gutting them through the throat and throwing them in this pot of court bouillon. The whole kitchen was full of water and trout on the floor. It was exhilarating. Just unbelievable. And they did turn blue."

FOR ALL THE FLUBBING and seat-of-the-pants improvisation, Chez Panisse was setting standards that not only had never been met in America but had never even existed. What Alice and Jeremiah were doing resembled in many ways the French approach to food, but they were doing it without the historical precedent, the formal training, and the infrastructure that made fresh, seasonal food second nature to the restaurateurs of France.

In France, chefs had it a lot easier. Alice had roamed the markets at Les Halles in Paris, marveling over what to her were miracles of freshness and variety and to the French nothing more than how things were supposed to be. "They always had this local distribution system," she explains. "So much wonderful food came from nearby, less than an hour away."

When the restaurateurs or their agents began their daily rounds before dawn at Les Halles, the fish were gleaming with life just departed, skin redolent of Mediterranean reef, deep Atlantic, cold swift river, or alpine lake. There were greens just cut from their stems in the cool of the late afternoon; ripe fruit picked one piece at a time and laid gently in straw; whole infant lambs from the salt marshes of the southwest; quivering whole foies gras from Quercy; blue-legged chickens that had grazed their way slowly to maturity in the open pastures of Bresse; wild mushrooms and strawberries gathered in the forests of the Massif Central; little cheeses from

Burgundy, the Pays d'Oc, Alsace, Normandy, Savoie, a hundred, a thousand places, each cheese an individual voice of an individual place, made on a farm by a person with a name. Could Chez Panisse ever be what she wanted it to become, Alice wondered, in the absence of a system like that?

It was the same virtually all over Europe, all over Asia, indeed in much of the world, where farms were still small and "agribusiness" was unknown. "But not here. Not in Berkeley, not in San Francisco or New Orleans or New York"—not anywhere in the cities of the world's leading industrial nation, the biggest producer and exporter of food on the planet.

"Some good things you could get in some places," Alice remembers. "Great beef in New York, fresh fish there and in some other port cities. There were roadside farm stands in the summer with lovely fruit and vegetables. There were the Chinatowns and other little ethnic enclaves."

Fancy French food, of a sort, could be had in most big American cities—at the Blue Fox or Ernie's in San Francisco, Quo Vadis or Le Pavillion in New York, the Maisonette in Cincinnati, the Pump Room in Chicago, Locke-Ober in Boston, Antoine's in New Orleans, Justine's in Memphis. Restaurants such as these worked hard to find decent ingredients, and the food there could be excellent. "Ah!" Alice sighs. "La Bourgogne in San Francisco! I loved that place. They had Dover sole flown in, and Maine lobsters cooked live, and Grand Marnier soufflé with two sauces, and the most fabulous Swiss waiters that you fell madly in love with."

But at a good many expensive French restaurants in the United States, the foie gras in the tournedos Rossini might well reek of tin, and the truffles were likely to have no taste at all. One could get *escargots bourguignonne,* but the snails were canned. Some of the most popular dishes were flamed with liqueurs—steak Diane, bananas Foster, (canned) cherries Jubilee—triumphs of spectacle over savor.

Even then, the customer often had to surmount the untranslated French of the menu and the leather-clad *carte des vins.* The *froideur* of the waiters intimidated more customers than they charmed. Then there were the mysteries of multiple tipping: of the captain, the waiter, the sommelier, the coat-check lady, maybe the bartender, maybe a bathroom attendant, sometimes a cigarette girl—and, worst of all, the magisterial maître d'hôtel, especially if one preferred a table out of olfactory range of the toilets. More often than not, these masters of condescension were French, and, says Alice, "They'd have been out of work in a week if they'd acted like that back home in France." What was worse, these restaurants were staggeringly expensive—two or three times the price of a meal at Chez Panisse.

Good, honest, even splendid meals could be had in a few Chinese restaurants if a party insisted emphatically enough that they liked real Chinese food. A few other old-fashioned ethnic restaurants produced authentic versions of the food of the old country—though more often it would be Americanized beyond the old country's recognition.

"You could also eat very well if you were lucky enough to get in on a midday dinner at an old-fashioned family farm," says Alice, "where the ham and the greens and the okra and the peaches in the cobbler had all been grown on the place and the homemade bread was hot out of the oven."

And thanks to Julia Child on TV, Craig Claiborne in the *New York Times,* James Beard's syndicated columns, and *The Joy of Cooking,* more than a few Americans were starting to cook serious food at home. Like-minded people were finding one another, giving long, leisurely dinner parties with plenty of good wine (which was blessedly cheap).

If one was fortunate enough to live near one of the serious food shops springing up in the largest cities—such as Balducci's in New York's Greenwich Village—fine olive oil, a wide range of cheeses, artisan bread, and imported pasta could now be had. Their produce would definitely not have been organic, and it was as likely to be out of season as in. Pesticide-laden fruit and vegetables imported from Mexico and Chile were common, but at least they were fairly fresh, and the shops took good care of them. A few of the great old downtown markets remained—such as the Reading Terminal Market in Philadelphia and Pike Place Market in Seattle—where local farmers and fishermen sold their wares directly to the public.

In most of America, however, the prospects for good food were getting worse. The family farms were dying off. The children of the immigrants who knew what good food was were growing up detesting the old-country stuff. "Little family restaurants that might have had a few good simple things were being plowed under to build McDonald's," Alice says.

Even in the moderately expensive restaurants, portion control—a rigid formula governing the amount of each item served—was becoming the order of the day. Chicken Kiev and shrimp "scampi" could be had in frozen heat-and-serve vacuum packs, and an innovation called the microwave oven could have the food out the swinging door in a few minutes flat. Frozen inventory meant nonspoiling inventory. Mass purchasing and mass marketing empowered the rise of chain restaurants above and beyond hamburgers, fried chicken, and pizza, with national brands for every niche—Benihana Japanese steakhouses for dinner-as-theater, Red Lobster and Captain D's and their heaps of deep-fried seafood, T.G.I. Friday's custom-tuned to the drinking crowd, Denny's to the nondrinkers, Bonanza and Ponderosa for cheap steaks, the International House of Pancakes and its many colors of syrup twenty-four hours a day. All these companies used sugar and fat in amounts much higher than in home-cooked food. Crabmeat and clams no longer needed to taste like themselves; in fact, they no longer needed even to be crabmeat and clams, as long as their simulacra were well-breaded, deep-fried, salty, and hot. America's journey toward obesity had begun. "It just made me want to cry," says Alice. "But mostly I just kept my head down. It wasn't till years later that I really saw what was going on."

For people who wanted to cook seriously at home, the raw materials available were also declining in quality. There was an increase in the range of choice, especially of packaged, processed foods. Fruits and vegetables that had been available only in season were now in the supermarkets year-round—grown half a world away; treated with pesticides, fumigants, and preservatives; refrigerated sometimes for months; leached of nutrients and of flavor. All this had been made possible by the consolidation of agribusiness companies, which controlled growing, shipping, marketing, and retailing: Their flawless-looking but half-dead produce was highly profitable, in part because it underpriced any competition from local, small-scale farmers, whose produce might be less perfect-looking but was certainly better-tasting. The proliferation of choice was an illusion. "If you wanted a peach that tasted like a peach," says Alice, "you pretty much had to grow it yourself."

Such was the culinary landscape outside the charmed refuge of Chez Panisse. "When I traveled"—which was rarely—"I had to bring food with me," Alice recalls. "My life-support kit. A bottle of olive oil, a bottle of vinegar, a loaf of bread, a little bag of salad, and some cheese." She would not darken the door of a McDonald's, either for irony's sake or as opposition research.

She was well aware of the decline in how America ate, but as yet she saw no hope of changing it. "All I knew was that Chez Panisse could be better than it was." If there were no farmers in northern California raising chickens comparable to the blue-legged beauties of Bresse, perhaps Alice could persuade a farmer to raise some old, nearly lost noncommercial breed of American chicken. There was no bread to compare to Poilâne's in Paris, but, Alice recalls, "We had a busboy on the staff who decided he was going to keep making bread till he got it right. Steve Sullivan. And he did get it right. We're still serving his bread. We lent him money to start up Acme Bakery." (In its four Bay Area bakeries, Acme now has sales of twelve million dollars a year, producing several dozen kinds of bread and selling them to some four hundred restaurants and retail businesses.) There were hippies raising goats up in the hills of Marin and Sonoma beginning to learn to make chèvre as beautiful as the small-farmstead cheeses of France. But of course they never advertised. They had to be found. Alice and Jeremiah were finding them—farmer by farmer, artisan by artisan. "We were starting to reach outside our own little circle, telling them, 'You can do this too.'"

The Chez Panisse ideal was coming to fruition—French techniques pepped up with jazzy improvisation, bright-flavored and utterly fresh California ingredients, purity of flavor, simplicity of presentation, seasonality: This was the birth of what came to be called California cuisine.

As Jeremiah explored the little-known masterpieces of the golden age of French cuisine, and Alice began to codify her complementary doctrine of seasonality, freshness, local sourcing, and unfettered creativity, gastronomy in France itself was moving in similar directions. It is safe to say that virtually no one of culinary importance in France had heard of Chez Panisse, but "we did have some notion of what was going on over there," Alice remembers, "through what we'd read and what our friends could tell us. I'd still not been back there." The most influential chefs of France were reaching at once back into forgotten classics and forward into experimentation—just as Alice and Jeremiah were doing.

The early 1970s in France gave birth to what the French restaurant critics Henri Gault and Christian Millau had dubbed *la nouvelle cuisine*. From the summit of their epicurean Sinai, Gault and Millau proclaimed ten new commandments:[3]

1. *Tu ne cuiras pas trop:* Thou shalt not overcook.
2. *Tu utiliseras des produits frais et de qualité:* Thou shalt utilize fresh, high-quality ingredients.
3. *Tu allégeras ta carte:* Thou shalt lighten thy menu.
4. *Tu ne seras pas systématiquement moderniste:* Thou shalt not be inflexibly modernist.
5. *Tu rechercheras cependant ce que t'apportent les nouvelles technologies:* Thou shalt nevertheless explore new techniques.
6. *Tu éviteras marinades, faisandages et fermentations:* Thou shalt avoid marinades, the hanging of game, and fermentation.
7. *Tu élimineras sauces brunes et blanches:* Thou shalt eliminate traditional brown sauces and white sauces.
8. *Tu n'ignoreras pas la diététique:* Thou shalt not ignore nutrition.
9. *Tu ne truqueras pas tes présentations:* Thou shalt not gussy up thy presentations.
10. *Tu seras inventif:* Thou shalt be inventive.

The chefs favored by Gault and Millau—Paul Bocuse, Alain Chapel, Jacques Pic, Michel Guérard, Jean and Pierre Troisgros, among others—were rather selective in their obedience to the commandments. Bocuse could not resist antiquarian presentations such as bass stuffed with lobster mousse, baked in pastry sculpted to look like the fish within, and sauced with beurre blanc, which, because it was not thickened with flour, did not, in his view, officially count as a white sauce. Chapel still loved such thoroughly non-light classics as chicken cooked in a pig's bladder with copious cream and truffles. Chapel also stuffed a calf's ear with sweetbreads and truffles and sprinkled it with fried parsley, and combined in one dish morels, crayfish, and the cockscombs and kidneys of young roosters. Jacques Pic was among the first to offer a *menu de dégustation,* a tasting menu—he called it his Menu Rabelais—consisting of eight courses plus cheese and dessert. None of these was anything like "lightening thy menu."

But Michel Guérard decamped from what he deemed the toxically froufrou atmosphere of Paris to build a luxurious weight-loss spa in the clear-aired southwest of France, where he perfected his low-in-fat, high-in-vegetables, visually stunning *cuisine minceur,* as well as his own take on the nouvelle cuisine, which he dubbed *la cuisine gourmande.* The Troisgros brothers were dragooning kids to hunt for snails, encouraging local farmers to grow things to the restaurant's specifications, insisting on absolute freshness, serving only what was in the prime of its season, and truly not gussying up their presentations[4]—precisely the practices of Chez Panisse.

"Jeremiah kept up with all the new styles and ideas coming from France," Alice states, "and I loved all that, and I couldn't wait to try it at the source."

While the French press and intelligentsia debated the philosophical implications of the nouvelle cuisine, most of the rest of France continued along in its sturdy bourgeois way, with its tradition-bound, delicious dinners at home or in its thousands of bistros, where the same clear notes rang again and again—Muscadet; Beaujolais; just-opened oysters; calf's liver with long-cooked onions; sole *meunière*; roast veal; thin pan-fried steaks with a little reduction of red wine, shallots, and butter; a little salad; a little cheese; a piece of fruit. To some American tourists, the servings seemed penuriously small, the hours spent at table painfully long. Conspicuously absent from many of the bistros' menus, but conspicuously abundant in French homes, were vegetables, nearly always local, fresh, and plainly cooked. "When I was first there," Alice says, "which was what? forty years ago? the poorest people always ate well, always had a salad and a beautiful soup with beans and cabbage and lovely things. It always tasted good."

. . .

"IN OUR BEST MOMENTS," Alice recalls, "Jeremiah would think of a menu, and I'd say, 'Well, I think maybe this would be better.' And he'd say, 'Oh, yeah, let's do it like that.' And then I'd say, 'Oh, God, you need to put a vegetable with that because *dadadada*.' It was like that all the time. It was a collaboration. It was fun for us. I was in the dining room, and I knew what things people were really liking, or how they were reacting to special little things that we'd try for just a few people, and I would feed that back to him. Sometimes I'd bring in something that I'd tasted, or some recipe I'd found, and Jeremiah and I would work through it, making it better, trying this and that accompaniment, till we were both satisfied. And we were both not easily satisfied. It was important for the sort of spiritual life of the restaurant that we be a little daring, that we not get too set in a path."

Alice and Jeremiah were attempting a difficult, even paradoxical expansion of the Chez Panisse experience: They wanted to maintain the restaurant's easy informality, its gemütlichkeit, and now to that they wanted to add a sense of festivity, of occasion—and more profit. That meant more special dinners, more-breathtaking cooking, more panache. "We cooked a wild boar outside, on the sidewalk in front of the restaurant, that we had gotten from Big Sur," Alice explains. "Jeremiah had some friends down there, and somebody had hunted this huge object. I think it was about four hundred pounds, and somehow we spitted this thing, and then it started to rain, so we rigged up a tent. The spit was turned by hand. It did draw quite a crowd."

Festivity also meant special consideration for the most festive members of the Chez Panisse circle. Tom Luddy's movie people were especially valuable. No matter how crowded the restaurant, no matter how late the hour, Alice would always have a table for them. The clientele was subtly changing. Chez Panisse was becoming chic.

"They were all so sexy," Ruth Reichl remembers. "Jerry Budrick was very sexy. I had a huge crush on him. He was really arrogant—and delicious. There were all these really good-looking people at the restaurant. In many ways, Jeremiah and Jerry were very similar—you know, bad boys.

Jeremiah Tower

And Tom Luddy also. The Swallow [a collective restaurant where Ruth worked as a waitress] was in the Pacific Film Archive, and Tom would come swanning through with Martin Scorsese and all these people with a sort of entourage. People who weren't important, he would bring to the Swallow. When it was someone important, you'd know they were going to Chez Panisse. We were earnest, Earth shoe. They were glamorous."

Jeremiah was feeling mounting pressure—much of it self-generated, but no less stressful for that. "Chefs have a reputation for bad behavior," he writes in his memoir *California Dish,* "in part because they have to play so hard to counteract the daily pileup of tension and fatigue. . . . For many of us, it was about how many oysters and great wines we could fit into a few hours and still get some rest before the work began again. . . . The mental onslaught was never-ending, even in sleep. . . . And drugs were easier to organize than sex, unless it was casual, which usually meant with one another."

Eleanor Bertino recalls, "Lindsey, of course, had this little shed in the back, and she'd go home at four o'clock. So at night there was nobody working there. I think there was a bed in there at one point."

During the week, living on oysters, wine, and the tiny bites he would taste at the restaurant, Jeremiah was half-starving himself. Then on his one night off, he would pig out at Trader Vic's in Oakland or Vanessi's in San Francisco, often till very late. On the verge of cracking up one night at Chez Panisse in January 1974, he suddenly burst into tears and announced that he had to have a vacation. He promptly fled to the Caribbean, not specifying a date of return.

It was just then that Anne Isaak appeared. (Here again is an example of the curious pattern in Alice's and others' recollections of the history of Chez Panisse. The right people seem simply to "appear" at just the right moment. It can be presumed that people who might have been right happened to appear at wrong moments, and hence never entered the history.) Anne had worked in professional kitchens—including a good one, with highly competent Chinese cooks, and also "the worst kitchen in the world, Elaine's in New York." Everything about Chez Panisse appealed to her. When she went to ask for a job,

there was nobody in the restaurant, and I went into the kitchen. There was this woman at a large sink, cleaning trout. Alice. She said, "Well, I'm cooking right now, because Jeremiah is away, but we're going to be trying people out for a sous-chef job soon." I went for a tryout, and she hired me just like that. She said, "The problem is, I'm only here temporarily, and you're going to be working with Jeremiah, and he doesn't like women."

My first job was to chop parsley, and I had had this great experience with the Chinese, learning how to chop parsley with two knives. No one was professional at Chez Panisse, so they were very careful about picking parsley off the stems, and everything was done kind of slow, and nobody had their own knives then. But I had my own knives, and they were sharp, unlike all the other knives in that kitchen. So I got all the parsley together and I went *hrruuummmm*. That gave them the impression that I knew something.

While Alice and Willy and Anne Isaak manned the stoves in Jeremiah's absence, Jeremiah's Caribbean vacation—with margaritas delivered to his hammock on the quarter hour, as he has recalled it—set his brain sizzling with new ideas. The regional French dinners were popular, and profitable, but he wanted now to build festival dinners on the work of the historic chefs of France—Escoffier, Prosper Montagné, Henri-Paul Pellaprat, and Urbain Dubois—and then lead up to the present with the British apostle of Mediterranean simplicity Elizabeth David and the American Richard Olney, who also espoused a style of French cooking considerably pared down from the liver-challenging classics Jeremiah had tended to favor.

After a few more weeks, Jeremiah came back to Chez Panisse eager to be doing new things. Elizabeth David and Richard Olney were all very well, but what really turned him on was when he could "go big, out-landish." For the hundredth birthday of Gertrude Stein, February 3, 1974, he took both text and recipes from *The Alice B. Toklas Cookbook* (Toklas was Stein's lifelong companion, and a San Francisco native). Willy Bishop designed the menu card, portraying Gertrude Stein as a stove with Alice B. Toklas in her oven:

Dining. Dining is west. **Mushroom sandwiches**
upstairs.
Eating. Eat ing.
Single fish. Single fish single fish single fish.
Sole mousse with Virgin Sauce. I wrote it for
America.

Everyone thought that the syringe was a whimsy.
Mousse and mountain and a quiver, a quaint statue
and a pain in the exterior and silence. **Gigot de la
Clinique** a cake, a real salve made of mutton and

liquor, a specially retained rinsing and an
established cork and brazing

Wild rice salad. She said it would suit her.

Cake cast in went to be and needles wine needles
are such. Needles are. **A Tender Tart.** That
doves each have a heart.

Nobody ever followed Ida. What was the use of
following Ida.

Cream Perfect Love.

Though tempted, Jeremiah refrained from putting hashish in the after-dinner cookies.

He had been avoiding marijuana since an incident involving the new, much more powerful pot coming onto the market. Egged on by the waiters, he had taken one puff from a fat joint. He then walked through the swinging doors with the intention of joining Alice and eight food writers at a table, but he made it only three steps before passing out cold. A quick glass of Champagne, administered by Willy Bishop, revived the hopelessly stoned chef.

For her birthday, in April 1974, Alice took off two weeks, to return, at last, to Europe. "That was when I really started to get it about French food, I think. I realized how relentless and how careful the scrutiny of everything was in the best places—and I don't mean necessarily the most expensive places. It was about caring."

Lindsey and Charles Shere went to Europe for their first time in the summer of 1974. For six weeks they immersed themselves in every manner of French restaurant, from the plainest to the fanciest. "Alice felt that people should be able to take these trips, to have time off to educate themselves. And it was an eye-opener for me," says Lindsey. "We went to the Auberge of the Flowering Hearth for the first time, and we went back and back and back. The cookbook that Roy Andries de Groot wrote based on the food at the Auberge was a tremendous influence on Chez Panisse. They were cooking regionally and seasonally before we were." The inn is no more, but the book *The Auberge of the Flowering Hearth,* while not well known, is a masterpiece. It informs the cooking of Chez Panisse to this day.

THEN CAME THE RESTAURANT'S first glimmer of national recognition. Marion Cunningham, then a food writer for the *San Francisco Chronicle,* brought James Beard to the restaurant. "And he," Alice recalls, "was the first one to say that this was really not like anything else."

"We went for lunch," Marion remembers, "and the first sentence Jim said was, 'This is not a real restaurant, Marion.' Meaning it was a home that took in money for food."

Characteristically, Beard's praise in his syndicated column was acidulated by a dash of reproof: "Recently, while dining in a fascinating small restaurant called Chez Panisse, in Berkeley, California, I had a perfectly cooked duck with green peppercorns, a lovely blend of flavors—but the peppercorns were floating around in the sauce. Had the peppercorns been crushed to a paste before being added, you would have savored their special flavor without having to bite into the peppercorns themselves, which is not as pleasant to the palate."

The complexity and the difficulty of Jeremiah's food were on a steep upward trajectory, and so was the labor required to produce it. Jeremiah and his staff were often at the brink of exhaustion. Then, in 1974, an effective (or so it was thought at the time) antidote to the pressure arrived at Chez Panisse: "It was cocaine that became the fuel for the energy that changed the way America dines," Jeremiah writes in his memoir.

"After work, we would drink until the bars closed, and then I would go home and be able to paint and go to bed at six or seven and go to work at one or two," recalls Willy Bishop. "And I was turning forty at the time, and they were all under thirty. I think the exuberance overtook everyone, and with coke you were able to do things you couldn't really do. Nothing was daunting.

"On Sundays, it was always slow. There were just three of us. Jeremiah and me and this boy whom Jeremiah was in love with. A pretty. He went off to Reed College in Oregon. We were doing nitrous oxide, the chargers. You could pass out. That kid fell down once. After that, he didn't do it anymore. I remember the time one of the busboys came through the door and fell down. He had stuffed opium up his ass. Too much. He just fell right down. That's the way to do it—it bypasses the digestive system, and that way it doesn't make you nauseated. The mucous membranes absorb it.

"We'd do acid on Sundays too. These were purple barrels. The purple barrel is a mild acid like a purple tab or windowpane. It was more like MDA [3,4-methylenedioxyamphetamine, a stimulant that made people so euphoric, and so benignant, that it was called the love drug]. Everything is good and happy, and you just work."

"You've got to remember that drugs were everywhere in those days, especially in the restaurant business," Alice asserts, "and we were no different. Actually, we were probably a little more disciplined, most of us. We all got into it, some more than others, but that period was very short. Certainly for me it was very short."

The year 1974 also brought Chez Panisse its first house wine, of an unofficial sort. Jerry Budrick had been making banana wine at home for several years: "It was quite good, light and fruity, shall we say, and almost free." That fall, a friend of his from Amador County suggested that Jerry try making real wine. The next thing he knew, his Amador buddy had presented him with five hundred pounds of zinfandel grapes.

"We had a big garbage can and some bricks that went down in the bottom of it, and then another garbage can at the bottom with holes drilled in it," Jerry explains. "My feet were too big, but Alice's were just fine. So she crushed, and we made wine from these five hundred pounds of grapes. And it was delicious. We let it age for a month or two, and then we bottled it. I used to bring a bottle when I knew some dignitaries were coming to the restaurant, some wine people, just to fool them. Darrell Corti is a famous wine guy from Sacramento. I said, 'I'd like you to try this wine. I'm not going to tell you what it is, you tell me.' He swirled it around, did the whole thing, and he said, 'Well, this is an Amador County zinfandel, and I've never had it before.' I said, 'How did you do that?' I was blown away. We've been friends ever since."

FRIENDSHIP, romance, casual sex, and serious commitment swirled through the population of Chez Panisse, in such complexity that sometimes the categories were hard to distinguish. Alice was still semiofficially the companion of Jerry Budrick, though not his cohabitant. "We never got to live together," Jerry recalls. "First I had a house with my wife in it, and that wouldn't do. Then in '74 I got divorced, and I bought another house, a fixer-upper that was in such disrepair that Alice couldn't stand it. She just wouldn't live there with me. She lived in lots of places. She lived in a garage for a while."

"Well, I mean, I did fix it up," Alice says.

"She lived in a ship captain's mansion."

"With a turret!" Alice exclaims. "Just like London, but much grander. It was a sensational house, historic. I had the whole first floor."

"Then there was that house on Delaware that she ended up sharing with Jeremiah," Jerry recalls, pointedly.

"Jeremiah wasn't my boyfriend," says Alice. "It was a very odd thing. I mean, no. He was interested in every young guy at the restaurant. But he indulged me to a certain extent. We always danced together. We always went out at night. We went on trips together. We had this whole romantic way of being together. I always wanted to dance with Jeremiah."

Alice and Jeremiah traveled to Nice, and drank Krug Champagne, he writes, "on the terrace of Venice's Gritti Palace in the moonlight." They were perfectly, dangerously balanced—in their level of aesthetic refinement, in their ambitions, and in their desire to be in charge of Chez Panisse.

Rivalry, romance, Champagne—whatever the Alice-Jeremiah elixir was concocted of, it was powerful. In those halcyon days, they seemed to see no limit to what they could accomplish together. In February 1975, Chez Panisse mounted a three-week festival of special dinners honoring a French gastronome and writer whom both Alice and Jeremiah delighted in—Maurice Edmond Sailland (1872–1956), who was known by the single-barreled pseudonym Curnonsky (a curious hybrid of Latin and Russian, roughly meaning "Whynotsky"). *"La cuisine, c'est quand les choses ont le goût de ce qu'elles sont"* was Curnonsky's most famous dictum: "Fine cooking is when things have the taste of what they are."[5]

Though Curnonsky is best known for his celebration of the provincial cooking of France, his masterpiece, *Cuisine et Vins de France,* published in 1953, goes in rather less for rustic *cuisine grand-mère* ("grandmother cooking") than for haute cuisine at its loftiest heights. Accordingly, Jeremiah and Alice's menus for the three weeks of Curnonsky featured such extravagances as *tarte à la moëlle périgourdine,* translated on the menu as "tart of beef marrow, butter, Madeira, and veal essence"; *canard farci aux huîtres,* "fresh duck stuffed with shallots, fresh oysters, and the duck livers, braised with aromatic vegetables"; and, on the last night, the *timbale épicurienne de Curnonsky,* "the great extravagant seafood 'timbale,' including, in one dish, cooked together, fresh Maine lobster prepared *américaine* (with veal essence and brandy), fresh shrimp *bordelaise* (with red wine, shallots, and beef marrow), oysters poached in white wine, cream, shrimp butter, and truffles."

About the Curnonsky dinners Jeremiah told San Francisco *City* magazine, "French food is family food. Even though it's an incredible amount of work, each thing in itself is very, very simple. That seafood timbale, for instance, was actually a very simple thing, even though it took a week to prepare, and unbelievable labor. When you opened the casserole, you could see immediately that there were oysters in their shells on top, with cream and white wine sauce, and then prawns and lobsters underneath, in their sauce. But that's simple—in a way."[6]

THE WINE WRITER and importer Gerald Asher represented an estate in Provence called Domaine Tempier, whose wine was made under the appellation of Bandol. This appellation was hardly known in the United States, and it had not been much better known in France until the Peyraud family took over at Tempier and began to produce some of the deepest-flavored, best-balanced wines ever to come from the south of France. When Lucien

Alice, 1975

and Lulu Peyraud came to visit Gerald Asher in San Francisco in the spring of 1975, he recalls, "I wanted them to eat at Chez Panisse. Alice loved them immediately, and wanted their wine." Much more would come, in due course, of this meeting.

The menu for Thursday, June 5, 1975, shows how far Jeremiah and Alice would go in those days for an "ordinary" weeknight dinner at Chez Panisse:

Gratin de queues d'écrevisses
(the classic, expensive, very time-consuming, and now rare dish
of shelled crayfish tails sautéed in Cognac,
covered with a cream and crayfish butter sauce and gratinéed)

Consommé de chou rouge
(duck consommé with puréed red cabbage and
sliced red cabbage cooked in walnut oil)

❧

Selle de porc sur le gril
(marinated loin of pork roasted over a charcoal fire with fresh herbs,
served with a fresh herb butter sauce)

❧

Salade chaude d'épinards
(salad of spinach wilted in olive oil and sherry vinegar)

❧

Fruit and cheese

❧

Crème Carême
(cherry sherbet)

❧

Coffee or tea

❧

$9.00

That's $34 in today's money.

Less than two weeks later, Chez Panisse served a British dinner, to commemorate the Battle of Waterloo. The menu was in English, archly accompanied by "a special translation for non-English-speaking diners":

Salmon cooked in white wine, pounded with butter,
then preserved in ramekins
(saumon braisé au vin blanc mélangé avec du beurre en ramequins)

❧

Either: veal kidneys cooked in butter, cream, and port
OR soup of veal, beef, lamb, and pigs' ears with vegetables
(soit rognons de veau braisés au beurre avec crème et porto
OU potage de pieds et oreilles de cochon)

❧

Roasted leg of lamb with pickled mushrooms
(gigot rôti avec champignons marinés)

🐛

Salad of greens, herbs, radishes, and spring onions
(salade verte aux herbes, radis, et oignons nouveaux)

🐛

Stilton cheese to eat with port
(fromage Stilton)

🐛

Custard with maraschino and "cuirasseau" with sliced almonds
(crème anglaise parfumée au Maraschino et Curaçao)

🐛

$9.00

IN JUNE 1975, Alice's old Berkeley friends Martine and Claude Labro had returned to their home in the Provençal town of Vence. A friend of theirs, Nathalie Waag, ran a quirky little restaurant there called Au Hasard (best translated as "Serendipity"), where she served whatever she happened to feel like cooking every day. Nathalie's boyfriend, a mathematician, was going to an IBM conference in San Francisco, and bringing Nathalie. The Labros told Nathalie that she absolutely must look up their great old friend the restauratrice Alice Waters, who also served whatever she happened to feel like cooking every day. "My first thought," Nathalie recalls, "was about the name of the town, Berkeley, which seemed so funny to me, because in French, *beurk!* is the noise in cartoon strips to mean throwing up. In any case, I went. When I met Alice, she was running out of the restaurant. I asked her if she knew Alice Waters, and she said, 'Yes, why?' And I said, 'I am a friend of Claude and Martine.' So she grabbed my arm and said, 'Come with me. I'm going to buy fish.' And then she said, 'Come for dinner tonight.'"

The dinner that night epitomized the what-the-hell over-the-topness of Jeremiah at his most extravagant and eccentric. Every course was accompanied by a Sauternes, the intensely sweet Bordeaux white wine that, according to custom, was considered appropriate only with dessert—indeed only with certain desserts, or with foie gras. And these were not just any Sauternes. These were among the rarest wines, of any kind, available anywhere. It can safely be said that no other restaurant in either America or France would have dared to present so voluptuous, so sybaritic a meal. "This was pure Jeremiah," Alice says. "I had nothing to do with it."

Jambon de Virginie aux pruneaux
(ham from Culpeper, Virginia, braised in Sauternes and served
with prunes stuffed with green olives)
1947 Château Caillou

Colombines de saumon Nantua
(quenelles of salmon with crayfish butter sauce)
1949 Château Climens
1949 Château Doisy-Daëne

Entrecôte de boeuf
(sirloin of beef, roasted,
potatoes cooked in butter and duck fat with mushrooms)
1967 Château d'Yquem
1955 Château d'Yquem

Pommes Chez Nous
(green apples filled with berries, served with crème fraîche)
1959 Château Guiraud

Salade Alice
(salad of greens, herbs, radishes, and spring onions)

Tarte chaude de fruits
(hot deep-dish fruit pie)
1959 Château Suduiraut

❦

Blanc-manger
(almond cream dessert)
1922 Château d'Yquem
❦

Noix caramélisés
(caramelized walnuts)
❦

Café
❦

$20

Three vintages of Yquem! It was, and remains, one of the most expensive wines in the world—though all wine prices were far lower then, including Yquem's. (Today a Château d'Yquem of an age and quality comparable to that of the 1922 in 1975, the 1953, goes for between $1,000 and $2,000 a bottle.)

Alice sat at the table with Nathalie throughout the Yquem dinner, each delighted with the other. Alice was looking for a farmhouse to rent in France that summer. Nathalie adds, "And I said, 'Well, there's my farmhouse in Bonnieux.' And she said, 'Yes, but will you be there?' And I said, 'I don't know.' She said, 'Is it big enough so that Claude and Martine could come?' And I said, 'Ah-hah! and we could play poker!'" The Labros had fallen in love with American poker during their sojourn in Berkeley, and had played a lot of it with David Goines and Alice. "Then she said, 'But how much?' And I had no idea. I had never rented my farmhouse. But I ended that beautiful evening with a lot of dollars in my pocket and a new friend. And I spent three or four weeks that summer in the farmhouse with Alice. She wanted me to be there too.

"I remember very well that on the twelfth of August [1975], she went to visit Richard Olney, and I acted as her driver." Richard was the author of one of Alice's culinary bibles, *The French Menu Cookbook,* and he lived only a few minutes' drive from Domaine Tempier, and was a close friend of the Peyrauds'. (Years later, when Lulu was known as one of the best home cooks in France, Richard would write the cookbook *Lulu's Provençal Cuisine.*) Through Alice, Nathalie too would come to be a friend of Lulu and Lucien Peyraud's, as would Claude and Martine Labro. These interlocking friendships assured for the future of Chez Panisse a permanent connection to that little corner of Provence.

Alice was entranced with Lulu's primitive kitchen and the glories Lulu produced in it. From that visit forward, Lulu Peyraud would serve as Alice's mentor, soul mate, and hero. Alice loved the simplicity of Lulu's food, and its dependence on the most perfect ingredients, as exemplified here in Alice's words:

· LULU PEYRAUD'S TAPENADE, SEA URCHIN TOASTS, AND SARDINES ·

Lulu always serves tapenade toasts as a little *amuse-bouche*, with those little Niçoise olives and garlic that are just pounded together in a mortar. Actually, sometimes she sneaks and does it in the blender. I still don't even know where the blender is in that house. But I always do it with a mortar and pestle. Garlic, olives, and olive oil—that's it. Lulu sometimes puts some savory in it.

My favorite thing that she does—well, I have two favorite things. One is that she gets her son to go down and get sea urchins in Cassis, fresh ones, dive for them. She'll have little pieces of a brown bread, and she'll spread them with butter and then take out the roe from the sea urchins and put it on the buttered bread, raw, absolutely raw. And you eat it right away.

My other favorite thing is her sardines. She'll just fillet the sardines right on the spot, and sometimes she puts them on a little plate, raw, with salt and oil. Or she'll just put them on a piece of buttered bread or a crouton, raw, or just slightly cured. She fillets

> the sardine right there, and you don't wait. Oil, salt, and lemon juice, that's it. You don't put any parsley on.
>
> At Chez Panisse, we get sardines fresh from Monterey Bay. They're not quite like hers. I mean, hers are still alive, and ours aren't quite that perfect, but we do get them within twenty-four hours. At the most.

AFTER THE SAUTERNES DINNER, Chez Panisse staged its own vacation, a figurative one. On the first of July 1975, the menu touted *TROIS SEMAINES DE VACANCES DANS VOTRE ASSIETTE:* A THREE-WEEK GASTRONOMIC TOUR OF FRANCE FROM YOUR DINNER TABLE. In those three weeks alone, there were special dinners featuring the regional dishes of Brittany, the Auvergne, Languedoc, Picardie, the Touraine, the Lyonnais, Champagne (again), Normandy, Alsace, Burgundy, Gascony; the Dauphiné (typified in "*truffade:* potatoes and tomatoes cooked as a cake in bacon fat"); Bresse, the Dombes, Bugey, and the Pays de Gex ("*caneton au beurre d'écrevisses:* roast duck served with a crayfish, brandy, and butter sauce"); Nivernais, Morvan, and Bombonnais ("*saupiquet des Amognes:* slices of ham sautéed in butter, served with a sauce of juniper berries and shallots reduced with vinegar enriched with butter and sour cream"); and Provence ("*Berlingueto:* hard-cooked eggs stuffed with fresh basil, anchovies, garlic, bread crumbs, parsley, and black pepper, set on a bed of the stuffing and browned in the oven with olive oil").

Immediately after that onslaught of butter, cream, and other fats, on July 22, 1975, the menu announced, "*Trois semaines de vacances ne suffisent pas—il nous faut quatre semaines (au moins):* A three-week vacation is not enough, so—a fourth week to more distant places." That single week took Chez Panisse to Switzerland and Savoie, to the county of Nice, to Corsica ("*la polenta de castagne:* chestnut pancake with heavy cream"); to Saintonge, Aunis, and Angoumis ("*la Migourée de Matata-Meschers:* various saltwater fish browned in butter and olive oil, heated in the sauce of butter, white wine, garlic, onions, and shallots"); and at last to Morocco and Tunisia ("*Shlada dyal Feyjel ou Lichine:* salad of oranges, radishes, orange-flower water, cinnamon, and romaine lettuce").

A sensible observer might have concluded that the Chez Panisse kitchen could not possibly get any more extravagant. A sensible observer, as happens so often in this restaurant's history, would have been wrong. After what he describes in *California Dish* as "a surreal holiday in Mustique," where he says Lord Colin Tennant tried to persuade him to stay as Princess Margaret's chef, Jeremiah was ready for more. He and Alice staged a two-week festival, beginning at the end of September 1975, in honor of "the divine Salvador Domenech Hyacinthe Dalí," the surrealist painter, who had published a cookbook of his own—a very strange one—dedicated to his wife, Gala. From it, the kitchen of Chez Panisse produced, among many other equally Dalíesque delicacies, "*un cannibalisme parfait de l'automne:* a prawn-cold parfait of crushed prawns with cream and garlic, served with hot sausages in pastry"; "*un atavisme des oxyribonucléique sans truffes:* a salad not composed by Alexandre Dumas of beets, celery root, and Maxim's sauce"; "*un délice petit martyr sans tête:* toast of avocado, brains, almonds, Mexican liquor, and cayenne"; "*un Spoutnik astique d'asticots statistiques:* love's apple consommé: frog and tomato consommé with Royalist flourishes"; and "*l'entreplat drogué et sodomisé:* leg of lamb injected"—by hypodermic needle—"with Madeira and brandy, roasted with garlic and herbs."

Fireworks like these could not fail to be seen from across the Bay, and from farther. Despite the Dada antics and the artery-clogging sauces and the narcissistic bravado, Chez Panisse was eliciting serious praise. In the combined Sunday edition of the *San Francisco Chronicle and Examiner* of September 7, 1975, Wade Holland wrote,

> Chez Panisse can be criticized for overly casual service, for culinary experimentation that does not always meet with universal approval, for refusing to give the guests a choice of menu items, and I suppose for simply being "too Berkeley." But after four years, it also just happens to be in my estimation one of the very best French restaurants in all of California and certainly the most innovative. . . . Chez Panisse's inestimable stature owes to unremittingly superb

quality in food preparation, innovativeness in menu planning, purchase of the finest of ingredients, and resolute attention to even the smallest culinary details.

Also in the fall of 1975, Alice and Jeremiah hired another young Harvard graduate, Fritz Streiff, who had been learning the fine points of the nouvelle cuisine at Jacques Manière's Au Pactole in Paris. Fritz was eccentric, brilliant, charming, deeply cynical, and just as sentimental. He fit in perfectly. Fritz was partial to white linen suits and bow ties. He wore round-lensed vintage thirties glasses. He was always depressed, though in his telling his depressions were often rather funny. He loved to see the bad side of everything. He remembers with pleasure disillusioning his bosses about the immortal Auguste Escoffier: "Escoffier was on the take!" Fritz told Alice and Jeremiah. "He and César Ritz cheated the Savoy Hotel [where Ritz was manager and Escoffier chef] out of a bunch of money. Escoffier was taking money on the side from suppliers. They both got sacked."

The restaurant sought out wine to match the swagger of the staff and the ambition of the cooking. Jerry Budrick had been so pleased with the homemade zinfandel that Alice's own feet had pressed that he proposed to make his next batch of it the official Chez Panisse house wine, and Alice agreed. He promptly contracted for six tons of grapes from Amador County and went looking for a winery to do the vinification. Unfortunately, the one he had counted on was fully booked. Because Pagnol et Cie's board of directors had declined to put up the money, Jerry owned those six tons of grapes. Then Bruce Neyers, the business manager of the brand-new Joseph Phelps Winery, came to dinner with his wife, Barbara; and Jerry, as he loved to do, fell into conversation with them. Both Phelps and the Neyerses would go on to fame as winemakers, but at this time they had plenty of excess capacity. And sure, they'd be glad to make some wine for Chez Panisse. They vinified some of Jerry's grapes in the then-popular style of Beaujolais Nouveau—fresh, fruity, unaged, and good for only a few months—while the rest became a sturdier, barrel-aged, longer-lasting wine. For a restaurant to have its truly own wine—not just a bottle of somebody else's with a custom label slapped on—was yet another first. It was good wine, too.

. . .

THEN CAME THE REVIEW that overnight elevated Chez Panisse to national fame. In the October 1975 issue of *Gourmet* magazine, Caroline Bates wrote:

> Chez Panisse is joyously exploring *la vraie cuisine française* in all its vigor, freshness, and variety. . . . One evening some months ago, while diners in restaurants the length of California were facing that unholy trinity of onion soup, duckling à l'orange, and crème caramel, we were occupying a window table in the enclosed porch off the dining room at Chez Panisse and discovering a ramekin of mushrooms in the style of Quercy, roast duckling with fresh basil, and an almond tart surely made in heaven.
>
> Like many creative young chefs in France today who have turned away from the pretensions of *la grande cuisine,* [Jeremiah Tower] strives for the simplicity and directness that characterize French provincial food, with its emphasis on fresh ingredients and the integrity of each taste.

"Well," says Alice, "that was when we knew we'd arrived. Really arrived. I wish I could say I felt better about it. Mostly what I felt was dread. Everybody and his mother were going to want to come in and see what all the fuss was about. Coming in with a chip on their shoulder. One of my dearest friends sent us a funeral wreath."

The review in *Gourmet,* just as Alice had feared, brought a whole new crowd of doubting, demanding customers to Chez Panisse. "In the last two months," wrote San Francisco's *Bay Guardian* in November 1975, "the modest Panisse has suffered two critical blows which have left the staff shaken and staggering.

"Since the reviews appeared in the *Chron* and *Gourmet,* Alice Waters calculates that near on sixty percent of the customers have been out-of-towners. . . . There have also been phone calls coming in at an average of one every two minutes, flooding Panisse's two lines. Unfortunately the surfeit of calls has resulted in a mixed excess of diners—Alice Waters estimates an average of ten to twenty no-shows per night."

After getting reviews that other restaurants could only have dreamed about, and being inundated with big spenders, Chez Panisse was doing less business than it had before its ascent to national fame.

Berkeley being Berkeley, backlash was inevitable. The *Berkeley Gazette* complained about paying ten dollars for "pork and beans"—the restaurant's prized *cassoulet*.

Willy Bishop was outraged. "That *cassoulet!* My God! We had to make goose confit. We had to make lamb stock, and duck stock for the beans. We worked probably twenty hours before we put it in the oven. Different-size casseroles—one for two, one for four. Different timing for each casserole, so it would be ready exactly on time. Perfect timing. Perfect bread crumbs on top. Oh, my God! That *cassoulet* was so rich and so fine! And that fucking guy called it pork and beans."

All through the fall and winter of 1975, Jeremiah's temper had been flaring more often and more nastily. Once, when he noticed that a busser had his fingers in the food as he headed for the dining room, Jeremiah's reproach was "What is it about 'keep your fingers out of the food' that your little cockroach mind can't grasp?"[7]

For Jeremiah, this was an opportune moment for a little sabbatical—and a chance to seek out Richard Olney in France. Richard was a culinary saint to him as much as he was to Alice. Perhaps more important, he was just the sort of whimsical, stylish, gay, and alcoholic sybarite Jeremiah adored. They shared an almost inconceivable capacity for wine. After a great banquet of the gastronomically elite Club des Cent in Paris in mid-October 1975, Jeremiah accompanied Richard to his house at Solliès-Toucas. "The long winter nights were filled with single-malt whiskey, old French music hall records, and talks about food," Jeremiah writes in *California Dish.* "All this talk of eating and love made me want to do a festival at Chez Panisse in celebration of [Richard's] new book, *Simple French Food*"—a book that would move Chez Panisse back toward its roots in the French countryside. Together Richard and Jeremiah planned a series of menus for a California Zinfandel Festival, to come the next fall. For the menus, Richard encouraged Jeremiah to think not only of French food but of the possibilities inherent in some traditional American cooking.

Richard also introduced Jeremiah to Domaine Tempier. Lulu Peyraud's cooking was rustic, highly aromatic, strong, and personal. She didn't care how anybody else did anything. She had her own, fiercely elemental way. She still cooked nearly everything on a wood-fired hearth (though she did have a tiny two-burner stove and oven in another room).

Jeremiah returned to Berkeley in December 1975, in time to concoct a New Year's Eve dinner worthy of Olney's sumptuous gourmandise.

La salade de Bugey, Lucien Tendret
(salad of lobster, chicken breasts, black truffles, squab breasts, mushrooms, and shrimp, with a mustard vinaigrette)

❧

L'entrecôte de boeuf, sauce périgourdine
(prime sirloin of beef with truffles, roasted and served with a truffled Madeira sauce)

❧

Le purée verte et la purée blanche
(purée of green beans and purée of turnips, leeks, and potatoes, with garlic)

❧

Le granité de Champagne
(Champagne sherbet)

❧

Tartelettes de fruits
(fruit tartlets)

❧

Bonbons Chez Panisse

THERE ARE A NUMBER of veterans of Jeremiah's time at Chez Panisse who dispute his memories. Kim Severson, reviewing *California Dish* in the *San Francisco Chronicle,* wrote, "To make it through former superstar chef

Jeremiah Tower's memoir, the reader has to suspend disbelief and accept three basic premises: 1) Everything was his idea. 2) Any culinary and financial reversals weren't his fault. 3) Everyone wanted to sleep with him."[8]

Patricia Curtan, the artist who has been part of the life of the restaurant for some thirty years, was particularly outraged, and she has good authority as a witness. She was a student of David Goines's in the mid-seventies as well as the lover of Willy Bishop. She worked as a bartender and occasional cook at the restaurant, and eventually became, like David, a designer of menus and posters for special occasions at Chez Panisse. She says that in *California Dish,* Jeremiah "took a story that was rich and nuanced and interesting, and he reduced it down to just this one version of himself at the center. It just diminished everything. He portrayed himself as this incredibly hardworking genius who worked twelve, eighteen hours a day, and that wasn't true either. There were so many people working really hard propping him up. Willy was an incredible workhorse. He didn't buy the prima donna act."

Greil Marcus, the writer who has been a partner in Chez Panisse since the beginning, also remembers the Jeremiah years as less than halcyon: "There was a time, maybe two years or so after Jeremiah started, when we didn't feel comfortable there, didn't feel welcome. It had become extraordinarily insular. A lot of the clientele were dope dealers. A lot of people were eating there for free. I remember saying to Alice any number of times, 'Alice, if we don't feel welcome there, and we're part of it, how do you think the general public is going to feel?' Jeremiah had a good deal to do with that, because that's his whole way of being in the world, to divide the world into those who count and those who don't."

Alice's former lover Tom Luddy, though he continued to dine at Chez Panisse and to bring his visitors from the movie industry, says, "I always felt that the food Jeremiah was cooking went against the philosophy of Chez Panisse, and Pagnol. It was getting back toward this Parisian, over-ripe, overrich, decadent, French high-class food that I never liked. I think Alice was intimidated by Jeremiah. Alice, God bless her, is not an egotistical, overconfident, arrogant soul. She's easily intimidated, and Jeremiah knew how to intimidate her."

Ruth Reichl, today the editor of *Gourmet* magazine, recalls, "Jeremiah had a much more sophisticated vision of what the food should be. And Alice was entranced by that. But she was influenced by other people too. It was a time when everybody was learning from everybody else. But I think that the uncompromising quality, the purity of the ingredients, is her. Jeremiah did not bring that to the table. For me, the epitome of the food at Chez Panisse was not the great Sauternes dinner, it was when you misread the menu and you thought you were going, you know, for some squid-ink fantasia, and it turns out to be chicken, and you're disappointed because it's not the meal you want, and then it comes out and it is the best piece of chicken you've ever had in your life. And that's not Jeremiah."

ONE NIGHT IN 1975—she does not remember quite when—Alice was savagely attacked in her home. "It was a huge, shocking, awful thing," she recalls.

I was living in a little cottage behind my friend Suzy Nelson's house, in a garage that I had made into a little studio. I was sleeping on a loft. I had thought many times that if somebody broke in, I would throw myself out the window. I had always thought up little scenarios. But I never imagined being awakened by somebody with his hand on my mouth in the middle of the night. I had always thought that I'd rather be raped than killed. But it turns out that's not true. I was willing to fight that hard. It was a real revelation about myself. I screamed bloody murder. I fought up to the point that he choked me until I passed out. I don't know how long I was out, but when I woke up, he was still there. When I thought about it later, I was pretty sure that he had lost his knife and was looking for it. He didn't rape me. I think he was looking for his knife, and he felt insecure without his knife. And he couldn't find it, and so he said, "Give me some money." And I said, "I don't have any, but I have a restaurant, I'll go." He was behind me. I never saw him. Then he said, "Well, go up to the loft." And I remembered my exit strategy. As soon as I got up there—he was holding on to my foot—I just threw myself with all my weight out the window. And he let go of me. The window was only one little story from the ground—probably eight or ten feet. I was down somehow, and I started running. And I escaped.

Alice was now afraid to be in the cottage alone. She quickly found another house, and Jeremiah gallantly offered to move in. Alice was grateful for his protective company, at least initially. "Ultimately," she says, "that's how it all kind of fell apart, with his moving into my house—and taking over my house. And the restaurant likewise. I just couldn't stand to be around him at that time." She had been so shaken by the attack that for some weeks afterward Alice exerted much less control over Chez Panisse than was her custom, and Jeremiah accordingly took up more psychic space in the restaurant, and she felt crowded out. In her home he had arrived as her protector, but she found his presence more irritating than comforting—so irritating that she moved out. "I just camped out with friends," she remembers, while Jeremiah continued to live in her new house.

Finally, Alice reached the limit of her patience, and one night, when Jeremiah was out, she reoccupied her house. Conveniently, Jeremiah had left his key there, and Alice locked him out.

7.

LAST
BIRTHDAY?

1976

In January 1976, in *City* magazine, Alice's old political mentor Robert Scheer wrote, "As a result of recent writeups in *Gourmet* and other magazines, the Orinda crowd has swamped the place and the regular trade of drug pushers and movie types is in danger of being squeezed out. . . .

"It is the best restaurant in the Bay Area. . . . Since my ratings include price in the judgment, a restaurant as expensive as Chez Panisse ($10 prix fixe) had better be extraordinary. . . . If an offering seems odd, as with the pig tails and ears last week, then we must assume that our sensibilities are still too limited." Scheer awarded the restaurant his highest rating, four stars.

Jeremiah took umbrage at a review that would surely have delighted any other chef, and on January 16, 1976, he wrote a letter to Scheer, reading in part:

Overcoming a desire to demand a proxy apology for [the] clientele of
Chez Panisse who reside in Orinda (for since when has the resident area
of anyone been a civilized reason for public condemnation?), and rising
above a desire to punch you in the nose for describing in slanderous fashion

*the "expensive ($10)" Chez Panisse as a hangout for "drug pushers" (who
would probably feel the restaurant far too inexpensive) and movie types
(for greater artists than you, Mr. Scheer, like Nick Ray and Kenneth Anger,
the restaurant could never have been a haven were it at all expensive or
did they mind the "Orinda crowd"), yes, putting these desires aside, I would
prefer to point out that there is no greater bore than the offense of a snob
who is uninformed, uneducated and cannot walk the fine line between
rudeness and a well brought-up and healthy contempt.*

Alice and Jeremiah in the fall of 1975 had hired a young Frenchman, Jean-
Pierre Moullé, to serve as sous-chef. Jean-Pierre was lean and graceful, strikingly good-looking, with a strong-cheekboned facial structure, shaggy hair,
a ready, roguish smile, and an unlimited store of charm. His manner was confident, but without arrogance. His formal French culinary training brought
a new professionalism to the Chez Panisse kitchen. "Jeremiah was inspired,
and he inspired me," says Jean-Pierre. "I was his tech support. He had no
formal training, you know. To get from point A to point B or A to Z he was
going zigzag. I said, 'Well, you can do it this way.' We worked well together."

Drugs and alcohol on the job were the curse of American restaurants
in the 1970s and well into the 1980s. And while they made the late, long
hours fun, they were a bad influence on the cooking. "I did enjoy it too,"
says Jean-Pierre. "I love Champagne. Cocaine, Jeremiah did a lot. I did
it for a year or two, and then I quit, because when you get tired, you get
more tired. It was bad. I remember once we were doing tastings and asking
everyone 'Okay, who's going to taste the dish?'—because with cocaine,
nobody could taste. And you're not hungry."

And so the Chez Panisse kitchen barreled along, heedless of burnout,
heedless sometimes, too, of the dining room, where impatience, irritation,
and disappointment were making themselves felt to Alice and the serving
staff. "There was a lot of carousing in that kitchen," remembers Lindsey
Shere. "And not even necessarily after hours. A lot of stuff went on in the
kitchen even during service, a lot of drinking and arguing. Often there was
a question about whose idea was whose. Jeremiah and Alice were definitely on a collision course."

Alice did not fire Jeremiah, but their relationship remained tense. In midwinter of 1976—not long after his intemperate letter to Bob Scheer— Jeremiah returned to France to join a gastronomic tour that Richard Olney was leading.

In Jeremiah's absence, Alice took over as chef. Two months later, when his money ran out, Jeremiah was ready to come home. Meanwhile, Willy Bishop had quit for good. "After it got written up," Willy says, "the food weenies came, the people with expectations and snobbery and criticism. After those reviews, the pressure just got to be too great. But it also brought an influx of new talent willing to work for nothing. Alice has always had a way of making people want to help her, do things for her."

Jeremiah returned from France with a host of new ideas. He proposed that Chez Panisse offer not one but four set menus every night, ranging from ten to twenty-five dollars a head. Since Jeremiah's advent in 1973, the former café upstairs had functioned as an extension of the main dining room on crowded evenings; now he wanted to establish a real café there, with its own full menu, simpler and cheaper than downstairs and offering a range of choices. Another inspiration from France was to offer a selection of special dishes that could be ordered a week in advance.

Alice's response to Jeremiah's café idea was that if guests were offered all that choice, the kitchen's focus would be diffused, and the unique identity of Chez Panisse would be at risk. She turned down all of his proposals flat, and stood ready for the consequences. Jeremiah decided he would finish out 1976 and leave.

While he remained, however, his ambitions continued to mount. He convinced the board of directors to raise the price of Friday and Saturday dinner from ten to twelve dollars. Though his departure was nine months away, he was already planning to go out in glory. At the beginning of March 1976, the restaurant posted this notice, in Jeremiah's unmistakable voice:

The last three weeks in March will celebrate a great master, a great pupil, and their followers. First, a week of Escoffier, who introduced the twentieth century to great French cooking and vice versa; followed by two weeks of menus devised for Chez Panisse by Richard

Olney, who renewed the passion and updated it. If the price for a particular dinner sometimes seems a bit stiff for the apparent humbleness of the ingredients, it is because of the immense care and labor involved. Following these three weeks, we will experiment with an à la carte grill-type menu and concept, emerging from Escoffier's innovations, so that the public may evaluate the two distinct styles.

And why did Alice, having already deflated Jeremiah's hopes for broadening the menu, ever allow the last statement to appear? "I guess he sort of sneaked it through," she says now. In any event, no "à la carte grill-type menu" ever came to pass.

The only change from the traditional set menu was a return to the *hors d'oeuvres variés* of the restaurant's earliest days. Jeremiah's versions, of course, were very different from the simple appetizers of 1971. On one menu he wrote, "The various hors d'oeuvres will include fish salads, mushroom brochettes, calves' brains vinaigrette, grilled kidneys with mustard, oysters sautéed in butter, duck livers, eggs with avocado, crab mayonnaise, and many others." He also provided diners with a densely typed page of Auguste Escoffier's culinary philosophy and a second page presenting capsule biographies of the legendary chefs Escoffier, Marie-Antoine Carême, Prosper Montagné, and Philéas Gilbert.

On April 1, 1976, Alice brought in an important late-night guest, Robert Finigan, the Bay Area's most authoritative restaurant critic. Finigan had been a classmate of Jeremiah's at Harvard, though they had not met there. He had bought *Jack Shelton's Private Guide to Restaurants* and had kept the name, though it was now Bob Finigan who wrote the reviews. By the time Alice and Bob and two others arrived, that evening's main course, roast leg of lamb, was down to three decent servings and a few trimmings that Jeremiah remembers as "some crisp bits that were delicious but totally unpresentable to paying customers." Jeremiah sent the waiter to ask if steaks would be okay. No. Alice had promised Bob Finigan lamb.

"I was entertaining three guests on this occasion, and their three portions were picture-book perfect slices of rosy meat," wrote Finigan in his newsletter of May 1976. "But mine had been assembled from inordinately gristly pieces hacked inexpertly from the leg. I quietly instructed the waiter to ask the chef for more appetizing slices. He was back in moments, the same plate in hand. 'The chef says, "Tough s——,"' he announced."

As occasionally happened at Chez Panisse, the waiter was just a friend of somebody's, not a pro at all, and it had not occurred to him that you shouldn't pass along remarks from the chef such as "tough shit" to a customer, especially if (a) he was a restaurant critic, and (b) Alice was at the table.

Finigan reported the incident, but his review ended, astonishingly, with this: "When I reflect on the pressures that weigh on Chez Panisse, I am amazed not that it stumbles occasionally but that it does not stumble more often. . . . The Chez Panisse experiment must be judged overall a resounding success."

A number of the faithful regulars of Chez Panisse who had predated Jeremiah had been gradually falling away throughout his four years there. His food struck many of them as fussy, overbearing, and excessively formal, and it seemed to them to be getting more so. Because of its growing fame, the restaurant continued to do good business, but many of the customers now were tourists, and many of them were more demanding than the local regulars, colder, sometimes even rude. The jovial egalitarianism, the camaraderie between staff and clientele that had defined Chez Panisse as much as its exquisite food, had deteriorated badly, and the mood of the staff was darkening. The longtime waiter Steve Crumley, for example, had taken to calling Jeremiah by Benito Mussolini's self-bestowed sobriquet—"*Duce.*" (Others, apropos of Jeremiah's lofty, sometimes prissy manner, called him the queen of England. For the restaurant itself, one wag coined the nickname Cheese Penis, which was quite popular for a while behind the scenes.)

Despite the discontent among the staff, the food had never been better. Somebody with a better head for business, thought Alice, might be able to make good money here. Chez Panisse was not yet five years old, but Alice was sick of the whole thing—the arguments, the lame-brained new clientele, the eroding spirit of the place. She conferred with the other directors—Jerry Budrick (still her boyfriend as well), Tom Guernsey, Charles and Lindsey Shere, and Jeremiah—but they could not come to an agreement. Eventually, however, Alice prevailed. She wanted to sell the place and get out.

On May 26, 1976, the *San Francisco Chronicle* reported rather quietly that Chez Panisse was for sale. The price was half a million dollars, not including the services of either Jeremiah Tower or Alice Waters.

And yet, such now was the restaurant's reputation that Jean Troisgros—co-owner, with his brother Pierre, of the Restaurant Troisgros in Roanne, one of the best restaurants in the world—asked if his nephew Michel might come to work in the kitchen at Chez Panisse. In *California Dish,* Jeremiah wrote, "I said to Michel, 'I should be studying under you.' And he said, 'Oh no, no, no, no. You've got it the wrong way around, because . . .' you know, because I didn't know any of the bad habits of the French." With Fritz Streiff and Jean-Pierre Moullé already there, the majority of the *brigade de cuisine* would now be French or French-trained, just at the moment when Chez Panisse had begun in earnest to Americanize its food.

It was typical of Chez Panisse that French and American influences would first oppose each other and then find a creative mutual accommodation. Jeremiah had been inspired by the Four Seasons restaurant in New York, the first fine-dining establishment since the nineteenth century to elevate American food and wine to parity with French, and Alice and Jeremiah were still seeking out more and better sources of local fruit, vegetables, and seafood. (Meat was still a problem, the wholesale market at that time being under the near-total control of the big national packing houses.) Spurning the American bicentennial, over which the rest of the country was making such a fuss, Chez Panisse decided that its next special dinner would be—very Berkeley—in honor of Bastille Day, the French equivalent of the Fourth of July. Every course would be based on garlic—a notion that would have repelled any French chef or gastronome. Only Americans would propose such a menu as that served at Chez Panisse on July 14, 1976.

Champignons à l'ail aux feuilles de vignes
(whole garlic and mushrooms baked with olive oil in grape leaves)

❦

Purée d'ail rôti, cuisse de poulet
(roast garlic puréed and served with baked chicken legs)

❦

Aïoli aux haricots verts et pommes de terre
(garlic mayonnaise served with green beans
and little red boiled potatoes)

❦

Nouilles fraîches, sauce pistou
(fresh pasta served with a paste of garlic, basil, pine nuts,
olive oil, and parmesan cheese)

❦

Tripes au pistou
(beef tripe with basil and garlic)

❦

Bourride aux tomates
(fresh fish poached in a fish stock with tomatoes,
with garlic mayonnaise thinned with the broth)

❦

Gigot rôti, sauce à l'ail saintongeoise
(leg of lamb marinated with garlic and wine, stuffed with
prosciutto, and served with a sauce with mint,
garlic, and wine that's simmered for hours)

❦

Purée de pommes de terre à l'ail
(potato purée with garlic-infused cream)

❦

Figues, fromage blanc, et miel à l'ail
(fresh figs, white cheese, and garlic honey)

❦

$15

It was a roaring success, to return by popular demand every summer thenceforward.

THERE HAS BEEN a sort of manic-depressive oscillation throughout the history of Chez Panisse, and despite reviews, new and unpopular customers, and never-ending staff conflicts, the *famille Panisse* was recovering its *joie de vivre*. Through the summer and into the fall of 1976, the dance of French and American influences went on. Chez Panisse continued to serve French dishes with French names, but increasingly derived inspiration not from Alice's and Jeremiah's forays into obscure old cookbooks but directly from the bounty of northern California's soil and waters. In August, when summer squash, green beans, basil, eggplant, and tomatoes were coming in, the accent was French, but the language was American.

"We were doing some of the simplest food we'd ever done, and I loved it," Alice says. "And the customers loved it. We had tomato soup with

David Stewart, a waiter since the earliest days
of Chez Panisse, and Alice

basil. Beet and red onion salad. Fresh pea soup. Steamed clams. Roast duck with bacon and onions. Salmon with beurre blanc. Virginia ham, all by itself on the plate. Vegetable salads. Avocado with walnut oil and lemon juice. Chocolate cake with ice cream."

Alice had always preferred local food sources, but Jeremiah's extravagant creations had sometimes required long-distance importation. With the new simplicity, however, both Alice and Jeremiah were discovering local resources much finer than what had been available to them just a few years before. "We were really foraging, and finding the most wonderful things," remembers Alice. "Crayfish raised in California. Wild salmon that was caught just outside the Golden Gate. People gathered wild mushrooms for us, and we just grilled them wrapped in grape leaves—Napa grape leaves. We were getting our oysters from Tomales Bay [just north of San Francisco]. More and more of what came out of that kitchen was about the fruits and vegetables that grew within just a few miles of the restaurant. Avocados, peaches, watercress, peppers, beans. We got rabbits from Amador County, squab from Sonoma, live trout from Big Sur. This was when the farmers' markets were springing up all over the place, and we got such beautiful things from them that we barely had to touch them."

From that summer of 1976 on, farmers' markets would be a fundamental element in not only the food but also the philosophy of Chez Panisse. The markets connected the cooks directly to the land. Alice's description of putting together a typical salad from the market demonstrates how ingredient-driven her culinary creativity had become.

· FARMERS' MARKET SALAD ·

I start by looking for really good textures and colors. In spring, I'm certainly going to have radishes in the salad, either shaved or quartered, and I'm going to have all those little spring greens. I'll get them from different vendors, from whoever has the best little wild rocket or whatever. I love those tiny little onions in the spring that are so small they're almost like a little chive. I'll put those in whole. The radishes can go that way when they're tiny as well. Fennel for sure. I love fennel in salad. You can chop up the little fennel leaves—they're beautiful when they're just new. And I like mustard flowers as a garnish. I might get farm eggs and put in some hard-boiled eggs that are halved.

Hard-boiled eggs are wonderful when they're really done right. I bring the water to a boil, and then I put in the eggs. And then I boil them for—well, it depends on the size of the egg—maybe eight minutes. The way I tell that they're done is I take an egg out of the pot and I'll just crack the shell slightly and press, and you can just tell. If it's too soft, you put it back in again. Just firm, and you know that it's done, and you rinse it in cold water.

I've had raw asparagus in a salad like that, but for vegetables, usually I'll make a plate that is more of a spring aïoli plate. I'll cook asparagus and artichokes and potatoes and carrots and fennel, and then make some green garlic aïoli with it. I crush the green garlic— the green and the white parts both—in a mortar, and then blend that into a homemade mayonnaise. Little piles of each of the vegetables, separate, not seasoned—dead plain. It's a beautiful lunch. It's my favorite lunch to make for friends—some variation of vegetables with either vinaigrette or an aïoli, and maybe with a tapenade and some toast.

For any salad greens, you're looking for the ones that have just been picked. Ones that have an aliveness about them. Ones that don't have any little discolored ends. I don't mind the ones that have a little dirt on them because they just came out of the field. They didn't even have time to wash them. You'd be surprised where you can find greens like that. If I lived on the Upper West Side of Manhattan, I would make friends right away with a gardener who was part of one of those community gardens.

The restaurant's fifth birthday, August 28, 1976, featured "oysters, roast pig, composed salads, pasta, our own pastry and ice cream, and other gastronomic treats; the Louisiana Playboys and late-night jazz perhaps; the Marcel Pagnol movies *Marius, Fanny,* and *César;* a new poster by David Lance Goines; et cetera." David's poster proclaimed "Fifth Birthday Celebration," in English, but the specially printed menu, also designed by David, was headlined with the ominous French words *dernier anniversaire*—"last birthday." It wasn't a joke.

The restaurant may have recovered its spirit, but Alice had not recovered hers. "I was just fed up," she recalls. "These new customers, if they decided not to go, they'd just not go—and not call. Of course that was costing us money. What was worse was the wasted food. Seeing our beautiful food go into the garbage! And empty tables—we weren't used to that at all. There's a particular feeling when everybody's in there together, and a big empty table absolutely spoils that."

As the far horizon of Jeremiah's tenure came into view, and with buyers bearing half-million-dollar checks so far nonexistent, Chez Panisse found itself in an identity crisis. Even if Jeremiah had been going to stay, it's doubtful how much longer the restaurant could have endured as a living museum of bygone French cookery, or as a madcap laboratory of surrealism, experiment, and irony. "We'd been the obstreperous teenager about long enough," says Alice. "It was getting time to try to grow up a little.

"One of the ways we were doing that was by simplifying, and by focusing more and more on what was local. We had a stronger sense of who we really were as a restaurant. We did a special dinner that fall that really showed what we were about. Looking back now, I can see that that was when our style was really finding itself. This could be a menu from last week as easily as thirty years ago." There was nothing clever about the title, nothing fancy about the food. The menu was all in the plainest of English—"and all Jeremiah's," says Alice.

NORTHERN CALIFORNIA REGIONAL DINNER
October 7, 1976

Spenger's Tomales Bay bluepoint oysters on ice

❦

Cream of fresh corn soup, Mendocino style, with crayfish butter

❦

*Big Sur Garrapata Creek smoked trout steamed
over California bay leaves*

❦

Monterey Bay prawns sautéed with garlic, parsley, and butter

❦

Preserved California-grown geese from Sebastopol

❦

Vella dry Monterey Jack cheese from Sonoma

❦

Fresh caramelized figs

❦

*Walnuts, almonds, and mountain pears from the
San Francisco Farmers' Market*

❦

$20.00

❦

WINES OFFERED BY THE GLASS $1.50

Schramsberg Cuvée de Gamay 1973
Mount Eden Chardonnay 1973
Beaulieu Cabernet Private Reserve 1970

Ridge Zinfandel, Fiddletown 1974
Mission del Sol, Harbor Winery 1974
Tawny Port, East Side Winery

Twenty dollars for dinner was expensive—sixty-nine of today's dollars—though certainly not unreasonable, considering the number of courses. But those $1.50 glasses of wine, adjusted for inflation, would be only $5.00 apiece today, and they came from some of California's finest bottlings. A bottle of six-year-old Beaulieu Cabernet Sauvignon Private Reserve, for example, now goes for about $80.00 retail. Restaurants typically price wine by the bottle at about twice retail, so the Beaulieu on a wine list would sell for $160.00. With wine by the glass, however, restaurants typically count on just four glasses per bottle, to allow for spillage, some spoilage, etc.—and they will price it at about two and a half times retail. Thus the Beaulieu Cabernet goes up to $200.00, which divided by four comes to $50.00 a glass!

Between 1976 and 2006, the real, inflation-adjusted price of dinner at Chez Panisse has slightly more than doubled. In the same period, that Beaulieu Cabernet Sauvignon Private Reserve has increased in price by a thousand percent, and other premium wines have risen comparably. The great Yquem dinner could not be repeated today except at exorbitant cost. Wine at Chez Panisse in 1976 was seen as one component of several that made up a nice meal, as Europeans have seen it for centuries. Rare now, however, is the high-end restaurant with more than a handful of bottles on its list selling for less than a main course, and affluent diners-out not infrequently spend as much on wine as on the entire rest of the meal.

AFTER A RESTAURANT gets rave reviews, there is usually a burst of demand, and then it slowly dies down as the many who chase the latest thing find the latest thing elsewhere. But that didn't happen at Chez Panisse. A full year after the reviews in *Gourmet* and the *San Francisco Chronicle*, the phones were still ringing all day. People were making reservations weeks in advance. The old-time regulars couldn't get a table unless they called Alice directly. "We thought for a while that perhaps we should close," Alice told *New West* magazine. "I just don't know how to express how torn we felt about the reviews, particularly the one in *Gourmet*. In a way, the review told us that this is the time to re-evaluate the way we see Chez Panisse."[1]

At Tom Guernsey's Sunday brunch, for which reservations were not taken, there were lines down the stairs, out the door, and along Shattuck Avenue, and the kitchen couldn't keep up. "One Sunday," says Alice, "I looked at Tom and asked, 'Do you want to do this?'"

"No," replied Tom.

"Well, neither do I."

And that was that. On October 12, 1976, the menu bore this note:

Two of the finest services we have provided for our amiable clientele have been our Sunday brunches and weekday coffee and croissant breakfasts. Therefore, it is with deep regret that we announce that, due to the impossibility of finding permanent employees in Berkeley who rise early and smilingly, we will not open until 11:30 a.m. from Tuesday through Saturday, and not at all on Sunday.

Tom was by now the de facto general manager of Chez Panisse, and everybody on the staff, including Alice, counted on his steadiness, his impeccable taste, and his ability to do any task the restaurant might require. Sometimes, nostalgic for Tom's brunches, Alice would implore him to make her one of his omelets. "Tom made the most perfect omelets," she says. "I'll never forget his *omelette aux fines herbes.*"

· TOM GUERNSEY'S OMELETTE AUX FINES HERBES ·

First you break three eggs into a café au lait bowl. He always used a café au lait bowl. You take a fork and stir the eggs around— not too much, but a little, so you can still see separate white and yolk. Stripes. Salt and pepper. You take one nice tablespoon of sweet butter—we used an iron pan, very seasoned—and swirl it around, over medium heat. Just at the moment when it began to sizzle, he would pour in the eggs. He would move very quickly, with a wooden spoon, moving the sides in and swirling it all around. And in a minute, not even a minute, he would flip it, and then on go the fines herbes—tarragon, chervil, parsley, chives. Then he would roll it out of the pan and fold it over. He'd put just a dollop of ever-so-slightly-whisked crème fraîche on it, and sprinkle that with fines herbes all over. Sometimes he'd rub down the top with a little butter.

Sometimes we would use the recipe from *The Auberge of the Flowering Hearth*. He loved that cookbook, and so did I. He would melt sorrel and put that in the middle, and roll it out of the pan so the sorrel would be on the inside. And then he made a little whipped cream with salt and pepper and a splash of Armagnac.

There's a dramatic difference in the taste when you use good eggs, no more than a couple of days old. And it's important that the butter be sweet, not a little sour as it can get so quickly.

What to drink depends on what's inside. I like those Friulian whites. I suppose if I had something that felt very Provençal, I wouldn't mind drinking a little Bandol rosé. But then I drink Bandol rosé with just about everything. What doesn't go with Bandol rosé?

We also do scrambled eggs at the restaurant with black truffles. We truffle the eggs the day before. That is, you store the whole raw eggs buried in the truffles, so the eggs taste like truffles to begin with. Then we chop the truffles very fine and mix them in with the eggs before we cook them. We serve them with very thinly sliced *levain* bread that's grilled and then rubbed with just a hint of garlic. And a little, very wintry mesclun salad on the side.

As Jeremiah's last weeks passed, he seemed to be summing up his four years at Chez Panisse. He honored the classics: *saucisson à l'ail en brioche* (garlic sausage cooked in pastry with a butter sauce), *cotriade* (effortfully explained as "fresh fish cooked with onions and white wine in a Brittany-style bouillabaisse"), *gigot rôti, sauce madère* (roast leg of lamb with Madeira sauce). He also tipped his hat to the nouvelle cuisine, with *boeuf mariné aux kakis et aux kiwis* (beef marinated in olive oil with green peppercorns, served with persimmons and kiwifruit—the latter just beginning to be known in America), *soupe de courge Paul Bocuse* (Paul Bocuse's pumpkin soup), *truite farcie Georges Garin* (trout stuffed with a truffled sole mousseline and poached in butter), and in tribute to the *cuisine minceur* of Michel Guérard, *gigot de poulette cuit à la vapeur de marjolaine* (described on the menu as "a seemingly simple but actually complex dish of chicken drumsticks stuffed with morels, sweetbreads, and mushrooms, with a garnish of celery"). He also continued to pay homage to Alice's emergent California classicism— cold Dungeness crab with an herb mayonnaise, sautéed Monterey Bay prawns with warm fennel salad, local oysters on the half shell.

On December 31, 1976, the last meal Jeremiah Tower was to present at Chez Panisse—or so he thought at the time—was remarkably restrained. No jokes, no *tours de force* or *de folie,* (except perhaps Lindsey's *croquembouche*), just pure elegance. The menu was printed only in French, but Jeremiah translates it as below in *California Dish.*

Soupe aux truffes, Paul Bocuse
(Paul Bocuse's truffle soup, which he did for the president
of France at the Élysée Palace)

❦

Cailles rôties au vert-pré
(roast fresh quail on a bed of watercress)

❦

Fromages
(California cheeses)

❦

Croquembouche
("one- and two-foot towers of pastry-cream-filled profiteroles
stuck together with hot caramel," in Jeremiah's description,
"[the] most festive of French desserts")

❦

Gâteau au chocolat, glace au nougat
(chocolate cake with nougat ice cream)

❦

Bonbons

❦

$25.00

Jeremiah and Alice, in a tempestuous four years, had created unique combinations of ambition and simplicity, of worldliness and hominess, and of old and new. Those qualities had become, and today remain, the foundations of the Chez Panisse style.

With the end of 1976, there having been no takers in the seven months it had been on the market, Chez Panisse was no longer for sale. And the era of Jeremiah Tower had come to a close.

8.

ENNUI AND
INSPIRATION

1977–1978

In January 1977, Alice Waters for the first time assumed the title of chef of Chez Panisse. Jeremiah's departure and her own taking sole charge reinvigorated Alice. She was full of ideas, and her sous-chef, Jean-Pierre Moullé, consummately professional, could cook anything she could imagine. Together they hired Mark Miller, a superlative cook who, when he left Chez Panisse, would follow a pattern that became typical of its alumni: opening their own restaurants, sometimes in multiples, all of them taking something from the Chez Panisse spirit, but none of them entering fully into it. Only one of them—Sally Clarke, in her eponymous London restaurant—has yet dared a no-choice menu. No one cares as little about profit as Alice. Mark Miller found fame first with the Santa Fe Bar and Grill in Berkeley and later the Coyote Café in Santa Fe, New Mexico. Miller also owns restaurants in Washington, D.C., and Sydney, Australia, and is the author of ten cookbooks. Meanwhile, Alice has continued to operate the one restaurant in the rambling old house in Berkeley. Jean-Pierre has come and gone, but he has run the kitchen at Chez Panisse longer than anyone else.

"Ah, Jean-Pierre," Alice says with a sigh. "When I worked well with him was when I was doing the menus and he was helping me execute them. That was divine. That's how we started out. We worked together. I did one course, he did one course. I would put things on the menu that I knew he did really well, and he would love that. And he did those just the way or better than I would have done them. It was a great arrangement."

It was not a stable one, however. "Just like Alice was in love with Jeremiah, in a strange way, before," says Jean-Pierre, "then it was the same thing for me. She was in love with everyone who was really interesting. She had passion for people because they had something, skills, whatever. The main thing is, I was striving for recognition, because I was running that kitchen. Even if she said no, I know I was running that kitchen.

"I am a little responsible for a lot of the mess, because I was chasing girls. You know, I am French. Actually, the girls were chasing me. The first six months I was here, I would go to a party, and girls would come to me. I couldn't believe it. I messed up a lot of things in the restaurant. Starting to go out with the flower lady, going out with the waitresses. Alice didn't like it."

Beginning on June 28, 1977, the menus at Chez Panisse were no longer bilingual. Only such untranslatable items as bouillabaisse were listed in French. "When the menu went into English," says Jean-Pierre, "I think it was for Alice a period of anti-French, because of me first, and because of a lot of things. We had fights about everything."

"He was wonderful as a right arm, and more than a right arm," Alice says. "But then he wanted to be in charge, and he just didn't have the personality to do that. What he lacked—it was certainly management skills, and it certainly was communicating with me. And culinary vision. He was a great cook, but I thought the things he chose were not necessarily the things that he did best. We just had a hard time."

Meanwhile, Jeremiah Tower was finding it more difficult to tear himself away than he had foreseen. Saturday afternoons into April 1977, he gave cooking lessons in the Chez Panisse kitchen. Alice and Jean-Pierre did turn out occasional special meals—suckling pig roasted outside on the sidewalk for Jerry Budrick's birthday in February 1977; a Richard Olney menu in March featuring the great Burgundies of the Clos de Bèze; another Gertrude Stein birthday party, with a menu much subdued from the wacky version of three years back; a sixtieth-birthday lunch for the composer Lou Harrison—but Alice's focus was less now on the celebratory event and more on refining her own cooking style and seeking out ingredients of ever higher quality. "If only a few people can taste the difference, that's enough," she said.

Jerry Budrick had bought 160 acres in Amador County, in the foothills of the Sierra Nevada, and there he and Alice planned a one-acre garden to produce the hot-weather crops that the backyard gardens of Berkeley and the farms of Marin and Sonoma counties were too cool to grow. It was going to be totally organic, a concept well known to hippies and vegetarians but at that time completely ignored by high-end restaurants. What organic produce there was to be had was usually tired, bruised, and old, sold in "health food" stores reeking of brewer's yeast and dietary supplement pills. "My idea of organic was to grow everything so, so carefully," Alice says, "pulling off the bugs by hand if you had to, and bringing the food to the restaurant so fresh it was really still alive. That's what distinguishes a great salad from a good one—a great one is alive."

The Amador garden, at first, was a delight. In June 1977, Alice featured a week of menus titled SPECIAL SALADS FROM OUR GARDEN— "summer salad of fresh crab with grapefruit slices, green and white asparagus, and baby oak leaf lettuces," "fresh salmon mousse surrounded by vegetable salads," "Richard Olney's salad of various lettuces, hyssop flowers, nasturtiums, garlic, shallots, and various fresh herbs." But the delight didn't last. "That garden was a disaster," Alice confesses. "We paid a farmer and bought the seeds and really thought something was going to grow, but the gophers got there first."

That July, the Bastille Day dinner became a weeklong festival of garlic-based dinners—culminating in "roast suckling pig from garlic-fed sows from the Dal Porto Ranch in Amador County." Giving credit to the grower in this fashion came naturally to Alice. Over the ensuing years,

Alice, 1977

a bastardized version of the practice would spread across America, with dubious statements of geographic origin ("Hudson Valley apples") or virtually meaningless descriptions ("fire-roasted") giving a little tweak of borrowed prestige to tired menus. "They didn't understand," says Alice. "All we were doing was recognizing our friends for doing good work."

ALICE, for whom extended stays in the kitchen were exhausting, needed a vacation—a good, long, proper European holiday. The last dinner of the summer of 1977, including a rather daring lamb's brain salad, was served on August 27. The next day was the restaurant's sixth birthday, but it was a Sunday and there was no party. Instead, there was to be an enforced vacation, for everybody. Alice shut down Chez Panisse altogether, and the restaurant stayed closed till the end of September. "I went to see Claude and Martine Labro in Vence," she recalls, "and then all of us descended on the Domaine Tempier. Jerry came over to join us. He loved that Bandol wine. Looking back now, I see just one endless meal, outside, under the arbor, with Lulu producing the most beautiful things, dish after dish after dish. She'd always go to the docks in the early, early morning, right when the fishing boats were coming in, so she'd get the widest choice and the freshest fish. They make some very serious wines at Tempier, these noble old reds, but it was hot that September and I think only of that cool, pink, wonderful Bandol rosé."

Alice and Martine traveled a long, zigzag route to sample the newest French cooking. Alice did not relax, exactly—Alice does not relax—but, "Oh, it was a recharge, and I was so happy to be with those friends. They seem to know so much, just instinctively, about how to live, how to be happy. My French was not very good, and Lulu's English is nonexistent, but we would talk for hours. There's a special happiness that I feel only with Lulu, I think. And then with Lulu's food, well, it was paradise.

"Of course, I did have to come home. But when I came back, I didn't want to be in the kitchen anymore." Ever social, she wanted to be back among the customers. She loved to see their reactions to the food, and she drew inspiration from their enthusiasms. When a particular dish was a big hit, she would dream up variations for Jean-Pierre and his brigade to try.

Starting in January 1978, therefore, Jean-Pierre would function as chef, while Alice, though overseeing the front of the house, retained the title. Jean-Pierre was annoyed, but he stuck to his stoves. This was an early instance of a phenomenon of which many observers and former staff members of Chez Panisse have complained over the years: Alice taking credit that others think she should have shared. "History," Charles Shere observes, "is littered with the bodies of men who feel they should have gotten more of the credit than Alice."

"I've thought about this issue a lot," says Greil Marcus. "I don't think Alice would be the focus that she is if she didn't enjoy it, if that wasn't important to her. There are many ways to avoid attention. On the other hand, Chez Panisse is Alice's idea. It's Alice's values. It's Alice's standards.

To the degree that it falls short, it's because her ideas and her standards are not being met. I've said for years that if she were hit by a bus, the restaurant would close. I don't think it would sustain itself. When Alice is in Berkeley, she is at the restaurant all the time, and there is never anything that is right. She is always finding fault, whether it's with service, or food preparation, or ingredients, or the way something is cooked. That's because she has a clear idea about every aspect of what the restaurant is. And nobody else does. Nobody else has the complexity of vision that she does."

"I try to give credit where it's due," Alice says, "and I know sometimes I've failed. It's hard to be successful and not have some people be upset with you."

GRILLING HAD BEEN part of the Chez Panisse style almost since the beginning, but in the early days it was improvisational at best—a home barbecue in the backyard, or sometimes on the front sidewalk, and then a fireplace indoors with a spit that never worked properly. In January 1978, however, the restaurant closed for two weeks for the installation in the downstairs kitchen of a massive wood-burning oven and grill. "It was an inspiration from Lulu," Alice says. "Also from the Royal Pavilion at Brighton, though scaled down a little bit." When the restaurant reopened on January 13, 1978, Alice wrote at the bottom of the menu, "This weekend begins a new era in culinary possibilities for us all."

Though its finances remained chaotic and profit elusive, Chez Panisse was becoming more and more a "destination restaurant." Many people came expecting perfection—something Chez Panisse, for all its skills, rarely achieved. When so many customers will never be seen again, as was the case with the many tourists determined to eat at the great Chez Panisse just once in their lives, staffs are tempted to treat them less well than the regulars who are the true source of life for a restaurant.

In France, under the stern eye of the red-covered *Guide Michelin,* the few restaurants accorded the ultimate rating of three stars must maintain not only the highest culinary standards but the warmest of hospitality.

There was no Michelin red guide, however, for the United States, and a certain arrogance was creeping in at Chez Panisse.

The columnist Herb Caen, in the *San Francisco Chronicle* of February 18, 1978, reported an example of the decline of civility among both the clients and the staff:

> Imagine Betty Friedan, the great Fem-Libber, trying to pull rank on a sister! At crowded Chez Panisse in Berkeley Fri. night, she swept in without a reservation and demanded a table. Told she'd have to wait, she snapped at the hostess, "Look, I'm Betty Friedan!" "Uh-huh," replied the hostess, "and I'm Suzy Nelson." La Friedan stomped out.

A story often ruefully repeated concerns Jerry Budrick, who in his capacity as headwaiter sometimes greeted arriving diners. A couple approached whose appearance, for some reason, he didn't like, and he met them not with welcome but with a stream of cigarette smoke, straight into their faces.

"Jerry Budrick would always correct my French pronunciation," recalls Tom Guernsey's former wife, Nancy Donnell Lily. "He let you know how he felt about you. Not always in a gracious way—that's one way of putting it."

"We were all drinking too much," says Alice. "Especially Jerry." Jerry still considered himself to be Alice's lover, and she did not deny his claim, but the distance between them was clearly growing.

Jim Maser was married to Alice's sister Laura; both of them were very close to Alice and Chez Panisse. Jim recalls, "I went to Alice, and I said, 'Alice, how can you have this person represent you? He is so arrogant.' And she said to me, 'Well, you need to have a little bit of attitude to deal with the public.'"

"On the other hand," says Greil Marcus, "Jerry was also an enormous asset to the restaurant. He was the first person we ever knew who considered being a waiter a profession. Jerry was a fantastic presence in the dining room, and tremendously knowledgeable. He demanded respect from the customers without placing a little card on the table at the beginning of the meal saying, 'I want your respect.' Just through his manner."

"The restaurant really was a club," Ruth Reichl recalls, "and until Alice became a friend, the food was wonderful, but it was very awkward. You always felt like you were nobody. It wasn't being put in Siberia so much as I'm sure what people still feel today, which is that eighty percent of the people in the room belong to a club that you're not part of. I remember the first time after I'd gotten to know Alice, Doug and I went to the restaurant as insiders, and it was so much a better experience. It was a feeling of, Oh, now we really live in Berkeley. And we'd lived in Berkeley for about eight years."

Drinking on duty by too many of the staff was still a problem, as was the restaurant's eternally miserable financial management. But the food was as fine as ever, and again it was evolving. With Jean-Pierre in command of the kitchen, and as a result of Alice's long tour of France, Chez Panisse was becoming more French again. Though there still were California flourishes, and the menus continued to be printed only in English, there is no mistaking the French provenance of asparagus with hollandaise sauce in puff-pastry cups; Gruyère soufflé; truffled saddle of lamb; *pot-au-feu Dodin-Bouffant,* described on the menu as "an elaborate recipe from Maxim's restaurant made with larded beef, marrow bones, chicken, pork, and veal sausage with herbs, veal knuckles cooked in Burgundy wine with vegetables and garnished with duck livers." In March 1978, there was a week of specialties of the Languedoc, followed by a week and a half of dishes from the Restaurant Troisgros. Then suddenly the menus were bilingual again—French first, followed by the English translation.

For the in crowd there were parties galore—birthdays, wedding receptions, and anniversaries, each honored with a special menu. For David Goines's birthday, every table in the restaurant got a free bottle of zinfandel in his honor, and the menu—in tribute to David's scholarship in the classics—quoted the Roman poet Marcus Argentarius:

Welcome, old friend, long-necked bottle,
Dearest companion of my table

And of the wine-jar, with your soft gurgle
And your sweetly chuckling mouth: welcome;
You secret witness of my poverty
(Which you've done little enough to aid),
At last I hold you in my hand again.
But I wish you had come to me undiluted,
Pure as a virgin to her bridegroom's bed.

"In those days," says David, "there was a very strong sense of community and involvement. People would come by and shell peas and talk. When it was decided that the restaurant needed a wine cellar, I dug it with my own two hands. When garlic week came around, people would come by and peel garlic and drink wine. They'd be there for three or four days, peeling garlic and talking."

A good example of how welcoming Chez Panisse could be in the late seventies, despite its occasional bad behavior toward people it disdained, is the story of a Stanford University art-history major named Judy Rodgers. Judy had spent her senior year in high school at the home of Jean Troisgros, spending every possible moment in the Troisgros restaurant's kitchen and taking copious notes, which she brought with her when she went to celebrate her twenty-first birthday at Chez Panisse in the fall of 1977. "I showed Alice my Troisgros recipes that night," Judy recalls.

We only talked a little, but I told her that I was bereft, ever since leaving Troisgros. I said, "I'd love to just come and occasionally spend a day in your kitchen, just watching." Alice was keen on that and said yes. We kind of negotiated—no, we didn't negotiate, it wasn't a negotiation. You don't negotiate with Alice. Nothing happens like that. It's always seduction.

At that time, Alice was alone doing Saturday lunch. She proposed that I just come up and help with that, and I was thrilled. So I would drive up each Saturday morning from Palo Alto and put together the lunch at Chez Panisse. We'd always have a soup and salad combo. We always had smoked trout from Garrapata, with different flavored mayonnaise every week. My job was just doing slight variations week after week. I had to make a soup every week, always a puréed vegetable cream soup. After just a couple of weeks, Alice trusted me to do it on my own—that's one of her characteristics, to trust people. She's less worried if you don't have the competence if your heart is in the right place and you're shooting for the right aesthetic. I got in over my head, as did Chez Panisse constantly. I'd never lit a fire in a grill in my life.

Then at some point Alice proposed to me that I actually become the lunch chef. I was blown away. I was twenty-one years old. So I signed on to cook lunch during spring break. After the first two days, Alice wasn't even there, and I was in my own little world in that kitchen. Every Saturday I'd look at the prior week's menus, and Alice would talk to me about making decisions. We'd go over to the Co-op and buy some chickens, and she'd show me how to cut them in half. Sometimes she'd talk me through what to do over the phone.

I don't think anybody would pretend that everything produced by that restaurant was stellar, three-star cuisine every day. What people loved about Chez Panisse was the generosity, the spirit. It was the same thing I'd seen at Troisgros. There was so much given to you, whether it was an idea of a dish, the conception of a menu— a sequenced meal that you couldn't quite understand why it was so satisfying. That meal made you happy the way great home cooking did. It reminded me of the meals that my aunts in France made, who would uncannily fashion these simple little meals out of almost nothing—a salad with a few chopped-up hard-cooked eggs that had never been in the refrigerator, so they were warm and tender and fragrant. And a few nice seasonal walnuts with a drop of walnut oil. Alice did that same kind of thing.

Judy Rodgers would go on to her own renown as chef and co-owner of the Zuni Café. Zuni is the closest thing San Francisco has to Chez Panisse—the food is straightforward, elegant, informal, and delicious— and it's often referred to as the city's favorite restaurant.

Though modest in manner, Alice had begun to recognize her kinship with the other most celebrated people in the food world. When they came to Chez Panisse, she went all out. A good example is this seventieth-birthday menu, served on July 25, 1978, for the food writer M. F. K. Fisher, manifesting the synthesis of French and Californian cooking that the writer idealized. The titles are those of four of her books.

SERVE IT FORTH!

CONSIDER THE OYSTER
Pacific oysters served on the half shell
Billecart-Salmon Champagne
꘠

MARSEILLES, A CONSIDERABLE TOWN
Fresh California snails with Pernod, tomatoes, and garlic
Bandol rosé, Domaine Tempier
꘠

Whole Pacific rockfish charcoal-grilled
with wild herbs and anchovies
Crozes-Hermitage blanc, Bruno Thierry
꘠

Young spit-roasted pheasant with new potatoes
Côte Rôtie, Bruno Thierry
꘠

Bitter lettuce salad with goat cheese croutons
Bandol rouge, Domaine Tempier
꘠

Three plum sherbets with orange rind boats
꘠

A CORDIALL WATER
Muscat de Beaumes de Venise, Bruno Thierry
꘠

Coffee & candies

At Christmastime 1977, Alice had said she didn't want to be in the kitchen anymore. A year and a half later, she wanted to be away from Chez Panisse altogether. Amid the unhappy Jean-Pierre, an intemperate dining-room staff, and her less and less familiar public, Alice was yearning again for Europe and its civilized ways. "I really needed to get out," she says. "I wanted four months. I wanted to taste, travel, take it all in, and just be away. I was uneasy leaving the restaurant for so long, but that didn't stop me. I'd been to a lot of wonderful places, but there were still so many more. So I asked Marion and Cecilia if they wanted to go."

Marion Cunningham was an early devotee of Chez Panisse who had gone on to be James Beard's personal assistant and had just finished a massive revision of the classic *Fannie Farmer Cookbook.* Having tested some seventeen hundred recipes ("Even my neighbor's dog got fat," she recalls), Marion was ready to eat somebody else's cooking for a while. Cecilia Chiang was the proprietress of one of America's first luxurious Chinese restaurants, The Mandarin, in San Francisco.

Alice, Marion, and Cecilia all agreed that it would be fun to ask Jeremiah Tower—bored stiff in the lonely wilds of Big Sur—to squire the three ladies to the greatest restaurants on the Continent. He was delighted to accept.

Then Jeremiah's mother died suddenly, and he had to drop out. Alice asked if he would like to come back to the old stand for the rest of the year. He said he would, and once more Jean-Pierre was pushed into the background at Chez Panisse.

For two weeks in September 1978, Alice, Marion, and Cecilia dined in a number of the best restaurants in Europe, often two a day. Starting in Brussels, they went to Comme Chez Soi, Galalou, The Crown, Witamers Bakery, and Ming's. In Paris, they took in Jacques Manière's Dodin-Bouffant (the successor to Au Pactole); the famed ice cream maker Berthillon; the elegant Quai d'Orsay; the very old and classicist Drouant; the beautiful, feminine Pré Catalan, in the Bois de Boulogne; the archetypal bistros Chez Allard and Au Beaujolais; the great fish house La Marée; and the paragon of three-star restaurants, Taillevent. They would travel to Alsace to experience what a long-established, seamlessly hospitable three-star in the country was like, at the Auberge de l'Ill; to Switzerland for the uncategorizable cuisine of Frédy Girardet ("The best food I had ever put in my mouth," Alice says); to the pastoral Chez la Mère Blanc at Vonnas, deep in the Burgundian countryside; to Roanne, where the Restaurant Troisgros was evolving along a path parallel to that of Chez Panisse but far above it in luxury; to Hiély-Lucullus in Avignon, where the traditional cooking of interior Provence was refined to its essence; and finally to the Champagne capital, Reims, and Gérard Boyer's Les Crayères, a magnificent château surrounded by extensive English gardens and serving the most classical of haute cuisine. "I don't know how my liver survived," Alice recalls, "but, oh, we did eat well."

For the first month of her absence, Alice had selected all of the recipes to be served at Chez Panisse, printing the menus well in advance to insure that Jeremiah stuck to the script. THE BEST OF CHEZ PANISSE, as the menu sequence was titled, was the first time that the restaurant had ever looked backward. Jeremiah's heart was not in it.

As soon as the rigid prescriptions of September were finished, however, Jeremiah tossed them aside with a flourish—free now to dish up calf's brains salad, pear soup with raspberry cream, blinis with caviar, *salmis* of quail, braised capon with two sauces, *civet* of duck with poached dried fruit, another all-Sauternes dinner. He did a week of tributes to his primary influences—Olney, Montagné, Escoffier, Elizabeth David, and "my Russian uncle." He did a week of white truffle dishes, a week devoted to Joseph Phelps's new vintage of zinfandel nouveau, a week of black truffles.

After Marion and Cecilia's departure, Alice remained and made her home base at Claude and Martine Labro's, from which it was but a short trip to Lulu and Lucien Peyraud's. Richard Olney's house was just down the road from the Domaine Tempier. Alice and Martine hit the road again. "We were still doing the three-stars," says Alice. "L'Oasis. Vergé. Les Baux. Chapel. Bocuse. But my favorite by far, after going to all of them, was still Girardet."

In October, Jerry Budrick came to Europe, leaving Jeremiah short another valuable (if volatile) veteran. Jerry, still believing in his relationship with Alice, flew to Rome with Bob Waks, of the Cheese Board, and Jay

Heminway, whose Green and Red zinfandel would succeed the Phelps zinfandel as the Chez Panisse house red wine. Alice met them in Rome, and they rented a Volkswagen for a drive through Italy.

Back in Berkeley, Jeremiah was turning out food as dazzling as ever, but he was unhappy with the state of Chez Panisse.

10/31/78

My dear Alice and Jerry,

I am sitting here in the office on Hallowed Eve, drinking Thivin, and wondering what to say . . . what to tell you about the restaurant. . . . Now I am going to scold you, hoping that it coincides with something in your head, though I fear not. I don't think the restaurant can go on in its present way. All the trade deals, maneuverings, decentralization of responsibility, laxness (laxative) of the staff to me spells ruin very soon. . . . I do not want to incur your wrath. But I hope you come back after having very, very serious thoughts about what must happen here in the next year or two. Maybe I am just spooked with ghosts and very fatigued with two or three jobs going at once, but it's really out of my hands now and I can't do much in these few months when I am really only an eccentric visitor at Chez Panisse. It will be strong when you return, that I can say. But it ain't mine no more. I am a stranger here, except for Suzy and, believe it or not, Tom, who has been nothing but total support. How have you let these staff learn such bad manners?

Carrie has had the same flower arrangement on the dining room mantelpiece for three weeks. DEAD LEAVES WITH BROWNING ORCHIDS. She calls every day at noon for her special order. My very sweet Alice, what have you let happen?

It really is time to do the next thing with yourself and the restaurant—they are probably the same thing. I feel apologetic for not having a brilliant idea. My need and only idea is to go on to do something else. But I am still in love with the fact that Panisse has survived and should go on for forty years. . . .

I feel cannibalistic, dark, Jeremaiad, and a son of the Semites. Hawk noses, smooth leather saddle bags. I smell horses in the desert when cooking,

with the obvious results: Mint is in everything. Peppers—but mostly the
varieties of the black. Melons with old Sauternes and black pepper.
Anchovies and figs with raspberries, with a tired old Margaux. . . .
And a return to the old bistro in the south of France. To the food we
did a year after I started. It appeals to me again. Fuck all this orange
peel julienne and pubic hairs of leeks. Give me some of Tempier's lunches.
Give me caviar and buckwheat and a lover of vodka-like appetite. . . .
Toast in bed in the morning with smoky tea and a hit of opium. Bitter
salads for lunch. Gin with violets at six. Guinea fowl over the coals with
pommes sarladaises, *rose ice, a whipping for dessert. . . . Do enjoy it all,*
do be naughty there so you can be straight here.

    Coquilles with possum butter,
    Love and kisses,
    Jeremiah

Meanwhile, stuffed into the Beetle, Bob Waks, Jay Heminway, Jerry, and Alice picked up a turkey in Florence for Thanksgiving, which they were going to spend at Jay's family's chalet in the Swiss Alps. Along the way there, they stopped in Turin, where they found precisely "the next thing" that Jeremiah couldn't think of.

The four had reservations for a late dinner at a fancy restaurant, but by three thirty in the afternoon they were ravenous. They stopped in at the first open place they found, a pizzeria. "We could see a fire burning inside," Alice wrote some years later, "and it pulled us in. And there I had my first pizza out of a wood-burning oven. We all thought it was the best thing we had eaten on the whole trip."[1] She asked to see how they did it. She was shown the fat oven with its firebrick floor and white-hot oak coals heaped in the corner. The temperature inside was a thousand degrees Fahrenheit. A pizza went in on a long wooden peel, was twirled once, twice, three times so that each side got the full blast of heat from the coals—"with flames swirling around under the ceiling of the oven"—and in less than two minutes it was ready to eat. "That moment was the real beginning of the café," says Alice. "Pizzas were so inexpensive to cook, and it was just so convivial, that little group of people hanging out."

A café upstairs at Chez Panisse, a simple café, with its own open kitchen and its own pizza oven. (The earliest version of the upstairs café had not had a real kitchen, and Jeremiah's recent proposal would inevitably have been fancier than what Alice had in mind now. Besides, that was Jeremiah's idea, and this one was Alice's.) It could mean the return of their friends, the regulars, the old-timers who had been priced out. There would be no compromise of Alice's standards. The ingredients would be as fine as those of the formal downstairs, and the cooking would be just as inventive and skilled, but there would be no truffles, no foie gras, no classic French sauces. The preparations would require much less labor. There would be a small menu, changing daily, according to what was best and best priced on the market that morning. You could order as little or as much as you wanted. You could hang out with your friends. It would be nothing less than the embodiment of Alice's original vision of Chez Panisse—something that from the first night forward had never really existed.

9.

CREATION AND DESTRUCTION

1979–1982

A s 1978 waned, Jeremiah became more preoccupied with his own future, and Jean-Pierre was once again, though still uncredited, chef. With the New Year Jeremiah departed, this time for good, and Alice returned. The great restaurants of France had inspired her deeply, and after four months there, she determined to reproduce their masterpieces at Chez Panisse.

The menus for the first three weeks of 1979 were titled SPECIAL DISHES FROM A RECENT GASTRONOMIC TOUR OF EUROPE. From the three-star Auberge de l'Ill in Alsace came "salad of rabbit and rabbit livers cooked with truffles, served with escarole and a sauce of olive oil, lemon cream, and black truffles," and a lobster soufflé. From Troisgros there were "sweetbreads and veal kidneys sautéed with black mushrooms, served with a spicy brown wine sauce"; from Girardet, "chicken baked in a sealed crock, with black truffles under the skin, served with a leek confit"; from L'Oasis at La Napoule, "duck liver mousse dusted with black truffles and served with a Champagne gelée."

Once again, rave reviews came pouring in. Patricia Unterman in the *San Francisco Chronicle* of April 8, 1979:

> For eight years now, Chez Panisse in Berkeley has been turning out a different menu each night. That's in the neighborhood of 3000 new dishes, and they keep doing it. What is so remarkable is that the food is always exciting, very rarely poor, occasionally merely good, and usually superb. . . . The palette of foods is so varied and complex that you usually taste something you have never tasted before.

The *International Review of Food and Wine*, for its first anniversary in May 1979, held an event in New York to showcase the talents of up-and-coming American chefs, and Alice was invited to attend. She wanted Jean-Pierre at her side. She called her artist friend Patricia Curtan and asked if she'd mind stepping in at the restaurant for a week. "I was stunned," Patty recalls. "I'd never been a chef! I said, 'Well, no, Alice, I can't do that.' This is an insight into Alice: She just said, 'Well, what do you have to lose? I have something to lose here, but what do you have to lose?'"

In the *New York Daily News*, Ella Elvin described the meal that Alice and Jean-Pierre produced at the New York event:

> Coin-sized oysters taken from the sea near Seattle the day before. Whole heads of garlic, baked to a butter, that, with slight pressure, eased out of their crisp skins and became a spread for country bread with white goat cheese. Spring lamb from a California ranch, grilled to perfection . . . accompanied by a zinfandel produced on the same ranch. A salad of four-inch leaf lettuce picked just a moment before serving from garden flats carried [in Alice's lap] on the plane from California. . . .
>
> Asked how she felt about the luncheon she had just presented, Waters, ever modest, used just one word—"Pleased."[1]

Alice and Patricia Curtan in the Chez Panisse kitchen

That lettuce was in fact mesclun, the seeds of which Alice had brought back from her sojourns with Martine and Lulu and planted in her backyard. Mesclun was second nature in Provence, but at the time unknown in the United States.

The *Daily News* had found Alice in a somewhat dreamy moment, quoting her, "I'd like to have a completely self-sufficient restaurant, a country inn. I think of having a spot in the Napa Valley. That's my goal. I'd produce my own olive oil, butter, grow my own little lettuces. We could do everything."

Alice was also pleased with Patty Curtan's work in her absence, and asked her to stay on. Patty worked part-time through the summer, and with Mark Miller's departure in September 1979, she became sous-chef to Jean-Pierre. "She was so unbelievably capable, and responsible," Alice says. "She was the only one who swept the floor between seatings. She wouldn't begin to work unless the floor was swept."

Lois Dwan wrote in the *Los Angeles Times,* "In some eight years, Alice Waters has made Chez Panisse a place of pilgrimage for all serious gastronomes," and she quoted Alice saying, "It's a wonderful feeling, wonderfully exciting when at six o'clock you can just pull something out of the air and say, Oh, no, the watercress needs a little of this or that—and it becomes just right. If it looks like too much cream in too many dishes, I can just stop midstream and say, 'We can't do that.' I cooked scallops the other night, maybe fifty times, and each time it was different. There was probably one person there at the end that got the perfect scallop dish."[2]

In *New West* magazine, Colman Andrews wrote, "If you could eat in only one restaurant for the rest of your life, Chez Panisse would be the one to choose."[3]

The restaurant's native exuberance seemed to be coming back to the surface. One signal occasion was a screening of Errol Morris's new film *Gates of Heaven,* which the director Werner Herzog years before had teased Morris that he would never finish. If it ever opened, said Herzog, he'd eat one of the shoes he was wearing at that moment. Now Morris was holding Herzog to his bet.

"I remember distinctly the cooking process," Alice recalls, "and the crazy idea I had—to put it in fat, cook it like confit, because I thought it would soften it up. I cooked it, and I cooked it, and I cooked it, and I cooked it, probably eight hours, and it never happened. That shoe was something formidable. It wasn't just some little Italian loafer. It was a serious shoe. I remember watching him bite into it. He chewed on it for a long time."

Another filmmaker, and one of the Chez Panisse family, Les Blank, had been struggling for some time to make a documentary titled *Garlic Is as Good as Ten Mothers.* He had documented the hellzapoppin' bacchanal of the Chez Panisse Quatorze Juillet dinners of the past three years, and now he had footage of Herzog trying to eat the long-stewed shoe. The film was to be shown at a Les Blank retrospective at the Museum of Modern Art in New York in June, but it still wasn't quite finished, and Les was out of money. Alice proposed a benefit dinner to raise the remaining funds (at $100 a head)—A SPECIAL GARLIC EVENT TO CELEBRATE *ALLIUM SATIVUM,*

FILM, MUSIC, AND THE VERNAL EQUINOX. The menu for March 21, 1979, was, of course, all garlic (except, this time, the dessert) and redolent of the baroque complexities of Jeremiah—executed now, however, by Jean-Pierre.

Galantine of pigeon, duck, and quail,
filled with layers of meats, livers, and garlic mosaics

❦

Whole baked fish, served with a garlic puff pastry
and lobster butter sauce

❦

Spring lamb with three garlic-infused vegetable purées

❦

Roquette salad with goose fat and garlic-rubbed croutons

❦

Poached figs in red wine with garlic-shaped meringues

In July 1979, the menu for the fourth annual garlic festival was headlined GARLIC FRENZY!!! The dinners featured garlic soup with garlic salad, whole baked garlic, garlic soufflé, deep-fried garlic cheese, garlic crépinettes with garlic potatoes, garlic eggs and garlic sausages and garlic brioche, and, not for the faint of heart, chocolate-covered garlic cloves flavored with rose water.

In the *New York Times,* Mark Blackburn published a piece headlined IT WAS THE FESTIVAL OF THE 'STINKING ROSE,' which read in part,

"Remember LSD?" said Tom Weller. "Garlic is the LSD of the 70s." Mr. Weller, president of St. Hieronymous Press, which prints posters designed by his partner, David Goines, was sitting in the garden of Chez Panisse, the French restaurant patronized by the Berkeley elect, waiting for his turn at table.

Several chairs away was Mr. Goines, in a white chef's jacket, recovering from eight hours of peeling garlic for the fourth annual Garlic Festival at Chez Panisse. His posters, the restaurant and the festival are all phenomena of the new Berkeley, which has taken up good living in lieu of revolution. . . .

"The third year it became outrageous," [Alice Waters] said, "and this year I almost didn't do it. People are flying in in Learjets from Los Angeles. It's become absurd. We're booked up three months in advance, and the regular customers can't get in. . . .

Will there be a garlic festival at Chez Panisse next year? "Who knows," she replied.[4]

A similarly dyspeptic reaction to the restaurant's fame and good fortune came from Charles Shere, Lindsey's husband. After *Playboy* magazine had put Chez Panisse on its list of America's twenty-five greatest restaurants, Charles wrote in the *Oakland Tribune,* "It's happened before, and it'll happen again. That sounds complacent, but it's not: it's resigned. . . . In every case the result is a brief upsurge in a particular kind of patron—the one who comes in with a show-me attitude. . . . People really concerned about food values tend not to eat out on *Playboy*'s recommendation."

The Chez Panisse culture's oscillation between joy and gloom was by now an inextricable component of its identity. Fame had come, and with it an increase in revenues; then Alice and the staff didn't want to have to live up to the glory. Sometimes, as when she cooked Werner Herzog's shoe, Alice was really happy with Chez Panisse and her place in the world. Sometimes, as when she flew the mesclun in her lap to New York and then started extemporizing to a reporter about moving Chez Panisse to the Napa Valley, she could revel in her idiosyncrasy while also communicating to those who knew her well a deep discomfort with what she and the restaurant had become. Sometimes she presented a big smile to the camera and privately wished she was anywhere else.

Alice's shifting moods were mirrored in those of the whole *famille Panisse.* Year by year the staff had grown smaller and more familial; by 1979, there were fewer than twenty full-time employees. But they were the core, and when things were going well, they were proud to be part of what had become perhaps the most famous restaurant in America, and they worked together in peaceful communion, following the Chez Panisse ethos of fairness, optimism, and excellence. Sometimes, however, in accord with Alice's sudden accesses of bleakness, the restaurant as a whole—for it was by now, it seemed, a single social organism—seemed to lose its *esprit de corps*. Nearly always, Chez Panisse managed to present a calm, contented face to the world. Nearly always, there was something going haywire behind the scenes.

By the time the restaurant's eighth anniversary rolled around in August 1979, Alice's dissatisfaction had become general, and it included Jerry Budrick. Their alienation from each other had grown slowly through time, but Alice had been too shy or too kind or too guilty—perhaps all of those—to break with him entirely. Now, however, she did it. Jerry, of course, had seen it coming.

Why did we break up? Well, I'm an old-fashioned kind of guy, and I believe in honesty and openness, and it turned out she didn't. I always suspected things, because she was off a lot on these trips, and I never knew what she was up to. I just couldn't take the not knowing, and not trusting and not believing.

She was always experimental, and I should have realized that that's how she treated life, with an attitude of "I'll try anything"— try a new restaurant, try a new food, try a new trip, try a new place to go—and that openness would naturally lead to that. I should have realized it when she took up with me. She was living with Tom Luddy. And once she took up with me, it seemed like she became monogamous with me. That's how it seemed.

People, when they meet me and they know I was at Chez Panisse, they ask me, "Well, how was it working for Alice?" And I have to try to explain that I never worked for Alice, I worked *with* Alice. We worked together. We made the plans, we made the schemes, we did all that together, renovations and gardens and wines and all that stuff. It was great, and we had a wonderful time doing it.

THROUGHOUT 1979 and the first half of 1980, the creation of the café occupied most of Alice's attention. "I was completely focused on the food. I don't really remember anything about the dining room, because I was just so absorbed in who was going to cook and how we were going to manage to do an à la carte menu. We knew we wanted to have food that was really inexpensive. I wanted to use all our leftovers. That was my theory, that if we didn't use it, we couldn't just throw it out. There were all those expensive cuts of meat downstairs, and that was one way we could save on food costs—use the unused things from the downstairs in the café the next day for lunch."

Alice's friend Cecilia Chiang recommended the architect Lun Chan and a kitchen designer named Bumps Baldauf. Kip Mesirow would contribute his design skills and expert Japanese woodwork to the interior.

The budget for building the café was about $200,000. Thanks to Pat Waters's signature, the corporation had obtained its first bank loan of $50,000. Pat had also borrowed $15,000 personally and lent that to the restaurant. Mary Borelli and Jeremiah Tower, however, each of whom held five hundred shares in Pagnol et Cie, had demanded to be bought out at $50 a share, and there had gone the $50,000. The subsequent sale of those shares brought only half that. Chez Panisse had managed to squirrel away $72,000 from its operating income. That left them $88,000 short.

Alice said, "Don't worry, it's going to be such a hit we'll wipe out that debt in no time." What mattered to her, as ever, were the aesthetics, and they were a dream. Kip's designs for the paneling and lamps melded Japanese design with California Craftsman and a hint of Art Nouveau. Alice hung huge posters for Pagnol's movies on the walls. The kitchen, running narrowly along one wall, was completely open to the dining room. Alice's idea was that the sounds and smells of frying, charcoal grilling, and the new pizza oven would drift throughout the dining rooms.

That oven, however, wasn't at all like the one that had inspired Alice's epiphany in Turin. "Bumps—the kitchen designer—came in," says Alice, and he didn't know anything about Italian pizza ovens, but he knew a German bricklayer. This guy had never even heard of a pizza oven. I was trying to describe what it should be like, trying to remember from that time in Torino. There was kind of a low opening, and a low arched ceiling with the flames licking the top. And he built us basically a German bread oven. Wolfgang Puck came up to see the oven shortly after it was put in, and he said, "Oh, I want one of these for Spago." And he hired the same German bricklayer, and he had the same problems we had.

We tried to adapt it for the next ten years. It used just ten times as much wood as an Italian pizza oven. It cooked a certain kind of pizza, which wasn't really a pizza in the way that an Italian would think about it.

Luckily, we found Michele Perrella. He said he was a pizza maker, and since we had no idea what making pizzas was all about and he knew how to make the oven work, I hired him. He was a shining light from day one.

Finally, we got our friend who did bread ovens out in Point Reyes, and he actually crawled into the oven to investigate. He upped the floor, and he changed some of the dimensions, but he was a bread-oven guy, too, and we had another bread oven. You couldn't get it hot enough. It's a matter of the dimensions, really allowing the fire to go over the top. It's not just a matter of low, it's a matter of the arch in the right proportion. Why it took us so long to get that done, I don't know. It wasn't until we brought an iron insert from Italy and put it in there that the oven really worked.

The Café at Chez Panisse, as it is formally called, opened—"perhaps appropriately," Alice says—on April Fools' Day of 1980.

In the name of informality, Alice didn't want to take reservations, but the café was immediately mobbed, and it wasn't long before people were waiting an hour and more for a table. Crammed into the tiny waiting area, they contributed gratifyingly to the bar income, but too many were getting tipsy or worse before they'd had a bite of food, and some of them, inevitably, would complain vociferously about the unendurable wait they were enduring. The money was rolling in, however, just as Alice had so blithely predicted.

The café menu had a relatively fixed format, but within each category there was constant variation, often even between lunch and dinner. There were always soup, salad, pizza, pasta, usually a poultry dish, usually a meat dish, and as often as possible—according to availability and perfect freshness (not always reliable in those days)—a fish or seafood dish. There had not been room for a pastry installation upstairs, so the half dozen or more desserts offered in the café meant a radical increase in the variety and productivity of Lindsey Shere's pastry department downstairs—which was now fully professional and fully indoors.

Very early on, there were a few café dishes so popular that they were exempted from the norm of daily variation: a salad of just-picked mixed baby lettuces—Alice's passion—with garlic croutons; the calzone that was the specialty of master *pizzaiolo* Michele Perrella, which came to be called simply *la crostata di Perrella;* Lindsey Shere's almond tart; and a cool salad

Alice and Lindsey Shere, with a poster from the Pagnol trilogy behind them

with a warm baked Laura Chenel goat cheese melting gently at the center—the quintessential Chez Panisse Café dish.

A native of Sonoma County, Laura Chenel had studied cheese making under the foremost authority on goat cheese in France, Jean-Claude Le Jaouen, and when she returned to California in 1981, she shyly approached Alice with her first American-made chèvres. She was, in fact, the first American ever to have attempted the French style of goat cheese. Alice loved it.

Alice's idea of warm goat cheese in a salad was apparently unprecedented. "There may have been baked goat cheese in France," she says, "but I don't think anybody had ever combined it with a salad." The salad has proved so popular that it is now seen on a good many bistro menus in France, and it has never been off the menu at the Chez Panisse Café, which buys fifty to a hundred pounds of Laura Chenel's cheese a week. The dish is considered a classic of California cuisine.

· BAKED GOAT CHEESE WITH GARDEN LETTUCES ·

This is really one of the easiest things in the world, but it can go wrong. I just get one of those logs of goat cheese. It doesn't have to be round, it could be square. You cut slices maybe an inch thick. We marinate those in a dish with some olive oil, pepper, and herbs—bay and thyme. You use pretty fresh goat cheese, not one day old, about a week old—fresh, young, light, not strongly flavored. If it's too strong-flavored, it gets kind of funky when it's cooked. You can just drizzle it with oil—you don't have to cover it, but we do cover it because we make so many at the restaurant. Marinate it in the oil and the herbs anywhere from a couple of hours to a couple of days. I'm not sure how crucial that step is, ultimately, to the flavor. We just got into the habit of doing it.

Then we make bread crumbs out of good bread, French baguette, crustless. We toast it very lightly, just beginning to get golden, and then grind it into bread crumbs. We pack the bread crumbs onto the goat cheese—it adheres because of the olive oil and marinade—and then we bake it at about four hundred, just until it's beginning to soften. You don't want it to be runny, you just want it warm. It's nice to have the cheese at room temperature before you put it in. It's really important that the cheese comes out really golden brown.

Then we make a little salad that goes along with it. That salad can vary according to the time of year and what you have. I rather like it with rocket [sometimes marketed as "wild arugula"]. I love it with figs in the summer, or a few little almonds in the winter. Greens always. Or if there don't happen to be any good greens, it's very nice with just some almonds and figs as a cheese course. I usually toast the almonds unless they're just fresh from the crop in the fall.

And vinaigrette, just very simple. Red wine vinegar and olive oil. Depending on the greens and what time of year it is, if they're a little strong, I might add a little garlic. Or garlic and anchovy. Maybe even a little mustard. If it needs sweetness, you can always put in a little balsamic vinegar. Not lemon juice, because you've already got some tartness with the goat cheese. Some olives would be nice with it. If you were in Nice, you would have Niçoise olives and a mesclun salad. You might do the same.

I don't put the goat cheese on the greens. I put it on the side of the plate, and I put the pile of greens to the side.

Whether or not such a thing as a California cuisine even existed was still being debated (indeed, still is today). In January 1981, in the *International Herald Tribune,* under the headline NEW WAVE CALIFORNIA CUISINE: A MARRIAGE OF MANY AND A MIME OF NONE, Patricia Wells wrote,

The cuisine generates an excitement about food, a sense of experimentation, plus an uncompromising concern for good food and good dining that seems to have been lost in much of America, where fast food, fake French, and fern bar spinach salads are about as haute as many menus get. . . . The new wave California cuisine is perhaps best personified by a little Berkeley restaurant called Chez Panisse.

Later in 1981, the California Culinary Academy convened a panel in San Francisco to consider the existence, or nonexistence, of California cuisine. Julia Child, California-born, chaired the discussion.

Alice, widely regarded as the mother of California cuisine, said, "It has not quite arrived. . . . We are now in the kindergarten stage." She went on to say that California cuisine would not truly exist until more restaurants were willing to deal directly with farmers and artisans. She talked about Sonoma goat cheese, vegetables grown without pesticides, yellow tomatoes, and the fact that Chez Panisse had planted its own gardens.

Julia replied to Alice:

There is not as much of a California cuisine as you chauvinists would have us believe. It is actually such a mixture that definitions cannot be made. Although you mention simplicity, I think menus can be so simple that they become dull. Sometimes I'm glad when I can go back to France, where they really do things with food.

You have an unduly doleful point of view about the way that most people shop for food. Visit any supermarket and you'll see plenty of fresh fruits and vegetables. And if you don't like the looks of what you see displayed at the market, complain to the produce manager. That's what I do, and it always gets results.

Alice's reply, if ever spoken, was not recorded.

"We remained friends in spite of that," says Alice. "I always had a little back and forth with her. She was the most influential culinary leader in America, and I think the whole organic movement could have moved along a lot more quickly if she had taken it up. But I utterly appreciated what she did do. She expressed the joy of cooking. No one else has been able to do that in the way that she did it. Who cares if she was a good cook or not? She had fun, and she shared it with everybody around her table. She brought people to the table. I always liked that part on her TV show when she sat down and ate."

Whatever it was called, and whatever Julia thought of it, what Chez Panisse did was attracting ever wider attention, most of it in the form of breathless praise. Arthur Bloomfield, in *San Francisco Focus* magazine, compared the calzone that emerged from the new pizza oven to "Toscanini conducting the finale of Brahms's Second or Schubert's C Major."[5]

Craig Claiborne, the United States' supreme arbiter of food, wrote in the *New York Times:*

Where American gastronomy is concerned, there is one commodity that is rarer than locally grown black truffles or homemade foie gras. That is a chef of international repute who was born in the United States. Even rarer is such a celebrated chef who is a woman.

There is, however, one here in Berkeley who could justifiably deserve such renown. Her name may not be a household word from Maine to California, but many culinary experts, both here and abroad, sing her praises without reservation. . . .

Miss Waters makes a cuisine française that is authentically bourgeoise, commanding the basic flavors, which she ferrets out with a passion and astonishing understanding, from good and beautiful products of her native land. . . .

After an altogether joyous lunch with Miss Waters, we insisted on going upstairs for a sample of what had been described by an outstanding East Coast gourmet as the best calzone in the world. . . . Our friend's enthusiasm was not unfounded; the calzone was a triumph of taste and imagination.[6]

What had been for Alice a swirling, ceaseless, sometimes incoherent rush of experiences—crises, inspirations, celebrations, days, weeks, years of

Alice did cook at Chez Panisse from time to time.

time flying by, punctuated by crystalline moments but always so briefly, an impossibly fast-motion film of lovers, waiters, chefs, customers, farmers, and friends blurring into and out of her life—that formless welter seemed now to be assuming a shape, becoming palpably one thing: Alice-Waters-and-Chez-Panisse. Alice, by nature ever attuned to impermanence, came uneasily but also with excitement toward the recognition that she should publish a book that expressed what the entity of Alice-Waters-and-Chez-Panisse was about.

She would model the book on one of her favorites, Richard Olney's *The French Menu Cookbook.* She would title hers *The Chez Panisse Menu Cookbook.* It had to be much more than a cookbook, however. It had to manifest what Chez Panisse was, both on the surface, in terms of ingredients and cooking, and deeper down. It had to express the philosophy and the ethics that were the heart of Chez Panisse, what made it fundamentally different from other restaurants. But the book had to be fun, too, and useful. Organizing it as a collection of menus made it a composition of compositions, like a volume of poetry.

Bob Scheer, Alice's old political mentor, was a friend of Jason Epstein, the distinguished Random House editor, and suggested to him that this could be something worthwhile. "Bob Scheer took me to Chez Panisse for dinner," says Jason. "I was skeptical at first, but bowled over by the meal. Alice joined us for dessert, and I offered her a contract then and there."

"All my friends were brainstorming how I would do this," Alice remembers. "And Linda Guenzel, who was this very obsessive and compulsive customer of the restaurant, as well as a friend, said, 'Well, Alice, you just talk, and what I'll do is record everything you say. Because you say it so well just saying it. And then I'll have it transcribed, and you can pick and choose what you want to put in the book.' So she began doing that, and that's what became the foreword. And I mean, she wrote volumes. But parts of it were written in an adulating way about me. Even though it was supposedly my voice, it was written in a way that I couldn't say it. And after she had transcribed all that, and embellished it, it was extremely painful for me to cut it back. She must have written twenty times as much as what was published as the foreword. It had become her book. She wanted the book! It was very hard for me to find the right tone after that. So I brought Fritz in."

"Alice knew exactly what she wanted to put in the book," says Fritz Streiff. "She knew how she wanted it to be arranged, and she knew what menus she wanted to put in. I was just working on the essay, and some of the other text—the material that Linda Guenzel had been amassing. Linda was extremely eccentric. She had grown up in, I believe, Mississippi gentry, so that when she was a little girl they were poor but they had old vintages of Lafite at the dinner table. She had an extraordinary palate despite the fact that she chain-smoked. Throughout dinner, actually.

"Her feelings were hurt when Alice snatched the manuscript away and gave it to me to finish. I remember doing quite a lot of cutting and rewriting, and adding more material. But please understand that I wasn't the writer. It was pretty much Alice's—taken down verbatim, a lot of it.

"Meanwhile, I also began working in the café, a couple of nights a week, as host. That was fun, but it was also difficult."

"After the café opened," says Alice, "we really had a whole new clientele.

We added four hundred people a day! We'd had a staff of about fifteen, and now all of a sudden we had fifty."

The new level of complexity, and the influx of thirty-five people, most of whom had not been inculcated with the Chez Panisse ethos, provided ample opportunity for conflict. Lindsey Shere's sister, Pat Edwards, had come aboard as business manager, and she remembers:

We began to have all sorts of problems with staff, because suddenly you had all these waiters and cooks and busboys, and we had to become a lot more serious about employee relations and following the laws. The busboys would be smoking marijuana between breaks— I could smell it wafting into the office—and the waiters would drink, and they'd be ordering meals for themselves from the cooks. People really didn't take to the idea, after having had such a loose organization, of being controlled in any way. They thought it was their right to do exactly as they pleased.

You would hear Alice and Jerry shouting out in the back at each other. She got to the point where she wouldn't come and ask me to write a check, but she had check-signing privileges, and so she would sneak in on the weekends and take checks. And I was supposed to control her. She didn't like me very much, because I took my job seriously.

There was a time when the law changed, and we had to start reporting the waiters' tips. That was pretty funny. They would claim some exorbitantly small amount. They made huge amounts of money, especially the downstairs waiters, and on top of that they were stealing. We didn't take charge cards at that time, so people were paying cash, and it was going out like water. So I gave them a specified number of guest checks at the beginning of the night, I counted them, and wrote down the serial numbers, and they had to give those back to me. It seems like the logical thing, doesn't it?

Sometimes I wonder why they ever hired me. I was just Lindsey's sister, and an organized person, and not particularly interested in food. I'd much rather grow flowers, actually.

Pat's office was "a tiny little hole in the wall. When they did the plans for the café, they forgot to put an office in. There was a filing cabinet and a desk. It was so small I had to use the handicapped bathroom for filing things. Eventually things got so bad that they rented a big long shed and made a slightly larger office for me in there. Out back. In a shed. Everybody and his dog used that office.

"The staff and I really got along very well. I was sort of like the mother to them. They would come and tell me their troubles and complain about Alice and whatever else was happening." Alice's criticism of the food was often sharp, albeit nearly always accurate. Some of the staff took her brusque manner as a given, knowing that it was about achieving excellence, and not about the person at all. Others, not surprisingly, were hurt or insulted.

Shelley Handler, the first café chef, sought Pat's counsel frequently. One of the cooks working under Shelley, Joyce Goldstein (who would also go on to her own fame), Pat says, was driving Shelley nuts. "Shelley would come into my office, close the door, and sort of say, 'Ahhh, a place of sanity.' Joyce was a very aggressive and very smart and determined woman, so eventually, actually quite soon, Shelley quit, and Joyce took over."

Alice's father had retired from his full-time job, and he and Marge had moved to Berkeley, where Pat now ran a consulting business from their house. The haphazard way in which Chez Panisse conducted its finances had always rankled Pat Waters, and now that he was on the scene, he offered to help see if they could be straightened out. Alice had always been devoted to her father, and she was very happy to welcome him into the business. He collected no salary or fee, and had no official title, but he had Alice's carte blanche to scrutinize whatever he chose, from books to staff management, and he was welcome as well to attend board meetings. There were those on both the board and the staff who were not so happy with Pat Waters's sudden immersion in the restaurant's affairs, but no one dared say so to Alice's face.

Pat asked for a professional appraisal, to be finished by June 30, 1981. To the astonishment of many, it was a remarkably sunny document. "In an interview with Alice Waters," the report said, "we asked about the success of the restaurant and to what she attributed it. Her reply was that she never compromised on ingredients or ideas and that she had a purist approach. She stated that she was not concerned with the cost." Salaries had been raised across the board, and management was "generous with bonuses," but the appraisal pronounced the restaurant financially sound, and set a value on the business of a million and a half dollars. The appraisers even attributed "the revitalization of the neighborhood" to Chez Panisse.

As Chez Panisse turned ten years old in August 1981, the business was prosperous enough for Alice to begin thinking of bigger things, and the great world outside. Alice was thirty-seven years old now, and she was returning to the cultivation of her social conscience. David Goines designed and donated a tenth-birthday poster, which in its first month on sale at the upstairs bar raised $5,000; the money went to an environmental group known as the Abalone Alliance, to help stop Pacific Gas and Electric's proposed construction of a nuclear power plant at Diablo Canyon. The effort failed—the plant was built—but it had reawakened the political passion that had first brought Alice and David together in the wake of the Free Speech Movement.

DISASTER CAME to Chez Panisse with the suddenness of an earthquake. While Jean-Pierre and his wife vacationed in France, Alice had taken over the kitchen. After midnight, in the early morning of Sunday, March 7, 1982, she did the final cleaning after the dinner service. She locked up and went home. In the middle of the night, her phone rang. Chez Panisse was on fire.

> My dad was the designated emergency contact. That's why he was the one who called. I came racing down, and I saw the flames coming out of the upstairs windows, and then I knew how serious it was. It was like your child's in there somehow. You couldn't go in. The firemen had completely cordoned everything off. Fire trucks, arcs of water, just a mess. I remember very vividly going in the next

day, when they had put out the fire, and the whole downstairs was dripping with water and completely charred. Everything.

We think it started by a live coal being put back into the wood box. Taken out of the fire and put back into the charcoal box again. I was on the grill that night, so who knows. I might have done it myself.

Being in a fire is something. It's a terrible, terrible mess. You can't get the smell out, you can't get the water out. You feel like you're never going to put it back together. We saved a lot of the upstairs. What we didn't save was any of the downstairs. That had to be rebuilt. Even the floors. We were within ten minutes of losing the building. It was close to getting the main beams, and when those go, the whole place collapses. But they caught it in time.

I really learned something from that fire. It was a big turning point, in that I kind of thought that restaurant was mine, you know? It wasn't mine. It was the people who came to eat there—it was theirs. They were part of it. I hadn't been paying enough attention, I think. I was in a little, narrow, inner-circle Chez Panisse world, thinking we could just do it all on our own. We're going to grow our own, do our own, be our own. But after the fire, I felt like we had to open up the doors and look outside.

This was a sobered, measured, mature Alice Waters. She would never lose her passion, but henceforth it would take considered and intentional form. When she opened up the doors and looked outside, she saw a world of opportunities to put the Chez Panisse philosophy to use.

10.

REBAPTISM
BY FIRE

1982

The blackened, reeking, dripping hull of Chez Panisse on the day after the fire drew crowds of grief-stricken onlookers. But Alice allowed herself no time for grief; there was work to be done. There remained quite a lot of food, wine, and liquor undamaged but legally condemned; it would be distributed to the staff. Alice wanted the whole staff paid during the reconstruction—everybody, down to the dishwashers—but there wasn't enough cash to go around. And she wanted the restaurant back in operation fast. To Alice, there was something strangely energizing about this destruction.

"The morning of the fire, at seven a.m.," Alice's old friend the wine merchant Kermit Lynch recalls, "Alice was at my door in tears. Two days later, she was beaming—dreaming of what she could do now."

"I read *A Pattern Language,* by Christopher Alexander," Alice remembers. In the book, Alexander proposed a radically new way of designing buildings and communities, with their residents as the primary thinkers and actors in their design, arrangement, and construction. "I realized there was so much we could do. That book was my bible. He was a friend of Charles and Lindsey's, and because I admired him so much, we met. And we talked for quite a long time about how to translate my ideas into the reconstruction of the downstairs."

There had been only a narrow single door between the kitchen and the dining room, but the door and the whole wall were gone now. Alice liked it like that. "I had always wanted to be connected, cooking and serving the customer in one room. So when that wall went down in the fire, I just said, 'Let it be.' Sometimes I almost thought I started the fire purposefully."

She asked Kip Mesirow, the master of Japanese woodworking who had been adding his subtle touches to the interior over the years, to conceive a unified design, derived from the style that had served Chez Panisse so well, but now more thorough, more integrated. At Pat Waters's insistence, the restaurant had been well insured, and reconstruction could begin immediately. Support poured in from the friends of Chez Panisse, the staff, and Berkeley at large—clearing out the remains, preparing lunch buffets for the workers, just showing up to pitch in.

The café was less badly damaged than the downstairs, and because it was the restaurant's primary cash generator, the board wanted it back in operation as soon as possible, but Alice wanted improvements, too—restoring the café bar, changing the ventilation, cutting in new windows, building a better waiters' station.

Members of the Cheese Board Collective, the restaurant's longtime friends across Shattuck Avenue, organized a benefit party for March 22, 1982. Chez Panisse would provide whole pigs and lambs to roast, and the Cheese Board staff would serve. Donated items would be solicited for an auction. All the proceeds would go first to the staff, and only then toward building Alice's (and Jerry Budrick's) latest dream, a grand new grill and wood-burning oven in a brick alcove just off the downstairs dining room.

With only ten days to solicit donations, and no advertising except word of mouth, the auction drew seven hundred people. There were many bottles of rare wine—magnums of vintage port, ancient bottles of Château d'Yquem, a Salmanazar (equivalent to eight bottles) of Pommery Champagne. Another lot was a sailing outing for six on San Francisco Bay aboard an eighty-two-foot schooner. Tom Luddy offered a private screening of Marcel Pagnol's *The Baker's Wife*, and Lindsey Shere would bring dessert. Alice, Tom Guernsey, and Jerry Budrick would cook dinner for six at the winning bidder's house. There were dinners at K-Paul's Louisiana Kitchen in New Orleans and Michael's in Santa Monica. There were lingerie, perfume, and a nineteenth-century sword-cane. Twenty thousand dollars was raised for the employees' fund.

The café was back in business on March 23, 1982, just over two weeks after the fire. The restaurant was serving again on April 27, fully remodeled, with a sparkling new kitchen open to the redesigned dining room. The customers could see the kitchen at work, and the cooks could see how people were reacting to the food. The dining room itself retained its golden glow, its redwood shadows, its mirrors and sprays of flowers, but the kitchen, which had always had a homey, cobbled-together look, was now a bright, clear, fully professional space. Its white luminosity and the staff's white shirts were a dazzling presence at the rear of the dining room. "It felt entirely different," Alice states. "To see outside, to see to the front of the restaurant. To see what was going on in the dining room and anticipate that people were coming in and what we had to prepare for. To see the sunset. It was fantastic."

CHEZ PANISSE had become her life, her family, her identity, but Alice was lonely. She began to think about getting older, even to the extent of half joking about a Chez Panisse retirement home in Sonoma County, where the superannuated geezers of the sixties could retire, keep their ideals alive, run a restaurant and maybe a hotel, and, most of all, keep working— together, as a family: "Apartments around a courtyard," she said. "People will gather in the courtyard to work together. Some kind of enterprise in front, facing the street . . . I'm not sure what . . . something useful for the community. And a big garden, of course. And we'll have to be attached to some other institution, with young people. We have to keep that connection. Selection, naturally, will be important. Maybe thirty people . . . I don't know. It has to be just big enough, and just small enough, to allow for—you know—eccentricity."

She was thinking about the present as well. "I was in my late thirties, and I was very aware that I would either have to have a kid or I wouldn't have one. Really aware of that, and I think the tenth birthday of the restaurant and then the fire were the end of a certain chapter. That was a really difficult moment in my life." She had yet to meet a man with whom she could imagine having a child. Her most recent lover was a cook at Chez Panisse, handsome and sexy and smart and focused—and fifteen years younger. (She had hardly ever found a boyfriend outside the restaurant, so total was her inhabitance of it.)

And then, one day that spring, Patricia Curtan and her boyfriend, Stephen Thomas, told Alice that there was someone they wanted her to meet, another Stephen. He was an artist, and he'd been fixing up a loft as his new studio, and he was having a housewarming.

"Patty Curtan said to me, 'I think he'd be really good for you, but I don't know whether you'll be good for him,'" Alice says. "She made lots of suggestions about it, for two or three weeks before this party. It was in May of 1982. I don't remember that I had ever laid eyes on him before. He had come to the restaurant many times before, but I didn't remember him. So he knew all about me, but I didn't know about him. And we met that night, and we never parted."

It seemed to be classic love at first sight. Stephen Singer was, like Alice, small of stature, elegant, stylish, and passionate. Also like Alice, he managed to find clothes that resembled nobody else's. There was an antic quality both in his wardrobe and underlying the intricate intellectual flow of his sentences. He was dark, with dark, intense eyes under thick brown eyebrows. "He had the most gorgeous complexion," Alice remembers. "This lovely red-brown skin.

"We moved in together right away. Not to the house I've got now. I was living in the musician's house—Alan Curtis—this beautiful Mediterranean-feeling house that I just adored, with three fireplaces." Curtis lived in Europe half the year, and his expectation for the other six months was that Alice would move to the basement. The latter half of the arrangement appealed to neither Alice nor Stephen. "So we were there for a bit, and then at Stephen's studio, and then about a year later we bought the house on Monterey Avenue. The one I'm still living in."

Stephen loved wine, loved food, loved travel and luxury. He also was younger. Alice had just turned thirty-eight. Stephen was twenty-seven. He was much more worldly, and wealthy, than an upbringing in Tulsa, Oklahoma, might have suggested. After visiting San Francisco's Chinatown at the age of eight, he decided that San Francisco was where he wanted to live when he grew up. Like Alice, he had taken time off from Cal to travel around Europe, though for Stephen the food was secondary to the art. He had also developed an encyclopedic knowledge of wine.

Alice was uncertain about monogamy, but at the same time she was quite consciously in search of someone who would make a good father. "I had a lot of sort of desperate, difficult relationships right before Stephen. Really just flinging myself around desperately. And they all ended in the same way. They began with this infatuation and this desire, and ended up not being satisfying in any other way. So I decided that desire wasn't at the top of the list, that I really wanted some other kind of relationship. I didn't know what that meant, but I was not going to be dismissive if desire wasn't the driving force of the relationship.

"What is that about?" she asks herself. "Maybe desire is an evolutionary error. Maybe we weren't supposed to live in such a monogamous way, either. Maybe we haven't evolved enough. I feel pretty certain we're not meant to be little twosomes off in a corner. I tell people I'd be happy to have an arranged marriage. If you're going to get married, an arranged marriage has just as much chance of success as finding somebody yourself."

THE CHEZ PANISSE MENU COOKBOOK was published by Random House on August 1, 1982, after two years of intense work by Alice and a

Stephen Singer

whole squadron of collaborators: David Goines had designed the book; Patricia Curtan had helped Alice develop the recipes; Jean-Pierre Moullé had cooked, tasted, and refined the dishes; Carolyn Dille had tested and retested the recipes; Linda Guenzel had transcribed Alice's rambling descriptions and tried to organize them into useful commentary; and Fritz Streiff had come in for the final weeks to polish the prose to a luster. The book was an immediate success, both in sales and in the press (and it has continued to sell in considerable volume through the years). David Goines's dust jacket exactly captured the heterogeneous style of the restaurant's entrance and front windows—part generic California bungalow, part Japanese tea garden, a little Arts and Crafts, a soupçon of Berkeley's own Julia Morgan. The introductory essay, "What I Believe About Cooking," states Alice's philosophy eloquently:

It is a fundamental fact that no cook, however creative and capable, can produce a dish of a quality any higher than that of the raw ingredients. . . .

The unfortunately widespread misconception that cooking that isn't complicated isn't cooking has sometimes proven to be a trap for me. In cooking classes we once gave at the restaurant, I was face-to-face with people's expectations of intricately involved and lengthy recipes. I sometimes felt foolish saying that good cooking meant having the freshest ingredients you could find, and then doing as little as possible to them. . . . I found that it required a tremendous interchange of information and lots of experience in order to convey what it takes to make simple foods succeed. One night, looking at the guests in the dining room as they ate slices from perfect, tiny melons, I began to wonder if perhaps the food had failed to live up to their expectations and that they had, horrifyingly, all come expecting to have filet mignon en croute; instead, all they saw before them was a beautifully faultless piece of melon. Anyone could have chosen a perfect melon, but unfortunately, most people don't take the time or make an effort to choose carefully and understand what that potentially sublime fruit could be.

One paragraph provides not only a guide to Alice's thinking about food but also a kind of character portrait:

When I cook, I usually stand at my kitchen table. I may pull a bunch of thyme from my pocket and lay it on the table; then I wander about the kitchen gathering up all the wonderfully fresh ingredients I can find. I look at each foodstuff carefully, examining it with a critical eye and concentrating in such a way that I begin to make associations. . . . Sometimes I wander through the garden looking for something appealing, absorbing the bouquet of the earth and the scent of the fresh herbs. Sometimes I butterfly my way through cookbooks, quickly flipping the pages and absorbing a myriad of ideas about a particular food or concept.

Jeannette Ferrary, writing in the *San Francisco Chronicle,* recognized in *The Chez Panisse Menu Cookbook* Alice's faith that having the right feelings will give you the results you seek—a very Berkeley, very sixties, very Alice notion: "Even in her most offhanded asides, the author articulates a distinctive California character. This is still frontier country, she implies, free from the constraints of stodgy tradition. Don't repeat eternally the one achievement you have mastered. . . . Never look back, burdening yourself with the memory of the dinner (or whatever it was) that didn't work."[1]

The book's publication set off a series of explosions that still resound through the debate about how much credit, in general, Alice should get. The first text in the book is a page of acknowledgments, opening with these words:

> This book would never have been written but for Linda Guenzel's belief in me and in Chez Panisse. She transcribed my ramblings, organized my thoughts, and overcame my doubts, all with tireless enthusiasm. I cannot thank her enough for the countless hours she has given me so generously. This book is as much hers as mine.

—except that Linda Guenzel didn't think that her work had been a gift to Alice. Linda thought she was going to be paid royalties. The contract with Random House did not include her, however—which she may not have known. In any case, she considered herself co-author. (The title page credit reads "by Alice Waters" in big type, followed by "In Collaboration with Linda P. Guenzel" in small type, and Alice's name appears alone on the copyright page.)

"Linda was hugely loyal to Alice and to Jeremiah both, and their ideal customer in every way. Linda's feelings were very badly hurt," Fritz Streiff explains. "I thought the work I'd done after Linda had done her part was all okay, all done with Linda's approval. Alice was mortified that she had offended Linda. And they made a deal—a cash payment to Linda—in partial recompense for the slight."

Linda Guenzel was not the only aggrieved party. At the tenth-birthday party of Chez Panisse, a spectacular picnic at the Joseph Phelps Winery in the Napa Valley, in August 1981—a year before the book's publication—Alice and Jeremiah had gone up in a hot-air balloon together. "He had some really nasty things to tell me while we were up in that balloon," Alice recalls. "Jeremiah thought he should have gotten much more credit than the manuscript gave him."

"We had sent Jeremiah the manuscript, and he showed up at the party with it," Fritz remembers. "He had made numerous corrections, and had various cavils, mostly in the section where Alice had reprinted various menus that had been done for special occasions, and she had been cavalier with assigning credit in some cases. And he had suggested corrections. It would be most interesting to look at his notes for that, because I remember going through the manuscript with Alice, and in every case where he wanted something changed, we either removed it entirely so that it didn't matter, or we made the change that he wanted."

In the book, Jeremiah was, in fact, lavishly credited. In a paragraph introducing the section of special menus to which Fritz refers, Alice had written, "Many of these menus were conceived and executed by Jeremiah Tower, who was the chef at the restaurant during its formative years. He developed the idea of regional dinners celebrating the food of provincial France (Brittany, Périgord, Champagne, Burgundy, Alsace, etc.), Morocco, Louisiana, and ultimately, our own region of northern California; his innovative and adventurous menus gave the restaurant its reputation for ambitious experimentation and exploration."

For all that, in *California Dish* Jeremiah refers to Linda Guenzel as "the person who actually wrote it." Also he writes, "I saw that some menus and events that were so obviously mine had been removed"—another way of saying just what Fritz said.

Alice was having personal clashes at the restaurant as well. Jean-Pierre Moullé says, "I was bad. I said I was the chef to a journalist for an article. I said, 'I'm the one who runs the kitchen.' And [Alice] really didn't like that. I was working hard, and I was doing all the work. When you run the kitchen, when you do the ordering, the hiring, and the menu, and run everything, I think you are the chef. And I was stupid enough to tell everyone that Alice was not really cooking."

"Something had to give. He had to go," Alice concluded. It wasn't going to be simple. They would have to buy out Jean-Pierre's contract, and he owned Pagnol stock as well. Nobody in-house was capable of replacing him, except Alice, who didn't want to. "He was unhappy," she says.

He didn't want my input. I felt like, You're really missing something important not to take my input, because I've been in the kitchen, I've been in the dining room, I know about this. It's a very personal decision I make about who's in that kitchen. It has to do with a lot of other things besides just being a great cook. I'm not even sure I know what they all are. They certainly have to do with a certain kind of diplomacy both in terms of customers and staff. Inspiring the staff, understanding the dynamics of how a kitchen works, trying to communicate with people upstairs as well as downstairs, not dividing the restaurant in two. Somebody who connects with dishwashers and the foragers and the office as well as the immediate staff.

There've been very few people who stayed here very long who didn't have a rapport with me, or if I didn't feel that their cooking was interesting in some way to me personally. I've compromised on other things, but I have never compromised on the cooking piece for very long. There have been a little six months here, a little six months there, when I didn't know what to do except pull my hair out. But even with impossible people—according to the staff—they were cooking well.

Jean-Pierre was (and remains) married to Denise Lurton, of the famous Bordeaux family—they own or operate some twenty châteaux—and both of them were homesick. Jean-Pierre began to look forward to some good simple labor in the wine cellars, to working on the house he still owned and restoring its old barn. He and Alice agreed that he would stay at Chez Panisse through September 1982, and—so he thought at the time—then leave and never return.

"THEN PAUL CAME," says Alice with a gesture of gratefully outstretched hands, as though receiving manna from above. This was another fine example of the classic Chez Panisse pattern: Just at the right moment, the right person seems to appear.

"I grew up on Chez Panisse," Paul Bertolli recalls. "When I came to study at Cal, Chez Panisse had just opened. I remember going in and smelling the smell. It smelled like my grandmother's kitchen."

Paul's maternal grandmother presided over his family's kitchen in San Rafael, not far north of San Francisco. She was Italian-born, from the foothills of the Alps north of Venice, and she loved to cook. Eventually, his other grandmother, from near Milan, came to live nearby, in El Cerrito. "Two different traditions, really," he observes, "two different accents, dialects, two styles of cooking. It was great."

He loved food, but music—lute, guitar, and most of all piano—seemed to be his destiny. He won awards at the San Francisco Conservatory of Music when he was still in high school. He graduated from Cal in 1977 with a double major in composition and piano. But in his postgraduate study under a master teacher in New York, he grew disillusioned about his prospects as a concert pianist. "There were these Taiwanese girls who were half my size and half my age who could play circles around me," Paul remembers.

I decided, Okay, I'm going to take my last six thousand dollars and go to Europe.

I settled in Treviso, and I got a job in a restaurant that specialized in mushrooms. I fell in love with Italy. I thought, This is the greatest place to eat or drink or look at food or be at a table. I was twenty-three years old, and I felt like I had discovered the world.

Later I lived on a farm near Panzano. I began to learn about discovering what's there already, in nature. I really got the idea that these people eat this way because they live here and nowhere else.

When he returned to California, Paul decided to try for a job at Chez Panisse, and persuaded Alice to come to lunch. "At the time, Patricia Curtan was cooking, with Mark Miller, Jean-Pierre Moullé, and Alice. They all came to lunch. The asparagus soup I cooked in an aluminum pan, and it turned brown. I undercooked these little cannellini beans. I had this salmon that was poached, and decorated—sort of the wrong direction for Chez Panisse."

"He cooked this salmon out in his backyard," Alice remembers. "He covered it with nasturtium blossoms, and I just thought, Oh, my goodness, this is just too-too."

In 1981, Paul got married and went back to Italy. "I worked in three restaurants in and around Florence, and then I worked as a private chef for Sir Harold Acton in his Villa La Pietra. It was a great job. He didn't know what to do with me; I wasn't really a servant. He had a butler who would dress him and bring his cherries and tea in the morning. I would show up at ten o'clock in his study, and he would tell me who was coming to dinner.

"I fed not only Sir Harold and his guests, but his staff, which was huge. There were something like fifteen gardeners. He had two women who did nothing but iron all day, and he had a woman who worked full-time taking care of his glass collection."

With his skills sharpened and his urbanity elevated, Paul returned to Berkeley in the late summer of 1982. Suzy Nelson, who had been a waitress at Chez Panisse and was a longtime friend of Alice's, was giving a luncheon party based on a sequence of fancy wines, and she wanted food good enough and simple enough to highlight the wines. She hired Paul Bertolli. Alice was among the guests.

"That meal really turned my head around," says Alice. "Paul made *vitello tonnato*, and he cooked lamb over fig branches. He pushed that smoke into the dining room, perfuming everything. I'll never forget that.

Jacques Pépin, Alice, and Paul Bertolli

The lamb was sensational. And he did this prune semifreddo with nocino, a green-walnut liqueur, which I had never tasted. *Mmm!* He got me."

"This time"—Paul laughs—"*she* called *me!*"

Alice says that the earthiness and clarity of flavor in Paul's food were "a breath of fresh air for me. I loved that he had such an instinctual way of cooking. It was a beautiful thing to cross the border into Italy, into the land of olive oil and garlic and anchovies and a whole other palate. Plus I was about to have a kid, and he made me feel secure."

It may be worth noting that Alice doesn't mention Stephen here. Despite her pregnancy, they were still not married. But with a child on the way, she knew that her involvement in Chez Panisse was bound to lessen, and Paul's easy assumption of authority was a considerable comfort.

Whatever amount of authority Alice loaded onto Paul Bertolli, he never bowed under the weight. "Smiling off my reluctance," he would write some years later, "she believed in me sooner than I did."[2]

· PAUL BERTOLLI'S TRIPE AND PASTA ·

Paul made a tripe pasta that was the best. The best. I've had tripe lots of ways, but his cooking of tripe absolutely rivals anything I've ever tasted. Paul did it, obviously, Italian style, Florentine style. He made a *mirepoix*—carrots and celery and onions—along with garlic and olive oil, and he cooked the tripe with that for a long time in chicken stock, with tomatoes and pancetta, till it was really tender. With parsley, bay, and thyme, probably. And a little cayenne. The tripe was in strips, and he made egg pasta that matched it exactly. He finished it with fresh chopped parsley, Parmesan, and a bit of butter. It was so good.

"At first," Paul remembers,

I had to send all my menus over to Alice for review. She'd come in and taste and criticize. Sometimes she wouldn't say anything, and you would just have to know how to read her. The frustrating part was that there was a last-minuteness to a lot of her decision making. People call her a visionary. I think she has reactions more than visions. She can see best in a moment of crisis. When everything was about to happen, and something wasn't right, she had no qualms about saying, "We've got to do something about this." Well, she could have done something about it three hours ago, too, if she had applied herself, but there is something about this live moment when she has a reaction and things have to change.

"It is important to remember that you are preparing food, not culinary artwork," Paul would write in *Chez Panisse Cooking,* published in 1988. "Cooking is a commonsense practice, not alchemy. Listening and watching closely while you cook will reveal a richly shaded language understood by all the senses—the degrees of a simmer, the aroma of a roast telling you it is done, the stages of elasticity of kneaded dough, the earthy scent of a vegetable just pulled from the ground—it is everything to mind these details."

In his insistence that the cook's primary—and most noble—goal is to prepare food, not art, and that cooking is not alchemy, Paul exactly captures the difference between the French and the Italian approaches to food—the difference, too, between Jeremiah and himself. In the three principal chefs of the first twenty years of Chez Panisse—Tower, Moullé, Bertolli—can be read the history of Alice's own gastronomic fascinations.

Until the arrival of Stephen Singer and Paul Bertolli, Alice's focus had been largely on the moment, on pleasure for its own sake, on aesthetic refinement and sensual satisfaction. Now she was thinking about the earth, about responsibility, about the future. She had begun to recognize that pleasure had a moral dimension. And as has always been the case, she internalized her concerns so thoroughly that they were immediately personal: She was asking herself what she, herself, should do.

Some of Alice's detractors accuse her of ignoring a moral conflict inherent in Chez Panisse. To achieve the level of excellence that it does, it has to charge high prices. Aren't those high prices—entailing as they do the exclusion of the poor and, in fact, much of the middle class, too—a betrayal of the counterculture's idealism?

"That's like saying that a really simple-tasting soup can't be as divine as blinis with caviar," Alice replies. "The excellence, the perfection of it, can be there. It's about a way of doing work. It's about a way of focusing. Having fine-tuned senses so you can make really right decisions. Anybody can do it."

"It's interesting, isn't it?" says Charles Shere. "There's always been a sort of tension between the peasant and the gentility in Alice's makeup. She loves grilling over an open fire in the backyard, but she prefers it if the backyard is behind a manor house. But she is basically a democrat. She's a person who sees everybody as being intrinsically on the same footing and of equal merit and worth, and she sees her mission as facilitating the intermingling of these equally footed people."

"My sense of the ethics and politics of food was coming to the surface.

I mean, those values were instilled in me during the Free Speech Movement, and my early travels in France. But it didn't really start to come together till the early eighties," Alice says. "It had to do with becoming friends with the farmers and understanding deeply that the food at the restaurant was as good as it was because the produce and the ingredients were as good as they were. The farmers were the people who really got it, about the ethics of food."

Alice had left some of her democratic idealism behind with the defeat of Robert Scheer in 1966. Because she was so drawn to beauty, and to excellence, she could never have identified with the radical egalitarianism of the sixties far left. But she was seeing now that the purity of her devotion to excellence could inspire large numbers of people. Her deepening understanding of the relationship between healthy land and a healthy society would provide the platform from which she could speak. And the child growing in her body was an irrevocable investment in the future.

"It all started with Fanny," she says.

11.

A WORLD
FOR FANNY

1983–1984

Pregnancy. Oh, my," Alice sighs.

It was amazing and mysterious, but I never got sick at all. In fact, I went to China when I was four months pregnant, and I ate everything. The trouble was that Fanny came early. Everything was fine until I went to New York to cook at my friend Anne Isaak's wedding in the heat of the summer. July 1983. They had this big party out in Sag Harbor, and I thought I could help grill. But apparently, Fanny didn't like that, because when I got back to New York, I just felt like, Oh, my God, something has changed. Something is really different inside. I went to the doctor when I got home, and she said, "You have to go to bed and stay there, because the baby is going to come too soon." She was supposed to be born at the end of September, and she was born the fifteenth of August, 1983. She was okay, she was just little. I had a cesarean birth. It was quite a trauma. But Fanny was great. The difficult thing was that she got colic two weeks later. I didn't know what that was about, but she couldn't sleep more than an hour at a time for three months. It took Stephen and me a couple of weeks to realize that we were the nurses in the emergency room, really—that we could never have a normal life as long as this child was unhappy. So he never went to work, and I never went to work. For three months.

Colic is an imperfection in the digestive system. Some little glitch, so every time the food comes to that point, it's very, very painful. They arch their back, and they become just inconsolable. We came to understand that the only way to make her happy was sort of sensory overload. We would turn on the shower in the bathroom, and I'd put her into her little Snugli, and I'd turn on the vacuum, and I'd sing to her all at the same time, and then she would go to sleep finally. All these things simultaneously. Which of course drove us over the edge, too. Every friend we knew came and helped take care of Fanny when she was crying. And she was crying for three months. And then she stopped, magically. And became the wonderful kid that she is. It took me a while to catch my breath, but I never went back to work in the same way. I couldn't.

Paul was cooking, and I was going to the restaurant a couple of nights a week, and Stephen would go to work a couple of days when I didn't go in to the restaurant. He had just started up a wine shop in San Francisco, called Singer and Foy. That's when Bob Carrau came into my life. He was Stephen's best friend, and he took care of Fanny while Stephen cooked dinner for them all and I went to work. He basically lived with us for fifteen years. I mean not really living there, but almost. He went on our vacations with us. He became Fanny's uncle/other father. He was always looking out to see how people were feeling. He's still that way.

"Stephen and I were friends at Berkeley," Bob Carrau remembers.

He was in two of my classes one quarter—a film class and an aesthetics class—and he talked so much that I kept thinking, This guy is either one of the smartest people I've ever met, or he's the biggest asshole I've ever met, and as Stephen said later, jokingly, "And I turned out to be both." I didn't really connect with Alice, because she and Stephen had this romance, and they kind of went off into her world. I saw Stephen every now and then. Then I remember seeing Alice when Stephen had an art opening. She wanted to do the food at his studio party, and I said I'd go help. That was my first experience with what she's like when she's all wound up in cooking things, and I was just a guy from the suburbs, not a very sophisticated person, so it was a whole new experience. I was like, Wow, what's going on here? I mean, whoa!

Stephen moved into Alice's house, and I went over there for dinner one night. It was just the three of us, and it was very uncomfortable for me at first, because Stephen and I, when we used to hang out, it was more like—you know, guys, smoking pot and drinking and goofing around. And now he had this woman friend who was very refined, in her own weird way, she's sophisticated, and she's a little older, and she has all this experience of traveling and knowing all these famous people, and she's almost European, and I was, especially back then, just kind of "Uh, hi."

She started shaving white truffles on something we were eating, like a pasta or something, and she was so excited, she was treating it like it was something precious, you know, and I remember thinking, This is an interesting smell. I had no idea what truffles even were. But I did like them.

Alice and I connected much more once Fanny was born. Stephen always wanted company being the father when Alice was working, and I was someone he could call, and I would just come over and hang out. It was always fun, because there was always good wine, good jokes, and he could cook too.

I get sad thinking back on that time, recognizing the naïveté of all of us, and all the stuff that was under the surface that we were all probably trying to express, but at the same time it was a very fun time for us. We traveled a lot together, and Alice and I could go someplace on our own, or Stephen and I could go someplace, or they could. I always related to Fanny as this clever and interesting person—not really as a child so much. She was as much a pleasure to be with as Alice was, or Stephen, so it was never like this issue of, Oh, I have to babysit.

And then I met Sue Murphy.

Sue was a professional actress and comedienne, and had to travel frequently, but having become Bob Carrau's lover, whenever she came back home to Berkeley she was now ipso facto a member of Fanny's team of caretakers.

I'm a gay person, but back then, I was kind of going all over the place. I had really strong feelings for Sue, and I said to her, "Listen, I don't really understand this totally, but if you're up for exploring this, I'd like to."

I liked being part of that family, and I think Stephen and Alice and Sue all liked it, too, and we actually grew into this kind of interesting foursome. In retrospect, I think I was facilitating what was going on between Alice and Stephen, but it was mostly a real pleasure for me.

Alice and her friends Patty Curtan and Sharon Jones remodeled Alice's garage into what Bob Carrau recalls as "an ad hoc day-care center for their kids." The mothers, and sometimes the fathers, as well as Bob and Sue, were all caretakers. It was a very busy place, and a great place to be a kid.

About this time a debate began among Alice's friends, which continues today, over whether she is too busy, overcommitted, in danger of burning out—a recapitulation of Tom Luddy's worry in the early days of the restaurant. Throughout the years of her friends' concern, however, Alice has virtually never slowed down.

She often seems so frantic, her mind on so many tracks, that she can't finish a sentence. Asked simply how she is, Alice cannot just say, "Fine," and be done with it. She stammers, hesitates, leaves half a sentence hanging, starts again, trails off—by which point her interlocutor tends to charge ahead with the conversation. The impression is of a brain about to boil over, or implode. Corby Kummer, a senior editor and food columnist at *The Atlantic,* is a longtime friend, and he says,

> Once, I had this idea of her as this fragile flower, always on the verge of bursting into tears. It took me a while to see her will of steel. In the early to mid-eighties there was a perception that she was always one step away from a breakdown, throwing up her hands and leaving the restaurant. People don't think about that now so much. She's more confident and straightforward now, while always keeping the seductive girlishness that is so much a part of her.

"After I had Fanny, I did change," Alice says. "I guess I mostly changed in relationship to the restaurant, although I'm sure Stephen would see it in a different way. Having a kid, always my mind was divided. Always my life was divided. Being a mother divided me from the restaurant. I tried to do everything and obviously failed on all fronts. Deeply. But I knew from the very beginning that Stephen and I couldn't bring up this kid by ourselves. I don't know what we would have done without Bob Carrau and Sue Murphy. It was great for them—they loved being part of the family— and it was great for us, because we loved having them there for us as family. That continued from '83 until '97. Then, when it all came apart, it was very hard. Very painful."

ALICE WAS HORRIFIED at the prospect of Fanny's growing up "without understanding what food meant to the survival of the planet." Most of the food on the market was tainted in some way by pesticides, or hormones, or antibiotics, or cruelty to animals, or bad farming practices, or poor treatment of farm workers. Finding genuinely untainted food—for the restaurant or for her family—was a continual struggle. Fortunately, she had a team of like-minded others as concerned as she was—friends and family close to home, and a growing grassroots movement on a national scale. In addition to improving the business practices of the restaurant, Alice's father had

Stephen, Fanny, and Alice

taken an interest in finding farmers who didn't use pesticides or other harmful chemicals. Pat Waters drove hundreds of miles through northern California in search of them, and found a number, though not enough to supply Chez Panisse on a regular basis with everything it needed.

"In 1983, we hired my friend Sibella Kraus—she was a line cook at the restaurant at the time," adds Alice. "She would go out and just comb the hills looking for farmers who would grow these particular varieties that I wanted."

Sibella remembers:

Alice had the fantasy that you'd have this total system where you were using up everything on the farm, and you'd have this ideal ecological and economic situation. Well, it didn't work. If a pack of aphids came, there went the salad.

We did have some wonderful suppliers, but getting the stuff to the restaurant was an incredible hassle. We would get Laura Chenel's cheese sent to the bus station. I'd call and say, "Okay, so-and-so, pick your corn now, the bus is coming in an hour." Alex Waag, Nathalie Waag's son, used to drive the van and fetch things from the bus. I had a car stained with blackberries. There was the joy of discovery, but most of the time I had no idea what I was doing. I would pick apricots that were sublime, but when I got them to the restaurant that evening, they were good for ice cream, if that.

Then I left Chez Panisse, and I went to study agricultural economics at U.C., and I started meeting farmers who were passionate about what they were growing. I'd meet people who were growing eight kinds of heirloom Japanese eggplant. These were products nobody had ever seen or heard of.

I went to Alice and a couple of other restaurateurs and said, "Hey, I'm meeting these farmers, and don't you think you would want me to try to hook you up?" So that summer, 1983, we set up the Farm Restaurant Project, to bring local farmers and chefs together. We produced a weekly distribution of produce available by direct order—that is, straight from the farmer to the restaurant. Nobody had ever done that. And that grew into an annual celebration called the Tasting of Summer Produce. A hundred people gathered to taste and compare the whole array of summer produce that had been donated by the growers, and the chefs prepared a wonderful meal. For the first time, the farmers and the chefs were talking to one another about their particular needs. It opened up a whole world.

It was a well-kept secret that Alice had actually been married once upon a time, very briefly—it was something of a marriage of convenience, to help a young French filmmaker named Jean-Pierre Gorin get into the United States. In 1978, Jean-Pierre Gorin had been able to return the favor by introducing Alice to a remarkable farm near La Jolla, California, where the Japanese-American Chino family was producing some of the most delicious fruits and vegetables Alice had ever tasted, in stupendous variety. The items available on one single day, as reported by Mark Singer (Stephen's brother) in *The New Yorker* of November 30, 1992, included:

beets (yellow, golden, red, white with red stripes), carrots (white, orange, yellow, golden, red, long-and-tapered, thumb size, in-between), turnips (white, golden, red, black, white-and-purple, round, long), radishes (white, red, red-and-white, purple, pink, daikon, red-fleshed Chinese, green-fleshed Chinese), celeriac, fennel, escarole, white endive, red endive, white cauliflower, Romanesque cauliflower (pale green with a stegosauroid architecture), mibuna, mizuna, bok choy, choi sum, cilantro, French thyme, winter savory, lemon balm, rapini, garlic chives, nasturtiums, basil (lemon, cinnamon, Thai, French, piccolo fino), Vietnamese coriander, Chinese spinach, Chinese long beans, French green beans as slender as candlewicks, purple cabbage, green cabbage, flat black cabbage, two dozen varieties of lettuce, a plastic tray of mixed lettuce hearts—and that's not all.

And that was in January.

For the produce of the Chino Ranch, Alice gladly broke her rule about using only local supply; this produce was just too good to pass up. Arrangements were made for a weekly delivery by jet. A Chez Panisse representative would meet the plane at the Oakland airport, pack the boxes into a waiting van, and race up the freeway to Berkeley. (For the less perishable items, there were also occasional deliveries by car.)

Sibella Kraus and Catherine Brandel, the restaurant's first official forager, found a number of unique, often eccentric farms. Foremost among them were Green Gulch farm, in Marin County (a venture of the San Francisco Zen Center) and Warren Weber's Star Route Farm in Bolinas. Warren was a perfect addition to the Chez Panisse community—a Shakespeare scholar with a doctorate from Cal, and one of the first growers to pursue all-organic farming. He had started Star Route with five acres in 1974 ("with a horse-drawn plow and a lot of long-haired ambition," he says), and had never veered from his dedication to grow organic produce that also tasted great.

Sibella says, "Alice's philosophy, and mine, was always to seduce and educate. 'Taste this peach. Now that the juice is dripping down your chin, let me tell you about the farmland where that comes from, and how endangered it is, and what you can do about it.'" Sibella explains,

The label for a box of Warren Weber's mesclun,
designed by Patricia Curtan

When you're around Alice, you understand the sensibility of "This bean might do for dinner today, but I know there's a better bean out there. Get me a better bean."

I remember distinctly a morning when someone had given me a hint about this farmers' market out in Stockton. The market was under a freeway. There were all these Southeast Asians, everyone sort of in Indo-Chinese costume. Chickens in cages. It was another world. I brought back things I had never seen. I remember bringing back a cardoon, and Paul Bertolli says, "Oh! cardoons! yes! Song of my heart, a cardoon!"

ALICE'S DIVIDED ATTENTION had its effects on the restaurant and on her personal life. Stephen was not getting the attention he felt he was due, and Alice was not feeling as committed to Stephen as she would have liked to feel. There was little overt conflict, seldom a raised voice, but a quiet dissonance was making itself felt.

At Chez Panisse, the front of the house seemed to be plagued by personnel problems, and once again there were mounting complaints about the service. A 1983 memo to the staff set out "five causes for immediate dismissal." The list paints a nice picture of the monkeyshines behind the scenes:

1. Stealing from the restaurant or employees
2. Being drunk on the job
3. Fighting on the premises
4. Throwing food on the premises
5. Smoking marijuana on the premises during hours
   of operation

It may be inferred from this that Alice's own behavior was by this time a great deal more disciplined than that which she once had tolerated and taken part in back in the early days of Chez Panisse. Her moral maturation had given her an enhanced appreciation of discipline, as well as a recognition that some kinds of what some people called fun could be truly destructive. She had seen it up close in two men she had been very close to—Jeremiah Tower and Jerry Budrick.

At the same time, in the back of the house, Paul Bertolli's kitchen was becoming a quiet, studious, professional workplace. "It was a new game when I got there," he says. "It was a real transition point in the restaurant, when it began to be run more like a business and less like an incestuous family. I don't think I was necessarily responsible for that. But there was new blood. A new generation of cooks started to come in who hadn't been part of the whole flower-people movement and how that mutated into the cocaine and nitrous oxide and all that excess."

"Some people will give you the impression that the place was in perpetual turmoil," says Alice. "In fact, by the eighties, everything was pretty stable, thanks to Tom Guernsey. Maybe one week we'd have some turmoil, but mostly it was pretty smooth. Paul Bertolli was also a stabilizing force. So was the birth of Fanny. The few who had big problems, or who've been disaffected, seem like big figures in the story, because that's where people's attention is drawn. There have been hundreds of people who've worked at Chez Panisse—many of them for years on end—who've learned, and been changed, all in a very quiet way."

As far as Alice was concerned, her father could do no wrong, and what Alice felt strongly about, the board nearly always went along with. In April 1983, Chez Panisse began paying a monthly stipend of $1,000 to Pat Waters's consultancy company, Organizational Dynamics. Chez Panisse needed all the help it could get. With the opening of the café, the publicity from the fire, and the publication of *The Chez Panisse Menu Cookbook,* cash flow was way up, but there still wasn't a penny of profit.

As long as there was enough money to pay the staff well and buy the best ingredients and put out the best food they could, Alice still didn't care about profit. Paul Bertolli and she were of one mind about that. "Alice and I had a real rapport," says Paul,

> inasmuch as Alice had ideas but not necessarily the way to get there technically. She would say, "Make this taste good." I remember this particular dish we were working on, a pasta with sweetbreads and green beans. She said, "Can you make this taste right?" and I did that. The problem with the way people were cooking pasta at Chez Panisse was that it was sort of a California sauté approach. Italians build flavor from the bottom up. You have to spend some time building that flavor. What I did that time was take some veal on the side and make a little *fond* [caramelized bits that stick to a pan in a sauté] in the pan, and I crisped the sweetbreads. I did a deglazing of the *fond* and used *mirepoix* in that, and used some of the braising liquid from the sweetbreads. I browned the sweetbreads, so I got another *fond* and then poured that over the first one, so I got this sort of double-consommé process. That's how you build flavor. And then I worked all the fresh ingredients in at the end, and a little splash of cream, and that worked pretty well.

Alice had some amazing flights of fancy. I remember I was on a Meals on Wheels thing with her in New York City, and she'd seen some James Beard cookbook—a book from the fifties, I think, on entertaining. He had these enormous ice cubes, like five-foot ice cubes, with vegetables floating around in them. Frozen in there. I don't know how. I remember arriving in New York at four thirty in the morning and taking a ride up to a very tough section of the Bronx where there was this giant ice cube factory. And there I was with boxes of beautiful Chino vegetables and wire and weights, trying to get these vegetables down into the ice blocks as they froze. It was just ridiculous. They kept floating up to the top, there wasn't enough weight, but Alice really wanted this to happen. I thought, This is nuts, this is really nuts, do we really have to do this? But somehow I did it. It didn't look very good, and it didn't really work, but we did it. A lot of stuff like that happened.

Alice compares Chez Panisse in the 1970s to "an unruly child, just like a kid from age one to ten—difficult to take care of. And we weren't very good parents. Everything was touch-and-go." In the 1980s, however, she says, "We were trying for a transition to a more stable time. Trying to become a real professional restaurant. Our traditions were developing. We were established, but still always pushing forward."

"We moved toward making everything from scratch," says Paul Bertolli. "I developed an understanding of a menu as a form like writing a sonnet. I came into conflict with the board of directors, who always wanted to have a garden salad on the menu. That was sacrosanct. 'We have a five-course menu, and the fourth course is always garden salad.' But if I'm getting dull on garden salad, that's going to communicate to the customer. Well, a member of the board came to me one day and said, 'You can't touch that garden salad. We've all decided. Just live with it.' So I lived with it. But it started to feel formulaic to me. That's the problem, obviously, with any form that you repeat—redundancies. To keep the thing alive, you've got to turn it upside down, turn it all around, and I wanted to do that."

Alice's freedom from hands-on involvement in Chez Panisse was not uninterrupted. When Joyce Goldstein, the café chef, left in late 1983 to start her own restaurant, Square One, in San Francisco, there was once again no one in-house who Alice thought could handle the job. The café had problems—bad staff morale, confusion about reservations, continuing theft by some of the employees, disagreements about the menu, space conflicts with the downstairs kitchen (where much of the café prep was supposed to take place in the morning but often ran over into the downstairs restaurant's allotted time).

Alice's solution was to hire not one but two chefs. "My idea," she says, "was that each of them would work three days on, Monday-Tuesday-Wednesday and Thursday-Friday-Saturday. They would have complete responsibility for the time they were there. The other three days they might come in for a meeting, but mostly they'd be free to go out and forage or think up new ideas, or just be with their families. There would be cooperation, and friendly competition, and exchange of ideas."

The first "co-chef" Alice brought aboard was David Tanis. David had been part of the old after-hours crowd and had worked at restaurants all around the Bay Area, including a couple of brief stints at Chez Panisse itself. He had just the right kind of background. Even as a little kid he had loved food. He had gone to Deep Springs College, a converted cattle ranch in the desert near Bishop, California, where all twenty students not only studied the usual college courses but also ran the ranch. They cooked, carried mail, fixed fences, milked cows, cleaned stables, fed chickens, made cheese, slaughtered animals. Serious European chefs would come sometimes and cook for months; there were also distinguished professors from elsewhere in California who would rotate through a term or two. After that, David recalls, "I began faking my way into restaurant jobs. I'm not sure how much talent I really had, except to reproduce what I saw the good cooks doing—monkey see, monkey do."

The second co-chef Alice hired was Claire O'Sullivan. For reasons that remain unclear, there was instant friction between Claire and David. There ensued what David recalls as "ten days of constant drama. Then Alice had her father fire me. I was devastated." That was classic Alice: She faces an emotionally fraught task, and somebody else executes it.

Claire's friction was not with David alone, apparently, for she resigned the next day. In twenty-four hours the Chez Panisse Café had gone from having two chefs to none.

It took Alice about a minute to decide to call David and beg him to return—to be café *chef,* not co-.

"Alice was not going to just turn me loose, however," David recalls. "She wrote all the menus for the first six months. She tasted everything, over and over. She criticized everything I did. There were days when I would just cry like a child. Alice was always fiddling with the food up to the last second. We were constantly reprinting the menu. It was 'Oh, let's change everything right now, I've had a better idea.'" And then she would disappear, rushing home to be with Fanny.

UNDER PAT WATERS'S fiscal discipline—and despite continuing problems with employees making off with wine, desserts, and nearly anything else not bolted down—Chez Panisse was finally making money. They weren't making much, but it was enough for Christmas bonuses, a couple of new cars, and satisfied auditors. Paul Bertolli and Alice Waters were each making $42,000 in salary, plus stock and bonuses. Alice had, in addition, a considerable income from book royalties, and then, in June 1984 came the second cookbook, *Chez Panisse Pasta, Pizza & Calzone,* this time carefully attributed on the cover to three authors—Alice, Patricia Curtan, and Martine Labro.

By 1984, Chez Panisse had become what Alice wanted, and more. With Paul Bertolli firmly at the helm, Alice was free to want more, to expand her horizons, to dream again. She never lost touch with old friends, however. Late-night phone calls out of the blue, invitations to pitch in on a dinner party at her house, a birthday meal with a beautifully printed menu card designed by David Goines or Patricia Curtan—she held on fiercely to friends and family. "Alice is a very loyal person," says Barbara

Fanny and Alice, with Bob Carrau
in the background

Carlitz. "She doesn't leave people behind. She continues to gather people around, but not at the expense of old acquaintances or old friends. She's very sure of herself philosophically, and not so sure of herself in terms of human relationships. She has absolute conviction, mixed with timidity, which is a beguiling style. I think that's what has made her the natural P.R. magnet that she seems to be."

In the spring of 1984, Alice helped her sister Laura Waters Maser, and Laura's husband, Jim, establish the tiny but instantly successful Café Fanny, serving breakfast, snacks, and lunch. Café Fanny was only a few blocks from Chez Panisse, cheek by jowl with the wine shop of Alice's longtime friend Kermit Lynch. Kermit went way back with Jim Maser, too, having been lead singer in Jim's rock band, the Roaches. Many of the customers ate their Café Fanny takeout lounging on their cars in Kermit's parking lot, and it was perhaps the closest thing yet to Alice's original vision of a hangout.

"And Fanny was growing up right there in the restaurant," Alice says happily. "She was part of it. Everybody there was her friend. They were wonderful babysitters. They liked to cook for her. They had the same set of values. And then she had Bob Carrau and Sue, who took her out into nature and did things for her that I couldn't do. She was a happy child, a really happy child. And she loved the food at Chez Panisse, including some things you wouldn't really think a little kid could even stomach, much less love. Anchovies!"

· ANCHOÏADE ·

The way we did it was sort of à la Austin de Croze [co-author with Curnonsky of *Le Trésor Gastronomique de la France,* published in 1933]—with dried figs, almonds, garlic, olive oil, and anchovies.

Always salt-packed anchovies. That's all we ever use. I soak them awhile, and then I fillet them quickly, and let them sit in water again to get some of the salt out. Then you make a paste with those and the other things with your mortar and pestle.

The best way to cook it is over fresh, green pine needles. You get a really wonderful, special aroma. We almost burned down the restaurant a couple of times, however. We put the pine branches right in the wood-burning oven, and they were too dry and caught fire. We didn't do that many times.

So you just grill some toast, and spread the paste, uncooked, on the warm toast. I think our latest version is to grill the bread and then spread the paste on the hot bread without cooking it. I always have to ask all the cooks about how they cook this, because we have advanced since the medieval days of the restaurant.

12.

ALICE
TAKES FLIGHT

1985–1986

The middle 1980s brought to Chez Panisse a maturing that characteristically mirrored Alice's own. In the spring of 1985, Alice's father proposed that Chez Panisse be completely computerized: the purchasing, the checks, the accounting, the financial analysis, reservations, everything. Alice, who hated virtually anything high-tech, was horrified, but she submitted, for it was by her own choice that her father, without a title, a staff position, or a seat on the board, had effectively taken charge of the business of Chez Panisse.

One manifestation of Alice's technophobia was that the restaurant still didn't take credit cards. With the café packed near bursting every night and the price of dinner downstairs rising rapidly—from $25 in 1980 to $40 in 1984 (a 60 percent increase)—there was a lot of cash flowing into Chez Panisse. And this cash flow was really cash, which can disappear without a trace if the malefactor is half clever.

No cash flowed through the kitchen. The worst a cook could do was to swipe a bottle or two of wine or a truffle, maybe gobble a furtive slice of tart in the walk-in refrigerator. The back of the house, therefore, was a world apart from the front, and since the arrival of Paul Bertolli in the restaurant and David Tanis in the café, the better angels of the restaurant's nature had been thriving in the kitchens both downstairs and up. A memo from David to his staff expresses the Chez Panisse ethos during this period at its best:

> We are all at different stages of development. Some of us are career cooks, and some of us are cooking our way through college: some of us are cooks because we haven't quite figured out what we really want to do—some because we finally have! Any of these can be good reasons for cooking at Chez Panisse . . . if [your] cooking is approached with passion, with an eye toward beauty, with care; if efficiency is important, if improvement and shared knowledge are important; if cooking in a "normal" restaurant would not be enough. . . .
>
> Learn to cut an onion beautifully, to reduce a sauce to just the right consistency, to grill a piece of bread perfectly. Know when the pasta is "relaxed," when to stoke the fire. Make your plates lovely and simple. Rub your salad leaves lightly and let them fall from your hands naturally. . . .
>
> If your technique is faulty, it may be because your appreciation of the medium is not refined. Conversely, if you are having trouble with a visual aesthetic, it might be because you haven't mastered a certain technique. Please avail yourself of the many resources here. Talk food, read, get involved. Cook the staff meal; cook at home. . . .

This is not how most chefs think. The refinement, the intellectuality, and the philosophical bent of David Tanis were the kinds of qualities that moved Alice most deeply. His memo makes clear why it is so hard for anyone who has ever cooked at Chez Panisse to cook anywhere else, and why it is so hard for Chez Panisse to bring aboard anyone trained elsewhere. Chez Panisse sends not only apostles into the world; it also sometimes sends out alumni who try to be explorers, who venture into the larger restaurant world and then flee back to the home that Chez Panisse has become for them. As a rule, Chez Panisse welcomes their return, even when their departures may have been awkward or worse. They return, of course, with new experience and often valuable ideas. In this way Chez Panisse fertilizes the wider world of restaurants and is fertilized in its turn.

As easy as it can be for an alumnus to return, it can be equally difficult for a newcomer to penetrate the Chez Panisse culture. A cook with however brilliant a résumé from somewhere else may be turned aside with little more than a glance and a few polite words from Alice. You've got to "get it" to work at Chez Panisse. And "getting it" is a very elusive quality: The "it" is the whole thing—the ethic, a commitment to being your best, the sense of style, the palate, the nose, the intellect, the instinct, the personal manners, the ability to sense intuitively what Alice is all about, even when she cannot put it into words.

By the mid-1980s, Chez Panisse was doing very well (in every aspect except the bottom line). *Newsweek* hailed the restaurant's food as "a revolution in American cooking."[1] *Vogue* described dining at Chez Panisse as "one of this country's most sensuously satisfying, highly personal eating experiences."[2] In *House & Garden*, Jason Epstein (Alice's editor at Random House) wrote, "She penetrates to the essence—the soul, you might say—of a quail or an oyster or even of a sack of flour or a bottle of oil."[3] The *San Francisco Chronicle*'s restaurant critic wrote, "I've never found the food at Panisse as consistently good as it is now."[4] Marian Burros wrote in the *New York Times*, "More than any other single figure, Miss Waters has been instrumental in developing the exciting and imaginative style that has been labeled New American Cuisine."[5]

Chez Panisse and Alice Waters were still (and are still) not to everyone's liking. In his *Private Guide*, Robert Finigan thought Paul Bertolli's cooking came nowhere near Jeremiah Tower's (it should be noted that Jeremiah had become a friend of his). Finigan demoted the restaurant from four stars to two and stopped going there. *California* magazine called Chez Panisse "fussy and self-conscious," with "all the verve of a requiem."[6] In *The Nation*, David Sundelson wrote, "The triumph of Chez Panisse represents a new privatism, a sad turn inward, away from public issues and commitments."[7]

Alice had become known as the mother of the New American Cooking, or California cuisine, as it came to be called. Was she the personification of this new movement because she grabbed credit from others? Was it because she always went running to the nearest camera or reporter's notebook?

The answer is not simple. Certainly she liked the attention, the admiration, the fame. What is determinative, however, is not so much Alice herself as contemporary culture, which demands that every story have a hero. If you're a writer, you'll find it very hard to sell an article about an idea unless that idea is embodied in a hero (or a villain). People don't want abstractions; they want flesh-and-blood heroes. In Alice, so soft-spoken, so passionate, yet also so flustered and inarticulate sometimes, people had found a hero who was also unmistakably, unheroically human.

"Total strangers," wrote *California Living* magazine in April 1985, "call her Alice."

Alice was not instinctively comfortable in the spotlight. "I remember flying to New York one time," says Charles Shere. "Lindsey and I were sitting three or four rows behind Alice, and somehow, the way the seats were, I could see through the spaces between the seats to Alice. I just happened to see her pick up the in-flight magazine. She opened it up, saw a full-page picture of herself, closed the magazine, and put it back in its pocket. And she was closing it in a real hurry lest one of the people next to her should see it. It was a very funny moment. She was embarrassed." But she also knew that she had a role to play that no one in her right mind would have spurned.

"It is the fact," says Barbara Carlitz, "that a large number of dedicated people have let it be Alice's show, and have not piped up and said, 'Wait a minute, Alice owns two percent of the restaurant at this point,' or something, or, 'But wait a minute, Alice had three partners,' 'Wait a minute, there's a board that really ran it,' 'Wait a minute, there's a manager,' 'Wait, there's a chef.' No one has ever done this, with the possible exception of Jeremiah. I presume it's partly for two reasons. One, she's so damn good at it, and the myth is probably more enchanting than the reality to people. And two, I have to presume that people genuinely respect Alice enough to let her have that."

There is also to be considered "the Matthew effect," which was first described by Robert K. Merton.[8] In a series of interviews with Nobel laureates,

Merton found, "They repeatedly observe that eminent scientists get dispro-portionately great credit for their contributions to science while relatively unknown scientists tend to get disproportionately little credit for compa-rable contributions." Merton gave the effect its name based on chapter 25, verse 29, of the Gospel According to Saint Matthew: "For unto every one that hath shall be given, and he shall have abundance: but from him that hath not shall be taken away even that which he hath."

IN JULY 1984, Jeremiah Tower opened his dream restaurant, Stars. In its chic and jazzy premises in the heart of San Francisco's Civic Center—home to City Hall, the library, the opera, the ballet, the symphony—Stars was in the perfect position to cultivate the rich, powerful, and publicity-seeking. The food was exciting, the atmosphere electric, and Jeremiah triumphant. On the wall he hung a framed letter from Alice, written in happier times, praising him profusely. Displaying that letter, he told the *Chronicle,* was "a little bit of malicious vengeance. People can see in her own handwriting just who is whose disciple."[9] He seems not to have known how self-degrading a gesture hanging that letter on the wall at Stars was.

In a piece in the *New York Times* by Marian Burros on September 26, 1984, Alice's words on Jeremiah show a vividly contrasting character:

> "He had a bold way of doing things," she said of Mr. Tower, who is now co-owner of the Santa Fe Bar and Grill in Berkeley and owner of the two-month-old Stars. "He was not hesitant," Miss Waters said. "His cooking is more elaborate than mine, more flamboyant and richer. I'm more garlic and olive oil—he's more cream and but-ter. But initially I was fascinated by his combinations, things I wouldn't have thought of."

There's perhaps a subtle little knife twist in that "initially," but the otherwise gracious tone is that of a smiling winner.

Alice had mastered her self-representation to the media—with the me-dia's helpful assistance—but she had yet to master Chez Panisse. An average of twenty main courses were going missing every night. An exchange of memos among the staff sought to identify the strengths and weaknesses of Chez Panisse at the moment. Paul Bertolli thought David Tanis worked too slowly and "wasn't a leader." David Tanis's riposte was, "Our food must not be compromised." Fritz Streiff, always a thoughtful analyst of Chez Panisse, thought the restaurant "needed a radical change, to attract people lost due to loss of novelty, lack of local reviews, lack of variety."

For the fiscal year ending June 30, 1984, total sales had been a robust $2.7 million. Twenty-three thousand dinners had been served downstairs, more than a hundred thousand meals in the café. And Chez Panisse had finally shown a profit. Two percent.

Any other business would have considered that barely scraping by, but at Chez Panisse it was cause for jubilation. Pat Waters got his computer system—$46,000 worth. The restaurant lent Jerry Budrick $12,000 to buy a car. Alice's salary was raised to $52,000 per annum plus 10 percent of net income. Paul Bertolli got a similar raise, and a three-year contract. Pagnol et Cie insured the life of Alice Waters for one million dollars.

In the restaurant downstairs—under Tom Guernsey's sole leadership, now that Alice had largely given up acting as hostess—the front of the house began to run nearly as smoothly as the kitchen. "Bill Staggs and Tom were the most perfect waiters," says Alice. "They were like ballet dancers together. Everything just *worked.*" Thanks to Pat Edwards's hawkeyed vigilance and Pat Waters's computer system, the finances had begun to make some sense. Alice's father claimed that the new system was saving Chez Panisse $10,000 a month. The service had regained its style of polite familiarity, hospitality, generosity, and casual expertise. The waiters were taking home a lot of money, legitimately gained. Was all this good news just another of the restaurant's habitual fluctuations, or was Chez Panisse growing up?

What was clear was that Alice was letting go a little. By late spring of 1985, she was sometimes coming in only once a week, to help set up the downstairs dining room and act as hostess for the evening. There were also times when she would whirl through to taste the day's fare—often every item on both menus—and offer her customary detailed and merciless advice. But the rest of her time belonged to her daughter, and perhaps, a

Charles and Lindsey Shere

bit, to her relationship with Stephen, and to a grand new project that foreshadowed grander ones to come.

Alice was proposing to turn the restaurant of the Oakland Museum of California into a living exhibition of her philosophy. Food would be as fundamental a part of the museum's mission as the art it showed and the history and science it taught. The landscaping would be transformed into a "teaching garden," where children and other museum visitors would learn how crops were grown and turned into food. Then, in the museum dining room, they could eat what they had just learned about. With Fanny turning twenty-one months old, Alice was particularly interested in children's food. She foresaw the museum snack bar "selling sack lunches for children. They could eat lunch on benches in the garden. I wanted a demonstration bakery, where people could watch tortillas being patted out by hand." When asked how much it might cost to get the project off the ground and whether she expected it to turn a profit, Alice answered, "There's always money for good ideas."

That same spring, Pat Waters found a person who he believed could run Chez Panisse like a real business. Two percent was not Alice's father's idea of decent profit. Moreover, an effective manager would give Alice all the more freedom to spread her wings. The board authorized $15,000 for a six-month trial of Richard Mazzera as general manager.

Barb Carlitz had long been a member of the Chez Panisse board, as well as a virtual member of the Waters family; her recollection of the advent of Richard Mazzera is this: "Pat Waters served as pseudomanager for a while, and he decided we really did need to have somebody. Richard Mazzera was very young, very ambitious, attractive, probably in his mid-twenties. Pat, I think, considered him in some ways the son he'd never had. He considered him certainly a protégé. Some people in the restaurant hated Richard, and some liked Richard. Everyone was very suspicious, after all these anarchic years of nobody with a title of manager."

Pat Edwards, who thought *she* was the manager, was incensed. As she fumed, her sister's attention was inevitably elsewhere: Lindsey Shere was about to publish *Chez Panisse Desserts,* with a very large first print run of sixty thousand copies. Patricia Curtan had designed the book, and the painter Wayne Thiebaud—famous for his lush depictions of pastry—had illustrated it.

Lindsey's retelling of one of her favorite recipes demonstrates the subtlety essential to making simple food extraordinary.

· LINDSEY'S FRUIT GALETTE ·

Peaches, nectarines, and plums are great for this. It's easily translated to apples and pears, too. One of the great things about a galette is you can make it any size you want. If you want something for two people, you can make a little one. You start with a *pâte brisée,* of whatever size you need for what you're making. The one I use, for six to eight servings, is a cup of flour, six tablespoons of butter, a quarter teaspoon of salt, and a quarter cup of cold water. You just put it together like pie crust, very quickly. I usually chill it then for a little while to let the flour relax a bit.

I roll it out really thin, as thin as possible, into a big circle. I usually bake it on a pizza pan, but it could be on a flat cookie sheet. If you've got a pizza stone, putting the pan on that would be an ideal way to bake it, because you want to get heat to the bottom of it very quickly.

So you roll out a big circle and lay it on the pan. Then I usually make a mixture of equal parts of sugar and flour. For this size I'd use about two tablespoons of each and spread that over the bottom of the galette, out to about two inches from the edge. It's there to sit under the fruit and thicken the juices. Sometimes I add macaroon crumbs, or even a thin layer of almond paste.

If I were using peaches or plums or nectarines or pluots [a plum-apricot hybrid], I would use about a quart of sliced fruit. You can either arrange the fruit in a fancy design on the dough or just scrumble it around. Peaches I peel usually, but not plums or nectarines.

Now this is the part where you have to make a judgment. I sprinkle the top with sugar—more if it's something like plums, and less if it's something like peaches. You can sprinkle it reasonably heavily, because those things become much more tart when you cook them. If you want to test it, what you should do is cook a bit of the fruit in a tiny little pot, and sugar it and see how much you need. I can't give you any measurement. It's just something you have to try.

When you've sprinkled the fruit with sugar, fold the edges of the dough up over the fruit. You can pleat them in or gather them in, depending on how good a seamstress you are. Then I brush those folded-over edges of the dough with water, pretty heavily, and then I sprinkle just the edges really heavily with sugar, so there's a thorough coating on it.

It goes into the oven to bake at four hundred degrees for forty-five or fifty minutes. You should rotate it in the oven, and watch to make sure that the caramel on the crust is not burning. The thing you want to be sure of is that the fruit is thoroughly cooked, and that it's boiling in the center of the galette, because that will cook the flour on the bottom.

When it's done, immediately slide it onto a rack to cool, so that the bottom doesn't get soggy. In the first five minutes or so, while the juices are still bubbling, I use a pastry brush to pick up those juices and glaze any of the fruit that looks dry. After that, the juices disappear into the flour, so you've got to be quick. And that's it.

WHATEVER SUBSURFACE friction there was between them, Alice and Stephen seemed determined to overcome it, if only for Fanny's sake. On September 23, 1985, with two-year-old Fanny as flower girl, Alice Waters married Stephen Singer in a simple ceremony in New York's Central Park.

Why there? "Part of it," Stephen explains, "was that it sounded exciting, interesting, unconventional, and part of it was that if we had gotten married in Berkeley, the social obligations would have been huge. We went to New York as a way to not have to invite anybody. It was just our immediate family, so there were about, oh, sixteen, eighteen, twenty people at the wedding."

"It was in the herb garden," says Alice. "It was quite beautiful. By a pond in the herb garden."

"She had all the Pagnol fantasies going on at the same time," recalls Alice's sister Ellen. "She named her daughter Fanny. When Alice and Stephen got married, she wore a dress that could have been a double for the dress that Fanny wore in the wedding in *César*."

On their return from a three-week honeymoon in Tuscany (with Fanny along), Stephen went back to work at Singer and Foy, and Alice found familiar troubles at Chez Panisse. Jerry Budrick was drinking on the job again, complaining about his salary, and having trouble at home, too. Alice

Alice and Stephen's wedding

and the board agreed that when Jerry started acting badly in the restaurant, there needed to be some way to get him off the floor, though they didn't say precisely who was to do it, or how. Any other business probably would have fired him, but this was Chez Panisse, and Jerry was family.

Alice defended Jerry as long as she could, but the board was adamant. His drinking while working was not to be tolerated. Still, they were remarkably compassionate. In the fall of 1985, Jerry was given a sabbatical of six weeks, with full pay. He began work on a new business, developing a spring water source in the Sierra Nevada foothills. To pursue that, he decided to take the full year of 1986 off, though he remained a member of the board of directors of Pagnol et Cie. In 1987, Jerry Budrick and Chez Panisse parted ways for good. He continued to own 14 percent of the restaurant for the next five years, however, and continued to serve on the board through the same period.

"Alice is very tough," says Greil Marcus. "She wouldn't be where she was if she weren't. But these board decisions sometimes took a very long time, because Alice had to be convinced that we had to be cruel about it, and that's not her way. And sometimes it gave her cover for getting rid of people. She could either convince herself that it wasn't she who was doing it—which would be true, it would be the board—or it could be communicated through other people: This isn't Alice getting rid of you, this is us. It took a long time to get Jerry Budrick out, to isolate him, to push him into his own venture, the water business that he was trying to start. But ultimately you slam the door, and there is no route back."

With the restaurant full every night, great reviews still pouring in, herself newly married, in the autumn and winter of 1985–1986 Alice was full of optimism. She hired Stephen, first as a consultant, to restructure the wine list, and then to take control of the whole wine operation (which was still losing five hundred bottles a month). She put her shares in Chez Panisse into joint tenancy with Stephen. She persuaded North Point Press to publish a special edition of Marcel Pagnol's memoirs to commemorate the restaurant's approaching fifteenth birthday, and wrote a foreword for it herself. Despite her mistrust of technology and any sort of large corporation, she acceded to her father's insistence that Chez Panisse begin accepting credit cards.

Never had Alice seemed so certain about everything. When her sister Ellen Pisor was planning a first trip to France, she called Alice. "I wanted to really experience some of these wonderful things that she'd been talking about for years, and I said, 'Where should we go?' And she said to me in her own declarative style that there wasn't anything worth going to in southern France anymore. It was all built up. The Parisians had come down and taken over all the windmills. It was overrun by tourists. It was ruined, ruined! I got off the phone, and I thought, Oh, my God, it's ruined, and I've never been there. I have nothing to compare it to, so will I think it's ruined? I was very discouraged. Then Alice said, 'Let me think about it.' About two days later, she called me at midnight—she always forgot whether I was three hours behind her or ahead of her—and she said, 'Okay, I've got a place for you. Nathalie Waag's. It's great. She's got a little house outside of Bonnieux, and she serves meals, and she'll take you to the markets, and blah, blah, blah. I'll send you some stuff on it.' And you know, it really was quite wonderful."

Chez Panisse was beginning to have fun again. One anonymous joke-ster created a bogus menu identical in style to the real one, and then he interleaved copies of the fake among the real:

Tuesday	Parrot leg tartare, beaks & guano
	Bird-face soup with pesto
	Grilled glazed parrot breasts with yellow and red feathers, sautéed parakeet feet
	Garden salad
	Feuilleté of flight feathers, back claws and budgie droppings
Wednesday	Mixed grill: Amazon parrots, macaws, cockatiel & conure with Chino Ranch peppers, pesto & grilled cat paws
	Pasta with sun-dried conure beaks, herbs & perch gunk
	Roast tenderloin of macaw breast with garlic sauce, warm guava & papaya
	Garden salad
	Warm guano & avocado gratin

. . . and so on, down to the pièce de résistance:

Saturday	Double yellow head & green bean salad
	Risotto with cuttlebone & shredded cage paper
	Young canaries grilled & roasted with red wine sauce
	Provençal stuffed birdy assholes & grilled vegetables
	Warm guano tart with lavender-honey ice cream

"Why parrots?" asks Alice. "I have no idea. Whoever it was slipped these in with all the other menus, so you never knew who was going to get one. They just put them in there, printed exactly the way that our other menus were printed. So at first we didn't find it. It was very cleverly done. We just laughed hysterically. I don't know how long it went on. I know I shouldn't have let it."

On the fifteenth birthday of Chez Panisse, August 28, 1986, the North Point Press's limited edition of Marcel Pagnol's memoirs, *My Father's Glory and My Mother's Castle,* went on sale at the bar. In the foreword, Alice expressed with particular clarity the Pagnolian dream that sustained her: "an ideal reality where life and work were inseparable and the daily pace left you time for the afternoon anisette or the restorative game of pétanque, and where eating together nourished the spirit as well as the body—since the food was raised, harvested, hunted, fished, and gathered by people sustaining and sustained by each other and by the earth itself." She ended the little essay with a recipe very much in the spirit both of Pagnol and of Chez Panisse:

· GRILLED QUAIL WITH WILD HERBS AND OLIVE TOASTS ·

Marinate the quail with olive oil, a little sweet wine from Provence, fresh thyme, rosemary, and sage for several hours. Salt and pepper the quail. Grill them over fairly hot wood embers about forty-five minutes on the skin side, until nicely browned. Turn over and cook a few more minutes. While the quail sit, toast thin slices of bread over the coals and spread them with a paste of olives crushed with garlic and made smooth with olive oil. Serve with a salad of bitter greens and a bottle of Bandol.

13.

DEATH
AND LIFE

1986–1987

I n 1986, it had been scarcely four years since the United States Centers for Disease Control had coined the term *acquired immune deficiency syndrome,* but AIDS had already torn its merciless way through gay communities across the country, nowhere with greater ferocity than in the San Francisco Bay Area. The disease was not a killer only of homosexual men, although they were by far its most numerous and most prominent victims. And Tom Guernsey had it.

"Despair doesn't begin to describe what we felt," says Alice. "I had never been so devastated, brokenhearted, there's no word strong enough. My dearest, sweetest, irreplaceable Tom. He was so afraid, and so courageous. He was going to keep working."

As the birth of Fanny had awoken Alice to the future, the coming death of Tom Guernsey awoke her to its fragility.

I felt I had to do something now. There was nothing we could do to save Tom, but the illness was so ghastly, such torture, it tore people's lives apart. People with AIDS were living alone, and dying alone.

Mutual affection à la famille Panisse: *David Tanis,*
Tom Guernsey, and Alice

And there were suddenly so many. Vince Calcagno, the owner of
Zuni Café in San Francisco (this was before Judy Rodgers became
partner), had lost five friends in one month, and he was organizing a
big benefit to raise money to help take care of people with AIDS. Tom
and I had to be involved. It was going to be called Aid and Comfort.

April 1987 brought two changes with long-term consequences for Chez
Panisse and Alice. She decided to give the two-chef idea another try, asking Catherine Brandel to be co-chef with David Tanis in the café. She also
hired Gerald Rosenfield to replace Catherine as the restaurant's forager.

"Ah, Jerry Rosenfield," sighs Alice, sadly. "He was a great writer, and
very important to me personally. I'd met him during the Scheer campaign.
He was a moral force. An M.D., a psychiatrist, but he hadn't practiced in
a long time. After Bob Scheer's campaign, we lost contact, and years later
he just appeared one day, with a bucket of mussels."

Richard Seibert, a longtime pizza chef in the café, remembers, "Doctor Jerry had been out at Bolinas harvesting mussels, and thought they were the most delicious ones he had ever had. So he put a few dozen of them into a Folger's coffee can, snuck up, dropped them in front of Alice's back door, rang the doorbell, and ran."

Alice recalls, "He was destitute, living on the streets, just barely making it. He'd had big depressions, and that had made him a whole different person. So I bought the mussels, and then he brought more, and then he brought more."

Jerry's first task as forager was to find meat supplies as good, and as pure, as the produce the restaurant was getting from Green Gulch, Warren Weber, and the Chinos. He threw himself into the job. He wrote rhapsodic reports on his travels, the farms he found, and the people. Typical was this one, of October 20, 1987:

> Tonight's lambs were raised by Lori Gibbs of Acampo, in San Joaquin County. These are registered Southdown sheep, and Lori's show animals have won prizes at country fairs, and one of her yearling ewes was champion at the California State Fair. Lori is twelve years old, and this is her 4-H Club project.
>
> [He goes on to describe the feed, the absence of medication, the heritage of the Southdown variety of sheep.] Perhaps it has something to do with their ancient lineage, but I have noticed, looking over the animals at the fairs, that the Southdown is characterized by a personableness and self-containment not seen in most other breeds of sheep.

"Every time Jerry brought something," says Alice,

> he noticed something about the restaurant that needed to be attended to. The way the staff was treated, or how they greeted people coming in, or how I presented myself out in the world. He was always thinking about the people who weren't being considered. He would remind me how people were feeling about working at the restaurant, and how I needed to not forget the people who were my real friends, and not get

carried away with the fame of the restaurant. He would stay and talk with the dishwashers late at night, and he'd tell me that I needed to pay them more, and pay them more attention.

He wrote me long letters about all these things. Handwritten, three pages. Who were the honest and worthy people to buy food from, who was trying to take advantage of us. Treatises on garbage—he got me out there standing in the garbage Dumpster one time, made me clean it out myself. And boy, we changed our system right after that. Ever since then I've been obsessed with compost.

"When I first started there," Richard Seibert recalls, "part of Jerry's job was maintaining the outside grounds. He was responsible for recycling all the wine bottles and for keeping the garbage cans scrubbed out. I found a note in my paycheck, I forget exactly when, that said [he reads]:

As summertime draws near, it behooves us to minimize the miasma emanating from our Dumpsters. Therefore, we earnestly request that any sacks containing organic matter with sufficient moisture to leak (which would smell if not refrigerated) be tied with string. For your convenience, ready-cut lengths of string may be found by the dishwashers' dumbwaiter and upstairs under the counter by the rear waiters' station.

"That pretty much sums up Jerry," continues Seibert. "He was very crazy. When he was sane, he was incredibly bright.

"As *famille Panisse,* we'd all take care of each other if we got sick. So a committee was organized, and groups of people would take turns with Doctor Jerry to help reintegrate him back into the world."

"Jerry was my conscience," Alice says. "He was very important in my life. But ultimately he was having these horrible outbursts in front of the restaurant, and we'd have to call the police to take him away. He was sinking, going way down. Having fits of anxiety and terrible anger. Psychotic episodes. He knew it himself. He knew he had to be restrained. He was a peaceful person, physically, but a raging in-your-face yeller. Over anything. Maybe somebody had left the remains of their lunch on a table out back. The littlest things. And I was a public figure, and he wanted me to make the world right. I wasn't doing it right, or as fast as he wanted me to do it. I think he would be proud of me now, but . . ." Her voice trails off.

With Jerry Rosenfield spiraling into madness and Tom Guernsey growing sicker, the imminence of pain and death inspired in Alice what, in an essay some years later, she termed "a deepened appreciation for the joy and life in food."[1] A salad, a carrot, a plum, at its best, perhaps mere hours from its plucking, was in a sense still alive, and gave life not only to the body but to the mind of its eater. A fish too long out of water confessed its deadness in its sunken eyes, its graying skin, the doughy slackening of its meat. A fish fresh from the sea glistened with aliveness, its eyes moist and full, its muscles firm, its scales still sparkling. The life in food, Alice believed, wasn't just a metaphor. "We have always seen the meal as a center of the human experience," reads the restaurant's official pronouncement on sustainability. "At the table we are nourished and gladdened, put in touch with the source of life. . . . It is central to both the deepest and the most joyous of human activities: generosity, companionship, nourishment, growth."[2]

Alan Tangren, who had been at the restaurant for years, became the next forager, and it was in that capacity that he grew into something of a Chez Panisse institution. He had grown up living part-time on a farm in the California Sierra Nevada, with a grandmother who was a great cook. Alan himself cooked all through college and graduate school, eventually emerging as a professor of meteorology. But he couldn't keep away from the stove. He began cooking for the famed gourmet Darrell Corti in Sacramento: "He would have dinner parties at his house, and after every course he would come into the kitchen with his critique of how the meal was going. He was a great teacher. I thought by then that I was ready to cook at Chez Panisse. But Alice didn't."

He persisted nevertheless, and was soon doing lowly tasks in the café under chef Joyce Goldstein. Joyce had introduced more regularity and less variation in the café menu.

"It was very codified," says Alan.

Joyce made all the decisions. I think Alice was sort of distracted at that time, with Fanny and traveling. We had actual recipe books. Joyce's recipes. There was less experimentation. It was still seasonal to a certain degree, but you knew that every Friday we would have the wild rice and beef tenderloin salad.

Then when David Tanis came to the café, I started doing all kinds of things. I was the café chef on Mondays, and then the rest of the week I worked either in the prep kitchen or on the line or whatever needed to be done. Chez Panisse has always cultivated that sort of pinch-hitter quality. It's Alice's way of letting people find their own place. She talks about tossing the cards in the air. In my case, it's meant I've been able to do lots of different things. It's why I've stayed here so long.

I'd had another job, finding these really obscure items for visiting French chefs at the Mondavi winery. So the chefs at Chez Panisse started asking me to find things for them. Unfortunately, they started asking for things that weren't in season. They were getting a little bit disconnected from the sources of the things they were using. I had worked with Jerry Rosenfield, who was so particular about everything, and we had really learned how to find things. We would set up cream tastings, beef tastings, everything, just to compare the producers and find what was best. So it was natural for me to become the forager.

"Alan did that job for ten years, and he was always marvelous," says Alice. "He loves to surprise people. You know, 'You think you know what a blackberry tastes like, but taste this one.' And *pow*! He has such an amazing palate for fruit that when Lindsey retired, he was the obvious choice for pastry chef."

"It really was a leap of faith on Alice's part," says Alan. "She just said, 'Oh, give it a try.' And it took me a year to learn everything. I was totally dependent on Lindsey's recipes, and the pastry sous-chef, Mary Canales, who knew much more than I did. And of course Alice was always reaching for the next thing, wanting to do something differently."

(Alan Tangren would leave Chez Panisse in 2006, after twenty-five years in which, in Alice's words, "he just always knew the right thing to do." He is now raising flowers on his family's old farm in the Sierra.)

Chez Panisse by now had relationships with a number of excellent farmers, but the restaurant remained dependent on their choices of crops, and their harvesting schedules. Alice wanted to work with a farm that would grow what she wanted, and when. Her father undertook the task of interviewing more than a hundred farmers, all within a hundred miles of Chez Panisse. With the help of agriculture experts at the University of California at Davis, he whittled the list down to eighteen, and then to four. Toward the end of 1985, when Pat and Alice Waters interviewed the finalists, the winner was indisputable.

Nobody could ever have dreamed up Bob Cannard, or his farm in Sonoma County. His crops were choked with weeds. Some of the weeds came in wild—rye, filaree, mallow—but some he planted himself—barley, vetch, triticale. It looked like total disorder: a tomato plant here, a pepper there, three cabbages, a cluster of carrots. When Alice walked Bob's fields, the ground was as springy as a mattress, so rich was it in organic matter. Bob would clutch a fistful of topsoil and shove it under her nose. "It's delicious!" he would proclaim, and pop some in his mouth. He talked nonstop. He would pluck a fruit or vegetable, carve off a piece, and, grinning, command, "Taste that." It would be, reliably, the best turnip, radish, apricot, carrot, or avocado Alice had ever tasted. "Happy plants!" he'd exclaim. Sometimes he sang to them.

And he loved to talk about them. "You can read the whole plant," he said. "It's right there before you, and if you pay attention to the nature of the bark and the quality of the leaves and the growth habits and all of the observable and smellable and tastable characteristics, you can see the past history of a plant. In its new growth, you can see its present. If it had a bad past and has a bad present, why, then, it's going to be pretty difficult for it to have a good future, but a sick plant is one of your greatest teachers. The most important yield, as far as I'm concerned, is that I have been able to become a true cultivator of nature. I can go out into almost any circumstance and grow almost anything. With health. With health."

Bob Cannard

When Bob bought the land, in 1976, it was in miserable shape, the soil compacted to hardpan, the creek dead dry.

I picked this place specifically because it's somewhat isolated. I wanted to be out of the eye of general humanity, and not having people tell me that I'm doing everything incorrectly. I wanted to do everything incorrectly. I wanted to figure out how to do it correctly by doing it incorrectly, because it's obvious that the conventional agricultural dictates are incorrect, because our soils are in decline, our crop quality and food quality are in decline.

The place had had forty thousand turkeys on it for forty years, and the soils were heavily eroded and toxified by turkey manure and pretty well poisoned off with herbicides. If I'd wanted to make money, I could have selected a very fine soil, and I could do things wrong and never know it, and I could do things right and never know it. But I wanted a soil that I would know by observing if I did something appropriate and if I did something incorrect.

Under Bob Cannard's care, the creek began to run year-round, thronged with turtles, salamanders, and the tiny smolts of steelhead trout. The farm comprises only thirty cultivated acres (a hundred and fifty more acres, not cultivated, serve as watershed), on which Bob produces some two hundred varieties of fruits and vegetables. Leading a visitor on a tour, he says,

Well, let's see, here we've got my olive trees, about six hundred of those, just getting started, really. Got about a hundred gallons of oil this year. Here are persimmons, plums, apples, favas, figs, lemon verbena—you know how Alice loves that lemon verbena tea— broccoli rabe, leeks, beets. Over here we've got our raspberries, and artichokes, chervil, rocket, various lettuces. Chez Panisse trucks all their organic waste up here, you know, and I put it to work. Table grapes. I don't know how many varieties of them. Every vine's a different one. I'm starting a little cow herd, a British breed called Dexter. They're good for beef and milk both. Chez Panisse is my only customer, except I do still go to the farmers' market over in Sonoma town, Tuesday evenings and Friday mornings.

My setup with Alice has changed a bit lately, because Alice wants to support lots of farmers, though we do have, in my perception, kind of a marriage relationship. I've been monogamous, but my partner hasn't been. But I can't be too critical. She's got other social support reasons. Right now, they're using a lot of my stuff because it's winter and a lot of the sunny-day farmers go away, but come summertime, when all the easy-to-grow, nice-tasting things like tomatoes come in, well, they get lots of stuff from lots of other people.

All this is wildlife habitat. Nothing's fenced except the cows. The deer don't bother me. I let them have what they want. Only real problem right now is the ground squirrels. Here's apricot, more plums, endive, escarole. If your plants are healthy, they'll coexist with the bugs. They turn out to be better food, too. There's a completeness about these plants that they share with the people who eat them.

A good farmer's got to know how to assess plant health. You see those dead leaves rotting? That's not a problem. That plant's feeding itself for the future. Some bugs help you, too. The cucumber beetle visits the zucchini flower—never poops in it, either—and then at night, when the flower closes, the bug protects it.

"Finding Bob Cannard was a thrill," Alice says. "I have always had an excitement about meeting people who were growing beautiful fruits and vegetables, all different varieties, and picking them at the right moment and bringing them to us. I can't think of anything that really excites me more."

· GOOD THINGS FROM CANNARD FARM ·

When we started work with Bob was when we began to grill scallions and leeks, because he sent us so many little tiny ones. You just put some olive oil and a little water on them, and some salt on the grill—a pretty hot grill—and you move them around for just a couple of minutes. Serve them in a little pile with, oh, prosciutto, or chop them up and put them in a frittata.

Bob used to bring us down cherries on the branch, and we'd just put the branches on the table.

He has sensational carrots. He claims they're ten times as healthy as anyone else's carrots. It has to do with the way that he nourishes his soil. Carrots are really his specialty. He made us all believers in carrots. And carrot juice.

For little kids who come to the restaurant, we make a salad that we call a dipping salad, where we take a little wedge of lettuce, like a little heart of romaine, and we'll do carrot curls from Bob's carrots, and serve that with a little bowl of vinaigrette. The kids dip and eat, which is a great thing to see.

Bob's carrots have certainly transformed our carrot soup, which is one of the classic Chez Panisse soups. It doesn't get much simpler

---

than this. But when you can get carrots as good as Bob Cannard's, it's just sublime. When I've got really perfect carrots like that, I don't use stock, just water.

I start by cooking some onions in butter or oil with a little bit of thyme for about fifteen minutes, until they're soft and sweet. You want enough butter or oil to really coat the onions. Then I add the carrots. They should be sliced all the same thickness so you don't have some overdone and some underdone. I add a little salt, and I taste.

Then I add water and just simmer till the carrots are tender. Not falling apart, but fully cooked. Always tasting to be sure. You've got to get the salt just right. Then I put it through the food mill. You could use a blender or a food processor, but I think the food mill gives it a nicer texture. The medium holes.

At the end, you can float a little butter or herbs or lemon juice on top, but you should be very careful that the garnish doesn't overpower that lovely, delicate flavor of carrot. I wouldn't use cream. We're not cream people when it comes to vegetables.

On a Sunday in October 1986, at the Stags' Leap Winery in the Napa Valley, the entire staff of Chez Panisse met for a retreat. The day began with the distribution of a questionnaire, a swim in the estate's lake, and a lunch of organic hot dogs and hamburgers. Then came the meeting. Grievances were aired; classes for the staff were planned in such subjects as butchery, knife sharpening, pastry, and wine tasting; representatives from each department were chosen for staff meetings. Fritz Streiff led a toast with his poem "Written in Honor of Richard Olney":

Food neither good to look at nor to eat,
Deracinated diet, dull in the extreme,
Carcinogenic, tasteless, incomplete,
Dehumanizing: this is the cuisine

We might be eating still had we not read
Elizabeth David and begun to think
About the better ways we could be fed.

     Our lives were changed forever. Food & drink
Became for most of us our raison d'être.
We cannot thank or praise enough. We only
Can lift our glasses to our two great maîtres,
To Mrs. David & to Richard Olney:
We toast you with the most profound emotion.
Rhyme can't contain our homage and devotion.

Alice talked passionately about the goals of Chez Panisse. "Our primary motive is not profit," she said. "Our number one goal is to educate ourselves and the public. . . . Why do so many people eat at Chez Panisse? Obviously for the delicious, real food; but they also want to feel like part of an extended family. That is another goal of the restaurant: to try to operate like a family." She laid heaviest stress on what was becoming her most cherished ideal: "our responsibility to the rest of the world."

Alice had always been generous toward members of the *famille Panisse* who needed a sabbatical, some psychotherapy, investment in a start-up such as Steve Sullivan's Acme Bakery, a loan for whatever reason. She also gave to public causes that touched her heart—the famine in Ethiopia, political refugees from El Salvador, local hunger programs, a synagogue's Hanukkah bazaar. But she had begun to realize that supporting good causes wasn't enough. Chez Panisse, in its very identity, stood *against* things, too— most notably, industrial agriculture and the ever-declining quality of what Americans put in their mouths.

"Those of us who work with food," she wrote in "The Farm-Restaurant Connection,"[3] "suffer from an image of being involved in an elite, frivolous pastime that has little relation to anything important or meaningful. But in fact we are in a position to cause people to make important connections between what they are eating and a host of crucial environmental, social, and health issues."

Chez Panisse and its extended family and like-minded people elsewhere were a very small force to stand up against the juggernaut of industrial agriculture. The situation was bad when Chez Panisse opened, in 1971, but it was radically worse fifteen years later.

Genetically modified corn had made possible the production of high-fructose corn syrup at vastly lower cost than any other sugar, and that corn syrup was now appearing not only in desserts but in an astonishing range of food products. Consumers often didn't perceive the added sugar, but they came to prefer the products that contained it. It was, in effect, addictive. And it drove people still further away from the somewhat bitter-tasting foods—broccoli, Brussels sprouts, leafy greens—that were the most nutritious. Fast-food companies, and soon other restaurants, discovered that portion sizes could be increased at low cost, and that larger portions were preferred by many consumers. The corporations were offering to school districts special deals that would reduce their food costs substantially; cafeterias that actually cooked and served real food, therefore, were being replaced by vending machines and microwaved, portion-controlled meals-ready-to-eat. High schools rarely required their students to stay on campus at lunchtime anymore, so it hardly mattered if they served nutritious food, because McDonald's and its kind were very often conveniently situated nearby. "These guys find where the exits are on the freeways before they've been built," says Alice, "and they buy the land next to the school!"

"High-fructose corn syrup," wrote the *New York Times*, "can hinder the body's ability to process sugar, and can promote faster fat growth than sweeteners derived from cane sugar. . . . Since the advent of the syrup, consumption of all sweeteners has soared; the average American's intake has increased about 35 percent. . . . A study in the *American Journal of Clinical Nutrition* showed that the rise of type 2 diabetes since 1980 had closely paralleled the increased use of sweeteners, particularly corn syrup."[4]

Americans were getting fatter fast. Fast food—high in calories, low in nutrition—was the fastest-growing segment of the food economy. It was cheap, and seductive. "Food shouldn't be fast," Alice insisted. "And it shouldn't be cheap."

There was profound moral reasoning behind Alice's adamance. The fast-food industry was part of a larger agro-industrial complex that was causing harm on a scale few Americans understood. "Factory farms," with thousands of acres producing only one crop, sustained by vast inputs of petrochemicals, were becoming the rule—and destroying their soil's natural productivity, destroying wildlife habitat, poisoning the water, wiping out thousands of family farms.

The processed food that occupied more and more supermarket space was much more profitable than mere fresh raw ingredients, and the agribusiness companies' marketing campaigns were persuading the public to buy more and more of these "convenience foods"—far less nutritious than simple fresh food, and far more expensive.

The little family farm, with a few head of livestock, some chickens, small plots of this-and-that crop, was the kind of farm Alice loved. Each was home not only to a human family but also to nesting birds, weasels, badgers, rabbits, quail, squirrels, sunfish, deer. (And many of these freeloaders were food themselves for the farm family, for free.) But such a farm was no longer competitive in the marketplace.

On agribusiness's strategic map, Chez Panisse and the few other food enterprises that acted more on the basis of conscience than on that of profit were nothing more than flyspecks. How could Alice Waters and her one little restaurant hope even to slow the agro-industrial juggernaut?

"Well, somebody had to do it," she says.

She knew that only as a public figure—one of greater stature than she yet was—could she hope to be effective. If it meant cultivating reporters and critics, if it meant membership in the mercilessly scrutinized, surreal world of global celebrity, and recruiting her fellow celebrities to the cause, she was going to have to do it. That was how you reached people in numbers sufficient to make a difference. Her increasingly public role, of course, decreased the time she could devote to her private life. She felt obligated to Stephen, grateful to Stephen, guilty about Stephen, but of the decreasing private time she had, she devoted most to Fanny.

Alice's path toward celebrity was abundantly potholed. In the *Oakland Tribune*'s gossipy "East Bay Ear" section on February 10, 1987, a little squib marked the end of Alice's great dream for the Oakland Museum, with its teaching garden, its revolutionized dining room, its organic sack lunches for kids:

> The French magazine *Cuisine et Vins de France* recently asked its readers to name the 10 best chefs in the world. And guess who made the top 10? Alice Waters! The Chez Panisse owner is not just the only Californian on the list, she's the only American. But is she good enough for the Oakland Museum? Naaah!

She had set forth an elaborate and passionate proposal, and had garnered a good deal of verbal support, but in the end the museum rejected the project in toto. "My interpretation of what happened," Alice explains, "was that there were factions within the museum all vying for the same pot of money. We were going through a group outside of the museum that was willing to finance the whole thing. But the fund-raising arm of the museum wanted to have a lot of influence on how the project was run, and the fact that we could bring so much money to it was a cause for jealousy within. The people on the staff never could see that this was something that would benefit everybody."

One of the aims of the museum project had been to reach children, to teach them the inextricably bound deliciousness and social values of good food. "It was disgraceful, the way children were being fed at school. Public and private. Still is," Alice says. Chez Panisse taught those lessons well, but a dinner at Chez Panisse, or for that matter lunch at the café, was not an experience remotely possible for the majority of the people of Berkeley, much less those from poverty-wracked Oakland. Within scant miles of Chez Panisse, "Children were going hungry! I had to do something."

So much for the museum. A new and much grander vision had come to her: an American Les Halles (the central market of Paris, now demolished), a great market in downtown Oakland, only a few miles from Chez Panisse. The produce would be local, seasonal, mostly organic, and of the highest quality, but because the farmers would be selling directly to the public, with no middlemen, produce prices could be lower than in the supermarkets.

Alice found a great location for the market—the seventy-year-old remains of Swan's, a fresh-food market that had thrived from the 1920s to the early 1940s, and then been driven out of business by the postwar exodus of the middle class from downtown Oakland. The new market would be a place where not just food and money were exchanged, but ideas, too. Sibella Kraus had provided a stirring example with her Tasting of Summer Produce, which had made it possible for the first time for farmers to sell their produce directly to restaurants and the public. The food at the Tastings was much fresher than anything from a wholesaler's warehouse, and the farmer collected all the profit. At the new market, the network of Bay Area farmers and cooks that had formed around Chez Panisse and Sibella's projects would be able to talk to one another face-to-face, sharing ideas and galvanizing their sense of common purpose.

There would be no single proprietor. Small local merchants, farmers, fishermen, dairymen, and ranchers would own shares in the market. Steve Sullivan had agreed to build a branch of his Acme Bakery. "I loved the thought of the smell of baking bread drifting through the marketplace," Alice says. The Monterey Market of Berkeley, the Bay Area's best greengrocer, had agreed to join in, as did the longtime fish supplier of Chez Panisse, Monterey Fish. Then, in one fell stroke, the financing collapsed, and the developer pulled out.

"I put all my best effort into making [the market] go, but thank God it fell through when it did," Alice says now. "I say 'thank God' because I was actually relieved. The construction costs were turning out to be so insanely high that there was no way it could have been affordable for the people I wanted to shop there."

She was soon involved with smaller but more effective means of getting good food to poor people. Share Our Strength was an organization of restaurants that distributed their leftovers and unused supplies to the hungry. Alice supported the local Daily Bread Project, with a similar mission. She supported the Food First Institute for Food and Development Policy, a think tank studying the root causes of worldwide hunger.

"It was very distressing, realizing that poor people were buying these highly processed industrial foods. They were much more expensive than good organic produce! We had beautiful farmers' markets coming in all over the Bay Area, all over the country, in fact, but most of them were in affluent areas selling to affluent people."

Over the next several years, Alice was involved in a number of experiments aimed at bringing less-affluent buyers into the world of farmers' markets and organic produce. Some were modest successes, but most were unable to surmount the social barrier that made poor people feel uncomfortable in the farmers' market milieu—the expensive foreign cars in the parking lots, the expensive clothing on the shoppers, the embarrassment for people who spoke poor or no English.

Yet Alice was learning that small gestures could set large examples. She was thinking long-term. Each attempt, even when it failed, brought new believers to the cause. Legislators could be lobbied, bigger sponsors sought, more communities involved. "You had to start somewhere," she says today, "and show that it could work. What we're missing—what so many people are missing—is an education of the senses. Poor people in this country, for the most part, eat badly because they are victims of an intense campaign to keep them eating industrial processed food. We've got to start countering that."

Reaching children was important not only because they might be changed for the rest of their lives, but also because the schools bought food in such immense quantities that if they changed their purchasing patterns, the effects on the landscape and the small-farm economy would be tremendous. "One lunch at a medium-size school uses two hundred and fifty pounds of potatoes. Multiply that by the number of school days and then by the number of schools in the district, and then by the number of districts in the state. Think of the organic farmers that could sustain! Think how much cleaner the air and the water and the earth would be! It could change the world."

Alice now saw clearly what was to be the mission of the rest of her life. It was all of a piece: from her father's garden to Montessori through the birth and growth and flowering of the Chez Panisse ethos, and ultimately, to the philosophy and practice of sustainability—ecological, agricultural, and social. Like Alice's own journey, it all began with gardens and children.

ON JUNE 8, 1987, a thousand people paid $250 apiece to enter the red-and-white fantasia that the Japanese designer Eiko Ishioka had created for Aid and Comfort at San Francisco's Fort Mason. Alice recalls,

> Eiko created this space that was just magical. It had a little bridge that you went over to come inside. The whole ceiling was covered with these gorgeous, billowing white parachutes. She wanted to suggest going into the body.
>
> Eiko didn't speak English very well at that time, but this is somebody who is a perfectionist. She wanted it all done right. And she was in Japan. So I had this really excruciating but enormously inspiring experience of trying to take her ideas and produce them. She wanted everybody working there to wear a red cotton apron, and she wanted them dyed exactly the right color of red. When they turned out to have ties on them that were made out of nylon, and the dye didn't take right, she said, "Get new ties and re-dye them." Which I did. I'd asked the dyer to do it as a favor in the first place, and then I had to tell them to do it again. I was using up every favor I had.

This was Alice's first experience with the big time outside the restaurant world, and she was at first daunted by the complexity of bringing it all together, but she also learned two important lessons.

> One of the important moments for me was when the fire inspectors came in the day before the event and said, "No candles in the stream." There were supposed to be candles floating in the water in this black tunnel. Eiko was uncompromising about this. "Alice, you get those candles." I spent all day and half the night trying to find out who could give us the dispensation. Finally, I found him. Some

top guy in the fire department. I had somebody, some politician, call him up in the middle of the night. He called back and gave me dispensation. And that's when I knew that you need to know the person at the top.

The other big thing I came to understand was that when you work with a group of people who all have experience and are professionals about what they do, you can collaborate and make something greater than the sum of its parts. You can let go. You don't have to have control over every part. You can trust it.

Chez Panisse, Zuni Café, and a dozen of the Bay Area's other best restaurants served a fourteen-course meal, prepared in four separate kitchens on-site. "The dinner," said the *San Francisco Chronicle*, "was sensational— not merely by banquet standards but by the standards you normally would apply at a great restaurant."[5]

Linda Ronstadt sang "Desperado." The Kronos String Quartet played Jimi Hendrix's "Purple Haze." Bobby McFerrin sang all the songs from *The Wizard of Oz* in ten minutes. Shirley MacLaine, notorious for her belief in reincarnation, said, "May I say that this is the best dinner I've had in four thousand years?" Joel Grey, Carlos Santana, Herbie Hancock, and Boz Scaggs performed. Michael Smuin of the San Francisco Ballet choreographed a pas de deux from *Romeo and Juliet,* accompanied by the full ballet orchestra. The show was broadcast by San Francisco's public television station, KQED. There were five hundred limited-edition portfolios of prints, each page printed by a different artist, with contributions from Richard Diebenkorn, Wayne Thiebaud, M. F. K. Fisher, and Diana Kennedy, on sale for $175 each.

Bill Graham, the famed impresario of the Fillmore auditoriums in San Francisco and New York, had produced the entire event for free. Tom Luddy had coordinated the production for free. Everyone who served, cooked, waited tables, built the sets, raised the funds, performed, and cleaned up—including Alice and a number of other members of the *famille Panisse*—worked for free. Over half a million dollars went straight to local AIDS charities.

"That was a disappointment, actually," Alice recalls. "We thought we were going to raise a million. We should have charged more."

For the finale, Chanticleer, San Francisco's highly regarded all-male chorus, sang "Lean on Me," as the hundreds of volunteers poured onto the stage to join them. The audience stood and sang along, many in tears.

14.

SUSTAINABILITY

1987–1991

‘

A lice had always demanded the best of everything, and through the late 1980s, her criteria for what was best were growing more precise. She had never compromised on the quality of the food she bought for the restaurant and for her family, but now she wanted the way it was grown, harvested, handled, and shipped to be virtuous too— that is, to be good for the earth and its creatures, and good, if possible, for society.

In August 1987, Fanny turned four years old. Her preschool classmates envied her school lunches, and sometimes she succeeded in acquiring from the other children some choice forbidden item or another, but for the most part Fanny preferred what her mom provided.

Jerry Rosenfield had a new burst of energy in 1987, and his madness seemed to be under better control. As a forager, he had seen the wide disparities between good farms and bad ones, and he still had a strong intellectual influence on Alice. She now insisted that meat for Chez Panisse come from livestock that was treated humanely. She started reading the poems and essays of Wendell Berry, whose strict standards far surpassed

· FANNY'S SCHOOL LUNCH ·

One of the salads Fanny loved was my Greek salad. I put a few romaine leaves in there just for some body, and other greens in the salad, whatever was good from the garden in my backyard. In summer I'd add slivers of colored peppers and whatever little tomatoes were around, gold or red or green. Even if I made salad for her several days in a row, I changed the colors or how I was cutting the greens and the vegetables. Often I added some olives. I usually used those Greek Kalamata olives. I got some feta cheese, and I would season it with chopped-up fresh oregano and pepper, and I would crumble it on the salad. Oh, and cucumbers. Sometimes you can do little wedges of those small Mediterranean cucumbers. I used the Armenian sometimes—they're kind of lime green, a great color. There were the little Japanese ones, depending on the time of the year and who had the organic ones at the farmers' market. That was the salad that I did many, many variations on. Usually, I would make garlic toast to go with it, and then have a little separate container with the vinaigrette in it. For dessert, usually a piece of fruit.

I would try to surprise her every day with something different. She always loved salads and loved vinaigrette. As she got older, sometimes I would put in things from the night before, some chicken breast or something, as part of the salad. She always had some sort of leafy greens and herbs.

Alice's: He still plowed his Kentucky farm with horses. She discovered Wes Jackson and his Land Institute in Salina, Kansas, which was looking for ways to reform agriculture systemically, with the aim of recovering the ancestral health of all the natural systems that sustain the growing of food.

At the same time, Alice was examining the life of Chez Panisse on the small scale. The beef they were getting was okay, the lamb was excellent, the pork was variable, but the chickens never came close to the rich, dense, muscular complexity of the famous *poulet de Bresse*. She began her search with letters like this, to Pat Bridges and Bart Ehman of Pine Ridge Ranch, the restaurant's primary chicken supplier:

> *Dear Pat and Bart,*
>
> *I am writing to let you know that we are engaged in a search to find, or to help develop, a chicken that has the qualities of old-fashioned chickens that some of us remember from our childhood and others have eaten in rural areas of Europe. . . . Two backyard growers in Sonoma County are planning to raise a small batch each of Buff Orpingtons and Plymouth Rocks. They will range on green pasture with up to 20 square feet per bird to the age of four or five months. . . .*

A new and highly accomplished cook, Christopher Lee, joined the staff in 1988, and soon was out foraging on his own. Chris's reports, like Jerry Rosenfield's, were exhaustively detailed. It's hard to know how useful some of this was for a restaurant, but it makes delightful reading:

> Enid and Frank Dal Porto raise crossbreed Suffolk sheep. . . . At its 1500′ elevation, the ranch is typical foothill woodland: undulating hillside and pastureland, wooded in spots with various oaks, California bay and lilac, gooseberry, and yerba santa. An intermittent stream, Big Indian Creek, runs through the land. The stream is usually dry by the 1st of July, though it ran strong and swift with mountain snowmelt the afternoon I visited the ranch. . . . From the Dal Porto hilltop home, the creeping housing developments of the Sacramento area can be seen to the northwest. . . .
>
> Frank mentioned several times the dependence upon nature which the farmer is subject to. . . . In the spring, when the water flows freely, the grasses are green and in some spots lush and thick. But soon, without runoff from rain or snowmelt, the pastures will dry. This will immediately affect the animals by reducing their feed, but will also subject them to injury by the dried, curlicued seedpods of

the filaree plant, a species of *Erodium,* which become entangled in the wool of the face and make their way under the skin.

The ranch seemed a placid, even idyllic spot, with the sun shining down, the stream flowing through, the sheep grazing, and Frank Sr. cutting his newly grown asparagus stalks for his evening supper. . . . It made one feel satisfied with life, its bounty, and that bounty's seemingly easy availability, we observers being blind to the hours and years of cultivation necessary to produce all this. . . .

The report was accompanied by photographs of Frank Jr., of someone bottle-feeding an orphan lamb, and of the green seedpods, the dried seedpods, and the skin-piercing corkscrew of the unsheathed seed of *Erodium cicutarium.*

Only at Chez Panisse. Only Alice would pay money—considerable amounts of it—to bind her restaurant to its suppliers in so lavish and poetic a fashion: Christopher Lee's and Jerry Rosenfield's foraging did discover some valuable new food sources, certainly, but they carried their tasks out as much like artists as like restaurant buyers, and the relationships they developed between Chez Panisse and the farmers went far beyond the commercial. They were weaving together an extended family.

Where Christopher's reports were leisurely and mellifluous, Jerry Rosenfield's were densely packed with research, not without their own lyric flair, and, perhaps, a bit manic. Ed and Gerry Jastrem were raising the Barred Plymouth Rocks and Buff Orpington chickens in which Alice had expressed interest. Dr. Jerry wrote:

By the time we—Chris Lee and I—encountered them they were nearly full-grown pullets, enclosed in a large yard built around three American elm trees. Vigorous and active birds, they were foraging in their yard which, though cleaned of green growth, still contained enough attraction to keep the birds pecking at it. . . . The Barred Rocks, proud of carriage, particularly exuded a sheen of handsome good health and vigor. . . .

At our behest, taking our cue from the fact that the renowned

Bresse chicken is fattened on corn and milk during its final weeks, the Jastrems have added a portion of dried milk and rice to the pullets' feed, the rice, also a high-starch grain, substituting for the corn. Although American poultry growers have never been enthusiastic about rice, even where it is grown, it was the Chinese who developed the big birds, the Cochins or "Shanghais," which were the sensation of the memorable Boston Poultry Show of 1849. . . .

"The memorable Boston Poultry Show of 1849"! Only at Chez Panisse.

In ADDITION to Alice's work for sustainable farming and social justice, there was social injustice that needed to be confronted at Chez Panisse. "For eighteen years," she wrote to her board of directors, "we have been struggling with the inequities and distortions of the traditional tipping system. At our restaurant the quality of the food and the skill and taste of the cooks are at least as central to our success as the quality of the service. Unfortunately, traditional tipping has created great disparities in earning between the serving staff and the cooking and support staff."

What was more, there was believed to be tax cheating among the waiters, who got the great majority of their income in cash. In the back of the house, income was fully documented and fully taxed. Alice's father believed that a fixed service charge could be accurately tracked through the computer system and equitably distributed to the whole staff, front and back of the house alike. Alice agreed. Her hope was that Chez Panisse, as in its earliest days, would again feel like one team.

In April 1988, frustrated by the lack of progress toward equity and order, Pat Edwards resigned. Alice's father was running Chez Panisse behind the scenes, and Richard Mazzera had the official authority of his title as general manager, while Pat was left to her own devices, with little to do—one of several methods Chez Panisse has developed over the years for sending messages that Alice doesn't want spoken aloud. "Alice was quite happy, actually, when I quit," Pat recalls. "She hugged me and said, 'Yes, it's time for you to go.'"

In 1989, after a year of highly charged internal debate, Chez Panisse adopted the system nearly universal in France and in many other European countries—a simple 15 percent service charge, to be distributed fairly to the whole staff. They even used the French descriptor *service compris.*

The waiters protested, but Alice's determination was iron. At first, the waiters made the system decidedly misleading: The service charge was shown clearly on the check itself, but the waiters would also leave the gratuity line and the total both blank on the credit card slip. Diners who had had some wine, or who may have tended in any case to dash off tip and signature without close examination of the bill, could easily be tipping 30 or 35 percent. In time, however, it was made a rule that whenever a customer left a tip significantly exceeding the service charge, the waiter was to point out the error. If some customers still wanted to leave big tips, that was fine, but at least they would be doing so consciously.

The grumbling eventually died down. The service charge rose to 17 percent. The system is still in place, the charge is now 18 percent, and the staff of Chez Panisse, front and back of the house alike, do very nicely. "It's another form of sustainability," says Alice. "If the restaurant's going to sustain itself, and do things right, everybody here has to be doing things right, including the business itself. That means we provide good medical insurance, and time off, and retirement savings plans, and understanding of people's difficulties. In return, we expect what we almost always get. People stay. They like working here. It's a good place to work."

As Alice had learned at Aid and Comfort, getting the very best people and expecting their best worked a good deal better than constant critical oversight. The next major cookbook, *Chez Panisse Cooking,* published in October 1988, comprised more than four hundred pages of precisely, sometimes elaborately detailed recipes for the earthy, robust, and uncomplicated food that was now the Chez Panisse standard. It was Paul Bertolli's book more than Alice's, a fact reflected in the byline "By Paul Bertolli [in large type] with Alice Waters [in small type]."

Fatigue: Tom Luddy and Alice

M. F. K. Fisher praised Paul's "artful use of information about how to cook." Richard Olney called the book "a celebration of purity. The food is imaginative but never complicated; it is"—despite Paul's own modest deprecation of the term—"art."

COMMITTED NOW TO WORKING on very large-scale problems, still making all the major decisions at Chez Panisse, maintaining what was becoming a more and more difficult marriage, raising Fanny, traveling, giving talks, Alice was starting to lose touch with something simple and basic inside herself. She had fallen into the situation that characterizes a great many people of very high accomplishment—so busy, so completely absorbed in their work, so resistant to any image of themselves except that of the supreme accomplisher, that they unconsciously sacrifice self-awareness, self-doubt, and the vivifying power of tranquil reflection. Many people who have known Alice through the years still have no idea what Alice's inner life is like. That is probably because nearly all her life has been lived on the outside, in plain view.

"I lived in a haze, almost," she says. "I would respond to things very spontaneously. I never thought about how I was feeling. I never had a sense of my physical body. It was almost like you're in a half sleep. Like you're being led. Driven. I wasn't in charge of my life. It was just unfolding before me. There were so many things coming at me, and I was responding, and I was moving, and I had things in my mind, and I made things happen, but I felt like what I was doing wasn't deliberate. It wasn't considered. I didn't have any awareness of myself. Everything always seemed fate."

And fate did strike its blows. In September 1989, a burglar broke into Charles and Lindsey Shere's house in Berkeley and stole Lindsey's purse. It would have been a crime of no great moment were it not for the fact that the purse held Lindsey's precious recipe book—eighteen years' worth of painstakingly perfected work stuffed into a three-ring binder. She had no backup copy. Lindsey had intended to publish a second volume of Chez Panisse desserts, but that was no longer feasible.

The *New York Times,* the *Wall Street Journal,* and dozens of other newspapers covered the story. Lindsey offered a no-questions-asked reward of $500, and the local sanitation crew let Charles rifle through their morning's harvest, but the recipes were never seen again.

In June 1990, Tom Guernsey died. "He was cremated," remembers Robert Messick, one of Tom's best friends and now head of the restaurant's reservations department. "We took his ashes to Tassajara"—a Zen meditation retreat in Big Sur—"and we scattered the ashes in a creek. Tim [Piland, Tom Guernsey's partner] said, 'Now this begins Tom's journey to the ocean.'

"The Monday after he died, a bunch of us gathered at Trader Vic's and had mai tais. Tom loved that old Trader Vic's in Emeryville, and he and a lot of other people from the restaurant used to go there a lot. We continue to do that, about ten or fifteen people, on his birthday, every year. Alice always comes if she's in town."

"Tom had brought a certain very California sense of aristocracy with him," Greil Marcus says. "He wasn't from California, but he carried himself in an unpretentiously princely way. He radiated confidence, and he was the mainstay of the restaurant. He could and did do everything, whether it meant fixing a toilet, dealing with a staff crisis, dealing with a food provider, bringing bonhomie to the dining room, radiating a sense of warmth and an eagerness to make any dinner a special occasion. The restaurant suffered horribly when he died, because we had lost this person whom everybody trusted, everybody relied on, and who trusted himself, who believed that he really could solve all these problems, and that the restaurant was his home."

At about the same time, although Jerry Rosenfield was still on the payroll as forager, his mental health was in decline again. He was throwing tantrums in the restaurant, yelling at people on the sidewalk, browbeating Alice mercilessly. Finally, Alice admitted that he had to go. Two weeks later, Jerry was in jail. On his release, he was ordered to report to the Berkeley Mental Health Clinic, but he came and screamed on the sidewalk in front of the restaurant, then charged inside and told the customers that the kitchen was trying to poison them. Only the threat of a permanent restraining order finally persuaded Jerry Rosenfield to stop harassing Chez Panisse.

"I tried so hard to help him," Alice recalls, on the verge of tears. "A lot of people here really loved him."

Jerry eventually moved to the small remote town of Albion, California, in Mendocino County. Bruce Anderson, owner and editor of the *Anderson Valley Advertiser*, remembers him as "very smart, very friendly, a very gentle soul." Jerry Rosenfield lived quietly in Albion until his suicide in the early 2000s (sources differ regarding the precise date).

SOMETHING WAS SLIPPING AWAY, some elusive, precious spirit. Alice didn't know what was wrong. Some kind of bipolar dynamic was at work again in the collective psyche of Chez Panisse. Whenever things were going tremendously well, it seemed, something terrible would happen and the good mood would crash. "I started thinking, Maybe we should just close the restaurant," Alice remembers. "Quit while we were ahead."

On the nineteenth birthday of Chez Panisse, August 28, 1990, Alice held a meeting with the board and the chefs for the purpose of candidly bringing to light all the strengths and weaknesses of the restaurant. Barbara Carlitz, as board secretary, recorded these cryptic notes:

Topic: What is good, what is bad at the restaurant, and what changes do we wish to enact?

What is good:
Great cooking staff
Many multitalented diverse people on staff
Wide clientele both upstairs and down; lots of regulars
Nineteen years of tradition and reputation
Best restaurant in comparison to others
Sense of family
Wonderful sources of foodstuffs
Two different spaces, one lively, one intimate—
Price not yet a deterrent
Own our own building
Most people find it an inspiring place to work

What is not so good:
The "family" has too many children
Failure to satisfy our own sense of mission
Lack of harmony between upstairs and downstairs
Lack of discipline and focus
Poor service because of lax management
Shaken confidence
Failure to foster independence in key staff
Too many bosses with no one in charge
Victimized by own reputation
Lack of spirit in downstairs dining room
Failure to utilize all of the facility
Dictated by clientele; not doing what we really want

Not responsive to changing taste in foods
Not responsive to changes in the Bay Area
Not making enough money

After-lunch topic: What scenarios are possible for change?
Consolidating into one restaurant
Cheaper set menu family-style downstairs
Café downstairs
Open seven days
Become a cooking and waiting school in conjunction with farm
Become an Indian restaurant, Chez Punjab?
Sell produce and prepared foods downstairs
Move to the country
Close at age twenty

Most of the "what is good" items, while true enough, were either the old clichés of Chez Panisse or of little real significance. The "not so good" things, taken together, were a collection of truly grave faults, especially that painful "no one in charge."

The "scenarios for change" were either trivial or fanciful, except for the last: "Close at age twenty." The meeting ended with no conclusions.

Alice was preoccupied with her different causes now, with being a devoted, attentive mother to Fanny, and with finding her way half-blindly through a fog of marital dissatisfaction. Stephen was physically present at home, but psychologically, most of the time, he seemed both to Alice and to himself far away. Both of them longed for a resolution, but neither made a move. They both seemed in some way paralyzed. And Alice's "half sleep" encompassed even Chez Panisse.

AID AND COMFORT II was set for September 22, 1990, at the outdoor Greek Theater on the Cal campus. September is almost always dead dry in the Bay Area, but just as the composer John Adams raised his baton to conduct the Berkeley Symphony and open the event, rain began to fall in heavy, lashing curtains. Alice had worked for months to plan and prepare a sit-down dinner for five hundred people at $500 a head; box lunches for six thousand; performances by Laurie Anderson, Bobby Short, the Kronos Quartet, Herbie Hancock, Bobby McFerrin, and Philip Glass.

"Bobby McFerrin and Laurie Anderson improvised this nonstop performance to keep everybody there in the pouring rain. And probably five thousand people stayed. Nobody else performed, but it didn't matter. It turned into a genuine happening—a kind of free-for-all, in the most beautiful way."

Robert Messick recalls, "It rained so hard, but it was all right, because somehow it made us think of Tom Guernsey. His ashes went into the ocean, and water from the ocean goes up into the air. I've always felt that it was Tom coming down on us in the rain after it had been recycled from river to ocean to clouds."

PERHAPS IT WAS Tom Guernsey's absence that was bedeviling Chez Panisse. Alice said the company needed to impose some discipline, but the fall of 1990 was an epic of indiscipline. The books were a mess: Richard Mazzera reported that since the advent of *service compris,* there had been an overall shortfall of $150,000 in the café alone. Despite complaints about the soaring cost of Carrie Wright's flowers, Alice insisted that Pagnol et Cie pay Carrie $1,300 for her medical insurance and $3,000 for a four-week vacation. Alice had spent $23,000 of the restaurant's money on Aid and Comfort II, not counting the considerable labor and food donated by Chez Panisse. In response, the board ordered a moratorium on charitable contributions for the remainder of the year—a ruling that Alice violated repeatedly, with, among other donations, a gift of $10,000 to local food programs. An early freeze wiped out 90 percent of Bob Cannard's crops; he owed Pagnol et Cie $10,000 and couldn't pay.

This was not sustainable. If it kept up, Chez Panisse was on its way to oblivion.

Nevertheless, with little to go on but faith, Alice decreed that Chez

Panisse would survive. Not only that, the twentieth-birthday celebration in August 1991was going to be the biggest party she had ever thrown.

What had happened? In 1990, she had bottomed out, not quite knowing why. And in 1991, still not knowing, she bounced back. It was classic Chez Panisse, and classic Alice Waters: Ignore the odds; never say die; in every crisis, an opportunity.

15.

STAR POWER

1991–1994

T he twentieth-birthday party, in August 1991, took the form of a gigantic farmers' market up and down both sides of the restaurant's whole long block of Shattuck Avenue, in honor of the farmers and other suppliers of Chez Panisse. "We had little booths for every sort of food," Alice says. "Inexpensive, so anybody could come—everything from fresh fruit to corn on the cob. Paul made spit-roasted pork sandwiches and manned his own booth. Originally, I thought we might have thirty or forty booths, and get, oh, a couple or three thousand people. We had fourteen thousand."

There was a grand dinner afterward at the Jewish community center for all the growers and purveyors, prepared and served by the staff of the restaurant. The whole celebration cost some hundred thousand dollars, yet Chez Panisse managed, miraculously, to break even.

That evening in the restaurant, which was open for business as usual, the menu served downstairs added one new course—the soup—and this time also listed the salad as a separate course, but it was otherwise a replica of the first meal Chez Panisse ever served:

Pâté en croûte

❦

Fish consommé with tomatoes, leeks, garlic, and parsley

❦

Roast duck with olives

❦

Garden salad

❦

Warm plum tart

There were two big differences. First, this dinner was rather more professionally and calmly produced. Second, the price of dinner on opening night in 1971 had been $3.95. Adjusted for inflation, that was thirteen 1991 dollars. The price of the twentieth-birthday dinner was precisely five times as much: $65.00.

Two weeks later, five Berkeley residents signed the following letter to the *San Francisco Chronicle:*

Editor: The recent display of self-indulgent consumption on Shattuck Avenue in Berkeley is testament to this city's gutless pseudo-progressive agenda. . . . Amazingly, there was not a coherent, observable statement in this "progressive" microcosm to the effect of our deteriorating environment's role in sustaining and supporting these foods! While our environment goes to hell, Lamborghini Leftists pig out on its fringe benefits. . . . This city is becoming a parody of itself and its purported ideals.

Lamborghini leftists! Was that to be Alice's constituency? Well, yes and no. The fact is that any non-profit-making movement must live on gifts. If the movement is to be large, so must the gifts be. Chez Panisse, with its high ideals and high prices, was well fitted to the task of attracting the most desirable sort of potential donors: rich people with fully functioning consciences. The movement for sustainability and conservation required funding, certainly, and therefore wealthy benefactors, but it also required people in large numbers, and they didn't have to be wealthy. Few if any of the fourteen thousand folks eating organic peaches and pulled pork at the birthday party had arrived there in Lamborghinis.

The word *foodie* had made its debut in 1982,[1] by which time there were already millions of foodies, many uncomfortable with terming themselves *gourmets*. By 1991, there were millions more. Not many of them seemed concerned with the ethical aspects of food, but they were nevertheless Alice's natural audience. She was in increasing demand as a public speaker, an interviewee, a celebrity chef for a benefit dinner. In 1992, the James Beard Foundation Awards—the food world's equivalent of the Oscars—named Chez Panisse the Restaurant of the Year and Alice Waters Chef of the Year. Increasingly, when Alice went to a food-related event, she was mobbed. Among foodies, only two people were such icons as to be known by their first names alone: Julia and Alice. "And I hate that word *foodie*," adds Alice.

As Alice grew more and more widely known, some old friends began to pull away, lamenting that she had no time for them anymore, all she wanted to do was hobnob with the rich and famous. Others argued that she was unchanged, as loyal and generous as ever. New friends did multiply, and some of them were in fact rich and/or famous. Alice grew weary of the traveling, and she was in agony in front of a crowd or a camera, but when she was called on, she nearly always accepted. As Tom Luddy had done twenty years before, her closest friends were begging her to say no once in a while, to slow down, relax a little—but when Alice spoke, she could feel the electricity of her audience's excitement, and she knew that meant that they were starting to understand how much meaning food had. She was a teacher again.

She studied public speaking and camera presence. There were more and more demands on her time—more than anyone could possibly commit to. She still clung to the idea of herself as a person of the restaurant, who cooked, who tasted, who organized, who heard the complaints and soothed the misunderstood geniuses of her staff. Jean-Pierre Moullé was back again, working under Paul Bertolli downstairs; Alice did not know how long she would be able to hang on to Paul, who was getting restless, and she worried about what would happen when, as was probably inevitable, Jean-Pierre would wish to be chef and so titled. David Tanis returned from a six-month sabbatical in September 1991 and told her that rather than resume his post as co-chef in the café he was moving to Santa Fe, and Alice was back at the stoves again until she found a replacement in Peggy Smith.

And still the invitations came, and still she said yes. Alice Waters—sometimes alone, or so it felt—was teaching the world what virtuous agriculture meant for the earth and posterity, and why there was healing magic in the simple gathering of family and friends around a table.

Such was Alice's vision; her own reality differed from it. In 1991, she and Stephen had been together for nine years; Fanny was eight; and both Alice and Stephen believed deeply in maintaining a real family for Fanny. When they traveled, they always brought her along. Bob Carrau often joined them, and Sue Murphy sometimes, too. They picnicked together, went to the movies, attended Fanny's school events together. But the nameless enmity between Alice and Stephen continued to fester.

Fanny spent more and more of her time at Chez Panisse. "What struck me," Fritz Streiff recalls, "was how seamlessly Alice made Fanny part of all of her life. Fanny was in and out of the restaurant all the time, and I think it's fair to say there was some bemusement amongst the staff, a little bit, because everything had to stop for Fanny."

As long as Alice was at the restaurant or at home, the illusion of family normality could be maintained. But she was ever more often away, as her public obligations multiplied. She was a star. The eleven-year difference in their ages, Stephen now says, "only became an issue in that as I grew into my sense of adult self, the needs that that presented were not so much in conflict with where Alice was in her own aging curve as much as where she was in her public agenda. And that public agenda wasn't really part of where Alice was in her aging—it's where the curve or the trajectory was in her life."

In a further effort toward togetherness, Alice and Stephen worked on fixing up the bungalow on Monterey Avenue, and converted the old "ad hoc day-care center" into a freestanding studio for Stephen. With the new studio, he resumed his artwork. He continued to be the wine buyer for the restaurant, but he had also decided to open a restaurant of his own. In partnership with the former Chez Panisse cook Jonathan Waxman, he opened Table 29 in the Napa Valley—a good forty miles from Berkeley.

Alex Witchel, in the New York Times of April 17, 2002, described Table 29 as "a short-lived disaster," but it did get Stephen away from Alice, which, more and more, is where he wanted to be.

For Alice, the gap between reality and what she imagined—whether France or family—was not as wide as for most other people. Whatever she imagined, she believed she could bring into being. Chez Panisse was the proof of that.

While her vision of her family life proved stubbornly resistant to actualization, Alice found comfort in revisiting her vision (or myth) of Chez Panisse in a new book project with Bob Carrau. It would be the story of the restaurant from Fanny's point of view. Published in 1992, *Fanny at Chez Panisse* evokes the mythical Chez Panisse, where "The inside of my mom's mouth knows how everything at Chez Panisse is supposed to taste," and "I don't know why they write menus ahead of time, because they always end up changing everything at the last minute," and "I can never tell who actually runs Chez Panisse." The fictional Fanny also says:

My favorite day at Chez Panisse is Bastille Day. Bastille Day is like the Fourth of July in France, only it's on the fourteenth of July. There's a big party every year and everybody gets real French and kisses each other, and since Bastille Day happens at the same time of year that all the new garlic comes in, there's always a big, special garlic dinner that night. Everything they serve has garlic in it: garlic soup, garlic butter, garlic mayonnaise, garlic pizza, garlic oil, and one time they even had chocolate-covered garlic cloves. I'm not kidding. At the Bastille Day dinner there's music and laughing and everybody sits at long tables and talks to each other. The Head Garlic Lover wears a big hat that looks just like a big head of garlic—all billowy and white. . . . My mom likes Bastille Day a lot because it makes her feel like she's in those old French movies she likes so much. Everyone gets together to eat and drink and laugh and talk and cry and sing and dance just like Fanny and Panisse and their friends did.

"I always wanted to communicate with kids about food," says Alice. "I loved those books about Eloise at The Plaza, and I thought a way to communicate with kids and with their parents would be to write a book that appealed to both. I had this idea for a while, but it wasn't until Bob Carrau volunteered to help write it that anything happened. He said, 'You write it, Alice, and I'll help you.' Well, he wrote it, and I helped him.

"Years later, my friend Joy Carlin and I had been talking about making some sort of film for children, and she said, 'I have a crazy idea. I want to make *Fanny at Chez Panisse* into a musical.'

"She'd already been working on it, with this musician named Joe Landon, who had been the playwright-in-residence at the American Conservatory Theater. And they came over, and Joe sang this little song, 'Arugula, arugula, arugula!'

Suki HILL - Bastille Day 2003

Le Quatorze Juillet

"I couldn't imagine that it would come to something, but it did."

There were songs called "Make Me a Pizza" and "A Little Emergency" and "Dessert." The character of Fanny had been somewhat changed— she was a teenager now—and the script, at Alice's behest, was more political than the book had been. Alice insisted that the show include her message that "if you make the right choices about food, it changes the quality of your life and changes the world around you." This was classic Alice, too—so *serious*—and hardly an enhancement of the show's value as entertainment.

"And, well," she says, "it certainly wasn't the huge roaring success that Joy had imagined. Later there was a full-scale production that ran for six weeks, but it started off as a workshop at this little studio in San Francisco. Jill Eikenberry played me. I thought it would just be great if she came over to the restaurant and played me all the time. I could leave."

It was a joke with an unfunny subtext. Alice wanted someone to play her role. So she could leave. She was caught up now in being ALICE WATERS, imprisoned in her public role. She knew she couldn't quit, of course; the cause was too important. "One thing that everyone loves about Alice but also drives everyone crazy," Bob Carrau says, "is how she's always into the struggle. It can be annoying to some people, because they just don't want to think of this stuff all the time. There's a kind of sad beauty in it all— her fixation on injustice and her relentlessness about it. I'm sure it also allows her to stay out of her interior, too. So there's that side to it—her fixation on social justice as a way to ignore personal fears."

The gap between the world imagined in *Fanny at Chez Panisse* and that of the actual restaurant was also stubbornly resistant to closing. "In 1992, September, I believe," Greil Marcus recalls, "Alice asked me to talk with Paul Bertolli, who was having a hard time with the fact that he was a great chef, he was doing innovative things, he had his own ideas, he had his own point of view, but he was feeling unfulfilled. One day he said that he was terribly frustrated with the fact that Alice got all the publicity, and that his contributions weren't recognized in the world at large. And what I told him was, 'You're right, you aren't getting the recognition that you deserve. Your contribution isn't appreciated by the public, by food writers, by feature writers, by television crews. And it never will be. There is no way that a shy, retiring man, regardless of his talents, can stand up to an infinitely charming, vivacious, articulate, eloquent woman. It will never happen.' And he quit two days later, which had not been my intention. I had no desire to get rid of Paul. Not at all. I was just telling the truth."

Confronted again with the Jean-Pierre conundrum, Alice decided to make him her co-chef, at least for the moment, knowing it couldn't last. Jean-Pierre surprised her, however. He distinguished himself, and by the spring of 1993, Alice felt free to leave the kitchen in his hands.

In 1993, Chez Panisse was probably the best it had ever been: The food was superb, almost consistently; the service was clicking; the spirit was joyful again.

In April, Lindsey Shere won the James Beard Foundation Award for Pastry Chef of the Year. Michael Bauer, of the *San Francisco Chronicle,* gave Chez Panisse his highest rating, four stars.

> If there's one restaurant that has become a cathedral of gastronomy in the United States, it's Chez Panisse in Berkeley. It is the birthplace of the "California Cuisine" movement, and just about every chef in the country has been inspired by Alice Waters. Its reputation is so exalted that it would be next to impossible for it to meet the myriad expectations we all have of it. But in many ways, Chez Panisse still does.[2]

Late on the evening of August 12, 1993, the junk-food-loving president of the United States phoned Chez Panisse from *Air Force One,* hungry. Alice was in San Francisco, but a phone call brought her back across the Bay Bridge at high speed. An hour later, Bill Clinton and company descended on Chez Panisse. Trying not to notice the forty Secret Service agents swarming through the restaurant, Alice did her best to set a scene of gracious hospitality, spreading before the president a late-night snack of golden nugget tomatoes, fettuccine with corn and crabmeat, a salad of green beans and chanterelles, pizza without cheese (it was not allowed on his diet), house-cured prosciutto, and, for dessert—the course she knew Clinton loved best—blackberry ice cream, blackberry shortcake, rasp-

Lulu Peyraud and Jean-Pierre Moullé

berries, strawberries, Gravenstein apples, and a lemon custard with wild strawberries. Alice wouldn't let him pay. The *Chronicle*'s coverage noted:

> Waters, who turned down an invitation to cook at Ronald Reagan's inaugural in 1982 (saying she didn't know where Washington was), took the opportunity to buttonhole the president about San Francisco's Garden Project, where prisoners grow specialty crops for sale to restaurants like hers—and how important it is to be "connected" to what we eat and grow.[3]

The *Chicago Tribune* picked up another part of the conversation.

> While Clinton ate, she says, she discussed her worries about assuring that future generations will have a wide variety of good foods. The president, in turn, told her there had been some talk of starting a vegetable garden at the White House.[4]

Clinton was almost certainly just turning on his customary charm, but to Alice Waters that was an opening wide enough to drive a tractor through. A garden at the White House!

This just happened to be a time when Alice was freshly charged with fervor. It had been only a few weeks since she had attended a meeting in Hawaii that gave birth to the first group ever to try to turn chefs into active environmentalists, the Chefs Collaborative. At that time, chefs didn't set themselves up as leaders, or philosophers, or moral paragons. Some of them considered themselves artists, but their medium was food—they didn't try to reshape society. The creation of the Chefs Collaborative meant that Alice's ideals were gaining a foothold in the real world.

Chefs have real power to influence food consumption patterns. About two-thirds of all the fish bought in the United States, for example, goes to restaurants.[5] If restaurants began to buy fish only from sustainable fisheries, the oceans would soon be very much improved. In February 2006, for example, the Compass Group, the world's largest food service company, announced that it would henceforth purvey only sustainably harvested fish and seafood;[6] that single decision is saving at least a million pounds per year that would have been harvested from unsustainable fisheries and fish farms.[7]

Presidents and chefs can have powerful effects, but Alice's thoughts always came back to children. Adults had to be persuaded; children simply learned. For years, every day when she drove home from work, she would pass the Martin Luther King, Jr. Middle School. "I thought it was abandoned, because it looked so run-down. Graffiti on the windows, burned-out grass."

Curious, she went in one day. She discovered that most of the students bought their lunch at a snack bar inside the school, which didn't even cook the food. Its "kitchen" was a microwave oven. Its menu comprised reheated pizzas and hamburgers, potato chips, and soft drinks. Alice expressed her distress to the principal and invited him to lunch at Chez Panisse.

"I think he wanted me to plant a garden and beautify the school. In fact, I didn't know what I had in mind. I just walked around the school, and then it just hit me. I thought, There are a lot of schools with gardens, and they teach a lot of little things around food. Not so many, but some. But what's really important, I was thinking, is the whole cycle from the garden, back into the garden. As an old Montessori teacher, I believed in the education of the senses. And what better way could we educate the senses than through a school lunch program that was designed to teach kids about sustainability?

"I talked to the principal; I talked to the school board; I talked to anybody who might make a difference. I'd tell them, 'Think. We need to know where our food comes from. We need to know how to take care of the land. We need to know how to feed ourselves, and we need to know how to communicate with each other. Because we all live here together.'

"Three-quarters of the kids in this country don't have one meal a week with their family. That's a breakdown in our whole culture. How do we pass on our information, our values, to our children? Around the table!"

The project would take years to develop, but in Alice's imagination it took shape quickly. She would create a garden at Martin Luther King, where the children, about a thousand of them, in the sixth, seventh, and eighth grades, could learn to plant, cultivate, harvest, cook, and serve food that they themselves grew. Each activity could be tied to something in the curriculum. "For instance, they're studying Egypt. They might be making Egyptian bread and listening to Egyptian music and gathering and cooking together." Moreover, the program could serve as a shaper of young citizens: The kids would learn table manners, cooperation, mutual consideration, and a love of beauty.

It's important to encourage all the other values that are beyond nourishment and sustainability and the basic things. Beauty. When you set a table, you know, take time to do that—teaching the pleasure of work—that's probably one of the most important lessons. It's also about diversity. It's about replenishing. It's about concentration. It's about sensuality. It's about purity. It's about love. It's about compassion. It's about sharing. How many things? All those, just in the experience of eating, if you decide you're going to eat in a very specific way. It changes your life, and it changes the world around you.

This is the first generation of kids who haven't been asked to come to the table. And we're seeing the results. They're out there not knowing where they are. They're wandering around, disconnected. Shockingly so. And when they're not being sensually nourished, nothing's coming in except the McDonald's information. Fast food not only comes with poisons inside the food and destruction of the environment, but with the values that are part of it. It says food isn't important. It's cheap, you can eat it fast, and you don't have to eat with your kids. Food is for entertainment, and it should be all the same. It's okay to drink Coke and eat hamburgers every day of the year. Things that aren't advertised lose value. Only things that are advertised are really what's important.

In such a world, Alice could hardly close Chez Panisse. It was her public platform, her private bedrock, her true home. And to nearly any person of stature or fame or influence—a person, that is, through whom the philosophy might be promulgated—an invitation to dinner at Chez Panisse as the personal guest of Alice Waters was a powerful inducement.

She always had plenty to say. "You begin with food," she would say, "because it's the essence of life. If you're seduced by something that's beautiful and nourishing, you want that experience again. You're looking for that, and you realize that it's growing right over there, and you want to take care of that thing right over there. I look at the median strips in the highway, and I want to plant them. And I wonder, Why are the roads so wide? You could have an acre of fava beans there."

Alice has always been an extraordinarily persuasive person. It is as natural a part of her as her hands, her girlish voice, or her blue eyes—all of which come into play in the exercise of her charm. She likes to touch people. She will rest her hands on your arm, draw you close, hold your attention. Her voice, which can turn curtly dismissive or cynically harsh when it needs to, rarely needs to; much of the time it is so soft that you have to lean in to catch what she is saying.

"Alice," says Greil Marcus, "is the person who says, 'Of course it's possible,' when everybody else is saying it's impossible. She'll simply smile and, without any agitation at all, say, 'It can be done, it will be done, it's going to happen, you'll see.' She really does believe that she can change the world, she can change individual people one by one, she can improve people's lives. This isn't just rhetoric that she trots out whenever she is given an award."

More than anything else she had ever wanted to do, the kids' garden at Martin Luther King would bring Alice's beliefs to life. A Montessori garden. She would call it the Edible Schoolyard.

Alice Waters was going to be fifty years old on April 28, 1994. She had achieved everything a restaurateur could ever hope for. This, then—the promulgation of her philosophy, especially to children—would give shape and meaning to her fifties.

ON MAY 31, 1994, Stephen Singer had a terrible accident. "I was riding near our house. I'm a very active bicyclist," he recalls. "I think what might have happened is a misplaced sewer grate left a gap that my tire went into at the bottom of a hill. I don't remember. I woke up in the hospital. It was a serious accident. Part of the reason I have a mustache is that I'm covering up scars. My lip was cut in two in a couple of places, and my nose was basically lifted off my face and put back on."

Sue Murphy remembers, "I believe Jim [Maser] brought Stephen back from the hospital. I remember distinctly sitting on that couch when Stephen walked in the door and I saw his face. I was going, Oh, Christ, because they didn't dress it, it had to be all open, and he had ripped his face off. He literally ripped his face off. He tore his lip up, all the way up here, up his nose. So they had sewn that back on, and it was just—he was deformed-looking. And he'd knocked out his front teeth. If he hadn't had that helmet on, he would have been dead. He didn't break the orbits of his eye, so they didn't bandage that up, and his eye was just open and leaking."

"Alice was in New York," says Bob Carrau. "I called her, and she did say, 'Should I come back or not?' I said, 'Alice, I really think you should.'"

"We explained it," Sue Murphy recalls, "but maybe we weren't as clear as we might have been. It was the type of thing where you get on the phone and go, 'He's okay, he's all right,' because you don't want to make her think he's going to die. Granted, if I was Alice, I probably would have gotten the first plane home. But I also defend her, because she had two people who were family who were saying, 'We're here.'"

"I didn't understand how serious it was," Alice says. "I had no idea. They should have said to me, 'You need to get on a plane right now.' They were trying to protect me."

"Sue and I both remember a moment between Stephen and Fanny that was quite tender, before Alice got home," says Bob. "It was pretty shocking to look at him, but Fanny kind of stepped up to the plate and was gentle, caring, and nurselike instead of freaked out."

Alice came home not the next day but the one after. "I remember picking Alice up at the airport," Sue recalls. "I remember her walking back from the gates, and I was thinking how tiny she was in her little black outfit, little black hat, motoring along at a thousand miles an hour down the corridor of the airport. And I remember very clearly, when we got in the car, before I started the car, looking at her and saying, 'You need to be prepared for what Stephen looks like.'"

"He was so concerned about what he looked like," Bob says. "The day Alice was coming home, I helped him get in the shower, helping him bathe. He wanted to get dressed, and he wanted to look all right. I can understand being freaked out about not wanting to scare people, but he really felt that it was his image on some level that was most important to Alice, and I thought, Not only is it a telling thing about their relationship and Alice, it's also a telling thing about how he feels about himself. What does it mean that in your most intimate relationship, what you're most worried about is your appearance?"

"I used to have a notion that I needed to be pretty self-reliant," Stephen says, "because if I ever really needed Alice, I wasn't sure if she would be able to even see that I needed her, let alone be up to the task, and I know that she thinks that she wanted to help me."

Stephen was in pain for months. Surgery followed surgery. Plastic surgery. Restorative dentistry. He was badly disfigured, and the healing was slow. "I really needed her to be there," Stephen recalls, "but she couldn't be there. I don't want to dwell on this very much, but there was a change in my thinking about what my needs were. I wouldn't say that our life went straight downhill from that moment, but some information was definitely introduced into our experience together that made me realize I wasn't getting what I needed."

"It was a horrible accident," says Alice. "And I think Stephen was never aware of what kind of post-trauma shock he had. We tried therapy. Just little bits and pieces. I had some curiosity about it, but I never really followed through."

Alice's principal response to the deterioration of her marriage was to take refuge where she knew she was loved. She occupied her public persona with greater comfort. Many of her admirers were more than admirers— they loved her. She had dozens of friends who loved her. And there was always *la famille Panisse.*

Alice was spending a lot of time in the restaurant again, planning menus, tasting, advising Jean-Pierre, fine-tuning. At home, she continued to function as Fanny's doting mother, as household manager, as hostess to friends who would all pitch in together on long, boisterous dinners in the kitchen or in the garden. Alice wanted Fanny's life to feel as normal as possible, despite the domestic tension. "We had lots of friends over," Alice says. "We ate at home at least a couple of times a week, and we brought Fanny to eat with us at the restaurant, too."

Drawing on one of her heroes—Lulu Peyraud—more and more often, Alice was cooking directly over a wood fire. Clearly there was a sort of solace in it, a mental teleportation to Lulu's older, more elemental world. One of Fanny's favorite things was what Alice just called "the egg," cooked in a heavy, long-handled iron spoon that Alice's friend the blacksmith Angelo Garro had forged for her.

· THE EGG ·

You make a little fire. A little fire. Two logs parallel and not too far apart, and then when that gets going, you lay a log or two over the top, and when that log across the top gets going, it's like a little salamander [broiler]. And then you need a spoon, an iron spoon that is not too cupped, more of a flat spoon, although you could do it in a cupped one, like a ladle. But it's better to do it in a flatter spoon. With a long handle. I've been going around to fireplace shops finding old utensils. I suppose you could use a stainless steel kitchen spoon, one that you don't mind destroying by putting in the fire that way. But it has to be a spoon that has enough density that it's not going to burn the bottom of the egg before the top of it puffs up and gets cooked.

You want the freshest possible egg, like it just came out from under the chicken, and you crack it in the bowl and add some salt, a little pepper. Sometimes I add a little hot pepper, a little Middle Eastern pepper that Paula Wolfert gives me. Marash, it's called.

So I put a little bit of olive oil in the spoon. Sometimes I put it on the fire to warm up a bit. And sometimes I don't. Then I pour the egg in the spoon, very carefully. If your spoon and the olive oil are already nice and hot, the egg begins to set right away, and so you're not so likely to have the egg spill off before you get it into the fire. You put it under right away, with the bottom right on the coals, and the burning log above. It all puffs up when you do that, and it browns a little, too. It's like putting it into a pizza oven. You're getting a really hot floor and a hot top, too. You keep it there for a minute or two, and then you have another spoon right handy, and a piece of warm toasted bread that's been rubbed with garlic and a little oil. You take the second spoon and loosen the edges and just slide it onto the bread.

Fanny and I like to eat it with a little salad of some sort. Sometimes we'll have some tomatoes in the summer. I love a little watercress salad. This morning I made the egg for a friend and served it with a parsley salad with a little bit of basil. I usually eat it with a fork and knife because it should be runny in the center.

Stephen remained in place, a good father to Fanny, living in the bosom of his family, but he and Alice were no longer occupying the same world.

16.

INTO THE GREAT WORLD

1995–2001

The Edible Schoolyard was not a new idea. Back when the University of California at Berkeley had a college of agriculture, a professor named Ernest B. Babcock had written a brochure titled "Suggestions for Garden Work in California Schools." Published in 1909, it looked back at school gardens of the century before—the Philadelphia Vacant Lots Cultivation Association, the First Children's School Farm in New York City, the Whittier Garden at the Hampton Institute in Hampton, Virginia.

In Ventura, California, in 1907, a teacher named Zilda B. Rogers had written, "The children will gladly leave their play to work in 'our garden.' . . . Since commencing the garden work the children have become better companions and friends. They have learned to respect other people's property and to feel that there is a right way of doing everything."

There was a right way of doing everything—a very Montessori, very Alice notion. "The school garden," wrote Babcock, "has come to stay." He was wrong. By the late twentieth century, the school garden was essentially extinct in the United States.

At the Martin Luther King Middle School, Alice had seen an opportunity for a magnificent rebirth of the idea. MLK had a campus of seventeen acres, most of it covered in asphalt. In its place, she wrote, would grow a "comprehensive solution to both the neglect and the underutilization of the physical plant and its surroundings . . . experience-based learning that illustrates the pleasure of meaningful work, personal responsibility, the need for nutritious, sustainably raised, and sensually stimulating food, and the important socializing effect of the ritual of the table."

Alice had learned from the grand successes of the Aid and Comfort and twentieth-birthday events that it was just as easy to think big as to think small. In her initial proposal for the Edible Schoolyard, she wrote:

> The core of the intended learning experience for the students is an understanding of the cycle of relationships that exists amongst all of our actions. The tangerine peel that gets tossed into the compost pile becomes a feast for the organisms that will turn it into humus, which enriches the soil to help produce the fruit and vegetables that the students will harvest, prepare, serve, and eat. The health and well-being which they derive from the garden is recycled back into their attitudes, relationships, and viewpoints. Thus the discarded peel becomes the vehicle which provides tomorrow's city planners, software engineers, artists, and master gardeners their first adult understanding of the organic concept of interconnectedness.

She recruited an army of volunteers—gardeners, contractors, artisans, bakers, general volunteer labor. She recruited curriculum developers. The Berkeley Horticultural Nursery offered to donate plants and to teach the kids to plant and cultivate them. The family foundation of a friend of Alice's gave $15,000 in start-up funds.

Alice saw the Edible Schoolyard as a local pilot project that could, in time, function as a global paradigm. Thinking big, she wanted the president of the United States to know about it. She had recently seen Bill Clinton again, at a fund-raising dinner that she and Chez Panisse catered in San Francisco. On December 9, 1995, Alice wrote a long letter to the president and the vice president, with a copy to the first lady.

Dear Mr. President and Mr. Vice President:

Our project, the Edible Schoolyard, plans to create and sustain an organic garden and landscape that is wholly integrated into the school's curriculum and lunch program. . . . Help us nourish our children by bringing them back around the table, where we can pass on our most humane values. Help us create a demand for sustainable agriculture, for it is at the core of sustaining everyone's life. Talk about it; promote it as part of the school curriculum; encourage the spread of farmers' markets; and demonstrate it with organic gardens on the grounds of the White House and the Vice Presidential Mansion. . . .

It was Hillary Clinton who replied first, on January 15, 1996:

Dear Ms. Waters:

I appreciate your writing and agree wholeheartedly with your views about the family meal. In my new book [It Takes a Village] *. . . I talk about the importance of this time-honored ritual and our efforts, no matter how busy we are, to dine together at least once a day. . . . We have established a roof garden here at the White House where we grow a variety of vegetables and herbs. . . .*

Sincerely yours,

Hillary Rodham Clinton

On February 1, 1996, the president wrote to Alice:

Dear Alice:

Thank you so much for your kind and interesting letter. I appreciate your words of encouragement, and I am delighted to learn of the Edible Schoolyard project.

*I agree that in facing the challenges of tomorrow, we must continue
to recognize America's deepest values and obligations—from helping our
youth prepare for the future and restoring hope in troubled neighbor-
hoods, to revitalizing the bonds of family and the spirit of community.
We must work together to make this country a place where opportunity
and responsibility go hand in hand.*

You have my best wishes.

Sincerely,

Bill Clinton

Al Gore wrote that he and Tipper had an herb-and-vegetable garden
and a greenhouse, and that they tried to eat together as a family as often
as possible.

A roof garden and a cloud of hot air about "facing the challenges of
tomorrow" were not what Alice had in mind. "I wanted a big, prominent
demonstration garden in full sight of the public." But she did now have
the ear of the president of the United States, his wife, and the vice president. And the president was calling her Alice.

In July 1996, Alice catered another private fund-raising dinner for Bill
Clinton, with thirty of his top contributors paying $25,000 apiece for
a Chez Panisse meal at a private residence. "I went through six cases of
peaches," says Alice, to find the thirty-one perfect enough for the occasion.

But this was only one of three dinners that Clinton had to go to that
night, and he skipped dessert. Alice did manage to put a peach in the
president's hand as he was leaving, and was later told that he had eaten it
on his way down in the elevator.

She told Marian Burros of the *New York Times,* "[Clinton] talks about
community all the time, but you can't just demand that of people. The
way you have that happen is when you eat and care about their nourishment around the table, and the bigger table is the community. He should
be planting a kitchen garden on the White House lawn."[1]

Burros also reported some telling details from her visit to Alice's home.
Alice, as ever, was helplessly candid:

"I know I'm on overload when I can't sleep at night, and my stomach hurts, and I can't stop for a second to have a conversation with Stephen, and Fanny is frustrated, and the people at the restaurant say they can't get a straight answer."

Her husband, Stephen Singer, an importer of Italian olive oil and the restaurant's wine buyer, complains that she doesn't know how to set priorities. "I'm asking myself to let unimportant things go," she said. "I'm really too critical." (At that, she got up from the chair and cleaned a spot off the kitchen wall.)

The Edible Schoolyard was coming together with amazing ease and rapidity. The new kitchen was in place, and sixth-grade classes were already cooking in it twice a month. The acres of asphalt were being removed. An Aztec dance group had come for a cover-crop-planting ceremony: Bell beans, fenugreek, crimson clover, oats, and two species of vetch were now enriching the depauperate soil. The outdoor pizza oven was under construction.

The more Alice thought about the subject, the less she was willing to give up on the Clintons. On December 17, 1996, she wrote again.

> *Dear Mr. President,*
>
> *The prospect of your second terms fills me with hope—hope that you'll seize this opportunity. . . . I continue to believe that the very best way to bring people together is by changing the role food plays in our national life. There is a growing consensus that many of our social and political problems have arisen because we are alienated from meaningful participation in the everyday act of feeding ourselves. . . .*
>
> *A program like the Edible Schoolyard ought to be in every school in the country. . . .*
>
> *Respectfully yours,*
> *Alice Waters*

On February 24, 1997, the president replied:

Dear Alice:

   . . . The Edible Schoolyard project . . . complements the steps my Administration has taken to improve the nutritional health of our nation's children through the Department of Agriculture's Team Nutrition initiative. . . . I'm proud to say that edible gardens are part of the curricula now being used in over 16,000 Team Nutrition schools. . . .

   Sincerely,

   Bill Clinton

Team Nutrition schools, indeed! Alice knew that the federal government's influence on school lunches was almost entirely negative; surplus cheese and other industrially prepared foods of the lowest quality were what school lunch programs got. "I think Clinton wanted to do something about it," she says, "but he didn't want to put any money behind it. The government did a lot of talking, and passing out of leaflets about how we have to pay attention, but the serious stuff was unfunded."

WHILE ALICE DREAMED of Edible Schoolyards multiplying around the globe, Chez Panisse ticked along in its usual way—wracked by occasional storms of employee dissatisfaction; still barely profitable, if at all; producing delicious meals week after week—and from time to time Alice had to tear her eyes away from distant horizons to focus on matters at hand. In 1996, she restored the two-chef system in the downstairs restaurant, promoting Christopher Lee, who had been a Chez Panisse cook and forager for eight years, to be co-chef with Jean-Pierre Moullé. Jean-Pierre was disappointed, but he made the best of it.

In the summer of 1996, Alice's assistant, Gayle Pirie, left to open a restaurant of her own, Foreign Cinema, in San Francisco. By this time Alice had much too much to do to function without an assistant. A friend recommended a young woman named Cristina Salas-Porras as a replacement, and once again one of the classic Chez Panisse patterns manifested itself: Just the right person had appeared at just the right time.

Cristina had grown up in El Paso, in a life of considerable privilege. She was the youngest of six children in a matriarchal, culturally Mexican family that owned a chain of movie theaters in the United States. Her mother served on the board of the Federal Reserve. Cristina spent her junior year in high school in Japan, and went on to a major in East Asian studies at Middlebury College and postgraduate work at Keio University, one of Japan's most prestigious institutions.

She also loved food. She had loved her grandmother's Mexican cooking, she loved to cook on the family cook's night off, and she loved the elegant, spare food of Japan. She had had a job looking after VIPs for the Hotel Park Hyatt in Tokyo—a place where VIPs are taken very seriously—and that had enabled her, she says, to taste "food that even the Japanese didn't have access to." When she returned to America, she didn't know exactly what she was going to do, but it had to have something to do with food. She and a brother-in-law began experimenting with olive oils, and their "O" brand of blended oils won an award at a major fancy-food show as the best new product in the United States. But when Alice called, Cristina saw an opportunity for "something I really, really wanted—an opportunity to be in a mentoring situation with someone I respected and who knew more than I did."

With her almost-black hair pulled sleekly back, her large, dark, frank eyes, and her pale olive skin, Cristina had the mien and the bearing of a Spanish noblewoman, though without the austerity: That wide, easy smile was pure American. Her manners were perfect, her gaze direct, her answers concise, her intelligence obvious. This was far more than Alice needed in an assistant, but she sensed in Cristina a kinship and sympathy that she needed more than administrative acumen.

"I just loved her manner," says Alice. "I loved her spirit, her beauty, her international focus—speaking Japanese fluently, and Spanish. And she was somebody who had worked in the hotel business and knew about hospitality. She was the youngest in her family and always was there helping her older sisters and brothers, and had such a close relationship to that extended family. She loved older people and loved little kids, and she just completely, completely won my heart."

Cristina Salas-Porras

Also in 1996, Alice published *Chez Panisse Vegetables*. It was a remarkably encyclopedic cookbook, not just a compendium of recipes. Each vegetable got its own introductory essay exploring its essential nature, its behavior under different cooking methods, its prime season, and its history.

For the twenty-fifth birthday of Chez Panisse, in August 1996, "I didn't want to have a big huge party like the twentieth," she observes, "so we had a week of parties, and every day we had them for a different kind of group of people." The first, on August 23, was for Alice's fellow restaurateurs and chefs. The next was for the Chez Panisse "family tree"—friends, lovers, ex-staff, and family. Sunday was for growers and suppliers; the Los Angeles chef Wolfgang Puck drove the Chino family up from southern California for their first-ever meal at Chez Panisse. Monday was for Alice's artist and film-community friends. Tuesday was for wine people, and Wednesday, August 28, 1996, the actual anniversary, was for "old and dear friends" from the early days of Chez Panisse.

"Every night was so full of celebration, it was like having six huge New Year's Eves," Alice says. "I nearly died. I was worn out. It was right at the time when Stephen and I were having huge problems. So I was in a state, and I think this series of parties kind of pushed us over."

Stephen was planning to open a tapas bar, to be called—dipping as his wife had done into Pagnol's Marseille trilogy—Bar César. It would be situated directly next door to Chez Panisse. To Alice's friends, that uncomfortable proximity seemed both dependent and defiant. Alice herself simply kept her distance, and her own counsel.

"I used to spend hours with Stephen in those days," Bob Carrau remembers. "He was so angry at her. We used to ride bikes together, and the whole time would be about, 'Alice better let me open Bar César or I'm going to leave her.' I just thought, He keeps saying he wants to be out of Alice's shadow, but he keeps standing in it. I kept saying, 'Stephen, why don't you open a place across town?' What really was going on is he wanted her approval, and she wasn't giving it."

It took another year for Alice and Stephen's problems to come fully to the surface. One day in the summer of 1997, Stephen told Alice that he had fallen in love with someone else, a friend of hers. Alice was devastated.

"It wasn't a mutual decision," Alice says. "He said he still loved me, equally, but he had to tell me. It was very hard. Very painful.

"Walking and talking with friends is a kind of therapy for me. It was really important for me then. Fortunately I had a kid, and fortunately I had a family at Chez Panisse. Fortunately I had some money. I don't know how people manage. I was really lucky. I called all my friends. I was crying for help from everybody. Anybody."

Sharon Jones was one of Alice's oldest friends, one of the restaurant's first waitresses, a veteran of opening night. In the mornings, she and Alice walked together, often for miles. "Having her marriage fall apart was the biggest unexpected thing that had ever happened to Alice," says Sharon. "It took her a long time to process it, but I'm really proud of the way she came through it. Two or three years after my marriage broke up, when I was complaining about not having another relationship that was meaningful enough, I can remember her telling me, 'I don't know why you can't just go out and find somebody. There are lots of people around here.' She was very glib about it. And I thought, You don't know what you're talking about. It's not so easy, Alice. Then when her marriage broke up, her ability to empathize with people grew enormously.

"Alice has something that the world, I think, associates more with males, which is that you can fix it. I mean, she's such an improviser and such a problem solver. But there are some things that you can't fix, and this was the first thing that she could not fix."

"She didn't go out with anybody for a long time," says Bob Carrau. "I think she felt totally old. There was a whole period when she kept repainting her bedroom and moving furniture around, and going like, It doesn't feel right. I kept saying, 'Alice, the reason it doesn't feel right, it's never going to feel right, it's not anything to do with what furniture is in here and what paint is on the walls, it's because your husband left you!' And I'd come the next week and there would be Chinese boxes all over the place, and then the next week she was thinking of moving her bedroom into the living room, and then moving the house. She didn't even want to cook for a while. She would go to the restaurant and do things, but you'd go over to her house and she'd either get stuff from Chez Panisse and serve it, or we'd walk in the kitchen and she would go, 'You guys make dinner,' which to me was great because it meant she was relaxed enough to just bail. But you know, ever since then, she hasn't really been involved with anybody. I think she's so wonderful and she could be, but she keeps herself really wrapped up in business, and she's really manic, and so it's hard for her."

Stephen and Alice agreed that they would divorce, though they continued to live under the same roof well into the summer of 1997, when Fanny turned fourteen. The fact that they managed to live together under such circumstances shows how deeply committed they felt to keeping at least the appearance of family, for Fanny's sake. They held off telling her till the last possible moment.

Fanny Singer recalls, "It was a shock. I must have sensed their discord, but for some reason I have very few memories building up to the moment they told me they were splitting up. Then it took me a while before I could really communicate with my dad. Anyhow, I never lived full-time with him after that. I stayed mostly with my mom at our house, which is still, to this day, very much my true home. My life was tied up in that place. And my life is still very tied up in hers."

"Things were very difficult for Stephen and me before then," Alice says, "but I thought we would be married forever. I knew he was unhappy. I knew he wanted me to change my life, and I know he felt like I made all the decisions about everything, but I don't know, I just thought somehow we could work it out. I was really, really unhappy. It was excruciating."

Another loss closely followed the loss of her husband. On October 14, 1997, Lindsey Shere retired as pastry chef. Lindsey had been the prototype of all that was gentlest and most straightforward in the Chez Panisse way. "I was just so sad," Alice says. "She was a real partner, and a mentor, and had a beautiful way with people." Charles would continue to sit on the board of directors of Chez Panisse, and Lindsey would continue to attend board meetings, so she was not lost altogether, but, Alice says, "I knew it would never be the same."

Alice's closest friends, among them Bob Carrau, Sharon Jones, Sue Murphy, Fritz Streiff, and her new friend Davia Nelson (a movie casting director whom she had met through Tom Luddy), all felt an almost parental responsibility for Alice. "Alice is one of the strongest people I have ever met," says Davia, "but she also needs people to help her, in the same way that she helps others to distill things. So many things are coming at her simultaneously. Alice is the opposite of a loner. There is a fragility and a vulnerability about her, but she is always part of a group. If Alice walks around the track—something she's been doing a lot of—she always walks with a friend, and that friendship is strengthened, because she is a woman of ritual, of movement, of connection."

Over her first year, Cristina Salas-Porras had grown from Alice's assistant to Alice's confidante and adviser. Cristina recalls that time:

At first it was just scheduling and press and stuff like that. Alice susses you out as you go along. I came here during probably the hardest time in Alice's life. I didn't know her. I was a stranger to her, and yet I had to be privy to all of this terrible private stuff. It was very stressful. Alice was very unfocused and unhappy. The first two years were very hard.

It was hard to focus Alice on all the different components of the office. There were no systems, there was no filing system, there was nothing, and so I pretty much got to build it from the ground up—creating a way of doing things in the office and giving some structure to the way Alice was working. But in the beginning I had to check every single thing with her, and it was hard to get her attention and hard to move things forward. She was doing too much. What became easier is that over time, as I gained her trust, she just let me make those decisions and she didn't even know they were being made. And sometimes I made decisions that she wasn't comfortable with, but she said, "That's the position I've put myself in, so let's move forward."

Alice had been doing some public appearances, but not nearly as many as she began to do. Over the course of the next few years, things really changed, for a combination of reasons: Alice was able to redirect her energy in some ways away from the restaurant. She was starting to realize that she wanted to take food out of the food context and take it more into the social and cultural context. So we started being a little bit more strategic about what kinds of things she would do outside of the restaurant. And maybe that meant doing a show on the Food Network that she would have never considered doing before, but we did it because it reached a bigger audience or a different audience, and we weren't always preaching to the converted. We started being more selective about the things she would do and wouldn't do, which was hard for Alice. We had to convince her sometimes that we had to start reaching beyond our group of followers.

"I needed Cristina so much that year [1997]," says Alice, "and she was wonderful. She also became a great friend to Fanny, and she still is. Cristina has been very important to Fanny."

With so much pain in her recent past, Alice was seeing herself in the future now, climbing a very high hill step by step. She knew that if she could reach the top, she would be in a position to see her ideas take hold on a very large scale. There would be obstacles, there would be setbacks, but Alice knew now that she was succeeding, and that success fed on success.

THE EDIBLE SCHOOLYARD was a magnificent success. Alice created the Chez Panisse Foundation to assure its funding and, in time, to fund like-minded ventures wherever they might be possible.

At the Martin Luther King Middle School, the asphalt had all been removed, and the gardens had been planted. Students were cultivating, weeding, fertilizing, learning. The first harvest had come in—mâche, arugula, mustards, lettuces, kale, bok choy, carrots, turnips, beets, garlic, fava beans, and tomatoes—and now the kids were learning to cook. They produced a lavish banquet for their parents. Ten students came down from the Uni-

In the Edible Schoolyard kitchen

versity of Montana to build a ramada (an open porch of logs), through which climbing plants would be trained to provide shade. Using Japanese joinery instead of nails, the students and a designer built a tool shed from a single redwood tree harvested from a certified-sustainable forest. There were new plantings, of citrus trees, apples, plums, ground cherries, black currants, hazelnuts, figs, raspberries, edible bamboo, kiwifruit, scarlet runner beans, chayote, and—for tea, fragrance, and beauty—hibiscus, jasmine, and passionflower. And they planted one of Alice's favorite things in the world, a mulberry tree.

Mister Rogers' Neighborhood and *The Oprah Winfrey Show* broadcast on location from the Edible Schoolyard. Eleven apple trees were trained to an espalier. Alice persuaded the Berkeley school district to phase out all foods derived from cows given bovine growth hormone and all foods derived from genetically modified crops. And the crops kept rolling in— corn, blackberries, lemon verbena, mint, gourds, tomatoes, onions, leeks, peppers, basil, parsley, broccoli, collard greens. The students were raising, harvesting, cooking, serving, and eating them all. They had come a long way from microwaved hamburgers and soda pop.

· MULBERRY ICE CREAM CONES ·

This is another favorite dish that I like to make myself. Once upon a time, at the restaurant we had been getting these mulberries from a particular farmer, and they were always fantastic eaten raw on the fruit plate. But then one of the cooks made them into ice cream, and it was an awakening for me. I went right down to the pastry department and I said, "I want this every day. Every day." They always hate that, when I say, "This is so good I want this every day on the menu." They do it for about a week and then it's gone, and I don't see it again until the next year. We made mulberry ice cream cones for the twenty-ninth birthday of the restaurant, and Fanny and her friends served them out in front of the restaurant. It was the best thing anybody had ever tasted for two dollars.

We made the cones, too. We used one of those sort of Swedish waffle irons. You make a batter with flour and sugar and butter and a little bit of vanilla, and I think it has a little milk. You put a little bit in the iron, and then you press it closed, and in a minute it puffs up like a little thin waffle. We've got a little cone made out of wood, and you just roll the hot waffle around the cone. I suppose you could make it on a griddle. You have to have it really thin.

For the mulberries, you take the stems out and crush the berries in a blender, and push them through a sieve. If you like a rougher texture, you just use a sieve with bigger holes. You make a custard with egg yolks and half-and-half and sugar and cream. You strain that, and then you chill it. When it's nice and cold, you fold in the berries and put the whole thing into an ice cream freezer, and there you are!

I like to pour a little chocolate in the bottom. It makes a wonderful surprise.

In 1998, an astonishing offer came to Alice, one that could dramatically extend the range of her influence. Hélène David-Weill, director of the Museum of Decorative Arts at the Louvre, asked Alice if she would like to establish a restaurant in that ancient palace. She had refused for twenty-seven years even to consider opening another Chez Panisse, but this was different. The first image that rose into her mind was of a vegetable garden in the Jardins des Tuileries, to grow the fruits and vegetables that the restaurant would serve. A teaching garden. The restaurant would have 330 seats—almost seven times the size of the downstairs dining room at Chez Panisse. "Were there no French chefs for such an undertaking?" asked the *New York Times*. "Mrs. David-Weill said she did not find them. 'Probably there are very good people in France, but they didn't come to us.'"[2]

Probably there are very good people in France? Imagine the *scandale.* The first restaurant in the history of the Louvre not in the hands of a Frenchman? Not even a Frenchwoman? Alice was in raptures. She drew up a mission statement:

> A platform, an exhibit, a classroom, a conservatory, a laboratory, and a garden. It must be, in a phrase, an art installation in the form of a restaurant. . . . Amidst the grandeur of the Louvre, the restaurant must feel human, reflecting the spirit of the farm, the terroir, and the market, and it must express the humanity of the artisans, cooks, and servers who work there.

And then she went to take a look at the space. There was room for ninety diners, not three hundred. The idea of a kitchen garden in the Tuileries was met in official quarters with a sharply raised eyebrow. The only place for a prep kitchen was a gloomy, low-ceilinged basement. In *The New Yorker,* Adam Gopnik wrote:

> After Alice left Paris, *Le Figaro* published an interview with her in which she gently reviewed her concerns about the Rungis market [the main wholesale food market that supplied most restaurants in Paris]. THE MARKETS IN PARIS ARE SHOCKING! was the headline on the piece, whose effect, from a P.R. point of view, was that of a Japanese baseball player who after a trip to Yankee Stadium is quoted in a headline saying, "YOU CALL THAT A BALLPARK?"[3]

"We were intending that it would be truly part of the museum, that it would be like an exhibit in the museum," Alice says. "But the administrative part of the Louvre gave me a contract as if I was opening a fast-food concession. I was so charged up I wanted to go ahead and do it anyway. But I had a lot of people advising me, and they all said, 'Do not sign that paper.'"

Did she regret the loss of that grand opportunity? "Not a bit. It would have been awful. Besides, by then I was into Slow Food, and that was so much more what I wanted to do."

. . .

THE SLOW FOOD MOVEMENT had been following a path that would inevitably cross that of Alice Waters. It was just a matter of time.

On March 22, 1986, a McDonald's had opened on the Piazza di Spagna, in the heart of Rome, within easy littering distance of Bulgari, Valentino, Prada, and the city's most expensive hotel, the Hassler Villa Medici. In the distant Piedmontese town of Bra, a thirty-six-year-old activist named Carlo Petrini was horrified. Soon Carlo and several dozen of his supporters were in Rome, marching up and down in front of that archetype of fast food, carrying bowls of penne and placards proclaiming, in McDonald's native tongue, SLOW FOOD!

Carlo Petrini had founded Italy's first radical radio station. He had established a folk music festival where the musicians not only played onstage but marched into people's living rooms. He abhorred the industrialization and standardization that were creeping into the Italian way of eating. He and his friends opened a restaurant in Bra to express their credo of honest, hand-made, regional food. They called it Boccondivino, "Divine Mouthful."

Bra lies near the vineyards of Barolo. The makers of Barolo at that time were among Europe's most stalwart upholders of viticultural tradition-alism (some of them still are, though others have succumbed to a specious modernism). The wine was made essentially as it had been for genera-tions. It was harsh and unforgiving in its youth, but after ten or twenty years of maturation, it was transformed into a velvety, richly aromatic wine as fine as any in the world. Barolo epitomized the central tenet of Carlo's philosophy, namely, that to those who attune themselves to time and the land, good things, in time, come. The first advocacy organization he formed was the Libera e Benemerita Associazione degli Amici del Barolo, the Free and Deserving Association of the Friends of Barolo.

Among Carlo's supporters was a group of Milanese intellectuals asso-ciated with the magazine *La Gola* ("The Gullet"). Together they and the Associazione Ricreativa Culturale Italiana (ARCI) helped Carlo form a bigger organization, Arcigola—a pun meaning, roughly, "archgluttony."

Arcigola opposed not only the right wing but also the Green Party, marijuana, and vegetarianism.

Arcigola Slow Food, as it renamed itself in 1987, caught on quickly. By 1989, it had a membership of eleven thousand in Italy alone, and chapters were springing up all over Europe. The Arcigolosi, as they styled themselves, published widely, most often in *L'Unità,* the Communist Party daily. Their mission was to convert their starchy, self-abnegating fellow leftists into fellow hedonists—in unconscious emulation of what had happened twenty years before in Berkeley.

Slow Food. In those Anglo-Saxon, seemingly nonsensical words Carlo saw the dawning of his life project. Slow Food International (which had dropped the incomprehensible "Arcigola") wouldn't be just opposition to fast food. It would be about how to live. The hurry and hassles of America had already infected Milan and were working their way south. Pesticides were poisoning Italian waters. Industry was turning Italian workers into automatons. Grandmothers' recipes and techniques were undergoing a mass extinction as the new generations of women left their stoves for offices. Psychotherapy, antidepressants, tranquilizers, and plastic surgery, all growing fast, were no match for the modern anxiety that was afflicting the rapidly, radically changing society of Italy.

The Slow Food movement precisely mirrored Alice's mission, and in Carlo Petrini, she recognized a magnetism, an energy, and a determination equal to her own. Slow Food was growing prodigiously, but it was still a mainly European enterprise, with only a skeleton office in New York, fewer than five hundred American members, and no particular American ambitions. But Alice saw immediately that there was no reason that Slow Food couldn't boom in the United States just as it was doing in Europe. It just needed leadership.

Carlo had come to dinner at Chez Panisse once, in February 1988, and Alice had met him then, but her own focus at that time was strictly local. By 1999, Slow Food was emphasizing biodiversity as well as cultural conservation, and Alice was thinking big about education and biological conservation. She heard Carlo give a talk in San Francisco, recognized the

Carlo Petrini and Alice

prospects for powerful synergy, and said to Cristina, "We've got to get involved with this."

Carlo and Alice hit it off instantly. He didn't speak English, she didn't speak Italian, but—sometimes with the aid of a translator, and sometimes without—they seemed to understand each other perfectly. They agreed that it was time for expansion in the United States. Patrick Martins, an American who had been working for Slow Food in Bra, moved to New York to set up a fully staffed office, one capable of handling the growth that Alice and Carlo hoped for. Alice joined the board of Slow Food USA, and the office at Chez Panisse became its de facto West Coast headquarters.

Carlo visited the Edible Schoolyard and promptly concluded that school gardens ought to be on Slow Food International's agenda. "Alice," says Carlo (through a translator), "is a person who distinguishes among people very quickly, sometimes in an eyeblink. And she is a person who reconciles sweetness and tremendous determination. She has a great capacity for building things, because she knows how to bring people together."

On May 20, 1999, Chez Panisse gave a dinner to honor Carlo Petrini and Slow Food and to inaugurate the Berkeley "convivium," or chapter, which Alice and Cristina had just formed. Jean-Pierre Moullé moved a butcher block into the dining room, along with a tank of live trout. Risking a recurrence of the famous blue-trout disaster of 1973, he killed the fish one by one with a quick blow to the back of the head, and immediately plunged them into boiling court bouillon. The diners cheered.

Apéritif & hors d'oeuvres
NV Prosecco di Valdobbiadene Brut, Adriano Adami

❦

Local Pacific king salmon with lime oil and basil
Santa Barbara warm white asparagus with an herb vinaigrette
1997 Grüner Veltliner Federspiel, Im Weingeberge, Waschau, Nikolaihof

❦

Live rainbow trout au bleu with beurre mousseux
Sierra morel and pea ragout with a taste of grilled squab breast
1997 Green and Red Vineyard Chardonnay, Napa

❦

Braised Crystal Creek goat with roasted garlic, new potatoes,
and Berkeley Gardens salad
1997 Dolcetto d'Alba, Priavino, Roberto Voerzio

❦

Bellwether ricotta cheese and rhubarb
Chino Ranch strawberry sherbet and rose petal granità
1995 Handley Brut Rosé, Anderson Valley

Every one of the ingredients, as well as the wines, reflected the shared creed of Carlo Petrini and Alice Waters: local, just in season, and the work of dedicated artisans.

. . .

RICHARD MAZZERA resigned as general manager of Chez Panisse in March 1998, and joined Stephen Singer and two other partners in opening Bar César. The board of directors of Chez Panisse called for a thorough audit, and discovered that once again, the restaurant was in a financial shambles. Mario Daniele was hired as the new general manager, and immediately began a program of industrious accounting, cost control, and close oversight. After two years of that, the restaurant was, for the first time, making real money—enough, by the year 2000, to donate nearly $150,000 to the Chez Panisse Foundation.

Also in 1998, David Tanis had returned, cooking at the restaurant and café as needed but occupied primarily in helping Alice write *The Chez Panisse Café Cookbook,* which was published in September 1999, shortly after the death of the man whose books had inspired so much of the café's cooking, Richard Olney.

After many tumultuous years as not-chef, not-quite-chef, sous-chef, chef, and co-chef, Jean-Pierre Moullé resigned again on February 1, 2000, and returned with his wife, Denise, to France, once more certain he would never return. Alice asked David Tanis to be co-chef with Christopher Lee.

David's hair was graying now. Behind his big dark-framed glasses and under his shaggy brows, his dark eyes seemed to have a newly sharpened focus. He loved Chez Panisse, and his style of cooking was in perfect accord with it, but he had become psychologically independent of the restaurant now, and he was good enough to cook wherever in the world he wanted. Bob Carrau says,

> It appears to me that Alice finds people to work with who have these interesting personal, and maybe idiosyncratic, ways of working. Like her suppliers, or a lot of the cooks, and the chefs, and the artists, they're usually local, found in her backyard, her life. Then she collaborates with them, and the process infuses them with a certain sense of self and vision and confidence, and then something happens—like their work gets better, better known, and so forth, and so here these

artists have been born, but they're not the same anymore. They're not the naïve individuals they once were. Many times they aren't comfortable collaborating with Alice in the same way anymore. They want more say, more control, more money. So Alice watches them flourish and bloom and ultimately has to watch them move on.

THE YEAR 2000 also brought a change that would be as momentous for Chez Panisse as the arrival of Cristina Salas-Porras had been for Alice: the ascendancy of Gilbert Pilgram to general manager. Cristina had brought order and focus to Alice's life, and had become indispensable to her. Following the recovery that Mario Daniele had wrought, Gilbert wanted to bring further order and profit to Chez Panisse. He, too, quickly became indispensable. What was most important to Alice, she finally felt entirely comfortable leaving Chez Panisse in someone else's hands. Gilbert Pilgram, Alice believed, would allow her to climb the vertiginous heights of her dreams without looking down.

Gilbert is tall, thin, with long, lank, prematurely silver hair and pene-

Gilbert Pilgram and Alice

trating gray-blue eyes. He nearly always wears a fitted Hermès shirt with single French cuffs and a bright, floppy Hermès bow tie. A Mont Blanc pen peeks from the pocket. Gilbert personifies what Chez Panisse has become: secure in his skin, conscious of being at the top, confident in the future.

He grew up in Mexico City, where his family, of German descent, had a chocolate factory. Intended by his family to take it over, he majored in food science at the University of California at Davis. While there, he discovered he was gay, started spending weekends in San Francisco, and decided against a career as a chocolate magnate. After a couple of unsatisfying jobs for big food companies, he went to work at a prestigious law firm, and went on from there to earn an MBA at Golden Gate University. "Meanwhile, I was cooking all the time," he says.

Everything I did was god-awful. When they thought I wasn't looking, my friends would throw the food out the window.

I met Richard [Richard Gilbert, his companion of twenty-three years] at the law firm. We knew a painter who was also a waitress at Chez Panisse, and she suggested that I see if I could get a place as an intern. Which I did. Thirty years old, and working for no money.

I'd have fired myself. Jacques Pépin came to be chef for a little while, while Paul took some time off to work on his book. Pépin took one look at my technique and told me to get lost. I worked at Campton Place in San Francisco, and I went with Judy Rodgers and Catherine Brandel to this wine expo in Europe. All unpaid. Thank God Richard was a lawyer. Then Catherine started cooking at Chez Panisse, and she got me a real job there, doing prep in the café. Six dollars an hour.

Eventually, I made it up to sous-chef, and finally co-chef with Russell Moore, in the café. Russ and I were going to start our own place, but then Mario left and Alice persuaded Russ and me to stay. When she asked me to be general manager, she offered me a share in the restaurant equal to her own.

I felt very lucky. This restaurant is a living thing, you know.

People have been here twenty years. Everybody really cares about what they're doing. From the menu meeting on, the cook has total responsibility for the dish. That's what makes our food so different. At Jean-Georges, you make Jean-Georges's food. Here you are a chef. It is your kitchen, your dish.

It was difficult for me to get across the idea of sustainability. I say we have to take care of ourselves. There's a difference between charitable and sustainable. Slow Food and the Edible Schoolyard are very well, but my concern has to be the people of the restaurant. We've got to be profitable enough to pay a living wage. Alice likes to keep the restaurant as affordable as possible, and so one of the things I need to point out to her every now and then is that we need to generate enough income that we can pay everybody well. It is not sustainable to do twenty benefits a year for the foundation. It is sustainable to do a couple of them a year, but to also do a couple of events for profit—what I jokingly call benefits for Chez Panisse. I think the restaurant has a responsibility to pay above market, because what we ask of people is way above market.

"Gilbert can be very hard to argue with," Alice says.

Another thing that makes us different [says Gilbert] is that you have the sense that people will take care of you. If you get into a bit of personal trouble, the restaurant will step in—observing your privacy of course—to help you. You know you are not simply punching in, punching out, and getting a paycheck. We do a very substantial contribution to the 401(k). It's not unheard of for us to do a contribution of a hundred thousand dollars at the end of the year. You also know that all our watching the bottom line and watching overtime means that at the end of the year, we can have a very generous sharing—to the tune of two hundred fifty, two hundred seventy thousand dollars. We have a system of points to divide the money. So if you're in the dish room and have been doing really good work, you get points for that. How long you've been here earns you certain points. Another is how many hours you've worked. And then there's merit, which is completely discretionary. A dishwasher who has worked here full-time and worked very hard through the year could get another three thousand dollars. In the restaurant business, especially at the low end of the pay scale, that's not small potatoes.

Pat Edwards, Pat Waters, and Richard Mazzera had all tried to bring a modicum of serious management to Chez Panisse, and Mario Daniele had succeeded, but none of them exercised power over Alice, and her unbossability limited how much even Mario could accomplish. When Alice wanted to spend money, or give it away, she did it, and nobody could stop her. Gilbert would not have official authority over Alice either; but he was determined to govern the business of Chez Panisse. "I knew that she was used to having her way about everything," he says, "and if I was going to do what I intended to do as G.M., that was going to have to change. Initially it was very difficult. I was always saying to her, 'Alice, am I running this place or not?'

"Finally we got to the point where I could say, 'Alice, you're driving me crazy, and this is why.'"

The perfect freedom Alice had foreseen for herself in the Gilbert era was turning out not to be so easily gained, simply because she could never quite let go of the restaurant.

The culture of Chez Panisse did not lend itself readily to Gilbert's governance:

At first, I rubbed a lot of people the wrong way, because tightening needed to be done. In the downstairs crew, you'd break for dinner while the seatings changed, and back then you would get to open a bottle of whatever you wanted. But if you were an upstairs cook, you didn't get to sit down and have a bottle of Château Margaux. At the end of the shift, sometimes, suddenly Champagne would start to flow. That came from everybody's pockets. And I got people to understand that at the end of the year, I would rather have three thousand dollars going into my 401(k) and six thousand come to me as a bonus rather than drink that money through the year.

We've also had a problem of misplaced generosity toward customers. The easiest thing for a waiter is to give a glass of Champagne to everyone at the end of a meal. I don't subscribe to that school of thought at all. Alice does. When you do it all the time, I think you devalue the gift. A restaurant can be generous in exceeding its customers' expectations. If someone has ordered two glasses of wine, and you see that they have finished their second glass and they still have a little bit left of their main course, well, let me just top you off a little bit. But if we're giving whole lunches and dinners away all the time—I joke with Alice, saying, "Well, what do you do when someone really has a reason to celebrate? Do you send them home with the staff member of their choice?" You have to husband your generosity, and then you can make the person really feel special.

"Gilbert can drive me crazy," says Alice, "but in a way that's what I hired him to do. He's turned Chez Panisse into a real business."
Gilbert explains:

Our revenue last year was almost seven million dollars. Profit is not as much as you would think—around ten percent. It would have been bigger if we hadn't given a quarter of a million in bonuses. It would have been higher if we hadn't contributed a hundred fifty thousand dollars to the 401(k). For health insurance we pay seventy percent, and the employee pays thirty. Our part of that annually is over a hundred thousand dollars. This is a very good place to work. And it's sustainable.

WITH ANOTHER BLOWOUT fund-raising dinner for the Clintons in March 2000, Alice's last chance was at hand: Less than a year remained in the president's term in office. The menu was spectacular, with three iterations of his favorite course, dessert:

Truffled risotto fritters and vegetable crudités

❦

Dungeness crab salad and Fairview Gardens white asparagus
with watercress mayonnaise

❦

Petaluma duck leg braised with new garlic;
fava beans with rosemary noodles

❦

Tangerine granità

❦

Warm chocolate fondant with pecan ice cream

❦

Candies, candied fruits, and mint tisane

Alice did not buttonhole the president at the dinner itself, but on March 20, 2000, she wrote him a letter more imperative than any she had yet dared:

Dear Mr. President:

Although these are the final days of your presidency, I still believe that Thomas Jefferson's dream of a government informed by the values of a nation of independent farmers can be realized through your example. Therefore I encourage you to show the world your concern for the environment with this simple and beautiful gesture:

Mr. President, plant that garden on the White House grounds! . . .
I can think of no more powerful way to ground your legacy than to leave behind you a kitchen garden and the compost pile to nourish it. . . .

With respect and admiration,
Alice Waters

On April 28, 2000, the president wrote back to Alice. Note that by now he was just plain Bill:

Dear Alice:

It was good to see you in California last month. I really enjoyed the evening—your cooking is such a treat.

Thanks for your suggestion about planting a kitchen garden on the White House grounds. Since I took office, Hillary and I have been interested in the idea of growing fresh herbs and vegetables here at the White House. But we decided that an informal kitchen garden would not be in keeping with the formal gardens of the White House and the historic planting guidelines developed in the 1930s. Instead . . . Hillary requested that the National Park Service plant and maintain a vegetable garden on the roof of the Executive Residence. In addition, the East Garden has been planted with garden herbs that our chefs use for our meals, and the National Park Service maintains a compost recycling pile at our greenhouse. . . .

    Sincerely,

    Bill

Two weeks later, on May 12, 2000, Alice fired back:

Dear Mr. President:

    . . . I apologize for being so insistent, but I have the impression that you and Hillary may have made up your minds about a different garden than the one I have been proposing. An informal garden would indeed be out of keeping with the traditional formality of the White House grounds, but . . . as you probably know, L'Enfant's original plan for the capital city was inspired by the layout of Versailles, and at Versailles the royal kitchen garden is itself a national monument: historically accurate, productive, and breathtakingly beautiful throughout the year. . . .

    Respectfully,

    Alice Waters

Bill and Hillary Clinton knew a thing or two about stubbornness, too. Neither replied, and that was the end of the correspondence.

FOR THE THIRTIETH BIRTHDAY of Chez Panisse, Alice was dreaming big. She knew that if she could gather into one occasion the whole history of Chez Panisse and of her other accomplishments, the immensity of her vision would be manifest to all.

I thought we should have probably about five or six hundred people. I was going to use the Escoffier model: For every hundred people, there would be a full kitchen and a head chef. Then one day I was just sort of spouting off to the chancellor of the university [of California at Berkeley], wondering whether there was any place on campus that could handle a number like that, and he said, "Well, you know, you might want to come and look at the main library." I thought, Oh, my God! I'd never expected an offer like that.

Then I was looking at a book about L.A. at the turn of the century, when there were farms in Pasadena. There was this picture of some sort of big reunion in Iowa. There were these big long tables and all these people sitting with their hats on. Outdoors, under the trees. That became my *idée fixe*. This young woman took me around the whole campus, and every location was better and better, and then I saw the campanile [a replica of the one at San Marco in Venice], and the plaza below it. And there we had it.

For a long while I thought our office could run it. I thought we were doing okay until I realized that we were not. We were in deep water. Well, then, thank God for Cristina, and thank God for Carolyn Federman.

Carolyn Federman is slight, pretty, and animated, with long dark hair and a broad smile. Her manner tends toward the amused. "I interviewed with Cristina first," she recalls,

and she had to talk Alice into interviewing me. I had never done anything like this before. I did coordinate this one event when I was just out of college, a three-day music festival, and there were a lot of components, and I had also planned my wedding. So I was familiar with—you know, you do the music, you do the catering, you do the blah blah.

My interview with Alice was funny. She had this binder with sheet protectors, with all these pictures of what she envisioned the birthday would look like, and all these little notes. And when she opened the binder, all the pages fell out, and she was also talking, and she couldn't concentrate on what she was trying to say, so I took the binder from her and said, "Why don't I do this while you talk?"

Right then, I knew that we were going to be a good combination.

Once again, Alice was taking a highly risky chance on someone who had scant qualifications ("I planned my wedding") but who seemed to "get it."

She told me all the different things she wanted to have going on, and I walked out of there thinking, This woman is absolutely nuts.

Alice was trusting everyone to do their thing. Well, she did change the menu the day before the event. We were sitting down, all the chefs, and I was trying to take charge of the meeting, and David Tanis just stopped the conversation. He said, "She's never worked with Alice, has she?"

I kept thinking, These people are crazy, but it turned out everybody really knew their stuff one hundred percent. You could just really trust that when they said they were going to do something, they would do it.

Sunday, August 19, 2001, was a hot day for Berkeley, broiling in the sun though, as always, chilly under the redwoods. There were six hundred guests, paying $500 each, with the proceeds going to the Chez Panisse Foundation. There were sixty cooks in all, and two hundred volunteers waiting tables (in twelve teams, each with its own captain). Fritz Streiff composed the invitation:

As the aromatic smoke of lambs turning slowly on spits wreathes the base of the Campanile, we will welcome you with a sparkling apéritif and a *panisse*. . . . Just down the hill at the Bancroft Library, you will have an opportunity to view an exhibition that in-

Tables set for the thirtieth-anniversary party, 2001

cludes original Chez Panisse art, posters, menus for special occasions, cookbooks, and other memorabilia, and you may join in a silent auction of Chez Panisse menus and other ephemera.

. . . A leisurely lunch will fade imperceptibly into dinner—a feast prepared outdoors by our extended family of chefs and friends and interspersed with toasts and entertainment by some of the wonderful writers, musicians, poets, and personalities who have brought such life to Chez Panisse over the years. We will converse, dance, eat, and drink until sunset.

Dress as if for a grand holiday picnic or a Sunday town square civic celebration. . . .

As we look back and celebrate thirty years of Chez Panisse with this idealized evocation of communitarian and agrarian values, we are also looking forward—to a delicious twenty-first-century revolution in education that will bring about a saner and healthier future for our children. . . .

The menu:

RECEPTION AT THE CAMPANILE
Dario Cecchini's pork specialties from Panzano
Panisses, radishes, and almonds

LUNCH À LA FAMILLE ON THE ESPLANADE
Summer vegetable salads
❦

Provençal fish soup cooked in the fireplace
❦

Spit-roasted barons of Canfield Farm lamb with chanterelles
Spicy lamb and mint sausages
Fresh shell beans
Herb salad
❦

Cheese from Jean d'Alos
Apple and plum jellies
❦

Mulberry ice cream cones
Friandises and tisanes

WINES DONATED BY KERMIT LYNCH, WINE MERCHANT
Prosecco brut Bosco di Gica, Adriano Adami
2000 Bandol rosé, Domaine Tempier
1999 Bourgogne Blanc, Côte Chalonnaise Les Clous, A & P de Villaine
1999 Gigondas, Domaine les Pallières
1999 Muscat de Beaumes-de-Venise, Domaine de Durban

Lunch began with the Prosecco at one o'clock, accompanied by baskets of figs, olives, cherry tomatoes, hot roasted almonds, and salty, hot *panisses* (the indigenous Marseillais chickpea fritters after which the Pagnol character was named). At two thirty, as the Baroque Philharmonic Orchestra blasted out fanfares on valveless period horns, the diners took their seats at the long, white-linened tables arrayed on the lawns. The Gigondas had come from Kermit Lynch's own vineyard, the Bandol rosé from Lulu's.

Dario Cecchini, the famously eccentric butcher from Panzano-in-Chianti, in clown-striped pantaloons and purple cowboy boots, recited Canto V of Dante's *Inferno* in booming Italian, from memory. Alice had asked the choreographer Mark Morris to sing the menu, but he ended up singing "Let's Have Another Cup o' Coffee." San Francisco Symphony conductor Michael Tilson Thomas banged out his just-composed "Marche Triomphale de la Cuisine" on an upright piano:

CHEZ PANISSE! CHEZ PANISSE! CHEZ PANISSE,
Haute cuisine of revolution!
CHEZ PANISSE! CHEZ PANISSE!
We're your veteran foody institution.
We lead off the ev'ning news with our stews and ragouts.
Our attention to detail is deft and manic.
We refine obscure old goop into ecstatic soup.
We won't serve a toothpick if it's not organic!

CHEZ PANISSE! CHEZ PANISSE!
Fighting fast-food assassins' wretched base crud!
CHEZ PANISSE! CHEZ PANISSE!
On our guard to redeem each virgin tastebud!
We won't serve what we suspect's not politic'ly correct.
We're immune from fickle fashion's shoves and pushes.
We won't whisk our meringues for those types who harangue.
It's not likely that we'll beat around the Bushes!

CHEZ PANISSE! CHEZ PANISSE!
Roast, sauté, simmer, sear, and fricassee!
CHEZ PANISSE! CHEZ PANISSE!
Marinate, steam, reduce, and you will see—ah . . .
What do you say after the blood and sweat and tears?
What do you say after these thirty years?
What do you say? What do you say
But a four-star Hip Hip Hooray!

It's more than just a restaurant!

It's a proud credo we can flaunt!

Doing our bit for food each night!

Keeping the torch of taste alight!

Bravo and Bis!

And if you please

We'll never cease!

CHEZ PANISSE!

CHEZ PANISSE!

Fanny and Alice at the thirtieth

*Theater and opera director
Peter Sellars and Lulu Peyraud*

Pat and Marge Waters, Alice's parents

Alice at the thirtieth

*David Goines and his
friend Tati Argue*

An instrumental quartet serenaded the tables with Pagnolian tunes. An honor guard of Alameda County sanitation men passed in clangorous parade, spinning their garbage cans into the air like majorettes' batons. U.S. senator Barbara Boxer read a tribute to Alice. There were messages of congratulation from Senator Dianne Feinstein and Bill and Hillary Clinton.

Christopher Lee supervised the chefs—Jean-Pierre Moullé, Judy Rodgers, David Tanis, Jonathan Waxman, and Chris's new co-chef as of 2001, Kelsie Kerr. Twenty hindquarters of lamb sizzled gently above ten charcoal grills.

It was a blazing day, but Cristina had thought of a countermove: A nurse in a World War I uniform made her way among the tables distributing sunblock. Alice was everywhere at once, kissing, laughing, receiving congratulations, proud—and dressed in high Alice style: "I was wearing a maroon sort of tunic, and sort of short pants under it. I mean not short pants, capri. There was a little handmade bolero top with colored flowers embroidered on it. And a little kind of, what would you call it? A little cloche, that my friend Jeanne d'Alessio made for me."

The stage set depicted the oak-savanna hills of California somewhat in the style of Grant Wood. Flushing bright pink, Alice took the microphone and paid tribute to four women who had informed her idea of what a great female cook might be: Marion Cunningham, her close friend, longtime assistant to James Beard, and editor of the modern *Fannie Farmer Cookbook;* Edna Lewis, the grande dame of southern cooking; Lulu Peyraud; and Julia Child. (Julia, ill, was unable to be there.) Alice seemed flustered, overwhelmed.

A number of Alice's friends were appalled by her rambling, disjointed speech, in which she gave credit to no one. "What I was was high on Bandol rosé," says Alice by way of reply. "There's a film of me speaking, but you can't understand a word I'm saying."

Davia Nelson, a veteran of radio and film production, sympathizes with Alice's sometimes extreme difficulties in front of crowds:

Alice likes to be a presence, but being on a stage just gives her vertigo, makes her levitate. We always say, "Did you stay in your body that time?" Sometimes I watch her words come out of her mouth like little birds getting hatched. It's so painful to watch her find her words. Just this little neck stretching up to the sky. I always think it's like one of the saints trying to get a vision, only she's just trying to get to the next sentence. I can hear it caught in her throat. When only the simple phrase "thank you" needs to come out, her nerves are jangling and she bumbles her next line, and she'll say, "I'd like to thank mmm . . ."—and it just gets lost.

Alice's dad recalled the unsteady beginnings of Chez Panisse. Fanny, just having turned eighteen, said a few quiet words of admiration. Various others from the far reaches of Alice's vast personal geography raised a good many toasts.

The day passed slowly—languid, joyful, loquacious, and a shade elegiac as the sun sank toward the Bay. As dusk came on, a film crew projected onto the white granite of the campanile a montage, edited by Tom Luddy, of scenes from Marcel Pagnol movies, and the guests, all sated, many exhausted, slowly dispersed.

17.

AN EXTRAORDINARY
DAY IN ITALY

2001–2002

W hen Yale freshmen and their parents arrive on the campus each September, the president of the university gives a party in the enormous backyard of his enormous house to welcome them. Fanny Singer was one such freshman in September 2001, and her mother, Alice Waters, was with her. Alice and Fanny had just taken a look around Commons, the cavernous dining hall where Yale's thirteen hundred freshmen and a good many graduate students take their meals; just the smell of it—that ineffable fragrance of steam tables and soup—turned Alice's stomach. When Alice made her way through the receiving line to Yale president Richard Levin, she shook his hand and said, "I'd like to help you with the food here at Yale."

"Well," she says, "I was probably the three-thousandth hand he'd shaken that day, and he was just in a zone." She asked him why the food at Yale shouldn't live up to the quality of the scholarship there.

President Levin's wife, Jane Ellen Aries, recognized Alice, and in a moment they discovered that both Fanny and the Levins' kids had attended the Mountain School, a one-semester program of Milton Academy, in Vershire, Vermont, where the students work and live on an organic farm.

Alice started in, rapidly firing off ideas for the food system at Yale, but this was a receiving line, after all, with hundreds of hands for the president of the university still to shake. "Can you come and talk to me about this?" he asked Alice.

"I think he was thinking that I might do a dinner at his house. Anyway I went, and I talked to him." She told him he should revolutionize the way students were fed at Yale. And on she went, about local, organic, seasonal, fresh produce, and growing it right there on campus, and integrating the garden work with the academic curriculum. Yale had some vacant lots, surely? She described the Edible Schoolyard, and Slow Food International's campaign for similar projects in Europe.

"He said we'd have to talk to the vice president in charge of finance.

"Okay, so I did. The vice president said, 'My family had a farm, and all the farmland is being paved over, and I'm interested in doing something to support the farmers in New England.' I didn't even have to propose this myself. There was already a student group called Food from the Earth with about five hundred members working to get better food served. So the timing was right, and it got going very quickly."

The big question was whether the money could be raised—that is, whether Alice could raise it.

Certainly she could, Alice said, having no idea how.

Her plan was to start with a pilot project at one of Yale's twelve residential colleges. A steering committee was appointed, and chose Berkeley College (the name was a coincidence).

The Yale Sustainable Food Project would be a first step toward preserving what remained of Connecticut's centuries-old farming and fishing cultures. It would conserve rural landscapes and wildlife habitat. Would students have to give up their burgers and pizza? Certainly not, Alice declared. "We're going to have grass-fed organic hamburgers and an outdoor pizza oven."

Alice was thinking of what replication of the project could mean for the small farmers and artisans who were the front lines in what she was now calling, in an echo of the sixties and the Free Speech Movement, the Delicious Revolution. She saw school and college programs proliferating rapidly across the country and abroad. Soon after starting work on the Yale project, she said, "At Chez Panisse we buy from about seventy-five farms, and for some of them we're the only customer. Just think when you multiply that out to twelve thousand!"

Carlo Petrini had said that doing food right was going to have to become fashionable, even glamorous, for the revolution to take hold. It was happening now.

By 2002, the Yale project had hired Seen Lippert, a former Chez Panisse cook, to develop its menus. The project manager found a neglected one-acre plot on Yale property, from which students soon were clearing dying hemlock trees and tangled undergrowth. Alice found an executive at Aramark, the giant industrial food distributor, who—miraculously, in view of the company's reputation for frozen industrial food—was willing to find local organic farmers and deliver their produce. The Yale administration was by now enthusiastically in favor of the project.

The Chez Panisse Foundation had recently received an impressive gift out of the blue, from a woman in New York who did not want her name made public. Alice had not met the donor, but she made a point of doing so on her next visit to New York. Alice left that meeting with a promise from the anonymous donor to fund the start-up of the entire Yale project single-handed, with a gift (in addition to her earlier one) of $800,000.

On October 2, 2002, Alice held a dinner at Berkeley College to announce the college's commitment to be serving 100 percent organic food by the following fall. It wasn't long before Yalies from all eleven other colleges were angling to transfer into Berkeley.

· TO FEED THREE HUNDRED YALIES ·

I've always thought that I wanted to do the chicken paillard. At the restaurant we just pound skinless, boneless, organic chicken breasts flat with a mallet, down to about a quarter of an inch thick. I don't know exactly how you would do them on a mass scale, but I think it could be done. Somebody could invent something that would pound those chicken breasts. I think it could be an easy thing in terms of service.

I think it could be done for hundreds of people. *Bang, bang,* two minutes on the grill and then just serve it up—off the grill and onto the plate. Throw some fresh herbs on it, maybe a little lemon juice. They do have a grill at Berkeley now. It would make a great sandwich.

I think they'd be really good with some kind of French bread. I spread a little aïoli, some rocket, what else? Maybe a little tapenade spread—just olive oil and garlic and olives. They could do this on a mass scale just as easily as I do it in my kitchen at home.

Something like long-cooked pork, pork shoulders, would be great for a school. You could serve it with some beautiful winter greens. At the restaurant, we kind of braise the shoulder. We start with a *mirepoix* with herbs and a little wine, and add a little water to the bottom of the pan and long-cook it, covered, at low temperature.

Then we open it and it can get a little brown, but it should be falling off the bone. You don't have to bone it beforehand; it bones itself. You can take off all the meat and either leave it in larger pieces and serve it as a main dish, or break it apart and use it for a sandwich. It makes the greatest sandwich. Sometimes we purée the vegetables, sometimes we just serve it with the vegetables in it and they're all sort of melted. Or you can strain it out and serve just the juice. If it's flavorful enough, you don't have to do anything. And if it isn't, you can reduce it a little—after you've taken the fat off, of course.

Requests for information and for visits were coming in to the Edible Schoolyard virtually every day from start-up school gardens across the United States. Hundreds of visitors to the project came away inspired. After much romancing from Alice, the Berkeley Unified School District set a goal of serving organic food in all its schools. "That's ten thousand students!" Alice says. "We raised a quarter of a million dollars for that. Every school is going to have its own cafeteria and a full-service kitchen. We're going to get the junk-food vending machines out of there." Berkeley's Center for Ecoliteracy produced a comprehensive *Guide for Creating School Gardens as Outdoor Classrooms*. By 2004, there were garden programs in four hundred school districts in twenty-two states.

Alice was in and out of Chez Panisse. When she was there, she remained the merciless taster and critic, the dust-speck inspector, the perennially fussing lighting director, the change-everything-at-the-last-minute menu reviser. "I was very happy with the restaurant," she says, "though I was never satisfied. What I liked most was that when I wasn't there, I could sense that things were going along just as if I had been there. Gilbert was on top of everything. Cristina was my lifeline. If a problem came up, Cristina made sure I knew about it, wherever I was. Of course, there was always pressure on the chefs. That never stops. Still, it's always a pleasure for me to work with such talented cooks."

David Tanis resigned in 2001, and Alice replaced him from within the *famille Panisse*, with the shy, pretty, cerebral Kelsie Kerr. Chris Lee remained as the other co-chef. Also in 2001, *Gourmet* magazine named Chez Panisse the best restaurant in the United States. "And all I ever wanted," Alice said, "was to be like a little Michelin one-star restaurant.[1] I still don't want people to come with such great expectations. But I should be grateful, too. They keep us full all the time. They keep us in the black."

When Alice was not at Chez Panisse, she was focusing with increasing clarity on the events that could have the most significant consequences. "I want to live the change I want to see," she said. "That's what Gandhi said. I try to express that in what I'm doing. When I write a book, I want it to be beautiful. I want it to be straightforward, honest, and authentic.

I want to express the values that are important to my life. I really work at doing that. I can't say that I always do that successfully, but I try."

In April 2002, *Chez Panisse Fruit* was published. The eighth book to carry the Chez Panisse name, it was the most beautiful yet, thanks in great part to Patricia Curtan's superb linoleum-cut prints. As in the vegetable book, each fruit had its own print and its own little essay. The recipes were mostly simple and straightforward, never disguising the fruit.

The particular freshness, candor, and congeniality of tone that characterize all of Alice's books were at their best in *Chez Panisse Fruit*. The naturalness and ease of the narrative voice certainly had its source in Alice's own voice, but it was the product of an elaborate interpersonal back-and-forth that is typical of how Alice arrives at her fully formed ideas. Most often her interpreter has been Fritz Streiff, though it's not uncommon for Alice to consult with Cristina Salas-Porras, Patty Curtan, and other friends who she knows "get it." Round upon round of dialogue and editing may ensue.

Two classic Alice themes emerge in this technique: first, relying on friends, never doing anything alone; and, second, like the cooking at Chez Panisse, producing an effect of apparent simplicity that is underlain by layers of experiment and subtlety. Fritz's touch is to be found in nearly every speech Alice gives, every paragraph she publishes. Though he's always paid for the major work, there are a lot of little chores that are just what Fritz wants to do, because he's a member of the family. He watches the restaurant's menus with a ruthless eye for bad French, misspellings, and off-kilter usage. His jaunty personal style—the white suits, the bow ties, the air of bottomless gloom beneath the cheer—is in itself a Chez Panisse institution.

Alice has always loved Fritz, in the way of an occasionally exasperated mother. Asked in her kitchen at home what she might make him for lunch one chilly winter day, she improvised this little scenario.

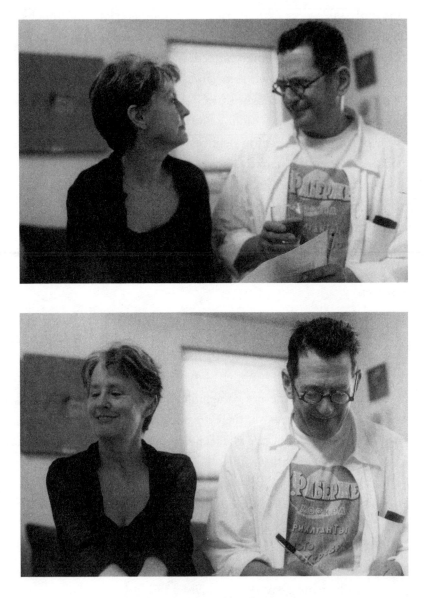

Frustration and resolution:
Alice and Fritz Streiff at work

· LUNCH FOR FRITZ ·

I have this beautiful ham, from Heritage Foods, this company that's trying to support all the rare breeds of pigs and cattle and turkeys and ducks around the country. So first I'd run out in the garden. My latest thing for making sandwiches is to pick whatever herbs are in the garden and chop them up fine and mix them sometimes with a little garlic, with a little vinegar and oil, into a sort of savory herb paste. It's interesting to have it change all the time because it's based on whatever is in the garden.

I really believe in toast. It's rare you can have bread that's beautiful, freshly made. So, okay, I'll dampen the bread a little and toast it on the grill. Then spread on the herb paste. Slice the ham, thin, on top of that. I have some great sweet onion marmalade, and I'd put that on top. Leave it open-face.

And I've got these different winter chicories from Bob Cannard for a salad. He has the most beautiful chicories in the world. I'd use little tiny bits of Treviso, and the Castelfranco, which is lime-green with little splashes of maroon. Right now there's something about the cold that really brings out the radicchio's deepest maroon. And the insides of the escarole are so yellow. It makes just a glorious salad.

And that's it, Fritz.

ALICE WATERS has lived in the same house for twenty-three years, and like Chez Panisse it has grown in subtlety and refinement without sacrificing its fundamental modesty. The house is a small, narrow bungalow built in 1908 in the Craftsman style. There is no longer a garage. Behind the house there is the studio she and Stephen built together. Behind the studio is a tiny guest cottage, just big enough for a bed and a little chest. "Sometime, if you have a little too much wine at Chez Panisse," she tells a friend, "come and stay here." The whole backyard is a garden, with raised beds, rows of tiny lettuces year-round, herbs, raspberries, Meyer lemon trees, swarming vines, and a towering hundred-year-old redwood.

Like many houses long lived in and loved, Alice's house has come to express the inner life of its owner. One's first impression on entering is apt to be of thorough old-fashionedness. It is darkish inside, as so many Berkeley houses are, its furnishings neither spare nor busy, its atmosphere deeply quiet. It smells of wood smoke, apples, old rugs. The living room is densely populated with books, pictures, flowers, a grand piano, memorabilia.

"I'm sure I'd have moved on by now, but Fanny will never let me," Alice explains. Fanny's bedroom walls are covered with a dense collage of photographs, clippings, memories.

Alice's bedroom is mauve, tidy, and bright. Adjacent is a lush Turkish bath. "That time I was traveling in Turkey, camping, in the late sixties, we went to a bathhouse. It was underground, with the hot water dripping from overhead, from a thermal spring. I wanted that feeling."

The heart of Alice's house, of course, is the kitchen, a very old-fashioned place indeed, reflective of her commitment to simplicity. Though when not at home, she is surrounded by all the beeping, bossy digital paraphernalia of the twenty-first century, Alice manages to thrive at arm's length from nearly all of it. She does not touch computers. "Well, I did get one, so people could send me photographs," she says, "but I still haven't been able to make it work. I can't even send e-mail. Have to get one of my wonderful assistants to handle correspondence." A friend will program her cell phone's auto-dialer. She does not own a microwave oven or a food processor. The highest-tech device in her kitchen is a little toaster oven, which she painted dark green to match the walls. Her favorite cooking devices—in the spirit of Lulu Peyraud—are the two wood-burning ovens and the open hearth built into her kitchen wall. She likes wire whisks, good knives, terra-cotta casseroles, *non*-nonstick pots and pans (especially the cast-iron ones). "My favorite tool in the world is the mortar and pestle. I love my mortar and pestle."

A big oval table topped with marble sits at the sunny end of the kitchen, surrounded by mismatched wooden chairs. A corner cabinet houses thick pottery plates, also of differing but harmonious styles. A bay

Alice in her kitchen at home

window looks out onto the garden through a tangle of vines. On the shelf below the window is a clutter of antique cookbooks, art books, baskets, bottles. On the walls are paintings—of a brioche, of a bowl of garlic—and photographs, one depicting the original cast of Marcel Pagnol's Marseille trilogy.

The inner kitchen—small, narrow, and ergonomically just right—has a copper sink, a butcher block, shelves crowded with bowls, plates, pots. Flanking the big professional stove is a long worktable, with plenty of room for people to prep and cook together. "I don't think I've ever had people over and made the whole meal myself."

The late R. W. Apple, Jr.—known to his friends as Johnny—was associate editor of the *New York Times* as well as a legendary gourmet and a longtime friend of Alice's. Recalling an incident vividly illustrative of Alice in her kitchen, he once said:

The *Times* asked me to get Alice to cook Thanksgiving dinner in advance, so we could run the story right before Thanksgiving. We went to her house, and the usual cast of characters was there. And then something required anchovies. And out came this gorgeous tin of salted anchovies. Big, round, discus-sized. And she couldn't find a can opener. So here's this turkey on a spit that she is basting with the branch of a rosemary bush, but there was no can opener. Finally she found one, but it was a ten-minute, fifteen-minute search for a can opener in the kitchen of the queen of freshness.

BY THE FALL OF 2002, when Slow Food USA was not quite three years old, it had signed up some seven thousand members and established about a hundred American convivia, as its chapters are called. Slow Food International had seventy-four thousand members in fifty countries. In Italy, Slow Food has been adopted into the regional governments of Emilia-Romagna and Tuscany and is guiding agricultural policies there. (If a similar policy revolution could be effected in American agricultural states, it would turn American farming on its head. For Alice, it would be a dream come true.) Slow Food formed a publishing company, Slow Food Editore, which has produced some sixty books. Slow Food Editore also publishes a quarterly journal, *Slow: The International Herald of Taste and Culture*, in English, French, German, Italian, Japanese, and Spanish. Recognizing that three-quarters of agriculture's genetic diversity and half of its livestock breeds were lost in the twentieth century, Slow Food's "Ark of Taste" program searches the world for endangered varieties of domestic plants and animals, farm products, and traditional dishes, and opens them to wider markets by means of what Carlo Petrini calls "virtuous globalization"—without which many would be doomed to extinction.

It is not commonly known that biodiversity on traditional farms is often higher than that found in national parks, wildlife refuges, and the other reserves that are usually thought of as the "arks" on which rare species are saved. Industrial agriculture, on the other hand, with its vast acreage of monocrops and its exclusion of virtually all other life from the fields, is one of the most powerful destroyers of biological diversity.

Recognizing the immense biological and cultural importance of traditional farming and inviting people into awareness of it through the pleasures of the food those farms produce are the guiding principles of what Alice calls the Delicious Revolution. Traditional conservation is based in considerable part on negative emotions—guilt and shame for the damage we have inflicted on our home planet, anger at those who continue to hurt it. Slow Food's and Alice's way is based on gratitude and joy—celebrating the beauty of the earth, eating its delicious bounty, participating as animals in its ecosystems. That is a revolution in conservation. It is powerful indeed, because it preserves the ways of human life that sustain biodiversity.

The writer Verlyn Klinkenborg lives on a traditional farm in upstate New York, celebrated in his editorial columns in the *New York Times*. Choosing to live as he and his wife do, he writes, "really comes down to living as close to wildness as we can. I realize that now. What makes it easier is that so many wild creatures don't mind living near us."[2]

In October 2002, Slow Food's biennial Salone del Gusto ("Hall of Taste") gave powerful proof of the movement's growing reach. Into a former Fiat factory in Turin—transformed in the 1990s by the architect Renzo Piano into one of the world's grandest public spaces—came 138,000 people to wander among more than six hundred booths and galleries representing eighty countries. There were literally miles of exhibitors—sausage maestros, cheese wizards, pig breeders, tomato conservers, olive orchardists, winemakers, bakers. All were artisans of the old, authentic specialties of local traditions around the world—Anglesey sea salt, herbed Scottish sheep cheese, kangaroo salami, organic Brazilian chocolates, Istrian truffles, Swiss cannabis pastilles, Genovese tuna belly, Wiltshire herb jellies, Tuscan chestnut cookies, goose prosciutto, hundreds of handmade beers, wines, and liqueurs. Most of these wonders were for sale; many of the artisans proffered free samples. There were little three-sided booths in which to sit down with a glass of wine, some cheese, and a piece of bread, few of them familiar beyond their regions of origin.

The Salone also comprised hundreds of tastings, exhibits, seminars, field trips, and superlative meals, foremost among them some sixty-five lunches and dinners at restaurants scattered across the nearby Piedmontese countryside.

On October 27, 2002, Alice and a brigade of cooks from Chez Panisse were to create a dinner at the Ristorante Real Castello di Verduno, near the vineyards of Carlo Petrini's beloved Barolo. Most of the Slow Food feasts were being prepared by the restaurants' own staffs, using familiar local ingredients to make classic local dishes. The Chez Panisse chefs, on the other hand, had seen the Verduno kitchen for the first time only that morning and, except for the bread and vegetables, had not been able to buy their own provisions.

The fish was lousy, and it was Sunday, with every fish market in Italy closed. Alice wanted the squab legs grilled, but there was no grill, or firewood. The pears were hard as bricks. The porcini were full of worms.

But each of those problems, over the course of the day, would be solved. When Alice arrived from Turin, she found her crew at work in the Chez Panisse way, quiet, intent, unhurried. Two chefs from the restaurant were there—Christopher Lee and Russell Moore—along with cook Amy Dencler and several Chez Panisse alumni temporarily lured away from their jobs elsewhere in Europe.

Conferring with Alice, and at six foot two towering over her, Chris Lee was mild-spoken in the manner that betokens restrained authority. After one look at the mass of pre-chopped sea glop meant to be the base for the fish stock, Russ Moole—with years of Chez Panisse experience—had thrown the whole mess out. They had planned to serve small portions of some meaty fish surrounded by an intense seafood broth, but none of the big whole fish they had was fresh enough. Russ said that if he could find some good little Mediterranean reef fish, he could make a *passato*—a thick soup passed through a food mill.

And then there were the Burlottos. These were the owners of the castle— the three sisters Gabriella, Elisa, and Liliana Burlotto, plus Elisa's daughter Alessandra Buglioni di Monale, the chef. The Burlottos were annoyed, and no wonder. They had waited up the night before to welcome the Chez

Panisse brigade, who didn't pull in till two in the morning. The team was late because they had stopped at Elena Rovera's Cascina del Cornale—an all-organic co-op, which was supplying the beautiful vegetables and bread for the Chez Panisse dinner—and Elena had insisted that they stay for dinner; then they'd gotten lost on the way to Verduno. They could have called, but they had not. Alessandra was now in her office with the door closed.

"Cristina?" whispered Alice worriedly. "You've got to talk to her."

With a long intake of breath, Cristina knocked, entered, and closed the door behind her.

Alessandra had curtly informed the Chez Panisse chefs that the only remaining possibility for fish was the supermarket. But Russ was now beaming at a just-arrived box of fat pink Mediterranean lobsters. Where had it come from? "I called a friend who called a friend."

Tall, wide-eyed, with a nearly constant thin, bemused smile and a shock of brown hair standing straight up at the summit, Russ moved with the meditative tranquility of a man who loves what he's doing. (He was until 2006 co-chef of the Chez Panisse Café.) His idea of the fish *passato* underwent a quick transformation: With the shells of those beautiful lobsters, some saffron, and some Pernod, Russ could make a rich, clear, bouillabaisse-scented broth. He would cook it on an open fire of oak and vine cuttings, which one of the cooks had scrounged up in the village, and the smoke would almost imperceptibly rusticate the aroma of the soup—an old *truc* of Lulu Peyraud's.

Leeks, onions, and fennel lay chopped in neat piles, ready for Russ's broth. Squab stock was simmering. In the main hall of the castle, under a high frescoed ceiling, Alessandra Buglioni di Monale and Cristina Salas-Porras, having emerged from the office, exchanged elaborate compliments. Alessandra looked no older than twenty, no heavier than eighty pounds, with the breastless body of a prepubescent boy. She had a fine-boned, elfin face, with prominent dark eyes, black hair, and translucent ivory skin.

The number of guests was supposed to have been limited to fifty-five, but Alice wanted to squeeze in another fifteen, including Carlo Petrini and her friend Mikhail Baryshnikov, whose White Oak Dance project was performing in Turin that week. "Alice wants there to be a particular spirit in the room," Cristina implored, adding, "We're very happy to be in this beautiful place."

"We also are very happy to have you here," replied Alessandra in lilting English, "but this is a problem." She had turned away friends and regulars of her own, she explained. Places were set for fifty-five, and no more.

Alice sniffed a pear and frowned, watched closely by Chris, Russ, and Amy. Amy Dencler, a cook from the downstairs kitchen at Chez Panisse, was tall, broad-shouldered, with wide-set, watchful eyes, short salt-and-pepper hair, and a shy, self-contained manner. The pears were her dish for tonight. They didn't have much of a perfume, and they seemed awfully hard, but Alice wanted pears and these were the best to be found.

Was Alice about to have one of her ideas? "She'll just say, 'Here's how I want a thing to be,'" said Russ, "and it's up to us to figure out how to do it. I try not to say no unless it's truly impossible." But no inspiration came to Alice this time, and Chris's and Russ's shoulders visibly softened.

"Now," proclaimed Alice, slipping into an apron, "I'm going to do the one little thing that I really like to do best, prep the salad"—especially when the greens are as vibrantly alive as these were: three kinds of radicchio, including the delicate Castelfranco variety—pale yellow speckled with pink—and *pane di zucchero* [sugar loaf], a creamy-green, tight-leaved chicory. A stillness came over Alice's features as she worked.

Cristina joined Alice in tearing the greens into casual but careful squares. "No luck?" asked Alice.

"None," said Cristina.

"There seems to be no way to get through to her," murmured Alice, meaning Alessandra. "She won't even look me in the eye."

In one of the dining rooms, Umberto I, king of Italy from 1878 to 1900, glowered down from a print on the wall, staring fiercely out the window at some of the best vineyard land in the world. On the sideboard below Umberto were arrayed eight bottles of the Castello di Verduno's wines, including Barolo, Barbaresco, Dolcetto d'Alba, Barbera d'Alba, and Verduno's own Basadone (which in Italian evokes "Kiss the ladies"), made from an ancient and genetically unique grape native to Verduno known as pelaverga piccolo, which was saved from extinction on that very estate.

These wines were the work of Gabriella Burlotto, Alessandra's aunt, a small, blue-eyed gentlewoman elegantly dressed *à l'anglaise* in tweed and suede. She is the first woman in four generations of winemaking Burlottos. She asked Chris Lee if he'd like to come down to the cellar for a little tasting. The wines were sensational, each one deeply true to its type, the Barolo brooding and earthy, the Barbaresco like velvet, the Dolcetto cherry red and cherry fragrant, the Barbera spicy and pungent, the Basadone pure, juicy, with a flavor like no other.

Chris's report on the wines elicited from Alice a pained wince. "Why aren't we serving *them*?" she groaned. "The wines for tonight are from Tuscany"—which in Italian terms, and according to the Chez Panisse way of thought, was as far away as the moon.

Alice and Chris assembled a trial version of the squab dish, the separated breasts and legs arranged just so on the salad—not architectural, just balanced. They studied the plate together, shifting a leg here, a leaf there. "I thought about julienning the greens," said Alice, "but then I thought, No, the hot squab might wilt them too fast, and anyway I like the colors like this. It's lovely, Christopher, don't you think?" She moved the squabs' ankles an eighth of an inch closer together, then put them back as they were.

An event such as the dinner that night would be a big money loser for Chez Panisse. But Alice had, as usual, bigger aims than profit: "It's important to express the philosophy of the restaurant." And a great Chez Panisse dinner might just inspire a wealthy and/or influential attendee to take up the cause of organic farming, enlightened consumption, healthy oceans, better European agriculture policies.

Meanwhile, Russ had improvised a cook camp on the gravel courtyard in front of the castle, crisscrossing oven racks across stacks of bricks to create a distinctly unsteady-looking grill. "It's going to be dark out here," he murmured, indicating the complete absence of lighting on the castle façade.

Alice appeared, smiling contentedly at the makeshift apparatus. "I'm going to skewer the legs," Russ explained. "It shouldn't be too bad."

"Can you use rosemary skewers?" asked Alice. "I love those."

Soon the stock was boiling away, lobster legs poking out haphazardly. Frustrated, Russ complained, "The pot's too small. So I've got to make the stock extra-strong and then dilute it."

Russ's girlfriend, Allison Hopelain, appeared, bearing two precious gifts: a glass of wine and a penlight.

In the kitchen, Alice began cutting yard-long strips of focaccia for the grill. Soon a test pear came out of the oven, looking dull brown and shriveled. Amy spooned an ivory sauce around a pear half. She, Chris, and Alice all took a taste. Alice pronounced the *crème anglaise* too sweet. She didn't like the almond stuffing, either. "It's too—something," she said, trailing off. Amy nodded as if she understood, and went back to work.

Five thirty. The kitchen door flew open, hard enough to bang against the wall. It was Chef Alessandra, catching nobody's eye, cruising between the tables and ranges, looking at this, looking at that, then cruising out without a word. Alice and Chris shared a quick uneasy look. The numbers issue was still not settled.

A bucket of sparkling-bright squid arrived, closely followed by Alice, grinning with delight. "Shall we fry them?"

The obvious question was where fried squid could possibly fit in tonight's menu, but Russ didn't ask it. He just said, "I'm not sure."

"Well, you know, you've got to do something with it."

Alice has a horror of waste, but she also has faith in her chefs. "I don't do anything, really," she said. "I'm not a chef. I just let them do what they do so well. They are the best, you know." She followed that statement with a soft, proud lifting of the chin. When Alice speaks with love, as she was speaking then, she tends to tip her weight ever so slightly forward, onto the balls of her feet, poising her body as though to rise, a shift from stillness to intention.

"It's nice squid. We'll have it ourselves, after service," said Russ.

Alice half tripped over a bag of potatoes. She held a potato under her nose, held it up in the light, turned it slowly around. Chris moved toward her warily. There were no potatoes on the menu either. "Ahhh," she sighed, inhaling the loamy scent. "Let's split them and boil them and roast them."

"We could grill them," suggested Chris.

"Let's grill them!" exclaimed Alice.

So now Russ's teetering crisscross of oven racks would be producing fish soup, grilled focaccia, grilled squab legs, and grilled potatoes—all in the dark. It didn't seem possible.

"This is my job," he said. "I can do it by feel."

An experimental assembly of the first course was ready—a cardoon salad with anchovies. The cardoons tasted curiously nondescript, though the anchovies, fresh from the Mediterranean that morning and marinated all day in garlic and olive oil, were sublime. Amy fiddled with the dressing: adding lemon juice, and then tasting; adding shallots, and tasting again; adding a little finely chopped anchovy and tasting yet again. She squeezed in more lemon, and tasted.

Then Christopher tasted the dressing. "Some parsley would be good," he said. "And there are beautiful chives in the garden." Alice grabbed a basket and scuttled toward the garden.

Russ, just in from the dark, called, "Alice, plus, while you're out there, we need herbs for the soup. Whatever looks good." She returned, aglow, with a huge bouquet of chives, parsley, lovage, rosemary, and mint spilling out of the basket.

As evening came on, Alice's posture grew slightly S-shaped; she looked softer, soft-boned, and then, as she seemed to catch herself sagging, she squared her shoulders and stood up straight, as if in resolution.

"I'm infusing the oil for the crostini with truffles," Chris reported.

Russ was chopping fennel and the small, flat red onions known as *cipolline*, which he would sauté and then mix with the chopped lobster meat. He lifted a steaming, just poached lobster tail toward Alice. "I thought, Just kind of herby, oily?"

Alice nodded serenely. Another Chez Panisse dish had been invented on the spot from materials at hand. A heap of the lobster mixture would ride a little raft of grilled focaccia floating on each bowl of broth.

Amy started in on the mountain of pears, halving and coring; the skin stayed on. Lindsey Shere materialized in the kitchen, a guest tonight but happily at home in the kitchen as well. She showed Amy how to cut a flat spot on the back of each pear half so it would be stable. Amy seemed to be moving remarkably slowly. Indeed, everybody did. Russ was slowly skewering the pigeon legs. Alice at that moment was off in a corner, slowly cleaning up the waste and trimmings from her salad greens.

It was six forty-five. The potatoes, once boiled, seemed awfully fragile. Russ broke one easily in half. "Maybe a vinaigrette?" he suggested.

"I think we can still grill them," said Chris. "Look." He halved a few more potatoes, then delicately threaded two skewers through each three halves, forming a compact, self-propping square.

At seven o'clock, the Castello dining-room staff, all of them women in white blouses and black skirts, came pouring into the kitchen. A grim chill seemed to grip the room. Suddenly, Cristina burst into song—a version of the song that Michael Tilson Thomas had written for the thirtieth-anniversary party: "Alice in a palace!" she sang.

"Chez Panisse!" chorused the whole *brigade de cuisine* at the top of their lungs.

"It's not just a restaurant, it's a proud credo we can flaunt!"

"Chez Panisse!" boomed the cooks.

After the boisterous song, calm returned. Alice withdrew with Cristina in her wake, and the preparation slowly continued.

Out in the halls of the castle, everything was still. Alice and Cristina descended from upstairs in impeccable dresses and makeup. Alice's coiffure was new, and rather shocking, with sprouts of blond and orange standing up amid her usual light brown.

Baryshnikov, smoking a cigarette, was the first to arrive. Soon the halls were thronged. A consul appeared in the doorway and paused there, his entourage lingering behind him. He waited on the threshold to be welcomed, then gave up and moved inside. A restaurateur from New York was quite sure it was all a fraud and the food was going to be lousy; she considered the reputation of Chez Panisse to be a fiction promulgated through the all-too-easily-gulled food media. Film people arrived, along with Slow Food members and staff, gourmets from half a continent away, a contingent of Alice's friends. It was a jolly and good-looking crowd.

Russell Moore, Alice, and Christopher Lee
at the Castello di Verduno

When the first course, cardoons and anchovies, was served, there were some sniffs of consternation. To many here it seemed awfully plain and unadorned.

In fact, it wasn't great. It was merely very, very good. It was indeed plain and unadorned—a few slices of poached cardoon, a sparkling anchovy, some mild green oil, and that was it. The fish soup, with its rafts of lobster, came next. It made a striking impression—deep and mysterious, powerful and delicate at once: indubitably great.

Out front, Russ was picking up squab legs with his fingers, tossing one here, another there, over the waning coals. He was out of firewood. But the legs were crisp and juicy—cooked to rosy perfection—as were the slightly rarer sautéed breasts with which they were reunited in the kitchen. The sauce of reduced stock was subtle but potent, a subliminal intensification of the meat's basic flavor. The potatoes were a bit dry, but a nice-enough foil for the rich, almost livery pigeon meat. The pears had never softened, but their flavor was intense, the stuffing was a contrastingly sweet sort of almond crunch, and the *crème anglaise* wrapped them in satin smoothness.

With the exception of the New York restaurateur, whose low expectations had apparently been met, the diners appeared quite blissful. The flavors had been pure and clear. The meal had not been heavy in the slightest. People had talked and laughed and made new friends. A few may have been revising their notions of what constitutes great food.

Alice, who had won the seating battle by sheer force of will, made sure that Alessandra shared in the praise. The crowd leaned forward, silent, to catch Alice's soft voice as she told them that all the ingredients tonight had been organic and local, that virtuous farming means better tasting food. "How we eat," she said, "can change the world."

18.

AN ORDINARY AFTERNOON AND EVENING AT CHEZ PANISSE

2003–2006

Jean-Pierre's coming back!" cried Alice in delight, and relief. It was July 2003, and Christopher Lee was leaving, to open his own restaurant in Berkeley. Jean-Pierre Moullé had returned from France once again, though he would be just filling in, as co-chef with Kelsie, until Alice and Gilbert found a replacement for him. But for once, the perfect person did not fall out of the sky into Chez Panisse at just the perfect moment. By the fall, after a couple of months of peaceful relations and superlative food, Alice realized that there was probably no one as creative, as disciplined, as intelligent, and as well versed in the Chez Panisse way as Jean-Pierre Moullé. Alice, Gilbert, and Jean-Pierre all agreed that he should stay.

This was a mellower, more mature Jean-Pierre. His hair was longer and had gone silver, but his body was still lean and compact, and his ready grin still flickered a hint of wickedness. He was getting along with

Jean-Pierre Moullé

Alice very nicely now. To a friend he said, flashing the grin, "It helps that she's here not very often."

Sylvan Brackett succeeded Cristina Salas-Porras as Alice's assistant in 2003, when Cristina resigned for full-time motherhood and part-time consulting. Cristina continued working on individual projects with Alice, and remains inextricably woven into Alice's life.

Sylvan had worked as a Chez Panisse cook and then as Cristina's backup since 2000. He seemed tailor-made for Chez Panisse and Alice: "At Reed College, I did my senior thesis on the emergence of the idea of taste in seventeenth-century France, and how that corresponded with the emergence of a distinct French cuisine. It was a rather cynical idea—that taste is something made up, to distinguish people from different classes."

Sylvan is not a cynic, but he is a close observer. Alice, he says,

Sylvan Brackett

doesn't use the jargon. She refuses to learn the table numbers. She'll say, "You know, the table by the window!" "The booths!"

I would say seventy-five percent of the stuff we do in the office is not affiliated with Chez Panisse. The money from the restaurant is funding the other efforts, and this is a point of contention. Gilbert is not a big fan of the Slow Food movement.

This sounds as if Chez Panisse might sustain itself more easily without Alice's being there at all. Sylvan:

I can't imagine Chez Panisse going on without Alice. But I can see her at ninety-nine, receiving people, looking over menus, and complaining about this or that. Saying she likes this person or doesn't like that person, and, "This waiter needs to cut his hair."

Alice with David Tanis after his return to be downstairs co-chef

In early 2004 Kelsie resigned to work with Alice on her next book and to spend more time with her young daughter. To preserve the co-chef system, Alice and Jean-Pierre created a new version of it: He would be chef—not co-chef, not quasi-chef, not chef-without-the-title, but *chef*—for six months, and then David Tanis would return for six months, and so on. Each would spend his six months off in France. The chef's work-week would be just five nights. On Mondays, when the downstairs restaurant serves its simplest dinner—often the old regulars' favorite—the longtime cook Phillip Dedlow would take the helm.

On Alice's sixtieth birthday, in April 2004, Cristina asked her what she thought she should be able to look back at ten years hence. Alice by then had the world for her stage. In 2003, the *American Masters* series on PBS, which for more than twenty years has been documenting "our most outstanding cultural artists," had broadcast a film by Doug Hamilton, *Alice Waters and Her Delicious Revolution*. Alice was the only chef ever to be chosen as an American Master. Also in 2003, she was elected vice president of Slow Food International, second only to Carlo Petrini. The Edible

Schoolyard and the Yale Sustainable Food Project were widely known, and just as Alice had hoped, similar projects were taking root in both America and Europe. What more could she hope to achieve? Alice gave Cristina's question a lot of thought.

The scope of her interests was global now. Alice's life now would be devoted to changing the world in the biggest ways possible. Her involvement in one new project after another meant that more and more of her time would be spent on airplanes and in places far from Chez Panisse.

All that involvement would also elicit criticism. What Alice's closest friends recognized as persuasiveness, others called manipulation. Susie Buell, a philanthropist and political activist, and one of Alice's true intimates, says,

Alice can't stop. She has to keep finding new things, and it's exhausting. She's very driven by her passions, her concerns, her curiosity, her anxiety about why we're not living better, why we're not taking care of ourselves. So she creates this character, this nonstop creator of everything. And it's true, it's authentic, it does come from within.

She's manipulative in a way, but she has to be. It's not a bad thing. That's the way you get things done. Every great person is manipulative. She does her little baby-talk thing, and she kind of pouts, and she wants things to happen her way. She has to convince people. And she adores men. She's the greatest little flirt. That's all very manipulative.

Some of her best friends won't talk to her sometimes for a while, because they feel that her expectations are too much, that they just can't be there for her the way she needs them to be so that she can have her way, have her thing done. But in the end, when the result comes, I don't think anybody would have done it any differently.

Davia Nelson sees good reason for Alice's increasing concentration on people of influence, but she insists that there is nothing exclusionary about Alice's circle, or circles, of friends:

Alice will worship heroes. They're in "the first circle." David Brower was in it, and Michael Pollan is. Wendell Berry. Carlo Petrini. And a Tibetan van driver and a butcher in Italy. Her first circle isn't about being famous, even though Baryshnikov is in it, and Peter Sellars. The first circle is about, Are you committed, are you passionate, do you want to change the world, are you a force for change?—even if you're a kindergartner. She recognizes that spark of passion in people.

ONE FRIDAY in the fall of 2004, a visitor came to observe an ordinary day at Chez Panisse. At one o'clock in the afternoon, Jean-Pierre went over the evening's reservations with Robert Messick. As usual, the restaurant was going to be full. There was a honeymooning couple, which always warrants special attention, and there would be a group from Slow Food. Glasses of complimentary Champagne were to be offered to the newlyweds and the Slow Food people.

Next Jean-Pierre checked his supplies. In the chilly air of the breezeway outside the kitchen door were stacked garden flats of root vegetables—turnips, carrots, rutabaga, parsley root, salsify, and Jerusalem artichokes, all just in from the Chino Ranch. The Chez Panisse van, having delivered its burden of compost to Bob Cannard's farm that morning, was expected back at the restaurant shortly. Jean-Pierre slid back the massive polished copper door of the walk-in cooler. In the walk-in hung a half dozen back halves of lambs, dark with aging. There was only one bag of fresh coriander seeds left. "These are hard to get," he said, "and it's not so many, but smell—powerful, no?" There were no Meyer lemons where they were supposed to be. He asked the pastry department if they could spare a dozen Meyers, and they could. A cook squeezed past with a hotel pan (a large, shallow, rectangular stainless steel container) filled with parboiled purple cabbage. Jean-Pierre grabbed a piece and munched. "Too salty," he said. Oversalting is the curse of many cooks' overworked, and therefore sometimes benumbed, palates.

Dhondup Karpo arrived with the van. He is Tibetan, one of a number of political refugees whom Chez Panisse has employed through the years;

there are also Afghans, Vietnamese, and Cubans. "Khalil Mujadedy," Alice says, "comes from an extremely prominent family in Afghanistan. The queen of England stayed at his family compound when he was young. But he came here as a dishwasher who hardly spoke English. Now he's become an indispensable part of the restaurant. He can fix anything. He can build anything. He's made copper railings, lamps, beautiful things.

"Dhondup—same thing—indispensable. These people work so hard. People who visit the kitchen don't see them, they're always behind the scenes, but Chez Panisse couldn't function without them."

Three cooks, including Jean-Pierre, hurried into the breezeway to see what the day's bounty would be. "Beautiful chervil," he said. "Beautiful, beautiful, tiny watercress." He took a small bite. *"Pow!"* he exclaimed. Just picked, it had a sharp pepper-and-licorice bite that would fade in half a day or less.

He ordered that the herbs and vegetables be taken immediately into the garde-manger—the room where cold food is prepared. "The café has been grabbing stuff early, because they're here first," said Jean-Pierre. "Look at this." He opened the heavy door of the dark room where house-cured hams, *zamponi* (stuffed pig's trotters), and salami were aging. "They put vegetables in here. That's why we have mold on the hams. I want them to use the wine room, but Jonno"—Jonathan Waters, the wine buyer (no relation to Alice)—"is resisting. Of course I'm resisting his wine list. Too many overextracted reds. Not enough Bordeaux." The grin flashed again— Bordeaux is Jean-Pierre's hometown. "Those giant wines, these zinfandels with sixteen percent alcohol, they overwhelm the kind of food we make. Where is my Savoy cabbage? You see? It's gone."

Michael Peternell, Russell Moore's co-chef in the café, came in to consult with Jean-Pierre about a sauce. Cal, as he is known, is tall, blond, elegantly well-spoken, and formally polite. Like many of his predecessors, he has been an artist, lived in Italy, and found a culinary home at Chez Panisse—while also able to live a real life at home with his wife and children. "I had time off when my son was born," he says. "Recently, I took some time to build my kids a tree house. There aren't many restaurants where something like that is possible. There's so little friction in our kitchen. Sometimes it amazes me how nice these people really are. And how good. All of them. How well the others like what I'm cooking, and the menus I write—that's the real measure, for me, of how I'm doing. And then they always have the opportunity to make changes in the dishes they're doing. So we've all got pride of ownership in what comes out of our kitchen."

AT NOON, leftovers from the day before were set out in a nook off the kitchen. Cooks, waiters, bussers, and office staff descended on them hungrily. These were not just any leftovers. There was a whole chocolate tart that didn't sell the night before. There were glistening slices of roast pork sprinkled with herbs; bowls of sparkling salads and vegetables. Staff lunch at Chez Panisse is one of the best meals to be had in the Bay Area. Unfortunately, everybody always seems to wolf it down in ten minutes. For these devotees of Slow Food, lunch is distinctly non-slow.

At two o'clock, the downstairs kitchen brigade took seats at an unset table in the dining room. In the low fall sunshine and without its golden lamps on, the room looked rather beat-up, the wood trim dinged, the chair legs gouged. Grass, leaves, string, and flower petals littered the floor: Carrie Wright and her assistant were improvising a new display of flowers.

Jean-Pierre took his seat not at the head of the table but modestly off to the side, studying a wrinkled handwritten menu and saying, "We pretty much have everything"—meaning that they could, if they chose, serve the same menu that was printed on the sheets stacked next to the front door and posted at www.chezpanisse.com.

"Okay, apéritif—Prosecco with a little Meyer lemon syrup." (There are always rows of bottles of fruit syrups in the walk-in, all house-made.) "Then we have"—he read from the menu—"warm salad of winter chicories with cèpes, pancetta, and eggs. Fish and shellfish soup with Dungeness crab, Atlantic cod, and fennel. I don't know about the fennel. Bob's chervil is so beautiful." He read again: "Grilled rack, loin, and leg of Cattail Creek lamb with fresh coriander seed sauce and roasted Chino Ranch vegetables.

"Okay. For the soup base we have fish, fish bones, shrimp, clams, mussels. Not too many vegetables, just leeks and fennel. The broth shouldn't be too strong—you want to taste the crab, eh? No aïoli, nothing like that. Maybe a plain crouton. Fennel tops or chervil. Beautiful chervil.

"For the roasted vegetables, we have turnips, carrots, celery root, beautiful cauliflower from Bob—you've seen what we have in the flats."

"I'd like to do the soup," Beth Lells volunteered.

"I'll take the lamb if it's okay," said Ignacio Mattos.

"The salad?" asked Paula Bock.

"Okay, good," said Jean-Pierre. "For the salad, Paula, a warm salad needs more acidity, maybe also mustard, not too much oil. Balance is very important, because when you dress it too much and then heat it, it looks greasy. So start with half the usual olive oil.

"The cèpes you want to sauté first with garlic and parsley, and for them a different vinaigrette. Or maybe roast them with the vegetables, covered, and crisp them at the end."

"I've never done this before," said Paula. "Do you think we could do one batch of the mushrooms for the whole seating?"

"I think maybe we work it out as we go," said Jean-Pierre, diplomatically avoiding direct contradiction. "Maybe small batches will be better. For the soup we have lots of crab—you can use five or six for the broth. And toast with that? I don't know. We decide later.

"The lamb, we make a marinade with dried coriander seeds, fresh cilantro, salt, pepper, thyme, garlic. I'm very excited about this coriander sauce."

Jérôme Waag—son of Alice's old friend Nathalie, and an artist when not cooking at Chez Panisse—said he would do the vegetables. Jérôme tends to look underslept, undershaved, terrible, thoroughly grumpy, till his sunny smile breaks through. "Maybe I do the turnips separately, eh? And roast the rootier things. I think maybe no potatoes. And we use that beautiful watercress to garnish, eh?"

"Some of these dishes," Jean-Pierre said to a visitor, "will evolve over the course of the day. I don't want to give directions too specific. I want the cooks to use their imagination. But it all has to pass my test—of course."

The Chinos' root vegetables were tiny, many no bigger than marbles.

Jérôme peeled them unhurriedly, creating hundreds of little spheres. The most senior cook in the room, Jérôme had taken the most menial task.

Jean-Pierre peeled the tiny salsify roots as patiently as Jérôme did his turnips. "When you're ready with the broth," he called across the kitchen to Beth, "I want to taste it." He started in on the very knobbly parsley roots. "These are a nightmare to peel," he said, working his way through dozens of them. This was scut work, which anywhere else would be done by interns or the lowest-ranking kitchen staff. But that is not the Chez Panisse way.

All afternoon, the downstairs kitchen was a quiet scene of the same operations repeated over and over: picking crab, shelling shrimp (glistening-fresh, harvested by a small-boat fisherman from one of the few remaining sustainable shrimp fisheries, but not local—they had been flown in over-night from Florida), stirring the lamb stock, turning the roasting bones in the oven, endlessly peeling the tiny root vegetables.

Ignacio broke down the lamb meat with quick strokes of his narrow, scalpel-sharp boning knife. He cut out every white trace of connective tissue. He made the marinade and then massaged it into the meat with his hands.

Paula dried small batches of salad greens with an ordinary plastic pull-cord spinner, always gently so that the leaves wouldn't be bruised or creased, laying the greens on soft white towels, dabbing at them till the last drop of water was gone. This was one place where the unseen pres-ence of Alice hovered—over Paula's salad greens—making sure that they would still look as alive in the dining room as when they arrived in the van.

Just after four o'clock, Jérôme and Ignacio shouldered the immense iron rotisserie out of the wood-burning oven and marched it out to the back, yelling people out of their way at every step. Two café cooks outside were digging into two five-gallon tubs of just-made ice cream—one hazelnut, the other pecan—happily taste-testing as they dug.

Jean-Pierre leaned against the wall with pad and pencil, composing the vegetarian menu, which it was quite possible no one would order: fennel soup with crème fraîche; roasted root vegetables; cabbage leaves stuffed with cèpes and other mushrooms; the same dessert, a Meyer lemon soufflé.

"We do have a problem sometimes," Alice says, "when people want something that's not on the menu. The vegetarians are no worse than anybody else. It's just that most of the time, there's not much we can do. We've bought the materials for that night's dinner, and that's it. Sometimes we can get something brought downstairs from the café, or vice versa, but it tends to break the flow."

By five o'clock, the vegetables, lightly coated with oil, each type separate, were roasting on sheets of parchment paper. A small fire was warming the fireplace. Beth debearded mussels while Jean-Pierre picked over the crab yet again, so that not a speck of shell would make it into the dish. Waiters arrived, in civvies, and started polishing glasses, folding napkins, setting the tables.

"Watch out for salt, Paula," Jean-Pierre called. "The pancetta, you know."

Paula, too intent on her work to look up or speak, nodded in silent acknowledgment.

Beth, stepping in to help Paula, peeled hard-boiled eggs, each yolk barely gelled at the center. The pace was picking up, the temperature in the kitchen rising into the mid-seventies, the cooks as they finished their prep work cleaning up quickly. At Chez Panisse there are no runners, no scullions, to pick up anybody's dirty pots; cooks must run them to the dishwashers themselves, and clean the counter themselves.

At five thirty, Jean-Pierre assembled the waiters and walked them through the menu with a detailed explanation of each dish. "In case anybody asks," he said with a hint of dismay, "yes, the cod is on the yellow list." (Both the Monterey Bay Aquarium and the National Audubon Society have been publishing guides to sustainable seafood. The aquarium's green list is "best choices," the yellow list "good alternatives," the red list "avoid." The Audubon list is rather more strict, green meaning "abundant, relatively well-managed species"; yellow, "significant concerns about a species' status, fishing methods, and/or management"; and red, for fish that have "a lot of problems—such as severe depletion, overfishing, or poor management.")

"But you know we have fishermen working in a way that it's okay to take them," said Jean-Pierre, "so I think it's all right. You explain to the customer if they ask."

The sourcing of fish for Chez Panisse has gone through a long evolution. In the early days, Alice would sometimes go down to the docks of a fishing port and buy directly from the fishermen, inspecting each fish personally. Along the way, she met Paul Johnson, who offered to buy fish for the restaurant. He focused on the finest of the fine, selecting individual fish out of larger hauls. Paul later, with Jerry Rosenfield, founded the Monterey Fish Company, which now has a substantial wholesale business as well as a retail shop in Berkeley. The company sells nothing but sustainably harvested fish, and acts as a sort of adjunct conscience for Chez Panisse.

"That Atlantic cod, for instance," said Phillip Dedlow as he watched Beth Lells poaching it for the soup:

> The species is on a couple of these red lists, but the conservation groups have to paint with a broad brush. Monterey finds a small fisherman with a small boat who's fishing with a hook and line, harvesting very small amounts. This whole thing is based on a chain of trust. We trust Monterey, which trusts the fisherman to be telling the truth and doing the right thing. What's important is that these are people who know and trust one another.
>
> Take monkfish. Most monkfish is harvested with these horrible drag nets that scrape the ocean floor—absolutely ruinous. But Paul Johnson has found a fisherman who uses what's called a tickler chain, which floats just above the bottom and stirs up the monkfish into the net but doesn't touch that whole ecosystem of the ocean floor. Also the guy rotates where he fishes—takes only a few fish from a given location, and then lets it rest. So we can feel pretty sure that we're doing the right thing with the fish we serve.
>
> It's the same with the beef, which I'm buying now for the whole restaurant. After we learned from Michael Pollan about all the horrors of feed lots and sick cows and all that, Alice decided she didn't want to use any more corn-fed beef, and we've been searching for

over a year now for grass-fed beef that tastes good. And it has to be humanely raised and killed. No chemicals on the land. Totally organic. It hasn't been easy to find. A lot of grass-fed just doesn't taste that great, consistently. What we've been buying from Magruder is the best we've found, but the quality seems to me to be also very dependent on *terroir*. As the grass begins to green up, the beef starts to taste better and better, and then toward the end of the summer when the grass is all going brown, there's a steady decline in flavor until the rains start again in the winter. Plus, we've been having to buy whole cows, and there are all these cuts that we don't know what to do with. It's a big learning process.

The old country-pine table that divides the kitchen from the dining room was hastily swabbed clean, and Shelley Mulhall, the hostess and dining-room manager, quickly arranged two still lifes on it, one of very earthy-looking root vegetables and the many-colored chicories, the other of round brown loaves of Acme bread. At five fifty-six Shelley called into the kitchen, "Four minutes!" Jérôme removed his dirty apron, put on a clean one, and returned to chopping his turnip greens.

Paula set up a sample salad for tasting. She heated the greens briefly in a bowl suspended over hot water while warming the mushrooms and pancetta in the *sautoir* and then sprinkling them with parsley chopped so fine it was almost a powder. The greens went on the center of the plate, and Paula set two quarters of eggs on either side. Jean-Pierre leaned over the salad and added an infinitesimal amount of salt and pepper. He didn't like the look of the eggs and suddenly attacked them with his knife, chopping them into uneven chunks that he then distributed over the top. He lifted a big forkful into his mouth, and five other forks plunged in after his. While they chewed, the cooks all watched Jean-Pierre, awaiting his reaction. He said nothing. Jérôme said, "The dressing is perfect, it just needs a little more. I think it should be a little warmer, and you should warm the eggs to room temperature. You can't taste them when they're cold like this." Jérôme was speaking with the authority of years of experience. Jean-Pierre nodded in agreement.

Jean-Pierre tasted each element of the soup separately. "The broth is too clean," he said, and Beth looked mystified. "A little more salt, I think. Don't worry about the broth. It will get better as the evening progresses."

The waiters donned their simple uniforms of white shirts and black pants. Two bottles of Prosecco were uncorked, and a pitcher of pale yellow Meyer lemon syrup set beside each. The main kitchen counter was wiped clean for plating. Jean-Pierre put on new whites, the fancy jacket with *Chez Panisse* embroidered on the chest. Shelley took her place at the podium.

ALICE WATERS was not at Chez Panisse that night. The regulars know by now not to be surprised if Alice isn't around. When she is, she will seem to be everywhere at once—up to her elbows in a sink washing lettuce; sticking a finger in a sauce and ordaining a dash of lime juice; shoving logs into the fire, and adjusting the rotisserie; inspecting the recycling cache behind the restaurant to be sure that the cans are spotless, the garbage odorless; sometimes in her trimly fitted kitchen whites, sometimes in one of her unique, unknowable-period dresses, making the rounds of the dining room, kissing friends on both cheeks, sitting two minutes here, five there, holding both hands of an admirer, pointing out to a busser a dusty inch of molding. When she is at the restaurant, she will taste every dish produced in both the downstairs and the upstairs kitchens, and she will not be hesitant with her criticism. There are 119 people on the staff of Chez Panisse, and not one of them, ever, argues with Alice's palate.

What is remarkable in Alice's absence is the continuing presence of that palate. Chez Panisse embodies a system of aesthetic discrimination of deep subtlety and hidden complexity. Alice's standards, her taste in everything from the quality of the light to the silkiness of the butter, her ethical standards, her sense of the restaurant as a family—all these stay behind when she is gone, as strong as when she is here. A common remark from one cook to another who has just tasted the first one's dish is, "Alice would love that." Besides the physical one, there is a virtual Alice Waters.

1517 Shattuck Avenue, 2006

THE FACE that Chez Panisse presents to the street is both plain and intricately expressive. Climbing or down-spilling vines weave through an arbor and screen fashioned partly of weathered redwood, partly of gray steel bars punctuated with little steel polka dots. A glass-fronted polished copper box displays the day's menus. Above the narrow entranceway is an arc of raw redwood on which the restaurant's name is jauntily, somewhat roughly painted. Behind the screen is a small enclosed terrace with three redwood benches, a potted camellia, and a Japanese maple growing through the brick floor with tiny violets at its base. An unruly wisteria sprawls upward into the second-story eaves. Strawberry plants line the pinkish concrete retaining wall. Squeezing through the sidewalk and towering over it is an enormous, rather bizarre-looking tree, which nearly

The downstairs dining room, looking west

The kitchen at Chez Panisse

Looking east, into the kitchen

everyone, including the waiters, calls a monkey-puzzle (*Araucaria arau-cana*, a native of Chile), but which is in fact a bunya-bunya (same genus, different species—*Araucaria bidwillii,* from Australia). All this artful jumble—the slow accumulation of Alice's refinements since 1971—does not conceal the building's beginnings as a humble, rambling old house.

That autumn evening in 2004, as the first customers approached, a waiter walked quickly across the terrace waving a delicately fragrant burn-ing branch of rosemary—the first of several subtle gestures of welcome devised by Alice.

It was one party's first meal ever at Chez Panisse. Handrails of ham-mered brass led them up six steps to a landing beneath layered raw wood gables. A heavy redwood door opened into a narrow foyer containing a bench, a small table, a rug, and a primitive space heater along the base-board. Two narrow windows peeked into the dining room. Double doors led to the second foyer, a warmer place, suffused with the golden light particular to Chez Panisse.

A beaten-brass vase was overflowing with autumnal flowers, vines, and leaves—manifestations of nature's abundance being another of Alice's customary gestures of welcome. A narrow stairway on the left led to the café upstairs. To the right was a redwood podium, behind which Shelley Mul-hall waited. Shelley found the party's reservation in her leather-covered book and noted the table location.

"Welcome to Chez Panisse," she said, and gestured toward the dining room.

Downstairs at Chez Panisse—the original dining room—is not an easy restaurant to get into. It is best to call for a reservation precisely a month ahead, preferably first thing in the morning. Robert Messick will answer the phone as he has been doing for the last twenty-two years: "Good morning, Chez Panisse." He reminds each caller that there is no choice on the menu, but that one can phone early in the week to find out what's planned, or look it up on the restaurant's Web site. He also tells the caller that what will actually be served may be what was planned, or may resemble it but differ; occasionally a course will have changed entirely.

Following Shelley into the dining room, the first-time diners slipped past a green velvet curtain and into an atmosphere both simple and studiously composed—foremost of aromas, floating from the open kitchen, of olive oil, garlic, wood smoke, pastry, roasting meat, something frying, something sweet, a mingling of the scents of haute cuisine and an Italian grandmother's kitchen. As yet unpeopled, the dining room seemed rather severe, with white plaster walls, redwood trim, copper sconces, a few mirrors, a couple of offhandedly rustic arrangements of particolor chicories and raw root vegetables. The room was gently lit, neither dark nor bright, except at the rear, which was open wide to the strong white light of the kitchen. The tables were set with plain flatware and glasses, plain white linen, plain white plates. The woodwork was faintly Japanese in style. The only immodest elements of the room were the spectacular bursts of flowers, all locally grown, all proclaiming the season and abundance and welcome.

At each place sat a small cream-color paper folder bearing on its front a delicate linoleum-block print by Patricia Curtan, of a bowl of tangerines. Inside was the night's menu:

CHEZ PANISSE

An apéritif

❦

Warm salad of winter chicories with cèpes, pancetta, and eggs

❦

Fish and shellfish soup with Dungeness crab, Atlantic cod, and fennel

❦

Grilled rack, loin, and leg of Cattail Creek lamb
with fresh coriander seed sauce and roasted Chino Ranch vegetables

❦

Meyer lemon soufflé

DINNER: SEVENTY-FIVE DOLLARS

TAX: EIGHT AND THREE-QUARTERS PERCENT

SERVICE: SEVENTEEN PERCENT

Over the next half hour, as all of its fifty seats were filled, Chez Panisse was transformed. The modesty of the dining room is the culmination of the thirty-three years of Alice's pursuit of an aesthetic so refined as to elude most conscious perception of the room as a physical space. What gives it life, in her intention, are people and their pleasure. That night there were shy young couples on important dates, gastronomic pilgrims from afar, wealthy tourists with prove-it looks, sweater-clad regulars leaning back in their chairs and laughing, and the Slow Food contingent, Europeans and Americans together. It was a highly heterogeneous crowd whom, if their common experience worked as Alice intended, the evening would conjoin in a brief community of delight.

To each table came a dish of olives, a basket of bread, and a small pot of butter; to each diner a slim glass of Prosecco, barely fizzy, scented with the house-made syrup of Meyer lemon—an apéritif concocted specifically to harmonize with that night's menu.

The wine list is neither short nor long, none of it cheap, though most of it reasonably priced. The waiters all know the wines well, but for each dinner Jonathan Waters, the restaurant's wine buyer, selects two whites and two reds that he considers particularly harmonious with the menu and good value as well.

A foursome of longtime friends of the house strolled into the kitchen to say hello to the cooks and the chef, and to see what was cooking. If a diner asks a question about the food that his waiter can't fully answer, the diner is likely to be invited into the kitchen, to talk to the cook responsible for the dish. The portions are adequate, but if someone especially likes something, and as long as there's enough, it's not a secret that the kitchen will gladly serve seconds.

The salad was a multirhythmic composition of textures, flavors, and temperatures: the fresh cèpes hot from the *sautoir,* slightly chewy, crisp at the edges, lightly garlicked, dressed with a very small amount of rather piquant vinaigrette, and sprinkled with infinitesimal flakes of parsley; the bits of pancetta warm, crisp, pungent, and salty; the leaves of the various crunchy chicories (red ones, yellow ones, Castelfranco freckled with pink, *pain de sucre* hued from pale at its center to bright green at its leaf tips) barely warm and softening slowly in the warmer vinaigrette, a milder one than that used on the mushrooms; and two quarters of boiled egg at room temperature, spotted with drops of bright green olive oil and glittering with crystals of sea salt.

After a pause came the soup. The stock on which it had been built was too complex for any but the finest of palates to tease out all the flavors, but it was not at all strong. Almost as light as water, it served merely to frame and focus the solid ingredients—half bites of pearlescent Dungeness crab, a small, tender square of house-salted cod, a few slices of poached fennel bulb, a sparse drizzle of finely chopped fennel fronds and chervil.

To drink with these, the waiter suggested a light-bodied white wine, perhaps a sauvignon blanc, a Muscadet, a verdejo—something with plenty of acid, he said, to stand up to the vinaigrette, and not too much fruit, in order not to blur the delicacy of the soup.

The three small slices of grilled lamb, each from a different cut, exhibited three palpably different textures, but they were uniformly rosy, slightly oak-smoky, and caramelized at the edges. There was not a strand of gristle, no silverskin, no rims of fat. They had been moistened with perhaps a tablespoon or two of intensely flavored lamb stock that at the last minute had been briefly infused with a bouquet of fresh coriander seeds. Despite its intensity and the exotic perfume of the coriander, the dark yet still transparent stock so discreetly deepened the savor of the meat that it was nearly imperceptible.

The tiny root vegetables accompanying the lamb were a palette of autumnal color—rust-orange carrots, pale green celery root, soft yellow rutabaga, cream-color parsley root, blue-white turnips, ivory salsify, apple-white Jerusalem artichoke, all bound with a little sweet butter.

Jean-Pierre Moullé favors aromatic, moderately extracted European red wines, with more finesse than power, such as classical Bordeaux and Burgundies, but he knows that the American fashion these days seems to be for the dense, thick, high-alcohol ilk of hot-climate zinfandel, syrah, and various reds from the sun-roasted slopes of southernmost France;

the Chez Panisse wine list offers some of each. The Green and Red zinfandel that is the Chez Panisse house red, which the waiter recommended to the first-time diners, nicely balanced power and finesse. It is the house wine for several characteristically Chez Panisse reasons. Its maker, Jay Heminway, has been a friend of Alice's ever since she was his daughter's teacher at the Berkeley Montessori School; the grapes are grown and vinified in entirely sustainable fashion; and the wine is delicious.

The diners' glasses were rarely empty, and never overfilled. The waiters will gladly chat, especially about the food, but if a party is deeply immersed in conversation, the staff becomes all but invisible. Look up, and someone will be there. There are no "zones"—any waiter will respond to any table.

As the food and the wine and the flowers and the staff did their work, there was more laughter, more talk. Strangers began chatting with one another. Old friends were changing seats. The newcomers, encouraged by the old-timers they had seen doing it, went in for a look at the kitchen and were welcomed.

As the meal wound down, so did the cooks and the waiters. Everybody was loosening up. The barriers of custom that separate stranger from stranger, server from served, frequently soften at this point in an evening at Chez Panisse, and sometimes they seem even to disappear.

Attentive observation by the dining-room staff determined when it was time to whip up the diners' soufflés and set them to bake. The soufflés arrived entirely unadorned. There were no cookies, no sauce—just a small individual bright yellow soufflé, sprinkled with powdered sugar, in the fluted white porcelain ramekin in which it had been cooked, sitting on a white paper doily on a plain white plate. When the first-time diners parted the tops with their spoons and the pure essence of lemon transformed into steam poured forth, they had made up their minds about Chez Panisse. At least a few customers may have shrugged, perhaps complained—portions too small! all this money for such plain food?—and they would probably never come back. But some of the people in the dining room that evening at Chez Panisse knew that they had had an experience they had never had in any other restaurant—somehow clearer, somehow clarifying.

OF THE PRECEDING seven weeks Alice had spent only six days at home in Berkeley. During her time away, she flew to North Carolina to raise money for the Edible Schoolyard; visited the Yale project; spoke at a dinner in New York for an organization that establishes community gardens in vacant lots throughout the five boroughs; flew to London, to meet with her new friend the Prince of Wales, an advocate of sustainable farming, whom she had persuaded to address some five thousand farmers, fishermen, artisans, winemakers, nomadic herders, and aquaculturists from all over the world at a convocation known as Terra Madre, an adjunct of Slow Food's biennial Salone del Gusto in Turin. From London Alice flew on to Turin to give a speech to Terra Madre herself, in which she asserted:

> I believe that the destiny of humankind in the twenty-first century will depend most of all on how people choose to nourish themselves. And if we can educate the senses, and break down the wall of ignorance between farmers and eaters, I am convinced—because I have seen it with my own eyes time and again—people will inevitably choose the sustainable way, which is always the most delicious alternative.

After a number of workshops, meetings, seminars, and more speeches, Alice introduced Prince Charles to the assembled multitude. "Slow Food," he began,

> is traditional food. It is also local—and local cuisine is one of the most important ways we identify with the place and region where we live. It is the same with the buildings in our towns, cities, and villages. Well-designed places and buildings that relate to the local-

ity and landscape and that put people before cars enhance a sense of community and rootedness. All these things are connected. We no more want to live in anonymous concrete blocks that are just like anywhere else in the world than we want to eat anonymous junk food which can be bought anywhere.

The prince is by far the biggest farmer in England, with well over a hundred thousand acres of land, on which he has been setting an example for an agrarian revolution perfectly in line with Alice's ideals—another pilot project, on an Olympian scale.

That evening, Alice returned to the village of Verduno—the scene of her triumphant dinner two years before—this time not as a harried chef but as the guest of the prince, at another restaurant owned by the Burlotto sisters, Cà del Re, which happens to mean "Castle of the King." The restaurant is in fact part of a modest *agriturismo,* a working farm that supplements its income by taking in guests. The next day, Alice and the prince visited one of Slow Food's most extraordinary projects, the University of Gastronomic Sciences—not a fledgling start-up but a complete university built from scratch. Housed in two beautiful old building complexes in the Piedmontese countryside, it has an international faculty of scholars trained in every possible field related to food, including soil science, anthropology, agricultural economics, food law and policy, microbiology, food service systems, plant and animal study, the geography of natural resources, the history of the agricultural landscape, cooking, tasting, and even the semiotics of food. Alice and Prince Charles also attended the annual Fat Ox Festival of a nearby village.

From Italy, Alice flew back to New York, to raise funds for the Chez Panisse Foundation, to lecture at the French Culinary Institute, and to meet with Gilbert Pilgram and David Tanis to ensure David's return as co-chef. Then it was on to Washington, where Alice was envisioning a temporary Edible Schoolyard as a living exhibit in the Smithsonian Folklife Festival. She saw it as a likely way to reach important members of the government and thereby to influence national school lunch policies.

The next day she was off to Ann Arbor, Michigan, to address a meeting titled "The Future of the Agrarian Adventure," and then, that night, to oversee a fund-raising dinner for the presidential campaign of Senator John Kerry, whose wife, Teresa Heinz Kerry, was rather more enthusiastic about a garden on the White House lawn than the Clintons had been.

And then, at last, she came home to Berkeley, for six days of nonrelaxation. Sylvan welcomed Alice to the Chez Panisse office with a bulging portfolio of obligations—dozens of phone calls, e-mails, restaurant decisions, foundation matters, personnel troubles, supplier questions, all clamoring for her immediate attention.

Those six days were a blur, and then Alice found herself on yet another long journey, this time to Nice, for yet another award, a banquet with the great chefs of Europe, a Bordeaux wine tasting, and—"Thank God!" she said—a couple of halcyon days at Bandol, in the sweet, soft, slow-moving world of Lulu Peyraud.

Paris was still to come, with a blowout seventy-fifth birthday party for Johnny Apple. The rest of the week was for herself, to eat, drink, breathe, and just *be in* Paris, where a bowl of soup, so long ago, set in motion the restless dream that became Alice Waters's life.

AS THE MONTHS rushed by, Alice seemed, impossibly, to be accelerating. The Edible Schoolyard became part of a broader campaign called Rethinking School Lunch. The Edible Schoolyard exhibit in Washington fed pizza—baked by kids—to a number of influential politicians, as Alice filled their brains with statistics. She changed the food service at the American Academy in Rome from steam-table cafeteria style to freshly cooked, seasonal local foods. The Chez Panisse Café turned twenty-five, with another big celebration. She lectured, she appeared on TV, she was photographed for *Vogue*. She started work on two new books. Gilbert Pilgram, exasperated at his inability to rein her in, resigned as general manager of Chez Panisse, and Alice threw him a grand, affectionate going-away party. He moved to Uruguay, but returned after a few months to buy Vince Calcagno's interest in the Zuni Café in San Francisco.

. . .

AND THEN ALICE BEGAN to take stock. The board of directors of Pagnol et Cie and she agreed that she was, for real this time, perilously close to being overwhelmed; the upshot was a six-month sabbatical—which in the event only slightly resembled a sabbatical. What it resembled was her normal life—office, meetings, phone calls, tasting, criticizing tiny but to her all-important details at Chez Panisse, more talks, more travel.

ALICE HAS TRAVELED somewhat more for pleasure than before, and at home she has begun to calm and clarify her life, with regular sessions of acupuncture, massage, yoga, and psychotherapy. She has lost weight, and toned up. Her friends say she has never looked so radiant. She believes that she has slowed down, though that is not always readily apparent to others.

Some of Alice's longtime friends still see the same little Alice they first knew, unchanged over the years. She does work hard to keep up with her old friends. Amid the swirl of her public life, she clings to private loyalties. She also makes new friends readily. Davia Nelson is a relatively new friend, and she sees recent change in Alice:

> She's more patient now, and more curious. More committed. The culture has caught up to where she has been all along, so these are the years when it's do or die for the planet, and she is part of that planetary crusade. So she is compulsively busy, but I think it's because she sees the sand in the hourglass.

Alice talks rarely of the past or her inner life. When asked when something happened, she often cannot remember. Her emotions are nearly always on the surface, open to anyone's scrutiny, and her mind, it seems, is nearly always on the present and the future. She sees the future in small things, highly specific goals, and at the same time on an almost inconceivably grand scale. "I'm completely dedicating this decade to public education," she says.

There are small things like writing a book and whatnot, but my immediate big hope is that we will have rolled out an organic lunch program in all seventeen schools in Berkeley. And that we will have integrated the curriculums of the grammar schools and the middle schools and the high schools with the school lunch program, and that ten thousand kids will be eating lunch as part of the academic day. And that we will be supporting any number of farmers and ranches and dairies that are within a couple of hours of the school district. And that we will have documented everything that has gone on. And that the children will have actually changed their eating habits, and that we will have stemmed the tide of obesity in Berkeley. That we will have our first graduates out, and that it will be so compelling and so delicious that the state of California will be contemplating a statewide program, and that they will be ready to take over the funding of the Berkeley program.

For Slow Food, my hope is that in ten years it will be a really

Alice and her Edible Schoolyard exhibit in Washington, D.C.

vibrant force for change in every country in this world. Slow Food for me is a huge commitment to seeing things in a global perspective. We can't talk about just the United States. We have to talk in this global way. A global vision.

The change in the scale of Alice's activities has been so great that the quantitative difference may be said to constitute a qualitative one. Yet she remains anchored to the old and the familiar: devoted to the same old restaurant and café on Shattuck Avenue, sometimes as chaotic behind the scenes as ever, nearly always nevertheless conveying an air of serene hospitality and serving a couple of hundred people every day some of the most delicious food they've ever tasted; devoted to Fanny, who has graduated from Yale and is studying art history at the University of Cambridge; devoted to her aging, ailing mom and dad, her sisters, her friends old and new; devoted to her garden, her mortar and pestle, the pleasures of talk and the table.

ACKNOWLEDGMENTS

My wife, Elizabeth, read this book in all its incarnations, including early ones that were pretty rugged going. She is my best critic, and she has been a patient, sympathetic, and loving partner throughout.

Alice Waters cooperated well beyond the scope of any possible obligation, and I will always be thankful for her generosity and sweet spirit.

Alice's friends and colleagues were also generous with their time and insight, especially Charles and Lindsey Shere, Fritz Streiff, Eleanor Bertino, Cristina Salas-Porras, David Goines, Barbara Carlitz, and the tireless, ever congenial Sylvan Brackett. The members of the staff of Chez Panisse were gracious and welcoming, even when I was endlessly underfoot in the kitchen. The chefs in particular—Christopher Lee, Kelsie Kerr, Russell Moore, Cal Peternell, Mary Canales, Alan Tangren, David Tanis, and Jean-Pierre Moullé—epitomized the Chez Panisse culture of intelligence and openheartedness.

R. W. (Johnny) Apple, Jr., who wrote this book's foreword, died on October 4, 2006. He was a dear friend to hundreds, and an inspiration to hundreds. He was both to me, and I will be forever grateful to him.

Colleen Bazdarich gave untold hours of time as my intern. I wish I could repay my debt to her in money, but it would never be enough. She and Wendy Jovero also put in many hours transcribing recordings of my interviews.

Susan Snyder guided me with care and caring through the labyrinthine mysteries of the Bancroft Library of the University of California at Berkeley.

I also owe gratitude to the various photographers whose work appears in these pages, some of whom are uncredited because I was unable to identify them.

I had two especially clarifying work-sabbaticals. The first consisted of two weeks at the incomparably tranquil Mesa Refuge at Point Reyes Station, California; to its creator and patron, Peter Barnes, my hearty thanks. The second mind-clearing interlude was a beautiful winter month at the home of my dear friend Miles Chapin in New York. His neighbor Sarah Black, with her talent for directness and simplicity, guided me toward a plainspoken voice in what until then had been a welter of contending styles.

Also in New York, Chip McGrath provided wise, cogent counsel at a time when I seemed unable to get a feel for the narrative as a whole. My first-ever and still-beloved editor, Bobbie Bristol, gave the manuscript a characteristically meticulous going-over. My agent, David McCormick, has been much more than an extraordinary business representative; his editing and editorial advice, though severe enough at times to be painful, prevented what threatened to be an embarrassing case of literary obesity.

At the Penguin Press, Liza Darnton, Alexandra Lane, Lindsay Whalen, and the boss, my esteemed editor Ann Godoff, have helped me in a thousand ways.

My father, Charles T. McNamee, Jr., ninety-three fierce years old, never let up encouraging me: "When are you going to finish that damn book, Tommy? Don't you want to get paid? Lord have mercy!"

NOTES

CHAPTER 2. SOUP, 1944–1965
1. Alice Waters, *The Chez Panisse Menu Cookbook* (New York: Random House, 1982).

CHAPTER 3. VERY SIXTIES, 1965–1966
1. See http://en.wikipedia.org/wiki/Sustainability: Wikipedia defines *sustainability* somewhat more elaborately, as "a systemic concept, relating to the continuity of economic, social, institutional and environmental aspects of human society, as well as the non-human environment. It is intended to be a means of configuring civilization and human activity so that society, its members and its economies are able to meet their needs and express their greatest potential in the present, while preserving biodiversity and natural ecosystems, and planning and acting for the ability to maintain these ideals in a very long term. Sustainability affects every level of organization, from the local neighborhood to the entire planet."

CHAPTER 5. VERY BERKELEY, 1971–1973
1. Alice Waters, "The Farm-Restaurant Connection," *The Journal of Gastronomy* 5, no. 2 (Summer/Autumn 1989).

CHAPTER 6. JEREMIAH, 1973–1975
1. Most people think of television as a much later invention, but the date here is correct.

2. The French here is incorrect, but it is what was printed on the menu. Correct usage would be *plat de fromages*.

3. See http://comenius.guymoquet.tripod.com/es1/cuisinier/corps.htm. Translation by the author.

4. Anthony Blake and Quentin Crewe, *Great Chefs of France* (New York: Harry N. Abrams, 1978).

5. This dictum is widely quoted in French gastronomic literature, but I have been unable to find the original source. Translation by the author.

6. Interview by Naomi Wise and Carol Field, *City* (San Francisco), April 16–29, 1975.

7. Jeremiah Tower, *California Dish: What I Saw (and Cooked) at the American Culinary Revolution* (New York: Free Press, 2003).

8. Kim Severson, *San Francisco Chronicle,* August 3, 2003.

CHAPTER 7. LAST BIRTHDAY? 1976

1. *New West,* May 9, 1977.

CHAPTER 8. ENNUI AND INSPIRATION, 1977–1978

1. Alice Waters and the cooks of Chez Panisse, in collaboration with David Tanis and Fritz Streiff, *Chez Panisse Café Cookbook* (New York: HarperCollins, 1999).

CHAPTER 9. CREATION AND DESTRUCTION, 1979–1982

1. Ella Elvin, *New York Daily News,* May 2, 1979.

2. Lois Dwan, *Los Angeles Times,* November 4, 1979.

3. Colman Andrews, *New West,* June 1979.

4. Mark Blackburn, *New York Times,* July 18, 1979.

5. Arthur Bloomfield, *San Francisco Focus,* March 1981.

6. Craig Claiborne, *New York Times,* June 3, 1981.

CHAPTER 10. REBAPTISM BY FIRE, 1982

1. Jeannette Ferrary, *San Francisco Chronicle,* August 1, 1982.

2. Paul Bertolli, with Alice Waters, *Chez Panisse Cooking* (New York: Random House, 1988).

CHAPTER 12. ALICE TAKES FLIGHT, 1985–1986

1. Charles Michener, with Linda R. Prout, *Newsweek,* November 29, 1982.

2. Barbara Kafka, *Vogue,* November 1982.

3. Jason Epstein, *House & Garden,* February 1983.

4. Stan Sesser, *San Francisco Chronicle,* November 25, 1983.

5. Marian Burros, *New York Times,* September 26, 1984.

6. Jeffrey Alan Fiskin, *California,* February 1985.

7. David Sundelson, *Nation,* September 25, 1982.

8. Robert K. Merton, "The Matthew Effect in Science," *Science,* January 5, 1969.

9. Blake Green, *San Francisco Chronicle,* August 14, 1984.

CHAPTER 13. DEATH AND LIFE, 1986–1987

1. Alice Waters, Chez Panisse sustainability statement, draft, 2000.
2. Charles Shere and the Chez Panisse Board of Directors, "Our Commitment to Sustainability," in *Chez Panisse Purveyors,* privately published, 2001. See http://www.chezpanisse.com/pgcommit.html.
3. Alice Waters, "The Farm-Restaurant Connection."
4. Mark Santora, *New York Times,* January 12, 2006.
5. Stan Sesser, *San Francisco Chronicle,* June 9, 1987.

CHAPTER 15. STAR POWER, 1991–1994

1. See http://www.etymonline.com/index.php?search=foodie&searchmode=none.
2. Michael Bauer, *San Francisco Chronicle,* March 17, 1993.
3. GraceAnn Walden, *San Francisco Chronicle,* August 13, 1993.
4. *Chicago Tribune,* August 13, 1993.
5. Monterey Bay Aquarium Seafood Watch: http://www.mbayaq.org/cr/cr_seafoodwatch/sfw_restaurants.asp.
6. See http://www.compass-group.com.
7. Rebecca Williams, Carol Ness, Carissa Remitz, and Deb Wandell, *San Francisco Chronicle,* February 15, 2006.

CHAPTER 16. INTO THE GREAT WORLD, 1995–2001

1. Marian Burros, *New York Times,* August 14, 1996.
2. Marian Burros, *New York Times,* June 10, 1998.
3. Adam Gopnik, *New Yorker,* October 26, 1998.

CHAPTER 17. AN EXTRAORDINARY DAY IN ITALY, 2001–2002

1. In October 2006, in its "red guide" for the San Francisco Bay Area, Michelin awarded Chez Panisse just that—one star.
2. Verlyn Klinkenborg, *New York Times,* April 30, 2006.

INTERVIEWS

In addition to these formal interviews, nearly all of them recorded, there have been many follow-up phone calls and e-mails.

Anderson, Bruce: September 23, 2005
Andrews, Colman: December 15, 2003
Apple, R. W., Jr.: December 31, 2003
Aratow, Paul: April 14, 2004; October 21, 2004
Asher, Gerald: November 10, 2004
Bauer, Michael: August 26, 2004
Bertino, Eleanor: April 10, 2003; May 10, 2004; May 17, 2004; October 27, 2004;
    July 29, 2005
Bertolli, Paul: September 30, 2003
Bishop, Willy: October 30, 2003; November 24, 2003
Brackett, Sylvan: March 3, 2004
Budrick, Jerry: October 29, 2004; November 17, 2004
Buell, Susie Tompkins: December 18, 2003; October 6, 2005
Cannard, Bob: December 19, 2003
Carlitz, Barbara: May 12, 2003; October 21, 2004; September 1, 2005
Carrau, Bob: October 10, 2003; January 19, 2004
Clarke, Sally: May 13, 2005
Constable, Ene: January 12, 2004
Cooper, Penny, and Rena Rosenwasser: November 22, 2004

Crumley, Steve: September 17, 2003
Cunningham, Marion: April 21, 2003
Curtan, Patricia: December 18, 2003
Danner, Mark: January 26, 2004
Dedlow, Phillip: October 18, 2005
Dencler, Amy: September 4, 2003
Donnell Lily, Nancy: April 20, 2004
Edwards, Pat: February 28, 2005
Epstein, Jason: December 10, 2003
Federman, Carolyn: September 26, 2005
Finigan, Robert: October 28, 2003
Flanders, Sara: July 26, 2004
Glenn, Carrie Wright: November 11, 2004
Goines, David: September 24, 2003; August 9, 2004
Goines, David, and Richard Seibert, September 6, 2005
Guerrero, Marsha: February 6, 2004
Gussow, Joan: December 10, 2003
Hamilton, Doug: December 30, 2003
Harrison, Jim: November 4, 2004
Heminway, Jay: June 22, 2004
Isaak, Anne: December 9, 2003
Jones, Sharon: May 8, 2003
Kerr, Kelsie: November 7, 2002
Knickerbocker, Peggy: December 19, 2003
Kraus, Sibella: March 25, 2005; September 26, 2005
Kummer, Corby: January 27, 2004
Labro, Claude and Martine: July 18, 2003
Lee, Christopher: February 13, 2003; September 4, 2003
Luddy, Tom: June 5, 2003
Lynch, Kermit: May 8, 2003
Marcus, Greil: June 22, 2004
Martins, Patrick: December 8, 2003
Maser, Jim and Laura: September 24, 2003
Messick, Robert: September 29, 2003
Meyer, Danny: December 9, 2003
Moore, Russell: November 7, 2002; July 30, 2003
Moullé, Jean-Pierre: October 8, 2003; March 7, 2005
Murphy, Sue: January 2, 2004
Nelson, Davia: May 3, 2004
Neyers, Barbara: July 5, 2006
Opton, Gene: November 11, 2004
Peternell, Michael: June 5, 2003
Petrini, Carlo: October 12, 2005
Peyraud, Lulu: July 17, 2003
Pilgram, Gilbert: September 4, 2003; September 26, 2005

Pisor, Ellen Waters: June 30, 2005
Reichl, Ruth: December 12, 2003
Rodgers, Judy: November 24, 2003; April 2, 2004
Salas-Porras, Cristina: September 12, 2002; November 7, 2002; February 11, 2003; March 3, 2004; October 10, 2005
Sandefer, Lee Ann: May 7, 2004
Savinar, Tim: May 5, 2003
Scheer, Robert: November 4, 2003
Seibert, Richard: November 10, 2003
Shere, Charles and Lindsey: July 15, 2002; April 2, 2003; October 17, 2003; November 29, 2003; March 6, 2004
Singer, Fanny: December 30, 2003
Singer, Mark: December 8, 2003
Singer, Stephen: June 3, 2003
Streiff, Fritz: June 23, 2003
Sullivan, Steve: October 31, 2003
Tangren, Alan: April 24, 2004
Tanis, David: July 24, 2003
Tower, Jeremiah: May 17, 2003; February 4, 2004
Trillin, Calvin: December 15, 2003
Waag, Nathalie: April 19, 2004
Waters, Alice: August 13, 2001; October 27, 2002; November 20, 2002; February 2, 2003; February 5, 2003; March 11, 2003; March 13, 2003; March 24, 2003; April 3, 2003; April 11, 2003; July 1, 2003; October 3, 2003; October 9, 2003; November 25, 2003; December 4, 2003; January 12, 2004; January 13, 2004; January 21, 2004; February 27, 2004; May 19, 2004; July 15, 2004; July 29, 2004; August 5, 2004; November 10, 2004; January 5, 2005; September 22, 2005; October 13, 2005; January 3, 2006; May 9, 2006; July 3, 2006; July 5, 2006; July 9, 2006
Waters, Jonathan: October 3, 2003
Waters, Pat and Marge: April 21, 2003
Waxman, Jonathan: February 2, 2005
Wise, Victoria (née Kroyer): October 20, 2003; June 11, 2004

BIBLIOGRAPHY

A number of the following works are not cited in the text, but all contributed to my understanding of Alice Waters and Chez Panisse.

Alexander, Christopher, Sara Ishikawa, and Murray Silverstein. *A Pattern Language*. New York: Oxford University Press, 1977.

Arnold, Ann. *The Adventurous Chef: Alexis Soyer*. New York: Farrar, Straus & Giroux, 2002.

Beard, James. *Delights and Prejudices: A Memoir with Recipes*. New York: Macmillan, 1964.

Berger, Frances de Talavera, and John Park Custis. *Sumptuous Dining in Gaslight San Francisco, 1875–1915*. Garden City, N.Y.: Doubleday, 1985.

Bertolli, Paul, with Alice Waters. *Chez Panisse Cooking*. New York: Random House, 1988.

Blake, Anthony, and Quentin Crewe. *Great Chefs of France*. New York: Harry N. Abrams, 1978.

Bocuse, Paul. *Paul Bocuse's French Cooking*. New York: Random House, 1977.

Brillat-Savarin, Jean Anthelme. *The Physiology of Taste*. Translated and annotated by M. F. K. Fisher. San Francisco: North Point Press, 1986.

Britchky, Seymour. *The Lutèce Cookbook*. New York: Alfred A. Knopf, 1995.

Caen, Herb. *Herb Caen's New Guide to San Francisco and the Bay Area*. Garden City, N.Y.: Doubleday, 1957.

Chabon, Michael. "Berkeley." *Gourmet,* March 2002. Reproduced at http://www.michaelchabon.com/berkeley.html.

Chapel, Alain. *La Cuisine: C'est Beaucoup Plus que des Recettes*. Paris: Éditions Robert Laffont, 1980.

Claiborne, Craig. *The New York Times Guide to Dining Out in New York*. New York: Atheneum, 1970.

Claiborne, Craig, Pierre Franey, and the editors of Time-Life Books. *Classic French Cooking*. New York: Time-Life Books, 1970.

Cooper, Artemis. *Writing at the Kitchen Table: The Authorized Biography of Elizabeth David*. New York: Ecco Press, 1999.

Curnonsky. *Traditional French Cooking*. New York: Doubleday, 1989.

———. *Traditional Recipes of the Provinces of France*. Translated and edited by Edwin Lavin. Garden City, N.Y.: Doubleday, 1961.

Daria, Irene. *Lutèce: A Day in the Life of America's Greatest Restaurant*. New York: Random House, 1993.

David, Elizabeth. *French Provincial Cooking*. London: Michael Joseph, 1960.

Davidson, Sara. *Spare Change: Three Women of the Sixties*. Garden City, N.Y.: Doubleday, 1977.

De Groot, Roy Andries. *The Auberge of the Flowering Hearth*. Hopewell, N.J.: Ecco Press, 1973.

Echikson, William. *Burgundy Stars: A Year in the Life of a Great French Restaurant*. Boston: Little, Brown, 1995.

Fernández-Armesto, Felipe. *Near a Thousand Tables: A History of Food*. New York: Free Press, 2002.

Fitch, Noël Riley. *Appetite for Life: The Biography of Julia Child*. New York: Doubleday, 1997.

Forbes magazine. *Forbes Magazine's Restaurant Guide*. Vol. 1. New York: Forbes, 1971.

Foster, Lee, ed. *The New York Times Encyclopedic Almanac 1971*. New York: The New York Times Book and Educational Division, 1969, 1970.

Frommer, Arthur B. *Frommer's Dollar-wise Guide to California*. New York: Simon & Schuster, 1966.

Girardet, Frédy, with Catherine Michel. *The Cuisine of Frédy Girardet.* Translated and annotated by Michael and Judith Hill. New York: William Morrow, 1985.

Goines, David Lance. *The Free Speech Movement: Coming of Age in the 1960s.* Berkeley, Calif.: Ten Speed Press, 1993.

Gourmet magazine. *Gourmet's France.* New York: Gourmet Books, 1978.

Hess, John L., and Karen Hess. *The Taste of America.* Urbana and Chicago: University of Illinois Press, 1972–2000.

Imhoff, Daniel. *Farming with the Wild: Enhancing Biodiversity on Farms and Ranches.* San Francisco: Sierra Club Books, 2003.

Jutkovitz, Serena. *SJ's Winners: An Exceptional Approach to Round-the-World Wining and Dining in the San Francisco Bay Area.* San Francisco: Russian Hill House Books, 1982.

Kimbrell, Andrew, ed. *Fatal Harvest: The Tragedy of Industrial Agriculture.* Washington, D.C.: Island Press/Foundation for Deep Ecology, 2002.

Kuh, Patrick. *The Last Days of Haute Cuisine: America's Culinary Revolution.* New York: Viking, 2001.

Levenstein, Harvey. *Revolution at the Table.* Berkeley: University of California Press, 2003.

Lovegren, Sylvia. *Fashionable Food: Seven Decades of Food Fads.* New York: Macmillan, 1995.

Lynch, Kermit. *Adventures on the Wine Route: A Wine Buyer's Tour of France.* New York: North Point Press, 1988.

Merton, Robert K. "The Matthew Effect in Science." *Science,* January 5, 1969, 56–63.

Montagné, Prosper. *Larousse Gastronomique: The Encyclopedia of Food, Wine, and Cookery.* New York: Crown Publishers, 1961.

Nabhan, Gary Paul. *Coming Home to Eat: The Pleasures and Politics of Local Foods.* New York: W. W. Norton, 2002.

Olney, Richard. *The French Menu Cookbook.* Boston: David R. Godine, 1970; rev. ed., 1985.

———. *Simple French Food.* New York: Macmillan, 1974.

Olsen, Alfa-Betty, and Marshall Efron. *Omnivores.* New York: Viking, 1976, 1979.

Pagnol, Marcel. *Marius Fanny César.* Paris: Le Club du Meilleur Livre, 1956.

Patrick, Ted, and Silas Spitzer. *Great Restaurants of America.* New York: Bramhall House, 1960.

Pellaprat, H.-P., et al. *The Art of French Cooking.* Translated by Joseph Faulkner. New York: Golden Press, 1962.

Pellegrini, Angelo. *The Unprejudiced Palate: Classic Thoughts on Food and the Good Life.* San Francisco: North Point Press, 1984.

Petrini, Carlo, ed., with Ben Watson and Slow Food Editore. *Slow Food: Collected Thoughts on Taste, Tradition, and the Honest Pleasures of Food.* White River Junction, Vt.: Chelsea Green Publishing Co., 2001.

Pico, Leonce, ed. *Restaurants of San Francisco.* Fort Lauderdale, Fla.: Gourmet International, 1963.

Planck, Nina. *Real Food: What to Eat and Why.* New York: Bloomsbury, 2006.

Rabaudy, Nicolas de. *La Cuisine de Chez Allard.* Paris: Éditions Jean-Claude Lattès, 1982.

Reardon, Joan. *M. F. K. Fisher, Julia Child, and Alice Waters: Celebrating the Pleasures of the Table.* New York: Harmony Books, 1994.

———. *Poet of the Appetites: The Lives and Loves of M. F. K. Fisher.* New York: North Point Press, 2004.

Robbins, John. *The Food Revolution: How Your Diet Can Help Save Your Life and the World.* Berkeley, Calif.: Conari Press, 2001.

Root, Waverly, and Richard de Rochemont. *Eating in America.* New York: William Morrow, 1976, 1995.

Rorabaugh, W. J. *Berkeley at War: The 1960s.* New York: Oxford University Press, 1989.

Ruhlman, Michael. *The Soul of a Chef: The Journey Toward Perfection.* New York: Viking, 2000.

Schlosser, Eric. *Fast Food Nation: The Dark Side of the All-American Meal.* New York: Houghton Mifflin, 2001.

Shere, Lindsey Remolif. *Chez Panisse Desserts.* New York: Random House, 1985.

Slow Food Editore. *Terra Madre: 1200 World Food Communities.* Bra, Italy: Slow Food Editore Srl, 2004.

Sokolov, Raymond. *Why We Eat What We Eat: How Columbus Changed the Way the World Eats.* New York: Touchstone, 1991.

Stein, Jean, and George Plimpton. *Edie: An American Biography.* New York: Alfred A. Knopf, 1982.

Theophano, Janet. *Eat My Words: Reading Women's Lives Through the Cookbooks They Wrote.* New York: Palgrave Macmillan, 2003.

Todhunter, Andrew. *A Meal Observed.* New York: Alfred A. Knopf, 2004.

Toklas, Alice B. *The Alice B. Toklas Cookbook.* New York: Harper & Brothers, 1954.

Tower, Jeremiah. *California Dish: What I Saw (and Cooked) at the American Culinary Revolution.* New York: Free Press, 2003.

———. *Jeremiah Tower's New American Classics.* New York: Harper & Row, 1986.

Troisgros, Jean and Pierre. *The Nouvelle Cuisine of Jean and Pierre Troisgros.* London: Macmillan, 1980.

Visser, Margaret. *Much Depends on Dinner.* New York: Grove Press, 1986.

———. *The Rituals of Dinner.* New York: Grove Weidenfeld, 1991.

Waters, Alice. *Chez Panisse Fruit.* New York: HarperCollins, 2002.

———. *The Chez Panisse Menu Cookbook.* New York: Random House, 1982.

———. "The Farm-Restaurant Connection." *The Journal of Gastronomy* 5, no. 2 (Summer/Autumn 1989): 113–22.

———. Foreword to *Lulu's Provençal Table: The Exuberant Food and Wine from Domaine Tempier Vineyard,* by Richard Olney. New York: HarperCollins, 1994.

———. Foreword to *My Father's Glory and My Mother's Castle,* by Marcel Pagnol. New York: North Point Press, 1986.

———. Foreword to *Slow Food: The Case for Taste,* by Carlo Petrini. New York: Columbia University Press, 2001.

———. "Tea and Cheese in Turkey." In *The Kindness of Strangers,* edited by Don George. Melbourne: Lonely Planet Publications, 2003.

Waters, Alice, with Bob Carrau and Patricia Curtan. *Fanny at Chez Panisse.* New York: HarperCollins, 1992.

Waters, Alice, and the cooks of Chez Panisse. *Chez Panisse Vegetables.* New York: HarperCollins, 1996.

Waters, Alice, and the cooks of Chez Panisse, in collaboration with David Tanis and Fritz Streiff. *The Chez Panisse Café Cookbook.* New York: HarperCollins, 1999.

Waters, Alice, Patricia Curtan, and Martine Labro. *Chez Panisse Pasta, Pizza, & Calzone.* New York: Random House, 1984.

Wechsberg, Joseph. *Blue Trout and Black Truffles: The Peregrinations of an Epicure.* New York: Alfred A. Knopf, 1966.

Wuerthner, George, and Mollie Matteson, eds. *Welfare Ranching: The Subsidized Destruction of the American West.* Washington, D.C.: Island Press/Foundation for Deep Ecology, 2002.

INDEX

Page numbers in *italics* refer to illustrations.

ILLUSTRATION CREDITS

ABOUT THE AUTHOR

Thomas McNamee was born in 1947 in Memphis, and grew up there and in New York City. He graduated from Yale University in 1969. His essays, poems, journalism, and natural history writing have been published in *Audubon, The New Yorker, Life, Natural History, High Country News, Town & Country,* the *New York Times,* the *Washington Post,* and a number of literary journals. He has written many book reviews for the *New York Times Book Review.* He wrote the documentary film *Alexander Calder,* which was broadcast on the PBS *American Masters* series in June 1998 and received both a George W. Peabody award and an Emmy.

The position of religion in the American state university is one of tacit compromise.

The state cannot champion religion. The university cannot ignore it. But state universities—government-created and tax supported—are responsible for more than half of the nation's higher education. What should they do, what can they do, in fact what do they do to live with this dilemma?

In lively, trenchant, often controversial chapters the experts tackle the question. A Catholic, a Protestant, and a Jew examine the setting. Leading educators deal with the history and the legal aspects of the problem, with religion as a way of knowing, with academic freedom, and with the role of religion in the teaching of the humanities, the social and the natural sciences, and the professions. Outstanding administrators, church leaders, student directors, and theologians describe the place of religion on some of the great state university campuses: the problems in counseling students, the functions of religious centers, the trend toward interreligious activities, the difficulties in interreligious understanding, the mythology of the present college generation.

Here, for students and all those interested in them—parents, personnel workers, community leaders, church leaders, religious counselors, college administrators—is the best current thinking on the place religion holds or should hold in higher education.

It would seem that the process of unmaking them is already importantly afoot. Protestantism, for instance, now feels its own inner discordant pluralisms as no longer an unqualified glory but as something of a scandal. And in the Ecumenical Movement it is in quest of its own unities. Catholicism in turn now feels that certain of its past unities were something of a scandal; there is, for instance, the unity asserted in Belloc's famous thesis that "Europe is the faith and the faith is Europe." In consequence the Church is asserting with sharper emphasis its own proper sacramental unity, altogether universal, altogether spiritual, not enfeoffed to any historical culture but transcendent to every culture at the same time that it is a leaven in all cultures. Again, Europe has realized that its modern pluralisms of many kinds, of which it was once boastfully jealous, are importantly the cause of its own present impotence. The "good European" has now emerged, and his quest is for some manner and measure of unity that will begin for Europe a new history and regain for it a due share of its lost significance in the realm of historical action. The Communist too, whether Soviet or Chinese, cherishes his own dream of a demonic unification of the world. And in the United States, finally, the problem of unity in its relation to the pluralisms of American society has begun to be felt with a new seriousness.

True enough, the problem is not seldom raised in a way that is false. One thinks, for instance, of the New Nativism, as represented by Mr. Paul Blanshard; or of the issue of "conformism," about which there is so much confused talk; or of the current anxieties about internal subversion, regarded as a threat to an American unity ("there are those among us who are not of us"). And so on. But even the falsities attendant upon the manner in which the issue of unity-amid-pluralism is raised bear witness to the reality of the issue itself.

The question has been asked: How much of the pluralism is bogus and unreal? And how much of the unity is likewise bogus —and undesirable? The more general question has also been asked: How much pluralism, and what kinds of pluralism, can a pluralist society stand? And conversely, how much unity, and what kind of unity, does a pluralist society need in order to be a society at all, effectively organized for responsible action in history, and yet a "free" society?

Similarly, certain words have now acquired a respectability that was long denied them—the word "order," for instance, which now is disjunctively coupled with the word "freedom," with the fading of the typically modern illusion that somehow "freedom" is itself the principle of order.

Finally, responsible and informed thinkers can now discourse about the "public philosophy" of America, considering it to be a valid concept which furnishes the premises for dissent, to be identified as dissent even though the public philosophy itself contains no tenets that would justify coercion of the dissenter. In the same fashion serious inquiries are now made into the American consensus—the question being not whether such a thing exists but what it is and whence it came and how it may be kept alive and operative by argument among reasonable men. Moreover, since every social consensus that supports and directs the historical action of a given political community is always to a considerable extent a legacy from an earlier age, questions have been asked about the American heritage and about the manner in which it has developed. Has the America of today been true to its own spiritual origins? Indeed, were the principles that lay at its origins ambiguous to some extent, so as to permit various lines of development, not all of them happy? Is the American man of today an "exile from his own past" (as Geoffrey Bruun said of European man)?

The central point here is that the quest for unity-amid-pluralism has assumed a new urgency in the mind of post-modern man.

In this connection it might be well to advert to the fact that, since St. Augustine's description of the "two cities," it has been realized that societal unity may, broadly speaking, be of two orders—the divine or the demonic. It is of the divine order when it is the product of faith, reason, freedom, justice, law, and love. Within the social unity created by these forces, which are instinct with all the divinity that resides in man, the human personality itself grows to its destined stature of dignity at the same time that the community achieves its unity. Societal unity is of the demonic order when it is the product of force, whether the force be violent or subtle. There are, for instance, all the kinds of force that operate in the industrial society created by modernity (irrational political propaganda, commercial advertising, all the assaults upon reason and taste that are launched by mass amusements, and the like). These forces operate under the device of "freedom," but unto the disintegration of the human personality, and unto the more or less forcible unification of social life on a level lower than that established, forever, by Aristotle's "reasonable man" and his Christian completion. The quest for unity-amid-pluralism must therefore be critical of its own impulses. Its stimulus must not be passion, whether the passion be imperialist (the will to power) or craven (fear and anxiety).

What then might be the attitudes and functions of the university in the face of the problem of pluralism as newly presented at the outset of the post-modern era? The premise of the question is the fact that the Basic Issues have come to matter to men in a new way. Does this fact matter to the university? Many of the commitments of modernity—shared by the university, because it too has been modern—have dissolved in disenchantment. Does their dissolution make any difference to the university? The positivistic universe (if the phrase be not a contradiction *in adiecto*) has come to seem a wilderness of disorder to the soul of man, which cannot be content to live in chaos since it is always aware, however dimly, that it is natively committed to the discovery of an order in reality or, alternatively, to the imposition of an order on reality at whatever cost both to reality and to itself. Is post-modern man's new commitment to order of any interest to the university?

I know, of course, that the word "commitment," used in regard to a university, raises specters. I am not myself fond of the word; it is more distinctively part of the Protestant vocabulary, which is not mine; and moreover the dictionary adds to its definition: ". . . esp. to prison"! In any case, some nice questions center around the word. Is the university, as a matter of fact, uncommitted? And in what senses or in what directions? Is "non-committalism" an intellectual virtue or is it what Gordon Keith Chalmers called it, a "sin"? Is a commitment to "freedom," understanding "freedom" to be a purely formal category, any more a valid premise of the intellectual life than a commitment to the Kantian *Moralprinzip*, understood as a purely formal category, is a valid premise for the moral life? "Handle so. . . ." Indeed. But *what* am I to do? And analogously in the former case, what is this "truth" for which I am to be "free" to search?

Leaving these interesting questions aside, I might better come to more concrete matters and venture a few assertions of a practical kind. First, I venture to assert that the university is committed to the task of putting an end, as far as it can, to intellectual savagery in all its forms, including a major current form, which is the savagery of the American student (perhaps the professor?) who in all matters religious and theological is an untutored child of the intellectual wilderness. Again, the university is committed to the task of putting an end to prejudice based on ignorance, by helping to banish the ignorance. Unless indeed the university wishes to commit itself to the prejudice that religious knowledge is really ignorance.

The assertion I chiefly wish to venture, however, is that the university is committed to its students and to their freedom to learn. Its students are not abstractions. And whatever may be the university's duty (or right, or privilege, or sin) of non-committalism, the fact is that many of its students are religiously committed. To put it concretely, they believe in God. Or to put it even more concretely, they are Protestants, Catholics, Jews. The university as such has no right to judge the validity of any of these commitments, so called. Similarly, it has no right to ignore the fact of these commitments, much less to require that—for the space, say, of four years—its students should be content to become scientific naturalists within the university, whatever else they, somewhat schizophrenically, may choose to be outside its walls.

The major issue here is the student's freedom to learn—to explore the full intellectual dimensions of the religious faith to which he is committed. He comes to college with the "faith of

the charcoal burner," of course. And it is the right of the university to require that his quest of religious knowledge should be pursued in the university style—under properly qualified professors, in courses of high academic content, in accordance with the best methods of theological scholarship, and so on. But this right of the university should itself conspire with the student's own freedom to learn, so as to create the academic empowerment that is presently almost wholly lacking. A college and university student is academically empowered to grow in all the dimensions of knowledge—except the dimension of religious knowledge.

What is the formula for translating the student's freedom to learn about his religious faith into a genuine empowerment? The question would have to be argued; and it might not be possible to devise a uniformly applicable formula.

In any case, the formula of the "religious emphasis week" is hopelessly inadequate; and when it becomes simply a piece of public relations it is also unworthy of a university. Again, the formula of a "department of religion" is no good, unless the "religion" of the department includes the major historic faiths, which is rarely the case. As for a "department of religion *and* philosophy," it chiefly serves to confuse the issue. In its most destructive concrete mode of operation it blurs the clear line of distinction that traditional Christianity has drawn between the order of faith and the order of reason. (Incidentally, it is not for the university to say that this line ought to be blurred, or moved from its traditional position.)

Whatever the concrete formula may be, it must reckon with the factual pluralism of American society, insofar as this pluralism is real and not illusory. There can be no question of any bogus irenicism or of the submergence of religious differences in a vague haze of "fellowship." And here, lest what I said above about the "unmaking" of modern pluralism should be misunderstood, I should add a clarification. It is not, and cannot be, the function of the university to reduce modern pluralism to unity. However, it might be that the university could make some contribution to a quite different task—namely, the reduction of modern pluralism to intelligibility.

This is an intellectual task. It bears upon the clarification of the pluralism itself. The Protestant charcoal burner today knows well enough that he differs from the Catholic charcoal burner, and vice versa. But it is not so certain that either could say why, in any articulate fashion. And if one or the other should undertake to give reasons, they would probably be mistaken, or distorted, or unclear, or even irrelevant. Anyone who has attended a run-of-the-mill college "bull session" will know this.

From this point of view I would specify two general academic objectives that a college or university could legitimately aim at in the field of religious knowledge as its contribution to a clarification of the problem of pluralism.

The first is a genuine understanding of the epistemology of religious truth—or, if you will, of the nature of religious faith. It is precisely here that modern pluralism has its roots. Karl Barth was making this point when he said, in effect, that it is no use discussing whether we believe in common certain articles of the creed, when we are in radical disagreement on what is the meaning of the word with which the creed begins, "Credo." It is in consequence of this radical disagreement that Catholicism and Protestantism appear as, and are, systems of belief that bear to each other only an analogical relationship. That is to say, they are somewhat the same, and totally different. One would expect the mature Catholic and Protestant mind to understand this fact, which takes a bit of understanding.

The second understanding—and academic objectives can be stated only in terms of understanding—would be of the systems of belief, precisely as systems, in their inner organic consistency (whatever it may be), and in their relation to other areas of human knowledge (insofar as these relations are intellectually discernible).

These two objectives are not unworthy of an institution of higher learning. They also coincide with the objectives that the student should be made free to reach. If he did reach them, he would be on emergence from college less a rustic than when he entered. And would not his college gently rejoice? The preservation of rusticities can hardly rank high among the preoccupations of the college dean.

When considered in terms of these two objectives, the practical difficulties appear less formidable than they are sometimes thought to be. There may indeed be some three hundred religious bodies in America. But there are not that many "styles" of religious belief. In fact, there are generically only three—the Protestant, the Catholic, and the Jewish. They are radically different "styles" and no one of them is reducible, or perhaps even comparable, to any of the others. And in each case the style of the epistemology is related to the structure of the theology (or possibly to the absence of a theology).

The academic content of possible courses would be no great problem, except as it involves selection from a wealth of materials. The Catholic theological tradition is a treasury that even lifelong study cannot exhaust. Judaism has its learning, rich and venerable. And today the Protestant has the task of assimilating the already great, and still growing, body of ecumenical theology. No college or university should have to worry about its academic standards if it were to turn its students loose, under expert guidance, into these three great storehouses of thought.

Under expert guidance—that might be the greatest practical problem. Specially trained men would be needed. One could only hope that they would become available as opportunities opened before them. For the rest, I should only insist on one principle. It was stated by John Stuart Mill when he said that every position should be explained and defended by a man who holds it, and who therefore is able to make the case for it most competently. This is, in a special way, a restatement of the principle upon which St. Augustine tirelessly dwelt: "*Nisi credideritis, non intelligetis.*" The communication of understanding supposes its possession. I do not myself accept the pedagogical canon that seems to be popular in university circles: every position ought to be explained by one who is sympathetic with it but who personally rejects it. It has never seemed to me that this is a canon of "objectivity" at all. Nor does it insure the communication of a critical understanding of the position in question, given the principle that only an immanent critique, as it is called, can lead to this desirable type of under-

standing. In any case, my own view is that the only path to genuine understanding of a religious faith lies through the faith itself. The possession of the faith is therefore the proper qualification of the professor who would wish to communicate a critical understanding of it.

These are but a few practical suggestions toward a definition of the role of the university in the face of the problem of pluralism today. In conclusion, it should go without saying that the function of the university is not at all messianic. It is entirely minimal. The Basic Issues, deeply considered, do in the end raise in the mind of man the issue of "salvation." But if post-modern man hopes for salvation, he must set his hope elsewhere than on the university. Henry Adams' gratitude to Harvard for its contribution to his intellectual development is the highest gratitude that the university can merit from man in search of salvation. Harvard, said Adams in effect, did not get in my way. But this is no small cause for gratitude when the issue at stake is salvation.

WILL HERBERG

The Making of a Pluralistic
Society—A Jewish View

CHAPTER II

In some sense, all societies, even the most monolithic, have
been pluralistic, for there has never been a society without a
wide diversity of interests, opinions, and conditions of life.
Yet when we speak of a pluralistic society, we mean something more. We mean a society in which these diversities not
only exist as a matter of fact but are recognized, accepted,
perhaps even institutionalized into the structure and functioning of the social order. In this sense, American society is
thoroughly pluralistic, but pluralistic in a very specal way, with
its own characteristic freedoms and limitations. The shape of
American pluralism helps define the underlying pattern of
American life, within which emerge the so-called "intergroup"
problems confronting us today, on campus or off, and in terms
of which they must be confronted and dealt with.

The pluralism of American society is the product of its
history, and therefore reflects its inmost being, for the inmost
being of men and their societies is essentially historical. From
the very beginning, America has been a land of diversity striving for unity. And from the very beginning too, the diversities
have been racial, ethnic, cultural, and religious, whereas the
unity striven for has been that of a new "way of life" reflecting
the "new order of the ages" established in the New World
(*novus ordo seclorum,* the motto on the reverse of the Great

Seal of the United States). This was the vision that fired the imagination of Hector de Crèvecoeur, the author of the celebrated "Letters from an American Farmer," who was so eager to interpret the new American reality to the Old and New World alike. "Here," Crèvecoeur proclaimed proudly in 1782, "individuals of all nations are melted into a new race of men, whose labors and posterity will one day cause great changes in the world." Thus early was the "melting pot" philosophy explicitly formulated, and thus early did the problem of unity amidst diversity, and diversity amidst unity, emerge as the perennial problem of American life.

The conception implied in the image of the "melting pot" (or the "transmuting pot," as George R. Stewart prefers to call it) has always been subject to a misunderstanding that is itself not without significance. When, at least until recently, Americans spoke of the "melting pot" (although the term as such did not come into use until the first decade of this century), they generally had in mind a process by which the foreign "peculiarities" of language and culture that the immigrants brought with them from the old country would be sloughed off in the course of Americanization, and a new homogeneous, undifferentiated type of American would come into being. Against this, the apostles of "cultural pluralism" protested; they stressed the richness of the immigrant cultures, deplored their threatening dissolution, and advocated a multicultural, even multinational society along familiar European lines. Both—the theorists of the "melting pot" and the "cultural pluralists"—gravely misunderstood the emerging pattern of American pluralism.

For American pluralism, through all its changes and mutations, has remained characteristically American, quite unlike the pluralistic patterns prevailing in other parts of the world. The sources of diversity have been different, and the expressions of it even more so. By and large, we may say that since the latter part of the nineteenth century, the sources of American pluralism have been mainly race, ethnicity, and religion, with section or region playing a diminishing, though in some cases still significant role. It is in terms of these that Americans have tended, and still tend, to define their identities amidst the totality of American life. The process of enculturation perpetuates the pattern. "When asked the simple question, 'What are you?'" Gordon W. Allport has noted, referring to certain recent researches, "only 10 per cent of four-year-olds answer in terms of racial, ethnic, or religious membership, whereas 75 per cent of nine-year-olds do so." "Race" in America today means color, white vs. nonwhite, and racial stigmatization has introduced an element of caste-like stratification into American life. For white Americans, ethnicity and religion have been, and still remain, the major sources of pluralistic diversity, though the relation between them has changed drastically in the course of the past generation. It is this change that provides a clue to an understanding of the present-day shape of American pluralism and of the place of religion in American life.

As long as large-scale immigration continued, and America was predominantly a land of immigrants, in the days when "the immigrants were American history," as Handlin puts it, the dominant form of self-identification, and therefore the dominant source of pluralistic diversity, was immigrant ethnicity. Religion was largely felt to be a part of the ethnic heritage, recent or remote. The enthusiasts of the "melting pot" were eager to eliminate this diversity as quickly as possible; the "cultural pluralists" were determined to perpetuate it; but both alike moved within the framework of a pluralism based substantially on ethnicity, ethnic culture, and ethnic religion.

Within the past generation, the picture has been radically transformed. The stoppage of the mass immigration during World War I, followed by the anti-immigration legislation of the 1920's, undermined the foundations of the immigrant ethnic group with amazing rapidity; what it did was to facilitate the emergence of the third and post-third generations, with their characteristic responses and attitudes, as a decisive influence in American life, no longer threatened with submergence by the next new wave of immigration. This far-reaching structural change has, of course, been reflected in the shape and form of American pluralism. Specifically, within the threefold American scheme of race, ethnicity, and religion, a shift has taken place from ethnicity to religion as the dominant form of self-identification, and therefore (as we have noted) also the dominant form of pluralistic diversity. Ethnic identifications and traditions have not disappeared; on the contrary, with the third generation, as Marcus Lee Hansen has cogently shown, they enjoy a lively popularity as symbols of "heritage." But now the relation of ethnicity and religion has been reversed: religion is no longer taken as an aspect of ethnicity; it is ethnicity, or rather what remains of it, that is taken up, redefined, and expressed through religious identifications and institutions. Religion—or at least the tripartite differentiation of Protestant, Catholic, Jew—has (aside from race) become the prevailing source of pluralistic diversity in American life. American pluralism is today (again aside from race) characteristically religious pluralism, and all problems of American unity and diversity have to be interpreted in the light of this great fact.

From this standpoint, the basic fact in the shaping of contemporary American pluralism is the transformation of America in the course of the past generation from a Protestant country into a three-religion country.

Writing just about thirty years ago, André Siegfried described Protestantism as America's "national religion," and he was very largely right, despite the ban on religious establishment in the Constitution. Normally, to be born an American meant to be a Protestant; this was the religious identification that in the American mind quite naturally went along with being an American. Non-Protestants felt the force of this conviction almost as strongly as did the Protestants; Catholics and Jews, despite their vastly increasing numbers, each experienced their non-Protestant religion as a problem, even as an obstacle, to their becoming full-fledged Americans: it was the mark of their foreignness. (This was true despite the much-esteemed colonial heritage of both Jews and Catholics, since it was not the "old American" elements in these two groups that influenced American attitudes but the newer immigrant masses.) In the familiar Troeltschean sense (that is, a form of religious belonging which

is felt to be involved in one's belonging to the national community), Protestantism, not any of the multiplying denominations but Protestantism as a whole, constituted America's
"established church."

This is no longer so. Today, unlike fifty years ago, Catholics
and Jews as well as Protestants feel themselves to be Americans not apart from, or in spite of, their religion, but because
of it. If America today possesses a "church" in the Troeltschean
sense, it is the tripartite religious system of Protestant-Catholic-
Jew.

This transformation of America from a Protestant into a three-
religion country has come about not as a result of any marked
increase in the ratio of Catholics or Jews in the population—
the Protestant-Catholic ratio has remained almost the same for
the past thirty years and the proportion of Jews in the general
population has probably been declining. It has come about, as
I have already suggested, as an accompaniment of the shift in
the pattern of self-identification, and therefore also in the
source of pluralistic diversity, from ethnicity to religion.

This religious pluralism, built into the very structure of
American life, receives explicit institutional expression in the
expanding interfaith pattern. The interfaith movement and,
even more, the interfaith "idea," articulates the new shape of
American life, and therein lies its characteristic appeal to the
American mind. Indeed, as the older ethnic identifications
tend to fade out with the appearance of a stabilized third generation, there is a growing feeling that unification along interfaith lines is the most appropriate way of expressing the
comprehensive unity of the American people. Since the pluralism of American life is so largely a religious pluralism, the
symbol of all-American co-operation in every good cause
naturally becomes "interfaith."

Thus, the "I am an American Day," originally observed to
demonstrate the American unity of the various ethnic-immigrant
groups that make up our population, is now celebrated along
interfaith lines. "Protestants, Catholics, and Jews, with a Negro
chairman, united to celebrate I am an American Day . . ." is
how one New York newspaper reported the event last Septem-

ber. Once Protestants, Catholics, and Jews are included, it is felt, then all Americans are included, and the way to include all Americans in any enterprise is to establish it along inter-faith—that is, tri-faith—lines.

This emerging pattern of American pluralism as religious pluralism would seem to be particularly significant for the campus community, for among the younger people on the campus the older forms of pluralistic diversity (ethnicity, re-gionalism) play a relatively small role, whereas the newer categories of religion, with their rich connotation of "heri-tage" and "belonging" along American lines, are acquiring a growing appeal. From this one may not draw any unequivocal conclusions as to the extent or quality of the "religious boom" on the campus or off; one cannot, however, overlook the fact that the problem of pluralism on the campus is (aside from race) a problem of religious pluralism, even more so than it is in the American community at large.

But before we can pursue this line of inquiry much further, we must raise another question. American pluralism, it has often been noted, is not simply plurality; it is also unity: it is, in fact, best designated by the term *pluriunity*—a unity in plurality as well as a plurality in unity. *E pluribus unum*: this phrase, which was originally employed to celebrate the unifica-tion of the thirteen colonies into the new nation, will serve very well as the formula for American pluralism as it has developed through the decades since the Civil War.

What is this unity that has supplied the centripetal force in American life, or (to change the image) the common frame-work within which the pluralistic allegiances find both their freedom and their limits? This unity is the unity of the Amer-ican Way of Life.

It is not easy to put into words just what the American Way of Life is, or how it functions to provide the over-all unity for the pluralistic diversity of American society. Perhaps the most important thing to say about it is that for the American, the American Way of Life is that by virtue of which he is an Amer-ican. Germans tend to interpret their common "Germanness" in terms of "race" (in the peculiar German sense); Frenchmen tend to interpret their common "Frenchness" in terms of "culture"; Americans, with their incredible diversity of race, culture, and national origin, find their unity, their common "Americanness," in their adherence to, and participation in, the American Way of Life. This provides them with their common allegiance and their common faith; it provides them, to use the words of the sociologist Robin M. Williams, Jr., with "the common set of ideas, rituals, and symbols" by which an "overarching sense of unity" is achieved amidst diversity and conflict. If the pluralism of contemporary American society is primarily a religious pluralism, the unity within which this pluralism is expressed and contained is a unity of the American Way of Life.

This means that in effect the "three great faiths" appear to increasing numbers of Americans as three alternative (though not necessarily equal) expressions of their common "Americanness." They are esteemed because they are felt to be at bottom three different versions of the same set of "moral and spiritual values of democracy," that is, of the American Way of Life on its religious side. Interfaith co-operation is understood as the co-operation of those who, whatever their belief, are after all Americans, sharing the same values and commitments. In other words, precisely because the pluralism of American life is so largely a religious pluralism, the overarching unity that contains this pluralism tends itself to be invested with a quasi-sacred character. What a philosopher like Horace M. Kallen states explicitly when he proclaims the "democratic faith" to be "the religion *of* and *for* religions . . . all may freely come together in it," is essentially implicit in the ethos of American life and finds expression in many of its social and cultural patterns.

The peculiar structure of American pluralism—religious diversity given unity through being interpreted as diverse expressions of the same overarching system of values and commitments —confronts Protestant, Catholic, Jew, and secularist alike with a series of complicated and perplexing problems.

The secularist naturally finds embarrassing the almost universal tendency of Americans to identify themselves religiously and to interpret their religious identification as the particular expression of their Americanness; for, under these circumstances, the man who refuses to "belong" religiously tends to be viewed with suspicion as somehow not truly American, very much as Catholics and Jews were looked upon until a generation or two ago. "There is a tendency," Sidney H. Scheuer, a leader of the Ethical Culture movement, recently complained with a great deal of justice, "to regard all people who are not committed to one of the three great faiths as being disloyal to American principles and traditions." This is true also on college campuses, even though on college campuses the proportion of those who refuse to associate themselves with one or another of the "three great faiths" is considerably higher than that among the population as a whole, and there is still a residual tendency, especially among the faculty, to pass off such refusal as evidence of enlightenment and nonconformity. Confronted with these pressures of the environment (soon internalized so that the deviant himself begins to feel something wrong with his attitude), and no longer so sure of the antireligious gospels and philosophies of yesterday, the secularist has, in recent years, tended to lose his fervor and to discover unexpected virtues of a social and psychological character in religion, provided it is not too "orthodox" or institutionalized for his taste. Thus what might be called a proreligious secularism has arisen in the wake of the great upsurge of religiousness that is sweeping the country today.

On the other side, Protestants, Catholics, and Jews who take their faith seriously are equally embarrassed by the way the religious situation is shaping up, though for rather different reasons. They find much of the religiousness that is engendered when religion comes to serve as a definition of identity and a vehicle of "belonging" in a pluralistic society to be shoddy, superficial, and void of authentic religious content. They are particularly perturbed by the current tendency in American culture to "religionize" democracy, Americanism, or the American Way by turning it into a great, overarching "common faith" to provide a quasi-sacred bond of unity for the multifarious diversity of American life. They see religion becoming progressively secularized in a climate in which secularism itself is becoming proreligious without ceasing to be secularistic.

This secularization of American religion was already well advanced by the end of the last century as far as Protestantism was concerned. "During the second half of the nineteenth century," Sidney E. Mead notes, "there occurred a virtual identification of the outlook of . . . denominational Protestantism with 'Americanism' or 'the American way of life.' . . . The United States, in effect, had two religions, or at least two different forms of the same religion, and . . . the prevailing Protestant ideology represented a syncretistic mingling of the two. The first was the religion of the denominations. . . . The second was the religion of the democratic society and nation" ("American Protestantism Since the Civil War," *Journal of Religion,* January 1956). As long as they remained foreign and therefore marginal, Judaism and Catholicism were little affected by this trend. As they became American, however, they fell under the same influences, and began to exhibit the same characteristic syncretism. What took place, and not in this respect alone, was the "Protestantization" of the non-Protestant religions of America.

It is necessary to understand these concerns of the secularist and the man of faith alike if we are to grasp the profound ambiguity of the present religious situation, reflecting the new type of American pluralism that has emerged in the course of the past generation.

While the new structure of American pluralism is becoming increasingly evident to all observers, it is envisaged rather differently by Protestant, Catholic, and Jew. The tripartite structure of American pluralism is thus reflected in a profound trilogue about the value and significance of the new reality. As Kenneth Underwood has recently pointed out, the three "faith groups" confronting the religious pluralism of mid-twentieth-century America tend to see and emphasize different aspects of it: Catholics "search for signs of a 'reintegration' of Western society" about the natural law, the "public philosophy," and the ageless wisdom of the Church; Protestants find evidence that a "vital diversity of religious groupings has been assured"; and Jews tend to stress the parity of the "three great faiths" in a three-religion country united by common "spiritual values." Perhaps my insistence on the transformation of America into a three-religion country as the key to an understanding of contemporary American pluralism may be traced to this Jewish "angle." I recognize that I am seeing and assessing American reality from a certain standpoint, but I do not think that this standpoint, while of course partial, constitutes much of a distorting bias; rather, I think, it encourages a fresh approach to what is after all essentially a new situation.

From this standpoint, one must recognize that there is great positive value in the contemporary three-religion pluralism. It is, of course, true that pluralism is not simply or unequivocally good, and a unitary society simply and unequivocally bad; no human order is ever simply and unequivocally either one or the other. Nor are the "liberal" arguments for pluralism—that in a pluralistic competition "the truth" will somehow prevail, and that diversity itself is a primary value and pledge of vitality —particularly impressive, especially as they relate to religion. Yet as a Jew, I do feel that the creative dialectic tension between Judaism and Christianity that I see implied in the divine purpose is, in many ways, advanced by our three-religion pluralism, though in other ways stultified; and as an American, I value pluralistic diversity (up to a point) as providing a kind of built-in system of checks and balances upon inordinate power: here I do but follow the logic of the Founding Fathers. It is true that religion is not to be reduced simply to its institutions or to be identified with its institutional power; yet religious institutions do exist, do tend to accumulate power and use it in ways that make limitation and control necessary in the interests of justice. A pluralistic setup, it seems to me, provides such limitation and control in a way that involves the least interference from the outside, and therefore the greatest freedom for religion.

Yet, as I have indicated, I do not regard pluralism or diversity as necessarily and intrinsically good, certainly not an unqualified good. Much of present-day Protestant enthusiasm for "vital and genuine diversity" in religion strikes me as simply an echoing and re-echoing of liberalistic naïvetés, with little relation to authentic Lutheran, Calvinist, or sectarian tradition. Here I find the Jewish position, somewhere between the Catholic emphasis on unity and the liberal-Protestant worship of diversity for the sake of diversity, more plausible, more viable, and more realistically related to the interests of religion and society. At any rate, it seems to offer a fruitful approach to the kind of religious pluralism that is emerging in America today.

The American college campus, particularly the state university, is in many ways a microcosm of the religious pluralism that characterizes present-day America. The tripartite division is taken for granted on the campus, despite a number of groups here and there that refuse to accommodate themselves to it. On the college campus, too, there is the so-called secularist element, a little more self-conscious perhaps, and certainly more numerous, than in the outside world. And in the background looms the "race question," which, though it does not concern us directly at this point, does after all constitute as basic an aspect of American pluralism as the religious pluralism we have been discussing.

I think it is fair to say that virtually all Americans who have given any thought to the matter are thoroughly dissatisfied with the present state of the relations between religion and education, particularly public education. This is true for all levels of the educational system, though it seems to be felt most disturbingly at the level of the elementary school. On the university level, the problems are, of course, very different, though perhaps even more complex, for it is on this level that the concern for objectivity and academic integrity is greatest and the fear of "outside influences" most acute.

It is by no means easy even to formulate the problem, but perhaps it may be put this way: the place that is granted to religion in the university scheme of things, at least on most campuses, does not correspond either to a sound conception of higher education or to the essential requirements of contemporary American religious pluralism.

Public education in this country emerged at a time when "nonsectarianism" meant the exclusion of any particular religious denomination from control or special influence, not the exclusion of religion as such; indeed, the public schools were for decades, and in some parts of the country still continue to be, what one might call generalized Protestant schools. With the increasing number of Catholics and Jews becoming part of American life, especially in the urban centers, this understanding of "nonsectarian" could not long remain viable; the phrase soon came to mean "nonreligious," since there seemed to be no way of meeting the obviously justified complaints of the non-Protestant minorities, who were compelled to send their children to what were essentially Protestant schools, except by altogether eliminating religion from education. This trend played in very well with the ideological secularism that toward the latter part of the nineteenth century began to make substantial inroads among the educated classes in this country. The extrusion of religion from education, especially higher education, was now justified on the ground that religion was of no intellectual significance, little more than an outmoded superstition and at best only the cultivation of private sentiments and ideals. It was in this period that many of the state universities came into being or received their definitive character; it was in this period, too, that many of the older colleges abandoned their church connections and transformed themselves into secular institutions, in this respect indistinguishable from the state universities. It was very much in line with the temper of the times, the temper of modernity.

The official theory ran that the university was neutral in matters of religion, not only as to the various kinds of religion to be found among the American people but as between religion and nonreligion, even antireligion. The university would have nothing to do with religion; let religion be taken care of, insofar as taken care of it must be, by denominational church groups off the campus. But of course this was a delusion; the extrusion of Christianity from the campus (there was as yet no question of Judaism) meant not the pursuit of the academic enterprise without any over-all commitments; it meant the replacement of Christianity by some secularistic pseudo-religion, usually some brand of naturalism or positivism, that soon began to acquire an almost official status. This suited the secularist intellectuals to a T and as long as the modern temper prevailed among the educated classes, the trend went un-challenged. The Catholics established their own institutions; and the Jews of the first or second generation who aspired to a higher education were even more secularist-minded than the rest.

But we are no longer living under the sign of modernity. Within the past generation, a profound cultural change has taken place in the Western world. The mind that has emerged from this change is a post-modern mind. It no longer takes the secularist philosophies of the nineteenth and early twentieth century as self-evident; to many these philosophies have be-come totally discredited, to almost all they have lost their earlier appeal. The collapse of modernity has not, or has not yet, led to any significant spiritual reconstruction; confusion, anxiety, and search are the marks of our time. But the pre-suppositions of modernity are gone and with them the presup-positions of religionless education.

It is no longer self-evident, especially among the younger and more sensitive people, that religion is simply emotion without intellectual content. On the contrary, the religious thinkers of today—I have in mind such men as Maritain, Berdyaev, Buber, Tillich, Niebuhr, and of course Kierkegaard, who is to all intents and purposes a contemporary—enjoy a remarkable prestige as vanguard thinkers, not only among "re-ligionists," but particularly among those concerned with so-called "secular" interests—psychiatrists, historians, political scientists, poets, educators, and literary critics. Religion—yes, theology—is recognized as having its intellectual relevance, and no institution of higher learning can be said to live up to its responsibility if it does not take this fact into account.

The philosophies of secularism can no longer claim pre-scriptive right in the university on the ground that they are not special commitments at all, but simply reason and science. They are special commitments, even quasi-theologies, and this is being widely acknowledged today. What the man of faith now demands, and this demand is beginning to make more sense than it has made for decades, is that his "philosophy," his *Weltanschauung*, his way of seeing and understanding things, his principle of integrating knowledge and experience, be given the same rights and privileges in the academic world as are the secularist philosophies, the same free course of learning and teaching. It is hard to find a ground, apart from the discredited dogmas of secularism, on which this demand can be refused.

If this is the first demand, the second is that the actualities of American pluralism be taken into account in relating religion to higher education. Catholics and Jews certainly have good grounds for complaint on this score. Most of the departments of religion in our colleges and universities (and even more, the administrative machinery of the campus religious work) reflect the older situation when Protestantism was America's "national religion," rather than the present situation in which the three religions of America are on a par, at least as far as public life is concerned. Rarely does a department of religion on a campus include a Catholic, and almost as rarely a Jew, even where large numbers of Catholic and Jewish students are to be found. This is surely indefensible, and the discrimination is not mitigated but rather compounded when the Protestantism that prevails is no more than a debased kind of "liberal religionism." It ought to be possible, and in a number of cases it actually has proved possible, to devise some form of tri-faith co-operation that would achieve the necessary unity and allow for the equally necessary diversity in the work of an effective department of religion. How effective any department of religion can hope to be under the present circumstances is another question.

But while the actualities of American religious pluralism must be taken into account, they must also be transcended. For American religious pluralism, let us remember, has two faces. On the one side, it brings the "three great faiths" together into a common framework; but, on the other side, this framework tends to be their common Americanness, more precisely the "moral and spiritual values" implied in the American Way of Life. These "values" are indeed worthy ones—some, in fact, are admirable—but religions that allow themselves to be defined in terms of the prevailing culture, however admirable, can never hope to be more than culture-religions, devoid of any genuine religious or prophetic power. This is the great danger confronting our historic faiths today, and it is a danger the more insidious because the threat comes from friend, not from foe. Those of us who are concerned about achieving a new relation between religion and higher education ought to be at least equally concerned about safeguarding and, where need be, restoring, the authentic content of faith, for otherwise the religion that is related to education will be little more than a spiritualized version of the current cultural values and convictions.

The "three great faiths" belong together, but they belong together not because they are "religions of democracy." They belong together because they are the religions of the Bible. The real and significant bond between them, in other words, is not that they are all American, but that they are all Biblical: we all, insofar as we are truly Christians or Jews, recognize Abraham as our father and the God of Israel as our God. The differences between the three religions are not trivial; they are very real and often of quite crucial importance, not to be dissolved into a generalized commitment to "religion" or "democracy." Yet they are differences within a common religious framework, usually designated as the Judeo-Christian tradition, and it is this common religious framework that, in my conception, gives ultimate religious meaning to the American tri-faith pluralism and to every effort to relate this tri-faith pluralism to the enterprise of higher education.

ROLAND H. BAINTON

The Making of a Pluralistic
Society — A Protestant View

The University of Michigan has long been dedicated to the view that religion belongs on the campus. Many another institution, in recent years, has been moving to the same conviction. All are confronted by the fact that their students are adherents of diverse faiths. In addition to the three main religions in America each with its own subvarieties, there is a fourth, which might be called the religion of Enlightenment, a Christianity attenuated as to doctrine and accentuated as to social idealism. Thomas Jefferson was its high priest and our democracy is its daughter. These three or four varieties have learned after wars of religion to co-exist. They do so because of the triumph of the philosophy of the Enlightenment. Start talking about religious differences with the common man and he will exclaim, "At bottom we are all the same. We believe in God. We believe in goodness; the rest does not matter." This is precisely the point of view, in the Renaissance, of Boccaccio, with his story of the three identical rings representing Christianity, Judaism, and Islam, a story re-employed by that great figure of the Enlightenment Ephraim Lessing as a theme for his play *Nathan the Wise*. It was the philosophy of John Locke, who averred that if he were on the road that leads to Jerusalem it was of no consequence whether he wore buskins, cut his hair short or long, ate or refrained from meat, or had as a guide one clothed in white and crowned with a miter. Such trivial points as these, said he, make implacable enemies of Christians, "who are all agreed in the substantial and truly fundamental part of religion."

This point of view is very prevalent, but it does not so far prevail as to make possible a unified religious program on the part of the three or four groups in the university. The Catholics, the Protestants (especially the Fundamentalists), and the Orthodox Jews will not admit that the points of difference are trivial. The liberal Jews and the liberal Protestants are closer to the philosophy of the Enlightenment, though they too, and notably today, would not relegate doctrine so blithely to the area of the nonessentials.

The degree to which this pluralism obstructs a program of religion in the universities depends somewhat on the reason for which the inclusion of religion is desired. One reason for introducing religion into the curriculum—and a perfectly valid reason—is that religion is a subject of universal interest with regard to which every educated man should have at least a modicum of understanding because religion has been so determinative in the formation of cultures. The number of religions is of no consequence here save to increase the amount and the complexity of the material to be studied. There may still be a question whether or not courses should be taught by adherents of the several faiths. For the most part this would be impossible on budgetary grounds, and even if it were possible to employ a Protestant, a Catholic, and a Jew as professors of religion, similar consideration could not be extended to teachers representing all the religions of the world. The most defensible technique would resemble that used for the languages where a philologian directs a course with the aid of native informants; thus an expert on comparative religion might supplement his offerings with lectures by members of the religions expounded.

But no one of the three main religions in our land is satisfied with only this approach. All would claim that religion is something more than anthropology or sociology or history and that one cannot really understand religion without being religious. The sincere adherent of a faith must desire ultimately, however adroit the approach, to make converts because he believes

that his particular faith has the answer to life's most fundamental questions and problems.

What shall we say of this our universe which increasing
knowledge discloses as ever more appallingly vast, whose extent is measured only in terms of light-years, and whose dura-
tion dwarfs the life of man to less than the span of an insect?
Evidence of staggering intelligence we see in its intricate
structure and delicate balance, evidence of purpose in its
dynamic, creative self-elaboration, and differentiation within
organic wholeness. But is there here any friendliness to man?
In the bleak recesses of stellar space, in the nuclear explosions
of solar radiation, in the erratic and devastating course of
tornadoes, in the eruption of volcanoes, and in the cooling of
planets, is there anything but the inexorable working of an
inscrutable purpose indifferent to mankind? Have we been
accorded by capricious fate a temporary haven on a sun-bask-
ing planet only that, after the mind of man has exploited every
resource for survival, we shall at last succumb when our earth
has become as extinct as the craters of the moon? And what
of all those who have gone before and of those who are yet to
come? What is the destiny of those who have labored in the
morning of man, carving bisons on the walls of their caves,
of those who for millenia followed unchanged the ancestral
ways of the forest primeval? Of those who throughout the
centuries have by searching found out some of the secrets and
added to the treasure house of knowledge? Are they now and
shall we shortly all be resolved into the dust from which we
came without the answers we crave to those riddles? And
what of the grave inequalities that life inflicts, the barbarous
torments that men have suffered at the hands of men? Is there
no vindication? And for those who have so sinned against their
fellows, is there no forgiveness? If we must answer "No,"
straight down the line, what then is the meaning of life and of
mortality? We may indeed say with the resolute poet brooding
over the recession of faith, "Let us be true then, love, to one
another." But how great a place have love and honor in a universe where man alone has evolved and cherishes such ideals?
And to come to our own situation, what is the point of foster-

ing universities and of acquiring more knowledge perchance with the consequence of hastening man's destruction? Or should we perhaps use our science to get it over with and not wait for the great freeze to encompass a burned-out world?

If religion has the answers to such universal questions, surely no subject could be more appropriate in a university dedicated to the quest of knowledge. But now comes a difficulty that is accentuated though not created by religious pluralism. Judaism and Christianity are religions of historic revelation. They announce a way to truth which is not that of the university, because revelation is conceived by all of these religions, at least in their more naïve stages, as something given in times past, a deposit to be accepted and elucidated, not to be questioned, whereas for the university truth is a quest where nothing is to be taken for granted and every hypothesis subjected to critical scrutiny. Truth as a deposit and truth as a quest, can these concepts coexist?

The notion of truth as a quest is derived from our Hellenic heritage. This was the presupposition of Socrates, of Plato, of Aristotle. The idea had a rebirth in the Renaissance when Erasmus applied it to the study of the Scripture. The classic formulation was given by that Renaissance Puritan John Milton, who declared that in theology as in arithmetic the golden rule is, "To be still searching what we know not by what we know, still closing up truth to truth as we find it." He was confident that in so doing truth would emerge. "Let truth and falsehood grapple; whoever knew truth put to the worse in a free and open encounter?" Father Murray asks us whether we can any longer be so naïve as to believe that. Now of course we have seen that the enemies of free encounter can so take advantage of free encounter as to destroy it. But the point was that among a company of seekers, all dedicated to free encounter, in which each would propound his hypothesis for the criticism of his colleagues, where each stood ready to convince or be convinced, truth would prevail. A further ingredient in this faith is that, "Truth crushed to earth will rise again." This second assertion is indeed a faith rather than a fact, and even the first does not admit of unexceptional verification. But it is the best method we have of arriving at truth, and it is the fundamental assumption of our universities.

The great religions claim that truth, though in some measure an object of a quest, in its most important phase (as it relates to the ultimate) is the subject of a deposit. Truth is given through a self-disclosure of God at definite times in the past and recorded in inspired sacred writings. The most unqualified form of this claim is made by the Roman Catholic church. Father van de Pol says:

Holy Scripture and the Church have always presented revelation as the making known by God of certain definite truths which before were hidden in the mind of God, but now, at the end of time, are announced and made known to all who believe. From the beginning, revelation, preaching, and faith have had a definite and unchangeable scope and content. These truths have always been proclaimed by divine authority, and it is precisely on account of this that they call for unconditional belief and unhesitating obedience on the part of man. The act of faith involves a complete surrender of man to the revelation of God, and to the authoritative teaching of the contents of this definite, final revelation.[1]

This is not to say that the revelation as given in scripture is explicit in every respect. Precisely because it is not, God has endowed the Church with the power of inerrant elucidation, and this power is focused on the pope. He is not an organ of revelation but only of explication. He is the unique recipient of that aid from the Holy Spirit which will so watch over his normal processes of reasoning that in making deductions from the revelation already given in the areas of faith and morals, when and only when he makes a pronouncement binding upon all Catholics, will he then be infallibly preserved from error.

The Catholic church claims, then, to be the custodian of the revelation given through Christ and recorded in the Scriptures, capable of formulation in doctrinal propositions and susceptible of further elaboration by inerrant deduction.

Is it possible, apart from religious diversity, to combine such a position with regard to the way to truth with that assumed by the modern university? It was done, of course, in the medieval university where theology was the queen of the sciences, and it was accomplished by a demarcation of sphere. Certain disciplines, such as physics, rest upon the inquiry of the human mind. Here the pagan Aristotle was regnant. Only theology proper dealt with revelation. Yet conflict arose even in the medieval university, and notably between philosophy and theology, when the philosophy in vogue came to be nominalism, which claims that reality consists of unrelated particulars, or more precisely, of particulars related only by contiguity in space and time. Difficulty arises when this view is applied to the doctrine of the Trinity, whose three persons transcend space and time. If, then, they have no relation save contiguity in space and time, the three persons in the Godhead become three unrelated absolutes, and the outcome in tritheism. The exponents of this view agreed that it did not comport with the theological teaching that the three are one. The solution was found in the doctrine if not of double truth at least of double logic.

The situation today is not vastly dissimilar. Catholic theology is compatible with natural science on the basis of a division of spheres, and many distinguished scientists are Catholic. In the area of philosophy only the Thomist's position is congruous with Catholic theology, and even in the natural sciences conflicts may arise and have arisen as in the case of Genesis versus geology and evolution. The pope has ruled that Adam was a real person from whom the human race is descended, an assumption with which no non-Catholic biologist would be ready to commence. One may wonder whether Catholicism can be genuinely at home in any university other than in a Catholic university. In any university whatever, Catholic theology could be taught but only by declaring itself to be at variance with some or at least an aspect of some of the other disciplines.

With regard to non-Catholics the case is different, and here it is that religious pluralism injects a difficulty at the most central point, the very concept of revelation. The Fundamentalist Christian and presumably the Orthodox Jew—as to Judaism I am less well informed than as to Christianity—find revelation in the Scriptures, which are taken to be entirely inerrant. Yet they do have to be interpreted, as the Roman Catholic church rightly insists, and what happens is that each Christian sect has its own scheme of interpretation. Once I sat in on an interchange between a Christadelphian and a Jehovah's Witness. They appeared to me to be of the same stripe, but they were quite unable to achieve common ground because of discrepant modes of interpretation. Fundamentalists are of course able in a university to do distinguished work in all of the disciplines not at variance with their own faith, and they may even fulfill the requirements of courses in a theology contrary to their own by mastering the body of information. A Fundamentalist can take a doctor's degree in religion in a liberal institution by being open to every fact and impervious to every idea. The purpose in so doing is to use the degree as a weapon with which to combat the point of view of the institution by which the degree was conferred. There may be some point in continuing such a situation because it does mean that in a measure a channel of possible communication is kept open. Yet one cannot but regard the case as sad if in religion the meeting of minds and hearts cannot go beyond the factual.

Those who belong to the liberal group among the non-Catholics entertain a view of revelation distinctly different from that both of the Catholics and of the conservatives in their own bodies. The term liberal is here used for those who have accepted the methods of historical criticism as applied to the sacred books and are not disposed in any case to think of revelation in terms that can be reduced to neat proposition. In this sense Barth, who has lavished so much criticism on Protestant Liberalism, is himself in many respects in the liberal camp.

Three examples may serve to illustrate differing views of revelation. The first is that of Berdyaev, a representative of the Russian Orthodox Church. He may be considered because he has been much read in American Protestant seminaries and because his point of view has its parallels in some phases of Protestant Liberalism as it did also in Catholic Modernism. "Revelation," says Berdyaev, "is not something which drops into a man's lap from outside and in which he has nothing but an entirely passive part to play." Berdyaev is the heir of that mysticism of the Eastern Church, not unknown to the Western, which finds the goal of religion in the union of man with God so that man himself is made divine. In the experience of union the distinction between faith and reason disappears because this belongs to the world of objectification. Revelation cannot be objectified. It cannot be formulated into propositions which in themselves are true or false. Revelation is a spiritual event. The truth which it communicates must be grasped integrally. Unless truth takes place in a man truth is not obtained. Revelation makes use of historical facts as symbols. "The Christian conception of the divine Incarnation ought not to mean the deification of historical facts. Christian truth cannot be made to depend upon historical facts, which cannot be fully attested nor ingenuously accepted as reality."[2]

This statement leaves one wondering as to the relation of faith and history. Is revelation the continuous self-disclosure of God in mystical experience for which the records of history provide only a garment of symbol or are we capable of receiving revelation in personal experience only because of the unique self-disclosure of God in the past? Berdyaev might respond to this question as he did to another: "There is," said he, "a question which is put by people who are wholly submerged in objectification and consequently in the spirit of authoritarianism. It is, 'Where then is there a fixed and abiding standard of truth?' And to that question I decline to give my answer."[3]

The second example is that of a Protestant layman, a Congregationalist and a natural scientist, Edmund Sinnott, who in his work *Two Roads to Truth* describes the one as the way of intellect, reason, science; the other as a way of insight, intuition, unreasoned assurance, instinctive feeling. The second way is strongly akin to aesthetic sensibility.

Beauty is a subtle, indefinable thing. Great art and poetry and music, nature's innumerable and radiant beauties—these set man's spirit singing. They warm his heart and wake within him a sense of glory and delight, lifting him to such ecstasy that, like the religious mystic, he becomes for a little while a higher sort of being, in tune with mysterious harmonies.[4]

The insight of the individual is incalculably indebted to the past—to the Hebrew and Christian past—yet is not to be restricted by the past. He continues:

Where all things thus are on the march it seems to the scientist the height of folly to try to tie up truth within the limits of a dogma, either philosophical or religious, and to deny the possibility of fuller understanding even of spiritual matters. Reverence for the past should never become a strait jacket for the present. Insistence on a truth that is certain and perfect, never to be changed, science repudiates. . . . Science respects the past, but builds upon it for a greater future. Why, one asks, should we not expect religion to have the same expansiveness, the same splendidly growing vision of the truth, as it explores mysteries deeper than science can ever probe? . . . He who told Simon to launch out into the deep would never counsel timid conservatism in such matters or seek to pour the truth's new wine into bottles of dogmatic certainty. "The worship of God," says Whitehead, "is not a rule of safety—it is an adventure of the spirit, a flight after the unattainable. The death of religion comes with the repression of the high hope of adventure."[5]

With this view of revelation the conflict between truth as a deposit and truth as a quest disappears. The difference lies between truth as sight and truth as insight.

The third example is afforded by Richard Niebuhr, a Protestant theologian, a liberal as to historical criticism, but with a much deeper feeling for revelation in history than one finds in Berdyaev's questing for obliteration of objective distinctions through union with the divine. Richard Niebuhr understands revelation as the disclosure of meaning in history and in life. The prophets by revelation illumined the history of Israel and gave to the men of their day an understanding of the memories of their people. Jesus, born in the fullness of time, brought to life the meaning of the convergence of the religion of the Hebrews and the philosophy of the Greeks.

Revelation continues ... The work has not been completed, for the past is infinite, and thought, even with the aid of revelation, is painful, and doubt assails the human heart. But for the Christian church the whole past is potentially a single epic. In the presence of the revelatory occasion it can and must remember in tranquillity the long story of human ascent from the dust, of descent into the sloughs of brutality and sin, the nameless sufferings of untold numbers of generations, the groaning and travailing of creation until now—all that otherwise is remembered only with despair. There is no part of that past that can be ignored or regarded as beyond possibility of redemption from meaninglessness. And it is the ability of the revelation to save all the past from senselessness that is one of the marks of its revelatory character.[6]

Such revelation cannot be set forth in a set of articles true or false. One does not assent to revelation as true simply by agreeing that it is so. The discovery of meaningfulness in life and history has to be felt, not simply believed, and it will not be felt unless there is first an inner transformation. "The response to revelation is quite as much a confession of sin as a confession of faith." What revelation

means for us cannot be expressed in the impersonal ways of creeds or other propositions but only in responsive acts of a personal character. We acknowledge revelation by no third person proposition, such as that there is a God, but only in the direct confession of the heart, "Thou art my God." We can state the convincement given in the revelatory moment only in a prayer saying, "Our Father." Revelation as the self-disclosure of the infinite person is realized in us only through the faith which is a personal act of commitment, of confidence and trust, not a belief about the nature of things.[7]

Such a view of revelation does not involve the discrepancy of the Catholic and Fundamentalist view as against the scientific, but it raises a much more profound question as to whether revelation can be taught at all. What will one do in a university with a course which must start with a confession of sin, and cannot the most untutored man make such a confession and receive the answer that gives meaning to his life and all that he knows of life? What then will one do with revelation in a university? The answer is that one can study the records of religious experience, the Bible as religious experience, religious biography as experience of religion. One can discover how others were brought to these moments of insight. An artist told me that he had no feeling for El Greco, but he looked and studied and observed and exposed himself until there burst on him an awed response to the clouds brooding over Toledo. It is the same with poetry and music. They can be studied by way of exposure. They will never be known until the spirit lists to blow.

If then there are differences so deep between the three religions and between varieties within these religions, how can religion be presented in a university where all three and more are present? Reconciliation of their divergent viewpoints is at present out of the question. Father van de Pol says that Protestants and Catholics must regard each other as heretics. He does not attach to the word all of the old invidious connotations. He is not issuing a summons for an auto-da-fé. He uses heretic in its primitive sense as one who is in error. Catholics hold out to Protestants no hope of reunion save by way of submission on our part, and we find the claims of Rome altogether untenable. The doctrine of papal infallibility is a great hinderance. We realize that the pope is claimed to be infallible only when he speaks on faith and morals, only when he elucidates previous revelation, and only when he speaks officially and makes his pronouncement binding upon all Catholics. He may in an unofficial statement be guilty of heresy as was Pope Honorius. Again Leo XIII pronounced the text in I John 5, which reads, "And there are three in heaven that witness, the Father, the Spirit and Son," to be an authentic part of this epistle, though not discoverable in any manuscript prior to the fifteenth century. Thirty years later another pope reversed this judgment. But this did not invalidate the infallibility of Leo in Catholic eyes, because he was not speaking officially. The distinction appears to Protestants very tenuous. Will the Spirit which bloweth where listeth so submit itself to that which is official? Even more repugnant to us is the claim that infallibility has no relation to the character of the pope. We can understand that a man does not need to be perfect in order to speak the truth, but that he should not only be immoral but even indifferent to religion and yet able to speak infallibly about religion taxes all credence. Leo X, for example, was a flippant pope more interested in hunting, gambling, and art than in religion. Yet the *Dictionnaire de Theologie E Catholique* reckons his bull, *Exsurge Domine,* as among the infallible pronouncements.

Even more grave is the preoccupation of liberal Protestantism with demythologizing, that is to say the endeavor to extract the religious core from the Scriptures while discarding the outmoded scientific thought forms of the first century, whereas Catholicism is occupied in making more mythology at variance we think both with history and with science, as for example the declaration of the Assumption of the Virgin. But this is not the place to air all of our differences. The point is that they are deep and not easily to be bridged. And they are lamentable because the very revelation which might bring balm to the world is discredited if the religions which profess to have received it are so at variance as to what it is. All of which is not to say that there are not great areas of agreement, and one is inclined to believe that the man who dishes out the hamburgers may be right in saying, "at bottom we are all the same, we believe in God, we believe in goodness, the rest does not matter." Yet it is easier for a Protestant to say this than for a Catholic, because for a Protestant what matters is not so much precise belief as interior piety and the Protestant is glad to testify that the Catholic has it. But interior piety or spirituality though esteemed by the Catholic is not sufficient without dogmatic rectitude. The gulf is still there. Happily some are striving to bridge it. Father Tavard, who has written a very understanding book about Protestantism, is seeking to make Catholicism more acceptable by a revival of the Augustinianism of the late Middle Ages as exemplified in

Saint Bonaventura, for whom the conflict of faith and knowledge was resolved in the vision of God.

Richard Niebuhr remarks:

There will be no union of Catholics and Protestants until through the common memory of Jesus Christ the former repent of the sin of Peter and the latter of the sin of Luther, until Protestants acknowledge Thomas Aquinas as one of their fathers, the Inquisition as their own sin and Ignatius Loyola as one of their own Reformers, until Catholics have canonized Luther and Calvin, done repentance for Protestant nationalism, and appropriated Schleiermacher and Barth as their theologians.[8]

The time for this has not yet come and until it does we shall not be able to organize a joint department of religion in a university. The only possibility is that a department of religion should offer courses given by Protestants, by Catholics, and by Jews working quite independently. They would be inculcating their own faiths. But this is impossible in a state institution because of the limitations imposed on education by the separation of church and state. What can be done is that religious bodies at their own expense may set up faculties of theology on the university campus and offer courses open to election by all students, for which the university will grant credits toward its own degree. In some places this is being done.

Yet this in itself is not enough, and no one of the faiths is content simply to give instruction. The impression must not be given that Catholics, because they can state revelation in propositions to be believed or rejected, are any less disposed than Protestants or Jews to say that belief must be more than intellectual assent if it is to be a saving faith. All of the three religions are concerned for the practice of religion alike in acts of worship and of social concern. The latter presents no problem. Fortunately, all three faiths experience no difficulty whatever in collaboration on such matters as social justice, opposition to racial discrimination, political immorality, and the like. This most important area does not require discussion here because pluralism offers no difficulty.

But worship does, and much more so for the Catholic than for the Protestant and the Jew. Because the Catholic feels that right worship requires right doctrine, and a liturgy acceptable to a non-Catholic cannot be satisfactory to a Catholic. The liberal Protestant and the liberal Jew place much greater stress on attitudes—reverence, awe, contrition, humility, adoration —and are willing to worship together with those who express these attitudes in other dogmatic terms. For us the dogmas have value more as symbols than as precise formulations of ultimate truth. That is why when I was in France with a Quaker unit of the Red Cross during World War I whenever we were in a village where there was no Protestant church I went to mass. Even on Catholic assumptions I cannot see why an occasional joint service of worship could not be worked out which would contain no dogmatic assertion unacceptable to any of the three. It could not possibly contain a full state-ment of the faith of each of the three, but it might center on common elements. As a Protestant I should have no difficulty in sharing with a Jew in a service drawn entirely from the Old Testament. He would have more difficulty in joining with me in a service including passages from the New Testament, but they might be so chosen that a liberal Jew would not feel obligated to withdraw. As a Protestant I could share with a Catholic in a service made up of scripture passages, of prayers from Saint Chrysostom, Saint Augustine, and John Henry New-man, hymns from Saint Ambrose, Jacopone da Todi, Saint Francis Xavier, and Gilbert Chesterton, and of meditations from Saint Francis, Saint Bernard, and Saint François de Sales. And I cannot see why a Catholic could not share in a service taken from the classics of Protestant devotional literature. I once gave a talk, by the way, on such literature over a Catholic radio program. Father Tavard says that: "Luther ranks among the most delicate devotional writers with his essay on *Chris-tian Liberty* and his very devout commentary on Mary's *Magnificat*."[9]

A Catholic chaplain of one of our state universities tells us that it cannot be and warns us not to embarrass Catholics by inviting them to do what they must refuse. A Catholic he says can pray with anyone save an atheist (that he thinks would be tough)[10] privately, but not officially. One would like to know, in the first place, whether this is a universal ruling. There are regional differences in such matters. The Bishop of Syracuse, for example, has forbidden Catholic students to participate in a Religious Emphasis program. But the bishops in other areas permit it. The present bishop of Connecticut has reversed the practice of his predecessors in permitting a priest in New Haven to take part on the platform in a public service of Thanksgiving with scripture, hymns, prayer, and sermon. But I am told that such joint services continue in other places. Here is a point on which we should be glad to be more precisely informed. If the bishop says, "No," we should not embarrass the priest, but there is no reason why we should not address ourselves to the bishop.

Admittedly, however, joint worship could be only occasional. Christians would not be satisfied with a chapel service all the year through which did not go beyond the Old Testament, and Catholics would not be willing to be continuously reserved in references to the Blessed Virgin and to the Saints. But if we can do so there is a point in holding joint services, because God is one and truth is one, and if we are sincere in our desire to worship the one God in truth, though manifestly since we disagree some of us must be in error, nevertheless we cannot go astray in joining in common adoration and petition for forgiveness and illumination from the Father of Lights, with whom there is no shadow of turning.

Neither should it be impossible to discuss our differences. Some of the interfaith movements have insisted that in all joint endeavors reference to dogma should be avoided and in no case should there be debate. This means getting together by avoiding fundamentals. But let us remember that students do not leave these matters alone. In private bull sessions no knuckles are gloved and no friendships are broken. Discussion on a public platform might indeed lead to acrimony, but what could be the objection to interchanges between representatives of the three faiths among small student groups? On the same level why might there not be informal unofficial services of worship in areas where bishops have forbidden collaboration in public worship? The chaplain mentioned above said that he could pray privately with anyone. Did he mean only with one, or might not a group of half a dozen, a cell in other words, engage together in meditation and prayer? Every avenue of collaboration at every level should be explored.

WALTON E. BEAN

What Is the State University?

CHAPTER IV

The position of religion in the American state university is a position of tacit compromise. On the one hand, there is the principle of separation of church and state. On the other, there is the fact that religion is inseparable from large areas of human thought and feeling and thus from higher learning. The resulting adjustment is perfectly appropriate to the general nature and circumstances of the state university itself, and typical of it. For like most American democratic institutions, the state university is a complex and ingenious product of the diversity, freedom, and flexibility of American society, and consequently it works in an atmosphere of healthy compromise.

Perhaps the supreme adjustment which the American state university has had to make is the adjustment between the proper nature of a university as an institution devoted to the free advance of the human mind, and the proper nature of a public institution, created by government and supported by taxation. This adjustment, though still imperfect, has fairly steadily improved. American state constitution makers and legislators have been substantially successful in devising a system which protects public universities from both the special dogmas of religious sectarianism and the special group interests of political partisanship. In America both religious beliefs and material group interests are indeed extraordinarily "pluralistic"; and a state university belongs to the whole people of an American state. It should be noticed that the high purpose of protecting such an institution from religious sectarianism no more implies the complete exclusion of religion as such than the necessity of excluding politics in the sense of partisanship means that it is desirable or even possible to make the state university other than an instrument of public policy, a major developmental agency of the state.

At the same time it should also be noted that balance and co-operation between public and private enterprise has been preserved in American higher education, just as in other aspects of American society. The similarities between state universities and private ones in America are much more numerous and important than the differences. Public and private universities share inseparably in the community of knowledge. So far as many of the major aspects of American higher education are concerned, the differences between public and private universities can even be ignored entirely, as in fact these differences quite properly are ignored in a number of the chapters in this book. It is widely supposed that different conditions governing the treatment and status of religion are among the essential distinctions between public and private higher education in America. It is true, in general, that private universities have schools or departments of religion and public ones do not, but there are major exceptions even to this generalization. The exceptions include both of the public universities of Iowa. There is a School of Religion at the State University of Iowa at Iowa City, and a department of Religious Education in Iowa State College at Ames.[1]

An attempt at definition or rather at classification of American universities is no easy matter. When Richard H. Ostheimber prepared his *Statistical Analysis of Higher Education in the United States*, as of 1949, he discovered that "if one attempts to get perfectly homogeneous classifications, one approaches the absurdity of finding that the number of classifications equals the number of institutions to be classified." The wide discretion left to the states by the federal government has permitted considerable diversity among "universities" both in name and in fact. At present, however, we may say that there are roughly sixty state universities in the United States and about the same number of private ones. Each of the forty-eight states has what it officially calls a state university. More than half of these institutions are "land-grant universities." That is, the land-grant agricultural college was made an integral part of a general state university. Moreover, in eleven of the states that maintain their land-grant colleges as separate institutions, these "state colleges" have now diversified their functions to the point at which they meet a reasonable definition of a second state university, and one of them, Michigan's, has recently received that official title. Any attempt at an exact census is further complicated by hybrid public-private institutions like "Rutgers University, the State University of New Jersey"; and by the fact that some states, most obviously California, include more than one full-scale university in a single state university system. There is also the question of whether some of the smaller state universities are truly of "university" scope, but here we can only give full faith and credit to the acts of each state.

A brief summary of the historical background is essential to an understanding of the present situation, for the story of the origins and development of American state universities does much to explain their characteristic adaptability to special needs and changing circumstances in American society.

The first American state universities were founded after the Revolution in the southeastern seaboard states, largely because no private colleges had been established there during the colonial period. In the region between the Appalachians and the Mississippi, state universities owed their original foundation largely to the fact that the federal government in 1787 had set the precedent of offering grants of one or more townships of federal public land for "seminaries of learning" in new states. The early "state universities" differed very little from the many private denominational institutions that were also founded on the pattern of the colonial colleges. The early American college curriculum, with its core in the classics of Greek, Latin, and Hebrew literature, had been designed for the training of ministers and gentlemen in an aristocratic society. The early state universities simply imitated this "literary" and "classical" college pattern, which remained almost static until after the middle of the nineteenth century. Neither public nor private institutions had succeeded in providing a system of education, let alone of research, which the American people could put to practical use, or which captured their imagination. College enrollments were actually declining in proportion to the population of college age.

The great potentialities of the state university first began to be apparent at Michigan in the eighteen-fifties under the brilliant presidency of Henry Philip Tappan, an admirer of the scientific achievements of the German universities. During the same period came the agitation that led to the Morrill Act of 1862, endowing state colleges of "agriculture and the mechanic arts" through federal land grants to the states. (These are the "land grant" institutions we speak of today, the earlier federal "seminary township" grants having now been largely forgotten.) Of the approximately sixty institutions that are reasonably classified as state universities at present, more than half owed their original organization to the stimulus of the Morrill Act agricultural college land grants. In the New England and middle Atlantic regions, where well-established private colleges and universities had pre-empted the field, the state university idea was resisted until well into the twentieth century, but in recent decades nearly all of the land-grant agricultural colleges in that area have become general-purpose state universities.

The American state university of today is intended to provide advanced general, professional, and technical education for the greatest practicable number of young men and women, largely at public expense. The proportion of students enrolled in public higher education in general is now larger than the enrollment in privately supported institutions, and this proportion, as well as that of college and university students in the general population, is virtually certain to continue a steady and rapid growth. Some of the implications and problems of this situation are certain to be of increasingly critical importance. College enrollments during the nineteen-sixties may be more than double those of the early fifties, mainly because in 1932 there were only about two million registered births in the United States; in 1943 about three million; and in 1950 nearly four million. Obviously, only the public purse can provide for the bulk of the enormous institutional expansion that will be required in the next decade. Where we shall find either the taxes or the teachers is an interesting question.

But find them we must and shall. For the role of public higher education as a central part of democracy, through its function as an avenue to greater achievement, service, and reward for the children of the common man is so familiar a fact of life in America that it is easy to forget its real meaning and importance. No one, perhaps, can truly comprehend the significance of mass public higher education until he has experienced the breath-taking contrasts between a society that has it and a society that does not. In this perspective the phrase "mass education" takes on an entirely new depth of meaning. For it becomes clear that the unprecedented and unparalleled achievement of mass public higher education in America has been not merely a result or a luxurious byproduct of the success of American society. It is rather one of the most essential causes of that success. The very heart of the plight of the underdeveloped nations lies in the limited number of their people who receive advanced general, professional, and technical education or are likely to receive it in the near future.

In the structure and the functions of the American state university a spirit of salutary compromise is everywhere apparent. In terms of structure and organization, there is constant compromise among the state university's constituent elements: faculties, administrations, governing boards, state officials, the public, students, and alumni. In terms of function, the state university performs simultaneously a maze of different services that are sometimes interrelated and complementary, but also sometimes in competition with each other. Thus there must be perpetual compromise, implicit and explicit, in the allocation of its energies and resources among the functions of teaching, research, and an infinite variety of services to the general public.

Although the state university functions as a human community rather than as a legal entity, an understanding of its special structure and form of organization under American state law is important not only as a part of its definition, but also for an understanding of the degree of freedom and flexibility that it has attained. Under the laws or constitutions of nearly every state, the state university is a semi-independent public corporation governed legally and to a considerable extent actually by a board of distinguished citizens, mostly appointed by the governor or elected by the people. This system, like the self-perpetuating governing board system of American private colleges and universities, is virtually unique and peculiar to the United States. In part, it grew out of quite accidental circumstances in early American history. No other country has entrusted its universities to the full legal responsibility and authority of external governing boards of "laymen," that is of men who are not primarily experts in educational matters. But although American university governing boards are often criticized as mainly drawn from the business community rather than from the entire community, the fact that every state has adopted this system and that none has seriously considered changing it indicates that in general it serves American purposes fairly well.

The governing board represents the interest of the public in the university, and it represents the university to the public. It has the duty both of keeping the university responsible to the public and of serving as a buffer to protect the university from unwise pressures. This is especially true in several states which, following the example of Michigan, have provided an important degree of corporate independence for their universities in their state constitutions. Theoretically such an institution is a kind of fourth branch of government, independent of and co-ordinate with the legislative, executive, and judicial branches, and this type of constitutional-corporation university was once defined by the Michigan Supreme Court as "the highest form of juristic person known to the law." Actually, of course, constitutional independence is somewhat compromised by financial dependence on the state legislature. But even in the states whose universities do not enjoy the protection of constitutional status, the institutions are coming to be regarded as a lofty and noble form of public trust, symbolized by the corporate governing board but shared also by the administration, the faculty, the students, and indeed by the whole body of citizens.

Several states define their universities for legal purposes as "the corporation known as the Regents," and an occasional regent may be found who seems to feel that he and his colleagues truly *are* the university in fact as well as in law. But even this extreme feeling is an understandable if not a pardonable form of pride. And moreover, similar feelings may be discovered among university administrators, professors, students, and even alumni.

In practice, governing boards have long since delegated much of their responsibilities to university presidents—a race of beings who must attempt to approximate superman. In the nineteenth century and the early twentieth, there was a critical stage in the evolution of American state universities when the development of the quality of each institution depended primarily on the wisdom and luck of the regents in selecting a chief executive. The net work of relationships, functions, and interests was becoming so complex that it was desirable to centralize responsibility in one man, and the "strong president" system was another American adaptation to special circumstances. In that stage, the American system of university administration was well described as "absolute dictatorship tempered by occasional assassination." Later, of course, as knowledge became more and more specialized and the number of university departments between art and zoology proliferated to about fifty (not including the number of departments within the professional schools), the president in turn had to delegate more and more of his authority and to rely much more heavily upon the advice of deans, department heads, and faculty committees. At present the list of administrative officers and faculty committees in the largest state university fills sixteen closely printed pages. It is difficult to keep the administrative camel from crowding the intellectual pilgrim out of his tent.

Even in this situation, however, the president remains a key figure. He must constantly mediate among all the diverse interests in an institution that is becoming almost as complex as the society it serves. For example, he must mediate between

the values and viewpoints of professors and businessmen—
between the scientist, the intellectual, the academic man on
the one hand, and on the other the corporation presidents,
bankers, lawyers, newspaper publishers, and farmers who make
up the governing board. This function is so delicate that many
state universities have a rule requiring all communications
between regents and professors to be channeled through the
president.

Thus the state university president has been rather accurately
defined as "a man who makes compromises for a living." Yet
he cannot succeed unless all his compromises are made on a
high level of principle.

In describing the state university as an institution, a social
structure, there is a tendency to overemphasize the relatively
external elements in its organization and control. Its most
essential components, of course, are not regents and administrators but teachers and students. A state university partakes
of the familiar definition of a university as such: "a community
of scholars." But even this definition is too narrow if it over-
emphasizes the idea of the faculty as an academic guild, if it
implies that research is more important than teaching in the
process of "scholarship," or if it forgets that a university is a
place in which youth forms its purposes in life.

Between its primary function of teaching and its corollary
function of research, the state university has in general achieved
a healthy interrelationship, a healthy balance and cross-ferti-
lization. A university has at its center an undergraduate college
providing broad general education in the first two years and
a partial specialization in the "upper division." In a university,
the "college" may be compared to the palm of a hand from
which extend the fingers of the graduate school and the professional schools. In all of these areas the process of research
constantly vitalizes the process of teaching.

A description of the life and work of the state university
must include the manifold services that it renders directly to
the public, as well as the public service that it renders indirectly
through teaching and research within its own walls. Through
university extension, agricultural extension, and other activities,

it has come to regard the whole state as its campus, and sometimes the nation and the world as well. There is a massive and constant interaction between the state universities and the whole complex of American economic and cultural life, and in several foreign countries teams of American professors are introducing or reorganizing instruction in such fields as public and business administration.

The intellectual freedom of the American state university has in general been fairly well protected against the damage it might receive from the constant stress upon practical service to the public. The effectiveness of this service has led the people's representatives in the legislatures of nearly all of the states to regard appropriations for state universities as venture capital of a remarkably valuable kind, for they are likely to produce anything from the Babcock process for testing milk, which revolutionized the dairy industry, to the atomic bomb, which revolutionized a great deal more. The practical results of university research are generally received with gratitude and sometimes with a kind of awe. They have made the public willing to allow universities a great deal of freedom to perform their more mysterious and abstract functions.

The majority of the public still does regard universities as rather mysterious, and professors often complain that the public does not understand what a university is. Occasionally, some wave of public emotion leads to drastic legislative interference in university affairs. Questions like those of "loyalty" oaths, or of the current attempts of several state legislatures to prevent racial desegregation, sometimes confront administrations and faculties with the delicate problem of whether they should oppose and seek to change an emotionally aroused public opinion on some major issue of state university policy. This can present a serious dilemma. As a distinguished professor of philosophy at a southern state university has recently pointed out, such a course may have the effect of inflaming instead of changing public opinion on the particular question; and it may also damage the general welfare by destroying that degree of detachment which makes the university's highest functions possible and which should therefore be preserved throughout all of its contacts with its various publics.

President Pusey of Harvard recently found it necessary to emphasize that the function of his university was that of "service without servility" to its constituents. This needs emphasis in state universities at least as much as in private ones. In American democracy the state university has become an important part of the mind of the state. To serve the state well it must be a free mind.

The constant proliferation of knowledge as well as the emphasis on its application to practical life have inevitably created real problems in the preservation of the values of broad, general, and liberal education. When, as someone has said, "the golden bowl of classicism was broken"—when the old homogeneous classical curriculum (in which religion was central) was replaced by one which recognized the demands of science, industry, and the professions, hundreds of new university courses were created. With the rise of the large university the total enrollment in the professional schools often exceeded enrollment in the liberal arts college, and even within that college the curriculum became increasingly complex. Many observers of American state universities, and many of the participants in them, feel that their curricula have become overspecialized and departmentalized. Some feel that they offer too many subjects that would be better left to technical and vocational institutions of lesser grade. Ezra Cornell expressed the intention of founding an institution "in which any student may find instruction in any subject." Cornell University is a private institution to which the state of New York entrusted its land-grant college, in an ingenious compromise between public and private enterprise.

Here again we see that there are few of the problems and shortcomings of American universities, just as there are few of their achievements, for which the blame or credit can be clearly ascribed to public or private institutions as such. The free elective system that permitted the student in the liberal arts college to browse at will among an ever-growing number of subjects, and under which the college tended to lose control of the curriculum to the departments, received its first great impetus not from the utilitarian demands upon public educational institutions but from President Eliot of Harvard.

In state universities as well as in private ones, a predominant recent tendency in reorganizing the curriculum has stressed efforts to reintegrate the knowledge that has been amassed in so many special fields. Private universities and colleges have more often taken the lead in this "general education" movement, but state institutions are making comparable efforts in it. It may be hoped that the reconciliation of specialism and generalism will be the foremost achievement, as it is perhaps the foremost need, in the next great epoch of higher education in America. It may well be that we are entering an age of reintegration in higher learning, and the various questions regarding the proper place of religion may well be considered in this context.

PAUL G. KAUPER

Law and Public Opinion

CHAPTER V

Writing to the Danbury Baptists Association in 1802, Thomas
Jefferson stated that the Constitution built "a wall of separation between Church and State." Whether the "wall" metaphor
was well chosen and whether government and religion can
be as neatly and completely separated as this statement suggested, it is true that Jefferson expressed a fundamental idea
that is generally accepted in American thinking and now
regarded as a key feature of our constitutional system.[1]

The handy phrase "separation of church and state" symbolizes an important facet of American pluralism; namely, that
church and state are to function side by side in American
society, that each is to pursue its own sphere of competence
and responsibility, and that neither has legal authority to
interfere with or control the other's operations. An implicit
result of this division is that the state, the politically organized
community, alone can exercise coercive power whereas the
institutions of religion must rest on a voluntaristic basis.

But the separation principle rests on something more than
an attempt to allocate spheres of responsibility in the interests
of efficiency and special competence. It acquires its substance
as a limitation in the interest of human freedom. Separation of
church and state as a jurisdictional principle can be restated
in terms of private liberty to mean that the state may not
execute its coercive power either to compel adherence to any
religious faith or creed, interfere with the free expression of
religion, or use its resources and powers either to prefer or

to discriminate against any religious group or organization. It is our conception that the religious life, as expressed both privately and corporately, flourishes best when divorced from both the compulsion and the restraint of political force.

Any discussion of the place of religion at the state university, both in terms of curricular considerations and the relationship of the university to the primary religious groups, must necessarily meet the issue posed by the separation principle. Is it even appropriate for a state university, admittedly an agent or division of the state, to provide opportunities both for instruction in religion and for primary religious groups to function more effectively on the campus?[2]

Before attempting any concrete answer to these questions by reference to explicit constitutional limitations that furnish positive grounds for legal application of the separation principle, it is appropriate to mention some basic considerations relevant to the constitutional aspects of the problem.

In the first place, it should be noted that the term "separation of church and state" symbolizes a generalized concept or principle and not a specific rule. Indeed, to the best of the writer's knowledge, this term does not occur in any American constitution. Insofar as the separation principle has been recognized as a legal limitation, it represents a judicial interpretation and synthesis of empiric provisions found in written constitutions. But legal limitations did not create the separation principle. They reflect the principle that has grown out of the experience and understanding of our people.

Viewed as a legal proposition, the separation principle lacks the historical depth and perspective that may give a solid core of meaning to such constitutional language as "due process of law." Moreover, when we look at American history and the practices sanctioned by history, some of which are now repudiated in the name of the separation principle while others continue unchallenged, all in the face of constitutional provisions that have remained unchanged, it is evident that we are dealing with an idea that in its application at any one time has no fixed or precise meaning. This idea, nonetheless, is sufficiently elastic to accommodate itself to new concepts and trends in American life and the popular understanding. It is true of law generally that to maintain its vitality it must be responsive to the needs of the day. And constitutional law even when fortified by judicial review under a written constitution has proved to be no exception to this. The whole history of constitutional interpretation makes clear that the Constitution is a malleable document, that the important limitations of the Constitution that rest on implication or on broad phrasings in the text do not lend themselves to precise technical rules or doctrinal absolutes, and that the judicial appraisal of underlying policy considerations and the pragmatic weighing of competing interests that deserve constitutional recognition become critical elements in the decisional process. In turn the current of historical movement and the climate of public opinion give life and meaning to the underlying values that either expressly or implicitly shape the course of judicial interpretation.

Turning now to the empiric constitutional provisions and their significance in respect to religion in the state university, we are faced at the outset by the pluralism within our constitutional system. In the continental United States we have forty-nine written constitutions, the Constitution of the United States and the constitutions of each of the several states. Plans and programs that may conform to limitations of a state constitution as defined by the state's supreme court may still be held to run afoul of the federal constitution as interpreted by the U. S. Supreme Court. In turn, it is also true that a plan or program may be held invalid under the state constitution even though found to be consistent with the federal constitution.

The variety of state constitutional provisions adds complexity to our study. And yet they go to the heart of our problem. State universities are instruments of state authority, policy, and power. They represent one of the proprietary enterprises of the state. The function, policy, and purpose of the state university are matters which should be determined by reference to the constitution and educational policy of the state, all responsive in turn to the forces of informed opinion within the state. Moreover, provisions of state constitutions that provide the legal scaffolding for the separation principle are usually stated with more precision and definiteness than the broad limitations in the First Amendment. Finally, it may be noted that these specific provisions of state constitutions have a long history. The results reached under them whether by judicial interpretation or by general acquiescence and understanding may be in the end a more reliable index to the meaning of separation as authenticated in American experience than what has been said by the U. S. Supreme Court in recent years in the few cases interpreting the First Amendment's brief and ambiguous language forbidding laws respecting an establishment of religion.

The state constitutions, as stated above, exhibit the greatest variety in the provisions relating to religious freedom and the use of public monies or appropriations of public property for religious purposes.[3] In general it may be said that the least restrictive provisions are found in the old constitutions of the states in the east, which simply affirm the general principle of religious freedom and freedom of conscience and worship.[4] But the constitutions of many of the states, in addition to affirming the principle of religious freedom, embody provisions forbidding appropriations of tax monies or public property for any church or sectarian purposes, and in many instances expressly prohibiting the use of public funds to support sectarian schools or sectarian instruction or to support a teacher of religion.[5] In some states the constitution prohibits sectarian instruction in the state's schools without relating this prohibition to the use of tax funds.[6] Although the usual provision is directed against "sectarian" education, it should be noted that the constitutions of the states of Washington, Arizona, and Utah prohibit the use of public funds "for any religious worship, exercise or instruction."[7]

Apart from these differences, the state constitutional provisions, while showing considerable uniformity in many respects, display diversities of other kinds.[8] Space does not permit a complete cataloguing of these variations, and it is hazardous to attempt to classify them or to base any generalizations upon them. The important point to be observed is that each state is master of its own house in this matter, and that the questions respecting the place of religion at a given state university must necessarily take into account the specific provisions of that state's constitution.

The state constitutional provisions have given rise to numerous cases involving public schools. The decisions are not very helpful in answering concrete questions raised with respect to the place of religion at a state university, but they shed some illumination on the general area under discussion and furnish some clue to what state courts understand "separation of church and state" to mean in the context of the positive limitations found in state constitutions. Bible-reading in public schools has frequently been challenged on the ground that this is a form of forbidden sectarian instruction since the Bible, depending on the particular version and the parts read, offends the religious or nonreligious scruples of some children and parents. The state courts have divided on this question. The majority of decisions, including some decided at a relatively early date, have held that Bible-reading is not constitutionally objectionable, particularly if objecting or dissenting students are excused from participation.[9] According to these decisions the Bible is not a sectarian book—its reading does not make the school a sectarian school and does not make the teacher a "teacher of religion" within the meaning of constitutional prohibitions. Other courts have reached the opposite result, and it may be noted that these contrary decisions have for the most part come at a later date. The reasoning in these cases is that the Bible is by its nature sectarian, and that the effect of reading it in school is to coerce the consciences of those who do not accept it as authoritative.

Programs whereby students are released from public school classes one hour a week in order to attend religious education classes conducted by representatives of the primary religious groups have also come under attack on the ground that the public school system was being used as a means of recruiting children for sectarian instruction and that the effect of the program was to place children under compulsion to attend these classes. But the few authoritative state court decisions dealing with the matter have upheld the released time program on the ground that attendance at the religious education classes was optional and that it was not inappropriate for the state to co-operate with religious groups in this way in the interests of religious education.[10]

Although it is futile to attempt to extract from the numerous state court decisions any commonly accepted definition of the term "sectarian instruction," a review of the opinions indicates that the courts in giving meaning to the term have been concerned with two primary considerations; namely, (1) that the public school classrooms shall not be identified with any type of religious instruction whereby the state in effect establishes an official creed and gives a preference to one religious faith over another, and (2) that the public school system shall not be used as a means of compelling students to accept religious instruction. Whether a given type of instruction or exercise does constitute an attempt at indoctrination in a particular religious faith and whether a given practice operates as a restraint on conscience are questions on which they have disagreed.

We turn now to limitations derived from the federal constitution. The First Amendment states that Congress shall make no law respecting an establishment of religion or prohibiting the free exercise thereof. In the *Everson* case (330 U. S. 1 [1947]), decided in 1947, the U. S. Supreme Court for the first time held that the effect of the Fourteenth Amendment, adopted in 1868, was to make this language of the First Amendment, adopted in 1791, equally applicable to the states and that the nonestablishment phrase ordains the separation of church and state. This in turn means, according to Justice Black's opinion in the *Everson* case, not only that government must respect freedom of conscience and worship, that it cannot prescribe official creeds or punish the dissenter and unbeliever, and that government cannot establish an official state church, but it means also that the state cannot give aid to religion even on a nonpreferential basis. "No tax in any amount, large or small, can be levied to support any religious activities or institutions, whatever they may be called or whatever form they may adopt to teach or practice religion."

One year later in the *McCollum* case (333 U. S. 203 [1948]) the Court, with only Justice Reed dissenting, held that the system of released time followed in Champaign, Illinois, whereby school children were released one hour a week for religious instruction given on the school premises by teachers supplied by the primary religious groups, violated the separation principle since in the Court's view the public school system was being used as a means of recruiting children for religious education purposes. Yet only four years later in the *Zorach* case (343 U. S. 306 [1952]) the Court by a five to four vote sustained the New York system of released time, which in its objectives and general features could not be distinguished from the Champaign system, except for the one circumstance that in the New York system the released-time religious instruction took place off the school premises. But even more remarkable than the slender ground on which the *McCollum* case was distinguished was Justice Douglas' majority opinion, noteworthy for its repudiation of the absolutism expressed by Mr. Justice Black in his prior opinions in the *Everson* and *McCollum* cases.

Space does not permit the extensive quotation from Justice Douglas' opinion needed to catch the full flavor of its thought. After pointing out that the First Amendment does not say that in every and all respects there shall be a separation of church and state, he asserted that in its provisions respecting nonestablishment of religion and the free exercise thereof, it studiously defines the manner in which there shall be "no concert or union or dependency one on the other." The problem like many other problems in constitutional law is one of degree. In short, according to Mr. Justice Douglas, in applying the separation concept the Court must follow the balance-of-interests technique and must engage in the familiar pragmatic process of weighing constitutional limitations against permissive ends within the range of legislative power. The state and its agencies may appropriately express a concern for religious education in view of the place that religion has occupied in the country's history. "When the state encourages religious instruction or cooperates with religious authorities by adjusting the schedule of public events to sectarian needs, it follows the best of our traditions. For it then respects the religious nature of our people and accommodates the public service to their spiritual needs. To hold that it may not would be to find in the Constitution a requirement that the government show a callous indifference to religious groups. That would be preferring those who believe in no religion over those who do believe."

The majority opinion in the *Zorach* case restored what appeared to many to be a sound perspective and judgment in the interpretation of the separation principle regarded as a constitutional mandate. The matter of separation cannot be approached in terms of verbal absolutes. Nor can a metaphor such as "the wall of separation" serve as an aid to analysis. The truth is that religion and government have been and continue to be interrelated, and that by hypothesis it is impossible to describe this situation in terms of "absolute and complete separation." Religious groups often exert a forceful influence in shaping governmental policy, and the spiritual and moral influences generated by religious forces have an important impact upon our national character and public life. In turn government has contributed much to religion. Our history bears witness to the numerous ways in which government has employed its powers and processes to provide more favorable opportunities for the exercise of religious freedom and the pursuit of religious interests without impinging upon the freedom of the nonbeliever and without giving a preference to a single religious group. The idea that the separation principle means that government cannot "aid" religion, if stated as a universal and absolute proposition, is not supported by precedent, history, or the common understanding.

The foregoing discussion, designed to give us the flavor of the federal and state constitutional limitations and the principal ideas that have emerged in their interpretation, furnishes the background for a consideration of the problems raised respecting religion at the state university.

At the outset, it should be noted that there is very little judicial authority dealing with these problems. Indeed, the only case directly in point is the decision of the Illinois Supreme Court upholding compulsory chapel services at the University of Illinois.[11] Possibly other suits have been brought to challenge certain practices at state universities but were not taken to the highest court of the state. No case involving religion in a state university has ever come before the U. S. Supreme Court for consideration and decision. The attorney generals of the states have on a few occasions given opinions on questions of this nature, but even these are scattered and for our purposes do not add much to the discussion. This picture is all the more surprising both because of the amount of litigation that has been brought regarding religion at the public school level and the extent to which our state universities over the years have offered instructional and other programs directly or indirectly concerning religion.

Indeed, if our constitutions require complete separation of church and state, and if, in turn, this means that the state university cannot take account of religion as a curriculum and teaching factor and that it cannot otherwise do anything to foster an interest in religious matters or afford opportunities to students for the cultivation of religious faith, it becomes extraordinarily remarkable to what extent our state universities for almost a century have engaged in unconstitutional practices. Or perhaps the more sensible conclusion can be drawn that these practices have given us a practical interpretation, founded on public approval and understanding and consistent with an understanding of the university's function, which is more vital and authoritative than logical conclusions drawn from abstract propositions. Here is a case where a page of history is worth a volume of logic, to use Justice Holmes's pithy observation. A brief look at history is here warranted.

We do well to remind ourselves that in the United States higher education was first instituted under religious auspices, and that our oldest colleges and universities owe their origin to denominational groups. And, when the tax-supported state university came into being, the religious influence was strong

there too and this, notwithstanding state constitutional limitations. Compulsory chapel services were the rule rather than
the exception in the early days of the state universities, and
attendance at Sunday worship services was often required.
Indeed, a number of state institutions continue to hold chapel
services at the present time. So far as the curriculum and
teaching programs were concerned, it is interesting to note that
state universities at an earlier day taught courses in such
subjects as Biblical Hebrew, New Testament Greek, and
Evidences of Christianity.[12]

Then came the movement that resulted in de-emphasis of
religion at the state university. Chapel services were abandoned
after a while at a number of state institutions. The courses
distinctively religious were dropped from the curriculum.
Compulsory attendance at worship services was generally
abandoned. In view of the practices previously followed, it
can hardly be assumed that these changes were in deference
to constitutional mandates. (The relevancy of the Fourteenth
Amendment in regard to some of these practices did not become apparent until 1947!) On the contrary, it appears that
these changes were attributable to a growing secularization
of society, the adoption of the elective system in institutions
of higher learning, the unpopularity of chapel services with
students, and the lessened intellectual respectability of religion
as the result of the new sciences.

But, in turn, the recent decades have witnessed a new
burgeoning of interest in religion at the state university.[13]
Novel, interesting, and diverse patterns have emerged and continue to develop in attestation of the state university's sympathetic concern for the religious understanding and religious
life of its students. New courses have been added dealing with
the intellectual and historical aspects of religion. Credit courses
in specific religions, often taught by scholars committed to the
religion they teach, are not uncommon. Or credit may be given
for courses taught by religious scholars off the campus. A
department of religion has been added by some universities.
Indeed, a School of Religions functions as a regular department
at the University of Iowa. A number of universities have

created the office of chaplain or co-ordinator of religion to assist in the formulation of the university's academic program respecting religion, to co-ordinate the university's program with those of the primary religious groups, and to counsel students. Student religious groups are in many cases permitted access to university buildings for meetings, and in a few cases chapels are maintained on university campuses for use by these groups.

During the course of the development briefly outlined above, the relevant provisions of state constitutions have for the most part remained unchanged. It is fair to infer, therefore, that constitutional limitations relating to separation of church and state have not been the primary factor in determining the role of religion at the state university.

What accounts for the apparent acquiescence in these programs at state universities despite the frequency of the objections raised when public schools interest themselves in religious matters?

Obviously, there are important differences between state-supported education at the public school level and state-supported education at the university level. Parents are compelled to send their children to some school, whether public, parochial, or nonparochial private. A child attending any of these schools may be said to be attending under compulsion of law. Moreover, the typical public school course, at least at the lower levels, is a required course in that all students are expected to take part in the same program. Even if dissenting children are excused from participating in religious exercises or instruction, they may find it embarrassing to state their objections and to find themselves separated from the other students because of this factor. Also, children at the public school level have impressionable minds and are more likely to accept as true what is told them, with the result that religious instruction of any kind is more vulnerable to the charge that it leads to indoctrination.

The foregoing arguments, usually advanced by those who oppose either any kind of religious instruction in the public schools or even that which affords some opportunity for religious instruction during the school week by means of the released time system, lose their force when we deal with religion at the state university level. Attendance at the state university is wholly voluntary, courses in religion in conformity with the general elective program are optional, the element of divisiveness is dissipated in view of the nature and size of the institution, and the maturity of students at this level, coupled with the general atmosphere of free and critical inquiry at the university, minimizes the risk of indoctrination as an incident of religious instruction.

The considerations mentioned above are adequate to demonstrate that the state university is in a totally different position from that of the public school in regard to religious matters, and that these differentiating factors are adequate to explain the paucity of litigation respecting religion at the state university, despite practices both past and present that show considerable involvement by state universities in matters of religious interest. In the end, however, the question whether the state university can properly teach religion and furnish opportunity for cultivation of the religious life must be answered by reference to positive considerations that are relevant to an appraisal of the university's function. What grounds may the university advance in support of such a program? Attention may be concentrated briefly on two primary considerations.

In view of the place that religion has occupied and continues to occupy in the life and history of man, its influence in the shaping of moral ideas, its impact on culture, and its significance as a unifying and integrating force that provides a high sense of purpose and motivation and opens up new vistas of truth, goodness, and beauty, religion must of necessity command some attention at any academic institution both as an intellectual discipline and as a way of life. This is especially true if it fulfills the role of a university in creating the educational milieu that evokes awareness and understanding of the ideas, values, and avenues to truth that are man's heritage. The university may well take the position that it is derelict to the high purposes for which it was created if it fails to deal in a positive way with religion as a vital force in the life and history of man. Indeed, it is fair to assert that for a university deliberately to exclude from its curriculum all courses with a positive religious content is not simply to fail to teach religion but in itself becomes a telling witness that religion is irrelevant to that process of cultivating the mind and spirit that we call higher education.

A second and corollary consideration is that by hypothesis it is impossible to exclude all consideration of religion, religious ideas, and religious institutions from any course of study at the university level, whether this course centers in the natural sciences, the social sciences, philosophy, literature, or art. Religion has played too large a part in man's history and thinking to be completely excised from academic consideration. Religious beliefs, theological formulations, and ecclesiastical institutions are frequently the subject of critical inquiry and discussion in university classes. Moreover, it has never been supposed that it was in any way inappropriate for a state university to teach such courses as Comparative Religion and Psychology of Religion. The real question then is not whether religion may be studied at the state university, but whether it deserves treatment in courses with a primary religious orientation. If, as the Supreme Court has said, the Constitution does not require the state to be hostile or even indifferent to religion, and if equality and evenhandedness are important facets of the separation principle, the university may well decide that in order to balance the scales and to afford religion an equal opportunity to be heard, it is necessary or at least proper that students have the opportunity to study religion, not simply obliquely or as a marginal adjunct to other courses, but in courses with a primary religious orientation and designed to afford opportunity for knowledge and understanding.

What conclusions may be stated then with respect to the limits on the university's freedom to teach religion and to afford opportunities for student religious groups to cultivate the life of the spirit? Some limitations are obvious. State universities may not discriminate against students because of religious or nonreligious beliefs. Adherence to an official creed may not be made a condition of admission or continued enrollment. Students should not be obliged to attend religious services. Even though the Illinois Supreme Court as late as 1891 (North v. Board of Trustees of University of Illinois, 137 Ill. 296 [1891]) upheld the validity of compulsory chapel services at the University of Illinois, it is safe to assert that such a practice would generally be condemned by courts today, unless excuses were granted to objecting students.

But to offer courses with a positive religious content should lie within the permissible range of the university's discretion in determining its total program. In deference to the separation principle, important limitations should be respected. Such courses, while properly given for credit, should be offered as electives so that the student's participation is wholly voluntary. Secondly, the principle of equality of opportunity should be observed. The state university should deal in a fair and even-handed way with all religious groups. If courses are offered to enhance understanding of specific religious doctrines and institutions, discrimination should be avoided. If opportunities are offered for various religious groups to supply teachers for courses in specific religious faiths, this opportunity should be open to all who are prepared to meet the university's academic standards. A third consideration is that the distinction should be observed between the teaching of religion to promote knowledge and understanding and that type aimed deliberately at indoctrination and commitment to religious faith. The teaching of religious ideas in an objective and fair way is appropriately a state university function. To win converts and seek commitment is outside its function and violates the separation principle. But in view of the intellectual climate that prevails at the university level, there is no compelling reason why a specific religious faith, whether it be Christianity (either in its general aspects or by reference to the various denominations and movements within it), Judaism, Islam, or Hinduism, cannot be taught fairly, objectively, and temperately for the purpose of presenting the doctrines, history, and nature of the ecclesiastical organization in the same way that the university may properly offer courses in the history, platforms, and organization of political parties without being subject to the charge that it has involved itself in partisan politics.

Whether the courses with a definite religious content are (1) offered as part of a definite program in religion, (2) given by several departments, (3) offered in a department or school of religion, or (4) taught for credit by regular members of the faculty or by teachers supplied by religious groups, the separation principle should not stand in the way of a state university's adoption of a program in any of these forms as long as the principles of voluntarism and equality are observed and the courses are taught to promote understanding rather than to indoctrinate and seek commitment. At least it appears that the First Amendment should present no obstacles.[14] To be sure, the Supreme Court has said that the state may not teach religion. But these statements were made in the context of cases dealing with the public schools and indicate that the Court's concern was with attempts to indoctrinate children with an officially sponsored religion. And it is worth remembering that the Court has said that the state may properly show an interest in religious education and accommodate its program to further this interest (Zorach v. Clauson, 343 U. S. 306 [1952]).

Substantially the same considerations apply in respect to most of the state constitutional limitations. Here the most acute question under many state constitutions is whether tax-raised funds are used for purposes of "sectarian instruction." This question is peculiarly relevant with respect to courses taught in specific faiths by teachers representative of the various religious bodies. Courts have not had occasion to define the meaning of "sectarian instruction" in the context of the state university teaching program. Historically, the term acquired its chief significance as part of the movement to keep the public schools free from control by religious bodies and to avoid use of public school classes as a means of compelling indoctrination in the religious tenets of a specific religious faith. To the extent that state constitutions extend the "sectarian instruction" prohibition to the state's institutions of higher learning, its significance must be determined by reference to the evils to be avoided. The principal considerations arising from the operation of the public school system in regard to this problem are irrelevant in the context of the university situation. As long as courses in religion are optional with the student, preference is not given to any single religious faith, the instruction is aimed at understanding and not indoctrination or commitment, and the university insists on observance of its usual academic and scholastic standards with respect to the teachers giving the courses, a persuasive case may be made that this program does not fall within the "sectarian education" category.

Certainly the term is irrelevant to courses taught by university professors aimed at study of religion in its central features. In any event the arrangement whereby religious groups pay the salaries of teachers offering courses in specific religious faiths seems to meet the type of constitutional objection which is directed against the use of tax funds, even if it is conceded that this is the kind of sectarian instruction embraced by the constitutional limitation. In the few states that prohibit use of public monies for any religious instruction, the breadth of this limitation may mean that no courses with a definite religious orientation may be given by teachers on the university staff, but here again it may be permissible for the university to give credit for courses taught by teachers supplied and paid by church groups. On the other hand, the constitutions of some of the older states in the eastern part of the country appear to place no limitations whatever on the teaching of religion at tax-supported institutions of higher learning as long as there is no compulsion that results in coercion of conscience and preference is not given to any particular religious faith or faiths.

Apart from courses in religion, a state university may also pursue a program designed to enlarge opportunities for cultivation of the religious life on the part of its students. The primary responsibility here, of course, is centered in the various religious groups that often maintain chapels and centers off the campus. But not all groups have such facilities. Again it appears to be a distortion of the separation principle to suggest that the university may not make its regular facilities available for use by voluntary student religious foundations or guilds provided that no preference or discrimination is practiced. Here the "aid" is not substantial and no appreciable out-of-pocket costs at the expense of tax-raised funds are involved.[15] Moreover, since a university usually makes such facilities available for various types of student activities, it is hardly warranted in discriminating against a particular student group because its interests extend to religious matters.

A more substantial question is raised if the university provides chapel facilities or a center to house the activities of student religious groups. A principal requirement is that the use of the chapel or of the center be open to all groups on a nondiscriminatory basis. A real problem is raised here, however, respecting the use of tax-raised funds. The provisions of many state constitutions forbid the use of such funds for purpose of a place of worship. It appears, therefore, that consistent with these provisions, the university will have to look to special funds to finance the construction of chapels, although it is not clear that these constitutional provisions bar the use of tax-raised funds to build student religious centers to house student extra-curricular activities so long as they do not come within the "place of worship" definition.[16]

In summary then, we may fairly say that consistent with the First Amendment a state university in the exercise of its discretionary authority may make a substantial contribution to religious education and to the furtherance of the religious life of its students, once it is recognized that the separation principle states no absolute rule, that the university in response to the felt needs of the time may accommodate its program to meet the student's total needs, and that the problem is one of a wise, fair, and sensible reconciliation of a legitimate and sympathetic concern for religion in the total educational process with the underlying values at stake in the separation concept. The same conclusion may be stated with respect to most of the state constitutions, although specific provisions of some constitutions may present real obstacles.

Granted that a state university has considerable freedom and a wide latitude in determining the place of religion in its total program, it must also be recognized that the determination of a concrete program concerned with the teaching of religion and the futherance of student religious activities is a matter within the discretionary authority of the administration and faculty. The university is under no duty to go as far in this matter as constitutional limitations permit. The constitutional considerations are important and the university must necessarily be guided by them. But first the university must determine what is its responsibility in this matter in terms of the university's total educational program and the demands properly made upon it. A number of considerations may lead the university to decide that it will not be wise or feasible to further the teaching of religion to the extent allowed by legal limitations. In case of serious doubt as to the propriety of a given type of program, the university as an institution which is expected to exercise a high degree of moral leadership and to show honest regard for the substantive values underlying the separation concept may well decide to resolve the doubt in deference to this principle. Likewise, with respect to certain types of plans that call for the teaching of courses by teachers supplied by the primary religious groups, the university may reach the conclusion that the risks entailed by way of possible contention or controversy between the various groups, exploitation of such teaching opportunities for indoctrination purposes, and weakening of the university's authority in control of its educational program are not worth taking. But on the other hand a fair consideration of the place of religion at the state university should not be obscured by an uncritical and dogmatic invocation of the separation principle. The problem in its total dimensions deserves careful and discerning study unhindered by a doctrinaire absolutism that ignores history, common understanding, and the public interest. We do well to remind ourselves that the life of the law, as Justice Holmes admonished, has not been logic but experience.

Religion and University Education

HELEN C. WHITE

What Place Has Religion in State University Education?

CHAPTER VI

Religion is of inescapable interest to any university no matter what the limitation of its faculties may be. Theology, the systematic study of religion, is one of the historical branches of learning, with its own distinctive field of inquiry, its own body of knowledge, its own techniques and methods, and its own objectives. But this fact has been obscured by the actual circumstances of the universities in which most of us live, and it is therefore easy for us to forget it.

Even in those private universities that have always had a faculty of theology, there has been a tendency to view the School of Divinity as something beyond and removed from the preoccupations of the ordinary faculty. Not long ago one of the great Protestant theologians of our day told me how he had challenged his university colleagues on their lack of curiosity concerning his field. It was assumed that the Divinity School professor would be interested in biology and psychology, for example, but the biologist and the psychologist on their side seemed to regard themselves as emancipated from any concern about the professional preoccupations of their colleague in theology. Much as many of us may regret it, the fact is that today in most intellectual circles theology is not regarded as the queen of the sciences.

There is, of course, a historical reason for this. Like so many other things in our American picture, it is part of a reaction to the period of theological controversy in the sixteenth and seventeenth centuries that nearly engulfed religion in Europe. The danger that the very life of religion might be destroyed in the theological battles that then rent Christendom was perceived by sensitive and thoughtful men at the time, but the fighting went on at every level until there were a good many people who came to feel that any concern about theology was a danger to the peace, and any extended consideration of theological issues a hazard to the higher life of religion. Such a reaction is quite understandable to anybody familiar with the extremes of oversimplification and vituperation to which sixteenth- and seventeenth-century religious controversy too often went.

But I suspect that there was another reason, too, for the popular reaction against theology, and that was the preoccupation with verbal expression that leads to jargon. The substantively preoccupied effort to define terms is, of course, one of the most important phases of human intellectual endeavor and one of the great instruments for the advance of human thought. But when the battle of words becomes a substitute for the battle of thought, and in itself an instrument of warfare, then all too often men take refuge in a jargon that removes the whole enterprise from the realities of ordinary life; and the average man, when he ceases to be awed by the incomprehensible words of the expert, tends to reject the claims of expertness. This is the more likely to happen when the issues do involve common human experiences with unavoidable opportunities for testing the relevance of the words. This phenomenon of jargon is, of course, not peculiar to theology. Many of those who have too easily rejected the realities of what is behind the jargon in the case of theology have not been equally alert to draw the lesson in their own fields.

But however understandable the common reaction to theological controversy and its battle of words, the results have been unfortunately narrowing for both religious and secular inquiry. We still have in intellectual circles a widespread suspicion of theology with an equally widespread ignorance of what it is all about. Yet those very sections of society that are the immediate concern of the university have still a great interest in what are essentially theological questions. This is especially apparent to anyone who has anything to do with young people.

Our age is an age of planning, and that fact is reflected in the findings of some of the surveys that have recently been made of student thought about the future. Some older people have been surprised at the materialistic vision of the future uncovered in these surveys. People who can recall the day-dreams of a more romantic youth are sometimes appalled at what seem the imaginative limitations of the new generation's planning. And yet every so often the shiny suburban surface of these plans gives way and one catches a glimpse of a very deep uneasiness, a fear that in the planning itself there may lurk an unsuspected booby trap. There is military service, for one thing, and afterward there is always the possibility of the never-quite-forgotten war of the nuclear giants.

Nowhere is the paradox of the modern world more apparent than here. In this society, so ingenious in eluding so many of the implications of man's mortality, there is everywhere a resolute disregard of the grimmer possibilities of life. And yet there is an uneasy awareness that, however morbid attention to them may be, they are still there. The immemorial wonders concerning the nature and destiny of man and the meaning of his life are no less inescapable because they are fenced off with plans that are more immediately engaging. The imaginations of the young are not calloused enough to shut them out forever.

This pervasive, even if unacknowledged, theological pre-occupation is particularly characteristic of the university. Whether or not there is a theological faculty on a particular campus, religion in the less specialized sense is certainly in the university because it is one of the great humanities to which the modern university is dedicated in its devotion to the study of man and his world. Religion is essential to any understanding of human nature that reaches beyond the most restricted laboratory experiment. Even the man who wishes to avoid religion on the contemporary scene cannot escape it in any approach to the past. The question of religious observance is one of the first to emerge from the very kitchen middens of lost peoples, and the names of the gods are often among the earliest words identified in the inventories of forgotten scripts. No secular enterprise but presently leads the investigator to religion in its not too remote antecedents. And many aspects of the latest developments on the contemporary scene are without meaning to one unaware of the religious elements in their genesis. Indeed, analysts of the present are not wanting who insist that the basic issues of our day are in their essence theological.

Certainly religion is necessary to any understanding of the works that are most expressive of man's nature—literature, the dance, music, the visual arts. They express religious conceptions, but what is even more important, they rest on religious assumptions and implications. Milton's *Paradise Lost,* to invoke one of the great poems of our language, is an obvious example; but the religious premises of Chaucer and Shakespeare, Wordsworth and Shelly, and even Swinburne are quite as essential to the understanding of their work. And religion must be reckoned with no less in our approach to contemporary literature. There is no escaping the necessity of an appreciation and an understanding of the fact of religion for the understanding of man and his history, the thoughts of his mind, and the work of his hands.

To some people, of course, all this may seem a chronicle of illusion and aberration. But then for them, a lot of human history must be a history of aberration, and much of what has most concerned man, illusion. Religion is simply a fact inescapable in any approach to man and the human world.

Yet religion is a good deal more than a humanity, a branch of study. Religion is something to be experienced. It engages not only the reason but the will and the imagination and the emotions. It involves not only the flash of insight, the decision, the conclusion, but also discipline and habit with its building of contexts. For religious life is dependent not only upon the individual insight but upon group support, not only upon the electric flash of momentary discovery and reaction but upon all the sustaining rhythms of the dear and the familiar. In short, religion is not only a matter of knowing but of living. Obviously, knowledge about religion is not enough.

It is not religion as a branch of knowledge that arouses the varying types and the varying depths of solicitude with which we are all familiar. It is not religion as a branch of knowledge that is worrying the parent at home who fears that his child in the university is not only drifting away from the religious life and observance of his family but is losing any contact with the whole moral and intellectual atmosphere in which he was brought up. What such a parent dreads is that it will not be possible for his child ever to come back home with any sympathy for the world in which his family lives. And so with the various religious advisers and guides. It isn't knowledge about religion that is the main concern of the Catholic priest who observes that a student is airily dismissing the claims of religion because his elementary-school command of religious ideas is inadequate to confront even his sophomore command of scientific ideas. Or the Protestant minister who, viewing with some understandable misgivings the bunch of cheerful heathen in the fraternity house next to his church, wonders how he'll ever get a little Christian influence into his incredibly inaccessible neighbors. Or the Jewish rabbi who sees a young man putting the rich tradition of his fathers behind him as something foreign and primitive to be forgotten in his rush for modernity. It is not knowledge about religion that is troubling all these. And one can sympathize with their desire to find some help in reaching the young people about whom they are so movingly concerned.

But this business of reaching another human being is a very delicate and complicated business at any age, and it is especially so at the university age. It is very often precisely those students whose parents are most concerned about their holding to family beliefs who are most eager to escape. It is precisely the type of young person who is apt to be swept off his feet by any new experience who is most enamored of the freedom the university offers. And here we must not forget that the basic principle of a university is freedom. Very much is offered at a university, often a bewildering array of possibilities. But the acceptance of these offerings is dependent upon the individual. It is the essence of the educational process as distinct from certain other human operations that the objects of educational attention can be influenced and led and guided and helped; but in the last analysis acceptance or rejection is up to the individual. The success or failure of the whole enterprise is at his mercy. No young man can be made wise or good in spite of himself.

On the other hand, the anxious elders should never forget the other side of the picture. The university age is an impressionable one and normally a generous one. As anyone who recalls his own youth remembers, a hint or a suggestion may count for a good deal. I still remember how a very wise man once received an outrageously glib and oversimplified historical summary which, I may hasten to add, was by no means original with me. He didn't waste any time trying to argue with some rather widespread illusions of that period. He merely said very thoughtfully with a tone of sympathetic speculation, "I wonder if you will always think that," and dropped the matter there. But I didn't. That was the beginning of a lifelong endeavor to understand certain historical relations which, I may add, has helped me to face the world in which I have lived better than that old and now quite outworn formula. One must never discount the ability of youth to take a hint nor forget that in a good many areas time is on the side of wisdom—if only the young man has not shut the doors of his mind too soon.

But religion is a good deal more than one interest among many. For a religious man it pervades and informs all his undertakings. It is the very air he breathes. It is the strength by which he lives. Particularly is this true of the higher intellectual life. No believer can think of that as alien to his basic preoccupation. And nowhere is the aid of supreme wisdom needed more than here. One might add, too, that nowhere is the worship through the exercise of the gifts which God has given more appropriate. When it is a matter of attempting to understand the natural universe around him, the structure of the society in which he finds himself, the community or the want of community among the peoples of the earth, and so on, then certainly the religious man relies on the Spirit of God within him; and in the exercise of his highest endeavors for the discovery of truth, he pays supreme Truth his highest tribute of honor.

This permeation of all the activities of the religious spirit is not, of course, confined to the scientific. Whether in the Platonic tradition or not, the worship of God has always been thought of as involving all the faculties of man, the love of goodness, and the enjoyment of beauty, as well as the pursuit of truth. It is at this point of the permeation of all life by the religious spirit that the church college, whatever its cost from other points of view, has an indisputable advantage. And it is at this point that the state university must admit its limitations. This is something that by the very terms of its relation to the state it cannot compass. It is at this point that we face, and might as well admit that we face, a very complicated situation.

Religion involves the individual in the most intimate fashion and, because it does, religion must take account of the tremendous range of individual differences. There are great variations in delicacy and range of sensitivity to things religious as to everything else. Individuals differ greatly in the intensity of their needs and responses and in the drive of their pursuit of an objective in this area as elsewhere. It is very easy for us here in America in the middle of the twentieth century with its middle-of-the-road atmosphere on problems of adjustment and balance to underestimate the wide range of human variation and by that underestimation to concentrate on the mythical center and forget about the rest. People who take up art, religion, or politics too enthusiastically for the prevailing temper may be great nuisances to others and very uncomfortable themselves. But we owe a great deal to their prototypes in the past, and we would lose a lot if we eliminated the possibility of their recurrence in the future. We are all safer in camp if there are at least a few scouts out in No Man's Land, and this is no less true of religion than of any other major field.

For the individual does not develop his distinctive tastes in a vacuum, even the most independent of individuals. And especially is this true of the balanced human being to whose production we seem to be dedicated today. Here it is well for us at the university to remember that there are other institutions—the family, the church, the synagogue, and a variety of societies that perform similar functions. Here, as in other fields of our society, we have an intersection of several institutions that are concerned with the same individual, but these institutions have a different character. The state, for example, is neutral to the various religious societies. But the family and the church or the synagogue are not neutral at all—in fact, they are highly demanding. In an age when great emphasis is put upon individual personal development—individual comfort, individual convenience, or what might be called accommodation to the individual—both family and church make demands upon the individual that are considerable. Both the egotism and the laziness that are catered to by other agencies of our society are here called upon to make great sacrifices. Indeed, so pressing are these demands that their fulfillment is possible only on the basis of a strongly consolidated personal preference —what may be defined as a genuine commitment.

The co-operation of the university and the church or synagogue or religious society must be thoughtfully planned for. That does not mean that it should be cramped by red tape or anxiety about jurisdictional jealousy. But thought should be given to certain principles, respect for which will facilitate co-operation. The two institutions can take pains to express their respect for each other. The recognition of church and synagogue in certain types of university functions is traditional. The participation of representatives of the local clergy in prayer and scripture reading on such occasions as commencement is a widespread, probably universal, example. The university can take pains to give recognition to religious leaders and establishments on other appropriate occasions, but all such recognition should not only avoid suggestion of preference but any hint of discrimination against the uncommitted. The university roof is a broad one, and no one who has a right to be under it because of his intellectual competence and scholarly commitment should be made to feel out of place because of any other consideration.

But while this recognition is important, it should never be

forgotten that the church or other religious body does not depend upon the university for the recognition of its status. It has its own dignity and methods, its own sphere, actually much larger than that of the university. And conversely, the university has its own mission and sphere and way of working—its own dignity, which the religious interests should take pains to respect.

There are a good many practical ways in which this co-operation can be implemented. The first and the most obvious is where the state university can find some place in its regular curriculum for the direct course in religion among courses in literature, history, and so on. Various types of general courses in religion are found in state university curricula. Some of those are long established, going back to a period when most of the clientele of the university shared a common religious outlook. Where such courses tacitly assume a common approach, they do not, as a rule, make much appeal to those who do not share that approach; and there is on all sides a considerable doubt as to whether such a solution is entirely adequate in an age when a good deal of emphasis is being put on the pluralist character of our culture. Nor is the "essentials of religion" or any type of least-common-denominator approach likely to be satisfactory to very many people.

After all, we get more from each other when we meet at our fullest and best. So there would seem to be much more scope for an approach that emphasizes common fields of concern in varying traditions and possibilities of co-operation between them on the basis of common interests. Expository courses in the religions of the world certainly have their place. In such courses it is possible to let the various religious traditions speak for themselves through their great books. They probably are easiest to manage when they deal with religious traditions that are more remote from our own. For it is easier to be objective in areas where one does not think that any of one's own commitments are threatened. There is no reason why an American citizen might not be a Moslem or a Buddhist. Indeed, some are, but they are still too few to elicit much response beyond friendly curiosity; so in the average American university community there will probably be less self-consciousness about an approach to oriental religions than to Christianity. Objectivity is something that the university is always working for, and it would be fatal if the university ever gave up that endeavor. But the difficulties of objectivity should never be minimized. It is easy to be blind or self-deceived here, as anywhere else, if we fail to take account of human limitations and the difficulties of transcending those limitations.

The field of religion is one in which the problem is especially acute. Any man who holds a position with regard to the tradition he is presenting is quite aware of the fact that the history of religion, for example, involves a very complex business of attention and interpretation. Two perfectly sincere inquirers may survey the same situation and find their attention riveted on quite different aspects of it. Two scholars on opposite sides may agree as to certain facts that have played a part in religious history—say, loss of original zeal or lack of contact with changing social conditions—and yet draw very different conclusions because of the different degrees of importance attached to various elements in the situation. It is only possible to handle this problem with great humility as to the limitations of any one man's approach and with great candor as to differences of perspective and value.

One does not have to give up the struggle for objectivity in this area to recognize that a man who believes in the religious tradition he is presenting will communicate a warmer and richer experience to his students than one who does not. It is for this reason that the arrangement which would probably be most satisfactory to the various religious groups concerned would be a system whereby each group offered its own instruction in the university with its own representative on the faculty, giving courses in its tradition which would be treated like any other courses. There is no question that such an arrangement would reassure the parent as to the university's concern about religion and as to the possibility of his child's having continuing access to his tradition and opportunity to mature in religious understanding as in other aspects of his intellectual relation to the world. There is no question either that such an arrangement would make it easier to persuade the indifferent or pre-occupied young man that the acquisition of religious knowledge is to be regarded as important. There would, of course, be problems of joint appointment. To draw attention to this is not in any way to suggest that the professional religious repre-sentative is not as intellectually competent and as well trained as the usual faculty member. In many cases he has undergone an even more extensive period of training. But the objectives of that training may be different as the criteria of selection in the first place may well be different. Justice would have to be done to two sets of standards.

The problem of judgment of work done would not always be an easy matter. The university has a responsibility for standards in any credit-giving, and its attitude toward and its concentration on values is somewhat different from that of the religious society. Moreover, if this pattern were developed, the great variety of religious commitments in this country would have to be taken into account. Particularly is this true with the groups who are usually rather summarily lumped together under the heading "Protestant." Any very high degree of specialization in these curricular offerings would inevitably lead to problems of representation. And the more seriously the whole thing were taken, the more considerable these would probably be. It is very doubtful if this arrangement would be possible in many places because of legal problems of separation of church and state and restrictions on denominational activities in the public institutions. But it has been possible to do this sort of thing successfully at an institution like Michigan State University in East Lansing.

There is also a possibility of co-operation between the uni-versity and religious bodies in the form of the School of Religion set up within the university. Here the university and the church and other religious institutions co-operate in main-taining an organization to which both can contribute and which both recognize. One such arrangement is the Bible College at the University of Missouri—an arrangement prob-ably possible only where there is a relative preponderance of one religious orientation in the population. A more inclusive and more widely applicable pattern is that of the School of Religion at the University of Iowa, which has for some thirty years now aroused great interest over the country. Here courses for the three major divisions of the American religious population, Protestant, Catholic, and Jewish, are offered by representatives of those traditions on the campus for full credit as university work. The success of the School of Religion at Iowa shows what can be accomplished where no legal or social barriers are raised and where the problems of representation and co-operation can be patiently worked out.

The University of Michigan, contemplating at present neither a School of Religion nor Department, sponsors activity in this area through an Office of Religious Affairs under the Vice-President of Student Affairs, and a faculty committee of professors from the College of Literature, Science, and the Arts. These two are roughly divided into that area of religion which is experience and that which is knowledge: the first co-ordinates the twenty-two student religious foundations in the campus community and has responsibility for the religious counseling services of the university; the second works closely with curriculum and the intellectual life. Needless to say, the Office and the Committee work in close harmony.

The Committee, responsible to the Dean of the College, is active in six main areas: (1) the degree program which, through requiring 18 hours of approved courses in religion in various departments and 18 hours in a single discipline, such as philosophy, history, anthropology, etc., provides a "major" in religion and ethics; (2) the securing of appointments to the faculty in particular departments to strengthen the program and enrich the intellectual life of the University; (3) the lecture program —in 1956-57, with a generous College appropriation, the Committee co-sponsored with appropriate departments eleven outstanding lecturers who expounded authoritatively the beliefs and values of various religions, represented stimulating points of view about religion to sizable lay audiences, and described significant research in the area; (4) encouragement of interdisciplinary thinking about religion among interested faculty members through monthly meetings of the "Faculty Colloquium in Religion"; (5) increasing the possessions of the general library in religion; and (6) co-operation on the university level with other agencies on the curriculum in religion in the state university.

The Office of Religious Affairs, newly established in May of 1956, is recognized as one of the Personnel Services of the University. Full attention is given to co-ordination, including such a program as may be necessary to the building of a climate in which co-ordination can be most effective. It also makes religious resources available in all the schools and colleges of the University and it emphasizes the relevance of religion to the educational process, moving toward the effective integration of the intellectual and the practical aspects of religion.

Another plan is the development of a number of credit programs in the various religious centers around the university—as at the University of Illinois and the University of North Dakota, where programs are well established and recognized. This makes possible wider representation of groups than the School of Religion and probably makes possible a freer hand for the religious group concerned. Such a program certainly demonstrates to parents and the community the regard of the university for religious instruction and leaves no doubt in the minds of students that from the point of view of the university this is as important as any other type of instruction. Such a program necessitates, of course, the maintenance at the religious center of a staff qualified for this additional work. There is the problem of maintenance of standards for work done in the atmosphere of other activities, and the problem of credit for work not under the university's control.

It is not, of course, always possible. Sometimes there is an explicit legal barrier; sometimes it is established custom and a prevailing climate of opinion that suggest caution. But barriers that are referred to as explicitly legal often have been revised by custom and public opinion. Where for various reasons these more direct provisions are not possible, the strong religious center—especially one that provides for both student and faculty participation—seems to be the most widely available solution. The religious center maintained by the church or other religious group at the university offers, of course, a full experience of religion as both material for study and a way of life. But there are problems of staffing. The ideal youth leader or the ideal counselor may not always be the ideal professor. And even when he is, he may be torn between the demands on his time. There are problems, too, of facilities, secretarial help, libraries, and student and faculty time. The student with a full schedule of university work, earning his way through school, may not have many hours left over for noncredit study. There are problems of contact with the university community. A good deal of the day-to-day administration of the university is carried on quite informally, even casually and incidentally. In such a situation, being in the middle of things is of great value. Anybody who lives in a university community knows how important the factor of constant communication is, so that it would not be surprising if the professional worker at the student center feels that he is left out on the sidelines. On the other hand, the student who has learned to pursue his religious education at the church center in a voluntary class is likely to keep up that process of self-education upon which the religious groups rely for the continuation of their lay leadership.

But whatever the possible situation on any particular campus, there is no question that the university and the religious groups can and do co-operate in the interest of the individual student. This co-operation between the faculty and administrative officers, especially those charged with counseling and guidance responsibilities, and the student pastors is a valuable thing on the campus of the state university and, I suspect, pretty generally appreciated. It is my experience that university officers are very glad to be able to call upon student pastors for help in individual problems, especially when they lie beyond the resources of the academic staff. And, on the other hand, the religious bodies look to university administrative authorities for understanding of special problems of students whose religious commitments bring them into conflict with university regulations and requirements. The conscientious objector in the institution with required ROTC, the Christian Scientist, the Seventh Day Adventist, the orthodox Jew with dietary problems, and so on, can usually count on a sympathetic understanding of his problems and help for their solution.

As for the general student community, it is very important that it should learn as early as possible that the respect for the individual on which we pride ourselves is likely at times to require some taking of pains for practical realization. More could be done, certainly, to promote communication and understanding. The contact of the student chaplain or rabbi with the faculty members in his own congregation is probably, day in and day out, the most reliable source of communication. On the other hand, the individual professor on any large campus is likely to be pretty much absorbed in his own academic and extracurricular obligations and not too much aware of what is going on in other corners of the campus beside his own. Any professor who travels at all has had the mortifying experience of hearing for the first time on a distant campus of something that's going on at home. Probably more formal occasions and conferences would help here, if for nothing else than to maintain contacts. Some central office on campus with provision of office service would unquestionably be useful, though on any campus there is a tendency for each new office to develop its own distinct sphere of activity that might make any administration hesitate about the expansion of claims on an already overstrained budget.

Various types of co-operation between the university and the church groups on common projects are found on different campuses. The faculty-student committees for religious activities are one example. They offer a good deal of opportunity for both understanding and co-operation. The religious sections in university libraries are another. The faculty member who sees that first-class religious books find their way into the library is performing a real service. Lectures give another opportunity not only for interchange between the students in the various religious bodies but for the university and the community around it. The visitor in a lecture series like that at Wisconsin usually meets not only with student groups but often with church groups in town, and the result is a very widespread stimulation of religious interest. Such programs as occur during Religious Emphasis Week stress the importance of religion and stimulate serious consideration of religious problems among a variety of groups—fraternities and sororities and dormitories as well as churches. And there are the various intergroup activities—programs, committees, conferences, week-ends, and so on. All of these have demonstrated very real values and possibilities. But, of course, there are problems of funds, staff, and so on. And student response is often incalculable. All education, however, is a sowing of seed of which the harvest is still some way off. Indeed, he who is not willing to cast his bread upon the waters should not embark on any educational enterprise, secular or religious.

There is no doubt that here, as usual in the vast possibilities of the state university, there is a good deal that we might do that we are not doing. Certain things should, I think, be kept in mind. There is a legal problem of state-church relationship in some states that stands in the way of explicit and formal inclusion of religion in the university curriculum. Even where there is some doubt as to the full extent of legal barriers, it must be asked whether the good desired is considerable or sure enough to justify the risk of strain in community relations. There are a good many situations where one may make more progress without forcing the issue. No palpable unfairness should stay unchallenged, but it would be a failure of traditional American enterprise to let any possibility of growth go unexplored.

Here we have a great variety of circumstances to consider, and it is characteristic of the human predicament that every set of circumstances has its disadvantages and its advantages. But the fact of difference of opinion is one that must be faced by young people in our society. They will need when they leave the university to know how to plunge into the varied common life of our time with quiet confidence in their own values but with respect for the different values of others.

Finally, from the point of view of the religious man or woman, student or faculty member, we should never forget that those human qualities which religion fosters—devotion to the things of the mind and spirit, respect for other people, love of justice, and charity—are things which are greatly needed in the university as in any other community. For these things the personal example is still the most potent witness, and that witness is not without power even in so large and so varied a community as that of the state university.

MARK H. INGRAHAM

Academic Freedom

CHAPTER VII

The claims of academic freedom, while including the freedoms which should be the right of every citizen, go beyond these to freedoms that institutions of learning and the scholars therein must possess if they are to fulfill their functions in society. The freedom that should be accorded the individual faculty member perhaps has had fuller treatment than the freedom of the student or the freedom of the institution as a corporate body. I deal with this first.

The Association of American Colleges and the American Association of University Professors formulated a Statement of Principles, accepted by both in 1940. Although modifications of procedure are being considered, this statement is still the commonly accepted standard. I shall quote from it, omitting the material concerning academic tenure, which of course is closely involved with academic freedom. After stressing the importance of academic freedom, the statement attempts to define it.

(a) The teacher is entitled to full freedom in research and in the publication of the results, subject to the adequate performance of his other academic duties; but research for pecuniary return should be based upon an understanding with the authorities of the institution.

(b) The teacher is entitled to freedom in the classroom in discussing his subject, but he should be careful not to introduce into his teaching controversial matter which has no relation to his subject. Limitations of academic freedom because of religious or other aims of the institution should be clearly stated in writing at the time of the appointment.

(c) The college or university teacher is a citizen, a member of a learned profession, and an officer of an educational institution. When he speaks or writes as a citizen, he should be free from institutional censorship or discipline, but his special position in the community imposes special obligations. As a man of learning and an educational officer, he should remember that the public may judge his profession and his institution by his utterances. Hence he should at all times be accurate, should exercise appropriate restraint, should show respect for the opinions of others, and should make every effort to indicate that he is not an institutional spokesman.

It is clear from the above that the scholarly profession claims a freedom beyond that which the scholars have as citizens. There is no constitutional guarantee that a man will not lose his job because of his expression of opinions. This is one of the essential guarantees which should be given to the mature scholar. There is no expectation that the ordinary citizen would be furnished a captive audience and a platform from which he can proclaim his opinions. These privileges are not accorded for the pleasure of the teacher or investigator. Rather freedom is the necessary condition for his maximum usefulness, stemming from the proper function in society of the scholar and also from, in the case of the faculty member, the purpose of the institution he serves.

Yet this freedom is not a freedom beyond that of the ordinary citizen except in the areas of special competence of the scholar. It is not a freedom to discuss the irrelevant in class. It is a freedom that presupposes the essential progressive character of scholarly investigation, the constant improvement of the tools of investigation, and the honesty of the scholar.

The independence of the scholar is needed by society in somewhat the same sense and for kindred reasons as the independence of the judiciary. In terms of his knowledge of the law, not limited by executive pressures, not controlled by any legislative act which may be unconstitutional, nor swayed by the biased points of view of the parties concerned, the judge interprets the law in the interest of society. The law forms a standard, yet a changing and developing standard, above the self-interest of various groups or individuals. The scholar also, through his scholarship, may bring to bear upon societies an insight more complete and more impartial than that of others. His findings also form a standard, both changing and developing, which in the field of his competence should be above self-interest and prejudice. One could say he also has a judicial function in society that is best when it is freely fulfilled. Or perhaps it would be more accurate to say that the judge is a scholar who, in the realm of his competence, must have the same independence that all scholars need in order to be of maximum use.

Not only truth but also diversity should be cherished. The university that does not promote the understanding and the development of the arts falls short of its purpose. The sky-scraper and the Parthenon, the sonnet and the epic, the abstract design and the genre painting, the Bartók concerto and the Gregorian chant, all contribute to the richness of humanity and to the heritage we bequeath our children. The university is an executor of the estate left to us by our fathers and augmented by ourselves for the enrichment of our children. The artist as a creator, the critic as an interpreter, require freedom as much as does the scholar as fact-finder and analyst.

Another aspect of academic freedom which should be borne in mind is distinction between freedom of thought and speech and freedom of action. Society, in its own interests, makes certain decisions as to how the individual shall act and legally enforces these through the police and through the courts. For instance, there may be a sixty-mile-per-hour speed limit for state highways. A driver going faster than this limit should be arrested and penalized. A driver driving with reasonable care within this limit should be exempt from penalty. It would be intolerable, however, if a citizen did not have a right to argue that this speed limit should be changed to fifty miles per hour or to seventy miles per hour. Academic freedom demands freedom of thought, investigation, and expression. The scholar's freedom of action is that of any other citizen.

Academic freedom is not all-inclusive; in particular it must be remembered, especially by the scholar, that it does not include freedom from criticism. The scholar who brings forward his own ideas in the hope that they will enlighten the subject matter of his field must expect them to be criticized not only by other scholars but frequently by the general public. Even an administrative officer, if he makes clear that he supports the scholar's freedom, should not be denied the privilege of criticizing the scholar's ideas.

The freedom that should be accorded the student in learning, in his organizations, in the speakers he listens to, and in his actions is a constant problem. In the classroom this is largely covered in connection with the freedom of his teacher. But this is not always the case. Unfortunately, there are teachers who, demanding freedom of their own to expound their subject, are grudging in allowing the student to form his own conclusions. Happily, such teachers are rare, but the students should be protected against them. However, it should also be remembered that students should be protected from the monopolizing of a class period by the persistent vociferation of the occasional exhibitionist in their own ranks.

The freedom of students and student organizations to bring speakers to the campus has been among the most discussed problems in academic circles. In general I believe that the limitations should be only those that state and federal legislation would impose upon all citizens and that we should strive to make this imposition light.

A community is something other than an aggregate, and the community of scholars that forms a university has a corporate identity and a corporate purpose. The university as a corporate body, especially the state university, is not free to define its own functions. It must be responsive to the needs of the state as expressed by its legislature; and, in general, the legislature determines the list of its component colleges. However, to agree that its function in society is largely determined by society does not mean that society should prescribe the means by which it fulfills its function. The state may determine that the university have a college of engineering. The university must determine the curriculum of this college, as well as the content of courses and the method of teaching. And if freedom is necessary in teaching, it is equally necessary in research. It is difficult to determine what portion of our knowledge best forms the content of a course. It is even more difficult to determine what paths we should follow when we explore the unknown. Within the broad limits, therefore, of areas of work that the state is willing to support, the university should have freedom of action.

Relevant to the freedom of the professor, of the student, and of the institution is a statement that those of us at the University of Wisconsin cherish, formulated by the Board of Regents in 1894 and now engraved in bronze of Bascom Hall, which proclaims that the University "should ever encourage that continual and fearless sifting and winnowing by which alone the truth can be found." Last fall this plaque was stolen, and just before its recovery, when it was expected that a new one would have to be cast, the Regents passed a resolution containing the following statement: "The search for truth is the central duty of the University, but truth will not be found if the scholar is not free, it will not be understood if the student is not free, it will not be used if the citizen is not free."

In respect to religion, however, the academic freedom of the faculty, students, and the university itself has been curtailed because most state universities are barred by constitutional provision from giving "sectarian" instruction. This is sometimes accompanied by a ban against "partisan" instruction. There is no question that such constitutional provisions limit academic freedom, but this limitation is probably wise.

It is now impossible to determine fully either the motivation that led to these restrictions or the meaning their authors would have attributed to them. I believe there was little antireligious sentiment involved. The doctrine of separation of church and state, as expounded by such men as Jefferson, must certainly have carried weight. Probably the zeal of each denomination and its jealous wariness of the others, as well as the desire to "keep peace in the family," were the major factors in barring sectarian instruction in both school and college.

In the state universities of the Midwest, for some time after the adoption of the state constitutions, compulsory attendance at chapel was the rule. This was succeeded by chapel services provided by the institution for those who wished to attend voluntarily. These chapel services were formed from the elements common to the dominant Protestant denominations. They were also a convenient vehicle for the expression of presidential opinions. The increase in the number of Catholic students as well as the number of students of faiths other than Christian would make any such services not supplemented by other types unacceptable at present. Such religious instruction, or at least religious exercises, were not considered unconstitutional. The constitutional provisions against sectarian instruction seem, in practice today, to be given a more narrow interpretation than immediately after they were adopted. It is almost certain that constitutional objections would be raised against any attempt to install compulsory chapel in state universities today. Even the provision of chapel with voluntary attendance probably would be subject to careful legal scrutiny.

These constitutional provisions chiefly restrict the program of an institution rather than the freedom of a faculty member. If medicine, for instance, is omitted from the list of colleges the legislature will support, this immediately limits the program of the university. To a large degree the barring of religious instruction is of the same nature. In at least two important respects, however, it differs from a determination not to support a medical school. In the first place, it is a constitutional provision that the legislature itself may not set aside. And, in the second place, it is a ban against a field that traditionally is a part of the liberal arts' curriculum while, at the same time, every state university contains a college of liberal arts. Thus it limits the freedom of the college in the choice of the relevant subject matter contained in its curriculum. (I still believe it might be disastrous to the support of the university and its relation to the public, if not to the curriculum, to remove this restriction.)

It is clearly recognized that the principles of academic freedom do not include the right of a professor to discuss at length in class materials irrelevant to his field. Yet in many fields the discussion of religion is essential. As it is integral to almost all history and central in the history of such periods as the Reformation, the teacher of history will inevitably discuss religion. The same is true of the philosopher, the anthropologist, the art critic, and a whole list of others. Although in practice wisdom, tact, and respect for the opinion of others is especially needed in dealing with religious topics, no scholar should be denied the right to give his own conclusions when they are relevant.

It is also clear, I believe, that state universities have the right to give courses in such subjects as the history of religion, the philosophy of religion, and comparative religions. If the treatment both as to exposition and as to emphasis of various doctrines is fair, one should not object to the students being told which of the many views discussed his instructor holds. There is no question, however, that the judicious handling of such material is more difficult than, for instance, the comparison of metrical forms. Instruction in these subjects is not sectarian. But neither does it fulfill the function of religious teaching.

Thus in law and in practice there are certain limitations on the freedom of the public college to develop a program of religious instruction. This is a major restriction on the corporate freedom of the institution. Since teachers of religion will not be employed under present constitutional provisions, these provisions are only a minor restriction on the freedom of the teachers at present on the staffs of the state universities. Unless religious instruction is supplied by other sources, especially the church, these constitutional provisions are an important restriction on the student.

Yet, despite this bar on sectarian teaching, religious groups have been actively interested in what takes place on the campus. It is very difficult to give the right balance to any discussion of the relation of religious groups to academic freedom, particularly in state universities. It would be easy to give the impression that there has been a constant struggle on the part of the state universities to protect their faculties from the undue pressure arising from religious sources to curtail their freedom. If one did this, one would be overlooking the fact that most of the defenders of academic freedom are themselves men of religious convictions and affiliations. Moreover, those who object on religious grounds to the statements or behavior of persons in the academic community seldom are speaking officially for any religious organization. Whether these persons are clerics or laymen, they are usually expressing convictions with which many in their own churches would differ. Nevertheless, it may be worthwhile to examine a few of the attacks that at times have been made in the name of religion on academic freedom.

Until shortly after World War I, one of the most frequent attacks upon the university has been in connection with the teaching of evolution. For those who believe in the literal interpretation of the Biblical story of creation, the teaching of the doctrine of evolution is the teaching of error; and because it throws doubt on the infallibility of the Bible, the error is important. This conflict of opinion was at its height during the formation and growth of our state universities. Our land-grant colleges, many of them parts of state universities, inevitably strongly emphasized the biological sciences. Practically all biologists, for well over half a century now, have been evolutionists. Attacks upon the freedom of public education through such laws as the antievolution laws in Tennessee and through such spokesmen as William Jennings Bryan lasted until the era of many of us still teaching. These attacks have to a large degree ceased—which is a triumph for the universities, particularly because it is a noiseless triumph. I believe they have ceased not chiefly because people have become convinced that all points of view should be fully taught but because the leaders in most churches have accepted the doctrine of evolution. In doing so they have discovered that the essence of their faith remains unchanged under the impact of biological science as under the impact of Biblical criticism.

Another area of attack has been upon outspoken agnostics in university faculties. Here the problem is somewhat more complicated. No one can possibly criticize churchmen for their own answers to agnosticism. They properly defend the creeds they believe and it is healthy that they do so. There is no reason why they should not criticize the points of view held by many of those who differ from them on the basic questions of religion. I believe it is unfortunate, however, when they criticize an institution for containing agnostics on its faculty who, in discussing philosophical problems, present their own points of view. When, as perhaps has occasionally been the case, this presentation becomes so insistent as to be essentially propaganda, one can understand how churchmen will declare that it is unfair in an institution which cannot give "sectarian" instruction to allow "antireligious" instruction. This is not an easy challenge to answer. I shall give my own reaction to it. A man who uses the classroom for propaganda purposes is acting improperly. I say this in spite of the fact that I believe a man, in trying to deal with all questions fairly, should not disguise his own beliefs and, if he is respected, those beliefs will carry weight beyond even the arguments given for them. This, however, is different from deliberate propaganda which, as I said above, is always improper.

There is much, however, that is improper that is not illegal; and the question always arises as to what degree should an institution use its authority to keep its own staff from acting improperly. This question has no absolute answer, for judgments of propriety are difficult to make and often dangerous to apply. I believe that universities should go a long way to refrain from institutional judgments that limit the freedom of the individual to act in accordance with his own judgment. The risk of limiting a scholar's freedom is so great that before any action is taken the administration should be convinced it is clearly necessary to step in. I have not myself experienced an abuse on the part of a faculty member in regard to a discussion of religion that I believed demanded administrative interference. Even so, I would not take the stand that such might not arise. For instance, a student's right to hold and express a particular religious point of view should be protected against the penalty of unfair grading or of ridicule. I also believe that in regard to occasional propaganda on the part of the faculty member, the greater danger is from its irrelevance rather than from the possibility of the unfortunate swaying of opinions. Most of our students are reasonably good at spotting propaganda, but they have no protection against the waste to their time that such propaganda represents.

The college-age period is often the last and sometimes the most painful in the long process of weaning. During this period independence of ideas and of action should be fully attained. As the uses of independence made at this time are sometimes rather foolish, the university is frequently attacked for not exercising more control over the behavior of its students. This is a different attack than the attack on the freedom of the scholar, although there are elements of the latter contained within it. For the university is often attacked for leading a student to doubt the precepts under which he was brought up by his parents and his church and for leading him to question social standards that are proclaimed, if not observed, by his elders. The university is also frequently criticized for being lax in the standards of behavior it permits. Again, the answer is one of degree—not an absolute.

The more strict institutions of the past seem to have had just as great difficulty with student discipline and individual student behavior as do the universities under the generally freer attitude of the present. I would not for a moment wish it to be thought that I am happy with the present situation. Cheating in university classes is prevalent and, to a large degree, uncontrolled by either discipline or student opinion. I believe that the moral standards of the university student community are somewhat above those of the general public. The difference, however, should be greater. To a large degree the blame must be shared by the home, the church, and the school. All of us must contemplate with reverence the possibilities of the human spirit but often be depressed by the actualities of the average. However, it would seem best, insofar as possible, to work toward higher standards within the framework of freedom rather than within the framework of restriction. We must remember that an enforced conformity will do little to improve the average and may do much to damage the ideal. Moreover, the conservative who criticizes youth without making distinction between standards of virtue and minor standards of good taste is inviting youth in its revolt against the latter to revolt also against the former. The university is in a very difficult situation in dealing with students on matters of conduct which we would not tolerate in the child nor interfere with in the adult. The home and the church can do more by intensifying their influences in the years before college and during college life than by asking the university to take a more restrictive attitude toward its students than the community in general takes toward its citizens.

I do not wish to be understood as advocating that the university should tolerate serious misbehavior. I do not! However, I believe the university should more consciously develop a sense of values in the students through example and through its faculty members being less reticent in presenting their own ideals and in showing their indignation with the selfish, the shoddy, and the dishonest. Many of us could usefully wear our hearts on our sleeves to a greater degree than we do now. I subscribe heartily to the faculty committee which wrote: "What are the qualities sought in a staff member? The first is integrity of character—the second, sound scholarship. Both must be present if a faculty member is to be useful to the University. Other qualities will enhance that usefulness."

Besides criticism of the university for explicit teaching in connection with such topics as evolution, or for agnosticism (which quite frequently has been confused with atheism), there is the vague charge that the state university is godless. I believe that traditionally this arose in the days when most private institutions were closely affiliated with particular churches. The degree of this affiliation frequently became somewhat more tenuous during the period when Carnegie pensions were being granted to persons in nonsectarian colleges. To a large extent the talk about the "ungodly" state universities died down. There is now a slight revival—particularly in terms of the appeal to wealth to give to private colleges, especially to church-related schools, rather than to public institutions. To only a certain degree this is connected with academic freedom in that it affects the ability of the institution to secure support for many of its programs from wealthy individuals, from corporations, and even to some extent from foundations. Moreover, at times it has been suggested that it was improper for a state institution even to solicit support for its work, especially its instructional program, from private sources. It is strange that the "godly" will sometimes use means to seek the dollar that the "ungodly" would shun.

We must make it clear that anyone has a right to state that he believes a professor in the university is mistaken and that the university policy in regard to teachers and even in regard to academic freedom is mistaken. Equally it is the obligation of the university and its administration to defend the academic freedom of the individual and of the institution and to try to persuade the public that attacks upon this freedom are—even if permissible—unfortunate, unwise, and mistaken.

There is no question that the state universities have been criticized, and I believe unwisely, by religious persons for the sciences they teach, for the opinions expressed by their faculties, and for the freedom they grant their students. It would be totally unfair to leave the impression that this was the only relation of religion to academic freedom. Religious groups have been among the staunchest defenders of academic freedom. An attack upon an institution by churchmen can generally be left for other churchmen to answer—frequently from the same denomination. And attacks also upon institutions' freedoms made by various political groups such as, for instance, veterans' organizations, are frequently offset by the strong defense that religious groups make. Let me give some illustrations.

Certain groups in the American Legion in Wisconsin urged the University not to allow student organizations on the Attorney General's subversive list to be registered at the University or to invite speakers from outside. There are many strong arguments for this point of view. I feel the strength of the case against it, however, is overwhelming. The University has not altered its original policy in this matter. Some of the strongest support the University received was from the groups of ministers within the State of Wisconsin. I quote, as typical of those received by the University from church groups or church men in support of its stand, a statement taken from the report of the Board of Social and Economic Relations of the Wisconsin Annual Conference of Methodist Churches:

"We commend the University of Wisconsin in its stand on freedom of expression. We maintain with pride our American heritage of freedom to study and express ourselves on even such a controversial subject as Communism."

A delightful experience that I had in regard to the attitude of churches toward academic freedom was soon after World War II, when the University was so crowded that we requested permission to give a course in political science in the local Congregational Church near the campus. This was granted when we assured the trustees that the University would be responsible for any damage to property and assured the minister that there would be "no limitation on the freedom of the teacher" in teaching this subject.

The history of the church would lead us to expect that religious groups would both limit and defend the freedom of the university and of the university scholar. The record of Christianity is an interesting mixture of conservatism and of revolution. An established organization such as the church is naturally conservative. Religious leaders—idealists, socially conscious, and frequently highly emotional by nature—are naturally reformers. This is why it is simple on the one hand to depict progress in western civilization as an expression of Christianity and on the other hand to have books written with such titles as "The Warfare of Science and Theology."

An established organization is also likely to be somewhat authoritarian. The reformer, religious or otherwise, naturally will break with authority. In some cases this break is merely an attempt to establish a new authority in the place of the old. The theocrats of New England did not wish to be under the authority of the King or the Church of England, but neither did they wish to give religious or intellectual freedom to the people of New England. On the other hand, such leaders as Roger Williams placed tolerance among the first of Christian virtues. Progress of freedom was first dependent on those who wished freedom for themselves without having generalized this to granting freedom for others, and then upon those who later saw that freedom as an underlying principle was even more important than any one of its individual uses. It is a mature social philosophy that accepts the principle of freedom as the first condition of change.

An institution must jealously guard those prerogatives without which it cannot fully serve society. The independence of the court, the church, and the university in each case is such a prerogative. The freedom of the scholar is another. Clearly among the pressures limiting the freedom of the state university and its faculty are those arising from religious sources. Yet I believe that at present these freedoms are to a far greater degree supported by religious influences. Today, as yesterday, much of the intellectual leadership and social conscience of the nation centers in the church and the university. Such leadership always seeks freedom for itself and latterly has come not only to grant it to others but to join in its defense. There must ever be a strong kinship between the university that seeks freedom in order to find the truth and the church that cherishes the text:

"Ye shall know the truth, and the truth shall make you free."

THEODORE M. GREENE

Religion and the Humanities

CHAPTER VIII

It is today a truism that the over-all purpose of education in this country is the enrichment of the life of the individual and the strengthening of our democratic way of life. The distinction between vocational and professional education, on the one hand, and "liberal" or "general" education, on the other, is no less obvious. We can assume that our school system will be expected to provide increasing facilities for the acquisition of specialized skills. The why and how of so-called "liberal" education, however, is much in dispute, not only among professional educators but also among liberal arts students and the general public. There is disagreement as to the kind of welfare which liberal education should seek to promote. If we approach this problem superficially, in terms of popular short-range objectives, present procedures seem reasonably efficient. The important controversial questions arise at the level of basic human needs and possibilities.

How today do most Americans conceive of the "good life"? Predominantly in "sensate" terms (to borrow Professor Sorokin's descriptive adjective), that is, in terms of physical health and comfort, passive entertainment, and economic and social security. Most of our fellow citizens seem to be willing to settle for a house equipped with the modern appliances, a car and a T.V. set, and the life of work and play that currently prevails in our big cities and their suburbs. Those who are more ambitious conceive of "success" in comparable terms, that is, in terms of a more responsible job at a higher salary which will make available a bigger house, a more expensive car, greater comfort, and greater local prestige. The type of person most respected and envied in our society is not the saint or the sage, not the scholar or even the brilliant scientist, not the military hero or the gifted athlete, not the great statesman, the powerful politician, the brilliant lawyer, or the shrewd financier, but rather the successful executive who is in a position to make "important" decisions and to control events within the framework of our competitive business-oriented institutions.

For this kind of life a minimal "general" education will suffice. Bare literacy and a slight knowledge of current events, national and international, make possible the casual reading of most newspapers and popular magazines. T.V. programs and the movies demand even less and so does most day-by-day social intercourse. American parents want the "best" for their children, and this "best" has come to include, wherever possible, a college education. But this education, insofar as it is general and not vocational, is chiefly valued by most parents and by most of their sons and daughters not for its potential enrichment of life but primarily because it provides useful social contacts, enlarges the field of marital selection, and thus opens a variety of doors to "success" in our society. When the value of general education is conceived of in these terms, it merits the half-hearted patronage which it presently receives from the American public. Small wonder that so many parents encourage their boys and girls in college to strive for athletic and social prestige, and that so many of our undergraduates exhibit little motivation for strenuous application to their non-vocational studies.

To take liberal education really seriously, we must raise our sights and define its objectives in a much more challenging way. We must envisage an ideal of human living which, though valid for all men in proportion to their capacity for response, will in fact capture the imaginations and enlist the loyalty of only a minority of our total student population. This may sound aristocratic. But only thus can we hope to safeguard our democracy and provide our abler youth with the enriching education to which they are entitled. It is in this realistic context that we shall discuss the proper role of the humanities and of religion in higher education today.

Let us start with the proper objectives of liberal education. These can best be defined in terms of basic human needs. What must we do and be, as human beings, not only to survive but to live a good life in the world as we know it today?

The answer is not far to seek. We are finite creatures living in an incredibly complex world not of our making to which we must adapt ourselves. Each of us is a composite being of body, mind, and soul (to use three vague but familiar terms) seeking to live in a composite total environment of nature, man, and God (to use three other familiar but ambiguous terms). Our total task in life is to know ourselves and our total environment as well as possible in order to discipline and develop ourselves for the most propitious response to the challenges and opportunities which objective reality actually offers us.

All men are also born into a society with a cultural legacy of language, customs, beliefs, institutions, and artifacts, both useful and aesthetically pleasing. We would be condemned to a primitive barbarism far closer to animal existence than obtains in the most savage human society were we not able to stand culturally on the shoulders of our predecessors and to benefit from their cumulative achievements. These achievements can be of great help to us in our response to the various impinging facets of our world. The richer the cultural heritage of a society, the greater are the opportunities for cultural assimilation and advance. A "primitive" society cannot provide its young people with the powerful linguistic instruments, the scientific procedures and knowledge, the technological skill, the wealth of artistic expression, the cumulative philosophical wisdom, and the enlightened religious beliefs of an "advanced" culture such as our own. We also have available to us today the cultures of other contemporary societies and the many great cultures which have arisen, flourished, and died.

What, then, are the chief attitudes and skills most conducive to our effective response to our total environment in the light of this cultural heritage? As regards attitudes, we need, first, an attitude of alert curiosity and wonder, a lively desire to discover all we can about nature, our fellow men, and the ultimate mysteries which have intrigued and haunted man since time immemorial. Equally important is what might be called the responsive attitude, that is, the cultivated impulse to get along with our natural, human, and Divine environment in the best possible way, through submission or accommodation or control. This responsive attitude finds its complement in an attitude of respect—the respect for nature which, until recently, was called "natural piety," a respect for ourselves as human beings and for our fellow men, and a respect, better entitled reverence, for the Ultimate as it reveals itself to us in philosophic wisdom and religious insight. An attitude of sincere respect tends, in turn, to arouse in us a sense of loyalty or obligation. Finally, the attitude which most perfectly complements a sense of spontaneous obligation is that disciplined abandon which characterizes human *creativity* in its myriad forms. These five general attitudes of curiosity, response, respect, obligation, and creativity, in combination, can put man into vital rapport with his environment. Without them he is unlikely to address himself to reality in the right spirit or to acquire the requisite insights.

There are four basic skills which together implement these five attitudes. The first can be entitled the logical-linguistic skill, that is, the ability to think clearly in one or more of the several languages, verbal and nonverbal, which man has invented to express and communicate his ideas. I couple the logical and the linguistic skills thus because of their absolute mutual dependence. We can think only as we articulate our thoughts linguistically; our use of language, in turn, makes sense only as it expresses clear thinking. The second basic skill can be labelled factual. This is man's ability to become factually informed and to distinguish between fact and fiction. The third generic skill is the normative, that is, the ability to discover and appreciate the value of whatever we encounter with informed and judicious sensitivity. The fourth and culminating skill is the synoptic, that is, the ability to rise above provincial prejudice, to widen our horizons, and thus to see life and reality more steadily and whole. We are well equipped for the task of human living in direct proportion as we approximate an ideal mastery of these four skills, that is, in proportion as we are literate, articulate and clear-headed in the several complementary languages of human discourse, as we are factually oriented and informed, as we are sensitive and mature in our normative responses, and as we acquire the capacity for synoptic vision.

These attitudes and skills are all prerequisite to an adequate apprehension of and response to our total environment. It is the responsibility of liberal education to cultivate these attitudes and skills as efficiently as possible.

But liberal education should also be focussed upon certain large distinguishable areas of reality and experience. To do so, it must be differentiated into several families of "disciplines" which differ in basic subject matter, that is, in the basic aspects of reality and human experience which man must systematically explore. These include the world of nature in all its complexity, human society with its multiple institutions, man's artistic artifacts, and, finally, the realm or dimension of ultimate mystery. The emergent disciplines are the natural sciences, the social sciences, the study of the arts and letters, and the systematic study of religion. These are the basic subject-matter disciplines of scholarship and of liberal education.

In addition to these four subject-matter disciplines there are two other types of discipline of major importance. The first of these embraces man's systematic studies of his own logical processes and of the various languages of human discourse, primarily the verbal languages. These studies include logic in its various forms and linguistics in all its ramifications. They can be entitled "skill" disciplines because it is these complex skills which are here the subject matter of orderly inquiry. The whole field of pure mathematics should be included in this family of disciplines.

The second type of discipline is oriented to synoptic vision. Scope and perspective can be developed along the two complementary axes of time and logic. The discipline whose basic frame of reference is time is, of course, history; the intensive study of reality as a whole in terms of its basic similarities and contrasts, and of the whole gamut of human experience, is philosophy. These can be called the "synoptic" disciplines. Neither of them has a unique subject matter of its own; both deal with what, as subject matter, is of equal concern to one or more of the "subject-matter" disciplines. What distinguishes them is their primary concern for inclusiveness or wide perspective, either temporal or logical.

A well balanced liberal education can best be defined in terms of these long-range objectives and these basic skills, attitudes, and disciplines.

Which of these disciplines constitute the "humanities"? The term "humanities" is very ambiguous today in academic circles. It is always, I think, made to include the study of literature and the fine arts. It often but not always includes philosophy, and, less often, history. It is usually distinguished from the social sciences and is always differentiated from the natural sciences. This usage is, I believe, largely indefensible but this is not the place to argue the matter. For convenience, we may list as humanistic disciplines the study of literature and the arts, history, and philosophy on the ground that they all deal specifically with human values and with man's attempts to express and assess these values. Let us now consider the proper role of the humanities, so defined, in a balanced liberal arts education, and how can they most effectively be taught.

Why is a meaningful introduction to literature *and* the fine arts an essential component of a liberal education? To answer this question adequately would involve a thorough analysis of art as such, of its value to mankind, and of the distinctive elements of strength and limitation in each of the arts, including literature. Here we must content ourselves with a bare enumeration of certain crucial facts. There is, first, the fact of sheer aesthetic enjoyment which, though always spontaneous, can also be cultivated by appropriate study. Secondly, it is a fact that the art of any culture and period is the most vivid expression of the ethos or temper of that period and culture. Thirdly, art at its best, and even at the level of honest competence, gives us the most poignant and immediate understanding of how the individual artist saw and assessed life and the world about him. Finally, these insights of unusually sensitive human beings into man's hopes and fears, triumphs and defeats, conveyed to us as they are with such moving eloquence in the successfully expressive work of art, can, in conjunction, give us an unrivalled comprehension of the values, secular and religious, which men cherish. Philosophers discuss values abstractly; the clergy and the moralists preach values; social scientists and doctors tell us by what means to realize many important values; the artist not only creates works of beauty but, in and through them, helps us to encounter the values which men prize and thus "brings them home" to us with unparalleled imaginative power. There is no study more conducive to the sensitive appreciation of human values than the study of the arts and letters.

It is important to add the study of the fine arts to the study of literature because each of the fine arts is unique and deserves to be studied in its own right. The medium of literature differs so greatly from the other artistic media that literary studies cannot serve as an adequate introduction to the nonliterary arts. The visual arts of sculpture and painting are most closely allied and both have much in common with architecture; these three arts can be studied together with profit in their historical context. They too, however, differ radically from music which, in turn, is most closely affiliated with the theater and the dance but which is, of course, an infinitely rich and unique art in its own right.

History as it unfolds is the concrete context of all cultures and human events. There is a history of everything and nothing can be understood apart from its history. Each of the disciplines should see itself and its subject matter in historical perspective. But only the professional historian weaves these specialized historical strands together—the artistic and scientific, and economic, political, and social, the military and technological, the philosophical and religious—and thus recaptures, in some measure, the concrete actualities of the past.

Philosophy is the systematic analysis and interpretation of all human experience and the assessment of all human beliefs regarding reality as a whole. The philosopher stands on the shoulders of his more empirically oriented colleagues. He studies their methods and inquires into their tacit presuppositions. He accepts and interprets these findings and tries to answer, as cogently as he can, the perennial questions of mankind concerning appearance and reality, the secular and the holy, the nature and criteria of beauty, truth, and goodness. Every reflective specialist is, of necessity, a lay philosopher, but it is the philosopher's task to help the specialist and the thoughtful laymen to see the innumerable details of human knowledge and experience in larger systematic perspective and to speculate as wisely as possible about life's ultimate enigmas.

History and philosophy, as disciplines, also need each other. The historian must select and appraise, and without philosophy his basic standards of selection and appraisal are bound to be naïve. Similarly, the philosopher who is unaware of his own place in history and of the fact of cultural conditioning is bound to speculate *in vacuo* and to imagine that he can indeed apprehend reality *sub specie aeternitatis*. There is a history of philosophy as there is a philosophy of history; each is an essential component of its sister discipline.

How can our undergraduates best be introduced to these two complementary synoptic disciplines? There are two approaches, both of which are feasible and profitable. The first is the "dispersive" approach whereby each specialist is, so far as he is able, his own philosopher and historian. The great merit of this approach is that the specialized studies are kept, for the student, in illuminating historical and philosophical perspective and are not sealed off from one another in insulated compartments. The other approach, which might be labelled "intensive," involves heavy reliance on courses in history and philosophy. This approach has the merit of giving the student a more concrete and unified account of specific periods and a sense of the continuous flow of history; it also more effectively introduces the student to the scope and the rigor of philosophical analysis and synthesis. These approaches complement each other and should, if possible, both be exploited.

We can now consider the vexatious problem of the place of religion in the college or university in the context of a balanced liberal curriculum and with due regard to the relation of religion to the humanities.

The first distinction to be made is that between religion as belief and worship, on the one hand, and the study of religion, on the other. The institution charged with responsibility for the former is the church; the chief responsibility of an educational institution in this area is for the study of religion. Much harm can be done by confusing the proper roles of these two complementary institutions.

A university or college does have a responsibility for the religious education of its students. But this responsibility cannot be restricted to scholarship and formal instruction for two reasons. Higher education, as we conceive of it in this country, though of course primarily concerned with its students' minds, cannot remain indifferent to their multiple needs and their total welfare. It should make appropriate provision on or near the campus for whatever religious activities are judged to satisfy a real religious need. Moreover, genuine religious insight and understanding cannot be achieved in a purely intellectual way, i.e., in formal study, but depend also on primary religious experience. Opportunities for religious worship and for religiously oriented activities should therefore be regarded as a kind of "laboratory" equivalent for the scientific laboratory, the art or music studio, or the practical social science project.

The importance of religious study is evident from the preceding account of the total goal and proper scope of liberal education. If a student is to be helped to explore all the facets of reality which impinge upon him so that he may properly adjust himself to them, the mysterious depths of reality which religion seeks to plumb cannot be ignored. Even if it be argued that man's age-old religious quest is based upon a gigantic illusion and that there are no such divine depths to explore, the student of human culture is still confronted by the undeniable fact that men in every human culture have, however mistakenly, taken religion seriously and that this religious concern has expressed itself in many fascinating ways and has profoundly affected their beliefs and their behavior. The most religiously skeptical anthropologist, sociologist, and historian must take religion, as a cultural phenomenon, seriously. So must the philosopher take seriously the problem of the validity (or invalidity) of religious belief. Similarly, the art and the literary historian cannot possibly ignore the whole body of religious art and religious literature and their great cultural importance. In short, religion must be accepted as an important part of the total subject matter of liberal inquiry.

Even if this be granted, however, the question must still be answered as to how religion can best be taught and studied in a university. Two alternatives suggest themselves: (a) The study of religion can be left to the several fields into which it intrudes itself in one way or another. If this is done, work will be offered by historians in the history of religion, by philosophers in the philosophy of religion, by psychologists in the psychology of religion, and so on through the whole list of germane disciplines. The value of such a multiple approach to a crucial subject is indubitable, and every well-balanced university is today, at least to some degree, already committed to this approach. The question is, is this sufficient? (b) That it is not sufficient should be evident at once from our current conception of what a responsible study of other major subjects involves. No one alert to the demands of historical study would tolerate the farming out of history to the other disciplines, despite the fact that all these disciplines do, or should, be concerned with the history of their own progressive inquiry and of its subject matter. Full-time professionally competent historians are needed to pull together the specialized strands of history into a total unified historical account of historical periods and of the whole sweep of history in all its complex concreteness. Similarly, a major phenomenon, like religion, calls for a discipline of its own and for teachers and scholars who, in conjunction, can provide competent instruction in it. In short, a "department" of religion is as imperative, from a strictly scholarly point of view and without regard for creedal commitment, as is a "department" of history or philosophy, or art or literature.

This still leaves unsolved three crucial problems. The first of these relates to the chief areas of, or approaches to, religion for which a well-equipped department of religion should hold itself responsible. On this controversial question I can only express my considered opinion.

1. I would strongly urge that undergraduates be introduced first to their own great religious tradition, that is, the Judaic-Christian. The present almost universal ignorance of this tradition on the part of our undergraduates today is a byword on every faculty and a great source of embarrassment to teachers in many areas such as art and literature. Courses should be made available on the Old and New Testaments and on the historical development of Christian and Judaic thought and practice.

2. A department of religion should also offer courses devoted to the systematic study of the psychology of religion, the philosophy of religion, and ethics in Judaic-Christian focus. These courses should provide thoughtful students the opportunity to raise and explore, in a disciplined manner, the many controversial problems relating to the nature and validity of religious insight and religious faith.

3. It is also highly desirable that undergraduates be given an opportunity to study primitive religion in at least some of its concrete manifestations and also to learn something about the other great religions of mankind such as Buddhism, Hinduism, and Islam. Without such study they can hardly hope to see and assess their own religious heritage in historical perspective and with philosophical objectivity. They should also have every encouragement to compare a religious approach to life with a secular or humanistic approach at its powerful best; indeed, every effort should be made to avoid the "special pleading" involved in the neglect of vital options or a narrow, provincial approach.

4. Students seriously interested in the study of religion should, finally, be encouraged to relate these intensive inquiries to the multiple expressions of the religious consciousness in art and literature. They should also explore the role of religious institutions, beliefs, and practices in various cultures and historical periods, as well as the impact upon religious belief, in-

formed and uninformed, of modern science and contemporary social studies.

The second problem which must be faced concerns the spirit in which religious phenomena are taught and studied. Here again the issue is highly controversial. There are those who believe that only the unbeliever is able to study religion objectively and without warping prejudice. Others argue, with equal conviction, that only the believer is in a position really to understand religion because it can be truly comprehended only "from within," by the committed participant, that is, only by the "agent" rather than the "observer." Finally, there are those who insist that the whole enterprise of teaching religion in a college or university dedicated to liberal studies and cultural scholarship is hopeless because religion is, in its very essence, dogmatic and illiberal and because it cannot therefore be taught in an open-minded liberal manner.

It would be most unrealistic to minimize these difficulties, both at the level of theory and of practice. I cannot, however, believe that the problem is insoluble. In principle it seems clear that the only way really to "encounter" and grasp any subject is to approach it with initial sympathy and involvement. To know what science is "all about" one must surely adopt the creedal point of view of the scientist and be willing to go with him, at least imaginatively, into his laboratory, interest oneself, at least vicariously, in his tried and tested scientific method, and thus see his problems, experiments, and findings through his eyes. The same spirit and approach, *mutatis mutandis*, are surely important for a true understanding of art and literature and of man's basic social and moral problems. It would indeed be strange if an illuminating approach to religion were less dependent upon real involvement or, at least initially, on a very sympathetic and concerned attitude.

But this is, of course, only half the story. For anyone who restricts himself solely to the sympathetic approach, especially if it includes genuine involvement and commitment, is doomed to prejudice and provincialism. The only escape is to combine the approach of the "agent" with that of the detached cultural "observer" who can dispassionately relate the subject in ques-

tion to other subjects and judicially assess conflicting inter-
pretations and appraisals. Man can hope to approximate to
authentic "objectivity" only by combining these two approaches
and by keeping them in fruitful dialectical tension. Either
approach alone is bound to be inadequate for real understanding. That it is difficult to combine these approaches must be
granted, and it may well be particularly difficult to do so in
the study of religion. But the outstanding scholars and teachers
of religion in our day and in the past prove by their work that
it is possible. A university should therefore try its best to
secure the services of scholar-teachers of this temper and
caliber.

The third problem which we dare not ignore concerns the
art of teaching in any controversial area and therefore the art
of teaching religion. We can assume that anyone of mature
stature will have definite convictions on matters of great human
concern, be they political or economic, moral or religious.
Should such a person, as a teacher of undergraduates, be
careful to conceal his relevant convictions, whether they be
affirmative or negative, in order not to prejudice the relatively
immature minds of his students, or should he express his convictions freely and openly? Many noted teachers still insist
on the first-mentioned policy as alone compatible with proper
academic "objectivity." I would myself plead strongly for the
second policy, both on the score of honesty and in the interest
of pedagogical effectiveness.

If one has real convictions on important issues germane to
the subject of a course and to one's own discipline it is, it
seems to me, only honest to reveal them and indeed defend
them to one's students, provided that one expresses these convictions not as dogmas or self-evident truths but with proper
humility and a lively sense of human fallibility. Such frankness,
in turn, has great pedagogical value for it not only helps the
student to sense the importance of the issues at stake; it also
enables him to discount the teacher's interpretation as much
as he sees fit in the light of what he feels, rightly or wrongly,
to be his "prejudice." But a teacher is also, of course, obligated
to try his best to do full justice to opposing views and thus to
exemplify the truly liberal attitude, particularly when he has

his own deep convictions on controversial issues. If he is successful, he will give his students an invaluable example (worth more than endless exhortation) of that reflective and open-minded yet sincere commitment which is the very essence of the spirit of liberalism. Our American undergraduates need, above all, to learn how to be both convinced and open-minded on vital human issues. If they can learn with our help how to have real convictions coupled with real respect for the opposite convictions of others in all the great controversial areas of our culture, they will indeed have benefited from their liberal education.

If religion is taught and studied in this spirit and manner, the resultant discipline surely deserves to be included among the great subject-matter disciplines of a liberal arts curriculum. It can also serve as one of the major synoptic disciplines because, as here envisaged, it includes careful consideration of such synoptic problems as the relation of time to eternity, of the infinite to the finite, of God to man, and the holy to the sinful, of the religious to all secular perspectives, and many other problems of comparable scope. Indeed, an exhaustive study of religion in all its ramifications would be a liberal education in itself. It is a sad commentary upon our contemporary culture that so many of our young men and women graduate from college with no inkling of the nature and value of this rich discipline and in almost complete ignorance of its subject matter.

Paul Tillich has said that religion is the substance of a culture, culture the form of religion. This is true only in proportion as both religion and culture are vital in a society. Our prime responsibility as educators is to help our students achieve a lively sense of religion as a vital force and of culture as a vital expression of the human spirit. A grudging study of religion and the "humanities" will not benefit our honest realistically minded undergraduates. What they need is inspired teaching by dedicated teachers. We must learn how to quicken their imaginations, challenge their will, arouse their curiosity, and evoke a passion for integrity, a real social concern, and genuine humility. This is the crucial task of all liberal education and of all the basic liberal disciplines. Only in this context can the distinctive values of the study of religion, and also the humanities, be properly appreciated and actualized.

I have deliberately avoided, in the foregoing analysis of religion and the humanities, all special pleading for the humanities or for religion. Such one-sided appeals are still prevalent, but they do more harm than good. They merely encourage an aestheticism which belies the power of authentic art and an artificial piety which is essentially irreligious. If we would be realistic and mature as human beings we must orient ourselves primarily to the whole of life and to reality as a whole. If education is to be vital it must be truly liberal; it must liberate us from ignorance, insensitivity, and provincialism. If any of the humanities are to perform their proper function they must, from first to last, do what they are uniquely qualified to do, that is, help to make man more truly human, more humane. No religion is worthy of our respect and allegiance which fails to provide us with a valid central objective, an "ultimate concern for the Ultimate."[1] Every human being has some sort of ultimate concern, but in most cases it reflects an idolatrous veneration for something merely finite. It is our prime responsibility in the university to direct our student's attention to the truly Ultimate and to help him to make his concern for the Ultimate as sincere, profound, and enlightened as possible. We can do so only in proportion as we help him to make his religion the vital core of his life and to relate it, both intellectually and existentially, to all of man's major inquiries and pursuits. The study of religion in a university is bound to lack the significance it should have unless it is made an integral part of the total curriculum and of the total life of the undergraduate.

The study of religion, so conceived, should make an essential contribution to each of the liberal disciplines; each of these, in turn, has its own unique value for religion. This is particularly true of the humanities. A great work of art in any medium is great because the insights it expresses are profound, and profundity depends upon the humility, scope, and deep involvement that characterize man's religious quests at their authentic best. This is no plea for any religious orthodoxy in art and literature or for an explicitly religious "subject matter." It is, rather, a reminder that all significant art reflects, in one way or another, man's "ultimate concern for the Ultimate." Truly significant art is thus absolutely dependent upon a religious orientation. But religion is equally dependent on significant art and literature. They are, par excellence, the most precise and eloquent vehicles for the expression and communication of man's religious insights and the necessary vehicles for his religious worship.[2]

A similar case can be made for the mutual dependence of the study of religion and the disciplines of philosophy and history. The study of religion is bound to be dogmatic, uninformed, and provincial if it is divorced from the historical record of evolving cultures and from judicious philosophical interpretation and appraisal. History, in turn, cannot with impunity ignore or minimize man's recurrent and manifold religious search and the rise and impact of religious beliefs in the course of human events. A dogmatic secularism and an exclusive focus upon religious beliefs and practices are equally one-sided and provincial. The discipline of history is significant in direct proportion as it avoids these extremes and studies the march of history with the realization that religion is indeed the essence of every culture, and culture the form of religion. Similarly, philosophy dooms itself to triviality when it limits itself to the sophisticated puzzles—logical, epistemological, and metaphysical—of the philosopher who has lost contact with life and with man's deepest anxieties and needs. Significant philosophy is focussed upon man's most vital problems, and these can never be divorced from his predicament as a finite mortal. In this sense, which contains no plea for any species of religious orthodoxy, philosophy at its best must be profoundly religious in its ultimate orientation.

All these sweeping generalizations are, of course, highly controversial and call for extensive development and defense. They must suffice, however, to indicate my own conception of the proper roles, and the supreme importance, of religion and the humanities in liberal education on every college campus, including the state university.

KENNETH E. BOULDING

Religion and the Social Sciences

CHAPTER IX

The great drama of man's history has a long and continuous main plot in which the principal theme is the tension between the sacred and the secular aspects of life. This struggle is not a simple dialetic in which, for instance, the secular enlightenment gradually overthrows the sacred gloom, but a complex web of interacting strands as first one, then the other aspect of life rises to dominance in constantly changing forms—priest over peasant, king over priest, prophet over king, priest over prophet, emperor over priest, pope over emperor, princes over pope, people over princes, preachers over people, professors over preachers. The development of man's whole image of the universe can be interpreted in terms of a tension between the heroic vision—the wild leap of the poetic imagination, the awe in the presence of Revelation—and the prudential vision—the common-sense view of things, the wisdom of practical men. On the whole this tension between the secular and the sacred has been a creative tension, each constantly reproving the excesses of the other, though there have been times when it has become excessive and destructive.

We are now contemplating a single scene in this enormous drama. The set is the campus of a state university in the United States; the time is A.D. 1957. (It is interesting to note that the number 1957 is part of a series with a sacred origin.) We have come late to the play, as inevitably we must; we find our seats— no, worse, we find ourselves pushed onto the stage from the wings, for we are not spectators but actors. We fumble for our programs: What has gone before? How much do we have to know of what has gone before, and of what is still going on in other theaters, in order to get the hang of the plot and to know what is going on now?

Our first clue is the set itself. The architecture is strangely miscellaneous; surely an amorphous mixture of the sacred and the secular. If there is an emotional center to the campus it is likely to be a bell tower with no church attached. This is deeply symbolic: the sterile phallus. There is likely to be some Gothic or quasi-Gothic architecture, recognizably a sacred type. The building, however, that looks like a cathedral turns out to be a library, and the one that looks like a chapel turns out to be a gymnasium. Detailed inspection reveals no building on the campus used primarily for religious purposes, except perhaps something called, enigmatically, a Y. The conclusion seems to be that we have here an institution in which the secular is completely dominant, and in which the sacred is present only in vestigial forms and organs. We must be careful, however. On the edge of the campus, pressing in on all sides, are buildings that are quite clearly sacred, both in form and in use. We count at least a dozen churches and perhaps two or three building. Furthermore, we find them crowded and prosperous, bursting with activity. Looking at the matter in some detail, we find that on one or two campuses there are even chapels, just built or projected. On other campuses there remains a certain hostility to religion; this, however, is diminishing, and the prevailing attitude toward religion might be described as a slightly bewildered friendliness. We might conclude that we are here witnessing a turn-of-the-tide phenomenon; that a high watermark of secularism has been reached somewhat earlier and that the tide of religion is once more coming in.

Now we must look at some of the previous scenes. The idea of a university itself comes from the previous high watermark of the Sacred, the thirteenth century. If we visit the older universities of Europe, we shall find them occupying the sets of the previous act, and at the center of the set is always a large chapel. The medieval university was primarily a religious institution, modeled on the monastery, and the monastic flavor lingers in the architecture and in some of the customs. Today, however, the chapel is little more than a tourist attraction—students rarely visit it, and it plays little or no part in the life of the college. Between the thirteenth and the twentieth century a great tide of secularism has washed over the whole world. The story is a familiar one—the Reformation, which broke the unity of Christendom and yet renewed the vigor of the society; the Renaissance, which was an infusion of a strong current of ancient secularism; the Discoveries, which brought the whole world into a geographical unity; the Enlightenment; the rise of nationalism and democracy, and finally the enormous enlargement of man's view of the universe and of his power over it through science. The American state university is a monument to nationalism, to democracy, to the separation of church and state, and to science and technology. Its saints are Copernicus, Galileo, Kepler, Newton, Adam Smith, Dalton, Darwin, Freud, and Einstein, and perhaps Washington and Jefferson.

Here again, however, the plot is not so simple as it seems. The tide of secularism is full of strange eddies; it not only draws its springs from sacred waters but carries them on its surface far and wide. Medieval Europe, which we westerners parochially think of as the then known world, was in fact a tiny peninsula on the edge of the great world of Islam, sprawling across the hemisphere from Spain to the Philippines. The cultural explosion that carried Europe to a position of world dominance by the ninteenth century is a good illustration of the creative tension between the sacred and the secular. It can be argued that it was a revival of religion in the Reformation and Counter Reformation that set it off—a revival fed continuously by the rise of new sects in Protestantism and new orders and movements in Catholicism. Even the saints of secularism are strangely religious; both Galileo and Copernicus were unmistakably Catholic Christians, Newton was obsessed by theology, Dalton was a devout Quaker, Faraday was a Sandemanian preacher, Priestley was a Unitarian minister, Darwin was a man of natural piety, Einstein a mystic. The apparent breakup of the medieval religious unity was in fact the beginning of the great age of world expansion of Christianity—to all the Americas, to important missionary enclaves in Asia and Africa. Coming closer to the present scene we find that one of the most striking long-run trends in the history of the United States has been the rise of organized religion. The United States was founded at the height of the Enlightenment; the founding fathers were almost to a man deists and rationalists. I have seen one estimate that at the time of the Revolution not more than 4 per cent of the people of the American colonies were actively associated with any organized church. This figure may be unduly small; however, there seems to be evidence for a very steady rise in the proportion of church members in the population from a rather small figure in the mid-eighteenth century to about 60 per cent today.

Where then—to come to the main topic of this chapter—do the social sciences stand in this complex historical pattern? The rise of social science is one of the most striking, and perhaps one of the most far-reaching, movements of the twentieth century. Its origins, of course, go far back into social thought and philosophy. The peculiar characteristics of the movement that enable it to qualify for the holy name of "science," however, are quite recent. I would argue that Adam Smith developed the first over-all "system" of social science in his theory of the equilibrium of a price system. Quantification comes even later. The modern census began in the eighteenth century, but it is not really until the twentieth century that the collection of social information becomes deliberate and massive. Statistics owes a great deal to, and has done a great deal for, the social sciences, but this, too, mostly in the twentieth century. Sociology, anthropology, and psychology, as organized professions and departments of learning, are creations of the second half of the nineteenth century. The twentieth century has also seen the rise of applied social sciences into professions with professional schools in the universities to propagate them. Schools of public administration, business administration, journalism, and social work, and institutes of human relations, labor relations, and international relations can all be regarded as applied social science institutions, much as schools of engineering are mostly applied physical science and schools of medicine and dentistry are applied biological science. Social science is even creeping into professions and professional schools that previously had little to do with it. Industrial engineering tends to become less and less distinguishable from business administration; schools of medicine get interested in social medicine, in public health, in psychosomatic and psychiatric medicine. Nursing is presumably at least half applied social science.

I think it must be argued that the social sciences historically ride firmly on the secular side of the secular-sacred seesaw, even more so than the natural sciences. It is extremely hard to think of antireligious persons or even nonreligious persons among the great names in the natural sciences. This is perhaps because the natural sciences compete with religion only at its periphery. Religions, especially those which rest on sacred books, have always tended to give sacred sanction to the ideas of the physical world which were prevalent at the time of their founding. These ideas of the physical world, however, are the accidents of religion—they rarely form its central core. Thus, while Copernicus and Galileo are upsetting to the church, in that they destroy the literal validity of much of the physical imagery of the Bible, they upset the imagery rather than the image, and insofar as the new ideas of the physical universe inspire awe and wonder at its grandeur, they are actually friendly to some of the deepest religious emotions. The extension of the universe, both in time and in space, away from the cozy three-storied, four- or five-thousand-year-old universe of the Bible into the billion-galaxied, four-billion-year-old universe of today's image should make man more, not less, ready to fall on his knees in wonder and adoration at such great majesty and splendor. As we penetrate more deeply into the intricate machinery of life, here again a sense of awe is neither unseemly nor unnatural.

The great object of study of the social sciences, however, is man. (A sociologist has recently described his science as the improper study of mankind!) The subject matter of the social sciences lies closer to the heart of religion than does the material of the natural sciences. The views which religion holds of the nature of man are not peripheral, for all religion concerns itself deeply with the regeneration, improvement, or salvation of man, and consequently its views as to what should be done about him must be rooted firmly in certain views about his nature. The possibility therefore arises of competitive relations between the views held on the nature of man by religion and by social science. A further possibility for competition arises because in their applications both religion and social science conceive themselves as performing a therapeutic role not only on the individual but on society as a whole. A church that lays down the law on usury runs into disagreement with the economist; a church that lays down the law on divorce runs into disagreement with the sociologist; a church that claims divine right for kings runs into disagreement with the political scientist, and a church that claims to divide human actions sharply into sins and virtues may run into disagreement with the psychoanalyst.

In view of the potential competition, therefore, between religion and social science, it is not surprising to find that on the whole the great figures in the social sciences have been frequently indifferent or even hostile to religion. Adam Smith, like his friend Hume, might be classified as a deist, but his attitude toward religion was at best quizzical. He looks at the church as a kind of spiritual business, meeting certain human needs which no doubt need to be met, but always in danger of creating an artificial demand for its products by arousing enthusiasm. His recipe for "that pure and rational religion, free from every mixture of absurdity, imposture, or fanaticism, such as wise men have in all ages of the world wished to see established"[1] is, as we might expect, free competition among sects so that each has to moderate its doctrines in the direction of sweet reasonableness in order to attract adherents from the others. I have never been able to detect the slightest interest in religion in Ricardo's writings. Malthus, it is true, was a clergyman, and this fact seems to have given him some slight qualms about birth control, but apart from this, religion seems to have made singularly little impact on his thought. Keynes was a thoroughly secular character. Marx, of course, like Freud, was actively hostile to religion.

The sociologists have been more interested in religion than

the economists, as one might expect, but apart from Max Weber[2] and Durkheim,[3] it is hard to think of outstanding figures who have paid much attention to it, and I doubt if there are more than a dozen sociologists in the United States today who regard themselves as specialists in the sociology of religion. The one sociologist who has taken religion very seriously is Sorokin, and perhaps partly because of that very fact he is looked upon with a good deal of suspicion by his professional colleagues. In psychology, likewise, there has been little attention paid to religious experience except when it takes pathological forms. There was very little follow-up from the pioneering work of William James's *Varieties of Religious Experience,* and apart from Allport's study of student religion,[4] there seems to be little interest in the matter among modern psychologists. Yet in spite of all this, religion flourishes as it has not done perhaps since the seventeenth century!

Anthropologists, by reason of their very subject matter, have been much interested in primitive religion, for religion, as one of the earliest parts of the intellectual life to develop, forms a large part of the culture of primitive peoples. With some exceptions, however, anthropologists have been also indifferent or hostile to the religion of their own culture—perhaps because of a certain habit of nonparticipation in the cultures which they have investigated and a not wholly justified identification of advanced with primitive religion.

The aversion or indifference of many social scientists toward religion may arise in part because of the difficulty of transferring from one abstract role to another when the subject matter with which the two roles are concerned exhibit so many similarities. The role of the scientist is marked by aloofness from the subject matter which he investigates and an assumption of an ideal of objectivity. By contrast, the role of the religious person is marked by deep involvement with the subject matter, by commitment and dedication to it, by reverence and obedience. The role of the scientist is like that of the musicologist and critic—a questioning, inquiring attitude, holding nothing sacred, approaching the object of inquiry as an "outsider." The role of the religious person is like that of the artist, identifying himself with his material, willing of course to use objective knowledge, but always being willing to transcend it in the act of identification. It is not surprising, therefore, that there seem to be few people who are capable of sustaining both roles, as they seem to involve contradictory values. Nevertheless, tolerance of apparently contradictory roles may be one of the principal sources of creativity in the individual.

My main thesis is that the traditional hostility or indifference of social scientists to religion is a historical accident, arising from the peculiar circumstances of the period when the social sciences developed, and that, if certain misconceptions can be overcome, we should be able to enter a period of mutually beneficial interaction between these two great areas of human life and experience. We can think of these two areas as slightly overlapping regions of our social space. Each consists of a "core" of more or less professional, full-time practitioners, with a penumbra of persons affected in greater or less degree by the web of interaction within the region. At present the "cores" of the two regions overlap little; there are a few Catholic social scientists; there is some interaction among social scientists and professional churchmen, both in the denominations and in such bodies as the departments of the National Council of Churches. There are also certain strong currents of ideas which permeate our whole society—the ideas of Marx, Freud, and Keynes, for instance, exercise influence on many who have never read them or who do not even know their names, and similarly the influence of Barth, Niebuhr, and Tillich spread out far beyond the relatively narrow circle of their own readers. On the whole, however, the overlap is small; economists, psychologists, sociologists, and anthropologists pursue their professions, teaching, reading, writing, meeting, without being much aware of what is going on in the world of religion (or even of what is going on in neighboring sciences). Similarly, the religiously minded go on their own way, preaching, teaching, writing, worshipping, conferring, without much regard to what goes on in the little world of the social scientists. The two areas differ in that religion has a very large penumbra, reaching out in varying degrees of involvement and interaction into almost the whole society, touching all classes, poor and rich, intellectuals and laborers, whereas the penumbra of social science is much smaller, reaching beyond the intellectual classes only in a very attenuated form, and consisting mainly of students, most of whom have only a very casual contact. The difference may be stated in the form that religion is sustained by a general, non-specialized community (the church); social science is sustained by a specialized community of academics and intellectuals. Social scientists have classes, social workers have clients, but only preachers have congregations!

Let us then explore some conditions under which a greater degree of interaction between these two social regions would be mutually beneficial. The most essential condition of such intercourse is a widely shared belief in the complementary, or at least noncompetitive, nature of the two areas. As long as even one side visualizes the other as a "threat," interaction will be discouraged, and defense will be sought in isolation. Important in this connection also is whether one party visualizes itself as a threat to the other. Here is an area where few or no studies have been made and where a little social-scientific inquiry might be very fruitful. One may venture a tentative hypothesis that on the whole the churches do not see themselves either as threatened by, or as a threat to, social sciences, either at the core or at the penumbra, whereas many social scientists visualize social science as something of a threat to the churches; hence, expect the churches to see social science as a threat and, hence, see the churches as at least potentially hostile to social science. Both the complacency of the churches and the arrogance of the social scientists may, of course, be due to ignorance; at the present stage of this interaction, however, one suspects that the obstacles lie more on the side of the social scientists than on the side of the churches. This may not last. As the churches become more aware of the "threat" of social science, their attitudes may harden.

In situations of this kind a clear delimitation of boundaries can lessen tension and prepare the ground for interaction. As long as each does not feel secure within a certain "home base," there will be mutual suspicions. This delimitation would take the form of a recognition of the different levels of abstraction at which the two processes operate. Social science on the whole is an attempt to apply mechanical and mathematical models to the behavior of men and societies. This is a useful abstraction, and the power of social science lies precisely in its ability to abstract from the immense complexity of the human organism those elements that permit the construction of rather simple mechanical models. The danger of abstraction, of course, is the danger of mistaking the abstraction for the reality and hence elevating the model into a metaphysic.

Religion on the other hand is not an abstraction, but a practicum—an area of human life, experience, and practice in all its complexity, both present, past, and to come. To revert to a previous analogy, that of music: there is a "science" of music, which includes both its physical mechanics and its social mechanics. There is a physics of sound and a sociology of the symphony. Both these are necessary to the full understanding of the phenomenon; neither are strictly necessary to the practice or the enjoyment of music. Religion similarly encompasses an area of experience—in prayer, in worship, in liturgy, in revival meetings, in meditation and devotion, and so on. This likewise requires a mechanics—in this case a mechanics of communication and emotion, of social involvement and individual values. The practice and enjoyment of religion, however, like that of music, is not necessarily dependent on the underlying mechanics. This is not to say that in both cases understanding may not lead to enrichment of the experience, though I have known cases where an overintellectual understanding destroyed the enjoyment of music, and there are even more cases where an obsession with the mechanics of religion has prevented the enjoyment of its practice. Where this happens, however, it is because of a failure to appreciate the difference between abstraction and reality, or because of a fear of reality which prevents a person from plunging into it and giving himself to it, and which leads to the substitution of the safe abstraction for the dangerous reality. To use still another figure, it is no doubt useful for a swimmer to know the mechanics of swimming, but nobody ever learns to swim by just studying the mechanics. To learn to swim, we have to get in the water.

There is here a very interesting problem of the relation of science to practice which might be described as the relation of explicit to implicit knowledge. The swimmer swims largely because of implicit knowledge. He could not formulate his knowledge of hydrodynamics in terms of differential equations, and it would not help him to swim better even if he could, in spite of the fact that his actions depend on the implicit solutions of some very complex equation systems. On the other hand, airplanes fly and submarines swim because of explicit knowledge; an airplane does not fly like a bird, nor does a submarine swim like a fish. This is because we have discovered that by the application of much simpler systems than are generally present in living organisms, it is possible to do simple things better than the living organism. Because living organisms have to do such enormously complex things as growing and reproducing, they have to have an immensely complex machinery, and because they then have to use this complex machinery for doing simple things like locomotion, they do these simple things rather badly. Hence, no living organism uses the wheel, the piston, and the screw as part of its biological apparatus mainly because devices which require a high degree of mechanical accuracy can only be made, they cannot be grown.

The business of science is explicit knowledge; the power which comes from this kind of knowledge arises out of the possibility of applying it at its own system level—that is, its own level of simplicity. Mechanics is very useful for making machines, but if we are ever to duplicate living organisms—as one day I expect we will—we will have to have explicit knowledge about the processes of life which we do not have at present. Art and skill, on the other hand, involve implicit knowledge—the application of unconscious systems in which the organism is able to control parts of its environment because of an elaborate system of information fed out from and back into the system. Thus, the potter who throws a pot on a wheel adjusts the pressure of his fingers to the feel of the clay by a complex "cybernetic" process in which deviations of the performance of the clay from the "ideal" in the mind of the potter are perceived and almost instantly corrected by movements of the hand.

One of the great difficulties in the application of the social sciences is that the subject matter of the social sciences largely consists of behavior involving the use of implicit knowledge of social systems. These systems, however, are immensely complex—quite beyond, in their complexity, the ability of simple mechanical systems to describe. On the whole, however, social science has not risen much above the level of simple mechanical systems in its theoretical models. The explicit systems of the social scientist, therefore, are very imperfect substitutes for the implicit systems on which most human behavior is based.

The church, like all social organizations, tends to operate with implicit rather than explicit knowledge of its social environment. The question as to what use can the social sciences be to the church then resolves into the question, whether there are any areas in which an explicit knowledge of social fact or relationship derived from the peculiar techniques of the social sciences can improve upon the implicit knowledge which comes out of common-sense experience and casual observation. The answer to this question would certainly seem to be "yes" in some limited areas. The survey method, for instance, can be applied to derive explicit information about the population of the area which is served by a church or a group of churches—information which may be of great importance in planning the work of a church, in visitation, in planning buildings or new locations, in identifying its "constituency," in pointing the way to needs which it might serve and which it is not now serving. These things may sound trivial, and perhaps they are. Whatever else a church is, however, it is also an organization, existing in a certain environment, drawing its sustenance from the fact that it meets certain human needs and is therefore able to attract resources to itself. There seems to be no loss in becoming more self-conscious of the nature and environment of the organization, even though all these matters may properly be regarded as secondary in the minds of the "core group" of the church.

The question of explicit knowledge of the internal functioning of a church organization is perhaps more delicate. In every organization there is a formal hierarchy of some kind, but also an informal system of communication and influence, and the two systems do not usually coincide. A skilled social anthropologist should be able to go into any organization, such as a church, and by studying the patterns of communication and influence, develop a picture of the organization as an explicit role structure. It might be doubtful whether he would find out more than a well-placed individual within the organization would know; on the other hand, it might well be that much more goes on than any single individual is aware of.

Another point at which the social sciences can be—and are —helpful to the church is in the field that might be called applied religious ethics. All religions include some kind of an ethic, and in the advanced religions the development and inculcation of the ethic is conceived as a major task of the church. Religion is thought of as containing a set of general ethical principles which have to be applied in the situations of daily life as well as in the observance of specifically religious ordinances. As the world changes around us, however, so do these applications of the religious ethic change—new techniques, new products, new ways of life constantly pose new ethical problems, and if the church is to remain in touch with the life of its people, it must help them to solve these new problems. This is perhaps less pressing in churches whose life consists mainly in ritualistic pursuits and otherworldly hopes, but for most American churches, the problem of social ethics has been one of substantial interest. It is interesting to note that the interest in this problem in the Roman Catholic church has closely paralleled the development of the "social gospel" in the Protestant churches, and also that a common interest in the social applications of Christian ethics has been one of the main sources of the ecumenical movement in Protestantism.

If the ethical judgment is to be mature and informed, it must be based on a firm knowledge of the consequences of various kinds of human action or political policy. It is one of the objectives of social science, however, to increase explicit knowledge of social systems and relationships, and this increased knowledge cannot fail to have an effect on the ethical judgment. As an illustration of this point, we might observe the change in the social doctrines, especially of Protestant churches, which has come about as the result of increasing sophistication in regard to economics. In the middle of the nineteenth century, the prevailing social doctrine was one of classical laissez faire; preachers united with economists to laud the benefits of free trade and the magic of property. Toward the end of the nineteenth century, "Christian Socialism" in various forms became popular. The roots of this are to be found not so much in Marx as in the "romantic" revolt against the coldbloodedness and calculatingness of capitalism—as represented, for instance, by Ruskin and Carlyle, William Morris, and Charles Kingsley. It is the contrast between the mechanical coldness of laissez faire market capitalism and the warm, familistic love ethic of the New Testament that really produces this revolt. By the end of the nineteenth century, this had produced the "social gospel" as represented by preachers like Gladden and Rauschenbusch, and by the various social action agencies of the churches. The British Labour party and the American "New Deal" owe much to this "social gospel" movement—British socialism has been described as Methodist rather than Marxist socialism, and the New Deal owes a great deal intellectually to a group of reforming economists of the early twentieth century (H. C. Adams, Ely, Commons), who in turn were much affected by the movement for "social Christianity."

In the mid-twentieth century again, the "social gospel," as represented, say, by the pronouncements of the Department of Church and Economic Life of the National Council of Churches or by the writings of leading Christian social philosophers like Reinhold Niebuhr and John Bennett, has become more sophisticated, partly of course under the impact of the momentous events of the times, such as the rise of Hitler and Stalin, but also under the impact of criticism from professional social scientists. Christian social thinkers have come more and more to realize that familistic forms of organization may not be suitable for large groups, that there is a real and difficult problem of power and responsibility in society, that a "profit system" does not necessarily imply Scrooge-like behavior, and that all problems are not solved by turning them over to co-operatives, labor unions, or the benevolent mother-state. The rise of the Keynesian economics has opened up the possibility of remedying the major defects of an unregulated market economy by the fairly simple means of government policies that do not involve serious loss of individual freedoms or the manipulation of men. Such a movement in social science inevitably has a profound impact on the judgments and preachments of social ethics.

In other areas also, a wider knowledge of the social field inevitably leads to modifications of the ethical judgment. In their teaching on sexual ethics and family life, for instance, the churches can hardly fail to be affected by Malthusian and Freudian theories, even though they would be under no necessity to swallow them whole. They can also hardly fail to be affected by the growth of explicit knowledge of the facts of sexual behavior as represented, for instance (however imperfectly), by the Kinsey studies. Ethical judgments on race relations, both inside and outside of the churches, have likewise been profoundly affected by the work of social scientists. Insofar as prejudice might almost be defined as judgments in social ethics derived from highly limited and restricted fields of experience, the expansion of the field of experience which the methods of social science opens up inevitably has a corroding effect on prejudice. The churches have to make their own adjustments to this widening of the field of knowledge. As it is hard for the church to move much ahead of its members, these adjustments are often difficult. They are, however, necessary and creative.

I now come to the very delicate and difficult problem of the contribution that religion can make to social science. The very suggestion that religion might make some contributions to social science will be resented by many social scientists, especially by those whose vocational drive into the social sciences arose out of a rejection of the religion in which they were brought up. It must be admitted also at the start that many excellent and creative social scientists have been indifferent or even hostile to religion. There is no law which says that a man must be religious in order to be a good social scientist. Indeed, there might well be cases in which devotion to religion actually stood in the way of that objectivity of mind and devotion to truth at all costs which is supposed to be—and sometimes is—the mark of scientific inquiry. This problem, however, is not peculiar to religion. If any ideology is held in such a way that a threat to the ideological system is perceived—even subconsciously—as a threat, either external or internal, to the person holding it, devotion to the ideology will be a handicap in the discovery of truth. This is true of the communist ideology; it is true also of materialist or atheist ideologies, as well as of religious ideologies. The strait jacket into which scientific inquiry is forced by the ideology of dialectical materialism is well known—the destruction of free scientific inquiry in Russia has been one of the most shocking fruits of communism. It is not so easy for us to see that we may have a strait jacket of our own—a kind of secular, nationalist materialism which likewise sets limits to scientific inquiry that does not follow the established high roads. There is a quasi religion of "scientism" which by rejecting all psychic or spiritual phenomena severely limits the scope of scientific inquiry.

Religion differs sharply, however, from these atheistic and materialistic "faiths" in that it consists not merely in an ideology but in a set of practices and special experiences. There is really no equivalent, for instance, either in communism, national secularism, or scientism for the practices of prayer and worship. These represent one of the worlds of human experience, just as music or art or science itself is a world of human experience. If this is rejected out of hand as invalid or uninteresting, this rejection severely limits the field of social-scientific study. We may say, therefore, that one important contribution of religion to the social sciences is to give it a field of study and inquiry. For reasons which may be found in the sociology of the social sciences themselves, this is perhaps the most neglected field in the whole subject matter of social sciences. Psychologists make very little attempt to study religion as an aspect of human behavior; sociologists have done very little work on the church as a social organization. A world of fascinating subcultures within the framework of American society awaits the social anthropologist, and religion, as an outgrowth of small group interaction, has been shockingly neglected by the social psychologist. Even the economist might find it profitable to look at the influence of the churches on economic behavior.

This neglect of an important field of study is merely one facet of a serious problem in the sociology of the social sciences, arising out of the narrow field of personal experience of the social scientist himself. Social scientists, like any other occupational group, form a subculture within the larger society. They are, moreover, a rather small and narrow subculture —not quite so narrow as that of the Amish, perhaps, but almost comparable. This subculture has its own sublanguage, its own rituals, such as the publication of articles in quasi-liturgical form (coefficients of correlation and statistical tests of significance are nice examples of social science liturgies), and its communications are very largely internal to the group —even casual and social communications. Furthermore, this subculture is middle class, academic, largely cut off from contact with wageworkers or farmers, and is transmitted from the old to the young through the power which the old have over the promotion and professional advancement of the young. As a result of this, the social scientist tends to have less and less firsthand, intimate, face-to-face contact with people in the other subcultures around him. He consequently tends to concentrate his investigations within his own or closely related groups—experimental human psychology and social psychology, for instance, is almost wholly confined to the behavior of college sophomores—or his contacts with other groups are made on the basis of such an impersonal relationship as the questionnaire or the interview. This inevitably leads to a narrowing of his field of social vision, and it becomes very hard for him to escape the prison of his own subculture. Of all the social scientists, anthropologists live most intimately with other cultures. Here, however, there has been a strong tradition of studying remote cultures, so that while we know a great deal about the Ubangi, we know very little about

Jehovah's Witnesses. Also, one wonders whether the limitations of the intimate personal experience of the anthropologist in the cultures of his own civilization do not at times blind him to certain qualities of richness and depth in more primitive cultures.

Few social scientists will quarrel with the proposition that religion should provide subject matter for social science investigations. Many will not follow me in the assertion that for the healthy growth of social science we need maturely religious social scientists. I base this assertion, however, on two grounds. The first is that, as religion is part of the whole experience of mankind, the social scientist who does not participate in it is cut off from a deep and meaningful area of human experience and is in this sense maimed. Now, of course, a maimed person may be a very good scientist; the blind and the halt also serve, and these deficiencies can be overcome. But who would argue that they are an advantage! Similarly, the social scientist who is deaf to music and blind to art may be excellently skilled in his profession, but there will be something lacking in his person. Not that I would press the argument too far—otherwise, we might find ourselves arguing that we must sin the more that knowledge may abound! But where a large area of human experience is rejected or neglected, surely it can be argued that there is a deficiency.

The other argument is that as social science develops, the problem of the ends of human activity become increasingly pressing, even for social scientists. Knowledge, we write over our schoolroom doors, is power, and power is power unto salvation or unto damnation, depending on how we use it. As long as man is relatively impotent, the problem of what to do with the power he does not possess remains academic. With the growth of power, the problem of its use becomes of increasing importance. We see this in the physical sciences, where the question of the use of the powers which knowledge has unleashed has become perhaps the most critical question of our age. The power which the social sciences may unleash, however, may be ever more terrible—power to control the minds and actions of men, both individually and in the mass;

the power of indefinite corruption of the integrity and individuality of sovereign man. We cannot therefore rest neutrally with the question, "How do people get what they want?" We cannot even assume that it is ethically neutral to help people to get what they want. As social science develops, the critique of ends becomes ever more important, and the question, "Do I (or does anybody) want the right things?" becomes insistent and inescapable. It is precisely this critique of ends, however, which is the great moral task of religion. The future of science, and especially of social science, may depend on our getting better answers than we now have to the question of when ignorance is bliss—or, as a matter of fact, what bliss is anyway! And bliss, curiously enough, is one of the great subjects of religion.

I am not, of course, advocating religious tests for the employment of professors of social science—religious tests, like so many others, test the test rather than the testee, and even from the point of view of the health and vigor of religion itself, the secularization of academic (and political) institutions has been a great gain. We have only to compare, for instance, the remarkable vigor of the Lutheran churches in this country with their debility in Scandinavia to see the futility of trying to impose religion by external sanctions. One does not make people musical by forcing them to go to concerts, nor does one make people religious by forcing them to profess religion. Religion must make its own way and be judged on its own merits; the very breath of coercion will destroy it. It is not necessarily a bad thing to have a few atheists around a university, even if it is only to prove that there is religious freedom (a few communists, incidentally, might also be used to prove that there is political freedom). But there is a great opportunity today for fruitful intercourse between religion and social science, and if the university should not force this, at least it should be able to provide some facilities.

The application of religion to the social sciences must be left to the social scientists themselves. With the application of social science to religion, however, the university might well be positively concerned. One can visualize, for instance, a research institute in this area, somewhat analogous, shall we say, to institutes of industrial relations, which would bring together social scientists from different fields for the development of both theoretical and empirical research in the area of religious experience, practices, and institutions. Such an institute would be difficult to staff at present, and it would run into some difficult problems of public relations, both inside and outside the university, for its members would have to deserve the confidence of both the academic and the religious communities. The development of such a research center would do much to encourage the kind of interaction which I have argued is desirable; it would also bring the university closer to its ideal of studying the universe.

G. E. HUTCHINSON

Religion and the Natural Sciences

CHAPTER X

In this chapter I shall explore what appears to me to be the most important aspect of the relationship of science and religion. Inevitably I write from the standpoint of one brought up in the tradition of Western Christianity, but I shall consider no dogmatic aspects of religion; the particular kind of problem discussed is presumably of equal importance to analytically minded people educated in various faiths.

No question of the traditional encounter between nineteenth-century science and nineteenth-century religion is discussed; we do not now live in that period, and its problems, however instructive in retrospect, are not those that we have to solve. The problem of the conflict between the account of creation in Genesis and that implied by palaeontology may still occasionally arise in the classroom, but it is not an important educational issue today. The problem of the nature of the human soul and its survival after bodily death, which in the past has frequently been an area of debate between primarily scientific and primarily religious people, is likewise not considered explicitly, though it is a source of anxiety to some. All such questions will be regarded as special cases of a much more pervasive and educationally significant problem: namely, to what extent does the method that we call scientific investigation give a true and a complete picture of existence?

The attempt to answer this question leads to the conclusion, firstly, that in studying increasingly large and increasingly small aspects of the universe, we probably have before us two fields of investigation that can never be completely known. Science is probably in this way inexhaustible. It is secondly also possible that science is inexhaustible in the same sense as mathematics is inexhaustible owing to the existence of unprovable propositions in mathematics, which could have physical models in nature. It is evident thirdly that, when we study human behavior by the ordinary technique of building conceptual models of various isolated processes, we run into difficulties of an epistemological sort owing to the fact that some of the conceptual models can actually be physically realized. The question whether an electronic brain thinks cannot be solved except by denying any kind of intuitively significant meaning to the word think, so that we have to admit that we do not know what we are. Fourthly, the only region so far encountered in the whole of empirical science which seems to bear on this last problem leads to such paradoxical results that it is not accepted at all by many scientists, and, if accepted, is admittedly at the mercy of a kind of uncertainty principle due to inevitable interference by the experimenter with the results of the experiment.

It is concluded that scientific investigation, though it leads to results that are convergently true, is certainly and probably permanently an incomplete mode of knowledge. Since we live in the universe which is incompletely known and probably incompletely knowable, we must live our lives using everything at our disposal and not merely the scientifically mapped part of reality. Statements outside the scientific body of knowledge are inevitably made in a language which is formally derived as metaphor from language describing the investigable world. Yet words will have different meanings in the scientific and theological languages.

It is obviously impossible to give, in a few paragraphs, an account of the present state of scientific knowledge as a whole. The aspects of the known external world to be presented are chosen because they appear to be relevant to the present discussion.

The universe accessible to investigation is, even by terrestrial standards, immense, of radius of the order of 10^{21} or 10^{22} miles.

It is uncertain whether it is better regarded as part of an open infinite system or whether it is closed though unbounded.[1]

The major, more or less discrete, objects in the universe are galaxies or enormous collections of stars and clouds of dust. The number of these systems in the accessible universe is of the order of billions. There is evidence of some sort of an irregular pattern in their distribution. They appear in general to be moving away from each other, giving the impression of an "expanding universe." This effect has often suggested that, initially, all the matter in the universe was collected together. Such a state would imply a creation at a specific time, or it could imply an excessively unlikely random collection of matter achieved in the course of infinite time. Dates for creation can be derived from other phenomena and are in general of the order of 6,000,000,000 years ago. It has, however, recently been widely held that such dates are specious. In an infinite universe which was apparently expanding locally, matter would seem to be disappearing. In order to maintain a steady state, matter would have to be continually created locally. This view has appealed to certain investigators on the ground that it permits the postulate that at any time and at any place the general large-scale features of the external world are the same. It does so at the price of introducing an entirely unexplained random creation of matter at an arbitrary rate, which is, however, so small that it is most unlikely that it could be directly detected instrumentally in the foreseeable future.

One galaxy, known to us as The Galaxy or Milky Way, has a moderate-sized star about halfway from its center and edge, which we know as the sun. Around the sun, a number of planets revolve and on one of them we live. It is very probable that on one other planet, namely Mars, there is a low form of life, which, if we could examine it, we should probably regard as vegetable. It is quite likely that several species of such organisms exist on Mars; their physiology must be most peculiar. The evidence for their existence is primarily the changing color of certain areas of the planet's surface in circumstances suggesting growth. The observed existence of life on earth, the probable presence of life on Mars, and the fact that, when a mixture of gases comparable to those likely to have formed an early atmosphere of a planet is subjected to a silent electric discharge or other source of high energy, a vast number of organic compounds is formed, all suggest that, given a suitable environment, living matter evolves spontaneously. That it is not observed to evolve in nature today is due to the fact that the earth is already populated with bacteria which would decompose the initial organic compounds, and to the fact that the oxygen of the air itself, largely a biological product, screens the surface of the earth from the short-wave radiation of the sun, which would be the required source of energy.

Once life has started, it appears to evolve by a process of variation followed by natural selection or survival of the more favored varieties. The variation process appears, within the limits available to an organism, to be essentially random. When we attempt to analyze the ordinary physiological behavior of organisms, in every known case an analysis in terms of the process of physics and chemistry appears to be possible.

In some of the less complicated physiological processes, such as that by which the energy in a molecule of glucose is converted into mechanical work by the contraction of a muscle, we now have a fairly complete account of what is happening. Though this is one of the simpler biological events, its physico-chemical description is extremely complicated. It involves at least twenty chemical changes in relatively simple organic compounds and a set of changes in the much more complex fibrous protein system of the muscle fiber which lead to those changes in position of the parts of the molecule that appear macroscopically as shortening of the muscle fiber. Though these changes in position are visually understandable in terms of models, when we inquire into the actual processes involving the forces binding together the constituent atoms, we enter a world in which visual macroscopic models are less and less significant. As soon as we want an analysis not in molecular terms, but in terms of subatomic phenomena, ordinary macroscopic modes of presentation become useless. Entities which are particles at one moment are waves at another, energy is no longer transferable in a continuous stream but only in discontinuous packets, and we can only make statements about the probability of an event and not its definite occurrence. There is nothing surprising in this. Our senses have evolved to deal with phenomena in a world of great size compared even with the largest molecules. What we regard as the true visual appearance of objects is determined by this. When we look at things we ask about phenomena which initially can be sensed directly. Later in the analysis, we reach a state when the properties of the smaller and smaller entities become increasingly unfamiliar. This is true of the nonliving as well as the living parts of the world. The results of the application of scientific method is to produce a series of explanations of increasing generality, in terms of well-defined relationships between increasingly abstract entities. Anyone who doubts this has merely to sit in the sun with a copy of the *Astrophysical Journal.*

In view of the fact that the methods of investigation available to us do not give us absolute and certain truth, it is legitimate to inquire how true the current scientific view of the world is likely to be. The answer is, I think, that over the field that is being considered something very like our world picture must be in a certain sense largely true. Quantitative details will certainly be revised, but in general such revision will tend to make the universe older, larger, and containing more subsystems. It is exceedingly unlikely that the apparent age of the earth or of any of the major systems used to determine "ages of the universe," would prove to be much less than the figure given. An age as low as 600,000,000 years is so improbable as to be hardly worth considering. An age for the earth as great as 60,000,000,000 years seems intuitively rather less improbable, but nevertheless is not at all probable. This is a matter of importance in the present context, because there has sometimes been a tendency to conclude that, since scientists are always changing their minds, their conclusions are of little general interest. Scientists certainly are always changing their minds, but within very definite limits; in any science developing healthily, the limits moreover tend to decrease.

Apart from the ordinary epistemological difficulties, such as the sense-data problem, it is evident that there are at least two major barriers, or at least areas of increasing difficulty, namely the study of the very large and that of the very small. In both cases the conceptual procedures become difficult, and there is no certain guarantee that they can be developed indefinitely. In the intermediate region it is usually supposed that the main difficulties are in matters of technique. I have, however, a very strong suspicion that there are really three main areas of increasing difficulty, the third being the study of events that are commonly spoken of as mental or psychological. The ordinary method of procedure in this area nowadays is to build theoretical models embodying sets of relationships between entities which are either unanalyzed or are believed to be reducible to physicochemical terms. In such models, the boundaries are regarded as spatiotemporal of an ordinary kind, so that whatever may enter or leave the system is considered to be a signal or series of signals bearing information, which at any moment is describable in any desired degree of detail in terms of ordinary physics. This method of procedure has proved extraordinarily successful. A monistic system accepting no postulates save those of the laws of physics as now known has sufficed, it is often claimed, to provide explanations of phenomena wherever they have been sufficiently analyzed. It is illegitimate according to the rule of procedure known as the principle of parsimony, or the simplicity postulate, or Occam's razor, to introduce any entity into a theory where it is not needed. It is, therefore, argued that, since nothing has been shown to be needed so far, apparent demonstrations of additional needs in limited areas are likely to prove specious. The whole position is of some interest in the present context because it is a special case of an argument also used to deny any validity to religion.

The most cogent argument that has been brought against religious ideas by scientists is that such ideas add unnecessary terms to scientific theory. The idea of God is held to be an unnecessary addition, either because, as to Laplace,[2] it adds nothing to an analytical explanation, or because it can be used to provide an unlimited number of *ad hoc* pseudo explanations. For this reason, it is important to consider as carefully as possible the simplicity postulate, or Occam's razor. The idea is certainly an old one. Occam (*de Corpore Christi,* 28) uses it quite casually in the form *non est necesse ponere*

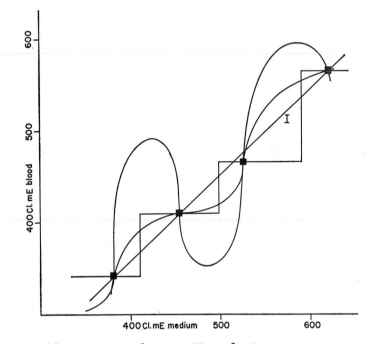

The Problem of Formulating a Hypothesis

Diagram illustrating the problem of decision in formulating a hypothesis to account for a set of facts. The actual data, which are irrelevant to the discussion, are the blood chloride concentrations of hagfishes in sea water of varying chlorinity.

talem . . . et ita frustra poneretur. Occam would have been horrified to have known that God was what it is not necessary to postulate, but very many people, apart from Laplace, have held such a view in discussing the universe. It will, however, be best to begin on a less grandiose scale.

Suppose we have a set of observations of two variables determined simultaneously in an experiment, which can be plotted as on the figure. It is possible to draw through these points an indefinite number of curves. Some of these curves have been drawn in the figure. The problem that arises is what criterion have we for deciding on any particular curve. Practically everyone would choose the straight line (I) and would be fairly confident that, if further observations were to be made, their choice would be vindicated. Since the straight line can be described by the minimum number of coefficients and involves only the first power of the independent variable, departure from it is equivalent to adding unnecessary postulates, which according to the rule must not be done.

If the rule is a valid one, it therefore appears that, before we have actually proceeded to construct any hypothesis, there is a certain prior probability that hypotheses of a certain kind, namely those with few terms, are more likely to be verified than those with many terms.

It would seem extremely odd if the universe actually were constructed in this way, and much more likely that the apparent high probability of the simple hypothesis is introduced into the argument surreptitiously by the investigator. If we suppose, given a body of confirmed theory T_n and a new set of observations relating to the subject matter of T_n, there is a infinite number of ways of proceeding to an increased body of theory T_{n+1} it is obvious that there must be a priori a distribution of probabilities so that some methods of proceeding are more probable than others. If this were not the case, since there is an indefinite number of ways of proceeding, each would have an indefinitely small probability of being true and we should never find a reasonable hypothesis. Actually, unless T_n gives us a lot of hints as to what the new data may mean, we should probably have to be content with a rather unsatisfactory empirical statement that the two variables look as though they are related in simple proportionality. The somewhat more complex hypotheses such as:

$$Y = k \left[(1-e^{-x}) - \frac{1}{15}(1-e^{-9x}) + \frac{1}{45}(1-e^{-25x}) \ . \ . \ . \right]$$

which would give for small values of x a graph hardly different from the straight line, are likely not to be tried, unless T_n predicted that this was the sort of relationship likely to be found in material of the kind treated in the theory. For example, if we are dealing with growth, a proportionality to a logarithm of some observable parameter would be the most reasonable simple expectation.

What the simplicity postulate really says is that early in an investigation we know less than when we have made further advances, and that the terms must be added one by one, if we want to keep erroneous theory to a minimum. The simplest hypothesis is to be preferred, because it makes the minimum number of statements and so reduces the chance that the whole hypothesis is wrong. At any given stage in the development of science, there will be regions of such great difficulty that no hypothesis of any predictive power can yet be invented. These may be approached stepwise often over a long period of time. The whole distance early in the investigation will seem impossible; the last step will probably, when all preceding steps have been taken, appear reasonably simple. There is no evidence that the whole of the universe can be investigated, merely experience that we can build up a body of generated information dealing with increasingly more of the universe. Occam's razor therefore merely clears the most practical path immediately ahead of us.[3]

This does not mean that, when we are confronted with the whole of experience, and must live our lives in conformity with such experience, the simplicity postulate is necessarily a good rule to follow. We can in fact be confident that what we cannot deal with analytically is likely to be as complex as what we can. Occam's razor, unless used discreetly and stepwise, certainly would let us down in the study of the investigable parts of the universe; how far it can help in facing what cannot be stated in the form of cognitive propositions, only experience can tell. It is certainly an abuse of the principle to use it to exclude the whole field of experience not so describable, or to attempt to use it to limit what we may try to think about.

I am here using the word "investigable" to indicate everything which can be described in a series of propositions constituting the language of science, S, publicly verifiable in principle, which may be either analytic or synthetic. The question of the existence of noninvestigable existents is obviously a difficult one because no constructive definition in S can be given of any such things if they exist. I am inclined, however, to regard all directly known sensations and images as at least containing uninvestigable elements, such as the quality yellow as it is perceived, as distinct from the publicly defined color of light of wave length about 5890 Å, or the electrophysiological changes that might be studied in the perception of such light. It will be apparent from the argument of the next two sections that the existence of such uninvestigable aspects of sensation is not as trivial or unimportant a matter as many modern philosophers appear to have thought. All statements that attempt to refer specifically to such uninvestigable subjective aspects of experience fall outside the S language, even though they make up a large part of what we attempt to say.

It is also just possible that, since it is now known that there must be undecidable problems in any well-developed consistent mathematical system, physical systems may exist that constitute special cases of models of undecidable problems. In such cases, no general scientific theory may be realizable, but only empirically known special cases which can be classified under some general inductive statement that cannot be properly explicated. The four-color problem on a plane, if it should turn out to be unprovable, would provide an instance of the sort of situation involved, though this is a trivial case scientifically, however deep it may be mathematically. At least these two kinds of examples should prepare us to accept uninvestigable aspects of reality.

At the present time there is an enormous technological growth of machines for performing operations that are ordinarily thought of as human. These may be of the nature of goal-seeking devices as in certain kinds of automatic weapons, or they may be computers capable of performing elaborate operations which formerly would have required impossibly large numbers of human arithmeticians. In practice we do not award posthumous decorations for valor to exploded missiles, and membership in learned societies is for the designers of computers rather than for the computers themselves. In practice, thoughtful people appear to be able to distinguish men from machines. A number of machines, however, are capable of quite dramatic learning, such as Shannon's maze-running electronic mouse and the various devices of Ashby and of Grey-Walter. It is, moreover, quite possible in theory to build a self-reproducing machine, though in practice the expense might well prove prohibitive. Machines can obviously be taught to answer nonoperational questions, such as "Are you conscious?" or "Are you aware of the presence of God?" in the affirmative. In spite of this, most people would feel able to distinguish in a practical way between men and machines. Actually it seems probable from the various discussions of the problem, that the criteria of distinction are empirical characters, such as chemical composition, size, shape, rapidity of output, none of which has any obvious fundamental connection with the problem.[4]

In principle, if we can build machines which can calculate, make decisions, embark on new courses of action, communicate with one another, make unverifiable remarks, exhibit neurotic behavior, and reproduce, there is no theoretical reason why a single machine incorporating all these types of behavior should not be built. It is indeed usually conceded that, if we really understand a process, we can in theory design a machine that will imitate the process. This proposition depends on the meaning of "understand," but in the ordinary reductive sense in which the word is commonly used in science, the proposition is certainly true. From a strictly empirical point of view, we should have to admit that the difference between such a machine and a living being would be that it was of an entirely different shape and size, was composed of metal, various dielectrics, and gas under low pressure, rather than of proteins in an aqueous phase, and that it used the sun as an energy source via the waterfall or heat energine and power station instead of the cornfield or the ox, and that initially it had been created by man.

Even though the machine should protest when tampered

with, no one at first would believe that it felt pain, and, if some people came to believe this, we should feel justified in regarding them as neurotic sentimentalists. The ordinary objection to regarding the machine and man as both living is that if the man says he is conscious of his own activities, we believe him, but if the machine were to say so we should not believe it. It is obvious that this criteria is completely nonoperational. It begs the question it asked in S, and can never be applied in making an actual decision.

It is evident to the present writer that, in the greater part of biology as in the sciences of the inanimate world, a reductive theory in which no concepts that are not ultimately based in physical theory are needed, is quite adequate for the present state of our knowledge. Occam's razor warns us that, if we attempt to stray from the reductive path, we shall run into a tangle of hypotheses of every degree of complexity and that, even if one happens to be truer than anything we have, we should have a very small chance of finding it in the tangle. The only way in which we might be able to discover if the reductive procedure can let us down is to start investigating those areas in which it seems least likely from previous experience that it will work. We must then make every effort to find a reductive explanation in such areas; only after such efforts are exhausted have we any right to conclude that something other than physical principles are operating.

Since we have run into an impasse about the consciousness of a machine built to imitate cerebral behavior, while no such impasse exists anywhere else in biology, it would seem worth while to consider whether in the study of purportedly conscious behavior[5] we might find nonreductive processes. Logically perhaps there is no reason why the epistemological difficulties of the conscious machine should suggest that reductive theory might break down. It is, however, reasonable to suppose that situations of this sort, since they involve to each of us experience of noninvestigable subjective elements, are likely to be fertile if faced imaginatively. This view, that conscious behavior involves something special, has been strenuously opposed by most academic psychologists, partly because they rightly feel that reductive theory must come first and partly because they are quite wrongly afraid, like so many primitive people, of sorcery.

The particular phenomena to be considered are what are commonly called parapsychological, a category including primarily the various kinds of extrasensory perception and of psychokinesis. The experimental basis for accepting extrasensory perception is largely that when certain people are asked to write down a series of symbols, there is sometimes fairly clear evidence that the frequency and order of the symbols is determined either by certain material series of marks that are not physically accessible to the subject (clairvoyance) or by sequences of images in other people's minds (telepathy). The experimental evidence for psychokinesis is based on the position of dice thrown at random when someone is wishing for a particular number or other kind of position. The effects can be positive or negative; in the case of dice-throwing significant negative results (i.e., statistically too few sixes when six is wished for) seem to be particularly common. There are sometimes curious displacements in time, so that later events reported in the mind of one person appear to have a statistical effect on earlier events in the mind of another.[6] In every case the experiments have to be described in sentences in some of which reference is made to reports, not in S language, by some of the participants.

Until recently, most investigators have tended to shy away from this field. More recently, it has seemed to many that only two alternatives are offered by the published data. Either the whole thing is a gigantic hoax, or the main results of the best parapsychological experiments are in the main valid, i.e., the propositions describing such results are with a very high degree of probability likely to be true.

The hypothesis that the results are a hoax involves systematic dishonesty on the part of a number of supposedly respectable people. It cannot ideally be proved untrue because, whenever anyone previously skeptical does an experiment giving ostensibly positive results, the remaining skeptics can merely claim that the experimenter has joined the hoaxers. It is claimed by those who adopt the hoax hypothesis that the latter is a priori much more probable than is telepathy, clairvoyance, or psychokinesis, that no amount of evidence in favor of these classes of alleged phenomena can counterbalance their negligible probability of existence.

This argument is hardly based on prescientific experience prior to scientific study, because the impression given in daily life due to coincidence, simultaneous reception of identical sensory cues, and the like, is that there is far more telepathy actually occurring than anyone who seriously studied the matter would claim.

From the standpoint of the present work, the important results of such researches are first, that it seems very unlikely that any reductive theory, based on our present understanding of the inanimate part of the universe, is likely to be of help here. Ultimately, some sort of unified theory including parapsychology may become possible, but it is unlikely to resemble the physicochemical theory believed to underlie most of biology. It must, however, be pointed out that it is not inconceivable that further progress along these lines may be virtually impossible owing to the phenomena being too sensitive to uncontrollable parapsychological influences of the experimenters. It would seem not impossible that a sort of uncertainty principle, presumably only faintly analogous to that encountered in physics, is involved. This possibility should not be used as an argument against research in this extremely important though often discouraging field. Even the smallest positive results, such as we now have, challenge the commonly accepted view of the content of scientific theory. The area should obviously be investigated far more intensively, but with the full understanding that the results may be very few, though enormously significant.

There is no guarantee that we can investigate everything that exists. The known existence of undecidable problems in mathematics and the possibility that some unsolved problems which may, like the four-color problem, be general models of physical situations in nature and may reflect some undecidable situation, suggests that uninvestigable areas may exist. It would seem that the criteria for discriminating between living systems of the highest degree of complexity and inanimate artifacts may involve properties such as shape, size, or kinds of atoms involved that a philosopher would hardly consider to be fundamental. The problem of the machine built to say that it is conscious raises the difficulty of how one knows that it is not.

Parapsychological phenomena which are apparently associated with conscious human minds seem to be nonreductive in the present state of knowledge. It is possible that investigation of such phenomena may lead nowhere should they prove to be, as by their nature seems almost inevitable, continually interfered with by the personality of the experimenter.

Wittgenstein's famous dictum "whereof one cannot speak, thereof one must be silent" has seemed hopelessly constricting to most people. Since it is apparent that communication of a nonverbal sort is continually going on even if we try to remain silent, it is not only constricting but completely impractical, even lethal.

Most people now recognize the propositions of religious belief and the sentences of religious ritual as continuous attempts to do what Wittgenstein told us we must not do and what humanity continually declares it must do. The justification of this behavior is obvious. We cannot neglect that part of reality about which we cannot make publicly verifiable statements. Being social and cultural animals, we want to transmit our insight into the uninvestigable parts of the universe no less than our discoveries about the investigable parts. We have a language in which publicly verifiable statements about the latter parts can be made. We borrow its elements, make them into metaphor, add everything we can think of, and fail to make ourselves clear when we try to deal with our insight in the inductively uninvestigable parts. *Introibo ad altare Dei* means one thing at the beginning of the Roman mass; it may mean something quite different at the beginning of Joyce's *Ulysses*.

At the present time all that I would as a scientist ask of the theologians and of the nonrigorous philosophers is that they make quite clear in what language they are talking. It is for instance extremely cruel to torture the minds of the young with problems relating to free will and determinism in which half the propositions employed relate to the scientific S language, and the other half to a metaphorical T language developed for theological purposes. In S, the dichotomy is presumably between determined and not-determined, and in some cases a continuum of partially determined states is permissible. In S, the not-determined is presumably random. The moralist not sure of his language is likely to protest, though in vain, that he wants nonrandom, nondetermined behavior on the part of responsible free human beings. But in the metaphorical language T, we may pray "O God, who art the author of peace and lover of concord, in knowledge of whom standeth our eternal life, *whose service is perfect freedom.* . . ." In such a statement as that italicised, considered as a statement in S, there is an obvious inconsistency, for the service of God at any given time, for any given individual, presumably presupposes a unique mode of behavior. Considered as a statement in T, the verification of which is a matter of individual experience, and in which the meaning of "service of God" and that of "freedom" are implicit in such a nonpublic verification, the statement can at least personally be known to be both true and nonparadoxical.

Margaret Masterman, moreover, has given indications (*Theology* 54 [1951]: 82-87) of a most penetrating and ingenious way in which statements of an apparently paradoxical kind in theological language can be submitted to a quite rigorous kind of logical analysis. The possibility of such an analysis is a matter of very great importance. There are far too many Christians who, catching desperately at St. Paul's remarks about "foolishness to the Greeks" and finding the existentialists easier reading than either the scholastics or modern logic, glory in the absurdity of their faith, until religion is regarded as shallow unless intellectually ridiculous, and intellectual activities immoral. To such ends surely we were not born.

GEORGE N. SHUSTER

Religion and the Professions

CHAPTER XI

Training for the professions has become the principal business of modern higher education in this country as well as in foreign lands. This fact probably more than any other differentiates our practice sharply from that of the past. It is noteworthy, for example, that so far as one is able to determine the Romans knew neither schools of architecture nor colleges of engineering. We are left to surmise that the men who erected such glorious functional structures as the aqueduct at Caserta and the Black Gate, the *porta nigra* of Trier, must have learned their craft as members of a guild fostered by the army. Of equal interest though of more recent vintage is the circumstance that during a century of discoveries as brilliant as those of our own, the Royal Society could bring together, discuss, and promulgate the findings of otherwise isolated thinkers, Newton and Halley among them, who to our way of thinking had been trained for mathematical studies only. Drawing generalized conclusions from such data would be perilous. They serve both critics and commenders of our time. Perhaps one may not injudiciously say that what is most novel and significant in this development is that a procedure has now been established for readily bringing the discoveries made by men of great stature to the attention of the many fledgling scholars so that they in turn can embed the meaning of these discoveries in a growing awareness of that "accumulated knowledge" which, as Dr. Conant has said, is another name for science. This knowledge has now become the principal source of dynamism in a highly complex industrial society.

So far-reaching in pertinence for the social well-being of the race has this change in educational method become and so difficult is it now to master the data made available to the student for a profession that several fateful consequences have ensued. First, professional education has forced its way back into the colleges by means of what has until recently been an ever-increasing demand for prerequisites, and at the same time it has forced its way into doctoral programs. Of course it has not everywhere succeeded in having its way, and there are even some indications of a change of heart. Yet who will deny, in spite of many protestations, that a "broad, general training" is favored by business and some of the professions, that for very many young people, male and female alike (as well as, perhaps, for most of their teachers), the vocation remains the solely significant consideration and that whatever hampers pursuit of it is likely to seem peripheral or even a waste of time? Second, the number of professions with which the college and the university are at present concerned has notably increased. To use just one example, training for "commerce" is now capped with instruction in business administration. Similarly, the "calling" of yore has become the "profession" of today. Thus home economists are no longer women who have learned to cook, sew, and mind the baby but are masters of the chemistry of nutrition and students of the sociology of family living. The third consequence is no doubt materialistic but, even so, important: the financial support required by the major kinds of professional education is tremendous, and in not a few instances the sums needed can be secured by university administrations only by curtailing other scholarly activities.

Although I am here discussing the professions as a single group, it is important to note a few of the contrasts among them. Most of the guidance professions—notably medicine, law, and teaching—are as old as recorded history, though new ones like social work and psychological counseling are seeking to establish themselves in our society and have to some extent succeeded. The technological professions, such an engineering and architecture, are relatively new, whereas those identified with administration, in a variety of forms, are quite modern. True enough, a number of European educational institutions, primarily the German *Handelshochschule,* have in the past manifested some concern with the arts of management, but this was usually casual and never systematic. At any rate, it seems rather significant that the guidance professions have had and still retain a greater interest in the liberal arts and specifically in religion than do the others, exception having been duly made in this country for the War College and certain other establishments for the training of government personnel. This is in part no doubt attributable to the fact that the guidance professions, as counseling agencies, must take into consideration every aspect of human life and behavior. It is not unrealistic to believe that teachers and students of the law may be concerned with Plato, or Kant's *Critique of the Practical Reason,* or the Canon Law. Yet no doubt the impact of modern life has also made itself felt in the trend towards exclusion of all but professional interests. Who would suppose, for example, that an up-to-date school of business administration would normally make a point of discussing Paul's Epistle to the Romans?

If, then, this is the situation—if the subject matter of professional education has become so many-sided, so hard to master, and so completely absorbing, and if there be that in the time which has seemingly dictated a retreat from concern with religious and humanistic subjects—how shall one counsel the university to foster a living interest in the literature of the spirit? Let us note first of all that whenever religion is of primary importance to an individual he will seek it out, even if need be by retiring in high dudgeon to a Trappist monastery. "Every spirit," said Emerson, "builds itself a house; and beyond its house a world; and beyond its world, a heaven." This is probably as true in Russia as it is with us. But our trouble generally, I believe, is hardly that most of us do not want a place for some kind of religion in our mansions, but that we think first of the plumbing, the furnace, and the kitchen. When we get round to planning a room with a shrine in it, all that is usually left is the attic. And of course there is forever with

us the fear that becoming too deeply immersed in religion
involves the danger of drowning. Or at least of having to wear
a special brand of bathing suit. "Philosophy," said Newton, "is
such an impertinently litigious lady that a man has as good be
engaged in lawsuits as to have to do with her." No doubt many
feel, secretly or overtly, that way about religion.

At any rate, religious issues or commitments currently play
a very minor role in professional education conducted under
public auspices. As a matter of fact, the lines assigned to them
are not particularly impressive in private institutions either,
even when these are directly associated with a church. Sometimes courses of formal instruction in what is called theology
are offered as are classes in philosophy; but conversations with
persons teaching these do not convey the impression that
students look forward to them with impatient enthusiasm. This
does not by any means indicate that the official attitudes of
the schools themselves are hostile or perfunctorily tolerant.
On the contrary. The prevailing frame of mind in publicly
supported institutions certainly appears to be one of benevolent
neutrality. While many administrators and professors think
they haven't time to bother with such matters, they usually
have a feeling that religion is something that quite reputable
people cherish, or that it is much better represented in thoughtful literature than used to be the case. Surely *Life* would not
offer its readers a series of expensively illustrated articles on
the great faiths of the world and then reissue these in a handsome volume costing a tidy sum if there were not "something
to them"! In addition the clergy, if not held in high esteem,
at least are likely to be tolerated or even befriended. With
us, for example, the popular institution of Masonry is not
anticlerical though it has been that in a number of European
countries. There is a good deal of criticism of the local priest
or minister, but so is there of the mayor and the Secretary
of State. On the whole, the American attitude seems to be that
a clergyman is at least a necessary evil. To paraphrase Voltaire,
if he did not exist it would be necessary to invent him.

But what is the educator to do about it? There is no campus
outcry for the healing of the spirit. The religious practice of

the professional student (even when he is in the strict sense a preprofessional student) naturally varies greatly, but is as a general rule an unperturbed reflection of commitments made during earlier years. Parental allegiances, young people's groups of many kinds, talks with clergymen, Sunday morning instruction—all these leave marks, more or less indelible, on the prospective engineer or chemist. But, exception having duly been made for elites, the average professional student's association with religious life appears to be shallow and perfunctory. In his better moments he considers it a valuable moral prophylactic agent but not a quest which can enlist in any notable way the active powers of his mind. That it might do him good he is likely to surmise, but that he might devote himself to it with gusto is another matter. To these conclusions one is led by a variety of forms of evidence, ranging all the way from public opinion surveys to sociological studies and to what is garnered through personal experience. There are medical students, for example—I have met some of them at Harvard and have been greatly impressed with their earnestness—who are on fire with zeal. But there are very many such students who do not greatly care whether the soul be in the pituitary gland, the cerebrum, or nowhere in particular.

That this constitutes a grave danger, quite apart from all considerations of an individual's well-being in the life to come, is obvious to anyone who believes that the assumptions of religion are correct. For with what moods and goals in view is a man to lead his life? It is fatally easy to fall into the habit of thinking that technical ends are good in themselves if ends established through contemplation of the transcendental are not normally, naturally, the firm props of one's spirit. It would of course be easy to buttress this view with quotations from saints and theologians. If Newman was right in saying that there are only "two luminously self-evident beings—myself and my Creator," a man to whom neither is at all "luminous" must be sitting in spiritual shade. But there are many more mundane commentators. How one could wish that many educators would read and ponder carefully *The German Catastrophe* by Friedrick Meinecke, the unforgettable teacher of a generation of

American historians! This little book chronicles step by step, as it were, the way in which the moral consciousness of a great nation's elite, engrossed with the power of doing, could descend irrevocably from awareness of ethical ideals to their complete insensitivity. No one can leaf through the great, tragic debate between the spokesmen for Nazism and their noblest antagonists without seeing how the descent to the abyss took place. Consider, for instance, a secret memorandum, recently come to light, which Heinrich Himmler wrote on the subject of the education of youth in conquered territories:

A basic question to be put when considering these problems [i.e., those of the Occupation] is, what is to be done with schooling, and therewith what is to be attempted in the supervision and sifting out of youth. For the non-German populations of the East, no higher school must be permitted to exist than an elementary school limited to four years.

The objective of such a school can only be to teach simple arithmetic to a peak of the number 500, and to expound the teaching that there is a Divine command to obey the Germans, and to be honest, diligent and considerate. Reading I do not consider necessary.

Apart from the school thus described, there are to be no educational institutions in the East. Parents who seek to secure a better training for their children at the elementary as well as at the higher levels must make application to the principal officers of the SS and the Police. Each such application will be considered in the light of whether the child is above criticism from the racial point of view and conforms with our other requirements. If we accept such a child as being of our blood, it will be explained to the parents that the youngster is to go to school in Germany and is to remain there permanently.

It may seem incredible that such sentiments could once constitute the official educational philosophy of a mighty power. But if one accepts Himmler's premises the conclusions are inescapable. German blood is the highest good; all other blood, particularly that of the Jews, is the property of menials; and accordingly the first is entitled to education while the second is not. This reasoning is no doubt based on lamentably bad genetics, and yet not too many years ago doctrine akin to it was widely credited in the United States, and not only because men responsible for it were antagonistic to the Negro. At all events, it was scarcely a wonder that almost the last and bravest deed of the illustrious physicist Max Planck was to speak eloquently to his students about the necessity for a theistic religion. Where else, in the laboratory or outside it, might one expect to find a convincing answer to the monstrously cruel abracadabra which was then bent on leading the world to destruction? And in a comparable, contemporary fashion, the same protests have been voiced against Communist rule.

Many Americans do not wish to consider this form of argument. They feel that it is lacking in validity insofar as the concrete present is concerned. I cannot refrain from saying by way of reply: what has happened elsewhere does as a matter of fact take place here. During the heyday of the Communist movement in New York, we saw that colleagues who were good, indeed in some instances first-rate, scholars and quite affable persons did not hesitate to undertake the basest acts of character defamation, dishonesty, and utterly indefensible cruelty if the party line demanded it of them. As a friend said of an especially agreeable comrade, after he was caught in an act of flagrant and harmful lying, had he been a commissar he would cheerfully have stood the rest of us with our backs against the wall. I recall that one amiable Communist said to me during the course of an animated conversation that he was devoting all his spare time to the study of Freud. A few weeks later, Moscow announced that thenceforth no party member in good standing would deviate from the teaching of Pavlov. Needless to say, the psychologist in question discarded Freud even as a moth does its cocoon and was soon exclusively engrossed in the works of the author of the conditioned reflex.

What interests our countrymen very much more at this time is the uneasy awareness that membership in the "managerial class," which is the ultimate social reward for having survived the particularly strenuous varieties of professional education, includes a gilt-edged subscription to "conformism." This phenomenon, as presented in dark outline by David Riesman and

William H. Whyte, may or may not be as disturbing as they maintain. It nevertheless is widespread, and as a result raises questions about intellectual and spiritual values that cry out for answers. Not a few of them are directed to our system of education, as Whyte in particular makes evident. If educators accept as the purpose of education the studious preparation of our most gifted men and women for "belongingness," they must inevitably assume responsibility for the results. So also, however, must religion. If the growing church membership in suburbia is just one more approved form of "belongingness," then it is surely incumbent on the churches to study carefully the social ethic of which they have become the staunch if sometimes unwitting supporters.

As Will Herberg, commenting on Whyte's book, has indicated, the problem to be faced is one of "personal authenticity in a world of all-engulfing mass heteronomy." Assuredly this problem is one which drives education and religion into at least an uneasy partnership. Is there something which they must, and therefore can, do together in order to foster the freedom of awareness which is the significant first half of freedom of conscience? Certainly this, whatever it is, will not be achieved by a proclamation, an addendum to the curriculum, or even a Religious Emphasis Week. It can only come into being as a result of a thoughtful, uncompromising study of the general spiritual situation in which we now find ourselves.

The few words of comment on this situation which I shall offer here form only a short and very meager prolegomenon to such a study. If they can evoke dissent and spur on thought they will have served their purpose adequately. We live in a world whose destinies are being determined by science and from which since the middle years of the nineteenth century religion has stood apart. It seems to me that the fundamental difference between the religious and the scientific attitudes is that the second inevitably rests on a principle of agreement, while the core of religious experience is differentiation, which upon occasion can be a very rugged kind of individualism or, indeed, heresy of no indecisive kind. As the lives of Pasteur and Einstein will illustrate, most newly discovered scientific formulae are, to be sure, born to the tune of disputation. But once established they are necessarily assented to, because they are adequate to account for the phenomena they describe. This is true also of certain areas in the social sciences. But every great religion is a corporate union of individual persons, each of whom has his wholly separate, startingly lonely, relationship with the Lord God. "The way to God is the way of God," Abraham Heschel has said profoundly, noting the awesome truth round which mystical theology revolves, namely that the adventure of faith belongs in the first instance to the Divine Huntsman seeking his quarry. The uniqueness of the religious experience will become still more apparent if one uses the word "ad-venture" in its primal Latin sense. "A coming to" God is not something anyone can arrange even for a friend. To realize this we have only to recall Augustine and his mother.

It seems to me that the basic reason why science and religion have been scandals unto one another is therewith laid bare. Men strictly brought up in accordance with what for lack of a better term is called "the scientific method" are first of all repelled by the fact that there are so many religions in the world all claiming to be true and evoking acrimonious discussion which cannot be resolved. They conclude, often regretfully, that since there is no way of bringing about agreement on one formulation, the verity that may be in the theologies can never be known. Or, alas, they may even decide that since Divinity is *Deus absconditus,* the hidden God, he is probably a fabrication. More generally they will feel that since the subject matter of religion is of a character wholly alien from that of science they should be content to leave it to others.

Religious men, on the other hand, are repelled by the absolutism—in their eyes a cold and sterile standardization—of science. They frequently tend, therefore, to fight it off, often hastily and angrily, whenever it seems to affect the core of the human personality. As a result, thought, which in the strict sense is not scientific at all—for example, the psychoanalytic procedures resorted to by Sigmund Freud—is rejected upon occasion as being an unholy concoction of the laboratory. But no doubt evolution is still the classic illustration. Because faith in Christ is historically allied with credence in the Scriptures, spokesmen for Protestant and Catholic churches permitted, during a fatefully long period, a very naïve and literal reading of Genesis to bar acceptance of facts that Darwin's studies of the origin of species had brought to light. This attitude was not merely obscurantist but foolhardy from the point of view of Christianity's own mission. Churchmen were correct, however, in opposing the truth they had learned through lives of prayer to doctrines which for a while seemed to be implicit in what Darwin and his associates were saying, namely, that all existence is at bottom only a fierce struggle for domination and survival. For through prayer, in its corporate historical forms and also in the actuality of personal realization, the truth of the reality of love is established.

The cleavage between science and religion cannot be surmounted by trying to prove that all faiths are, when one gets down to bedrock, the same. Arnold Toynbee has devoted his genius as a historian to this task, coming eventually to the conclusion that love for one's fellow men, as expressed in a purified Christianity and one form of Buddhism, is the fundamental religious commitment. Aldous Huxley's "perennial philosophy" establishes a comparable thesis with different argumentation. But interesting and useful though their speculative essays may be as expositions of religious positions arrived at by modern men of great talent, they do not help to dispose of the problem. It is true that Jesus Christ taught that the noblest commitments were to the love of God and of neighbor, but He also said with the strongest possible emphasis that there was no way to the Father save through Him. This "way" He outlined with dramatic clarity. It leads to the Cross, and there is no other route for Christians. Therefore, however deeply he may revere men who subscribe to other faiths and hold them in unwavering affection, he cannot escape the conviction that the roads down which they travel are the wrong ones. No one can doubt that the "exclusiveness" of Christianity is one highly important reason why science and religion have been in conflict. The Western world has been the cradle of scientific inquiry. It is also, uniquely, the area in which the basic cultural questions have for two thousand years been these: did Jesus have the right to say of Himself what He did say; and, if so, am I walking in His footsteps as he would have me do?

It may also be useful to consider briefly certain aspects of Christian history that appear to reinforce what has been said. The "existentialist" revolt against established Protestantism and the philosophy of Hegel that was set in motion by Sören Kierkegaard resembles in impressive ways the Protestant revolt against the Catholic church and the Scholastic philosophy that had its greatest spokesman in Martin Luther. In both cases the dominant convictions were that the ecclesiastical organization had become bureaucratic and therewith spiritually dull, that prosperity had paved the way of the Cross with asphalt and set up roadside inns on Calvary, and that acceptance of a philosophy (for Luther the target was Aristotelianism) making claims to universal validity crushed the personalism of religious experience. For many reasons it is unfortunate that Luther's uprising could not have assumed the form of a major house-cleaning within the Church, just as it is that the drastic, uncompromising Kierkegaard should have possessed so limited an awareness of the social framework within which life is necessarily lived. But both do make clear that religion, even the Christian religion, is not a tranquilizer but an explosive, not just another prerequisite for club life in suburbia but a going out alone to the rim of the world, not soft music played at funerals merely but also a sudden clash of cymbals in the night and a man answering on his knees, "Depart from me, O Lord, for I am a sinful man!"

Of course, the religious community may also most legitimately be identified with warm human experience. Indeed, with us how regrettable that it is frequently not so associated —that the parish church is often like a doctor's office, to which one goes at regular intervals for a checkup; that usually the congregation is preached at and not talked with; and that the expression of love for others that normally accompanies worship is dropping a dollar into the collection basket. From this point of view certain trends in suburbia are promising and might be aped on the campus. In their rescue of the individual Riesman and Whyte outdo Kierkegaard. However greatly one may disapprove of "belongingness," the fact remains that man is not only a gregarious animal but a friend seeking friends. It may be too bad that suburbia is serenely Catholic, Protestant, and Jewish. But one surmises that even so it is better to live in White Plains than it was to reside in Magdeburg during the Thirty Years' War.

The conclusions to be drawn are not at all simple. Men need in an age of the masses to deepen their awareness of personality and conscience. They are driven also to find community with their fellows on a basis that transcends material interests and recognizes the worth of profound and holy aspirations. From both points of view the race has never known any substitute for religion. But the architect of the time is science—a builder with whose genius we cannot dispense, for if he took his hand away for an hour the edifice already erected would collapse. On its ability to supply a steady stream of well-trained scientists our society depends not merely for its well-being but for its survival. Unfortunately, there is a gulf between the man of science and the man of religion. This is not due to any gainsaying of the one by the other, but to the undeniable fact that the intuitions of the one are not those of the other. This is a hard verity. Even harder is its corollary: if the two are not conjoined, a man will be only half of himself.

So much for the prolegomenon to a study which, let us hope, someone will sometime undertake. I am led by it to believe that the task of the educator in any school for professional men and the task of the teacher of religion is—to use a phrase not unlike some of Luther's—to stick pins into each other until they are awake and sufficiently agitated to do something together to prepare young people for a nobler world than one in which the best-tasting toothpaste is sold with the help of the latest group dynamics by the glibbest advertising agency. After they have got through eying each other askance, they will have to reckon with the fact that young people will not acquire religion by stirring a spoonful of it in their tea. A number of uncomfortable facts will also have to be faced. The most immediate of them has already been alluded to— the plain, simple, sober truth that most of the young people under consideration have their eyes on a ranchhouse within commuting distance and often on precious little else.

The first remedial step is obviously to put religious teachers on the campus and see what they can do. In other words, Mark Hopkins must come and he will need a log to sit on. But when one tries to draw a blueprint of the characteristics of such a teacher working on a campus dedicated in whole or in part to professional education of first-rate quality, a number of queries present themselves. First of all, the man must have been adequately trained in his own theological discipline, which of course means that he will practice and expound a creed and not a common denominator of creeds. Second, if he is to succeed as a teacher his right to membership in the faculty must be based not on courtesy but on unimpeachably evident intellectual stature. He will possess insight into at least some of the philosophic and methodological implications that the habit of quite wholly absorbed living in the world of science has for the men and women about him. It seems to me self-evident, for example, that if he be stationed at a university or college where his principal concern will be with meeting students specializing in education, he will have made himself familiar with behaviorism as professed in many branches of psychological study, and with its achievements and limitations. All this does not mean that he is to bandy phrases about with the profession or to engage in useless controversies. What matters is that he knows intellectually those he meets. And finally, as a thinker in his own right, he will realize, with whatever measure of sadness, that engrossment in science has crowded out of many lives the practice of dialectic in virtually all its forms; and dialectic, whether it be that of Socrates or Aquinas, of Kierkegaard or Martin Buber, is the method by which religious insight has traditionally developed from naïve belief to intellectual realization. Ingrained habits of "positive" thinking are bound to be a theologian's major impediment to success.

When one tries to visualize whence religious teachers of such description are to come, and how they might be induced to undertake their mission with intelligence and enthusiasm, one is squarely face to face with a major conundrum. Such men are to be found, but they are very busy in theological seminaries, religiously affiliated colleges, editorial offices, or research institutions. The fact that in the United States theology is never a discipline in a university under public auspices (as it often is in Europe) is of major importance. If it were, teachers of the kind indicated would develop naturally on the campus. Therefore, if the study of religion is to acquire rank and status in our professional schools, particularly those on the graduate level, church sponsors have no choice save the education of trained and experienced representatives. They must also be ready to take for granted an environment that will not take kindly to old-fashioned interconfessional philippics. Conflict cannot be avoided altogether, but open and venomous warfare is a scandal to the young and a topic of derision for their elders. No doubt Americans do too often believe that sitting round a table will solve all problems of an intellectual character, but these faults cannot be corrected by highhanded and in a real sense scurrilous conduct.

We shall now assume that the requisite religious teachers have been found and that places have been made for them on the campus. What is the situation they will normally encounter? Administrators will be affable and attempt to reveal as little as possible of their traditional stuffed shirts—which are usually no more than the standard appendages of diplomacy and decorum. Inwardly, of course, they will feel a bit constrained or even worried lest something go awry and thunder be heard in distant episcopal sees. A few members of the faculty will lend ardent support, and a comparable number will prove irreconcilably hostile. But the great majority will pay no more attention to the representatives of religion than chemists do to astronomers, or the devotees of pedagogy to instructors in the "content subjects." There will be a student flock, sometimes prodded into membership by anxious parents, and also upon occasion, thank God, spurred on by their own deep convictions and ideals. In almost every instance, the religious culture of young people, as distinguished from religious practice, will have been developed prior to entering the professional school. This means that startling variations will appear. Sometimes, especially if a student has attended a good college, awareness of religious history and values will be quite adequate. But in general the training received will have been rudimentary, however satisfactory young people themselves may consider it; and unless a good deal is done the roots of faith will wither, sending up no shoot other than the instinct for "belongingness," which is unfortunately responsible for very much of what we currently term the religious revival. I think therefore that the initial stage of the academic mission must be the building of a community round the center of worship. This will make it possible for those less well prepared to be stimulated and encouraged by their better-trained companions, even while meeting the teacher in a familiar environment.

It is my profound conviction that once the community has been established, the first-rate religious teacher will find a deeply interested audience, like Newman's at Oxford or—in a quite different mode—Alain's in Paris. Granted such a following, there will be no barrier to the desired goal—namely, that courses in religion be offered for credit to students who wish to take them. For the most part, however, the student will come of his own volition to the religious center, in which we hope vigorous and fruitful discussion of life issues and problems is habitual. We very much need this kind of discussion for graduate students in particular, who are now the abandoned sheep of American university life. Let me add that at least a minimum of discreet and friendly co-operation between the protagonists of varying creeds is desirable (as indeed Pope Pius XII has indicated), though a perfunctory display of sham solidarity may well do more harm than good.

Now what of the campus as a whole? There are, I believe, two principal ways in which concern for religion can be developed on the campus, and these we shall now explore. First, habits of intellectual formation fortunately exist in professional schools that afford opportunities to religion, odd and paradoxical though they may at first sight seem. Let me give an example. American observers of medical practice returning from tours of exploration behind the Iron Curtain were struck by the impersonal, quite mechanistic approach to the patient as compared with our own, which when it is at all contemporary in spirit holds that therapy must begin with a consideration of the patient as a person. This difference some of the observers have attributed to the influence of psychotherapy on American medicine as contrasted with Communist reliance on a strait-laced version of Pavlovian psychology. Now it is well known that the art of psychoanalysis (for despite its use of scientific pigments it is an art) was at the outset definitely antireligious. The reasons why this was so were many and certainly included evidence (of which a great deal was made) that many neuroses could be traced to fears and inhibitions suggested by religious precepts. But as time has passed the fact that sound faith and good psychotherapy both establish the existence and paramount importance of the personality as an indubitable if always inexplicable entity has led many soundly trained and widely experienced medical men to conclude that the healing process of sublimation can be aided by religious practice as by nothing else. This is not because such practices are "tranquilizers," but because they assist the individual in probing to the depths where his decisions are formed. It is quite strikingly true that although some clerics still fulminate against Freud, much of the most penetrating comment on religious writing is currently made by practicing psychotherapists.

Such confluences, and they exist in a number of professional fields, need careful exploration and irenic discussion. An additional illustration from the realm of educational theory may be adduced. Many religious people tremble at the mention of John Dewey's name as they might on the approach of Satan himself; and it is of course true that this philosopher's later discussions of "scientific pragmatism" were as "a-theistic" as can well be imagined. They clearly reflected the crisis of belief which set in after the turn of the century. Yet that which is essential in the pedagogical theory of Dewey and his associate

Kilpatrick stems from the days when both were religious men who employed the old American concept of the community co-operating for good ends in formulating a philosophy of education which in essence wanted children to be given a chance to become part of a functioning community while in school. Wherein does this differ radically from the wisdom of Pestalozzi, Montessori, and others who were as deeply Christian as human beings could well be? The proper critique of Dewey, insofar as his practical pedagogy is concerned, therefore will not be based on antipathy to his cloudy metaphysics but solely on whether the "school community" he envisioned gets its work done and whether the number of policemen and tax collectors in it ought to be increased.

The second way that opens before us is formal instruction in religion. Certainly this is very badly in need of revamping, particularly if it is to be effective within an environment so greatly influenced by scientific inquiry and methodology as ours is. Comment so astringent may at first seem unwarranted. There can be no doubt that the books available today on all the major faiths are vastly superior to the dull, schematic outlines in vogue half a century ago. Major seminaries have likewise given a great deal of thoughtful attention to the problem. The trouble as I see it is that instruction is given as if the young person interested in law, engineering, or some other profession were in fact preparing for the sacred ministry. He is expected to respond in a personal way to material which would be entirely appropriate were he in a theological seminary. On the other hand, the teacher of religion to lay college or university students tends to feel that his discipline will lose its pertinence and value if he proceeds in any other fashion.

Here no doubt European experience can be of value to us, not because of cultural inferiority on our part but because a long period of corrosion of the religious sense, as well as decades of devastating warfare that gave prominence to the problem of evil even while destroying long-established communal solidarities, has compelled teachers in the Old World to revise drastically their concepts of the mission to intellectual men and women. What Romano Guardini and Joseph Pieper have done in Germany, or Yves Cougar and his associates in France, or the indefatigable Jesuits of Liége in Belgium has set an example that needs only to be followed imaginatively on the American scene. Professor Guardini's *Glaubenserkenntnis* (Realization of Faith), for example, presents a course of lectures in dogmatic theology which, while quite orthodox from the Roman Catholic point of view, are nevertheless vividly modern in feeling and concern. The fact that more than a thousand students, of varied church allegiances and academic disciplines, go to listen to them clearly indicates that when the sheep have pasture they will feed. I hasten to add that these lectures are substantial, having nothing in common with peace of spirit or televised dramatics. Even so, religious teaching could undoubtedly take a leaf from the book of modern education and discover the usefulness of audio-visual materials.

For my part I believe that it is not the religious commitment of the young man or woman which has been subjected to fearsome erosion—for as Augustine has said the human heart remains unquiet always—but the intellectual acre in which that commitment must be planted if it is to flourish. The problem we face, therefore, is how to enrich the soil. Accordingly, religion must not shy away from using the treasure made available to it by the centuries during which it has been so important and creative a force in the shaping of liberal culture and ethical reflection. These may not seem to an exacting theologian much more than exercises designed to discipline the mind so that it may be ready for contemplation of Divine mysteries. But today they assuredly provide far, far more than the normal ration of spiritual food. The standard program of the European humanistic secondary school, with its emphasis on the moral teaching implicit in literature, is likely to seem to many of us merely a somewhat sublimated version of McGuffey's readers. But if our generations are fed on the cereals of utility only, thereby limiting their imaginations to the horizons of science, how can one expect them to hang over the ledge from which alone one can see eternity in time?

The liberal arts have a way of living up to their origins. That T. S. Eliot could pack a great hall at the University of

Minnesota with people anxious to hear him lecture is not without its significance for religion also. The more room we provide for the liberal arts in high school, college, and professional school, the less need we shall have for being worried about the specifically religious part of the course of study. But worry we should have to, even then. For however diligent his man Friday, the master theologian is indispensable. Take, for instance, the problem of justice. What is this, for which the whole world cries out, and to what does it obligate a man? What are the major areas of modern life which it affects? How is the individual to shoulder his own responsibility for its attainment? We can and should endeavor to deal with these questions in historical, legal, and philosophic terms. But is not Emil Brunner right when he contends that justice means giving every man his due, and that as a consequence it is the realization in action of that love of neighbor which religious contemplation confronts as a divine demand? Such love is either a movement outward into the world of the religious spirit or it is a delusion with which one must deal logically, mechanistically as do the Communists. Was not the initial appeal of their doctrine rooted in the widespread irritated conviction of the masses that those who professed the Judaeo-Christian faith did not practice what they said they believed? Yet it is now made manifest that the repudiation of justice in its totality by the atheistic on pantheistic totalitarians is not accidental. Justice was discovered, revealed, for us in the Scripture. It is to be found nowhere else. And so, do we not see here the outline of a course that the American professional campus badly needs?

There are certainly any number of worth-while things which might be tried not with a view to stripping religious teaching of all respect for systematic treatment but in the hope of clothing the bones of the "system" with recognizable flesh and blood. If this is done, young people will gladly leave their mathematics texts and their treatises on anatomy for precious hours during which their awareness of themselves, of their obligations and their destinies, can take them beside still waters more profound than any others. I am optimistic enough to believe that in the development of this awareness the gulf between scientific inquiry and religious belief can be crossed by very many. As I have tried to say elsewhere (in a talk given at the University of Michigan during the summer of 1946), there is a point of light at which meet the great men of science and the saints who are the final teachers of religion this side of God Himself. This is the point at which the demonstrated integrity of both is made evident. Yet one must remember that for our time the discovery of it is far from easy. As I then said:

To ask the saint and the scientist to give an account of themselves is not to suggest that either will immediately be believed. For those of us to whom the ancient Christian and Jewish faiths bring not defeat but joy, not doubt but confidence, it may be difficult to understand why the urge to holiness which glows so warm in our tradition should be so invisible to many. The Christian is aware that the Beatitudes, eight in number like a round of dancers, are fruits hung too high on the tree of life for him to pluck. None the less it seems to him that nothing more glorious was ever said of man than that some day his reach might attain even unto them—that he might be rich because he was poor, and mighty because he was humbly selfless. But he must be patient. He cannot help knowing that a curtain has fallen between him and the rest of men. He must give them an example before he can furnish them with a doctrine.

An example shown in patience, not with furor but in quietness! That is the essence of the religious education program for the professional school also. While making it evident that religious thinking can color all human reflection and add a needed dimension to science, the teacher must remember that he too sees through a glass darkly. Perhaps in the end the follower of Newman will meet in friendly company with the disciples of Newton and Blacktsone, Pasteur and Horace Mann. At least of this one can unfortunately be certain: our time will not have a soul until it is shown what having one means.

The Community—Campus Life

ROBERT M. STROZIER

Analysis of the Student Community

CHAPTER XII

In many ways the personalities of the American colleges and universities are reflected in the buildings that house them. The classrooms in which the teaching occurs stand alongside the elaborate hospital systems, the complicated new science institutes and laboratories, the libraries, the efficient administrative headquarters, and the chapel spires. Among these buildings on most campuses are numerous others in which teaching and research occur less frequently, if at all: the oval of the football stadium, the rows of fraternity and sorority houses, the blocks and blocks of dormitories, the sleek and streamlined student union buildings. The campus is a place of learning. In our definition of "campus" we usually do not make exclusions. I have sometimes observed the puzzled look on the face of a visitor from abroad as he has inspected the various rooms of our strange house. Occasionally, a guest from another land will be so bold as to ask what the bowling alley, swimming pools, and ballrooms have to do with scholarship. This is a fair question.

The personality of higher education in the United States is dominated by an important political fact and emotional attitude. In theory and generally in practice the American college campus is open to everyone as a matter of right. In every nation the institutions of learning play an important sociological role. In the United States the colleges and universities selfconsciously play a socializing role. Our campuses are not only congregations of minds dedicated to the pursuit of scholarship. They are also communities of bodies and souls, complete with all the material and physical paraphernalia and shortcomings attending human life.

The right to learning is one of the expressions of the strong American drive toward equality of economic and political condition. The attempt to provide learning opportunities for millions undoubtedly has had an effect upon the quality of the education ultimately provided. In any event, the millions have carefully policed their political right, and the masses have naturally been articulate about the results they expect educational opportunities to achieve. Colleges and universities in the United States are sensitive to the popular will, which largely accounts for the multiplicity of purposes assigned to higher education in this country. There is strength in a multiplicity of purposes. The plethora of our purposes, however, often seems to paralyze our ability to assign an order of values to the various things we do. Student life on the campus puts to a test our value structure.

The United States is still a nation of great economic and social mobility. Mass higher education plays a vital part in keeping things mobile. The public in this country thoroughly appreciates the relation between advanced education and economic and social mobility. Those who support the colleges and universities with taxes and contributions, and the students who come to partake of the education, not only expect the educational experience to equip people for fuller and more prosperous lives, but also to duplicate roughly the lives they already know. The American success story is broadly understood. Most American students need only look at their own parents, relatives, or neighbors down the street to observe some phase of the story in action. How natural it is for these young people, when they leave home for the collegiate experience, to take along with them the prejudices and expectations to which they have been conditioned. The mood of the general American public is directly injected into campus affairs through the conduct of the students.

The student community, therefore, is a ramification of the

adult community. The character of student life is always colored brightly by the events of national history.

The Roaring Twenties produced a generation of students who also roared. The campus life of these students could only have existed in a national climate of bewildering expansion. Prohibition, raccoon coats, jazz, and the gentlemanly "C" did not, of course, characterize or mold the majority of the students of this decade. They simply accented an underlying attitude. The Veterans of World War I thought themselves sophisticated. They had seen gay Paree, and they read and aped F. Scott Fitzgerald. Their younger brothers and sisters, like all those who copy the original, produced a kind of superficiality under the guise of sophistication which today seems ludicrous. This was not a decade of democratic spirit in student life. Still, the campuses drew more students to them than ever before, setting the stage for what was soon to follow.

The contrast between the twenties and the thirties is striking. The unhappy Depression Years brought a new sobriety to the campus. Matters of social importance were natural for young men and women whose parents had lost everything and were unable to finance a higher education for them. Campus jobs, snobbishly avoided in the twenties, became the order of the day. Glittering social functions were few and unpopular. The schools themselves suffered severe financial pangs, and the students in the schools were acutely concerned with their own future economic security. Young and idealistic minds toying with all the popular political panaceas and isms and the faculties existing on substandard incomes were part of the prevailing tone. Our campuses were populated by intense people.

World War II broke suddenly on the United States, and its impact on the campus was immediate. The older male students began to leave. Those who were on call were restless and frustrated, often unable or unwilling to study. Younger men were eager for their time to come, anxious not to miss the Great Adventure. School officials suddenly found their student bodies decimated and upset, and their budgets hopeless.

Many colleges and universities were saved from financial

disaster during the war by the establishment of military train-ing programs on the campuses. The strict discipline of the armed services' program contrasted sharply with the general university atmosphere in the larger schools, whose student bodies consisted mainly of the young, those physically unable to enter the armed forces, and the women. Teaching and research—except for that carried on in the government pro-grams—fell to a low ebb.

As the war drew to an end the leaders of the colleges and universities began to anticipate with mixed emotions the pros-pect of thousands of returning veterans. Preparations for their return assumed that the veterans would be a problem. Wash-ington assured the universities that demobilization would be an orderly process, and that the "problem"—whatever else it might become—would not be one of sheer physical chaos. Things did not work out that way. Men who had served gladly were unwilling to remain in the armed forces when the conflict ended, and their sentiments were effectively articulated by their parents, and thus by their congressmen. When it finally rained, it poured, and for a while it seemed that the campus would be inundated by the returning flood.

A problem existed in the years 1945–49 on most campuses, but the veteran was not the problem. His numbers helped to create the problem, which had been inadequately foreseen. Additional students created immediate needs for faculty, hous-ing, equipment, and services. Men and women who had faced the fire of battle, who confronted futures already foreshortened, returned in a serious frame of mind, naturally impatient with petty rules and red tape, poor instruction, inefficient adminis-tration, and the supine acceptance of anything whatsoever. They were young people in a hurry, definite in their aims, mature in outlook, and quite realistic in judgment. Some of the best students this country has ever known were present in this veteran group, and many of them would never have had the opportunity for higher education had it not been for the War and its unique educational aftermath—the "G.I. Bill."

In their eagerness to recoup financially, many institutions admitted more students than they could effectively instruct or accommodate. Fly-by-night trade schools flourished briefly, taking advantage of the five-hundred-dollar government allotments for tuition. Adequate controls for the approval of study programs were not instituted by the government, and there were many abuses of the opportunities afforded by the G.I. Bill. Despite these abuses, the impact of the bill on the educational scene was profound. The result persists, long after the majority of the veterans have exhausted their benefits under the law.

Local, citizen control of education in the United States is a deep-rooted tradition. Federal interference has long been avoided, and the fear of federal control—of a uniformity imposed by support from the national government—is a live and effective force in American politics and society. The G.I. Bill served as an example of federal economic support free from federal political control of educational policy. Those who most feared federal intervention in education came to realize that this particular federal legislation had democratized education in a way which many thoughtful people had considered impossible. The G.I. Bill brought this whole issue to the campus at a new level. What has since happened makes some administrators schizophrenic. On a grand scale, this unique instrument opened the door to higher education to young Americans from every economic and social stratum.

After this experience, colleges and universities were both ready and eager to absorb the returning veterans of the Korean action. Thus the wars at mid-century thoroughly democratized the opportunities for higher education in the United States. From this adversity blossomed into reality one of the great American ideals, and no one can understand succeeding student communities in this nation without first appreciating this monumental fact.

Religion assumed a more important role on the campus after World War II. The scepticism and agnosticism, prevalent in the twenties, had been succeeded by a marked concern with social issues during the days of the depression. Where independent thinking in the past had seemed to lead the student away from religion, it has, in recent years, seemed to bring him closer to it. State and private institutions have seen a great increase in participation by students in the religious groups. Students are just as much interested in matters of social import but less likely to substitute such interests for religion. The larger religious groups have their own centers on campuses. They co-operate closely with the personnel officers and contribute to the extracurriculum and advisory programs. If the representatives of the various faiths felt in past years that they were only tolerated by the administration, today they feel welcome. It might be added that the quality of the men and women assigned by the religious groups to campus positions is quite superior generally.

The student body constitutes one important link between the institutions of higher learning and the general community. On still another front colleges and universities meet the public directly in an influential context. This is the economic front —the sector in which the educational institutions fight their battles to finance their operations. The ebb and flow of this battle also helps to shape the forces that both expand and restrict student life. For most schools this battle is fought in relation to three major sources of power—government, the great private foundations, and private foundations and private industry.

The relationship between the federal government and the colleges and universities remains ambiguous. Land-grant schools have been recipients of the largess of the government for many years and have worked out a *modus vivendi* which seems to have left their policy-making powers completely intact. Not all state universities have been so happy in their relationships with their own controlling legislatures.

The participation of the federal government in research during and since World War II has been enormously expanded. Almost all the larger universities and many colleges have obtained grants from the government for special research activities. This represents a natural—though often difficult—union of interests and talents. In an atomic era, the government naturally has need of research for which it lacks human talent, technical equipment, and resources. Academicians usually prefer to remain in their professions rather than to join government service. Academic participation in such vast projects as those at Los Alamos and the Argonne National Laboratories are only the most spectacular examples of a trend very much in effect today.

To the extent that the government may give or withhold its resources for specific research objectives—and may always, of course, withdraw its support at the expiration of specific contract periods—the influence of the federal agencies is felt sharply on the campus. An abrupt decline in government support would seriously cripple many excellent educational institutions. On some it would have a disastrous effect.

Moreover, the interests of the national government have predominantly concentrated in the applied sciences. This fact has had a variety of mischievous effects on work going on in the other disciplines. It has created gross inequalities in faculty salaries. It has directed the use of academic resources within the science fields themselves. These concentrations of monetary power and resources within the university naturally influence the quality and the numbers of students who take up those disciplinary pursuits.

Federal influence in higher education at this level presents a very different set of problems and consequences from those implied by the federal scholarship program symbolized by the G.I. Bill. Those who remain adamant in opposition to all federal assistance often fail to honor the distinctions involved.

No college of quality can rely wholly on tuition income for financial security. In most institutions tuition-free income accounts for one-half or less of the total operating costs. No modern business or industry can escape the increasingly acute need for college and university-trained leadership and personnel. On the basis of this mutuality, the educational administrators have turned increasingly to business and industry in recent years for financial support. By and large, industry has responded to this situation generously and wisely. The Ford Motor Company has established its own educational program, as have DuPont and many other corporations. Each year finds new examples of either private programs for the children of employees or direct, general support of the colleges and universities. In their fund-raising efforts the schools have, with increasing frequency, turned to the medium-sized and smaller industries.

Quite aside from the influential role the leaders of industrial corporations play on the governing boards of universities and colleges, reliance on industry for direct grants presents new issues concerning the independence of the educational institutions from the particular interests represented by industry and business. Industry—like government—has its special concern with the applied sciences and with a relatively few other disciplinary areas. Industry has stepped up its campus recruiting activity, and through a variety of doors enters the campus in a manner which influences the choices that both students and faculty members make regarding study and career pursuits. The modern college curriculum reflects the specialized and vocational needs for success in the American industrial and commercial organization. Modern student life reflects the cultural patterns resulting in a society in which business success is the dominant model.

Foundations for educational purposes are not new, but the emergence of the Ford Foundation, with its galaxy of subsidiaries, has been a matter of national importance. Universities turn with more frequency than ever before to the large foundations—Ford, Rockefeller, Carnegie, and Kellogg—for special project support. At the same time, hundreds of smaller foundations have been and are being established with more limited areas of interest. The present tax policies in this country make gifts to foundations favorable to persons of large fortunes who are seriously interested in promoting education. The $500,-000,000 grant by the Ford Foundation in 1955 to private colleges and universities was the largest ever made, and it set a new pattern for foundation giving. Instead of grants of from three to five years' duration for special projects which the school is often committed to continue—assuming they succeeded—the Ford gift was both for endowment and operational purposes. Administrators have long argued that the colleges and universities have greater need for unallocated funds than for special project grants. In any event our schools are now, more than ever, dependent upon foundation support for the continuance of important segments of educational programs.

Curiously, the postwar national prosperity has in some ways adversely affected the economic welfare of educational institutions and their students. Inflation, the explosive growth of national population, and the broadening educational opportunities for our young people have revolutionized the financial situations of the students themselves. Tuition costs in our schools have advanced from an average of around $500 in 1950 to more than $1,000 per year in many of our private institutions. The state universities have also uniformly found it necessary to increase their fees. The student activities fee has become an accepted part of student expense at almost all institutions. It usually includes tickets to athletic contests, support for student publications, and social events. This taxation has led to a strong student voice in the distribution of funds. The associated student organizations in the major schools on the West Coast have almost exclusive representation in financing and controlling the extracurriculum.

Consequently, almost all institutions have been subjected to sharp pressures to increase their funds allocated for scholarships, fellowships, and aids for students. The state schools have expanded their resources for these purposes through special grants from the legislatures and private sources, and the other schools have drawn from unendowed funds as well as from industry, private individuals, and government. Many scholarship programs have been established on a nationally competitive basis—of which the National Merit program is an example.

In 1950 tuition at Harvard College, in the oldest university in the United States, was $600. Today it is $1,000. As President of Harvard University from 1933–53, James Bryant Conant established scholarships on a national basis with competition conducted in regional areas. Alumni who had previously recommended promising young men to Harvard now were asked to assist the Admissions Office to locate talented young men regardless of their financial circumstances. Thus, the scholarship program at Harvard has had a liberalizing effect upon the make-up of the student body of the College. The increased demand for student financial assistance, and the vigorous efforts of the colleges throughout the nation to meet this demand, have been additional factors accelerating the democratization of higher education in the United States.

At the graduate level the size of the fellowships given has increased markedly with the national inflation of the 1950's. The National Science Foundation, the U. S. Public Health programs, and other grants are larger than most universities have been accustomed to award. Competition for the qualitative science students, as a result, has been very keen. This is the day of the multiple applications from students for admission as well as for grants-in-aid. Member institutions of the American Association of Universities by common consent do not announce graduate fellowship awards until the first of April each year. Then they are confronted with a period of anxious waiting for acceptances by the more promising young scholars. Obviously, the quality of the educational institutions is affected by the outcome of such competition. The American universities not only compete for faculty members and general public support, but also for superior students.

The economic affairs of national life frame acute problems for the institutions of higher education in the United States and add an important dimension to the character of the student community. Through these problems the campuses are subjected to a variety of pressures. All segments of national life compete for the attention and talents of the academic world. Indeed, in obtaining competent teachers in the sciences, the academic world is itself a competitor with the government and industry. This intense competition not only affects the kind of educational opportunity ultimately presented to the students, but also has an impact upon the decisions students make about their career futures.

Because the typical American student is young, generally without dependents, and during his school years not engaged in full economic productivity, it is sometimes felt that his immersion in campus life is artificial, detached from the main currents of the general community. National and international events, however, reach into campus life and shape what the students do and think. Occasionally, campus affairs become national events. Though most campuses are separate plots of ground, they are not isolated. They could not be isolated, even if they wished it that way.

Long before the U. S. Supreme Court decided that equal educational opportunities meant something more than the provision of separate but similar facilities, this issue was vigorously faced by the American campus. Since the Court's opinion, this issue has focused on the South, where the great battle against segregation is still in progress. But the plight of minority groups has long concerned American society and the universities.

The segregation of the Negro is central. Discrimination against Jews has been less discussed, but its existence is tacitly recognized. The private quotas of many colleges have been relaxed. In the social life of the campus, integration of the various races has been rapid. The fraternity facet of student life is an example of recent progress.

During World War II the fraternity system in America suffered, and many educators thought it probably would never return to its former strength. This has not been the case. Fraternities provided much-needed postwar housing for many returning veterans. The veteran, tired of the disciplined life of the military, found gaiety and relaxation in the unstructured environment of the fraternity house.

Thanks largely to the influence of these returning veterans, a plan originated among the students at the University of Michigan designed to deny the use of campus facilities to student groups who practiced membership and social discrimination. The plan, which stipulated a given period of time during which the student organizations could alter their practices before censure, gained national importance through its sponsorship by the National Student Association. This proposal stimulated intensive debate within the American student body, and it spurred many colleges to examine more closely the rigidity of their social groups, fraternities, sororities, and clubs.

At the present time many Jewish students are initiated in the traditionally "Aryan" fraternities. Some formerly restrictive fraternities have pledged and initiated Negro members. Many national fraternal organizations have officially removed restrictive clauses from their constitutions. This legal action does not always insure perfect practices, but it does testify to the growing impatience of students with discriminatory practices. The shape of things to come is demonstrated by the keen sensitivities of our students, sensitivities often keener than those of their elders, the alumni, whose student days now rest in a remote and very different past.

Another important result of the postwar veteran ferment was the emergence of a genuinely representative, national student organization. While national student unions are traditional in other parts of the world, the scope and diversity of the American continent operated against such a federation. The U. S. National Student Association now has a history of ten years. It has grown to represent more than two hundred student bodies of more than a million students. In its formative years NSA experienced a rare and mature leadership and reflected accurately many national political tensions. Veterans were in the majority from 1946–50, and a struggle developed between extreme leftist and conservative student elements. With maturity a middle-of-the-road policy evolved, which has greatly enhanced the influence of the organization. The evolution of NSA has afforded hundreds of student leaders an extraordinary, practical education in the political dynamics of American life. But many American educators, trained in a different age, still look askance at student interest in practical politics.

Aside from its efforts to stimulate student interest in international student affairs, the most important consequence of the national organization has been its encouragement of campus student government. The development of vigorous self-government encountered a paternalistic tradition in many colleges and universities. While the curricula of our schools preached the democratic doctrine, little opportunity for the practice of democracy existed in campus life. Today student government is judiciously and calmly accepted. As the students have matured through the intelligent acceptance of the responsibility which accompanies increased freedom, so the administrative authorities in most schools have matured by permitting greater freedom to the students. The regulation of student life itself is now frequently placed within the jurisdiction of student government. On some campuses student government is encouraged to share faculty deliberations concerning what is taught and the methods of teaching. But on almost all campuses through committees, through round-table discussion and debate, the lines of communication between the students, the faculty, and the administration are firmly established. The paternalistic approach is no longer tolerated. The paradox of attempting to teach students to think, while directing their every act, is fortunately passé.

Even at a much earlier point in our national history, De Tocqueville observed the American passion for joining organizations and participating in public political and social affairs. He saw these peculiar American propensities as manifestations of the democratic spirit, the conviction among our people that each man was as good as his neighbor and thus entitled to mix fully in all aspects of public life. But one of the prices of equality, said De Tocqueville, was loneliness. The equalization process, he thought, erected impersonal mass models, which motivated the American to join with his fellows in public and social endeavor in an attempt to escape from his feelings of isolation.

Taking modern student life as a whole, perhaps the two dominant qualities are its informality and the way it seeks to encourage broad participation in a variety of activities.

Informality is the keynote to the social life. The student union movement has provided a central meeting place for all students. It has broken down the barriers between formal social activity and the more frequent, unstructured mingling of students of all backgrounds in social intercourse. Clubs and activities on the campus now follow easily the natural, ever-changing interests of the students rather than set and traditional patterns.

The spread of coeducation has accelerated the demolition of social convention and tradition on the campus. The women's colleges in the Eastern region still flourish, but there has been little expansion of these schools in recent years. In fact, some smaller women's colleges have become coeducational, and others have ceased to exist. The finishing school for young ladies has shown a marked decline in the East and the South —the only areas where it ever had importance. The woman's role in American society is reflected in campus life. Women students move with ease into student leadership positions on the newspapers, in the governments, and in the national student movement.

Campus attitudes toward sex have altered considerably. Aberrations which formerly could not even be discussed now are faced for what they usually are—symptoms of deep-seated maladjustments. Sex education and preparation for married life are subjects found either in the formal curriculums or in informal lecture and discussion series on the campus. These subjects are received by the students with frankness, intelligence, and curiosity.

In the athletic programs, attitudes are changing too. Many of the older traditions persist; football remains king of the campus, though some smaller colleges and a few larger institutions have withdrawn from intercollegiate competition. Two major team sports—football and basketball—attained a measure of notoriety in recent years as a result of some abuses: gambling, the excessive subsidization of athletes by the colleges, and promiscuous recruiting practices.

But the most important change is the resurgence of intramural competition. In most schools today participation is at a high level in the intramural programs. This is a manifestation of the desire to shift emphasis from spectating to participation. While the spectator sports are for everyone—particularly for the alumni—modern sports programs are aimed at the individual, not only while he is a student but as a preparation for his active, maturer years. While team sports remain popular, the present trend emphasizes anew the individual sports— handball, tennis, golf, swimming, squash, fencing, gymnastics, and skiing.

Notwithstanding the informality of student life, conformity is still apparent. The crew cut, the white buckskin shoes, and the skirts and sweaters suggest an even greater conformity than actually exists. Conformity in social groups is much less marked. The independence generated by an active student government is the result, not the cause, of this intelligent informality.

With social informality has come a relaxation of outward standards of conduct, which in another day would have seemed to produce immorality. The restrictions on hours for women students have been relaxed in almost all colleges. Smoking, long forbidden, then tolerated in restricted areas, is now casually accepted for women almost everywhere. Drinking is still taboo, but practices vary considerably in the different regions of the country. Most universities leave this indulgence to the discretion of the older students.

Prefabricated houses, trailers, and temporary housing of all kinds emerged after World War II to accommodate the veteran population, many of whom returned to the campus married. Universities have recognized the phenomenon of early marriage and replaced the temporary housing units with permanent apartments for student families. Until the late forties few colleges permitted married students to attend, and many had regulations which automatically dismissed students who were married during the educational term. This has all changed during the fifties. The baby carriage has become familiar on the campus.

The growing concept of residential education in America illustrates best the blending of formal and informal education and the all-permeating nature of the collegiate experience.

The residence halls and dormitories were once considered places where students slept and ate—necessary but distracting services on the periphery of the main educational experience. Today the planning of the residential units is as much of an educational programing task as it is an architectural one. The modern residence hall is seen as a focal point of the student's life in which the arbitrary line between the extracurriculum and the curriculum disappears.

In most American universities, even in the urban areas, the majority of the students in attendance reside in the university community rather than at the residence of their parents and families. Thus, the typical American undergraduate severs the home tie at the age of eighteen and, given the geographic breadth of the United States, this break means that the distance between the youngster and the adults who formerly supervised his conduct is great.

A major shift of this supervisory responsibility has occurred from the home and church to the campus and the dean of students. The college houses the student, feeds him, oversees his moral development, and attends to his emotional and physical health problems as well as to his intellectual maturation. In addition to all of this, as curriculums have expanded and specialized, the college assumes an important role in guiding the student through the academic complexities of the institution. Many students come to college under extraordinary economic pressures which cannot be ignored. Finally, as the student terminates his education in college, his introduction to a productive career is often facilitated by vocational guidance and placement.

To manage these affairs many schools have established deans of students with general responsibilities for this administration. These deans are assisted by staffs of experts: psychiatrists, psychologists, religious counselors, residence hall counselors, veterans' advisers, and vocational guidance and placement consultants. In addition to these there are special counselors for various student activities plus the managers of the student union buildings, the dietitians for the restaurants, and the people who operate the dormitories and the fraternity houses. The titles of dean of men and dean of women are still current, indicating in some places different procedures for handling the two sexes. The dean of students in coeducational schools recognizes certain areas in which women's affairs are different, and his staff includes women in prominent positions.

As a general rule the student's use of these various services is a matter for his own discretion. No one forces him to seek the advice and counsel that the services represent. On the other hand, many schools require students, before they reach their legal majority, to reside in the residence halls rather than off campus. In the event of a serious emotional or physical illness that affects the student's academic status, the use of a particular service may be prescribed. Academic counseling is generally required for all students—at least at the undergraduate level.

It may be argued that these services have very little to do with scholarship itself, that they detract from the central theme of university life and consume unnecessarily both the time and energy of student, teacher, and administrator. To some these accommodations appear to be coddling—crutches which weaken the initiative and independence of the student.

The wise use of the special services on the campus enhance the student's ability to make a wider range of intelligent choices. Students today—in a large, diverse, and free society—are, after all, confronted with a monumental range of decisions. In the totalitarian society many of these decisions are made for the student by his superiors. Others may choose for him his life's work, the field of his university study, his social station. In our country the student must choose for himself his wife, his job, his cultural pursuits, and religious affiliations. But free decision-making should be wise, and a step toward wisdom is the assembly of the relevant facts. Student services principally are mechanisms for the assembly of the facts. Given the best facts available, the decision is still for the student to make.

Educational exchanges of an official character began on a modest scale after the Boxer Rebellion. They were stimulated by World War I, leading to the creation of a national clearing house—the Institute of International Education in New York. But it was only after World War II that exchanges became a large and important affair in which almost all colleges and universities are engaged. At present more than 35,000 foreign students are studying on American campuses, and there are thousands of students from this country abroad. The year abroad for Smith College juniors was established between the wars, and today dozens of schools sponsor special programs of foreign study.

The Fulbright Scholarships established by our government have given a tremendous impetus to the exchange idea. These awards are based on an open national competition and offer study opportunities in nations with which we have concluded reciprocal agreements. Established as a means for the payment for surplus commodities remaining in allied countries after World War II, the program allows students from the United States to study abroad and to receive their scholarships in the currency of the foreign country. From its inception this has been an admirably conducted program. It has made campuses aware of the resources and talents of the universities abroad. It has encouraged faculties to share with their peers abroad the fruits of teaching and research. It has brought to the United States campus a real sense of being a part of the educational process which knows no boundaries and has no restrictions.

The presence of foreign students from almost all countries of the world on campuses has been accepted intelligently and happily. No longer are the people from overseas exploited because they are different. They have become a regular and accepted part of the educational scene.

Barriers remain for the students behind the Iron Curtain. Efforts begun in 1956 to effect exchanges between Russia and the United States have so far been fruitless; the situation in the Middle East may have set this effort back for some time in the future. The Hungarian Rebellion and the consequent admission of thousands of its people to the United States have aided these people, but have not decreased the tensions between the East and the West. Also, no relationships are now established between this country and China.

The World University Service conducts successful annual campaigns for funds on our campuses; fraternities and sororities welcome foreign students into their houses; the Seminars for International Living bring together earnest, dedicated young people; inter-country associations, like the English Speaking Union, the Alliance Française, and the American-Scandinavian Foundation, sponsor educational programs; the Marshall Fellowships, the Rhodes Scholarships, the Lafayette Fellowships, and innumerable other programs all support and extend the spirit of exchange and unselfish dedication to true educational principles.

The international responsibilities assumed by this nation after World War II have awakened American students to their increased responsibilities as citizens.

We have been discussing student life in a prosperous, mass democracy which has quite recently assumed tremendous new responsibilities around the globe, a nation whose power rests on a highly industrialized base, and whose society is mobile, fluid, and free.

Higher education in the United States is a major focus of the cultural and intellectual problems flowing from freedom, materialism, and the necessity to use wisely unprecedented power.

The student community contains all of the tensions that are generated in such a society. In the political life of the United States liberty and the pursuit of happiness have alway been linked to the proposition that learning and education are the keys that open the doors to wealth and success. Material achievements are intimately related to a political way of life—to the ability to think and act freely. Notwithstanding its wealth this is a nation where illiteracy is viewed—even among the uneducated groups—as socially undesirable; where democracy has so thoroughly permeated higher learning that attending college is a standard aspiration among all economic strata.

There are many basic unresolved issues in American higher education; specialization and general or liberal education; the sciences versus the humanities; vocationalism and generalism; conformity and freedom; materialism and spirituality. The exciting thing about students is their eager, fresh, dynamic concern with the important unanswered questions.

SEWARD HILTNER

Religious Counseling

CHAPTER XIII

Jerry is in the office of Pastor Holmes, Director of the Blank Denominational Foundation, which serves the students of a large state university. A brilliant graduate student, Jerry is reflective and articulate but is making no secret of his agitation.

"It was a letter I got yesterday," he is saying, "that made me decide to try to talk with you. Let me try to tell you the story. Especially since I came here to study, I suppose you could say I've been fighting against believing in God. Recently I thought I could end that fight, really believe, and then pray. But I can't. My younger sister is mentally deficient. It isn't that this has hurt me personally, except inside, and my parents have been wonderful about it although it's been hell for them. But ever since I can remember, I've been asking God for an answer to this kind of waste and human tragedy. But I've never had one. I've read, and listened to a lot of preachers, some of them good. I think I know that I ought to be able to see beyond this suffering. But I can't—because it's so senseless. I realize this must be tied up with my personal problems in general, and on those I've been getting some real help over at the Student Personnel Center. But it seems to me now that I need both religious and psychological counseling at the same time."

Jerry made it clear that he did not want discussion merely or mainly of his personal problem but of the religious view of suffering and human tragedy. Pastor Holmes complied with this. Recognizing that Jerry had already heard "the answer" many times without absorbing or accepting it, he attempted to help Jerry think through the deeper situation out of which religious answers have arisen. They discussed, for example, the freedom given men by God in relation to God's sovereignty, the relation of individual and collective sin to human tragedy, and the function of chance in connection with freedom and the creatorship of God. The next week Jerry returned, and reported a counseling session he had had with his counselor at the Student Personnel Center.

"I believe now that I've been asking God to change things so that I would have no occasion for bitterness, and no guilt over my bitterness—rather than facing up to guilt and bitterness as my own emotional problems. I think I must do this before it will be possible for me to accept an answer to the question I put to you last week."

Jerry's was, certainly, a deeply religious problem. But it was so bound up with Jerry's total personal problem as to be insoluble outside that whole personal context. In this instance the primary counseling job was being done by the student personnel service. In another, Pastor Holmes might well have done the counseling, both personal and religious, himself.

Charles, a student in the same university as Jerry, is talking with his faculty adviser, Dr. Hall, about his courses for his next and final year of undergraduate work. He is majoring in Dr. Hall's field of economics. As they have discussed available courses, it has become clear that two crucial decisions depend in large part upon whether Charles will go into business on graduation or will take a master's degree and enter a particular field of public service. Both opportunities are rather clearly open to him. At this point Charles says:

"I see now that I'll have to make some kind of decision, even if I change my mind later, by next fall. I don't know. It seems so mixed up. I do think public service is important, and I'm interested in this form of it. But I think you can do a lot of good in business too. Of course, some people think a businessman can't be concerned with any human values at all, only with his profits. Sometimes I think I'd prefer to get into business if somebody could assure me I'd be able to stand up against pressures of the wrong kind. At those times I feel public service would be safer for my conscience. But then, at other times, I think public service would do more good and be more satisfying. And then I think maybe I'd just be evading the moral issues that I'd have to face as a businessman."

Dr. Hall recognized rightly that this problem of occupational decision now confronting Charles could be aided not only by additional information but also by helping Charles to clarify his personal views about economic life in the larger sense. His helpful counseling with Charles proceeded in that direction. But beneath that specific dilemma, Dr. Hall sensed the deeper religious question of vocation. God might indeed call one man to public service and another to business; but each man should know which. At the conclusion of their discussion, Dr. Hall asked Charles if he had considered discussing this aspect of his decision with the student pastor. It had not occurred to Charles that the problem might be more than technical and personal. But he saw the point, and shortly had three valuable sessions with the pastor.

Here was, on the face of it, an occupational problem containing some technical and some personal elements. The proper decision, even tentatively, could not have been reached if Dr. Hall had not aided Charles with both the technical and personal elements. But either decision Charles would have made at that time, if he had not also had the pastor's counsel, would have left him feeling like a moral coward. If he had decided to enter business, but with a feeling of impending moral defeat, he would have been unnecessarily torn. If he had decided on public service, with the fear that he was more interested in safety than in service, that too would have meant conflict. Above the technical and personal counsel, it was vital that he consider his decision in the larger context of religious vocation.

In the case of Jerry, we saw an obviously religious problem which could, however, be dealt with only by first giving personal and psychological help. In Charles' case, we have seen a technical and personal problem which was, however, handled effectively only by religious counseling accompanying the other. Few student problems are purely and simply religious, and many problems that do not appear to be religious in the conventional sense require consideration at a religious level if they are to find proper solution.

On every large campus hundreds of poignant human problems arise that are religious in the traditional sense, such as that of the boy and girl of different religious faiths who are considering marriage. Here are a few excerpts from a typical situation of this kind described by William E. Hulme.[1] Protestant Ted is talking with the campus pastor about his relationship to the Roman Catholic girl he wants to marry.

"She's all a guy could want, if it weren't for this religious angle. My folks are really up in the air about it—my mother especially. Every time I step into the house it's an argument. . . . They're just downright unreasonable. Oh, I suppose they're right—Protestants and Catholics probably shouldn't marry each other. But they're going at it in the wrong way. . . . It just makes me all the more determined to keep seeing her. . . . I never realized how prejudiced some Protestants can be against Roman Catholics until I'd been going with Esther. . . . [After reviewing the documents he would have to sign if he proceeded to marry Esther according to the Roman Catholic regulations.] That's about what Esther said it was. . . . There's sure nothing fifty-fifty about that. It doesn't seem fair. But Esther just takes it for granted . . . It seems there's only three things—or four, that can happen. Either I turn Catholic, or she turns Protestant, or we have a mixed marriage with our children raised as Roman Catholics—or we break up. . . . I love Esther and she loves me. . . . Yet there doesn't seem to be any good answer."

Rightly enough, every clergyman must adhere to the regulations of his own faith in such matters. And most clergy of all faiths, knowing the probability of future complications beyond the vision of the couple in love, tend to be pleased when, as in the case reported by Hulme, the decision is against proceeding with the marriage. But our society and its universities are heterogeneous. The decision is very often in favor of the interfaith marriage; and every religious counselor, while faithfully executing his responsibility as assigned to him by his church, bears also the responsibility of helping the couple to confront realistically the special hazards to follow from their decision.

A variety of types of problems with an obvious religious significance are initially presented to counselors on the campus today. The following examples of such problems range from the more obvious and external types to the less obvious and internal types.[2] First there is the conflict aroused with old forms of religious faith or unfaith by newly acquired knowledge. The usual form of this is the threat posed to immature faith by findings of the sciences. But increasingly common is the problem of a student with no previous training or commitment in religion who is suddenly confronted by something vital about religion in his study of history, or the humanities, or even the sciences.[3]

Second, there is the situation aroused by negative events; for example, the student's new wrestling with religious faith because of the death of a parent or friend. As described above, Jerry's problem was of this sort.

Third, there are the problems of vocation not only in the economic but also in the moral and religious sense. Charles' problem was of this type.

Fourth, the problem of relationships among members of the several faith groups is illustratively suggested by Ted's story.

Fifth, there are the many sorts of moral problems plainly associated with religion. One aspect of these was seen in the moral dimension of Charles' conflict about what occupation to pursue. Problems of relationship between the sexes fall also into this category. Even the Kinsey findings show that there are very few persons on a campus who regard sexual behavior as devoid of moral significance.[4]

Finally, we shall note the problems of meaning and of meaninglessness. Studies like those of Philip E. Jacob, as well as common observation, suggest that the present student generation, on the surface at least, is more "conformist" than its predecessor, in relation to religion as to other things.[5] This is, after all, only the student reflection of the more general social situation, with the churches having larger memberships than at any previous period. But on the campus as in the local church, we soon learn that beneath the surface there is more anxious or wistful search for meaning than was evident at first glance.[6]

In the previous generation, the troubled skeptics and doubters either evaded all religious counselors except neutrals, or else presented their views with a kind of aggressive challenge. Today the search for meaning is quieter. Questions are more indirect. Indeed, they may be missed altogether if one is not steadily sensitive to what is conveyed beyond literal verbal meaning. But the problems are there, and, however indirectly, are being often posed.

For example, even apparently remote problems such as inability to concentrate may be symptoms of confusion and indecision about lifework, and this may in turn have a dimension involving religious vocation. Just as the clergyman needs to be prepared to deal with many kinds of problems in order to give help in the religious dimension, so the teacher or student personnel worker needs to be prepared for the possible emergence of unsuspected religious dimensions of a problem.

Since the business of a university is education and the advancement of learning, it is especially important that we ask about the relation of religious counseling to that. Granted that such counseling may be important according to the purposes of the several churches, is it nevertheless only peripheral to the university?

Properly understood and effectively executed, religious counseling is vital to the educational process itself.[7] Any counseling may at times have to become therapy in the sense of reestablishing a basic floor that has been seriously threatened. But most religious and other counseling of university students is more than therapy in this sense. It aims at clarification of meaning, at bringing together emotion and intellect, at better symbolization of genuine experience, at deepening or enlarging the perspective from which problem situations are viewed. Where the focus of the counseling is religious, then by our definition there is an attempt to grapple with deeper and more ultimate concerns and meanings. Unless there is some such clarification, the total personal functioning of the student may be impeded to the extent that he cannot pursue the purposes of the university itself. Good religious counseling, when needed, promotes the mind and the intellect no less than the person and the feelings.

On the campus of any state university two groups of people engage in religious counseling. The first are the professional religious workers: co-ordinators of religious affairs, faculty members teaching religion, nondenominational or interdenominational religious workers, denominational religious workers, and pastors of local churches near the campus. Their main concern is religion. While interested in all aspects of the students' welfare and education, their focus is on the religious needs, problems, and searchings.

The second group is the administrators, faculty members, and student personnel workers. Their focal concern with the student is his education. Their counseling of him is as a part of the educational process, to facilitate his learning. Their professional focus is not on his religion. Yet like it or not, since so many personal and educational problems have a religious dimension, they are inevitably engaged at times also in religious counseling.[8]

With reference to those religious needs of students that can best be met by counseling, what relationship do we find between these two groups on the campuses? Occasionally we find open hostility or suspicion. Most often we find a kind of noninteractive parallelism—you help students in your way, and I'll help them in mine. Latterly there seems to be emerging from both sides a desire for active co-operation, though it may be too early to call this a trend.

Each group—the clergyman on one side and the student personnel workers on the other—has been guilty of misreading the other's counseling function. The clergy have accused the personnel workers of being mere technicians, or of being willing to settle for the reduction of tension, or of neglect of spiritual values. The personnel workers have regarded the clergy as inevitably biased in their counseling, of having the answers even before they know the problems, or of focusing on souls divorced from body, personality, and the educative process.

Whatever grains of truth there may be in such projections, there are serious distortions on both sides. And the most important corrective agent to such misunderstandings is being found in counseling experience itself. Among student personnel workers there is increased attention to values, growing conviction that the counselor is unlikely to be helpful unless he likes and respects the person he would aid, and more interest in the person as a whole rather than merely in one's professional slice of him. Among the clergy there is a renunciation of any form of coercion without sacrificing conviction, renewed attention to the wholism inherent in both Judaism and Christianity, and recognition that religious problems and personal problems are intimately interwoven. Wherever there has been opportunity for honest mutual discussion of fundamental questions, both understanding and co-operation have thereafter increased. We anticipate no revolution but a gradual increase in understanding and co-operation.

Understanding is also increased through intelligent referrals. No counselor can handle everything, and an important part of his professional equipment is knowledge of those who can do something better than he. Included in this are such obvious needs as the clergyman's referral of a psychotic student to a psychiatrist, the teacher's referral of a brilliant but failing student to the personnel services, and a dean's referral of an interfaith marriage situation to the proper clergymen. But referrals are needed in many situations less obvious than these. For illustration look again at the situations described at the beginning of this chapter. No counselor should profess to skills he does not possess; but he can have knowledge of his ignorance only as he learns of the skills of others. Referrals are potentialities not escapes. Indeed, the clergyman referring the mentally sick student to the psychiatrist ought still to make a pastoral call upon him; and the teacher rightly expresses a continuing interest in the brilliant but failing student whom he has referred to student personnel. Each group has a focus of function, but each group is also interested in the whole student. If all groups remember this, then the specialized counseling services of the large campus really help without fragmenting the student.[9]

It is our conviction further that better mutual understanding, co-operation, and referral will come about to the extent that both groups see their counseling as a part of the educative process. We sometimes act as if professional religious workers were interested only in a compartmentalized soul, student personnel workers only with extracurricular emotions and technicalities, administrators only with budgets and discipline— and as if only the faculty were concerned with education. But since education is the real business of the university, every service must, in some basic way, be evaluated for its contribution to the educative process.

It is reasoning of this kind that makes us believe the faculty, as the very heart of a university, has a greater contribution to make to religious counseling than has often been assumed. This includes of course the counseling of individual students by individual faculty members, as in our case of Charles and Dr. Hall. Just as important, however, may be the lesson that the faculty member's counseling is, in one basic sense, the norm for all religious counseling in the university. It begins from the concerns of intellect appropriate to the subject matter under consideration. It progresses to personal and perhaps religious issues but with the primary focus still on education. It may indeed need to be supplemented by specialized counseling services. But it shows the proper context for all counseling of university students.

The clergyman who really believes that the best ultimate service to his church lies in the best counseling of the student to maximize his learning cannot possibly possess the counseling vices sometimes attributed to him. The student personnel worker who believes his best service to the student lies in the best fostering of the capacity to learn is similarly protected from the sins of which he is at time accused.

As John and Sue go off to begin study in one of our great state universities, Mother and Father back home may wonder if help and counsel will be available in the event John encounters some apparently godless scientific opinion, or Sue falls in love with someone of another faith, or either of them confronts basic questions of morals or vocation. On the fundamental fact let Father and Mother be assured. If the student will but take the initiative, the right kind of counsel is available on or adjacent to every such campus. Let it be admitted that he may not hit it right the first time. If he establishes contact before a shadow falls, he will be much wiser. But the resources, few though they are in comparison to the quantity of students, are there. And their quality is steadily improving.

We are soon to have, however, a great increase in student enrollment in the state universities. Can the services of religious counseling move ahead in spite of the growing number of students, or can they even keep up with it? The answer to this appears to be less encouraging. In the last analysis, the answer may be "Yes" only if Father and Mother, through their contributions to the church as well as by their taxes, make it so.

Let us look first at the professional religious workers who serve students. The religious co-ordinators, university officials charged with co-ordination of all religious services to students, do much helpful counseling. But the more students, programs, offices, problems, and dimensions there are to be co-ordinated, the less time they are likely to have for counseling. Something similar may be true for the pastors representing the various faiths and denominations. The larger the program, the less time for personal work. Even the pastors of churches near the campus may be swamped by the increased faculties brought to serve the larger student body, and have little time for counseling.

In all such offices on or near large campuses, there is a move toward the creation of more adequate staff so that, with no neglect of necessary program and administration and teaching, there can yet be significant amounts of time left for individual counseling. For most expansion of this sort, financial reliance must be upon private contributions to the church or related agencies such as the YMCA. Although most national church bodies have increased their support to this work in recent years, in none do the professional workers feel that support is sufficient to meet the needs that lie ahead. Because of its quiet and unspectacular nature, it is religious counseling that may suffer most when the staff is insufficient to carry out all activities.

The general prospects in the field of student personnel have been surveyed in another paper. Our question is: in the future are more faculty members, administrators, and student personnel workers likely to be able to help as needed for religious counseling? We doubt very much that the increase in the number of such people will do more than keep pace with increased student enrollment. If, then, there is no more time to be spent, proportionately, will it be expended better? The answer, we believe, is likely to lie in the perceptiveness with which these persons view the student's religious counseling problems within the context of the whole educative process. And that in turn is likely to depend upon whether something significant about this is included in the professional education or in-service training of these persons. There are encouraging signs in the work of several foundations concerned with religion in higher education, in several programs of the American Council on Education, and on many particular campuses.

If we ask whether the professional religious workers are learning more about their counseling task, the general answer is an unqualified "Yes." Among all faith groups there is a marked increase in both the quantity and quality of such training as a part of professional education. The opportunities for later in-service training are also increasing. And research in religious counseling of college students by the clergy is beginning. All these signs are positive.

Against these generally optimistic statements of the prospect for religious counseling must be set three negative factors. Each is formidable but not unconquerable. The first, and perhaps finally the most important, is the tendency for any professional group to become fixed in its ways and contacts and to interact with others only superficially, occasionally, or when compelled. We have suggested strong reasons why such discussion and co-operation are desirable and some bases upon which they can proceed. But without vision and leadership, professional isolationism usually prevails.

The second factor is the sheer problem of size of the schools, especially when the anticipated growth is considered. Bigness often becomes more efficient, and ultimately may even protect individual interest. But there must be a limit. And bigness that is constantly growing bigger is different from settled bigness.

The third problem is financial. Especially in a time of rapid growth, it is the quiet and unspectacular services that tend to be upgraded last. This is human; but unless it is guarded against both in university and ecclesiastical budgetary councils, it is inevitable. Against all these dangers it is not only the professional workers in university and church who can make the difference, but also Father and Mother.

Religious counseling certainly includes the action of the church in following the student from home to university, so that perplexing problems arising in the new context may not isolate him from the church in which he was born and to which, in one place or another, we hope he will return. But it has been our contention that religious counseling, even by the professional religious worker, is more than that. It is counsel given by any responsible professional person concerned in the life of the student and seen within the primary context of the student's education and learning. So viewed, concern for the religious dimension of counseling is shared by the clergy with faculty, administration, and student personnel. It is the private property of none. Attempts at mutual understanding and co-operation are, therefore, not optional but mandatory. Perhaps such a conception in itself may advance the prospect of religious counseling in the state university.

GLENN A. OLDS

Religious Centers

CHAPTER XIV

Few phrases are as multiple in meaning and diverse in description as "religious center." This may be taken to mean (1) a building in which religious work is housed and carried out, (2) a fellowship of students and faculty held together by a central religious concern, or (3) the ultimate loyalty, basic commitment, or framework of faith of a person's life that serves to shape and integrate it. The first is a matter of geography; the second, of function; and the third, of philosophy. No definition would be complete without all three, and each, in turn, is complicated.

How shall one describe the rash of religious centers that has "broken out" on or near the university campus from the turn of the century, and so dramatically since World War II? In round numbers the Catholics list 500, the Jews 200, the Lutherans 400, the Methodists 350, the Baptists 300, the Episcopalians 200, to mention but a few. In value these centers range from modest "homes" to multiutility buildings worth upwards of $2,000,000.[1]

The centers are as varied and versatile in type as the strategy of our pluralistic religious culture over the last fifty years.[2] (1) There is the home, among the earliest, the most economical and persistent forms. Intimate and informal, it houses the priest, rabbi, or pastor, serves as a center for fellowship, small study groups, classes, and activities, and occasionally houses students or small co-operative eating groups. (2) There is the clubhouse, functionally designed for fellowship, recreation, discussion, and study, as at the Lamar Technological Institute. (3) There is the chapel. It may contain offices for counseling, choir, and modest study room facilities; but its form and function are shaped as a "sanctuary." (4) There is the combination, with the intimacy and actuality of the "home," the social utility of the "clubhouse," and the sanctuary of the "chapel." (5) There is the church center, situated in and with the local church on campus. (6) There is the common center, bringing together several or all religious groups in one building with multi-purpose meeting rooms, offices, chapel, and social hall.

How shall one describe the function of these religious fellowships? Up to 1900, in the predominantly Protestant era of higher education, these were primarily "voluntary associations" of, by, and for students. They were bound together not so much by theological agreement as by personal, moral, and religious earnestness. They knew a deeper wisdom of the relation of "wholeness" and "holiness," and sought to translate into the larger life of the campus and the world the implications of their own dedication. Many, if not most, of the services to students later incorporated into official university responsibilities were cradled and carried out by these societies.[3] Walls between students of different races, sexes, classes, and conditions were challenged, scaled, and broken. These fellowships were nonsectarian and nonclerical, having no connection with parent church bodies. They were patterned chiefly as YMCA or YWCA associations which by 1900 numbered "some 700 associations for men and 600 for women, with membership totaling over 100,000—almost half of the students then enrolled in the colleges and universities."[4]

By the turn of the century the communities of faith entered the field through provision of professional and financial help. As early as 1887 the Presbyterians and the Episcopalians had begun work at the University of Michigan.[5] Shortly after 1900, full-time university pastors were provided at Michigan, Wisconsin, and Illinois, both Catholic and Protestant, with a first full-time rabbi at Illinois in 1923.

The phenomenal development in professional leadership, national associations, and co-operative programs and agencies in more recent years has diversified in breadth and depth the nature of these fellowships. The early conferences on "Church Workers in State Universities" at Michigan in 1908 and at Cleveland in 1915 defined the need and scope of trained leadership in the field, collaborated with the new Religious Education Association (1903), and sought to enrich the "content" of these groups. Growing concern with the intellectual content of faith in the life of these groups and the university gave rise to the development of Bible chairs as early as 1893, short-lived interdenominational "schools of religion,"[6] the University of Iowa School of Religion,[7] and the establishment of the National Council on Religion in Higher Education to select and train fellows in all fields of higher education. Miami University prior to 1930, and the University of Michigan in 1934, brought full-time religious directors to their staffs, followed in fresh resurgence since 1945 by Ohio State, Minnesota, Maine, Florida, Georgia, Mississippi State, Louisiana State, and others.[8]

By 1920 and onward, experience of these groups with one another prompted attention to interreligious understanding and co-operation; the founding of the National Conference of Christians and Jews; co-operative religious programs at the University of Pennsylvania, the University of California at Los Angeles, Cornell, and on other campuses; various national student religious bodies—denominational, ecumenical, and international—and the demand for increasingly competent student religious workers. These workers have increased from a handful in 1900 to some 200 by 1938, and to more than 1,000 by 1953, the last official record available.[9] They exhibit a diversity in function and outlook natural to diverse theological backgrounds, personal capacities, and local peculiarities.

The nature of the religious concerns that bind the groups together is equally complex and reflects a comparable development. The early societies stressed personal piety, missionary recruitment, and service; the "middle period," social activity, civic responsibility, recreation, and student services; and contemporary groups are bound together by theological interest. Through all phases these groups have reflected an amazing vitality, versatility, and adaptability.

How shall one describe the meaning of "religious center" in terms of man's ultimate loyalty, basic commitment, or framework of faith by which life is integrated and made whole? Clearly, there is no common core of agreement concerning the particular content or form that such a loyalty or faith takes. There is, however, recognition that religion, from the Latin *relegere,* does mean "to bind together," and that the university, from the Latin *unus* and *versum,* does mean "to turn into one." In intent, both bear witness to man's deep need to unify his life and thought around some ultimate principle, object of loyalty, or subject of faith. In practice, psychological and historical analyses bear witness that most men, institutions, and cultures have their "center" in this sense, which functionally, if not theologically, defines their religion.

The origin and development of the religious center in the two meanings already discussed, as building and fellowship, can only be truly understood in terms of this view of man's nature and need. In the earliest period of the modern university, when theology was queen, religious form and content provided a "center" for the curriculum and life of its students. Even in the state universities of the earlier nineteenth century, the products of a predominantly Protestant culture, concern for the cultivation of man's religious knowledge and commitment was central, through required chapel, courses, and activities.

The steady erosion of this pattern through a growing self-consciousness of religious pluralism, difference, and a consequent emphasis on separation of church and state could not help but alter the role and function of religion in the life of the state university. The growing separation of religious faith and liberal learning, and the qualification, criticism, isolation, and displacement of the common presuppositions and values of Biblical and classical religious faith in the development of the state university required a fresh strategy on the part of the community of faith.

The appearance of the religious center, in its complexity and diversity, bears witness to the experimental response of religious faith to this new and altering university scene. It reflects the confidence that, although the state university cannot enthrone any theology as queen or champion, its students and faculty alike will and must live by some basic loyalty, some kind of religious faith, if not explicitly, then implicitly. The religious center becomes thereby a symbol of this central fact, not as queen but as servant of man's persistent need to "be made whole." It is a place where persons meet, loyalties are found and fixed, faith seeks understanding, and the community of faith ministers to students in search of a "center" for life or fidelity and growth in that already found. It is a fellowship of persons, bound by common concern, steeled and stretched by study and service, and transformed and empowered by worship and love. It is the bearer of a persistent philosophy, meant to complement the mission of the state university.

The philosophy of the religious center, in whatever form, is more than a set of ideas. It is a way of life as well, for religion insists that idea must issue into act and vision into character and community. No simple analysis can do justice to the rich diversity in religious thought and practice that characterizes the religious centers of American college campuses. Still, we need some way to come to terms with a dynamic process. Within the compass of this brief chapter there is room to mention only three features of the basic philosophy of religious centers. They characterize (1) the climate, (2) the functions, and (3) the ideas that constitute a living philosophy informing the religious centers of American campuses.

Religious centers on state university campuses are not so much the product of a finished or fixed philosophy as they are the experimental expression of communities of faith trying to meet new problems in the changing religious atmosphere of the state university. To be sure, the experiment is not without its informing ideas, but its initial intent was nurtured by a general yet persistent sensitivity to growing student needs in the fast-developing state university.

These needs, at once personal and practical as well as theological, called for some strategy fashioned from the message and ministry of the community of faith, with concerns that are intimate, ultimate, and inclusive.

The intimate concern was to meet and minister to human

need at its most personal, decisive, and inward ground: the ground of self-acceptance, self-understanding, self-direction, and self-fulfillment. In the growing state university, numbers had begun to impersonalize and fragment, common worship was often precluded, relationships were increasingly anonymous and academic, and motivation for learning officially void of the religious dedication to God and neighbor in the service of love. How could the religious community minister to the intimate personal and practical need of the student to be a responsible, significant person?

The ultimate concern was to meet the student's growing confusion over what is truly Ultimate[10] and worthy of his complete commitment. How could the religious community keep the ultimate questions alive in a community in which they were precluded or given marginal or minimal attention?

The inclusive concern was to meet the student's hunger for wholeness in thought and life in an inclusive community, a real *uni*-versity. In the state university, frightful fragmentation of both curriculum and community had begun to replace the earlier more homogeneous constituency and objective. How could the religious community, precluded general academic relevance, presume to offer any help? How could it introduce the student to an inclusive community in which all barriers between man and man, and man and God must fall? How could it mediate an inclusive concern to bring all the scattered truths of man's specialized studies into one community of truth?

The ways in which the religious centers sought to implement these persistent concerns in plans, programs, practices, and personnel range over the entire spectrum of human interest and activity.[11] In one of the larger centers, where fourteen religious groups are housed and work together, a recent survey revealed over fifty different kinds of co-operative activity and programs and well over one hundred different activities and programs at the religious group level.[12] The scope of this chapter does not permit even rehearsing the variety and range of these functions. It is possible, however, to discern a few central functions which the centers perform, around which much of their activity can be organized and understood. Oversimplified but illustrative are three central functions performed in every kind of center and type of program, large or small, and irrespective of wide theological variation. They are the creation of continuity in life's values and goals, the maturing of life's loyalties, and the clarification of life vocations. To be sure, other institutions and the university share in these functions; but in a special way they derive from the religious concern of the center.

The center creates continuity. When a student goes to college, he makes one of the most dramatic breaks of his life. Discontinuity is encountered at the "center" of his life, involving the pattern and authority of the character-forming agencies of home and church. The religious center, as a bridge of continuity from one authority to another, from infantile dependence to responsible freedom, from home to a freely chosen community, assists this transition. It seeks to help him build upon the best he brings, without the folly and arrogance of rejection in the name of a fictional freedom. The center provides continuity with the wider spiritual family, the community of faith, without restricting the critical freedom of the student's new status and independence.

The center is especially sensitive to the critical climate of a university, the discipline of doubt in the process of understanding, and the particular period of independence through which its students are passing. It seeks to avoid the peril of religious habit void of meaning, symbol void of sense, and it nurtures in critical understanding the inner meaning of outer form, the religious significance of sacrament, practice, and creed. The continuity it provides is creative and open alike to the past and the future, to the stable values the student brings, and to the creative opportunity for self-determination that the university expects and provides. In the end, its preoccupation is with its students, whose creative passage from youth to maturity symbolizes the flexibility of this function of the center.

The center seeks to help its students mature their life loyalties. The center seeks to clarify the religious conditions that surround life's basic loyalties and to make them sacramental.

The sanctity of sex, the faithfulness of love, the integrity of an ultimate commitment, are not only the subjects of conversation but the climate of life pervading the associations of the center.

Citizenship is also made sacramental in this setting. Not only in its leadership training and nurturing of responsibility, but in its prophetic voice regarding practices and policies of the campus and wider world, the center seeks to translate the moral vision of its faith into the loyalty of its life. One of the dramatic witnesses to this latter function is the way in which the student leadership in these centers across the South has sought to challenge and heal racial segregation in our time.[13]

The center helps to clarify the student's choice of vocation. One of its rationalizations for the wide variety of activity emphases lies here, in providing a climate of student initiative and concern where, free from parental pressures and undue social prestige, God's will, human need, and personal capacity are discovered and related.

Virtually all the activity of the center is designed to provide not only needed help to others, but occasion for self-discovery in a wide variety of vocations through which one can express fully his richest capacities and religious faith. The center's range of activities helps to overcome the persistent notion that only one kind of activity, that of professional religious work, can be a religious vocation. It seeks to show the religious dimension of all useful human activity and serves to recover the dignity of work and the re-creation of play.

Difficult as it is to simplify the concerns and functions of the rich variety of centers at state universities, it is even more difficult to simplify their basic ideas. The different theological traditions, definitions of the "community of faith," conceptions of liturgy and priesthood, authority, and responsibility, make the task in this brief compass virtually impossible. Still, careful study of publications, practices, and judgment of the professionals makes it possible to isolate at least three basic ideas at work in all religious centers. They are these:

1. The self-transcendent reference in the center's life and work derives directly from its religious function, concerned as it is with God. To be sure, man's understanding of the objective

character of God, the Ultimate Religious Object,[14] will vary widely from the religious liberal to the more orthodox. Implicit, however, in all its forms is the "ontological reference" of high religion: the concern to bring man into relationship with what is Ultimately Real and Supremely Significant. To have faith is to be thus oriented.

This serious concern of the religious center—to come to terms with God—serves to judge and instruct man's claim to truth and constitutes a real contribution of the center to the university community. The conviction that all one's seeking and finding is grounded in what is Ultimate, however misunderstood, provides a striking unity to the intellectual enterprise and the mental integrity of the student. All the "truths" found in the university must somehow finally relate to the "Whole Truth." To be sure, this whole truth can be premature, forced, arbitrary, and idolatrous, but not for long. The judgment of expanding experience as well as religious affirmation bears witness that God's mystery outruns man's mastery, and ultimate meaning transcends immediate comprehension. Such judgment, nurtured in natural piety and honest humility, is a permanent warning against idolatry, religious or secular, and narrow compartmentalization of thought.

Free acknowledgment of such self-transcendence judges and instructs motivation for learning as well, saving from subjective self-seeking while at the same time permeating knowing with concern. All religious knowledge is "concerned knowledge." The religious man knows in order to do. His seeking is morally earnest, not neutral, subjectively concerned, not objectively detached. His knowing relates to his being and doing in a radical fashion that gets at the roots of motivation. He who loves God with his whole mind has achieved a condition, through love, whereby the mind is freed of fear of failure, the greed of possessiveness, the pride of performance, and the exploitation of others in the seeking.

Finally, this self-transcendent reference provides a touchstone and offers a corrective to a fragmented university community. In its mature expression it is always unitary and universal. It serves to warn against confusing the idea of God with God, the form of faith with the object of faith, man's broken religious and academic communities with the purpose of God. It symbolizes in ideal a unitary reference toward which the divided communities of faith and learning must move in truth and life.

2. Personal responsibility is the condition for religious discovery. Religious concern cannot be coerced. The self rises to its own self-discovery and personal integrity in the response of its ultimate concern. Religious commitment is the counterpart of freedom disclosing at once something beyond and within. Before God man is most radically and really himself. There is no place for retreat, deception, or duplicity. To respond to God is to leave the crowd for the awe-ful freedom of one's own selfhood. Here is the clearest clue to real responsibility. The religious center understands that this fact is the secret of the substantial student initiative and "finishiative" that characterize the life and work of the center. The voluntary nature of all its activity feeds the freedom essential to mature self-determination. This expectation draws the student from a passive spectator role to that of a real participant. Testimony of students would confirm the view that this is a condition, as well, of all true learning, and offers a suggestive clue to the perplexed educator.[15]

3. Religious maturity requires the interpenetration of worship and work. The center rejects the haunting dualisms that mark the modern world, of sacred and secular, theoretical and practical, and affirms that they belong together in the perfection of whole persons in real community. This rejection is the consequence of the religious acknowledgment that if God is of any importance He is of supreme importance and relevant to the whole of life. It requires that study and service, praying and playing, curricular and cocurricular activity be dynamically related in a total life and whole person. The emphasis is a prophecy not only of religious integrity but of mental health and the possibility of becoming a *uni*-versity community.

These basic ideas are not fixed or final. They are self-creative and self-corrective. They plot out directions and emphases, broad enough to permit the rich particular content of different faiths and diverse programs and functions.

Few religious centers are at the center of the campus. Their location is often a prophecy of their function, linking as they do the community of faith and the community of learning. They are creations of a "boundary situation," with all the torment, frustration, and creativity of borderlines and boundaries.

Their situation is further aggravated by sizable diversities in both the communities of faith and the communities of learning. In the former they are due to theological, historical, and practical differences from extreme left to right; and in the latter to local, political, and institutional differences making easy or difficult this relating. The uniqueness of each is expressed primarily in the way in which the message, ministry, and strategy of each center are bound up in a host of local circumstances, personalities, and attitudes making up its life. Survey of the history of different centers reveals no clear pattern of building type, program function, personnel and staff, or official status on campus by which a tidy classification of significance can be made. The persistent function of counseling bears little correlation with the type of building or activity program and reflects more the competence and accessibility of the student worker and co-operation with allied university services. The various types of interreligious co-operation correlate only vaguely with the kinds of centers involved. As one might expect, the importance of persons in student and professional leadership, in determining the center's role and significance, is substantial.

How, then, shall one arrive at any useful analysis of pattern and function? The "bridging" function of the center, between the community of faith and the community of learning, is suggestive. How these two communities, with their own centers of gravity, interests, and objectives, do relate becomes a means of organizing an analysis of the patterns. This should not be taken to mean that the vitality or value of the relation and work performed is given in the pattern, but only that the pattern furnishes a clue to emphases and possibilities. To be sure, the writer's own "slip of faith" is unpardonably showing. Though the analysis is not meant as "progression in value," there is an underlying conviction that an implicit value and philosophy is contained in the pattern of the relation of the center to the university.

There are seven discernible patterns. They are characterized not only by building location and fellowship emphasis, but by an underlying philosophy regarding the relation of the community of faith to the state university.

1. The center is adjacent, independent, and isolated. It is not only off campus, but is unrelated in sympathy and fact with the so-called secular university.

2. The center is peripheral but penetrating. It may be off campus, but its ministry is to the campus.

3. The center is marginal but co-operative. Although it may be on the edge of the university, it seeks to work in its midst. It recognizes points at which genuine co-operation is not only possible but necessary. These include collaboration in counseling, campus services and charities, supplemental help in moral and morale problems, and minor ministries attending major university events of a quasi-religious nature.

4. The center is informally recognized and complementary. It is informally part of the educational mission of the university, an acknowledged ally in the total enterprise. The center's own autonomy in program, personnel, and support remains unaltered, but it is no longer merely an outsider.

5. The center is formally recognized and officially important. It has official status and administrative recognition. The university frequently provides a building, or space, or helps the religious organization achieve both. At Minnesota and Ohio State, the university has provided a nonsectarian religious officer to facilitate liaison with and co-ordination of the different religious centers enjoying this status.

6. The center is organically important and officially responsible. It figures naturally in the educational process, fulfilling its religious role responsibly. This pattern reflects a long history of co-operation, appreciation, and confidence between the religious centers, and between the centers and the university. Examples of this type are found at Michigan and Florida.

7. The center is integral and central. It symbolizes recognition of the central importance of religion, its integral relation to learning, and its "essential" mission "in the university."

Its best example is found at Cornell University. There the revolving altar in the chapel respects the integrity and difference in the form and freedom of worship yet retains the fellowship of a wider charity and work. The entire center, with its multipurpose public rooms and auditorium and its private offices for chaplains and religious groups, constitutes a bona fide division of the university, guaranteeing religious freedom but insuring an integral religious function in the university.

But if it is difficult to discern a progression in the patterns of center-university relation, how much more difficult it is to spell out functions. This is aggravated because the religious center affirms a "wholeness" to life that makes distinction and separation of function difficult. Beneath the wide diversity of buildings, programs, and activities is a steady protest against the fragmentation and segregation of modern life. The communities of faith knew, in founding their centers, that intellectual brilliance apart from humility and reverence and unrelated to morally responsible action can be bleak, irrelevant, irresponsible, and dangerous.

This cycle in different forms and tempos, in different theological traditions and university settings, can be discerned as a permanent part of the center's life and function. The cycle carries within itself the deeper rhythm of the religious life— worship, wisdom, and work, the movement from aspiration to illumination, to action, the interpenetration of reverence, reason, and responsibility. It is precisely because the religious center has no final option on these dimensions of life and expressions of the human spirit, however central they are to its function, that problems arise in the university.

Problems arise precisely because sometimes, and in different ways, and almost always in isolation one from the other, the university in its own way is involved in all three. This is illustrated in worship. Many of the state universities in earlier predominantly Protestant days had their own chapels and chapel services.[16] Even in states with strong Catholic and Jewish population this was the pattern and practice. Led by the president and professors, the services were nonecclesiastical and frequently nonclerical. Some schools developed nondenominational or nonsectarian chapels led not by university personnel but by visiting preachers. Still others employed a chaplain to care for the public worship.

As university populations became more heterogeneous, reflecting the religious pluralism of our culture, and as, in more recent times, there has been a resurgence of religious orthodoxy in form and practice,[17] the problem has become more acute. The diverse patterns in location and function of the altar in religious centers reflect the uneasy tension in this area. Those centers located in church or synagogue solve the matter simply. Worship is in the sanctuary. Some centers have no chapel for public worship as such but refer the student to the nearest local church or synagogue as his center for worship. Others develop student churches with the total life of a religious parish. Others provide student chapels as part of the equipment and service of the religious center. Still others co-operate with the university in providing several services—Protestant, Catholic, Jewish, or any other distinct type represented in large numbers in the university—as a total university ministry to the campus.

In the last plan there is no longer an inclusive university worship service, but rather several worship services for the university in keeping with its heterogeneous religious population. At this point problems arise. How are these university services to be designed and led and how are they to be related to the local churches and synagogues and the religious centers? Or should they be abandoned and returned to the religious community and centers?[18]

Even more complicated, though not so difficult to solve, is the matter of study. Obviously this is the primary emphasis of the university, but in the area of religion and in the state university this is complicated indeed. Although more than three-fourths of the state universities have some form of official instruction in religion, the pattern varies immensely.[19]

In response to this varied pattern and local contingencies the religious centers have developed their strategies. Religious instruction in matters of faith and morals is a central emphasis not only of the Catholic Newman clubs and the Jewish Hillel foundations but virtually of all the other religious groups as well. This may vary from loosely organized informal Bible study and discussion classes to formal courses offered by the center for credit,[20] co-operative Bible colleges supported by several religious groups and centers,[21] institutes or schools of religion separate but recognized[22] or as an integral part of the university under a director.[23]

Beyond this formal study lies the hinterland of discussion groups, cell groups, social action groups, lectures, panels, and conferences that constitutes much of the life of the center. Varying from the "juicy" and popular "Love, Courtship, and Marriage" series to spot talks on "Fissure and Fusion," the pattern of study seeks to involve and help the student at the level of his interest and need, and in terms that his crowded time will permit.

The problems that lurk here are those of duplication of effort, exploitation of students' time, relative degrees of competence, and the age-old tension between propaganda and persuasion, the intent to convert and the intent to inform. Can you teach about religion without being acquainted with it? Can you be committed yet objective in religious study? How much responsibility shall the university assume in dealing with religious illiteracy, with diverse religious traditions, with religious ethical systems related to pressing social problems, with the framework of meaning and ultimate claim of faith(s)? Shall religious centers give courses? Shall they be for credit? By whom shall they be given? How shall they be administered? Shall religion be taught as part of other disciplines and in other departments? Shall it be taught as a department of its own or as an interdepartmental discipline?

Finally, the most prolific and perhaps perplexing function of the center is in its work, translating faith into action. It has already been noted that many, if not most, of the student services initiated by religious societies have been taken over by the university as part of its student personnel services. These have included employment and housing services, orientation programs, freshman handbook, student directory, campus chest, counseling services, and virtually the entire range of student personnel services. Most state universities have a lively sense of the practical implications of their research and teaching and the service component in all of their work.

The problems here again are those of relation, duplication, and administration. The student union and the social clubs have their recreational side. Shall the religious centers omit this feature from their program, or is recreation essential to the "wholeness" of the center's emphasis? How shall the service projects for relief, community service, and international outreach, and to special students and special needs be administered and related? What should be the relation of the religious center to the student council, the interfraternity council, the foreign student adviser, the deans of students' office, and the president or his representative in student affairs?

Most centers insist that the faith they profess must be embodied in significant human service, that love of God entails love of neighbor and vice versa. But shall the center organize as a religious group to work, or shall it work to have the campus organize to serve? Shall it insist on the religious motive for significant human work, or shall it work to make any human service significant, whatever the motive? These are growing questions requiring radical rethinking.

The acceleration of developments in this field makes prediction about the future as precarious as it may seem foolish. The center's phenomenal recent development in number, staff, buildings, and budget[24] has been matched by growing interest and concern on the part of the university.[25] Nor does this trend seem likely to be changed soon. Within this general development, however, certain local trends with potentially far-reaching significance are discernible. Space permits only their mention, description, and the suggestion of implications. We will consider general trends and particular trends relating to the threefold function of the religious center—worship, study, and work.

Concerning general trends, it may be said that there is:

1. Growing distrust of the segregation of religion and liberal learning.

2. Growing awareness that deepening of the center and widening of the circumference of the religious life must go hand in hand.

3. Growing concern that the large group of students not being reached and awakened by the deepest claims of both communities be found and helped. Certain types of such students stand out in bold relief and persistent challenge. They are: (a) The questioning but suspicious. (b) The indifferent. (c) The apathetic. (d) The unquestioning. (e) The questioning but fearful.

If these students are reached, a radically new vitality and leadership for good will be released within the university. If they are missed, we may expect even further erosion by conformity and mediocrity, with mounting numbers and dwindling moral resources. In any case, both communities have a fundamental stake and complementary role to play in this process.

Concerning particular trends, the following points may be made:

1. Worship. The trend seems away from the late liberal notion of the nineteenth and early twentieth centuries that differences in forms of faith and practice are really not decisive or important.

It is now generally recognized and accepted that for most religious communities worship reflects the highest art and deepest integrity of faith. Here form and content blend into one. For this reason, differences in worship are recognized and respected. This imposes new difficulties and deeper opportunities for the religious center in educating and the university in serving its students. An all-university worship service will likely progressively fragment at least into predominantly Protestant, Catholic, and Jewish student services, and such others as numbers may warrant. There is real gain and real loss in this trend. The gain is in the recovery of religious literacy and integrity respecting the inner form and content of faith and its expression.[26] The loss is in the concession to that deepest of all ironies of religious history—that what represents the highest religious art should be the most deeply divisive.

2. Study. Within the religious centers there is a new and healthy emphasis on theology, the worship of God with the mind. It raises the pertinent religious question regarding the vocation of a student and reinforces with religious significance the intellectual mission of the university. Within the university community are stirrings of special significance for the study of religion. The myth of complete objectivity and value neutrality has been significantly challenged by natural and social sciences alike. The university is coming to recognize that all of its significant undertakings proceed from some value presupposition, some standpoint of faith. The effort to preclude religion from the curriculum on the grounds that it is a faith to be affirmed, not taught, has been weakened by this new mood. Interest in ideology has revived the interest in the psychological and sociological role of religion as well as a concern to understand the motive and meaning of faith itself.

With this trend has gone the awareness that the effort to deal with "religion in general," to avoid sectarianism or any show of partisanship, has frequently led to missing the very nature of religious faith that makes it meaningful in life. A noticeable trend is away from the general treatment of religion and toward a treatment of particular faiths "from without" and often by not only a professional but a "professing" religionist, as at the University of Iowa, Columbia, and more recently at Harvard.

Finally, there is growing awareness that interest in "religion in general'" was evidence of a deeper wisdom concerning a general religious dimension of all life not easy to isolate or segregate. This trend seeks to discover and articulate the religious dimension of man's varied activities and interests, and, as at the University of Michigan, to incorporate within different departments of the university study of the religious phase of history, psychology, sociology, etc.

These trends are equally ambivalent. Theological interests of the center may deepen the life of the mind and the intellectual integrity of faith, or they may tend to substitute intellectual exercise for personal commitment. Recovery of the "faith standpoints" in all our knowing may alert us to a deeper dimension to all our knowing, but it may also become the apology for a new irrationalism with critical consequences for both communities. Interest in particular faith content may enrich an earlier religious abstraction, yet it may negate the important effort to discern fundamental unities where they exist, and return to a provincial Western religiosity. The imperative to understand the cultures of the East and the Middle East requires exposure to these traditions often given in the older "comparative religion" courses.

3. Work. There is a growing convergence between the religious center and the university in the area of student services. The trend is toward conversation, collaboration, and, where possible, co-operation. This is critically apparent in counseling but also at the activity and program level. Although there is a trend toward incorporating university responsibility for co-ordinating religious activities within the dean of students' office and area, there is a countertrend that I believe will be eventually more decisive. This trend recognizes serious jeopardy to the religious counseling and pastoral functions of the religious staff associated directly with administrative offices, which handle disciplinary and discretionary matters. It resists the temptation to reduce the work of the religious center to "student activities" alone, and bids for a wider relevance to the whole student and the total university.

Only close and continued collaboration at national, professional, and local levels between these groups will provide clues about how this development will and should proceed.

No appraisal can do full justice to the facts or be even tolerably acceptable to differing theological perspectives, educational philosophies, and personal standpoints. At best, an appraisal can lift again to bold relief broad principles that illuminate the nature and value of the religious center in the university. These will be gathered around three frames of reference: educational, theological, and cultural.

Educationally, we are able to see that though we may seek to separate religious faith and learning in an institution, we cannot do so in the life of a student. It is unsound to suppose that in all other matters the student should aim for integration but that in this decisive area he must subscribe to segregation. As a psychological impossibility, the effort creates chaos at the center of life. For better or worse, the university cannot fail to deal with the matter of religious faith in its students, and the religious center cannot fail to be in some sense an "educational enterprise."

The task here is twofold: (1) We must train a new kind of chaplain and university religious worker. With few exceptions, theological seminaries are too specialized, isolated, and insulated from the main currents of thought in the disciplines of a university to do this job. Yet the campus religious worker must understand and deal with the impact of these different disciplines on his students and their faith, all in fresh ways and with a marked degree of competence. He must know the university as well as the content and resources of religious faith. In his graduate training he must be exposed systematically to the presuppositions, outlook, method, and implications of the central disciplines of the university. In this task the best minds of the university can be engaged. They must be brought to bear on the issues where religion and the university meet, converse, and challenge each other. (2) We must develop a new kind of university faculty person alert to the twin demands of religious faith and liberal learning. The National Council on Religion in Higher Education and more recently the Danforth Foundation have been breaking ground in this area, but the need far outruns the results to date. What is required is a fresh wedding at the graduate level of theology and the other disciplines, such that the creative interpenetration required of the students at the practical level will have been grasped in some measure theoretically.

Theologically, both the university and the religious center stand in danger of the perpetual sin of idolatry and the peril of segregating God. Any thoughtful person knows, as indicated earlier, that if there is a God, if He is of any importance, He is of supreme importance and relevant to the whole of life. The difficulty is that both religious and university communities tend to force an impossible segregation of the sacred and the secular. The product of such segregation in the religious center is either irrelevance or presumptive pride, and in the university, value-neutrality and emptiness or some form of idolatrous faith.

The saving feature of our religious pluralism and democratic culture is the guarantee against any form of religious despotism capturing the state university. The plurality and particularity of faith that makes impossible uniformity in authority makes equally impossible ready identification of religious faith with any "watered-down" version of "democratic culture" or other forms of religious idolatry.

The task here is twofold: (1) We must translate the theological renaissance of the past quarter century into relevance to the contemporary educator who is perplexed by problems centering around (a) the nature of man, (b) the relation of knowledge to virtue, ignorance to sin, and (c) the religious roots of the institution and practice of democracy. (2) We must translate valid educational methods and liberal humanism into the practice and programs of the religious centers, rendering them more effective without displacing their religious motivation and ministry.

Culturally, both communities realize more than ever that our pressing problems are primarily ideological. They concern the faiths by which men live. Our problem is to discover how to deal with totalitarian "faiths," their power and efficiency, without succumbing to their methods or sacrificing the freedom and plurality of our own. We know no faith is more fanatically powerful than religious faith. Can we learn how to co-operate and federate our religious faiths without watering them down, rendering them instrumental or idolatrous, or robbing them of their free vitality? If there is any hope of learning how to do this, it should be in the state university, mirror in miniature of our complex culture. Can we discover how this can be done? Can we learn how to wed intellectual competence and religious commitment, the critical community of learning and the dedicated community of faith?

Our task here is twofold: (1) We need basic research concerning the relation of faith and culture, religious belief and social behavior, theology and practical ethics. The newly formed institute concerned with these relationships at Wesleyan University is an important experiment in the right direction. It needs expansion in new directions in other settings, including the graduate school of a large university. We have not begun to use the religious center as a laboratory in research-action, to which it would lend itself readily and well. (2) We need pilot faith-action projects aimed at reducing cultural tension, promoting creative intercultural and interreligious understanding. Too little has been made of the role and resources of religion in providing paths and bridges to this understanding. Religious centers collaborating with instructional units in the university are uniquely designed for such projects at home and abroad, more imaginative in character and wider in scope than traditional service and work camp experience.

Finally, whatever else the religious center and the university may do, they must help the student recover and reconstitute a valid center for his life through which life can be seen steadily and whole, and in terms of which both communities may realize their deepest intention as *uni*-versity and religious center.

ARTHUR J. LELYVELD

Interreligious Relations

CHAPTER XV

Several levels of motivation for interreligious co-operation exist on the college campus. They range—or they rise, if you will—from the inescapable practical demands of the campus situation to the distinterested effort to apply brotherhood ideals in the milieu in which they should be most naturally at home.

Whatever the motivation, interreligious activity in some form and in varying degree is omnipresent in the state university and, like all co-operative activity, it seeks structure and machinery and it demands accommodation. Its origin may be the need felt by the administration to present to the community the university's religious "face" despite its heterogeneous religious and ideological features. Or it may be the recognition by campus religious leadership that compelling common objectives are a counterweight to cherished differences, that the menace of shared peril and the tokens of multidenominational failure must neutralize sectarian competitiveness.

There is a growing and healthy unease about the shared peril, a growing recognition that despite swelling membership rolls and the quantitative success of external religion in the community at large, we are not doing too well. If we are transmitting our value traditions to the college generation at all we are doing so largely in terms of vague verbal affirmations; we are not evoking genuine commitment or a will to religious action.

Philip Jacob's excellent compendium of surveys of student attitudes[1] has given wide currency to disturbing conclusions which, though they are admittedly generalizations, probably apply to 75 to 80 per cent of college students today[2] and come as no surprise to those intimately acquainted with student life. Here the religious forces confront together a picture of a composite student who though "nominally religious" is "essentially secular," who is "gloriously contented" and "unabashedly self-centered."

What is more, Dr. Jacob jolts the religious forces by a hint that they are not to be too sanguine about their capacity to change this situation. Indeed he cites evidence purporting to show that the less "religious" the student, the less prejudiced and the more humanitarian he is likely to be.[3] But Dr. Jacob offers no comfort to the social scientists. He adds that there is no proof that a larger dose of liberal education or of social science produces "a more sensitive regard for the humane values."[4]

These facts, along with the prevailing societal attitude that makes material gratification a chief goal and the pursuit of self-interest a common characteristic of our time, are an invitation to humility. They demand that campus religious workers and the university community concerned pool their resources in the effort to introduce students to factors of enrichment and to moral and spiritual values. In this task, they will at the same time be combating a major menace: the multiplication of mass men who take their values from each other and whose goal in life is security within the protecting uniformity of the group.

In this context, religious differences are a good. The cultivation and appreciation of distinctive traditions not only protect society against reduction to universal grayness, but they are also important tools for the preservation of the group sources of societal ideals essential to democracy. Interreligious activity must, therefore, be of such a nature as to make possible the continuity of group distinctiveness and of valuable differences.

What we have been saying makes sense only if we are speaking of dynamic religion, the disturbing kind, not the anodyne kind, the revolutionary kind of thought found in the prophets and the gospels, the kind that makes demands on people. Lack of campus antagonism to religion—and there are no significant, committed antireligious forces today—may well be a danger sign. The university may comfortably make a *pro forma* bow in the direction of the church through the invocation by a religious dignitary on a stated occasion and through other equivalent amenities, when its benign attitude rests on the assumption that religious forces will not be strong enough nor religious convictions deeply enough held to constitute a problem.

The variant religious groups working together may contribute to the revitalization of religion and its acceptance of an effective role in society; they may introduce meaningful commitments into the lives of students, and by the reality of meaningful differences they may slow down the march of conformity.

In the state university, for legal as well as for human and moral reasons, this co-operation must be voluntary. But though it must grow out of the will of the groups themselves and remain free of "interference" by state agencies, the university cannot afford to ignore a development that crisscrosses the campus and lies so close to the heart of its own concern. This creates a dilemma that may belong in the category of those problems that never get solved but only get older. The university must walk the thin line between its constitutional responsibilities and its responsibilities to its students in an area increasingly recognized to be crucially important.

One approach to this dilemma on state campuses today is a technique called "co-ordination" of religious activities. In the proliferating area of student "personnel" services, the university that cares for the physical and mental health of the student, that provides counselors for his emotional and financial problems and guidance officers for his vocational uncertainties, may with equal propriety concern itself with his religious needs.

This approach was fully developed and first applied at the University of Minnesota where, under the leadership of Dean Edmund G. Williamson and Dr. Henry E. Allen, a rationale and a structure within the field of student personnel work was developed. The University of Minnesota Office of Coordinator of Students' Religious Activities was organized in 1947 and its "bureau history"[5] gives this description of its origin:

As the University grew in enrollment, and as the multiplicity of diverse faith groups became more apparent on the Campus, it was clear that a University-sponsored chapel service or the appointment of a University Chaplain could not be satisfactory when there existed diametrically different approaches to worship. Logic seemed inevitably to spell out a policy whereby the cultivation of spiritual growth among students was to be left to private organizations. . . . The advising and counselling of these faith groups was plainly the responsibility of the national denominational or interdenominational organizations with which the student groups were identified. Most churches designated a chaplain or counselor with responsibility to minister to the needs of these student "congregations."[6]

Since, however, these diverse student religious organizations were an integral part of campus life, there needed to be 1) a pattern of liaison which would show the University's appreciation for the contribution of these religious programs and 2) a method of making sure that the contribution of these groups and their advisers would be constructive. Student religious groups like all other student organizations were under the guidance of the Student Activities Bureau, but because of the recognition of religion as a basic motivating force, together with a full appreciation of the autonomy of religious activity in the American pattern of church-state separation, the establishment of a special bureau to coordinate religious activities was indicated.

One key to an understanding of this development is the phrase, "as the university grew in enrollment and as the multiplicity of diverse faith groups became more apparent." Life on the pre-World War I campus was relatively simple and nowhere more so than in its religious life. The student body was so overwhelmingly Protestant that the small Catholic and Jewish minorities could be overlooked without unfriendliness or irresponsibility.[7] The academic environment made for a liberal, ecumenical approach to Protestantism itself, and the minority religions could be invited in all good will to participate in "interdenominational" services or in the religiously motivated, secularly expressed activities of the Protestant YMCA

and YWCA's to which the care of the University's religious
life was frequently delegated. The fact that this did not meet
the religious needs of minority groups was not uncomfortably
evident as long as their representatives were few in number
and their own communions neglected them.

In 1913, however, the first Newman Club for Catholic students on non-Catholic campuses was founded in Philadelphia,
and there are today some 800 units in the Newman Federation
of America. Then, after World War II, the Hillel Foundation
for Jewish students came into being at the University of Illinois
and later, under the aegis of B'nai B'rith, spread to more than
200 campuses, serving a Jewish student population of almost
200,000. Quite unsurprisingly, the major concentrations of these
non-Protestant religious groups were on state university
campuses.

The value of this change in the religious life of university
communities was soon felt. Where formerly an official chapel,
intended to include all and offend none, may have been leading
to religious stagnation or impotence, the rise of religious differences helped the process of probing and re-examination that
has been characteristic of much twentieth-century religious
life. There was a dawning understanding of the benefits of
religious pluralism.

The greatest contribution to this development was made
by the disruptions of university life produced by World War II.
The campus was invaded by G.I. students who were more
mature in years than the average college generation and who
were returning from experiences that had shattered provincialism and opened their eyes to the multiplicity of human types,
human beliefs, and human responses. Among them were a
host of religious workers whose ministry had been remolded in
their service as chaplains to the military forces and who had
chosen student religious work as a form of expression analogous
to what they had done in the army and in the navy. They, too,
brought views broadened by their personal involvement in
cataclysmic events.

They had not only heroically served the needs of men of
diverse faiths in the midst of razor-keen tensions and soul-

smothering violence, but the best among them had also come to recognize, with a clarity sharpened by crisis, how inadequate were their ministrations to men of religions other than their own. In their fellowship with chaplains of other groups they learned that a minister might serve under the emergency circumstances of the battlefield as surrogate for a rabbi or a priest but that he could no more take their places than they could take his—that each faith group possessed depths of tradition, significant shades of difference of associations and meanings, which the outsider could strive to understand, to respect, and to appreciate but could never wholly appropriate while he retained the identity of his own faith. What is more, there was a new conviction among many that each faith deserved to flourish in the wholeness of its own continuity and through the contributions of its own scholarly interpreters.

One such individual, among the many I had the opportunity to observe, came out of military service and by the power of his own understanding revolutionized the chapel structure of a tradition-bound ivy-league school, securing quasi-official chaplaincy status for the professional head of each denominational religious agency. This sort of influence, combined with that of administrators governed by the American tradition of respect for equality of privilege and the rights of groups as well as of individuals, produced comparable changes on many state university campuses. Official chapels that had been taken for granted were now abandoned and several "interdenominational" Student Christian Associations became Student Religious Associations.

These changes have not taken place without understandable pockets of resistance and inevitable awkwardness. Indeed, the vestigial remains of earlier untroubled times frequently produce a measure of benevolent amusement. This is primarily true of the effort to find structural devices in new buildings that will evenhandedly accommodate all. There are three-way revolving altars, occasionally with one-third unsanctified by the church for whose use it was designed, and even four-way altars with one-fourth dedicated to completely innocuous, generalized religiosity.

On one campus where the wishes of the donor made necessary stained-glass windows not wholly acceptable to one faith
group, specially designed window shades carrying symbols
acceptable to that group were installed. The administration
of another state school succumbing to the anachronistic impulse
to build a chapel for all its students whatever their religious
backgrounds was surprised and even a bit offended to learn
that a motif of crosses in the brickwork made it difficult for
conscientious Jewish students to use the building. On another
campus where a new "meditation chapel" was built it was
equipped with offices for each of the "associate chaplains,"
making it necessary for some of the satellite agencies' leaders
to leave the comfort of their own well-equipped buildings to
make a periodic bow to the new structure in the name of unity
and good will.

The students of another tax-supported school have been
provided with an interreligious building—three-layer cake
in design so that there is a floor for each faith—the ground
floor of which is the scene of an annual struggle conducted
with restraint and yet with firmness about display space—for
the convictions of the group which displays madonnas will not
permit the madonnas to associate with the symbols of the Feast
of Lights, and the followers of the Feast of Lights are unwilling
to be relegated to an upstairs corner while Christmas takes
charge below.

Only one school, a privately supported one, has made the
logical response to the demand of the times for evenhandedness
without the watering down of significant differences. Brandeis
University has built three separate and equal chapels around
an interfaith area where a common altar is the focus of official
University events such as the annual baccalaureate service. But
this bold solution is obviously not without its own complications—nor could it be easily imitated by state universities.

In all this the Jewish minority, as the only non-Christian
group in substantial numbers on campus, has a special problem.
It is not one that is the result of ill will or of a fault in the
organization of activities; it is one that grows out of the situation itself. It is the problem of the unconscious dominance of
the majority culture. The Jewish minority is affected by it

even in its popular understanding of distinctive Jewish traditions. More frequently than not, they are identified by untutored Jews in Christian terms: Passover as a kind of Jewish Easter, the "sefirah" period between Passover and Pentecost as a kind of Jewish Lent. The very structure of society is undergirded by Christian assumptions.[8]

Thus even the liberal administration of an official chapel will inevitably reflect the Protestant tradition of worship—the underlying Protestant assumptions, for example, as to what prayer is, what its role should be, what the mood of worship should be, and even as to the character of reverence itself. With the best will in the world, a liberal dean on a campus where there is a large body of students representative of strict Jewish orthodoxy finds it difficult to plan a weekend retreat at a resort or camp away from the campus at the beginning of each school year, although she regards it as indispensable to the kind of thoughtful planning together that will make possible a year of meaningful activities. Her wish to provide conditions that will make possible both strict observance of the dietary laws and strict regard for the Sabbath runs counter to her wish to avoid setting up distinctions that would detract from the unity of the group experience. There is no simple solution for her—it is a situation that requires patience, respect for conviction, and above all a willingness to recognize that differences do exist and are important.

This kind of respect for difference, which frequently demands exercise of the Christian virtue of "going the second mile," is part of the moral responsibility of the dominant majority that is frequently more difficult to bear than the legal responsibility. This is the responsibility to recognize that deviations from the dominant norm may have intrinsic value; that they must not be crushed by the weight of numbers. It is of vital importance if we are concerned about the almost irresistible march of society toward monolithic, deadening uniformity.

Fortunately, this problem has won respectful attention, as may be seen by the wide variety of forms of interreligious organization with which state university communities are now experimenting.

The first such form is the appointment of official university co-ordinators of religious activity, to which we have already alluded. This experiment is in process at Minnesota, where it originated, at Michigan, and at Ohio State. It is noteworthy that these three schools are all large midwestern state universities each with a population of more than 20,000 full-time students of diverse backgrounds. Each has been well served over the past three decades by professionally staffed voluntary religious work agencies, many of which have fine physical facilities on the perimeter of the campus. Indeed a building boom during the last ten years has resulted in the multiplication of new, modern structures for the religious foundations on these and many other campuses.

At Minnesota, there are twenty-three such student religious work units, inclusive of the YMCA and YWCA, on the Minneapolis campus alone—from the large Lutheran Student Association, the Wesley and Westminster foundations, the Newman Foundation, the B'nai B'rith Hillel Foundation, the Pilgrim Foundation, and the Canterbury Club, through all the denominations and faith groups to the small Eastern Orthodox and Buddhist student fellowships. This is the situation into which an academically appointed co-ordinator, now holding full professional rank, was introduced—not to "originate religious programs but . . . to assist groups of all faiths to fit harmoniously and constructively into campus life."

As one of the "student personnel services" under the office of the dean of students, the co-ordinator's office serves as an information center and provides an "interreligious reading room." The co-ordinator is described as a "liaison official." His post is "in no sense . . . a directorship or a chaplaincy." Among the present functions of his office are (1) the processing of voluntary religious census cards, (2) providing a program consultation service for interreligious activities of a co-operative character, such as Religion-in-Life and Brotherhood Week programs, (3) arranging seminars for the professional workers of the voluntary agencies to increase their "student personnel" skills, (4) offering "impartial guidance" to students with personal religious problems, (5) occasional teaching of courses and "arranging institutes concerned with religious values," and (6) speaking on interreligious understanding and interpreting the University's attitude on religious matters.

I have quoted extensively from Minnesota's own statements concerning this office, not only because it is the pioneer bureau providing a pattern for other campuses, but also because even this sketchy outline of its functions suggests the care needed in any effort to nourish religious forces while avoiding favor or the appearance of favor to any religious group. The restraint in the outline hints at the way in which this kind of effort may arouse and indeed has aroused what Thomas Jefferson called the "asperities" of interchurch competitiveness. The new office is being watched most conscientiously, particularly in respect to the area of guidance to the so-called "uncommitted," and it has even been the target of attack by advocates of the "high wall of separation" between church and state. And indeed, when a university bureau presumes to seek to create "a method of making sure that the contributions of these (voluntary religious) groups and their advisors would be constructive," even those groups that co-operate officially in the program will be vigilant to protect their own freedom of action.[9]

This is given point by the fact that such efforts are motivated not only by a need to "co-ordinate" but also by the will to fill a gap and to provide a kind of nondenominational, "non-religious" counseling service, to serve those who cannot be reached by, or may be dissatisfied with, the existing sectarian campus agencies. It is the product of dissatisfaction with "un-official" religious work and its presumed ineffectiveness when left totally outside the structure of the university itself.

What co-ordination there is at Minnesota is carried on through the Council of Religous Advisors on the professional level and the Student Council on Religion on the student level. Working with the co-ordinator's office this latter council sponsors the religious emphasis programing in special weeks, freshman orientation, and the like. There is common agreement that the co-ordinator's office has facilitated interreligious co-operation by its administrative contributions, has opened the door to contact with official university life for the student pastors, and has placed the helpful stamp of official university recognition on the work of the religious agencies.

The recently established Office of Religious Affairs at the University of Michigan is like Minnesota's bureau in that it is headed by a co-ordinator and is part of the personnel structure of the University. Along with the Health Service and the offices of the Dean of Men and the Dean of Women, it is under the jurisdiction of the University's Vice-President for Student Affairs. The pattern of operations and of relationship to the separate religious agencies is similar to that at Minnesota, but the Michigan office stresses the fact that it regards University-sponsored program-planning and program-counseling as an important adjunct of its task of co-ordination. Two staff members of Michigan's Office of Religious Affairs give full time to the effort to stimulate and create interreligious programs. They work primarily with student government and major campus organizations. In this effort to influence the campus directly and to build a "climate" favorable to religious activity, the Michigan office may simply be carrying out the implications of its own background, for it grew out of an earlier, University-sponsored Student Religious Association operating under professional direction, which itself was the depression-born successor to a University Student Christian Association.

Here, too, there is co-ordination at the top through professional and student representatives of the voluntary agencies but little actual interreligious activity on the student level. Although the structure at Michigan is still too new to be evaluated, the consensus of those concerned is that the development is constructive and promises to be increasingly helpful as it establishes itself on the campus.

The Co-ordinator for Religious Affairs appointed by the University Board of Trustees at Ohio State in 1948 works with a University Advisory Board for Religious Affairs, which is composed of representatives of the University administration, the faculty, and the student body, along with the professional religious workers and local ministers drawn from the three major faith groups, all appointed by the President of the University. The administrative role of the Co-ordinator's office is similar to that of the office at the University of Minnesota, already described. All twenty voluntary religious work agencies surrounding the campus are represented on two subgroups: the University Religious Council composed of the professional workers and the Student Council for Religious Affairs. It was at the request of the University Religious Council that the University Advisory Board was appointed in 1949.

As on other campuses, this development has elicited some criticism: there are those who regard it as an overorganization of religious interests, which they claim has splintered adult participation and slowed down intergroup religious activities. On the other hand, there is general recognition of the value of the co-ordinator's work in liaison and in executing major interreligious activities such as the annual Religion-in-Life Week, the Convocation for new students, the "Recognition Banquet" for student religious leaders, and campus religious programs on radio and TV. One innovation at Ohio State is a distinguished Festival of Religious Music and a Festival of Religious Art which have served to broaden the area of interest in interreligious activity and to demonstrate the creative relationship between religion and the arts.

One would have expected a similar development of university administrative procedures in religious affairs at the University of Illinois. Illinois was the major laboratory for the birth and growth of off-campus religious foundations in the years immediately preceding and following World War I. Illinois pioneered in this form of response to religious needs, with what has been called "planned maintenance of church and university separation," which at the same time enabled the university to provide hospitality and encouragement to religious groups. However, the development of a University Office of Religious Affairs and the appointment of a University religious co-ordinator have not been contemplated at Illinois, and the organization of a new University Religious Council has encountered difficulties.

This may well be the result of a general university satisfaction with the pattern of leaving religious work to the individual voluntary foundations. Significantly, these foundations at

Illinois have always held a quasi-official relationship to the University through the accreditation by the University of the frequently popular and well-attended courses in religion which the foundations offer. A University Religious Council did exist from 1942 to 1953, but it died of inanition, and recognition was withdrawn from it at its own request. With it, the effort to observe Brotherhood Week with joint activity or to conduct a Religious Emphasis Week also died.

The proposal for a new University Religious Council, which functioned for a time although it had not been officially recognized, grew out of the desire of some of the professional religious workers appointed by the voluntary agencies to foster the development of co-operative activity. It has not been the result of any University-engendered program of co-ordination. The new group sought to be an official body under the supervision of the University and composed of representatives of the campus religious organizations, the residence councils, the faculty, and the administration. Its major function was to have been the planning of campus-wide interreligious activities. But the opposition of the representatives of several religious groups has led the Dean of Students to recommend a postponement of action on the proposal "pending further study." Some of the groups that oppose the plan have requested a final veto power on joint programing, fearing that a University Religious Council may take control of campus religious activities out of the hands of professional advisers and may "disquiet the minds of their students." They are reported to be "a vocal minority, mistrustful of student initiative in the field of religion."

Meanwhile, the Religious Workers Association, composed of the staff members of the eighteen voluntary religious work agencies, which is the major instrument for co-operative religious activity at Illinois, continues to probe the question of what kind of additional interreligious organization, if any, will meet their specific campus needs.

"Definitive and conclusive patterns will not emerge for a year or two and these are initial stages," writes one correspondent. "There is a good deal of groping for the right means."

This kind of "groping" is present even on campuses where

the response to the problem is the antithesis of the Illinois program of "maintenance of separation"—state universities where the pattern of an official university chapel persists. Notable among these are Pennsylvania State University, where a conscientious effort to adapt the old form to the new pluralism is being made, and the University of Maryland, where the chapel idea was introduced after World War II and where a new chapel building was completed some five years ago.[10]

At Penn State, the University Chaplain has been given the additional title of Co-ordinator of Religious Affairs, and the University provides him with an assistant whose function it is to plan interreligious programs. Both the University Chaplain and his assistant are ordained Protestant ministers. But the University tries to mitigate this appearance of favoring one faith group by officially designating several of the full-time religious workers who serve the voluntary religious institutions of the University community as "chaplains to the University." These are ordained clergymen representing the three major religious traditions on the campus. Of course, the chaplains to the University, in contradistinction to the University Chaplain and his assistant, are supported by their own denominations or faith groups. In addition, the University, using private contributions received for that purpose, has built a new "all-faith meditation chapel" whose permanent decor and pattern of use have not yet been fully developed. The pattern at Penn State, as described by the Chaplain, is tri-faith: tri-faith in its official literature, tri-faith in the University's Committee on Interreligious Affairs, tri-faith in the credit course in religion offered by the University, and in every area in which such participation is feasible. But the tri-faith pattern breaks down in the official chapel itself, which by nature and tradition remains Protestant. This is so despite the liberal extension of invitations to non-Protestant preachers and despite the fact that in 1956, of the 92.5 per cent of the entire student body that filled out voluntary religious census cards, 30 per cent noted a non-Protestant religious preference.

There is general agreement at Penn State that the atmosphere of interreligious relationships is "wholesome," but that the student response to interreligious activities is "lukewarm"; the conventional Religion-in-Life Week program has been abandoned in favor of periodic lectures by outstanding Protestant, Catholic, and Jewish leaders under the sponsorship of the Committee on Interreligious Activity and an annual Brotherhood Dinner, which is assured of attendance because of its organization on the basis of official representation of fraternities, sororities, and other student organizations.

On other campuses, the Protestant YM and YWCA's, still playing their traditional role, are important factors in the emergence of a new form of interreligious relationship. At Colorado the regents of the University approved the appointment of a "theologically trained person" to serve as co-ordinator for the Religious Workers' Association, half of the salary of the "co-ordinator" to be paid by the University and half by the YWCA. Then, as the last academic year ended, the post of co-ordinator was abolished and in his place the University appointed a "religious program counselor" who, serving the University half time, employs the other half of his time as a "Y" staff member. The counselor's responsibilities have not yet been fully marked out, but he will advise on Religion-in-Life Week and will work with the student government Sub-commission on Spiritual Development. This latter body is currently seeking to establish a small meditation chapel as well as a Department of Religion on campus and is fostering a program of year-round visits to the campus living units by "chaplain-faculty teams."

Some observers have found evidences, at Colorado and on several other campuses, of an incipient rebellion against the "tri-faith" approach, manifested in a refusal of Protestant groups to be "lumped together." "Some of our problems stem from a feeling of a plurality larger, much larger, than three," one correspondent writes.

A period of experimentation marking the transition from a traditional "Y" setup to tri-faith interreligious activity is also in process at the University of Texas where an officially recognized University Religious Council has been formed to work in co-operation with the office of the Dean of Student Life.

The "Y" itself acts as a clearing house and is conscientiously serving the development of genuine pluralism. In the past, student representatives and faculty joined the professional religious counselors in the wholly unofficial University Religious Workers' Association. Now the setup has been reorganized to create a student-run University Religious Council, making its headquarters in the "Y" and on which the members of the Religious Workers' Association serve as "advisory representatives." In addition, there is a Faculty Committee on Religious Life appointed by the President of the University. Texas' major interreligious activity is an annual Religious Emphasis Week but increasingly, it is reported, functioning committees of the University Religious Council are facing up to significant problems of human relations and campus tensions and to the tasks of religious orientation and education on a year-round basis. Through them, the Council is beginning to exercise a direct influence on campus life and values.

The structure at the University of Wisconsin has points of similarity to that at Texas. The "Y" groups, however, do not play a central role at Wisconsin, and the traditional Religious Emphasis Week has been abandoned in favor of quarterly lectures in the Student Union by representatives of the major faith groups. Wisconsin's dissatisfaction with Religious Emphasis Week is reported to have stemmed from the feeling of some that its program tended to be "evangelistic," and of others that its sessions "although well planned and favorably attended . . . presented a false 'united front' of religion to the campus."

The other end of the spectrum from the highly organized University of Minnesota response to the challenge of campus religious pluralism is to be found at the University of North Carolina, where there is neither organization nor the feeling of need for it either among students or denominational workers. An active Campus Christian Council represents the ten Protestant groups and the University administration has customarily looked to the "Y" as the focus of religious affairs. Nevertheless, the influence of Minnesota is felt—at least, verbally—for just last year the University of North Carolina requested the Associate Director of the University YMCA-YWCA "to assume the additional title of Coordinator of Religious Activities."

The problem of interreligious relations has different dimensions at the University of California at Los Angeles and at New York City's Hunter College where off-campus religious centers house all the voluntary religious work agencies.[11]

U.C.L.A.'s University Religious Conference, now housed in a beautiful new building, is a tri-faith venture that has existed for thirty years. It has won remarkable co-operation from lay leaders, clergy, and students of all groups. U.R.C. sponsors not only the usual Religious Emphasis Week at U.C.L.A. but also courses in religion, a School of Religion, and special projects such as its well-known "Panel of Americans" and its adoption of a university in India as its special concern.

Both the University Religious Conference and Hunter's Sara Delano Roosevelt Memorial House are corporate bodies independent of the tax-supported institutions they serve.

A most significant pattern, which has itself been the subject of specific study,[12] is that of the State University of Iowa, where a School of Religion, supported by private funds supplied by the major faith groups but wholly recognized by the University, not only gathers an academically qualified tri-faith faculty for the teaching of credit courses in religion but also serves as the focus of campus religious activity. Supporting its current tendency to place more and more emphasis on its academic function, the School has been encouraging the University's Office of Student Affairs to play an increasingly important role in coordinating the activities of the voluntary religious agencies.

At the University of Connecticut, encouragement of the religious agencies has been furthered by the fact that the University has managed to set aside a block of its land on a strategic edge of the campus, parcels of which have been deeded to the individual voluntary groups. As a result, several attractive religious centers have been built.

Through all these variant forms of interreligious organization one finds a surprisingly uniform pattern of programs and problems. The religious forces everywhere confront the crippling indifference of the mass of students, the lack of genuinely deep religious concern in administrative circles, and the secular and sometimes overtly antireligious attitudes in teaching staffs. But something is stirring. As Father Robert F. Drinan said in a recent issue of *America* (December 15, 1956), the "old campus gods of science, progress, secularism and humanism are undergoing an agonizing reappraisal" and educators are asking how the Judaeo-Christian heritage may be presented to college students in a manner more effective than religious organizations or religion courses seem to make possible.

For many years the chief reliance of interreligious programing on state university campuses has been the Religious Emphasis Week program, initiated by the University Christian Mission and recently influenced by the National Conference of Christians and Jews. We have already alluded to instances where this form of program has been abandoned and campus religious forces are actively searching for new techniques that will be freed of the more obvious defects of so-called Religion-in-Life Week approach. Those defects are the once-a-year, formal, and occasionally perfunctory character of this kind of program and its failure to make a meaningful impact on student lives. The new approaches are aimed at creating a year-round, week-to-week program in the campus living units with the stimulation provided by the visits of some of the most forceful personalities on the religious scene.

On one large campus, where Religion-in-Life Week persists, the featured orator last year was the most popular speaking personality of the denomination with the largest representation on that campus. The University's largest auditorium, capable of seating thousands, was set aside for his appearance. But when the great night came, the attendance totaled 150, not all of whom were students.

"Despite fine words, the University says 'no' to religious activity," one observer said in explanation of this disappointment. "After Homecoming Week, Greek Week, and Snow Week, the students are exhausted and barely able to muster up enough energy to study for finals. It is at this point that we come along and cruelly dragoon some student into taking the chairmanship of Religious Emphasis Week, doomed to failure before it begins."

There is, however, one "action project" of national character which is religious in its origins, religiously motivated on the American scene, and struggling to relate its religious values to its program of philanthropy and education. This is the work of World University Service, which annually raises hundreds of thousands of dollars for aid to overseas student communities and for a program of education in international understanding. Sponsored in the United States by the national student work organizations of the three major faiths and by the National Students Association, it has experimented in recent years with a "core" program on several campuses through which it has tried to enlist the energies of local representatives of the national sponsoring groups in activity and discussion related to the meanings that undergird the Service's fund-raising program. This effort has not proved to be easy. American students give, but they give through typically American, organized campus chests that inevitably obscure the causes for which money is contributed. The chests by their very nature substitute "promotion" for education and rely on ballyhoo and time-tested machinery and new "gimmicks" to extract student gifts.

"The Campus Chest contributes quite a large sum of money to World University Service, but though some of the church groups on campus may possibly educate their own students as to the purpose of WUS, they are not vitally connected with the central campus chest committee which is handled by the Student Government," one correspondent writes.

The dilemma is sharpened by an antithetical situation at another school where the campus chest committee dropped WUS and "the University Religious Council has picked it up and has done a much better job of education for it, but has not been highly successful in actually raising funds."

But this is after all the heart of the very dilemma with which campus religious forces must continue to wrestle: to find the means of linking participation with understanding, machinery with meaningful content.

Intergroup and interreligious activity acquire meaning when

they emphasize both service to common objectives and the application of shared social ideals. An interchange that possesses the dimension of depth becomes possible only when it is founded on the integrity and increasing understanding of each individual group, which are then reflected in the program of joint activity.

The organized attention which this problem is receiving is a recognizable new factor in university affairs. The first consultative conference to this end by state university administrators and faculty and religious leaders was held at Minnesota in 1949.[13] This meeting set off a process of continuing exploration and by its example stimulated the holding of several similar conferences. Nourished by the National Conference of Christians and Jews,[14] a conference of university personnel and religious workers at twelve midwestern universities was held at the University of Illinois in 1955.[15]

The fact that these conferences have not failed to recognize the difficulty of the problem and the impossibility of finding a simple solution is encouraging to those who believe that it must be confronted in all its complexity. The difficulty inheres in pluralism itself. The voluntary religious agencies representing as they do the variant individual faith groups must be the foundation for any interreligious structure, and, though there is some justification for dissatisfaction with their present effectiveness, the university must recognize them, encourage them, and thus help strengthen them or it faces the danger of building its new approach in a way which will violate cherished traditions of separation of church and state, infringe upon the freedom of action of individual groups, or offend the sensibilities of the minority denominations.

Sensitive understanding of this danger was expressed at the Allerton Park Conference by Allyn P. Robinson, who said:

A religious group derives its reason for being from its religious faith. This faith is rooted in its heritage . . . To ask a group to disregard or slur over its religious commitments in the interest of "cooperation" or "brotherhood" is to ask a group to do what it cannot do and maintain its integrity . . . Intergroup activities involve more than saying "My door is always open, anyone may come in." Too often this means that the majority groups determine the basis on which cooperative activities are conducted and minority groups are placed in the position of conforming or withdrawing. And if they do the latter, they may be quite unfairly considered "uncooperative." The ethics of a pluralistic society requires new norms, new appreciations, and new skills.[16]

We are today at the very beginning of the task of finding those new norms and new skills. But the hope that a "community of values" can be created is encouraged by Philip Jacob's finding that in certain group situations and in certain colleges where there is "unity and vigor of expectation" there is a "peculiar potency" to counteract the wound-down mediocrities of our times and to lead students toward meaningful and enriching life goals.[17] In carrying forward the effort to build that potency in the state university situation, we bear the overwhelming obligation to grasp both horns of the dilemma. The struggle to provide deep and significant religious educational opportunities must never infringe upon the absolute religious freedom which is the keystone of the American structure and is, at the same time, the expression of a supreme value.

FILMER S. C. NORTHROP

Students from Other Lands

CHAPTER XVI

The presence of students from other lands calls for exceptional religious and educational statesmanship. The task will
be misconceived if it is thought of merely as the chance to
acquaint them with our religious and social values and to
provide them with the facilities here for sustaining their own
religious faith. The opportunity is present also to educate
American and foreign students alike in interreligious, intercultural, and international understanding and collaboration.
President Eisenhower has noted that man now has it within his
power to destroy mankind. Either we learn to understand one
another and to restrain our culturally and religiously inspired
nationalisms and imperialisms or we perish.

The masses of Africa, the Middle East, and Asia are rebelling
against Western imperialism. This development includes insistence upon their own indigenous cultural laws. Since the
separation of politics from religion is foreign to any people
who have not passed through the Protestant Reformation or
come under modern Western secular political philosophy, this
native cultural renaissance is also a resurgence of their own
religion. Note the recent Islamic religious reaction in Turkey
against Atatürk's modern secular reforms. Read Prime Minister
U Nu of Burma's exposition of Buddhism in *An Asian Speaks*.[1]
Consider the similar synthesis of Buddhist religious values with
constitutional democracy in Thailand. Recall Ghandi's statements, "Such power as I possess for working in the political
field [has] derived [from] my experiments in the spiritual field"

and the Hindu Bhagavadgita is "the book *par excellence*" spiritually. Read Esther Warner's *New Song in a Strange Land*[2] and hear the contemporary Liberian say, "All we got to live under two laws. We got to live under the Liberian government [Western] law. They got plenty soldier. We don't give our heart to that law. The other law is the law of our people where the chief is the big man. That one we give heart to."

Clearly, the era in which religious statesmanship is conceived in terms of converting the world to one's own religion is over. It is by cultivating a respect for one another's differing cultural and religious traditions that religious statesmanship in today's world will find itself. As the Hindu Swami Akhilananda has suggested, "Teachers should not attempt to convert students from one religion to another." The deepening of each student's insight into the richness of his own religion and the expansion of his imagination, intellect, and heart to enter sympathetically and with understanding into the spirit and novel merits of other religions is the wiser course. In any event, it is the only practical one, the mood of non-Western people being what it is.

In fact, their present tendency is to affirm that the Judaic-Christian West, however inspired may have been its founders, is obsessed with material wealth and instrumental gadgets at the expense of the intrinsic religious values necessary to control them. Vice-President Radhakrishnan of India speaking out of his Hindu-Buddhist background, like Iqbal of Lahore speaking for a reconstructed Islam, concludes that the hope of the world centers in the religions of Asia, or of Islam, which, not drawing such a sharp division between the religious and the secular, keeps the details of daily life more continuously and intimately rooted in the spiritual. A recent study of Indian students on an American university campus shows that they leave, even after three years including visits in religious homes, with a conviction that Americans lack a proper appreciation of spiritual values.[3] Even European students often share this opinion. One need not accept these judgments in order to see their practical consequence, which is that the West, and especially the United States, is on the defensive with respect to its religion.

Another fact points in the opposite direction. The people of

Africa, the Middle East, and Asia are demanding both (a) the right to build their social institutions in the light of their own indigenous religious traditions and also (b) the higher standards of living and the democratic political control of their lives which they see the peoples of the modern West enjoy. These two demands generate spiritual conflicts and raise problems which must be understood if the needs of foreign students on American campuses are to be met or if American students are to make correct judgments concerning the introduction of Western beliefs and ways into non-Western lands.

The ways of native non-Western people before the modern Western imperialists and Christian missionaries came were not those of liberal, constitutional democracy. As Sir Henry Maine showed in his *Ancient Law*[4] and as the comparative philosophy of the world's cultures reaffirms, any people not influenced by Western law or religion live under the religion and ethics of "the law of status," and not under the religion and ethics of "the law of contract" from which liberal, constitutional democracy derives. In a perfect law-of-status society, the selection of political leaders is not made in an election guided by a contractually introduced constitution to which all people have in principle given their consent and before which they are all equal, after the manner of the religion and ethic of a perfect law-of-contract community. Instead, all leadership is set by status of sex and priority of birth within the family and by color-of-skin, familial, or caste status vis à vis the tribe, determined by whether one is of the predominant sex from the first family of the tribe.

For example, in a purely patriarchal, law-of-status religious community, the head of the nation or tribe is the eldest son of the first family of the tribe, according to the rule of primogeniture. In a purely matriarchal society, the eldest daughter is both the political ruler and the head of the family by the same principle of biologically bred status. Consequently, family, caste, and tribal loyalty become the primary moral, religious, and political obligations. Furthermore, religious worship is not congregational but focuses around the privacy of the family hearth and the ceremonies of the tribe.

Such was the religious, political, and personal ethic of the ancient cities of Rome before the creation of Western legal science by Roman jurists who were Stoic Roman philosophers or heavily under the influence of this philosophy. The African in Esther Warner's Liberia spoke truly when he said that he gave his heart to "the law of our people where the chief is the big man." In this statement he showed that their morality and religion is that of a law-of-status community. The laws of ancient Hindu India are called the Laws of Manu because Manu was the founder of the Aryan-Hindu tribe. Under the laws of this Hindu religious community, only patrolineal descendants of the first Manu enjoyed political, moral, or religious leadership. The same law-of-status ethic operates in Shintu Japanese society, in the Califate, in many local families in unreformed Islamic society, and to a predominant, though lesser, extent among families in Confucian and Buddhist societies.

This is why the people of Islamic Turkey and Pakistan and of Hindu-Buddhist Thailand, Burma, and India have had to introduce a law-of-contract constitution and a legal system imported from the West in order to bring their domestic affairs under their own democratic control and to introduce the reforms necessary to begin the lifting of their standards of living. But this is to begin the shift, initiated in Western civilization following the Stoic Romans, from the religious ethic of status to that of contract. The effect of this shift is to disassociate moral, political, and religious man from color-of-skin, family-centered, and tribally bred man, and to identify him with universal or cosmopolitan man, that is, any man whatever, standing equally with all other men before contractually constructed and freely accepted universal legal principles.

In the West, with the decline of the Roman Empire, this new religious ethic of the law of contract passed on the one hand to the eastern empire and Justinian and on the other hand into the Roman Catholic Church, thereby creating Western Stoic Roman Judaic-Christian civilization. (In fact, the literal meaning of the adjective "catholic" in the Christianity of the Roman Catholic Church is "universal.") Kant's categorical imperative, to the effect that only that conduct is good which can be expressed as a universal law for everyone, is an example of this ethic. The Declaration of Independence of the American colonists and the Bill of Rights of the Constitution of the United States and the Indian Bill of Rights are other examples.

Because the shift from status to contract cannot be made instantaneously, the Stoic, Roman Catholic, Judaic-Christian ideal historically tended in considerable part to be filled in with the law-of-status content. Consequently, Roman Catholic Christianity became associated with hierarchically ordered aristocratic and regal institutions rather than with democratic and egalitarian ones. The same is true of the Protestant Christianity of Luther's Germany, of Calvinism, and of the Church of England of Hooker, Elizabeth, Sir Robert Filmer, and of the latter's biological descendants, the First Families of Virginia. Hence, if the Stoic Roman Christian ethical ideal was to be achieved, it became necessary to reform not merely the Roman Catholic Christianity of Saint Augustine and Saint Thomas but also the Protestant Christianity of Luther, Calvin, Hooker, and Sir Robert by means of the more democratic values of (a) Nonconformist Protestantism and (b) modern secular natural and moral philosophy, particularly that of Newton, Locke, and Jefferson.

In their zeal, however, to locate the source of religious and political authority in the conscience and freedom of the individual, Nonconformist Protestant Christians tend to lose the Roman Stoic factor in Judaic-Christian civilization. Consequently, for them, unlike Roman Catholic Christians or followers of Islam, legal norms seem to be merely instrumental and to be irrelevant for intrinsic personal moral values or for the religious life; also, political nationalism tends to be fostered at the expense of lawful universalism and of faith in the need for the spiritual foundations of international law. It is no accident, as I have shown elsewhere,[5] that many of the major leaders in the achievement of the transfer of some national sovereignty to the Western European economic, military, and political community have been vital Stoic Roman legal thinkers and Roman Catholic Christians.

These considerations point up the fact that Protestant and

Roman Catholic Christians need one another. Interreligious understanding and collaboration on the university campus is as important, therefore, domestically as it is internationally.

Both Christian groups also need modern secular natural and moral philosophy. Witness the adherence of many Southern Nonconformist Protestants to the color-of-skin law-of-status ethic (derived from Sir Robert Filmer through the First Families of Church of England and Calvinist Virginia) and their resistance to the universal ethic of the law of contract by the Supreme Court of the United States in its recent unamimous decision on segregation in education. Clearly, the reform of Roman Catholic and Conformist Protestant Christianity by Nonconformist Protestantism is not sufficient to achieve the religious and moral shift from biologically bred status to a society in which Judaic-Christian man is universal man. All too often the Nonconformist Protestants, taking the Bible as the literally dictated word of God, go to certain parts of the Old Testament containing the patriarchal and tribal ethic for their criterion of the divine and the good. A third factor has been necessary, consequently, in order to approximate the initial ideal of Stoic Roman Judaic-Christian civilization. This third factor is modern secular, natural, moral, and political philosophy, especially that of Newton, Locke, and Jefferson and the Kant of the categorical imperative.

The foregoing role of the Old Testament in this story shows that Jews as well as Christians need the reforming influence of Stoic Roman legal science and modern secular science and philosophy. Otherwise, more and more Jewish students, persuaded by the latter subjects and convinced of the validity of the universal ethic of Western legal science, while they see many of their fellow religionists pursuing the religion and politics of the law of status, are going to be increasingly alienated from their religion. This, in fact, is the domestic problem of the secularized leaders of contemporary Israel from Western Europe when, in their introduction of a law-of-contract constitution, they are confronted with the religiously orthodox Jews from Morocco and the Arabian Peninsula who outnumber and outbreed them.

It appears, therefore, that if the natives of Africa, the Middle East, and Asia want to retain their indigenous religious and cultural traditions while also achieving the democratic control of their own affairs and the more democratically distributed higher standards of living which they see peoples in the West enjoy, they must amend the law-of-status religious and social ways of the masses in the light of a deep understanding and acceptance of the quite different law-of-contract religion and ethic of the Roman Stoic Judaic-Christian, the Nonconformist Protestant Christian, and the modern secular West. Clearly, the modern West has not merely its efficient instruments, but also its unique intrinsic spiritual values. A wise religious and educational statesmanship on the American university campus will insure that American and foreign students alike have the chance, inside as well as outside the curriculum, to learn what they are.

The Africans, Moslems, and Asians must master these values also if they are to achieve their present insistence upon the more universally spread standards of health and wealth which they see in the Modern West. These medical and economic aims require the introduction of scientific medicine, agriculture, and machinery and the latter's high capital investment. Such finance requires (a) the introduction of law-of-contract control of banking and investment at the federal level and (b) the moral integrity in the handling of finance by public officials who, abhorring nepotism, give greater loyalty to the law-of-contract norms of a dull legislative statute or an abstract constitution than to the concrete blood ties to the members of one's own family and to the first families of one's tribe—a type of financial integrity upon the part of public officials which a family-centered and tribally centered law-of-status morality and religion does not provide, and which only the universalist ethic of the Stoic Roman law-of-contract religion and society insures.

The latter ethic, as the Stoic Roman jurists and philosophers made clear, goes back, as does modern scientific technology, by way of Greek philosophy to Greek mathematical physics with its conception of any truly known individual thing as an instance of a formally universal law. This freed the essential properties of any truly known individual from such sensed properties as color, thereby preparing the way for the Stoic Roman jurists, and the Roman Catholic Judaic-Christians following the jurists, to disassociate moral, religious, and political man from color-of-skin, family, caste, and tribal man, and to identify him with universal man. It follows that if non-Western people want the widely distributed standards of health and wealth, they must introduce not only Western scientific instruments but also Western law-of-contract religious and moral values. Similarly, if Western religious and educational leaders are not to betray their spiritual heritage, they must radically reform their present conception of the relation between the humanities and natural science, breaking down departmental lines by revealing the common philosophical and scientific way of knowing from which both derive and upon which both depend for their validity and effectiveness. This is as important for American as for foreign students.

One final consideration remains. Countless Americans are emotionally disturbed and spiritually empty to the point of sickness. This is the case frequently, notwithstanding a religious upbringing and even attendance at Jewish synagogue or Christian church. Every state government is plagued with the endlessly mounting cost of providing care for the insane and the mentally sick. It is difficult to escape the conclusion that this points to something spiritually lacking in the religion of the Hebrew-Christian world and in the ethic of the modern secular West.

The central place which emotion occupies in these ills suggests that it may be here that for Western man the more intuitive religion of the African Negro, the Islamic Sufi, the meditating Buddha, the nondualistic Vedanta Hindu, and the warmhearted Confucian *jen* come into their own. In any event, Swami Akhilinanda of the Ramakrishna Hindu Society of Boston reports that American students, professors, and businessmen who are eminently successful come to him spiritually unsatisfied and emotionally at odds with both themselves and their mates. May it not be that the religious worship in which they participate in synagogue or church is too much concerned with group sermons, group ceremonials, and pastoral visits and confessionals and not enough given to nonverbal private meditation and direct intuitive communion in silence which religions such as Buddhism and nondualistic Vedantic Hinduism provide? Perhaps, also, the modern West needs those psychological techniques discovered by Asian spiritual investigators which so shift and transform the content and focus of a person's emotive experience that he becomes one with the existentially immediate, undifferentiated, and, hence, timeless and infinite component of himself and of all things. If so, the provision on the university campus of the religious symbols and practices of Africa, Islam, and Asia beside those of the Judaic-Christian West may be as important for Jews, Catholics, and Protestants as it is for enabling foreign students of other faiths to sustain and deepen and discover what is still valid, after the reforms by the ethic of the law of contract, in their own religious traditions.

In this connection, the new modernistic chapel at Massachusetts Institute of Technology is very much to the point. In this building there is but one chapel, completely devoid of symbols from any religion whatever. On the floor below the chapel there are several little rooms each containing the symbols of one of the major religions of the world, Oriental as well as Western. When one religion is scheduled for the main chapel, its symbols are taken there.

In one respect, however, this admirable practice leaves something to be desired. It makes the error of supposing that all religions are congregational, bringing people together to worship as a group. This is true of Judaism, Christianity, and Islam and also of Westernized forms of Buddhism and Hinduism. In her book, *The Hindu Temple*,[6] Stella Kramrisch reminds us, however, that congregationalism is completely foreign to [non-Westernized] Hinduism. The same is true in major part of Buddhism, Janism, Confucianism, and an important part of Roman Catholicism as the presence at any moment of the day of a person worshipping alone before a side altar in a Roman Catholic church demonstrates. Consequently, if the authentic religions of the Orient, in their non-Westernized forms, are to bring their intrinsic, intuitive, emotive values to their own adherents or to others on the American campus, special permanent rooms with their respective symbols, isolated from all outside noise, must also be provided for each of them.

For followers of Islam, the chapel at the Massachusetts Institute of Technology with its blank, modernistic interior is ideal. To a Moslem, the presence of any symbol whatever within the place of religious worship is regarded as idolatry and as religiously shocking. Also, the floor of any chapel should be level throughout and without any slope. Otherwise, the Moslem worshipper runs the risk of being unable to return his body to an erect position when, with his knees on the floor, he swings his trunk forward and touches his forehead to the floor. All pews or seats must be removed if followers of Islam are to worship there. At most, only a huge rug or many rugs should be in the room. Before the single chapel for all congregational religions is built, an astronomer might well be called in to orient it so that its front interior points toward Mecca. In campus meals or invitations to luncheon or dinner, where Hindus are included, the provision of an adequate meal containing no meat and composed largely of vegetables is of equal importance.

Such attention upon detail may seem overdone; yet their neglect may produce unnecessary embarrassment and result in more harm than good. Also, Oriental religions should be presented in their pure, non-Westernized, authentic forms. This does not prevent Westernized versions of Oriental religions from holding congregational forms of service, after the manner of the Ramakrishna Hindu Mission and certain Westernized Buddhist groups. Probably, however, the modern West has enough of such religious worship without going to Westernized Hindus and Buddhists for more. What we, in our hectic, oververbal, overpreached, and overlectured world need is the more private, silent type of intuitive meditation and contemplation that brings the emotive fulfillment and spiritual equanimity which the statute of the meditating Buddha, his eyes half open, half closed, or of the meditating Ramakrishna, conveys. The Oriental philosophical and psychological methods of analyzing and directing attention and modifying its content, described in part by Premier U Nu of Burma in his aforementioned article, need to be introduced by Asian experts and studied by Western analytic, radical, empirical philosophers and psychologists. French philosophers and scientists are already doing this.[7] Such study might revive an interest in and a respect for religion upon the part of faculty and students for whom religious philosophy means merely Hume or Wittgenstein and religious psychology suggests merely Pavlov or Freud.

Cultural anthropologists and philosophers have found that the behavior and ceremonies of one culture seem meaningless and even silly to an observer from a different culture unless the observer learns to understand what he sees in the observed culture's terms. Because very few religious people have learned how to do this, the observations of the missionary of one religion upon the meaning and merits of another religion are, with rare exceptions, of little worth. The same is true of most politicians and laymen in their judgments of a foreign nation's secular behavior. Contemporary social scientists who describe a foreign culture in terms of the concepts of recent Western behavioristic or Freudian psychology commit the same error. If we do not want students on the campus to react similarly to modes of worship or meditation other than their own, the religious and educational leaders must learn from the philosophical anthropologists.

The latter have found that to understand the people of a foreign culture one must think about what one sees or hears them do from the standpoint of their own way of thinking about it, rather than from the standpoint of one's own culture. When anthropologists such as Paul Radin and Clyde Kluckhohn did this, even for people who have no written language, they found themselves confronted in each case with a complete and novel philosophy. Recently the anthropologist Professor Hoebel has made a study of the legal norms of seven different so-called primitive peoples. So different are the norms of any one of these seven people from those of the others that he finds it necessary to set up seven sets of basic conceptions to describe them.[8] Interreligious understanding requires the same approach.

Practically, this means that the authentic presentation of the

major religions and their practices on or near the university
campus is not enough. The mentality or philosophy behind
each must accompany the presentation. To appreciate and
understand Roman Catholic worship, one must interpret what
one sees in terms of Roman Catholic doctrine and philosophy.
To evaluate and gain respect for Islam, one must, in addition
to observing Moslems at worship, read the Koran and some of
the Sharia (laws), while also having some appreciation of the
Greek, Arab, and Persian philosophy of a very high order which
has gone into their interpretation. Likewise, to understand the
Buddhist's Nirvana, the verbal and nonverbal practices of its
Zen sect, the Hindu's Brahman, or the psychological and gym-
nastic techniques of a Hindu Yogi, something of Buddhist and
Hindu philosophy and especially its epistemology must be comprehended. To present the authentic practices without the indigenous theory necessary to understand them is to fail
practically.

It follows that ministers, priests, and lay religious leaders
must be closely associated with the faculty. The resources in
the departments of anthropology, philosophy, area studies,
comparative law, and religion must be drawn upon. Perhaps all
of these departments will have to be expanded, becoming less
culturally provincial in the philosophy, law, and religion which
they teach. Also, foreign and American students who are authentic representatives of their respective faiths should be encouraged to expound to one another the inner meaning of each
religious tradition.

Since the major point in the coming of any foreign student to
the United States is to obtain an authentic understanding of
our culture, it is best that they live isolated from one another
as far as possible, with American students, so that they see
what we do from our specific spiritual standpoint. Otherwise,
the differing spiritual mentalities of the different foreign cultures which they represent will tend to reinforce them in the
error of judging the United States in spiritual terms other than
its own, and instead of achieving an objective understanding of
our particular spiritual values, they will leave, after the manner
of the Indian students in the aforementioned University of

Pennsylvania study, with their initial, provincial religious and political prejudices concerning the United States reinforced. Hence, the regular university union should be used to bring students together, and a residential international house is probably unwise.

It is, however, wise to have some official person or committee whose responsibility it is to see that foreign and American students alike obtain the experience and training in the inter-religious, intercultural, and international collaboration which our contemporary troubled world so desperately needs. This need is so great that the undertaking is one which merits the attention and aid of every university and public official, every faculty member and student, and every religious and lay leader in the surrounding community.

Campus Myths

History is a kind of vertical anthropology. The quiet gulf fixed between any two generations is paralleled by the psychological discontinuity between contemporary but widely separated cultures.

When an American from the suburbs of Chicago journeys to the Navajos or the Dobus or even to the dying villages of northern New England or to the sharecroppers of the deep South, he is enough of an anthropologist to recognize another world. But when, after he has turned forty, he observes his own children with their friends, he is less able—or less willing —to concede that here also is another world. Time, even a few decades of time, can make for discontinuity. The failure to recognize this fact is at the heart of the ever-present suspicion and malice existing between the generations. Each generation expects the new one to be a slightly modified version of itself. The breakdown of understanding will be greatest in periods like our own, when a wholesale psychological mutation and shift of values has occurred in the brief span of thirty years.

If anyone of middle age doubts that a real gulf is fixed between the generations, let him chaperon a college dance. He goes with nostalgic memories of exciting evenings. His social tradition had been one of rugged and sometimes jungle-like individualism. His was the era of prearrangements among men to make sure that the girls were "cut in on" an adequate number of times during the evening; it was also a period when social prestige accrued by dating a variety of persons rather than being always seen in the same company. The present reality, except in a few places where old traditions die hard, is utterly different.

The chaperon notes with growing bewilderment that the same couple dances together all evening, or at least until, in apparent ennui, they leave early for the nearest tavern. Very rarely is there any exchange of partners. No stag line loiters against the wall. It seems exceedingly dull to the chaperon and to his wife. For their part, they rekindle ancient embers to a mild glow by trading partners with other faculty couples. The students, observing this polygamous conduct, are gently shocked, as though a breach of decorum had been publicly committed.

The changed customs of the dance floor are merely by-products of a far deeper revolution. The old tradition of dating as many different persons as possible, and postponing the day of commitment, has been replaced by its exact opposite— "going steady." Perhaps the college where I teach represents an extreme development, though a fair amount of experience lecturing on other campuses makes me doubt even this. At any rate, in that college the period of "random dating" hardly extends beyond the third date with the same girl. From then on, there is the tacit or explicit assumption that they are "going steady." This status is somewhat vaguely defined, but it seems to be definite enough so that the young man or woman who casually seeks other dates is likely to encounter social ostracism. "Going steady" leads, sometimes slowly but often with great rapidity, to "pinning," which is usually defined as "being engaged to be engaged." This is an important rite of passage, particularly on those campuses that abound in Greek letters; there may be serenades and special listing in a column reserved for this purpose in the student newspaper. Formal engagement can follow soon or be deferred—this often depends on the two families—but once the "pinning" stage is reached there is a clearly defined status—monogamous dating and the presumption of eventual marriage. Not surprisingly, the percentage of students who marry while in college is steadily increasing.

The older pattern of dating put the emphasis on adventure;

the newer pattern puts it on security. A girl who is "going steady" can be sure of a date whenever a date is called for, and her boy friend has the same assurance. Neither may be the dream ideal to the other, but each has two legs and a pair of eyes and can be depended upon to answer present when summoned.

I have no apology for this somewhat extensive treatment of dating and courtship. Nothing in life tells more about the values by which people live. One should, however, add some mention of the markedly more serious attitude toward marriage now found among college students. If they are less starry-eyed and less inclined toward theories of "finding the only one in the world for me," they seem much more willing to work hard and systematically to create stable and satisfying marriages. When the sociology department, in response to student clamor, offers a course in Marriage and the Family, there are certain to be many pinned or engaged couples taking it together. One sees them afterwards at the student union, decorously discussing what Professor X said about sexual adjustment and the merits of the Okinawa system of child-rearing. The latter topic is not a theoretical one to them: they are counting their children before they are conceived and drawing up lists of suitable names.

The professor also discovers that certain jokes, which were once tried and true for classroom use, are no longer well received. He learns to mention marriage with proper respect and sex with due reserve. A certain neo-Victorianism is evident on the campus. I suppose the job of personal emancipation was done so thoroughly during the 1920's that the students today feel a greater need to put some of the wreckage back together and build a durable habitation for their future lives. This is all the more true because many of them come from broken homes and know from personal experience what it means to be sacrificed upon the private altar of their parents' "self-expression" and "right to happiness." In the new campus mood, even Mrs. Grundy is granted a minor but honorable role. It is perilous to make predictions, but the odds seem good that the oncoming generation, with its new earnestness, will score a better record of marital success than its immediate predecessors.

The more one examines the daily life of the campus, the clearer it becomes that security is the dominant ideal. This is not news to attentive observers, but it is perhaps worth while to spell it out in further detail. Take, for example, the college senior who is looking for a job. During the 1920's, the emphasis was still enough on adventure to lure the senior into taking chances, such as accepting that rather shaky job as a bond sales-man in the hope of making the quick million. To learn first-hand how great is the change in mentality, talk with any "com-pany representative" as he makes his rounds from campus to campus in the late winter or spring and interviews promising seniors. One of them, an apoplectic man in his early fifties, once burst forth to me, "I told this boy about the opportunities in our company; I told him there were real risks but if he had the right stuff, he could rise to the top. Then I asked him if he had any questions. Do you know what he asked me? Do you know what this twenty-one-year-old boy, hardly old enough to shave, asked me? He thought a while and then he asked me, 'What's the retirement age and what kind of pension system do you have?' "

To the company representative this seems a failure of char-acter, a downright un-American refusal to embrace the road of high commercial adventure. The college senior views it otherwise. He sees the business world more and more domi-nated by corporate giants which have lost their swashbuckling splendor and now increasingly resemble civil service. Theoreti-cally, he might aim at heading one of them, but the possibility is so remote that he settles for the comfortable and secure niche, the annual increment, a well-padded retirement.

All that I have said is obviously a generalization and an oversimplification; there are always the nonconformists in any period who go their own lonely way. But in broad terms, it is clear that security is as much the key concept in job-hunting as in dating and courting. It is also one of the prime motives in the somewhat changed attitude of college students toward religion. I do not think it is the only motive. There are deeper currents, and from a long-range viewpoint these are the more important. But in any case, part at least of the changed attitude toward religion clearly stems from the quest for security.

The change in attitude is evident on most campuses. Callow wisecracks about religion are not as good form or as funny as in previous decades. The prevailing attitude is to say that religion is a pretty good thing and the churches are useful institutions. True, the theological content of "religion" is rarely specified. Students are more open to "religion" than to Christianity or Judaism—or Hinduism. When the values of religion are discussed, as they incessantly are in bull sessions organized or unorganized, this is likely to be in purely social or subjective language—"what religion can do for society," "what I can get out of religion." The latter is customarily defined as peace of mind. Religion, thus viewed, becomes an added means to security, this time social and psychological security. Belonging to a religious body gives a social anchorage, and the subjective fruits of religion can be a greatly desired lessening of inner tension. God, in such a religion, is to be sought as one reaches for Miltown; His church is a decorous Sunday morning country club. God is to be used, not served or necessarily loved. I add once more that there are deeper and more abiding currents than this, but part at least of the current friendliness toward religion stems from the desire to use God for social and psychological ends.

At this point, the "other-directed" man described by David Riesman in *The Lonely Crowd* begins to come into focus. He abounds on the campus. He does not abound there only. He has been mass-produced throughout America in recent decades. The public schools, to name only one social institution, have labored mightily to produce him by their emphasis on co-operation, group adjustment, social adjustment, every species of adjustment. The changed emphasis in the schools is probably only a by-product of something more deep-seated in America's psychological and sociological evolution, a really massive shift in values. In any event, the "other-directed man," with his sensitive antennae for receiving the responses of his fellows, is the dominant type on most campuses.

The historical predecessor of "other-directed man" was "inner-directed man," who followed his conscience. That conscience might be a very erroneous one, filled with abominable absolutes, and the net result could equally well be a saint or a robber baron, but in any event he looked to his conscience for guidance. The other-directed man has a different absolute, the peer group. Uncertain whether there is a God who really means business, timid about committing himself to any metaphysical ultimate, half-convinced that the conscience is no more than a superego created by society, he seeks psychological security by craning his neck to see what his fellows are doing and saying. In time, he develops an exquisite skill at this, almost a kind of mind-reading. He can divine other people's thoughts before they think them. By behaving in such a way as to evoke favorable reactions from his peers, he wins acceptance. Being accepted, he has the warm sense of belonging. He is shielded from the leering aloneness of having to consult his conscience or his God too often.

I have no wish to compose a sentimental elegy for inner-directed men. In retrospect, as his era fades into history, it seems that he was more than human size, both for good and evil. Other-directed man is humbler, more the normal size of a man. He is inconspicuous, because he chooses to be so. You do not spot him in a crowd. At first glance, it seems that other-directed man has perhaps the moral and spiritual edge. He is likely to be friendly, helpful, considerate of others, less given to trampling them underfoot at the dictates of his unique conscience. His conduct often appears to grow out of the traditional religious virtues.

The truth is that no simple black-and-white evaluation is possible. Everything depends on what the attitudes of the peer group are. If they are such as to reward high standards of conduct, the individual may be lured and led to a way of life above his natural inclinations. If the attitudes are of another kind, he will be pulled down. The way to be accepted by demons is to become a demon. But whatever the level of the peer group—good, middling, or low—there is nothing to encourage the daring innovator who wishes to introduce new values.

In reality, it is fruitless to compare the outward behavior of the two types and try to draw significant conclusions. More important is the difference in motivation. Generally speaking, the enduring ethical systems of mankind have been built on one or more of three bases. A person behaves in a particular way (a) because that way is traditional, or (b) because reason or intuition demonstrates it to be the right way, or (c) because God has revealed that the way is His will. In all of these systems, there is the conviction that a particular kind of life and conduct are objectively right, without regard to the subjective effect they may have upon the individual who follows them.

Superficially, it may appear that other-directed man is a traditionalist, but actually he is not. Mutations of outlook sometimes occur with great suddenness in the group, and he "adjusts" to the changed outlook rather than clinging to what seemed a traditional pattern of values. No, his absolute is not tradition, not reason or intuition, not the will of God. It is the approval of the group.

Inasmuch as other-directed man constantly seeks approval and acceptance, he is daily tempted to use other people. He does it quietly, subtly, and often without knowing what he is doing. He may seem to subordinating himself to their wishes; he is really manipulating them by his own adaptability—manipulating them into accepting him. He is winning friends and influencing people. The "silent leader," who by acting meek and looking wise is rising to power on some campuses, is a good example of how to succeed politically through apparent lack of ambition.

Perhaps, however, this discussion is going into speculative depths that are not too relevant here. It is sufficient to recall the main point, which is the dominance of security as the goal of college students. Its primacy is revealed almost everywhere you look—dating and courting, job-hunting, much of the religious urge, the dedicated quest for acceptance and "adjusting to the group."

I believe it was *Life* which popularized the epithet, "the silent generation," and I find no reason to quarrel with it. After the flaming twenties and the raucously political thirties, the present generation of students seems curiously subdued.

I do not observe many of them passionately excited about anything. When they flame, it is discreetly and with a subdued
glow. They tend to be apolitical and exceedingly cautious about
taking strong stands on any important issue—the recency of
the McCarthy period is undoubtedly a subduing influence,
but the political and social quietism was already apparent
before the late senator mounted horseback to slay any available dragons.

It is not my purpose to attempt a historical explanation of
the underlying causes for the total change in the campus
mentality and mood. It is worth mentioning, however, that the
nation as a whole has changed in the same direction. Until the
1930's, the tradition of rugged individualism held sway in
America, though the frontier had long since dwindled to insig-
nificance, and year by year the nation was becoming more
urban, more industrialized, more dependent on infinitely complex patterns of co-operation. During the 1930's, the inevitable
and necessary adjustment was made all along the line. With a
splendid if slapdash empiricism, the New Deal remodeled the
political, social, and economic structure of the country, and
did the job so thoroughly that no important faction seriously
proposes that the reconstruction be undone. From the 1930's
on, rugged individualism of the nineteenth-century brand,
though still invoked on solemn occasions, has not been the
living reality of American life. We have moved far toward
group consciousness, toward a more collectivistic way of life,
toward the welfare state. The individual finds increasingly
that his well-being and survival depend on co-operation rather
than on the rules of the jungle. Security and group-mindedness
may be two sides of the same coin. If the nation has moved,
haltingly but surely, in this direction, it should not surprise us
to find college students advancing a few paces farther than
their elders and embracing a less ambiguous faith in security
and social adjustment.

I think there is more to it than this. The peculiarly subdued
quality of college students has something of shell shock about
it or of the hushed waiting in the cyclone shelter. My own
generation, men and women in their forties, can remember

the relatively carefree 1920's, when prohibition seemed the most momentous of human dilemmas. But consider a college senior. He was born during the latter stages of the Depression, about the time that Prime Minister Chamberlain journeyed to Munich and betrayed Czechoslovakia. A year later Hitler invaded Poland and World War II began. The present college senior, at the age of eight or thereabouts, asked his father what was this atom bomb he heard mentioned on the radio. He entered high school as the Korean War began. From that time on, it has been one crisis after another. He is aware that the Fascist threat has been replaced by the steadier menace of world Communism. He knows that in all likelihood the cold war is here for most or all of his life. More immediately, he is faced with the personal disruption of military service.

Born into such a world, it is natural for the student to aim at modest goals. How can he control the atom bomb? What wisdom does he have to solve the problems of the Near East? Can he indulge in collective bargaining with the draft board? The broad decisions, literally of life and death, are not in his hands. A kind of fatalism grips him. If he cannot shape the broad course of human affairs, he can at least build the most comfortable cyclone cellar possible and hope that the cyclone will not pass directly overhead. His cyclone shelter is not to be disparaged. At its center is a wife and children. It also includes friends and a means of livelihood. The mentality of the cyclone shelter may not produce a Socrates, a John Brown, a Thoreau; it can and does produce good husbands, good fathers, good members of the community.

It is tempting to assume at this point that the mood of the campus has been adequately sketched. But all schematic presentations of human realities are false, particularly when great numbers of persons are being forced into conceptual molds. To make the picture slightly more three-dimensional, other factors should be mentioned. One in particular seems to call for special attention. It is nothing new, but rather a frame of mind which has been powerful for some decades. For lack of anything better to call it, I shall use the term popular positivism.

I have chosen the phrase popular positivism to emphasize that this mentality is not usually the result of austere and technical studies in logical positivism or anything else that emanates from the modern centers of philosophy. It is rather a way of looking at life, knowledge, and experience which "is floating in the air." It has little to do with educational level. Popular positivism is simply the belief that something is real if you can bang your shins against it. Every other kind of reality is suspect. Less tangible experiences are usually put in their place by a "nothing but." Love is "nothing but sex," the response to the arts is "nothing but private emotions." God, in slightly more sophisticated forms of popular positivism, is "nothing but a wish fulfillment."

The great success story of the past few centuries has been science, and undoubtedly its triumphal forward march has helped generate the cast of mind I have been describing, though I hasten to add that I do not think the scientists—particularly the really great ones—have been generally guilty of embracing and disseminating popular positivism or positivism of a more rigorous kind. It is simply that science, especially on its simpler levels, seems so very precise and capable of verification, whereas morality, the arts, and religion by contrast appear to occupy a subjective and cloudy realm. There are doubtless other factors than science—one suspects that industrialism and the growth of cities have worked in the same direction—but the priestly role of science in modern life has certainly been a key factor.

Some campus observers would prefer to speak of "the conflict between science and religion," but that is putting it too narrowly. The arts, ethics, and the meaningfulness of personal relationships are in the same boat with religion. The crucial question is whether they have their own logic and rationality (though not that of Euclid), or whether they must be consigned to a domain of pure subjectivity, where anything goes and there are no guideposts except whim and untutored emotion.

Whatever the historical reasons for popular positivism, many students bring it to campus with them, and their classes and laboratories often powerfully reinforce it. This may not be the design of the individual professors. It is the precision and elegance of the scientific method which seem to confirm what has been more vaguely held as true. The counteracting influences are, in most cases, considerably weaker.

The student can react in one of three or four ways. If he has enough imagination and courage, he can take stock of his total knowledge and total experience, which will include everything from Physics 1 to memories of watching a sunset and listening to Vivaldi. He can then try to make sense of everything, without using the escape clause of "nothing but." If he does this, he will be driven to seek a way of thinking that will grant as meaningful a place to love and beauty and wonder and awe as to the pointer readings of the laboratory or the tautologies of pure logic.

Probably few students do this. A more common alternative is to move from popular positivism to a thoroughgoing and intellectually rigorous positivism. The final result can be the conviction that nothing is meaningful except the propositions of pure logic or statements capable of empirical (i.e., scientific) verification. The whole world of love, personal relationships, art, and religion is permanently banished to a sort of limbo where it can be cherished for its emotional satisfactions but denied any real rationality.

The attempt to be a consistent positivist does not, however, necessarily end at this point. Once in a while a student positivist is really consistent, with whatever agony to himself. One by one, he discards everything that fails to meet the standards of positivism. His religion, his moral convictions, his belief that T. S. Eliot is a greater poet than Sara Teasdale—these drop by the way into the wastebasket of mere subjectivism. But being driven by a passion for consistency, he goes yet further. Along the way he is troubled by the surrealistic quality of the newer physics and disturbed by non-Euclidian geometry. Finally, he becomes aware that the vast scientific enterprise rests upon staggering acts of faith—the existence of the material universe, the uniformity of nature, the "law of parsimony," and others, none of which can be proved. He is now staring into a genuine abyss. Nothing is provable. Even his own ability to gaze into the abyss finally falls under question, for if everything else rests on an act of faith, how can he be sure of his own reality as the observer looking down into nothing?

I have not been tracing a merely hypothetical evolution. I have seen it happen with an occasional student, though quite rarely. The intellectual passion and rigor that are required are more than most people, students or otherwise, can summon up. But when it does happen, there are two ways out—frank despair or the sober determination to re-examine all possible acts of faith, making sure that those of science and logic have no inherent edge over those of religion, personal relationships, and the arts.

Most students are content to drift philosophically and avoid the sharp and ultimate questions. If a student has come to the campus a vague popular positivist, he most often remains one, and becomes a little more so. From force of habit he may cherish some lingering belief that there is meaning and rationality in things other than science and logic, but he can't put his finger on it. Insofar as he still takes religion, love, and the arts seriously, he is haunted by the suspicion that he is blindly carrying on an outworn tradition. The practical consequence is that though he may not go all the way toward a consistent positivism, his commitment in realms of experience not vindicated by the positivist canons of genuineness are likely to be wavering and weak.

I have spoken of popular positivism as a legacy from the past. At the same time, it has a curious kinship with the emergence of "other-directed man," who, as we have seen, is engaged in a quiet and infinitely subtle attempt to manipulate his fellows so as to win their approval and acceptance. There is a certain detachment and calculation to his relationships, no matter how much he may appear to be another bee in the hive. As for the person who follows popular positivism, he also is encouraged toward "objectivity," psychological distance, and a refusal to make the complete commitment of the personality to anything or anybody. I should not wish to press the kinship of the two things too far, but they do seem to have this much in common. Both mentalities make it easier to analyze—and use—one's fellows than to know them in a completeness of mutuality.

I do not wish to end without one final impression. There is a pervasive wistfulness on the campus. One finds it is much in the campus leaders and paragons of adjustment as in the occasional nonconformists. It is as though, on a deeper level, a hunger arises for something more than mere security, mere comfort, pleasant social acceptance. There is the suspicion that life is being sold short, for limited and relatively trivial prizes. This restlessness, this yearning without a clearly defined object, may not often find words; it is something which must be sensed by long experience on the campus. But it is there, I am convinced, and growing. It may be the necessary prelude to a further stage in the never static life of the campus—a stage when it will be discovered that security and acceptance and all the standard goals are infinitely desirable as long as you are striving for them, but not enough once you have them.

WILLIAM K. FRANKENA

A Point of View for the Future

CONCLUDING STATEMENT

This final chapter cannot be a conclusion of the sort that may come at the end of a book written by a single author or by a group of closely agreeing authors. It cannot simply summarize what has been said, draw inferences from it, or pull loose strings together. The preceding chapters, while relevant to the subject and helpful to those working at state universities or trying to understand the position of the state university with respect to religion, are too varied in their topics, approaches, and conclusions for any such happy ending to be possible. The best that one can do here, then, is to read them and write another essay, with the future in mind, saying what one thinks needs still to be said or perhaps repeated. But I am a philosopher teaching at a state university; hence what I shall say will be mainly philosophical, and, while it does not represent the official position of my or of any other public university, it will be said from what I take to be the point of view of such universities. Thinking Americans, says Herberg, are dissatisfied with the state of the relations between religion and public education, and they ought to be, not only because an insufficient amount of attention is given to religion by our public universities, but also because the attention is sometimes given in forms that are inappropriate in such universities. This state of affairs, as Bean suggests, is due to a tacit compromise between conflicting tendencies, and, if it is unsatisfactory, our only recourse is to get back to principles, being careful to consider only what is relevant to the problem of the state university.

Such a recourse is all the more imperative because there is, in Herberg's words, a "great upsurge of religiousness . . . sweeping the country today." We may look forward to a period of increasing concern about the treatment of religion in state universities, and we must, therefore, get our philosophical principles straight, as well as our history and our constitutional law. For the question is not merely what our founding fathers and their successors intended, nor what we can get away with in the eyes of the law or the public, as many seem to imply; the question, as Kauper sees, is what "positive considerations . . . are relevant to an appraisal of the university's function" in the area of religion.

I shall take some time, therefore, to state what I regard as the philosophy which must guide a public university in dealing with religion. Much has already been said here about this by Greene, Northrop, and others, but few if any of their discussions are complete or pointed enough in my opinion, and some of them are not restricted to the subject of education in a *state* university. I cannot, however, try to justify the philosophy in question in the space allotted; I can only seek to formulate it, and then go on to make a few more practical observations which seem to follow from it.

The main consideration involved is that of "the separation of church and state." But what, if we take it at a philosophical level and not merely at that of political expediency or even of constitutional provision, does this principle assert? Ostensibly it says that the state is not to establish or otherwise favor any one institutionally organized religion as against others; it must be neutral with respect to the "churches." Now, most influential religions are institutionally organized. Many individuals, however, hold views which are properly speaking religious, without being members of a church, or at least without fully accepting the official creed of any church. Many others, moreover, take positions which are antireligious—agnosticism, atheism, scepticism, etc.—but which incorporate some kind of answer to ultimate questions, as religions do. These positions are not church-related, and it is only confusing to call them "religions" on the ground that they embody answers to ultimate issues or are what a man does with his solitude; they are not views of the kind that are traditionally associated with religion and are better called philosophies, though of course philosophies may also be religious. Indeed, discussions of religion in state universities are often misleading because "religion" is sometimes used to mean any ultimate attitude or belief, and sometimes to mean only the kind of attitude or belief which is associated with the historic religions. In this chapter, unless otherwise indicated, I shall use "religion" only in the narrower sense.

My point, however, is this: philosophically considered, the question of the relation of church and state involves a more basic issue, namely, what is or should be the relation of the state to whatever ultimate attitudes or beliefs its members may have or come to entertain? And the answer entailed in the separation principle is that the state is not to "establish" in any way any such ultimate attitude or belief, religious or nonreligious, rational or revealed, private or institutional, prevalent or esoteric. This is the full meaning of "freedom of conscience" or "freedom of religion," if we add freedom to perform the overt acts which are called worship. It means that here is an area in which the state is to be neutral, an area which is to be left to the control of reason, morality, aesthetic taste, or prophetic or mystical insight, an area in which the individual is to be left alone with his God, his church, or his universe. That this is what is meant was forgotten even by Locke, when he wrote that "those are not at all to be tolerated who deny the being of a God." It is no less forgotten by those who talk as if only three primary faiths need to be taken seriously by a state university, and propose that a privileged position be given by it to representatives of these faiths as against others and as against nonfaiths. But God, if we may believe Jeremy Taylor, does not forget it.

We can now see in general terms what is the resulting position of a state university with regard to the treatment of religion in its academic program. A state university is an organ of the state whose function is to provide, for those who wish it, a liberal or a professional education. We shall assume here that the creation and maintenance of such an institution by the state is justified, but it should be noted that this is an assumption, for the logic of many who discuss our topic seems to point to the conclusion that there should be no state universities. As an organ of the state, however, the university must provide an education under the terms of the above principle, and, as Ingraham points out, this involves a limitation of its freedom as compared with private universities. The problem is not only the relation of the state university to religion but to all ultimate creeds, and the answer entailed by the principle of separation is that it and its staff members cannot in their official capacities serve as the organs of any church, religious faith, or ultimate belief; it and they cannot seek in any official way to inculcate or propagate any religion or other form of ultimate attitude in preference to any other. Private institutions may do so, but not public ones. These cannot in any way establish or prefer any ultimate creed to any other—not by giving financial support, by giving or withholding grades, credits, degrees, tenure, advancement, or salary increase, or by any other official act of their staff members or administration. This means, as religious writers have often pointed out, that they cannot enshrine the "religion of secularism" any more than that of Catholicism, but it also means that they cannot choose any three religions and give them any preferred status, however prevalent or well-organized they may be, as the same writers sometimes propose. It means, further, that the state university cannot prefer religious to nonreligious forms of ultimate belief, or natural religions to revealed ones. It must accord to all of them, to atheism and secularism as well as to Protestantism and Catholicism, an equal status and tolerance. It and its representatives cannot support one by their official acts or obstruct another (except when it violates the law or common morality or contradicts the established findings of science or history). In fact, they must protect each, no matter how weak, against the others, no matter how strong, and maintain a free atmosphere in which new ones may come to life and possibly even triumph over the old.

The state university, then, must be neutral or impartial as

between religions and ultimate views. But, it may be argued, if it cannot in any manner inculcate or propagate any one such creed, then it must inculcate or propagate them all and so maintain a kind of neutrality—indoctrinating the students in Catholicism in one course, in orthodox Judaism in another, in atheism in a third, in Marxism in a fourth, etc., and leaving always one place where some wandering St. Paul may preach an Unknown God. This is rarely, if ever, explicitly advocated, but it is logically implied in one sort of argument that is given for the three-faith approach, and is suggested by those who hold that the university must not stand apart from the present conflict on basic issues. It seems clear, however, that this approach can only be hopelessly confusing in practice, and the three-faith plan is sometimes offered as a compromise which goes part of the way toward this "ideal" but is still feasible. But, if we must compromise, it would seem better to do so in another way, namely, by giving up the effort to inculcate or propagate religions or other ultimate credos at all. This way has rightly appeared, though it is not always consistently or rigorously maintained, in many discussions of the teaching of religion in state universities. The opponents of the three or many-faith approach have naturally emphasized it. But even the proponents of this approach have often disowned any effort to indoctrinate or proselyte, resting their case on the claim that students must be informed about the various religions and that only one who holds a position is really competent to inform them about it.

This second conception of neutrality or impartiality in the treatment of religion has been well-stated by John Stuart Mill in his Inaugural Address as rector of St. Andrews University. Speaking of the teaching of moral philosophy and religion, Mill writes:

> . . . it is not the teacher's business to impose his own judgment, but to inform and discipline that of his student. . . . The proper business of an University is . . . not to tell us from authority what we ought to believe, and make us accept the belief as a duty, but to give us information and training, and help us to form our own belief in a manner worthy of intelligent beings, who seek for truth at all

hazards, and demand to know all the difficulties, in order that they may be better qualified to find, or recognize, the most satisfactory mode of resolving them.

It would be unfair, however, to regard such a conception as merely a compromise due to the impracticability of an equal propagation by a single university of all the conflicting world-views. For it is doubtful, as a matter of principle, that it is the function of a state university to inculcate or indoctrinate at all, at least in the region of ultimate attitudes and beliefs. All such propagation, one may reasonably contend, belongs to the home, the church, church-related schools, and personal contact between free individuals, and is not the proper province of an organ of the state. This is the burden of the old theme of rendering unto Caesar and God, respectively, the things that are theirs—of delegating temporal power to the state but leaving the spiritual realm to churches and other voluntary associations or to the individual in his solitude. As Father Murray puts it:

> . . . the function of the university is not at all messianic. It is entirely minimal. . . . if post-modern man hopes for salvation, he must set his hope elsewhere than on the university.

The state university must remember this, and if necessary remind its students, their parents, and the religious denominations that the primary responsibility for the concerns of the spirit is not its but theirs. To quote Mill again:

> The various Churches, established and unestablished, are quite competent to the task which is peculiarly theirs, that of teaching each its own doctrines, as far as necessary, to its own rising generation.

Must the state university, according to this conception, be secular as well as impartial and neutral? The term "secular" is ambiguous. A public university must be secular in the sense that it must not put its official weight behind religious world-views, or in opposition to nonreligious ones. This does not mean, however, that its administrators and professors need to be agnostics or naturalists, though they may be; it does not mean that they must be irreligious in their private views or even neutral with respect to religions in their personal lives. Neither does it mean, of course, that the university must be officially against religion. A private university may, but a public one may not, be secular in the further sense of being opposed to religious faith, to revelation, or to what is not susceptible of scientific verification or objective rational treatment. To the extent to which state universities have espoused the ultimate creed of scientism, or any of the "philosophies of secularism," their neutrality may be rightly criticized as malevolent by those who are religious. But, for all this, they must welcome the antireligious as well as the religious student and tolerate unofficial opposition to religion in members of its staff; they must never allow themselves to be put into the position, because of pressure or because of the plans which they adopt for dealing with religion, of having to appoint or dismiss a man, admit or expel a student, or withhold any degree, grade, or preferment for anyone because of his ultimate beliefs. They may do so only on the basis of his other qualifications, even in the case of the "religious co-ordinator," or on the basis of incompetence, or of overt acts of treason, moral turpitude, and the like.

The task of the state university, then, on its academic side, is to "inform" and "discipline" its students in order to provide them with a liberal or a professional education. Here "to inform" means to pass on to them the generally accepted results of objective inquiry. "To discipline" means to train them to carry on such inquiry for themselves, and in general to develop their critical, imaginative, and intellectual faculties, as well as their moral character and aesthetic sensibility—and, on request, to train them for a vocation. This is why it has the right and the duty to teach history, mathematics, the sciences, the humanities, languages, and professional skills. But if it is fully to carry out its obligation to inform, it must also give an important place to courses about religion and other kinds of ultimate attitudes or beliefs—courses in the history of the

Judeo-Christian faiths, in comparative religion, in the psychology, sociology, and anthropology of religion, as well as in philosophy. This point has been made by Greene, Father Murray, and others, and need not be elaborated here. If the university does not offer an adequate program of such courses, then again it can be accused by the churches of being malevolently neutral, since it will be giving the student the impression that religion and philosophy are of little import in the past or present life of man. Of course, it must see that such courses are objective and scholarly, else they do not inform but mislead or proselyte; but, so long as they are, they are not in the least jeopardized by the principle of separation or of rendering unto Caesar, as Kauper has shown. As Mill has it:

Why should it be impossible, that information of the greatest value, on subjects connected with religion, should be brought before the student's mind; that he should be made acquainted with so important a part of the national thought, and of the intellectual labours of past generations, as those relating to religion, without being taught dogmatically the doctrines of any church or sect?

However, Greene, Father Murray, Miss White, and others are not content with courses *about* religion, courses designed merely to remedy the religious illiteracy so prevalent in the student body. They desire a yet more benevolent neutrality. Is it possible and desirable for a public university in its academic program positively to aid and encourage religion, as well as to inform about it? Not, as we have seen, if this means preferring religious to other forms of metaphysical or ultimate beliefs, and not if it means indoctrination in some religious faith. Yet it is true, as Shuster says, that without any ultimate perspective or center of some kind, "a man will be only half himself." May we assert then that even a state university, if it is to contribute satisfactorily to the development of its students, may and should aid them in the formation or selection of a philosophy or religion? It seems to me that we may, if we are careful in our assertion.

The public university cannot seek to lead its students to one kind of ultimate commitment rather than another, but it may encourage them to choose or work out some world-view and to commit themselves to it, although with tolerance for others; and its professors may even in class, and certainly in private, make clear their own positions with their reasons, so long as they do so undogmatically and without propagandizing. This in itself would be an important contribution, for many in recent years have accused our liberal universities of preaching agnosticism or scepticism, of propagating a kind of noncommittalism. But if the university takes this approach it must remember that atheism, naturalism, and scepticism are permissible ultimate positions as much as any others, so far as it is concerned. It must not beg any questions about what is "really ultimate."

It must remember also that even by offering its students information about the various philosophies and religions of the world, their history, psychology, sociology, their grounds and methods, the university is helping them to arrive at more enlightened conclusions about ultimate questions. If I may quote Mill again:

All that social and public education has in its power to do, further than by a general pervading tone of reverence and duty, amounts to little more than the information which it can give; but this is extremely valuable.

There is, however, a "little more." As part of its task of "discipline," the university can and should give its students training in how to think intelligently, both critically and constructively, about ultimate issues. In what will be my last quotation from Mill, he contends:

If teaching, even on matters of scientific certainty, should aim quite as much at showing how the results are arrived at as at teaching the results themselves, far more, then, should this be the case on subjects where there is the widest diversity of opinion among men of equal ability, and who have taken equal pains to arrive at the truth.

Here indeed, lies the main point of teaching philosophy in a state institution, in particular, moral philosophy, the philosophy of history, and the philosophy of religion. But courses in the history of philosophy, in comparative religion, and in the sciences of religion also have their disciplinary side, and give training in dealing with various kinds of questions about ultimate commitments. It is hard to see how any course with a more "positive religious orientation" can be designed to cultivate intelligent thinking about religious and other basic issues, without being too specifically religious for a state-supported college, but it should be possible to devise courses in the history or comparison of theologies which will do so.

Art and literature also have a contribution to make, which must not be ignored here. The study and appreciation of poetry, fiction, drama, painting, and so forth, have their own function in the aesthetic education of man, which is one of the tasks of a university, but they can also serve to supplement the studies already mentioned as informing and training the student's mind with respect to ultimate questions. For they can give him a feeling for and an imaginative realization of the essence of any given religion or philosophy as this is experienced by one who lives by it, and they can do so without inculcating or propagating it, because, as has often been remarked, the understanding of the meaning of a work of art involves a "willing suspension" of belief and disbelief in any dogmatic sense. Here then is a kind of spiritual enrichment which the state university may provide and which can do much to meet the desire for more than courses *about* religion.

These seem to me important ways in which a public university can and should teach subjects relating to the formation of or commitment to ultimate faiths or views. In these ways it can help to give its students the knowledge and the discipline which they need to make their world-views, whether they are already chosen or not, more enlightened and more intelligent than they would be otherwise. More it cannot do on its academic side, so far as I can see. That is for the individual himself to do or his church if he has one, except for what the university can add through its counseling and extracurricular programs.

In these programs the same goals may and should be pursued subject to the same guiding principles. Here too are many ways in which the university can foster a serious concern for ultimate questions and promote the relevant information and discipline, for example by inviting outstanding representatives of different faiths and philosophies to interpret their positions in occasional lectures or discussion groups. But here also there are many more ways in which the university can helpfully co-operate with parents, religious centers, and other voluntary organizations which may be concerned with "spiritual" matters. These have been outlined in detail in some of the earlier chapters. In extracurricular activities and discussions, furthermore, it is possible and appropriate for a member of the faculty to exert a more positive personal influence on a student's attitude and thought about basic issues than he can in class, as long as he makes it clear that he is not acting in his official capacity and behaves in a manner consistent with his belonging to a community of scholars. Finally, in its provisions for extracurricular affairs the university can do much to initiate or facilitate co-operation between the various student religious groups connected with the campus. It must, of course, leave them free, as Lelyveld insists, but even so it may and should seek to foster democracy, tolerance, reasonableness, and mutual understanding. As Father Murray emphasizes, it must not promote any "bogus irenicisms" or any religions of the common denominator, for then it is espousing a certain ultimate creed. It should, however, draw foreign students and their religions or philosophies into the picture, because Northrop is right when he says that it is both practically necessary and spiritually rewarding for us to understand the spirit and the values of their cultures.

Various plans for dealing with religion, both in and out of the curriculum, have been proposed for or adopted by state universities; and certainly it is wise that such universities should experiment with a variety of arrangements. It is not possible to discuss them at length here in the light of what has been said so far in this chapter; I must simply hope that the application of what has been said will be reasonably clear. Some existing plans, however, do seem to be of doubtful propriety in a public university, and I shall therefore venture a few remarks. As I said before, it seems clear to me that such a university cannot properly adopt any scheme which involves appointing a man because he holds a certain kind of ultimate creed or dismissing him if he changes his mind. It is also inappropriate, in my opinion, for it to adopt a plan which it is not ready to pay for out of state funds. It would likewise seem questionable for it to answer pressure by giving credit for courses taught in religious centers which are not fully accredited colleges, for if they are such that it can properly give credit for them it can also properly offer them itself. As for giving credit for courses on religion transferred from denominational colleges, it should do so only if upon scrutiny they are clearly taught in the spirit and with the competence which it would ask of its own teachers if they were to teach them. About the three-primary-faith plan I wish to add two observations. The first is that Catholicism, Protestantism, and Judaism are not the only live options in the western world; there are also existentialism, Marxism, and democratic secularism which may well claim to be represented in such a program. The other is that, if Northrop is correct, then Buddhism, Islam, and perhaps still other religions must also be represented. As was indicated earlier, however, I have grave doubts about the validity of any such plan. The argument that only a man who holds a certain position is competent adequately to present it is weighty, but not conclusive, in its favor.

It is sometimes suggested, for example by Greene, that a university should provide opportunity for primary religious experience as a kind of equivalent for the scientific laboratory or the art studio. Now, it is not clear that Greene is thinking of public universities when he makes his suggestion, but to me it is doubtful that such universities can themselves sponsor religious services. Perhaps it may do so if it makes clear that these services are only religious exhibits, but if they are performed in this spirit will they be bona fide expressions of religion? It would seem better for all religious services to be sponsored by churches or student groups, perhaps with some encouragement by the university, which might then remind interested students of the opportunities thus provided for seeing various religious faiths in action.

However, if some existing plans appear to go too far, there are others that do not go far enough, for example, those which include little or no university-sponsored academic work or extracurricular activity relating to religion. Such cautious plans are hardly required by the present state of public opinion or by philosophical principles. Where they are or appear to be dictated by the state constitution, it may be necessary for interested people to petition for a constitutional amendment. This would have to be carefully stated in terms of an adequate philosophy of the role of the state university, and its success would require its supporters to go about educating the public in this philosophy. Indeed, since there are those who are proreligious and those who are con, those who ask too much of the state university and those who ask too little, such a program of education is imperative anyway even where no constitutional amendment is necessary. In such a program the state universities must take the lead, and their spokesmen should be chosen from their faculties and administrations proper; they should not allow themselves to be represented only by those who have a vested interest in religion, as they so often have in the past. But, of course, they should enlist the co-operation of the many able and friendly religious leaders who are willing to help them.

Whatever the scheme adopted, the crucial problem, as several previous writers have seen, is to find the right men to do the teaching, counseling, and co-ordinating that is involved. The right man can make almost any plan satisfactory which is consistent with the above principles, the wrong man can cause even the best-laid scheme to "gang agley." The right man is, first, one who accepts the state university point of view, which I have tried to interpret here; second, one who is unusually able and objective as a scholar, thinker, teacher, counselor, or administrator in subjects and activities relating to religion and ultimate issues, whatever his own basic commitment may be. Such men are hard to find, and it is imperative that careful thought be given by the universities and by religious leaders to the discovery and training of people to work in religion at public institutions, and that interested young men be carefully advised about their preparation. The need must be met, but it must be well met. And again a caution must be added: while it is desirable that these people understand religion and philosophy well, and perhaps that some of them be sympathetic with religion or even personally committed to a certain religion, it cannot in a public university be a condition of their appointment or tenure that they subscribe to any particular kind of ultimate belief.

I fear that this chapter will be regarded as hopelessly "liberal" and "modern" by those who believe that we are in "the postmodern age." Perhaps we are in a new age which is to be guided by other ideas than the previous one, if by any ideas at all. If so, the state university must, of course, be realistic and take cognizance of this fact, for it must keep abreast of the times. But it should lead and not merely follow; in Pusey's words, quoted by Bean, it should give "service without servility." The mere fact, if it is a fact, that historical events have pushed us into a new era does nothing to establish the invalidity of earlier ideas. Historical change does not in itself justify the new either in philosophy, in science, or in morality. It may well be then that, in being a leader, the state university must drag its feet somewhat in response to "the current upsurge of religiousness." This upsurge is itself to a considerable extent a product of historical events, of the hot and cold wars, and political uncertainties of recent decades. It must not be presumed to be permanent; theologians themselves have often decried the superficiality of much of this newly acquired religiosity. In any case, the public university cannot take this upsurge as calling it to take on a religious mission itself, even though it may construe it as a call to do something more about religion than it has been doing.

Yet the point of view of this chapter is not really "secularist"; it does not advocate that the state university may or should embody and teach "the religion of the Enlightenment" or "the philosophy of secularism." It holds, rather, that such a university should strive to be neutral in the sense explained above with respect to such an ultimate creed as well as with respect to religious ones. So far I am ready to go with those who reject "modernity" or "secularism." This step of disowning the "secularist" conception of the state university is all that I find plausible in the arguments of the postmodernists, and it seems to me merely to involve drawing the logical consequences of one line of thinking in the democratic liberalism of the past. If the postmodernists reply that the neutrality described here is impossible, I can only say, "I am not convinced, but, as we believe in democracy, let us try in our state universities to approximate it."

Notes

Chapter III

1. W. H. van de Pol, D.D., *The Christian Dilemma* (New York: Philosophical Library, 1952), p. 21.
2. Nicolas Berdyaev, *Truth and Revelation* (London: Geoffrey Bles, 1953), pp. 47-48.
3. *Ibid.*, p. 40.
4. Edmund W. Sinnott, *Two Roads to Truth* (New York: The Viking Press, 1953), pp. 44-45.
5. *Ibid.*, p. 192.
6. H. Richard Niebuhr, *The Meaning of Revelation* (New York: Macmillan, 1946), pp. 112-13.
7. *Ibid.*, pp. 153-54.
8. *Ibid.*, p. 119.
9. George A. Tavard, *The Catholic Approach to Protestantism* (New York: Harper and Brothers, 1955).
10. Robert J. Welsh, *Religious Education,* Nov.-Dec., 1956, p. 426.

Chapter IV

1. See M. Willard Lampe, *The Story of an Idea: The History of the School of Religion at the State University of Iowa,* State University of Iowa Extension Bulletin No. 704, March 1, 1955; Henry E. Allen, "Practices of Land Grant Colleges and State Universities Affecting Religious Matters," *School and Society,* December 6, 1952; Edward W. Blakeman, "Curricular Religion in Our State Universities," *Religious Education,* July-Aug., 1953; Walton Bean, "Historical Developments Affecting the Place of Religion in the State University Curriculum," *Religious Education,* Sept.-Oct., 1955.

Chapter V

1. For general treatments of the legal aspects of the problem, see A. P. Stokes, *Church and State in the United States* (New York: Harper and Brothers, 1950); L. Pfeffer, *Church, State and Freedom* (Boston: Beacon, 1953); A. W. Johnson and F. H. Yost, *Separation of*

Church and State in the United States (Minneapolis: University of Minnesota Press, 1948).

2. For discussions of these questions, see the papers by C. P. Shedd, E. F. Waite, and L. Pfeffer in H. E. Allen (ed.), *Religion in the State University: An Initial Exploration* (Minneapolis: Burgess, 1950); also L. Pfeffer, *Church, State and Freedom*, pp. 421-23; M. Cuminggim, *The College Seeks Religion* (New Haven: Yale University Press, 1947), pp. 123-30.

3. The provisions of the state constitutions are collected in C. H. Moehlman, *The American Constitutions and Religion* (Berne, Indiana, 1938).

4. See, e.g., Maine Const., Art. I, Sec. 3; Conn. Const., Art. I, Secs. 3-4, Art. VII; S. C. Const., Art. I, Secs. 9-10.

5. See, e.g., Ill. Const., Art. II, Sec. 3, Art. VIII, Sec. 3; Mich. Const., Art. II, Sec. 3; Mo. Const., Art. II, Secs. 5-8, Art. XI, Sec. 11. Apart from constitutional limitations, the charters under which a number of state universities and colleges operate forbid sectarian instruction.

6. See, e.g., Col. Const., Art. IX, Sec. 8; Mont. Const., Art. XI, Sec. 9.

7. Wash. Const., Art. I, Sec. 11; Ariz. Const., Art. II, Sec. 12; Utah Const., Art. I, Sec. 4.

8. Thus it may be noted that while in some states the constitutional provisions directed against sectarian education apply only to public schools (e.g., Col. Const., Art. IX, Sec. 8; N.D. Const., Art. VIII, Sec. 152), the constitutional provisions of other states bar sectarian instruction in all of the state's educational institutions. See, e.g., Nebr. Const., Art. VIII, Sec. 11; Mont. Const., Art. XI, Sec. 9. The Wisconsin Constitution (Art. X, Sec. 6) expressly forbids sectarian instruction at the university.

9. For a discussion of the state court decisions pro and con on this question, see A. W. Johnson and F. H. Yost, *op. cit.*, pp. 41-73.

10. *People ex rel. Lewis v. Graves*, 245 N. Y. 195 (1927); *Zorach v. Clauson*, 303 N. Y. 161 (1951); *People ex rel. Latimer v. Board of Education of City of Chicago*, 394 Ill. 228 (1946); *Gordon v. Board of Education of Los Angeles*, 78 Cal. App. (2d) 464 (1947).

11. *North v. Board of Trustees of the University of Illinois*, 137 Ill. 296 (1891). In a suit brought by a taxpayer against the University of Minnesota to enjoin the University from permitting use of its facilities by student religious groups, the Minnesota Supreme Court, without reaching a decision on the merits of the question, dismissed the suit on the ground that the taxpayer should first have presented the matter to the institution's governing board. *State ex rel. Sholes v. University of Minnesota*, 54 N.W. (2d) 122 (1952).

12. See C. P. Shedd, "Religion in the American State Universities: Its History and Present Problems," in H. E. Allen (ed.), *op. cit.*, pp. 20-21, 23; H. P. Van Dusen, *God in Education* (New York: Charles Scribner's Sons, 1951), p. 111.

13. For a summary survey, see C. P. Shedd's paper cited in note 12, pp. 23-26.

14. Substantially the same conclusion is expressed by Leo Pfeffer in *Church, State and Freedom*, p. 453.

15. The U.S. Supreme Court has held that a taxpayer as such has no standing to question Bible-reading exercises in a state's public schools as long as he does not show that this practice involves added out-of-pocket costs at the expense of tax-raised funds. *Doremus* v. *Board of Education*, 342 U.S. 429 (1952).

16. See the opinion of the Michigan Attorney General, July 7, 1950, No. 1256, holding that tax-raised funds could validly be used to build a student center at a state college in conjunction with a chapel built with funds received by gift.

Chapter VIII

1. See Paul Tillich, *Protestant Era, Courage To Be, Systematic Theology,* etc.

2. See my "Art as the Vehicle of Religious Worship" in *Religion in Life,* VII (1938): 93-105.

Chapter IX

1. Adam Smith, *The Wealth of Nations* (Modern Library edition), p. 745.

2. *The Protestant Ethic and the Spirit of Capitalism* (New York, 1930).

3. Emile Durkheim, *The Elementary Forms of the Religious Life* (London, 1915).

4. Gordon W. Allport, *The Individual and His Religion: A Psychological Interpretation* (New York, 1930).

Chapter X

1. The idea of a closed but unbounded system is best grasped by the novice by considering the surface of a sphere, which is of limited area but as a surface has no edges. If we consider not a surface on a three-dimensional figure but a volume on a four-dimensional figure, we should have the required model of a closed unbounded universe.

2. At least according to legend; various estimates of Laplace's own position have been published.

3. The argument of this section, as Chaninah Marienthal reminds me, leans heavily on C. S. Peirce.

4. J. C. Eccles in *Nature*, 168 (1951): 53-57, however, suggests that complexity per unit volume, which is probably greater in the human brain than anywhere else in the known universe, may, in some way not yet understood, be profoundly significant.

5. By conscious behavior, I mean behavior involving report in some explicit language of subjective elements such as images, perceptions,

or any kind of effect. The fact that these elements may succeed one another in an incoherent way is irrelevant to the argument.

6. The best account of telepathy is that of S. G. Soal and F. Bateman, *Modern Experiments in Telepathy* (New Haven, Conn.: Yale University Press, 1954). The best experiment in psychokinesis is perhaps in R. A. McConnell, R. J. Snowdon, and K. F. Powell, "Wishing with Dice," *Journ. Exper. Psychol.* 50 (1955): 269-75.

Chapter XIII

1. *Face Your Life with Confidence* (New York: Prentice-Hall, Inc., 1953), pp. 173 ff.

2. The reader should note that the six categories mentioned here are about "presented problems," or the immediately felt needs. They are useful if this fact is understood. They do not attempt to distinguish, for instance, the student whose underlying problem is gaining independence from his parental home, or the student who has developed compulsive trends that pervade his life and work, or the student who is in danger of alcoholism. As presented problems, felt needs, or symptoms, these have plainly a religious significance; but other people may have religious problems also at a deeper level, even if the religious aspect is not obvious at first inspection.

3. As recently as 1947, a responsible discussion presented the first form but wholly omitted reference to the second. See Kate H. Mueller *et al.*, *Counseling for Mental Health* (American Council on Education, Series VI, Student Personnel Work, No. 8 [1947]), p. 63.

4. See my *Sex Ethics and the Kinsey Reports* (New York: Association Press, 1953).

5. Philip E. Jacob, *Changing Values in College* (New Haven, Conn.: Edward W. Hazen Foundation, 1956), especially pp. 3-4.

6. For a thoughtful psychological analysis of some aspects of the current religious "revival," see the article by Milton J. Rosenberg in *Pastoral Psychology*, Vol. 8, No. 75 (June, 1957).

7. I discussed this question at greater length in the Allerton Park Conference Report, a document issued for limited circulation by its editor, Milton D. McLean, of Ohio State University. This reported on a joint conference of religious workers and student personnel workers from the Big Ten universities of the Midwest, held in 1955.

8. Still notable for its general approach to religious counseling of students, including the responsibility of those who are not professional religious workers, is *Religious Counseling of College Students*, by Thornton W. Merriam, *et al.* (American Council on Education, Series VI, Student Personnel Work, No. 4 [1943]).

9. The fragmentation danger emerging out of increased specialized services is warned against by E. G. Williamson in *The Teacher as Counselor* by Donald J. Shank *et al.* (American Council on Education, Series VI, Student Personnel Work, No. 10 [1948]), p. iii.

Chapter XIV

1. Figures are not available for the total building investment of all groups, though the helpful, unpublished 1953 study of Parker Rossman, "Church Student Work Since 1938," for the Department of Religion in Higher Education, Yale Divinity School, lists some interesting figures. For example, in 1953 the Methodist centers were valued at $8,715,312, the Jewish at $4,500,000, and the Lutheran at $2,000,000. The Catholic centers recently completed were valued at Minnesota at $600,000, at Colorado at $500,000, and at Arkansas at $300,000. The Interfaith Center at Cornell, the gift of Myron Taylor, is valued at more than $2,000,000.

2. See the mimeographed study by John Peter Thomas and Malcolm A. Carpenter, "Religious Centers for Student Work: A Yale Study," (rev. ed.; New Haven: Yale Studies in Religion in Higher Education, 1947).

3. See C. Grey Austin's paper tracing this development at the University of Michigan, "A Century of Religion at the University of Michigan" (Ann Arbor: University of Michigan, 1957), and Richard Henry Edwards' *Cooperative Religion at Cornell University* (Ithaca, N.Y.: Cornell University, 1939).

4. Seymour A. Smith, *Religious Cooperation in State Universities* (Ann Arbor: University of Michigan, 1957), p. 4.

5. Austin, *op. cit.*, gives this whole development.

6. *Ibid.*, p. 24 ff. for this development at Michigan.

7. See M. Willard Lampe, *The Story of an Idea: History of the School of Religion at the State University of Iowa* (Bulletin No. 704, State University of Iowa, March 1, 1955).

8. Smith, *op. cit.*, p. 76.

9. Rossman, *op. cit.*, Table II.

10. The reader will recognize the influence of Paul Tillich in this definition of man's religious concern. See his *Love, Power, and Justice* (New York: Oxford University Press, 1954), pp. 109 ff., and *Dynamics of Faith* (New York: Harper and Brothers, 1957), especially chap. I.

11. For a general survey, see Smith, *op. cit.*, and Austin, *op. cit.*

12. A recent unpublished study made by the staff at Cornell University.

13. Note the way in which local and regional YMCA's and YWCA's in Georgia, Texas, North Carolina, and Florida, as well as other denominational and faith groups, are making slow but steady inroads on the problem. This is frequently in the face of deep and divisive opposition from religious groups and parent bodies, as well as of political and university pressures.

14. The term "object" may be misleading. God is not to be thought of

as an object among other objects in space and time. The term here is used as a referent only, and not as a clue to God's nature.

15. See the suggestive study bearing out this general conviction of the religious center regarding responsibility and learning in Philip E. Jacobs' *Changing Values in College* (New Haven, Conn.: Edward W. Hazen Foundation, 1957). See also the report prepared for the Commission on Student Personnel of the American Council on Education by Harry H. Lunn, Jr., *The Student's Role in College Policy-Making* (Washington, D.C.: American Council on Education, 1957).

17. See Will Herberg's study of the sociology of this development in *Protestant, Catholic, Jew* (Garden City, N.Y.: Doubleday, 1955).

18. Penn State, Kansas State, and the University of Maryland have sought to solve the problem through erecting interfaith chapels with changeable altar and liturgical appointments in order that each faith might worship with integrity in accord with its own tradition.

19. See the unpublished manuscript by Jeanne S. Brown, "Religion in the State University and Colleges" (Yale Divinity School, 1952).

20. University of Illinois.

21. University of Missouri.

22. University of Kansas.

23. University of Iowa.

24. In Rossman's study, *op. cit.*, in 1953 there were 2,971 religious groups on college campuses, 852 full-time and 1,008 part-time professional religious workers, building investments upwards of $20,000,000, and national and local budgets well over $5,000,000.

25. This has been reflected in the amazing increase in number of administrative appointed positions in university religious work, from around 40 in 1945 to well over 225 at the present time.

26. How often has the sensitive Jew been offended by being asked to read a Christological Biblical passage in the university chapel, for instance?

Chapter XV

1. *Changing Values in College* (New Haven, Conn.: Edward Hazen Foundation, 1957), p. 3 ff.

2. *Ibid.*, p. 5.

3. *Ibid.*, p. 22. (This conclusion has been attacked as a statistical finding based on a preconceived and narrow definition of the term "religious," unmodified by any study of attitude changes in the individual.)

4. *Ibid.*, 7 f.

5. University of Minnesota: Office of the Dean of Students. Bureau History: Coordinator of Students' Religious Activities. August, 1954. p. 2.

6. See Cuninggim, *The College Seeks Religion* (New Haven, Conn.: Yale University, 1947).

7. See Edmund G. Williamson, in *Religion in the State University: An Initial Exploration*, Henry E. Allen, ed. (Minneapolis, Minn.: Burgess, 1950), p. 2.

8. An interesting sidelight from the perspective of a Catholic student worker is supplied by Robert J. Welsh, chaplain to Catholic students and Professor of Religion, School of Religion, State University of Iowa (*Religious Education*, Nov.-Dec., 1956, p. 425 f).

    "Very often, without thinking about it (and I suppose they might be shocked if they thought they appeared that way) these campus religious councils actually do presume that their organization is a Protestant organization. This is perhaps due to the fact that, numerically, the Protestants are so much greater than Jew or Catholic and because, traditionally and historically, their place in the university antedates our own. . . .

    "I have often thought that if I were a Jew sitting in on a meeting of an interreligious group which simply presumed that the statement 'Christian' took care of everybody, I probably would feel that justice was not being done to me."

9. Henry E. Allen quotes a response from one tax-supported campus in which the threat of control is made overt: "The University should insist upon approving the various religious workers assigned to campus groups . . . If college chapters of religious organizations are to function on a campus, it is imperative that the University set up some means of active coordination and integration and, frankly, control." *School and Society*, Dec. 6, 1952, p. 363.

10. The President of the University of Maryland explained that "No appropriations from tax funds have been used in the erection of the chapel. The maintenance of the chapel will be budgeted along with other University buildings. The chapel is to be used for religious purposes exclusively. The University will not assume responsibility for any religious services of a denominational nature, but will conduct, at stated intervals, non-denominational services for all . . ." Quoted by Henry E. Allen in "Practices of Land-Grant Colleges and State Universities Affecting Religious Matters." *School and Society*, Dec. 6, 1952, p. 362. The anachronistic character of this arrangement is made clear in the discussion above.

11. Cornell University has a similar setup in its new Anabel Taylor Hall, but since Cornell is not a state university it has been able to place the hall in the center of the campus as an integral part of the University.

12. See Marcus Bach: *Of Faith and Learning* (State University of Iowa, 1952). The Bible College founded by the Disciples at the University of Missouri has a similar structure.

13. The papers presented at this conference appear in *Religion in the*

State University: An Initial Exploration, Henry E. Allen, ed. (Minneapolis, Minn.: Burgess, 1950).

14. Se Allyn P. Robinson, ed., *And Crown Thy Good: A Manual on Interreligious Cooperation on the College Campus* (New York: NCCJ, 1954).

15. "Religious Pluralism on Campus," The Allerton Conference Report in *Religious Education,* Nov.-Dec., 1956.

16. *Religious Education,* Nov.-Dec., 1956, p. 421.

17. See Philip Jacob, *op. cit.,* chap. VI, p. 99.

Chapter XVI

1. Available on request from the Embassy of Burma, Washington, D.C.

2. Boston: Houghton Mifflin, 1948, p. 36.

3. Marvin Bressler and Richard D. Lambert, *Indian Students on an American Campus* (Minneapolis: University of Minnesota Press, 1956).

4. London: Murray, 1908.

5. *European Union and United States Foreign Policy* (New York: Macmillan, 1954).

6. Calcutta: University of Calcutta Press, 1946.

7. Jacques Masui, ed., *Yoga; sicence de l'homme intégral* (Paris: Les Cahiers du Sud, 1953). See also Pitirim A. Sorokin, ed., *Forms and Techniques of Altruistic and Spiritual Growth* (Boston: Beacon Press, 1954).

8. *The Law of Primitive Man, a Study in Comparative Legal Dynamics* (Cambridge, Mass.: Harvard University Press, 1954).

The Authors

ROLAND HERBERT BAINTON is the Titus Street Professor of Ecclesiastical History at Yale University. Author of *Here I Stand, A Life of Martin Luther, The Reformation of the Sixteenth Century, Hunted Heretic: A Study of Michael Servetus,* he is also a frequent contributor to religious journals.

WALTON ELBERT BEAN is Professor of History at the University of California at Berkeley, an expert on United States history and on the history of the American state university. He is the author of *Boss Ruef's San Francisco.*

KENNETH EWART BOULDING, Professor of Economics at the University of Michigan, was the recipient of the Clark Medal from the American Economic Association in 1949 and is the author of *Economic Analysis, The Organizational Revolution, A Reconstruction of Economics, There Is a Spirit* (The Naylor Sonnets), and *The Image.*

WILLIAM KLAAS FRANKENA, Professor of Philosophy and Chairman of the Department of Philosophy, University of Michigan, has contributed a number of articles to *The Dictionary of Philosophy* and many to current philosophical journals.

THEODORE MEYER GREENE, for several years Professor of Philosophy at Yale University, is now the Henry Burr Alexander Professor in Humanities at Scripps College, Claremont, California. He is the author of *Liberal Education Reconsidered, Arts and the Art of Criticism,* and *Our Cultural Heritage.*

WILL HERBERG is the Professor of Judaic Studies and Social Philosophy at Drew University, where he teaches both in the Graduate School and in the Theological School. His most recent book is a sociological study entitled *Protestant-Catholic-Jew: An Essay in American Religious Sociology.*

SEWARD HILTNER, Professor of Pastoral Theology at The University of Chicago, has served as Executive Secretary both for the Council for Clinical Training of Theological Students and for the Department of Pastoral Services of the Federal Council of Churches of Christ in America. He is the author of *Religion and Health, Pastoral Counseling, Self-Understanding, The Counselor in Counseling,* and is at present a consultant to the *Journal of Pastoral Psychology.*

GEORGE EVELYN HUTCHINSON is the Sterling Professor of Zoology and Director of Graduate Studies in Zoology at Yale University. He has served as consultant in biogeochemistry for the American Museum of Natural History and as a consulting geochemist for the United States Geological Survey. He is the author of *The Clear Mirror, The Itinerant Ivory Tower,* and numerous scientific papers on aquatic insects, limnology, and biogeochemistry.

MARK HOYT INGRAHAM is Professor of Mathematics and Dean of the College of Letters and Science at The University of Wisconsin. He is a former president of the American Association of University Professors and a frequent contributor to mathematical journals.

PAUL GERHARDT KAUPER, Professor of Law at the University of Michigan and a member of the Board of Higher Education of the American Lutheran Church, is the author of *Cases and Materials on Constitutional Law.*

ARTHUR JOSEPH LELYVELD, Executive Secretary of the America-Israel Cultural Foundation, has served as Rabbi for congregations in Ohio and Nebraska, as National Director of B'nai B'rith Hillel Foundations, and in various positions with many other community and religious agencies. He is an outstanding lecturer and a contributor of articles to the *Universal Jewish Encyclopedia* and to numerous periodicals.

JOHN COURTNEY MURRAY, S.J., is Professor of Theology at Woodstock College and editor of *Theological Studies.* He was formerly an associate editor of *America,* and in 1950 was the recipient of the Cardinal Spellman Award from the American Catholic Theological Society.

FILMER STUART CUCKOW NORTHROP is the Sterling Professor of Philosophy and Law at Yale University and Professor Extraordinaire at the National Autonomous University of Mexico. He is the author of *Science and First Principles, The Logic of the Sciences and the Humanities, The Taming of the Nations, The*

Meeting of East and West, and *European Union and United States Foreign Policy.*

GLENN A. OLDS, Director of United Religious Work at Cornell University and former Professor of Philosophy at Garrett Biblical Institute, is a Fellow in the National Council on Religion in Higher Education and the author of *The Christian Corrective* and of articles in the *International Journal of Ethics* and other periodicals.

GEORGE NAUMAN SHUSTER, President of Hunter College, has served as an adviser to the State Department's Division of Cultural Relations, as a delegate to UNESCO conferences, and as Land Commissioner for Bavaria. He is a contributing editor and former managing editor of *Commonweal* and the author of *The Catholic Spirit in America, Religion and Education,* and *Religion Behind the Iron Curtain.*

ROBERT MANNING STROZIER, until recently Professor of Romance Languages and Literature and Dean of Students at The University of Chicago, is now President of Florida State University. He has served as President of the National Association of Student Personnel Administrators and of the International House Association.

CHAD WALSH is Professor of English and Poet in Residence at Beloit College and Associate Rector of St. Paul's Episcopal Church in Beloit, Wisconsin. He is the author of *C. S. Lewis: Apostle to the Skeptics, Early Christians of the Twenty-first Century,* and *Eden, Two-Way.*

ERICH ALBERT WALTER, formerly Dean of Students at the University of Michigan, is now Assistant to the President and Professor of English at that University. For a number of years he was editor of *Essay Annual.* He is also editor of *Toward Today.*

HELEN CONSTANCE WHITE is Professor of English and Chairman of the Department of English at The University of Wisconsin. She is the author of *Tudor Books of Private Devotion, With Wings as Eagles,* and co-author of *Seventeenth Century Verse and Prose.*

Acknowledgments

This book is published to mark 100 years of student religious programs at the University of Michigan. The editor gives his best thanks to the many authors that have contributed to this volume. He gratefully acknowledges the help he has received from the University of Michigan Centennial Commission on Student Religious Work. He thanks particularly the members of the Publications Committee: William P. Alston, C. Grey Austin, DeWitt C. Baldwin, Ronald Freedman, William Haber, George B. Harrison, and Frank L. Huntley—all from the University of Michigan; Allen P. Farrell, S.J., of the University of Detroit; Milton D. McLean, of the Ohio State University; Herman Weil, of Wisconsin State College; and Helen C. White, of the University of Wisconsin. To the resident members he owes a special debt for their willingness to read and reread the manuscripts as they were submitted and revised.

The preparation of this book—as well as of two other publications, *Religious Co-operation in State Universities: A Historical Sketch* by Seymour A. Smith, and *A Century of Religion at the University of Michigan* by C. Grey Austin—has been made possible through the generosity of various donors. Among them, a special acknowledgment is made to the Allen Industries Foundation, Inc., the Holly Foundation, the Kresge Foundation of Detroit, the Lilly Endowment, Inc., the National Conference of Christians and Jews, and the Development Council of the University of Michigan. The Centennial Commission expresses its kind thanks to these donors not only for making the publications possible, but also for the assistance which their gifts have lent to all the other phases of the Centennial program.

E.A.W.